ESSAYS IN EIGHTEENTH-CENTURY HISTORY

from the English Historical Review

arranged by

ROSALIND MITCHISON

BARNES & NOBLE, INC.
NEW YORK
Publishers · Booksellers · Since 1873

Published in the United States
in 1966

by B ARNES & N OBLE, I NC.
105 Fifth Avenue, New York

This collection © Longmans, Green & Co. Ltd 1966
Chapter 12 © G. C. Gibbs 1958
Chapter 13 © Peter D. G. Thomas 1959
Chapter 14 © N. C. Philips 1961
Chapter 15 © G. C. Gibbs 1962

Made and printed by offset in Great Britain by
William Clowes and Sons, Limited, London and Beccles

Table of Contents

Introduction

THIS volume originated in a conversation in the common room of Aberdeen University in May 1964 on the difficulty of providing books for students in the expanding Universities. Especial emphasis was laid on the problem of past volumes of learned journals and on the fact that in some cases these could not be bought by Universities since they were out of print. A scheme was worked out for a series of volumes of papers reprinted from one of the leading historical journals, dealing with either a single topic or a single period, and collected simply on the basis of the level of existing demand by students. This demand would be decided by asking a panel of University teachers which papers they most frequently inserted in students' reading lists.

This scheme was put before Professor Denys Hay, then editor of the *English Historical Review*, and taken up by him with the publishers. It was agreed to see what the response would be to a volume of papers from the *Review* confined to eighteenth-century topics, and produced as cheaply as possible. The main task of correspondence and selection was carried through by Professor Hay on the basis of the opinion and practice of a large body of eighteenth-century specialists. The lists of papers most frequently in demand showed a surprisingly high level of agreement and, when those already reprinted in other collections were eliminated, the fifteen here reproduced stood forward as the obvious candidates for reproduction. The consent of their authors, or in some cases of the authors' executors, was secured, and copies of the printed papers bought or borrowed for photographic reproduction.

This account of the origin of the volume is given so that the purpose and method of selection of the papers can be understood by those using them. There have been no alterations, and almost no corrections to the text as it was first printed. (*Errata* for essays 12 and 14 are given below.) The papers have not been brought up to date, but merely reproduced. It was felt that the dates of publication would remind readers that some of these papers could not now claim to be the last word on a subject, but must be studied in their context in the historical literature of the period. If this volume is found useful in Universities, the thanks of readers should go to the authors for their assent to reproduction, to the anonymous panel of selectors and to the editor and publishers of the *English Historical Review* who have carried through the bulk of the work.

ROSALIND MITCHISON

ERRATA

Essay 12. Page 265, line 6, for ' guarantee ' read ' guarantor '.
Page 271, footnote 4, for ' Lord Peter King ' read ' Peter Lord King '.

„ 14. Page 302, line 30, for ' electrick ' read ' elastick '.
Page 305, line 25, for ' much ' read ' must '.
Page 311, line 16, for ' Attorney-General ' read ' Solicitor-General '.

The London West India Interest in the Eighteenth Century[1]

THE character of society in the West India Islands in the eighteenth century was, in some respects, very similar to that of Maryland, Virginia, and the Carolinas. Their trade was not competitive with that of the mother country ; they had a staple product, sugar ; their cultivation was carried on by slave labour. But between the society of the West India Islands and that of the southern colonies of North America there were two principal differences : in the West India Islands there was greater disproportion between the negro and the white populations, and amongst the proprietors of the plantations absenteeism was far more rife. These differences made the protection given by the mother country essential to the islands, as preventing not only foreign aggression, but also rebellion at home. The prevalence of absenteeism had also another result. The absentees formed at home a wealthy and influential body of men. In the London West India organizations of the eighteenth century they were an element which can have existed only to a very small degree in the societies connected with the North American colonies. The amalgamation of the West India planters in England with the London merchants trading to the West Indies

---

[1] The main authority for this article is a collection of minute books in the possession of the West India Committee (15 Seething Lane, E.C.). These are in two series and are dated as follows :

(*a*) West India Committee, Minutes, West India Merchants : vol. i, April 1769–April 1779 ; vol. ii, June 1779–August 1783 ; vol. iv, August 1794–December 1802. These are the minute books of the Society of West India Merchants, founded *c.* 1750 and continuing to 1843. They are referred to in the foot-notes as Merchants' Minutes.

(*b*) West India Committee, Minutes : vol. i, May 1785–December 1792 ; vol. ii, February 1793–April 1801. These are the minute books of the standing committee of West India planters and merchants, founded *c.* 1782 and continuing to the present day. They are referred to in the foot-notes as Standing Committee's Minutes.

Information has also been obtained from the records of a firm of West India merchants trading to Barbados, Messrs. Wilkinson and Gaviller (34 Great Tower Street, E.C.). These records comprise entry books of outgoing letters and account books ; they commence in 1739/40 and are almost complete for the remainder of the eighteenth century. The firm is referred to in the foot-notes as Messrs. Lascelles and Maxwell, the name used in 1739/40.

gave to the society which they formed a strength that enabled it to exert an influence over British politics far greater than that of its contemporaries. And that society has had a continuous life to the present day, through all the economic and political changes through which the West India colonies have passed.

Certain definite results can be traced to this influence in the eighteenth century. Professor Pitman [1] has indicated its importance in the cases of the Molasses Act of 1733 [2] and the Sugar Act of 1739,[3] and it was seen again in 1764 when the policy of the act of 1733 was further developed.[4] Yet, if these acts could have been enforced, the result to the prosperity of the New England colonies would have been serious. With the same object in view—the maintenance of the prosperity of the sugar plantations by increasing the demand for British sugar—opposition, by this time no longer uniformly successful, was organized to Pitt's Irish resolutions of 1786,[5] to the founding of a British company for trading at Sierra Leone in 1791,[6] and to the introduction of East India sugar in 1792.[7] Two other important objects of the West India interest can be traced in the eighteenth century. In time of war, constant representation to ministers of the danger to the islands, the necessity for increased squadrons and for convoys for the trade, had at any rate a considerable part in saving the islands from foreign conquest. And in the latter years of the century from 1788 onwards the whole force of the West India interest was employed to oppose the attacks then made on the slave-trade.[8]

Of this West India interest there were, as has already been indicated, two main sections, the planters resident in England and the London merchants trading to the islands. A third element must be mentioned, connected sometimes with one or the other of these two, that is the colonial agents. The first colonial agent [9] of any West India island appears to have belonged to Barbados. The history of his appointment is

[1] *The British West Indies*, pp. 254–63, 181–3, 187.
[2] 6 Geo. II, cap. 13.   [3] 12 Geo. II, cap. 30.
[4] 4 Geo. III, cap.15.
[5] Chatham Papers, 352 (Public Record Office), Resolutions of West India Planters and Merchants, 24, 26 February, 9 March, 22 April, 6 May 1785. Also Standing Committee's Minutes, vol. i, 18, 31 May, 7, 14 June 1785. See also Holland Rose, *William Pitt and the National Revival*, pp. 255, 260.
[6] Standing Committee's Minutes, vol. i, 11, 13, 14, 17, 18, 19, 20, 23 May 1791.
[7] *Ibid.*, vol. i, 14, 20, 24, 28 February, 9–12 March, 17, 19, 20, 22, 31 March 1792.
[8] A sub-committee was appointed at a meeting of 7 February 1788 to deal with this matter, and its sittings are recorded at various periods during the remainder of the century (Standing Committee's Minutes, vols. i and ii).
[9] The term colonial agent has been used in its strict sense to indicate the representative resident in England of the planters and merchants of the islands : in most cases the appointment of an agent of the governor can be traced earlier.

interesting.[1]   Already in 1670 there were a considerable number of gentlemen planters of that island resident in England, and certain of these wrote a letter to the deputy-governor, council, and assembly in December of that year giving an account of some matters in which they had been acting in the interest of the island and suggesting that an agent should be appointed.[2]   They recommended that the assembly should

allow a Sallary to a person of some quallity who shall constantly attend the general Councelle and from time to time give notice to us what is in agitation Relating to Barbados and with our Advice draw up and prepare such things as are necessary, keepe a Register of the Orders drawne upon your treasury for money, and from time to time Remitt Coppyes of them to you.

The assembly took the advice, and in April 1671 a letter addressed to the gentlemen planters stated that an agent had been appointed. The first reference to an agent for Jamaica that has been found is dated January 1676/7,[3] and even then his position is not clear, for it was not until 1682 that the custom of 'raising money for soliciting the affairs of this his majesty's island in England' commenced.[4]   For the Leeward Islands the first trace of the agency appears in the year 1677.[5]

The gentlemen planters of Barbados in 1670 said that they advised that the agent should be some one whose interests were in Barbados : and this principle was fairly consistently followed for all the islands.   The fact that the agent was so often an absentee planter or a merchant made the consultation by him

---

[1] The record of the correspondence here quoted is given in the Journals of the Assembly of Barbados, Colonial Office Papers 31 (2, 7 March 1670/1 and 20 April 1671).

[2] Voluntary action by planters and merchants in London appears in the cases of all the islands to have preceded the appointment of a paid agent.   See Act appointing Commissioners and an Agent to Negotiate . . . the Affairs of the Leeward Islands . . . 8 Nov. 1690, Plantation Book, i (1677–1700), 163–5 ; also Colonial Office Papers 391 (1, 13 January 1675).   See also Edward Long, *History of Jamaica* (London, 1774), i. 135–6.   It is interesting to note that the merchants and planters of Jamaica in London appear to have suggested in the first instance the instruction to the governor of Jamaica to consent to the raising of money to pay the expenses of soliciting the affairs of the island in England (Colonial Office Papers 391 (3, 16 December 1680)).

[3] Colonial Office Papers 391 (1, 31 January 1676/7).   Sir John Griffith is the agent referred to.

[4] *Journal of the Assembly of Jamaica* ;   Colonial Office Papers 140 (2, 34 Car. II, 4 October 1682).

[5] Colonial Office Papers 391 (2, 10 May 1677).   An account of the negotiations resulting in the appointment of an early agent is given in J. C. Jeaffreson, *A Young Squire of the Seventeenth Century*, London, 1878.   The book is compiled from a letter-book of C. J. Jeaffreson, a planter of St. Christopher, who came to England in 1682 and acted as agent for the island.   The practice of appointing agents for single members of the Leeward Island group became general later ; for Antigua it begins in 1698 (Plantation Book, ii (1700–2), 13–14).   C. J. Jeaffreson was later (in 1690) appointed one of five ' commissioners ' for the Leeward Islands (Plantation Book, i (1677–1700), 163–5).

of other persons interested in the island a simple and natural matter. Thus in 1707 the lords commissioners for trade and plantations applied to the agents of Jamaica and others interested for their opinion as to the time and strength of the convoy for the Jamaica trade, and the answer was signed by the two agents (Sir Gilbert Heathcote and Bartholomew Gracedieu) and twenty-four other merchants trading to Jamaica.[1] Two years later the agents and other merchants submitted to the lords commissioners for trade and plantations a proposal for forming certain settlements in the island of Jamaica.[2] In 1737 it appears that the agents of the sugar islands were directed by the lords commissioners to consult the merchants interested on the subject of certain negotiations with the court of France.[3] Other similar occasions could be cited throughout the century.

It does not appear probable that in the early years of the eighteenth century these agents and planters and merchants had any permanent organization. When necessity arose meetings were held so that joint action could be taken, but there was no continuity in their history. Before a permanent society could come into existence there were several interests which had to be reconciled one to another. There had to be harmony between the resident planters, whose representatives the agents were, and the absentees; and between the absentee planters and the merchants. There had, moreover, to be unanimity between those concerned in the various islands : no evidence has been found that the last point was the occasion of any difficulty.[4]

The only institution connected with the West India interest which is known to have been in existence at this time was the Jamaica Coffee House, in St. Michael's Alley, Cornhill, whose foundation dates probably from the last decade of the seventeenth century.[5] Here the masters of ships engaged in the Jamaica and Guinea trade called to collect letters, and were to be seen by merchants or others at stated hours. To this coffee house letters were addressed to the agents and probably to other merchants and planters from their correspondents in Jamaica,[6] and no

---

[1] Colonial Office Papers 138 (12, 13, 16 May 1707).

[2] *Ibid.* 30 May 1709.

[3] Brit. Mus., Add. MS. 22676, fos. 122–5.

[4] A possible source of difference is indicated in a letter-book of Messrs. Lascelles and Maxwell, 1752–4, letter dated 1 May 1753 to Thomas Stevenson & Sons : ' a Bill is ordered . . . for the better peopling and Cultivating the Lands of the Island of Jamaica, which the Ministry seems to have much at heart. If that can be compassed effectually, a plenty of sugar may hurt yours and the Leeward Islands in time. . . .'

[5] *General Advertiser*, Tuesday, 18 December 1750. Notice headed ' To all Persons Concerned in the Jamaica Trade ', where reference is made to the existence of the coffee house for sixty years past.

[6] *Ibid.*, and Brit. Mus., Add. MS. 12431, fos. 116–17, 120–1.

doubt meetings were sometimes held here, to consult on the business of the island. But there is no indication that there was any
regular organization for the transaction of affairs.

In the case of Jamaica, at any rate, there were serious difficulties in the way of a permanent organization. In the first
place, the absentee planters and the merchants were far from
being in agreement. There were occasions when, though they
both took action on a matter, their influence was exerted in
opposite directions. In 1709, when, as has already been mentioned, the merchants drew up proposals for settling certain
people on the island, a counter-proposal was submitted by two
persons ' on behalf of themselves and other planters '.[1] But we
get the most authoritative statement on this point in 1725 from
James Knight, an agent of Jamaica.[2] He writes from London to
a correspondent in Jamaica an account of ' the method that the
Virginians take, in managing their affairs, which are under the
best regulation of any of the colonies '. The colony of Virginia
had two paid agents

who constantly meet the planters and merchants twice a month, and consult with them what is proper to be done for the Service of the Country : they
very Justly Consider their Interest the Same and dependant on each
other, therefore go hand in hand, without any clashing or Jealousie :
a Treasurer is Appointed to pay the Charges, and receive the Contribution
of a C[harge] per hogshead on every hogshead imported.

The agent says that he does not think such a plan possible for
Jamaica, owing to the ' Suspicions and Animosities, when the
Gentlemen of our Island in England and the Merchants meet
together '. He suggests that his correspondent may be able
to think of some means for overcoming these difficulties, ' especially if the assembly have a greater regard to the trading Interest,
which is most capable of serving the Island here '. Apparently
it was some years before the expectation of James Knight was
fulfilled. In 1745 we still find traces of antagonism between
merchants and planters : this time the evidence comes from
a merchant trading to Barbados,[3] and he is speaking of the
islands generally, so perhaps we may conclude that Jamaica
was in no way peculiar in this respect. He complains that the
planters in England, although they ' have certainly no authority
from the People residing in the plantations to act as their
representatives here . . . seem to assume it to themselves as

[1] Colonial Office Papers 138 (12, 2 and 3 August 1709).
[2] Brit. Mus., Add. MS. 22677, fos. 1–2. The letter is unsigned, but is the same hand
as the following letter which is endorsed as being written by Mr. Knight. It is also
referred to in the catalogue of Add. MSS. and more definitely in the index to the
catalogue (1854–75) as by Mr. Knight.
[3] Letter-book of Messrs. Lascelles and Maxwell, 1743–5.

a right '.[1] Yet more decisive is a reference of a group of planters
in the same year to the ' many . . . Instances . . . where the
Planting and Mercantile Interest Clash '.[2] No later trace
has been found of this lack of harmony, and it probably disappeared soon after this date. There remained, nevertheless, the
other great difficulty which delayed the growth of the West
India society which we find later in the century—the disputes
between the resident planters and the absentees. In 1750 there
were numerous hearings before the lords commissioners for
trade and plantations of the agent for Jamaica, John Sharpe,
on behalf of the resident planters, and a certain Mr. Paris on behalf
of the absentees. The point in dispute was the so-called Deficiency
Acts passed by the legislature of the island ; these required
that a certain proportion should be maintained on every estate
between the whites and the slaves, a fine being exacted as
penalty ; and where the owner of the plantation did not reside
on the island a larger proportion of whites was prescribed.
The absentees argued that the acts were contrary to an instruction
issued to the governors of the islands in 1748. For a long time
the matter was discussed, until finally in 1764 it was decided in
favour of the absentees.

Although it is true, however, that these disputes had to
be settled before the final form of organization could be developed,
they did not prevent some degree of organization in earlier years,
nor, as we have already seen, joint action by planters and merchants when occasion demanded. In 1733 and again in 1739
the West India interest secured strong support from parliament.
Details are lacking as to the means by which these measures
were obtained. We can trace, indeed, the petitions of the
planters and merchants, the evidence given by them, and we
know their final triumph : but at the manner in which the
influence at the disposal of the petitioners was manipulated we
can only guess. Valuable assistance is afforded by evidence
relating to the years 1740 to 1745.

At some time previous to 1740 there came into existence
the Planters' Club. William Beckford, writing to James Knight
from Spanish Town on 11 October 1740, says :

I am glad to find our Club at Lebechs continues. It is very proper that
a Number of Gentlemen should meet together in order to consult on Everything that shall be thought of for the good of their Country ;[3]

and again, ten months later, ' I am glad to hear our Club still

---

[1] Letter-book of Messrs. Lascelles and Maxwell, 1743–5, p. 249, letter dated
2 March 1744/5 to John Fairchild.

[2] Colonial Office Papers 177 (5, 16 October 1745).

[3] Brit. Mus., Add. MS. 12431, fos. 116, 117.

subsists '.[1]   That this is the institution generally referred to as
the Planters' Club is confirmed by the account given of its origin
by the club itself in a letter received by the council of Montserrat
in 1745 :

The sugar planters that Reside in England being Desirous to promote
the Interest of the Sugar Colony's in every Branch of it, as far as Lay in
their Power ; and to put a stop to many abuses that had Crept into the
Sugar Trade, thought that the first step to be taken for promoting these
ends, wou'd be, for the Gentlemen belonging to the several Islands, to
Unite into one Body ; and Accordingly they did some Years ago, form
themselves into a Society in London, which takes the Name of the
Planters Club.[2]

The letter was signed by twenty-eight persons, amongst them
William Beckford and James Knight.[3]

The Planters' Club was probably at this time the only permanent organization of the West India interest in existence.   But
in the year 1743/4, only a few years after the great triumphs of
1733 and 1739, we have a detailed account [4] of the method taken
by the planters and merchants to attain their ends, and it is
clear that the Planters' Club, although it joined in the business,
was by no means the predominant element.   The leaders
were John Sharpe, the agent for Jamaica and Barbados, and
Samuel Martin, the agent for several of the Leeward Islands.
The incident to which the description relates is well known : [5]
Pelham proposed to place an additional duty of 2s. 6d. per cwt.
on all sugar imported, and on 13 March a motion to this effect
was introduced into the committee of supplies.   Long before
this the duty had been ' much talked of '.   William Beckford
wrote to James Knight from Spanish Town on 18 June 1743,
' should the parliament propose laying an additional Duty of 2/4d.
[sic] per cent. [sic] on sugar Adieu to all new settlements '.[6]
Six months later the danger had become urgent and vigorous
measures were taken to withstand it.   The merchant trading to
Barbados, whom we have already quoted, describes what these
were.   First, a case was drawn up showing the grounds on
which the tax was opposed, and the agents presented it to
Mr. Pelham.

[1] Ibid., fos. 120–1.
[2] Minutes of Council of Montserrat, Colonial Office Papers 177 (5, 16 October 1745).
The club was supported by voluntary subscriptions.
[3] See also Journals of Assembly of Jamaica ; Colonial Office Papers 140 (33,
21 Geo. II, 16 April 1747), where the agent is directed to consult certain members of
the Planters' Club, including Beckford and Knight.   Further references to the club
exist in Colonial Office Papers 177 (5, 26 August 1745 ; and 9, 20, 13 February 1748/9).
[4] Letter-book of Messrs. Lascelles and Maxwell, 1743–5.
[5] See Pitman, The British West Indies, pp. 187–8, n. 67.
[6] Brit. Mus., Add. MS. 12431, fos. 125, 126.   Cf. letter published in the London
Evening Post, Thursday, 16 February to Saturday, 18 February 1744, under same date.

He said, he would carry it with him into the Country, where he was going during the Holy Days, and read it ; but whatever his own sentiments might be, the rest of the ministry were of opinion that an additional Duty upon sugar, would be born by the Consumers, and it was resolved therefore to bring a Bill for that purpose into the house, the case was then published. . . . The printed case has been sent to the respective house of every Member of Parliament in Town. The Agents, Planters and Merchants, have also agreed and divided themselves into several small parties to attend upon the several Members, and many of them have already been addressed upon the Subject and every one of them will be solicited personally, before the Bill comes into the House, All people that have any Interest with such as have Influence with Members are also Courted, and People in general seem to think as we do, in opposition to the Bill. Copies of the case have also been dispersed to the several sea ports of the Kingdom, besides publishing it in the Evening Post, and nothing shall be wanted to make the clamour popular, and if possible to get this d——d Bill as much abhored as the Excise Scheme.[1]

In another letter of the same date, 17 January 1743/4, the merchant states that ' there have been for some weeks passed frequent meetings of the Agents, Planters and Factors, interested in the Sugar Colonies '. One of the partners of this firm of merchants was a member of a ' Committee ' which went round to visit the members of parliament at their houses. A letter describes their experiences :

Our George Maxwell with three more, had the City Members in their beat this morning, and really some of them are odd people, but they were all of our side, but not to be much regarded, as they are of the Minority that oppose the Court. We found a d—lish staunch Man for us, whom Mr. Knight used to call by the name of forty-one Heathcott, but that Man would have been of our side without any regard to the merit of our Cause meerly to gratify his own natural propensity to opposition.[2]

The next day

George Maxwell with the same three deputies had the Quarters of 30 and odd Members to beat up. . . . The Courtiers were extremely civil, and said they had read our Pamphlet, which they thought well wrote, but as they were not versed in the knowledge of Trade, they must suspend their opinion till our arguments came to be debated in Parliament, and they assured us they had great tenderness for Trade, and especially for that of the Sugar Colonies.[3]

Among the members visited were two of especial interest, Dodington, of whom we learn that ' he wants as much to be a Courtier again as any one, and was they say refused, absolutely by the King to be taken in upon the last Change, because he had

[1] Letter-book of Messrs. Lascelles and Maxwell, 1743–5, pp. 82–3, letter dated 17 January 1743/4 to General Applewhaite.
[2] *Ibid.*, p. 85, letter dated 17 January 1743/4 to James Bruce.
[3] *Ibid.*

treated Lord of Orford with the utmost ingratitude ' ; [1] and Admiral Vernon, who said he would support the tax ; he knew that ' the Duty would fall upon the Planter ', but ' they would otherwise be for raising money by a Tax upon the People here, which would effect [sic] himself, and concluded that his shirt was near him, but his skin was nearer '.[2] He ' is not heard of scarcely, but in the house of commons, where he is a frequent but a very bad speaker, and there they will hardly bear to hear him, although he makes a noise, and declares he will be heard, and the house grows thin as soon as he begins '.[3]

After all these efforts the planters and merchants were not at all certain of victory. They secured the support of William Pitt, ' the leading Member of the Opposition ', and drew up a brief for him to speak against the tax. Further, they obtained a promise of help from the Scottish and Irish members. The latter were gained by an undertaking, given apparently by the gentlemen of the Planters' Club, to support in return a tax on foreign linens which would serve to protect the Scotch and Irish linen industries.[4] The combination of interests was succesful : the motion was carried against the ministry. The picture is clear : the merchants and planters divided into groups ' beating up ' the residential parts of the city ; their well-written case, with, as some one comments, more assertion than argument, the ministerial party professing to be unable to understand it until they have heard the debates in the house ; their difficulties in the face of the intrigues of Dodington and the vociferous declamation of Admiral Vernon. But this is not all. The organization was merely temporary : the time was not yet come when the old jealousies were laid aside, and a permanent society could be formed including both planters and merchants.

Fifteen years later, the first definite trace appears of an organization of the West India interest other than the Planters' Club. This organization was generally known as the Society of West India Merchants, a title that suggests analogy to the Society of London Merchants trading to Virginia and Maryland which seems to have developed at about the same time.[5] The

[1] *Ibid.* See also *Walpole Letters*, ed. Toynbee (Oxford, 1903–5), i. 154, n. 6, 165, 188–9.

[2] Letter-book of Lascelles and Maxwell, 1743–5, p. 119, letter dated 12 February 1743/4 to George Hannay.

[3] *Ibid.* The letter continues : ' He uses many expressions peculiar to himself. He says Cardinal Fleury was an old Jesuitical son of a ——— . . . that no Nation this side H—l is so much in Debt as this Nation, and was himself a single Man he would leave it and go to new England, which he calls the Land of Canaan, and he foresees this country will be ruined very soon by exorbitant Taxes.'

[4] *Ibid.*, p. 95, letter dated 17 January 1743/4 to John Fairchild ; and p. 249, letter dated 2 March 1744/5 to John Fairchild.

[5] Reference to this society is made in the Chatham Papers, 95. See also Merchants' Minutes, vol. i, meeting of 4 July 1769.

first reference that has been found relates to the year 1760.[1]
Under that date there is a letter among the Newcastle Papers in
the British Museum in which it is stated that ' The Agents of
the Colonies and the West India Merchants ' wished to be permitted to wait on the duke of Newcastle with a memorial. The
letter is signed ' Beeston Long, Chairman of the West India
Merchants '.[2] Six years later the West India merchants invited
the duke of Newcastle to a dinner, and a letter on the subject
has been preserved from the duke of Newcastle to Mr. Long.[3]
These letters could not perhaps be taken as proof of the existence
of a permanent and organized society of the West India interest
if it were not that from 1769 onwards there have been preserved
the minutes of its meetings. These are now in the possession
of the direct descendant of the society—the West India Committee.

The first entry in the minute books is under date 11 April
1769. By that time it is evident that the society has been in
activity sufficiently long for its constitution to be taken as a matter
of course. All our conclusions as to the form of the society
have to be deduced from a study of the business transacted, the
methods by which the society worked, and the information given
as to the persons present at the meetings. It is characteristic
of the whole development of the organized West India interest
that there is no trace throughout the eighteenth century of any
rules other than those of custom : in 1829 and again in 1843
there were constitutional reforms, but these are the earliest on
record. Nevertheless, we can get from the minutes a tolerably
clear and detailed account of the nature of the society. The
meetings were held normally once a month, but departures from
this practice appear to have been frequent. There was no
regular locality for the meetings, a room at the office of the
Marine Society [4] being the most usual meeting-place. The
exact basis of membership of the society is difficult to determine ;
probably there was no definite system of admission until the last
ten years of the century.[5] By 1792 it had become usual for the
names of new members to be proposed and seconded by existing
members at a meeting of the society, and then after the lapse

[1] It is possible that the society had been in existence since 1746 or earlier, and that
only its political activities are new in 1760 ; see below, p. 383, n. 5.

[2] Brit. Mus., Add. MS. 32902, fo. 458.

[3] Brit. Mus., Add. MS. 32975, fos. 416, 430. See also letter from Stephen Fuller,
agent for Jamaica, Add. MS. 32975, fo. 400.

[4] A charitable organization for ministering to the widows and orphans of seamen :
it was established in 1756 ; its present office is Clark's Place, Bishopsgate.

[5] At a meeting of 2 April 1771 it was resolved that ' the question of the admission
of members to this meeting ' should be considered next month, but when the time
came the matter was postponed (Merchants' Minutes, vol. i, meetings of 2 April and
7 May 1771).

of a few weeks the new members were declared to be admitted. The title of the society indicates that the membership was confined to merchants. No doubt this was so, but it is very difficult to make any further decision as to the scope of the membership. A consideration of their own interests would probably, however, lead all the prominent merchants to attend the meetings. The attendance varied considerably ; there were six or eight members in the early years of the society who were usually present, and there were also a very large number who attended more rarely, some very seldom indeed.

From the rule that all members of the society should be merchants even the colonial agents do not appear to have been exempt. One of the most constant attendants at the meetings was Stephen Fuller, the agent for Jamaica, and Richard Maitland, agent for Grenada, St. Vincent, and Tobago,[1] was also a member ; but the agent for Barbados, George Walker, does not appear.[2] Stephen Fuller and Richard Maitland we know to have been merchants, and George Walker was an absentee planter, so it seems safe to assume that the agents were admitted as merchants and not in virtue of their agency. Nevertheless, the merchants who were also agents had a very prominent place in the society, and matters were frequently referred to them on the ground of their position as agents.[3]

The chairman of the society, in its early years, was, as has already been indicated, Mr. Beeston Long, of the firm Long, Drake and Long. There was a paid secretary, James Allen, without whose signature, it is stated in the minutes of the year 1776, no advertisement by the society should be taken as authentic.[4] The treasurer was a member of the society, Mr. Samuel Long, of the same family and firm as the chairman. The fund of which Mr. Samuel Long was treasurer gives a most valuable indication of the nature of the society. It was not merely a group of traders combined to further their own interests and to regulate the conditions of their trade : it was not merely the counterpart for the merchants of the Planters' Club. It shows a definite advance towards the fusion of interests that resulted in the formation of the West India Committee. The origin of the fund was the charge on trade,[5] an imposition similar

---

[1] Tobago after 1772.

[2] George Walker and his successor Samuel Estwick appear later when there are joint meetings of planters and merchants.

[3] e.g. in 1770, when the agent for Jamaica had submitted to him a petition relating to exorbitant fees said to be exacted at Savannah-la-Mar (Merchants' Minutes, vol. i, meeting of 2 October 1770).

[4] *Ibid.*, meeting of 2 April 1776.

[5] The charge had been levied for some time ; in the year 1746, ' to prosecute the Fellows called Lampers, when detected in stealing sugars on board ' (Letter-book

to that which James Knight describes as having been paid by the
Virginia interest in 1725.[1] It was a charge of, normally, 1*d*. per
cask of sugar or puncheon of rum or 1,000 lb. of coffee and in
proportion for other goods brought into the port of London from
the West India Islands ; there was also a charge of 1*d*. per ton
on the shipping employed in the trade : [2] the merchants paid it to
the treasurer of the society. In the year 1777 it was stated that
some gentlemen had omitted to pay it, and the secretary was
directed to write to them impressing upon them the necessity
for contributing their share of this ' the sole fund ' of the society.[3]
But though the merchants paid the charge it was the planters
on whom the main burden of it ultimately fell. The merchants
in all their transactions acted as the factors of the planters.[4]
The sugar, &c., was shipped to the merchants at London, and they
shipped back to the planters the goods required on the plantations ; they sold the sugar and other goods at the best price
they could get and sent accounts of sales to the planters, showing
the various charges to which they had been subject and the net
proceeds of the sales and how far these were exhausted in the
value of the goods exported. And in these accounts of sales
one item was ' pierage, primage and trade ',[5] the last the import
charge to which reference has been made.

of Messrs. Lascelles and Maxwell, 1745–8, letter dated 14 June 1746 to John Frere).
A year earlier the Planters' Club stated that they had thought their expenses might
be paid from ' the Old Fund of One penny per Hogshead ' levied ' whenever it was
called for '. They had abandoned the plan because in their care for the general
interests of the islands they were sometimes at variance with the merchants : Colonial
Office Papers 177 (5, 16 October 1745). Possibly before this time the charge was
collected only on such occasions as the Sugar Act agitation, although for this some
at any rate of the cost was paid by the islands through their agents. The Planters'
Club in 1745 concerned themselves with the prevention of plunderage, and this suggests
that the charge was paid to them in 1746 ; but their statement in 1745 seems to
preclude this view : possibly the merchants had some form of association of which
traces have not been found. Cf. the evidence of James Allen in 1796 before the
committee appointed in that year on the trade and shipping of the port of London
(*Reports of Commissioners : Port of London*, 1796, pp. 170–1). The West India Merchants raised a fund ' to defray the Expence of Prosecutions for Thefts committed
on the River, and on the Quays, of West India Produce ' : and employed two constables on the quays to detect thieves.

    [1] See above, p. 377.
    [2] There are very few references to this charge on shipping in the extant minutes.
The only references are : Merchants' Minutes, vol. i, meeting of 7 July 1778 ; *ibid.*,
vol. iii, meeting of 23 May 1797 ; *ibid.*, meeting of 22 May 1799.
    [3] Merchants' Minutes, vol. i, meeting of 6 May 1777.
    [4] This was stated categorically by the merchants in a document drawn up by them
in 1799 on the occasion of the loan made to them by the Bank of England (Minute
Book of Committee appointed by a Meeting of the West India Merchants, 3 October
1799, meeting of 15 November 1799).
    [5] The accounts of sales from which I have taken this information relate to the
early years of the nineteenth century. There is a volume headed ' Barbadoes,
Accounts, &c.' belonging to Messrs. Lascelles and Maxwell, which gives an example
of an account of sales in 1806.

We have other evidence that the import charge was paid by the planters. In 1788 the anxiety caused by the attack on the slave-trade resulted in great activity on the part of the West India interest in London. It was found that the income resulting from the normal charge was not sufficient, and it was decided in 1789 to increase the rate from 1*d*. to 6*d*. and later to 1*s*.[1] From 1792 to 1796 there were annual meetings to determine the amount of the charge ; these annual meetings were of planters only, the merchants who paid but did not bear the brunt of the levy were not consulted. Further evidence still is afforded by negotiations carried on at this time with the out-ports. It was decided by the London organization [2] that application should be made to the societies at Liverpool, Lancaster, Glasgow, and Bristol for contributions to the expense of opposing interference with the slave-trade, and the contributions were to be obtained by a charge on imports. The merchants and planters of Glasgow objected ; of Liverpool the most that can be said is that they were lukewarm, and, apparently, the attempt was dropped.[3] In 1799 it was directed that a request should be made to the planters whose goods were sent to the out-ports to pay the charge due to Mr. Long.[4] There can be no doubt that the only function of the merchants in connexion with the import charge was its payment to the treasurer.

As to the charge on shipping nothing very definite can be said. There is no reference of any increase in the charge until 1797, when it is raised to twopence.[5] The increase on this occasion was voted at a meeting of merchants, and not at the annual meetings of planters at which alterations in the rate of the charge on imports were made, and it may probably be inferred that the charge on shipping was paid by the merchants.[6]

It must be noted in connexion with the charge, that there

---

[1] Standing Committee's Minutes, vol. i, meetings of 24 April 1789 and 16 May 1792.

[2] *Ibid.*, meeting of 16 May 1792, and *ibid.*, vol. ii, meeting of 1 June 1793.

[3] In Bristol the charge was levied for a time. It was decided at a meeting held at the Merchants' Hall on 3 June 1789 that a charge of 6*d*. per hogshead should be collected. This appears from a minute book now in the possession of the Society of Merchant Venturers, Merchants' Hall, Bristol. No evidence has been found as to the length of time for which the charge continued to be levied. The ordinary expenses of the Bristol West India Club (as re-established in 1782) were paid from an annual subscription of 5 guineas from each member.

[4] Standing Committee's Minutes, vol. ii, meeting of 20 May 1794.

[5] Merchants' Minutes, vol. iv, meeting of 23 May 1797.

[6] The only other class by which this charge could have been paid is the owners of vessels. There is the less likelihood of this, however, since there was a ' Society of Owners and Masters of Ships belonging to the Port of London, Associated for the Protection of Shipping of the said Port ', consisting in 1785 of ' upwards of One hundred and Seventy Members ' (*Journals of the House of Commons*, 25 Geo. III, 30 May 1785, xl. 1033).

was no absolutely impassable line between planters and merchants
and shipowners. Sometimes, possibly frequently, the merchants
were also owners of vessels employed in the trade, and sometimes,
probably not very often, they were planters. It seems likely,
however, that this double interest in the West Indies was less
common in the eighteenth century than it was later. At any
rate, it does not appear to have been sufficiently usual in the
eighteenth century to account for the fact that a fund to which
the planters were the main contributors was administered by
a society of merchants. The explanation lies, more probably,
in the fact already stated that the merchants acted in business
and private affairs [1] as the representatives of the planters, and
therefore it was regarded as natural that they should act as their
representatives in the use of this fund. The main point at issue
between the resident and the absentee planters—the Deficiency
Laws—had been settled in 1764 ; the quarrels between the
merchants and the absentees had disappeared. It was possible,
therefore, for the Society of West India Merchants to act as the
executive of the whole West India interest.

A consideration of the business undertaken by the society
leads to the same conclusion. To a certain extent the meetings
were taken up with matters of trade ; they fixed the rates of
freight outwards to the colonies, they concerned themselves
in the prosecution of thieves on the wharves ; later in the century
they played a very prominent part in the institution of the marine
police office.[2] But these were not their sole functions. In these
early years they dealt with all kinds of business affecting the
sugar colonies : for example, in 1770 they appointed a committee
to promote the passing of the bill ' for the better enabling Aliens
to recover Money lent in all His Majesty's Colonies in America' : [3]
and frequently sums of money were subscribed for the sufferers
from a fire or a hurricane in one of the islands, or for the printing
of some pamphlet on a subject in which the colonies were
interested. The Society of West India Merchants did not falsify
its trust.

In 1769 the Planters' Club was still in existence. Probably,
however, it was always more social than political in character,
and now that the merchants had developed so strong an organization it fell gradually into insignificance. In 1771 it was reported
at a meeting of the merchants that some of the merchants had

---

[1] The merchants played a prominent part in recommending planters with whom
they were connected to be members of council in the islands or holders of offices
there. This appears from the Letter-books of Messrs. Lascelles and Maxwell and also
from the Colonial Office Papers, especially Colonial Office Papers 391 (Board of Trade
Journal).

[2] Merchants' Minutes, vol. iv, meeting of 12 January 1798 *et seq.*

[3] *Ibid.*, vol. i, meeting of 4 December 1770.

discussed a matter connected with the trade with a committee of the Planters' Club;[1] but this is the last reference that has been found. Within a few years of this the club either disappeared, or altered its character and name by the admission to its membership of merchants.[2] And in 1783 a notice was inserted in the press suggesting that planters should meet at a dinner to discuss the formation of a club, ' to consist of planters only '.[3]

For some years, then, the planters left the main share in the organization, by which the interests of the islands were promoted, to the merchants. Yet they were by no means idle. In the minute books of the merchants' society there are recorded, besides the monthly meetings of the merchants, and the meetings of committees appointed for some special purpose, certain general meetings of planters and merchants. These general meetings were apparently regarded as necessary when any alteration in the freight homewards from the islands was considered desirable ; they met also when matters of particular interest or importance were afoot. There were other meetings of a similar character, which, for what reason we do not know, were not recorded in the minute books. An example of this occurred in the year 1775, when a series of meetings was held to consider what measures were necessary in view of the events that were taking place in North America. The history of these meetings is worth recording as illustrating the development of joint action by planters and merchants at this period.

At a meeting of the merchants on 3 January 1775, Mr. Long reported that he had received a letter from a number of ' Gentlemen of the West India Islands living in London ' asking that the Society of West India Merchants would join with them in calling a general meeting of planters and merchants.[4] The merchants agreed, and next month it was reported that several meetings had been held. A general meeting was advertised for 18 January at the London Tavern, Bishopsgate Street :[5] and apparently a preliminary meeting was held on the 5th inst., when it was resolved that the London merchants and planters would join with the ' merchants, traders, &c., in the West India business, residing at Bristol ' to concert what measures should be taken.[6]

---

[1] The nomenclature of all the societies dealt with is very varied. In the minutes of the merchants' society the same meeting is definitely referred to as having been requested by ' the British West India Society at the Thatched Tavern ', and held with the committee of the Planters' Club (*ibid.*, meetings of 1 January and 5 February 1771). This looseness is indicative of their very gradual crystallization.

[2] In 1779 Admiral Keppel was invited to a dinner by ' the Society of West India Planters and Merchants ' (*ibid.*, meeting of 23 February 1779).

[3] *Morning Herald and Daily Advertiser*, Thursday, 13 March 1783.

[4] Merchants' Minutes, vol. i, meeting of 3 January 1775.

[5] *Gazetteer and New Daily Advertiser*, Thursday, 5 January 1775.

[6] *Morning Chronicle and London Advertiser*, Friday, January 6, 1775. Statement

On the 18th the general meeting met, Mr. Beeston Long being the chairman : a committee was appointed to prepare a petition to the house of commons ' representing the alarming situation in which the West India islands are placed by the resolution of the congress, held at the city of Philadelphia in North America on the 5th of September 1774, and praying their interposition ' : the committee was to report to another general meeting to be held on the 25th inst.[1] This meeting was held and the petition agreed to ; it was determined that Mr. Alderman Oliver should be requested to present it and that the committee before appointed should prepare evidence in its support. A third general meeting was held on 31 January, and this is noteworthy because it resolved that the committee should meet from day to day, adjourn as they thought fit, and call a general meeting when they considered it desirable.[2] On 6 February the power to summon a general meeting was exercised ; and a notice was inserted in the press that a general meeting was to take place the next day. The notice was signed by the members of the committee, eight in number ;[3] five of them (including the chairman) were among the gentlemen planters who signed the request to the merchants asking for a general meeting ; a sixth, George Walker, we know to have been a planter and the agent for Barbados, and of the remaining two neither was an attendant at the meetings of the merchants' society. If it be true that these eight members were the whole committee, the absence of merchants is noticeable, and lends some colour to a letter which appeared in the *Gazetteer and Daily Advertiser* of 17 January, violently condemning the merchants for their subservient relations with the planters.[4] It is, in any case, clear that it was far from being true at this time that the influence of the planters was overshadowed by that of the merchants.

No evidence has been found that the committee had anything but a temporary existence. When it again became necessary that general meetings should be held the matter proceeded very much on the same lines as before. In April 1778 two general meetings of planters and merchants took place, and at the second of these a committee of planters and merchants was appointed. On this occasion the chairman of the committee was Mr. Long, in whose house the committee met ; and several merchants were among the members.[5]

by Mr. Samuel Vaughan to ' American Merchants, assembled Wednesday at the King's Arms Tavern '.

[1] *Gazetteer and New Daily Advertiser*, Thursday, February 16, 1775.

[2] *Ibid.*   [3] *Daily Advertiser*, Monday, 6 February 1775.

[4] *Gazetteer and New Daily Advertiser*, Tuesday, 17 January 1775. Letter signed J. Massie, addressed ' To the Merchants trading to, or interested in, our North American Colonies '.

[5] Merchants' Minutes, vol. i, meetings of 28 April 1778 and 29 April 1778.

These committees appointed at general meetings [1] show the direction in which the development is tending. From the repeated general meetings and their committees gradually a permanent organization is being built up, its activities supplementary to and in no way superseding those of the merchants' society. In 1782 we get another step towards the final form of organization. In the minutes of the meeting of merchants of January of that year there is inserted the copy of a petition of the West India planters and merchants to the king ; the first signature is that of ' Nathaniel Bayly, Chairman '. Hitherto the chair at general meetings has always been taken by Mr. Long ; he is here superseded by Mr. Bayly, who was a gentleman planter. In June of the same year two more general meetings were held, and at neither of them was Mr. Long in the chair : at the earlier of the two the chairman was Richard Pennant ; and from this time there does not seem to have been a general meeting at which Mr. Beeston Long presided, and whenever Mr. Pennant is present he is in the chair.

At one of these meetings of 1782, there is a reference to the standing committee of planters and merchants, appointed presumably at one of the previous meetings. During the years 1782 to 1784 this organization takes permanent shape, and we get thus the standing committee, with Mr. Pennant (created Baron Penrhyn in September 1783) as chairman.

It is impossible to give the exact date at which the standing committee became a definite permanent institution, for unfortunately no minutes have been preserved to the West India committee for the period August 1783 to May 1785.[2] Certain manuscripts among the Chatham Papers [3] in the Public Record Office give evidence of the existence of a committee of West India planters and merchants in February and March 1784 and again in the same months of 1785. In March 1785 the names of the members of the committee are given ; Lord Penrhyn was chairman, and Mr. Beeston Long one of the members. In April there was a meeting of ' the select committee ', but there is no means of judging its relation to the former committee. The same term is applied to two meetings in May, after the minutes commence again, and then in June there was a meeting of the standing committee, henceforth the kernel of the association.

It is, as we have suggested, probable, though not certain,

---

[1] For the sake of clarity the term general meeting has been used to indicate a meeting of planters and merchants. In the minutes the term is used not only for this purpose, but in reference to ordinary meetings of merchants only or planters only as contrasted with committee meetings.

[2] See list of minute books, p. 373, n. 1.

[3] Public Record Office, Chatham Papers, 352.

that the standing committee was appointed in the first place at a general meeting. Additions to it were, we know, made from time to time by general meetings. It had, therefore, no constitutional connexion with the meetings of the merchants' society, though many of the members did in fact belong to both. This is an interesting point. The merchants' society had been in existence for over twenty years ; its members had been active in promoting general meetings, but it received no recognized position at the constitution of the standing committee.

The standing committee, if we can judge from the minutes that have been preserved, did not meet regularly, but rather as business required. The chairman continued for the rest of the century to be Lord Penrhyn, the secretary was, as for the merchants' meetings, James Allen, and the treasurer, Mr. Samuel Long. The fund appears to have been the same as that from which the expenses of the merchants' society were paid.

The minute book in which the meetings of the standing committee are recorded contain also general meetings of the planters and merchants. These could meet only by summons from Lord Penrhyn.[1] There are also the meetings of numerous sub-committees appointed by the standing committee to deal with matters of special interest ; the most important were those formed to deal with the agitation respecting the slave-trade and the scheme, finally brought into operation, for the construction of wet docks for the exclusive use of the West India trade.

Enough has been said already to indicate that with the growth of the standing committee of planters and merchants— the predecessor of the present West India Committee—the meetings of the Society of West India Merchants did not cease. The business undertaken by their meetings lessened considerably in scope during the last decade of the century, gradually becoming more and more confined to the regulation of trade : but the organization, however, continued as before. On the death of Mr. Beeston Long early in 1785, he was succeeded as chairman by Sir Richard Neave, Bart., who had been for some time deputy chairman ; and Mr. Beeston Long's son, another Beeston Long, became deputy, and in turn succeeded Sir Richard Neave as chairman. The treasurer was still Mr. Samuel Long, and the secretary James Allen, son of the former secretary of the same name. The only meetings recorded in the minute books of the merchants' society are the monthly meetings and meetings of

[1] The earliest evidence for this statement is in connexion with a meeting of 21 December 1792 (Standing Committee's Minutes, vol. i). General meetings had formerly, however, ever since the beginning of the minutes of the standing committee in May 1785, been summoned by Lord Penrhyn.

sub-committees appointed by them : general meetings are recorded in the books of the standing committee. The merchants' meeting continued to have its separate organization until 1843 ; it was resolved at a meeting of that year that the continuance of a separate society was no longer necessary, and that such of its members as were not already members of the standing committee should be transferred to that body. Its long continuance is an interesting example of survival : the disagreement between planters and merchants resulted in the existence of separate meetings for nearly a century after the disagreement had disappeared.

The position during the last twenty years of the eighteenth century was then briefly this : there was a joint organization of planters and merchants ; there was a separate society of merchants only ; there were occasional general meetings of planters alone for specific purposes. There were also throughout the eighteenth century occasional meetings of the planters and merchants interested in one island or group of islands only.[1] These are sometimes recorded in the minute books, but sometimes we get no indication of them from this source. Frequently they were called by the agents in connexion with some business of special importance which was being transacted with the government. Perhaps the most interesting of these cases was in 1783, when the planters, merchants, and others interested in the island of Tobago held meetings to consider what action should be taken in view of the proposed cession of the island to France by the treaty of Versailles. The earl of Shelburne had recommended the appointment of an agent by the planters and merchants to represent the interests of the island at the court of France ;[2] the advice was taken and assurances were obtained from the French ministers that favourable treatment should be accorded to the British planters.

Thus from various sources grew up the West India Committee, a powerful influence on British politics. In its final form it appeared only during the last eighteen years of the century ; but long before that its way had been prepared by the practice of holding meetings to draw up petitions to the government. For many years nothing more definite than these occasional meetings could be developed owing to divergency of interest and

---

[1] See Minutes of the Council of Jamaica, Colonial Office Papers 137 (32, 18 and 19 December 1760) ; Journals of the Assembly of Jamaica, Colonial Office Papers 140 (46, 12 Geo. III, 20 November 1771) ; Merchants' Minutes, vol. ii, meeting of 28 November 1781. For the earlier half of the century the only evidence is the petitions and representations of the planters and merchants interested in the islands, the most fruitful sources for which are the series Colonial Office Papers 391 (Board of Trade Journals) and the *Journals of the House of Commons.*

[2] *Gentleman's Magazine,* vol. 53, January–June 1783, pp. 173, 535.

differences of opinion, but gradually these obstacles were removed and a society grew up in many respects similar to that of the present day. Many changes have, indeed, taken place in its constitution, but none so great as to break the continuity of development from the time when Lord Penrhyn was chairman of the standing committee, and James Allen carried round his minute books to the London Tavern, or the Marine Society's office, or the King's Arms Tavern in Cornhill.

Among the societies formed in the eighteenth century by the unincorporated branches of commerce, the West India Committee alone has survived to the present day. The history of its development is therefore interesting as throwing light on the methods by which such societies attempted to secure their ends in English political circles. It does not in itself wholly explain the peculiar success that attended the activities of the West India interest ; for this an investigation must be made of the membership of the West India organizations, and of the attendance recorded at general meetings, an investigation which would produce evidence to show the great strength in the house of commons commanded by those concerned in the West India Islands. There is, however, another interest that attaches to the narrative. Although in many ways the West India organizations, especially the Society of West India Merchants, were comparable to the numerous ' meetings or clubs . . . of the Turky and Italian merchants, the Spanish, the Portuguese, the French . . . ',[1] they had an importance shared only with ' the Virginia, the Carolina, New York, and New England merchants ' in that they were connected with a group of British colonies, and an importance in which they had no rivals in that these colonies were not lost to Great Britain at the break-up of the old empire. The presence in London of the West India organizations ensured that the interests of the colonies should not be violated by the home government through lack of information : to make certain of this was primarily the function of the colonial agents, but a much smaller measure of success would have been attained had it not been for the assistance afforded by the other planters and merchants with their wide influence and constant communications from the leading inhabitants of the islands.

LILLIAN M. PENSON.

---

[1] *The Universal Spectator and Weekly Journal*, Saturday, 10 August 1734.

The Excise Scheme of 1733

THE history of Walpole's excise scheme and the circumstances of its defeat were narrated by Coxe more than a century ago, and his account, followed by that of Lord Mahon, remained for a long time the basis of most others. A better account was that by Lord Hervey, intimate friend and admirer of Walpole, which was not published until long after his death and after Coxe had written his *Memoirs of Sir Robert Walpole*. The publication of the Historical Manuscripts Commission's *Report on the Carlisle Manuscripts* in 1897 supplied additional information, corroborated the narrative of Hervey, and further invalidated that of Coxe. The episode of the excise is memorable not so much because a wise scheme was undone by political machination, but because it is one of the most striking instances in former times of a powerful minister being coerced by clamour and opinion. The force of this public feeling was aroused and displayed, as had often been the case before, in innumerable little pamphlets, and, perhaps for the first time, in the newspapers of the day. It is particularly from the newspapers and pamphlets in the British Museum, largely brought together since the time when Coxe composed his biography, that I propose to study this subject again and attempt to discover what was the public opinion of this time and the devices by which it was influenced.[1]

Walpole had long desired to reform English taxation in such manner as to relieve the landholders from the heavy burdens laid upon their estates.[2] At the beginning of 1732 he proposed to revive the inland duty or excise upon salt, which had recently been abolished, and to reduce the land-tax by one shilling in the pound. His proposal encountered bitter opposition. 'This seems to be a step towards introducing a general excise, which is inconsistent with the liberties of a free people,' said one speaker. 'This tax upon salt is . . . a dangerous precedent,' said another;

---

[1] This article was written independently of M. Vaucher's book *La Crise du Ministère Walpole*, and was in the Editor's hands before that book reached Professor Turner. It has therefore seemed best, although the two to some extent cover the same ground, to publish the present article without inserting references to M. Vaucher's work and without substantial modification.—*Ed. E. H. R.*

[2] *Parliamentary History*, viii. 944, 945, 968, 970, 1048.

' it is one step towards a general excise ', which would destroy the liberties of England and overturn the constitution. Ministerial speakers rebuked their opponents : ' As for a general excise, I never heard of any such design ' ; ' I am persuaded that no man ever thought of introducing a General Excise into this country.' But Walpole did declare that it would be a beneficial thing ' if all or most part of our customs were converted into excises '.[1] ' Who ', asked a writer, ' will have Cause to complain against reasonable Methods for improving the Revenue, and easing the People, by turning the most burthensome of the Customs on Importation, into Excises upon Home Consumption ? Our Liberties can be in no Danger from such Excises.' [2]   A skirmish of pamphleteers now began,[3] and the leaders of the opposition either believed or affected to believe that there was danger of a general excise or at least a considerable extension of such taxes.

> Ask you why Phryne the whole auction buys ?
> Phryne foresees a general excise.[4]

The bill was presently passed, but not without protests from the lords who dissented.

It may be said that these leaders were constantly seeking to discover some means of attacking the minister and most probably exaggerated their alarm ; yet the ease with which they afterwards spread this alarm shows that it must have existed of itself. Excise had been commended by some of the foremost financial writers of the past, but the detestation in which it was held appears in many a pamphlet of the sixteenth and seventeenth centuries.[5] ' The very word " Excise " has always been odious to the people of England,' said Pulteney.[6] Apprehension was further aroused when the salt duty yielded so little that Walpole, in order not to reimpose the shilling which had just been taken off the land-tax, was forced to encroach upon the sinking fund to supply the current service of the year ; and it was realized that thereafter some permanent device must be employed to supply the deficiency.[7] It was not difficult to believe that Walpole was considering an extension of the excise.

In October a writer in *The Craftsman*, that able but unscrupulous paper of the opposition, said that excises had contributed

---

[1] *Ibid.* cols. 949, 951, 953, 956, 960, 961, 972, 973.

[2] *A Letter to a Freeholder, on the Late Reduction of the Land Tax* (London, 1732), p. 62.

[3] [William Pulteney], *The Case of the Revival of the Salt Duty* (London, 1732).

[4] Pope, *Moral Essays*, iii. 120 (1732).

[5] E. R. Turner, ' Early Opinion about English Excise ', *American Hist. Rev.* xxi. 314–18.

[6] *Parl. Hist.* viii. 1299   [7] Hervey, *Memoirs* (Philadelphia, 1848), i. 168.

to destroy the liberties of France, and declared that he would discuss the subject in later numbers. ' God forbid that We should ever see *Those* also established in this Country.' [1] He hastened to make good his promise, so as to begin discussion before the meeting of parliament. Excise was enforced without trial by jury. Since goods might not be removed without consent of an officer there was intolerable confinement of property and restraint of trade. A vast number of officers must be quartered upon the population to administer the law. Excise legislation was commonly made perpetual or for a long term of years. Nor were the benefits claimed for the system real. It did not prevent smuggling, but merely tormented the fair trader. Excise would not relieve the landholders, but result in a perpetual burden upon them under another name. He did not know that any minister would propose a general excise, but a minister had before suggested this in lieu of the land-tax, and followed it up by reducing the tax on land one shilling in the pound, and then renewing the excise on salt. It might well be that the process would go farther. There was now a long list of commodities subject to excise, and for a long time the number had been increasing, so that there certainly was a tendency towards a general excise. This was very dangerous.[2] These articles, written by Pulteney, Bolingbroke, and their associates, were the beginning of an attack which was throughout more vigorous and successful than the defence that was opposed to it.[3]

Ministerial journals answered at once. *The Daily Courant* declared that *The Craftsman* had no means of knowing whether such a scheme would be laid before parliament. This paper always found something for an attack on the ministry before parliament opened : ' We are now to be terrified with the Apprehensions of a *General Excise* ; and the Monster is painted in the most tremendous Manner imaginable.' Excise might not be bad, however. It was very necessary that something should be done to lessen smuggling, whereby those who cheated the government were able to undersell those who paid lawful duties. Many customs officers had been barbarously mangled and murdered. There was no doubt that excise laws prevented smuggling ; and also that they yielded a greater revenue than customs.[4]

The opposing writers ' affect to dissemble the Knowledge of

[1] *The Country Journal : or, the Craftsman*, 21 October 1732.

[2] *Ibid.* 28 October, 4, 11, 25 November, 2, 16 December 1732.

[3] Writing later Delafaye says : ' Some blame Sir Robert Walpole for omitting to have something printed to explain his Scheme ; for my part . . . I think it a Proceeding more becoming the Dignity of the Government, to let the Thing justify itself, and the People see, how they have been imposed upon by Incendiaries.' To the Earl of Essex, 18 January 1732/3 : Brit. Mus., Add. MS. 27732, fo. 94.

[4] *The Daily Courant*, 28 October, 11, 21, 25 November, 12, 16, 23 December 1732.

any *such Project*, tho' the whole Town rings with it, and a *certain Gentleman*, as I am informed, hath even publickly avowed it,' was the reply.[1]   ' The Report of intended Excises is spread far and near,' said another.[2]   Sinister stories of the doings of excise-men now appeared.[3]   The result was that meetings of merchants and importers began to be held, in which it was resolved to oppose the extension of the excise by any lawful means,[4] while letters were written to members of the house of commons and deputations appointed to wait upon them.[5]   ' Your Excy. will have seen in the Prints, what caballing there has been, all over the Kingdom to stirr up the People against it, there is not a Cobler but is made to believe that he is to pay an Excise before he eats his bread and Cheese and drinks his pot of Beer,' wrote Delafaye, under-secretary of state.[6]

Parliament was opened on 16 January 1733.   The king asked the members to take such measures concerning the revenue ' as will most conduce to the present and future Ease of those you repre-sent '.[7]   Walpole's project had not yet been announced, but Delafaye wrote :   ' The intended turning the Customs on Wine and Tobacco, or part of them, into an Excise, is what is likely to give the most occupation this Sessions,' and added that he was persuaded ' it will not be attempted without being sure of Suc-cess '.[8]   Newcastle looked for little opposition.[9]   At the same time, however, meetings continued to be held to oppose an excise, and ballads, pictures, and papers were dispersed in all parts of England.   *Britain Excis'd* was sung from a sheet with a picture of Sir Robert in a carriage dragged by a monster devouring the substance of the people.[10]   Among the characters in a scurrilous opera he was put down as ' A compleat Villain '.[11]   But Henry Pelham was convinced that the clamours raised by the opposition were local, ' and will be easier quel'd, than even those they have formerly been foil'd in '.   ' Excise will be the grand affair,' wrote Newcastle from his country seat, ' but as it is right in every

---

[1] *Craftsman*, 25 November 1732.   [2] *Fog's Weekly Journal*, 18 November 1732.

[3] *The Daily Journal*, 20 December 1732 ; *Fog's Weekly Journal*, 23 December 1732.

[4] *The London Evening-Post*, 19 December 1732 ; *Daily Journal*, 23 December 1732, 12 January 1733 ; *The Grub-street Journal*, 4, 11 January 1733 ; *The London Journal*, 13 January 1733 ; *The Universal Spectator, and Weekly Journal*, 13 January, 17 February 1733.

[5] *The London Evening-Post*, 6 January 1733 ; *Daily Journal*, 8 January 1733 ; *The Daily Post*, 10 January 1733 ; *Fog's Weekly Journal*, 13 January 1733 ; *The Weekly Miscellany*, 13 January 1733.

[6] Brit. Mus., Add. MS. 27732, fos. 93, 94.   [7] *Lords' Journals*, xxiv. 165.

[8] Brit. Mus., Add. MS. 27732, fos. 93, 94.   [9] Brit. Mus., Add. MS. 23627, fo. 45.

[10] *Britannia Excisa : Britain Excis'd*, &c. (London, 1733).   *A Sequel to Britannia Excisa, a New Political Ballad*, &c. (London, 1733), and *The Countryman's Answer to the Ballad, Call'd, Britannia Excisa* (1733), were written on the side of the ministry.

[11] *The Fox Uncas'd : or, Robin's Art of Money-catching.   A New Ballad Opera. As it is privately Acted near St. James's*, &c. (London, 1733).

respect, it gains every day, and will certainly be carried by a great Majority in both Houses.' [1]

Meanwhile the war raged in pamphlet and fly-sheet. *The Craftsman* continued its attack so that there was thought of prosecuting it for libel,[2] and other opposition papers vied with it. The controversy which had been begun in the press was taken up by a multitude of pamphlets, so numerous that one can neither use all of them nor be sure of having discovered them all. Upon their faded pages are arguments which the leaders used in the house of commons, and which were amplified day by day in the newspapers. Many of them, indeed, were first published in whole or in part serially in the papers, and then embellished or reprinted in pamphlets to be spread broadcast through the streets of London and in remoter places where newspapers were not yet carried.[3] Constantly these pamphlets were announced in the papers as they were published, or advertised beforehand, and repeated notices of them sometimes make up the larger part of the newspaper advertising. Letters sent to members of parliament asking them to oppose the excise were collected in pamphlets or published in the papers.[4] Even newspaper articles were advertised or announced in other papers.[5] All this marks, I think, the widest use of advertising for controversial purposes in English political life up to this time.

Extraordinary pains were taken to distribute this writing as widely as possible. The pamphlets were published at sixpence or a shilling, but they were also given gratis, while it was asserted that the government prostituted the post office in sending its writings about the country.[6] The work of the opposition provokes irate comment from one of the minister's friends : [7]

Besides the regular Infatuation from daily and weekly papers, little *Hand Bills* were dispersed by thousands all over the City and Country, put into Peoples Hands in the Streets and Highways, dropped at their Doors, and thrown in at their Windows ; all asserting that Excisemen were (like a foreign Enemy) going to invade and devour them, and ready to enter their Houses ; into all Houses, private or public, at any time, by Day, or by Night. They might as well have asserted, that these Excisemen were to be invested with Power of Life and Death.

Such as could not read, were informed by such as could : and all were ready to inform, and mislead, and enrage one another. It was the Theme

[1] Brit. Mus., Add. MS. 27732, fos. 95, 125, 126.

[2] *State Papers, Dom., George II*, xxix, 17 January 1732/3.

[3] *An Argument against Excises ; The Reply of a Member of Parliament to the Mayor of His Corporation*, p. 10.

[4] *Fog's Weekly Journal*, 24 March 1733.   [5] *Daily Journal*, 24 March 1733.

[6] *Reflections upon a Pamphlet, Entitled Observations upon the Laws of Excise*, p. 27 ; [Pulteney ?], *A Review of the Excise-Scheme*, p. 4.

[7] *A Letter from a Member of Parliament for a Borough in the West*, pp. 9, 10.

of Coffee-Houses, Taverns, and Gin-shops, the Discourse of Artificers, the Cry of the Streets, the Entertainment of Lacquies, the Prate of Wenches, and the Bugbear of Children.

In the streets the attack was carried on with vigour and success. Scurrilous ballads were cried about and sung.[1] Simple folk were delighted with pictures of the wicked Walpole in his iniquity and his power.[2] Emblems were displayed in shops, and wooden shoes were imported from the Continent to be carried about on poles that the people might see to what a dismal state they were coming.[3] There were meetings in all parts of the kingdom, particularly in London, and numerous letters drafted to be sent to representatives in parliament, or recounted in opposition papers.[4] Even the borough of Lynn ordered such a letter to be sent to its representatives, Sir Robert Walpole and Sir Charles Turner.[5] It must be said that some of the instructions thus sent were publicly disavowed.[6]

What the anti-ministerial writers were attempting appears in a dialogue of this time : [7]

Squat : You can be no Stranger, sure, Sir *Andrew*, to the Conspiracy that 's form'd against us.

Sir Andrew : Bless us ! What Conspiracy ? What are they going to do to us ? Is there a *Proclamation* to be issu'd against *Trade* ? Is our *Privilege* of being govern'd by *Parliaments* to be taken away ? Is *Ship-money*, or *Tonnage* and *Poundage* going to be levy'd upon us ? Is a *Star-chamber* to be erected ? Is the *Habeas Corpus* Act repeal'd ? Or is the *Pretender* and *Popery* coming in upon us ?

Squat : Psha ! those are mere Trifles ; *Popery* is as good as any *other* Religion, and the *Pretender* is nothing but a *political Scare-Crow.*—No, Sir, 'tis something more terrible than any thing you have mention'd. We are to be *Excis'd, Excis'd, Excis'd*, Sir !

.   .   .   .

Sir Andrew : Good lack ! I profess I am sorry for it. I had only heard that there was a Scheme on foot to *levy the Duties* upon *Wines* and *Tobacco* by way of *Excise.* But——

Squat : But what, Sir ? S'death and Furies ! is not that enough ? Is destroying our Trade, rifling our Houses, and striking at the Root of all National Liberty, nothing at all then ?

Sir Andrew : Dear Squire, don't always think and speak in a Passion.

Somewhat before had appeared a bitter attack upon evil ministers, bearing on its title-page lines which Cicero once had spoken

---

[1] *Grub-street Journal*, 18 January 1733.   [2] *Craftsman*, 10 February 1733.
[3] *London Journal*, 17 March 1733.
[4] *A Collection of Letters ; Daily Post*, 16 February, 13, 14 March 1733.
[5] *Fog's Weekly Journal*, 20 January 1733.
[6] *Daily Journal*, 3 February 1733.
[7] *A Dialogue between Sir Andrew Freeport and Timothy Squat, Esquire*, pp. 5, 6.

against Catiline, and a speech from Addison's *Cato* which used to thrill the audiences of London : [1]

> Is there not some chosen Curse,
> Some hidden Thunder in the Stores of Heaven,
> Red with uncommon Wrath, to blast the Man,
> Who owes his Greatness to his Country's Ruin ?

The tale was told of how Portugal was rescued from slavery by the assassination of an odious 'Prime Minister'; [2] and also the story of prime ministers in England from the Conquest to the Restoration, showing that some had come to their end by the halter and some by the axe, that some had gone into exile, and some been thrust into prison. [3] It was asserted that a general excise would be imposed. [4] Ministers had as yet announced no new excise whatsoever.

The effect of the agitation became very evident. ' Sir Robert is thought by many to be in a declining way,' wrote Lady Irwin at the end of January. [5] He did, indeed, postpone his announcement in hope that the clamour would die down, and it began to be believed that he would abandon his scheme altogether. [6] On 23 February, however, in the debate about appropriating part of the sinking fund, Pulteney asserted that another project, ' that monster, the Excise ', had struck terror into the minds of the members. Walpole admitted that he cherished a plan, but nothing evil. ' Let it be what it will, I am resolved to propose it,' he said ; ' and if I have but a very little time, I shall lay it before you for your consideration.' And four days later : ' It is certain that I have a Scheme which I intend very soon to lay before you.' [7] In face of the storm which was now gathering some of his friends advised him to give it over ; but he declared that he was too far embarked, that it was known what he purposed, and he was resolved therefore to carry it through. [8]

At length the matter was brought up in the commons. On 7 March the commissioners of the customs were ordered to prepare an account of the frauds in importing wines and tobacco. Walpole now spoke for the first time about what he intended, and in the opinion of a friend was heard with more general approbation than could have been expected after all the noise without doors. [9] A committee of the whole house was to consider the better

---

[1] *The Norfolk Sting : or, the History and Fall of Evil Ministers*, &c. (London, 1732).
[2] *Fog's Weekly Journal*, 10 February 1733.
[3] *A Short History of Prime Ministers in Great Britain*, &c. (London, 1733).
[4] *Daily Courant*, 2 February 1733.
[5] *Historical MSS. Commission, Carlisle MSS.* pp. 98, 99.   [6] *Ibid.* p. 102.
[7] *Parl. Hist.* viii. 1203, 1205, 1228.   [8] Hervey, i. 169.
[9] Delafaye to the earl of Essex, 8 March 1732/3 : Brit. Mus., Add. MS. 27732, fos. 131, 132.

security of these revenues on that day week.[1] Excitement grew
as the day came for the committee to sit. Constables, beadles,
and a reserve of horse and foot guards were ready to prevent
tumults and riot. The prince of Wales, the Spanish ambassador,
and most of the foreign ministers were present to hear the
debates.[2] 'There scarce ever was a greater Appearance of Members in the House ; nor a more numerous Crowd in the Court of
Requests, Westminster Hall, and the adjoyning places.'[3] It was a
long sitting with reading of numerous returns and reports.[4] Shortly
after midday the debate was begun by Walpole. In a speech of
more than two hours he explained the project which the government was putting forward.[5] His plan, he said, was for the better
security of the revenues charged upon tobacco. A struggle over
this would be a contest of the unfair trader with the honest one,
the planter, and the public. Ultimately, indeed, it was the landed
interest which suffered most from the frauds now rampant. He
alluded to the slanders that he would propose a general excise,
and denied that such a thought had entered his mind. He had
only considered wine and tobacco, and would for the present
confine himself entirely to the latter. An excise upon tobacco
instead of customs duty would probably give relief to the
oppressed planters of America ; it would also benefit the fair
trader now injured by frauds. He then proceeded with evidence
in detail showing that such great frauds were committed by under-
weighing, false declaration, and corrupt connivance of customs
officials, that despite high charge but little revenue came to the
government, while great advantage came to the unfair trader in
underselling or forestalling his honest competitor. A small duty
was still to be paid on tobacco imported, but he proposed now to
substitute for previous customs aggregating $5\frac{1}{3}d.$ per pound an
inland duty of $4d.$ per pound, to be paid when the tobacco was
withdrawn from bonded warehouses to be sold for domestic consumption. He then made answer to some of the objections which
had been raised, and which were afterwards much harped upon,
and concluded by declaring that this scheme would not only
benefit merchants and help the revenue, but make London a free
port and by consequence the market of the world.[6]

   Walpole spoke 'with so much perspicuity and strength of
Argument, that it was allowed to exceed any Speech he ever

---

    [1] *Commons' Journals*, xxii. 77.   [2] *Daily Journal*, 15 March 1733.
    [3] Brit. Mus., Add. MS. 27732, fo. 137.
    [4] *Commons' Journals*, xxii. 89–91. 'My head is confused this morning, after
having sat twelve hours in so hot a House, as we had yesterday ' : Colonel Howard
to Lord Carlisle, 15 March 1733 ; *Carlisle MSS.* p. 104.
    [5] Brit. Mus., Add. MS. 27732, fo. 137.
    [6] Coxe, *Memoirs of . . . Sir Robert Walpole* (London, 1798), i. 385–99, who obtained
it from the Orford Papers. *Commons' Journals*, xxii. 92, 93.

made '.[1] He was answered by the leaders of the opposition, who
heaped denunciation and invective upon his proposal. Frauds
in the customs were not so great as represented. Planters were
not oppressed by the factors. The scheme tended towards a
general excise, and towards the entire overthrow of the constitution. It deprived men of the right to trial by jury. There would
be great increase in the number of officers, oppressive to the
people and dangerous to the liberties of the country. It could
ease the landed interest only at the expense of others.[2] ' The
best Speech was Sir Wm. Wyndham's, who made the Most of
a bad Cause and spoke extremely well . . . Mr. Pulteney's much
below his usual manner of speaking.' [3] The minister's friends
replied that here was no question of endangering the constitution,
but of remedying grievous frauds.[4] Walpole at last closed the
debate, and ' was in as high Spirits when he spoke last, as at the
beginning of the day '.[5] The number of members present was
471, ' as full a House perhaps as ever was known '. The question
was put after midnight, and carried by a majority of 61.[6] ' This
Event will shew that neither the Ministry nor the Parliament are
to be deterred by popular Clamour from doing what is for the
King's and the Country's Service,' wrote Delafaye.[7] Great numbers
of those interested in the wine and tobacco trade, ' the like not
seen in the Memory of Man ', had congregated in the court of
requests to influence members of their acquaintance, and when
at last the debate was over the exasperated crowd threatened
Sir Robert with violence.[8] On 16 March the report of the committee was presented, and the debate was resumed with increased
bitterness. ' Never was there a Spirit of Contradiction raised,
more irrational or unaccountable.' [9] The house agreed to accept
the report by a majority of 60, and a committee was directed to
bring in a bill.

Meanwhile the controversy raged with undiminished intensity.
The Craftsman fought a bitter contest with *The Daily Courant* and
The Daily Journal. From all over England corporate towns sent
deputations to London against the scheme.[10] Pamphlets appeared
so rapidly that the most zealous partisan could scarcely have read
them all. Nevertheless there was now for the leaders a lull while
the houses adjourned for the holidays.[11] On 4 April Sir Charles

[1] Brit. Mus., Add. MS. 27732, fo. 137.
[2] *Parl. Hist.* viii. 1281-7, 1291-5, 1296-1304.
[3] Delafaye to Sir Thomas Robinson : Brit. Mus., Add. MS. 23787, fo. 303.
[4] *Parl. Hist.* viii. 1287-91, 1295, 1296.   [5] Brit. Mus., Add. MS. 27732, fo. 138.
[6] *Ibid.* ; Coxe, iii. 129.   [7] Brit. Mus., Add. MS. 27732, fo. 139.
[8] *The Grub-street Journal*, 15 March 1733 ; *Fog's Weekly Journal* and *The Universal
Spectator*, 17 March 1733 ; Coxe, i. 402.
[9] *Daily Courant*, 19 March 1733.   [10] *Daily Journal*, 28 March 1733.
[11] Brit. Mus., Add. MS. 27732, fo. 143.

Turner presented, according to order, a bill for repealing several subsidies and for granting an inland impost. Objection was made that parts of the bill were not in accord with the resolutions ordering it, but opposition was voted down by substantial though diminishing majorities, and the second reading was to be that day seven-night.[1] 'Probably it will be a long Sessions,' wrote Delafaye, who recorded the extraordinary contest on first reading.[2] Conditions meanwhile had become worse, and now wore an ominous aspect. Letters from the boroughs to their representatives came pouring in.[3] ' Last Week, and about the Beginning of this, there were Deputies arrived from most of the Cities and principal Corporations in England, to sollicite against any new Excise.' [4] Representations came to the commons from great trading cities, and the sheriffs of London presented the petition of the city, which feared ' that the most fatal Blow which ever was given, will be given, on this Occasion, to the Trade and Navigation of *Great Britain* '.[5] Under this storm of protest Walpole receded. He did not propose, as he had intended, to excise wines ; [6] and on 11 April, the day for the second reading of his bill, he moved that this be postponed to 12 June, ' which you know is equivalent to dropping it entirely for the Sessions ', wrote a correspondent.[7] And so it was, for men understood generally that the house would rise before that time. Though contrary to expectation this did not come to pass, the commons adjourned over that day, and the excise bill was not brought forward again.[8]

The causes which led Walpole to abandon his project were not properly understood by Coxe, and were misrepresented for a long time. Coxe, believing that the true motive was unwillingness to carry any measure marked by popular disapprobation, accepted an anecdote long famous, that Sir Robert, realizing that in the present inflamed temper of the people the act could not be executed without an armed force, declared at a meeting that there would be an end of the liberties of England if supplies were to be raised by the sword, and so withdrew his measure.[9] Coxe believed also that the decline of the minister's majority from 61 to 17 afforded no explanation, since his friends did not join the

[1] *Commons' Journals*, xxii. 104.
[2] Brit. Mus., Add. MS. 27732, fos. 147, 148.
[3] *The Weekly Register ; or, Universal Journal*, 7 April 1733.
[4] *Fog's Weekly Journal*, 7 April 1733.
[5] *Commons' Journals*, xxii. 108, 109, 114.   [6] *Carlisle MSS.* p. 107.
[7] Edward Weston to James Dayrolle, 20 April 1733 : Brit. Mus., Add. MS. 15868, fo. 161 ; *Commons' Journals*, xxii. 114.
[8] Coxe, i. 403, 404.
[9] There are good reasons for doubting whether any such meeting was held : Croker's note in Hervey, i. 206. Apparently the conversation attributed to Walpole by Morley (*Walpole*, p. 174) is made up from that given by Coxe (i. 404) added to that in Hervey (i. 194), and is a paraphrase of them both.

opposition.[1]   In the light, however, of contemporary accounts,
which were published after the time of Coxe, it may be said that,
while Walpole was no doubt swayed by considerations of benevolence and moderation, nevertheless he abandoned his scheme
because he was compelled to do so.

There is no great amount of contemporary correspondence
bearing upon this. Walpole's associates merely explain that the
project had aroused such opposition that it was deemed advisable
to drop it.[2]   At first the court party had no doubt of their ability
to carry the measure, or at least they so pretended. On 15 March
Delafaye wrote to a friend : ' The House is now sitting upon the
Report, and fighting the Battle over again, but there is no manner
of Danger.'[3]   Four days later another declared : ' The main
labour of that affair is over, though it must be carefully attended
in all its steps through both houses.'[4]   A few days more and
Colonel Howard wrote to his father : ' It 's inconceivable the
clamour and spirit of opposition there is. . . . It 's thought we
shall not have finisht the two Bills next month.'[5]   On 1 April
Lady Irwin said : ' 'Tis certain Sir R. is pressed so extremely
every day in the House that 'tis thought he would be glad to
resign quietly, and has even desired it of the King.'[6]   The king,
whose civil list was to be increased, and the queen were taking
great interest in the event, and were growing more and more
alarmed as the days went on. Lord Hervey told the king that
he had never known the opposition so strong, so sanguine, and
so insolent.[7]   On 9 April Lord Scarborough told Walpole that
the clamour was so great that in his opinion the administration
ought to yield, that dislike of the scheme was universal, and that
even the soldiers, believing that the price of tobacco would rise,
were ripe for mutiny.[8]   And to the queen, when she asked his
advice, he said : ' I will answer for my regiment against the
Pretender, but not against the opposers of the Excise.'[9]   Scarborough, Chesterfield, and a number of prominent members of
the court party now declared against it.[10]   On the evening of the
ninth, it is said, Walpole conferred with the king, and it was
resolved that the bill should be dropped.[11]   Next day, on the
question of receiving the city's petition, with parliamentary precedent against petitions concerning money bills, government had
a majority of only 17. ' I believe it 's most people's opinion that
the Bill has met with its fate tonight,' wrote one member.[12]

[1] Coxe, i. 403, 404.
[2] Brit. Mus., Add. MS. 27732, fos. 152, 153 ; Coxe, iii. 131.
[3] Brit. Mus., Add. MS. 23787, fo. 303.   [4] Coxe, iii. 131.
[5] *Carlisle MSS.* p. 105.   [6] *Ibid.* p. 106.
[7] Hervey, i. 183.   [8] *Ibid.* p. 186.
[9] Maty, *Life of Chesterfield*, p. 124.   [10] *Carlisle MSS.* p. 107.
[11] Hervey, i. 188.   [12] *Carlisle MSS.* p. 107.

Opposition now looked for the immediate disgrace of Walpole
and the total overthrow of his administration : [1] ' it may happen
to prove like Dr. Sachevrell's affair, and produce a change in the
Ministry.' [2] ' It is over,' said the queen, when she heard the
news, ' we must give way ' ; and that night at supper Walpole
declared to his intimate friends that the bill would be given up.
' This dance it will no farther go, and to-morrow I intend to
sound a retreat.' [3] Sir Thomas Robinson, who wrote a detailed
account of the progress of the bill in the commons, and who
recorded the ministry's dwindling majorities as the days went by,
says that on the day appointed for second reading many of those
who had deserted Walpole but not voted against him, ' came
down with a resolution openly to join with the enemy '.[4] In 1742,
when Walpole had at last been driven from office, William Pitt,
speaking upon the motion to inquire into the conduct of the late
administration, said : [5]

I come now, in course, to the excise scheme, which the hon. gentleman
says ought to be forgiven, because it was easily given up. Sir, it was not
easily given up. The promoter of that scheme did not easily give it up ;
he gave it up with sorrow, with tears in his eyes, when he saw, and not
till he saw it impossible to carry it through the House. Did not his
majority decrease upon every division ? It was almost certain, that if he
had pushed in any further, the majority would have turned against him.

It may be that popular demonstrations had something to do
with the event.[6] There were riotous scenes about the house of
commons. Members were hissed and cried at as they came out.
A great crowd filled the lobby and the court of requests. Once
Sir Robert left by the back way through the speaker's chamber ;
but when the bill was given up, he came out surrounded by
friends and guarded by constables. There was a struggle to come
at him, and much beating of sticks. One fellow caught him by
the collar, and had he been thrown, he must have been trodden
to death, but he got away at last safely to his chariot.[7] Next
day the commons solemnly resolved that such behaviour was

---

[1] ' Sir Robert Walpole . . . was never more struck with any defeat or less able to
disguise his being so than this night. He stood some time after the House was up,
leaning against the table with his hat pulled over his eyes, some few friends with
melancholy countenances round him, whilst his enemies with the gayety of so many
bridegrooms seemed as just entering on the enjoyment of what they had been so long
pursuing.' Hervey, i. 192.

[2] Lady Irwin to Lord Carlisle, 12 April 1733 : *Carlisle MSS.* p. 108.

[3] Hervey, i. 192, 194.   [4] *Carlisle MSS.* pp. 108–10.

[5] [John Almon], *Anecdotes of the Life of . . . William Pitt . . . with His Speeches
in Parliament,* &c. (London, 1810), i. 69, 70.

[6] A ministerial pamphleteer takes pains to state explicitly that Walpole was not
terrified : *A Letter from a Member of Parliament for a Borough in the West,* pp. 31, 32.

[7] Brit. Mus., Add. MS. 23788, fo. 79 ; *London Evening-Post,* 12 April 1733 ;
Hervey, i. 181, 196 ; *Carlisle MSS.* p. 108.

' a most outrageous and dangerous Violation of the Rights of Parliament, and an high Crime and Misdemeanour '.[1]

How inflamed the populace was may be judged from the wild rejoicings that followed. In London there was crying of uproarious ballads,[2] ringing of bells, great fires, burning of Walpole and the queen in effigy, and shouts of ' No Excise, no Wooden Shoes '.[3] At Liverpool two excisemen were burned in effigy, and guns were fired in honour of those who had voted against the bill.[4] At Bristol was a holiday for school children and great rejoicing.[5] Throughout England there were drinking of healths, illuminations, and hanging and burning in effigy.[6] According to an opposition paper the ' Rejoycings ' were ' more General, than ever were any since the Restoration of King Charles IId ' ; while in Scotland they ' were greater than ever were known upon any Occasion whatsoever '.[7] Probably this joy was exaggerated by those who reported it, and apparently there was in some places regret that the scheme had been abandoned.[8] A list of those who had voted for and against the excise bill was circulated,[9] and members returning home were received with ovation or opprobrium.[10] At the end of the session the king in his speech referred to ' the wicked Endeavours that have lately been made Use of, to inflame the Minds of the People ', and the ' Tumults and Disorders, that almost threatened the Peace of the Kingdom '.[11]

Certainly the victory was hailed as a great triumph for the opposition. A writer in *The Craftsman* said : [12]

We have seen an *insolent, domineering Minister* reduc'd after all his Defyances, to the wretched Necessity of recanting his *abusive Reflections*, and giving up his *infamous Projects*, with Tears in his Eyes, which seem'd to flow from an equal Mixture of impotent Rage and Pusillanimity. We have seen Him hurried, by the Consciousness of his own Guilt, into dreadful Apprehensions of Danger, and skulking through *private Passages*, for the Security of his Person.

[1] *Commons' Journals*, xxii. 115.

[2] *The London Merchants Triumphant : or Sturdy Beggars are Brave Fellows. A New Ballad Proper to be Sung on the 12th of June*, &c. (London, 1733) ; *The City Triumphant : or, the Burning of the Excise-Monster. A New Ballad*, &c. (London, 1733) ; ' R—b—n in the Suds, or, a Hue and Cry after the Bill of Excise ', *Ballads and Broadsides, Haslewood Collection*, p. 65.

[3] *Fog's Weekly Journal* and *The Universal Spectator*, 14 April 1733.

[4] *London Evening-Post*, 19 April 1733.   [5] *Daily Courant*, 19 April 1733.

[6] *Fog's Weekly Journal*, 21 April 1733.

[7] *Ibid.*, 21 April, 19 May 1733.

[8] *Daily Courant*, 3 May 1733 ; Brit. Mus., Add. MS. 27732, fo. 155.

[9] *Fog's Weekly Journal*, 7 July 1733 ; *Some Observations upon a Paper, Intituled, the List*.

[10] *State Papers, Dom., George II*, xxx, 13 July 1733.

[11] *Lords' Journals*, xxiv. 311.   [12] 28 April 1733.

And 'his memorable Overthrow last Spring' was mentioned by a pamphleteer afterwards.[1] Some said that Walpole had been forced to drop the bill,[2] and others that he should not have been allowed to abandon it so easily.[3] The truth is, however, that the triumph of the opposition went no farther than causing the scheme to be given up. They did not venture, as they desired, to move that it be rejected with condemnation,[4] and shortly after an attack on the existing excise laws, in a petition from dealers in tea and coffee, was easily defeated. Futhermore, in a struggle to elect a committee to inquire into the frauds in the customs a decisive victory was won by the ministerial party.[5] ' I believe Sir Robert has stood a trial that no Minister besides himself could have done,' said an observer.[6] Such was the constitution of cabinet government at this time that Walpole, retaining the personal favour of the king, found his power little shaken, but was able to take summary vengeance upon those who had failed him or joined with the opposition.[7]

When the bill was dropped the controversy by no means came to an end. The opposition was loath to let the fury which they had raised die out, and the supporters of the ministry redoubled their defence in paper and pamphlet. ' The close of this Session will probably be attended with a Shower of these Poison'd Arrows,' wrote an informer about libellous pamphlets ;[8] and, indeed, an attempt was made to fan the spirit of faction by asserting that the government would shortly bring forward its excise plan anew. ' The *Projector* hath not yet laid his *Scheme* aside ; and only waits for a proper Opportunity to *revive* it,' said *The Craftsman*.[9] Throughout the year 1733 and also in the earlier part of the following year a great number of writings continued to appear. I propose to examine together the arguments which were advanced in the transient publications on the two sides during the course of the controversy.

In the bitter accusations which were hurled from one side to the other each party accused the other of acting in bad faith. Ministerial writers affirmed that some opposed the excise from engagement to party, some out of resentment to ministers, and some through apprehension of popular commotion ; that some

[1] [Pulteney ?], *A Review of the Excise-Scheme*, p. 4.

[2] *A Second Review of the Late Excise Scheme*, p. 3 ; [Pulteney], *An Humble Address to the Knights, Citizens, and Burgesses*, p. 18.

[3] [Pulteney], *The Late Excise Scheme Dissected*, p. 1.

[4] The opposition desired ' that it should be rejected, and a mark put upon it to prevent any future Minister ever undertaking another scheme so greatly detrimental to trade and to the liberties of the people ' : *Carlisle MSS.* p. 110 ; Hervey, i. 194, 195.

[5] Coxe, i. 403–5 ; Brit. Mus., Add. MS. 27732, fos. 162, 163.

[6] *Carlisle MSS.* p. 113.   [7] Brit. Mus., Add. MS. 23788, fos. 99, 134.

[8] *State Papers, Dom., George II*, xxix, 17 April 1733.   [9] 26 May 1733.

who had formerly been zealous for excises now cried out against the scheme as a badge of slavery ; that the principal opponents were vintners and tobacconists : [1] ' They who gain by cheating the Publick, would cheat it still, and account it high Injustice to be forced to be just.' [2] Some were those who profited by frauds in the customs, others those who would oppose every measure of the administration.[3] Caution was given that such poisoning of the mind of the nation might make the Hanoverian dynasty less secure, and bring back popery and arbitrary power ; [4] while as the contest waxed more desperate and bitter the opponents were traitors, papists, Jacobites, non-jurors, and enemies of country and church.[5] The anti-ministerial writers, catching the public ear first, busied themselves rather with attacking the scheme itself, but they represented their opponents as ' Hireling Scriblers, and such Gentry '.[6] In this contest of wits Walpole took some part with strong, clear, and well-reasoned writing, but not so much as Pulteney, who, with Bolingbroke, used bitter and violent but clever arguments.

Generally speaking, Walpole's adherents declared that excise was a desirable mode of taxation. ' Whilst there are Men and Evil in the World, there must be Laws and Taxes,' and the business of government was to see to it that they were carefully and equally laid.[7] Taxes ought to be such as could be most easily borne by the body of the people.[8] Excises tended to the true interest of trade, the relief of land, and the increase of public revenue ; [9] and they were preferable to customs duties.[10] Every thriving nation in the world now chose to raise revenue by inland duties rather than customs.[11] The whole question in dispute was

[1] A Letter from a Member of Parliament for a Borough in the West, pp. 13, 19 ; [Walpole ?], A Vindication of the Conduct of the Ministry, pp. 14, 15.

[2] [Walpole], Some General Considerations Concerning the Alteration and Improvement of Publick Revenues, p. 24.

[3] A Letter to William Pulteney, Esq., p. 12.

[4] The Thoughts of an Impartial Man, pp. 4, 5.

[5] ' The M——l Writers, unable to defend their Proceedings by Reason, have gone another, tho' not so candid a Way to work, and represented all that oppos'd them as Jacobites or Republicans ' : [Pulteney], A Letter from a Member of Parliament, p. 27. For example, [Walpole], A Letter from a Member of Parliament to His Friends, p. 18 ; The Landed Interest Consider'd, pp. 3–6 ; The Rise and Fall of the late Projected Excise, pp. 60, 61 ; London Journal, 17 March 1733.

[6] Fog's Weekly Journal, 13 January 1733.

[7] [Walpole], Some General Considerations, pp. 16, 17.

[8] [Walpole], A Letter from a Member of Parliament, p. 10.

[9] The Reply of a Member of Parliament, p. 16.

[10] ' The nearer the Duty upon any Commodity is paid to the time of Consumption, the Consumer may be afforded that Commodity the cheaper ; and as the Consumer is the Person that pays all Taxes, in that Respect the Tax is itself lessened by its being collected as an Excise ' : Considerations Occasioned by the Craftsman upon Excises, p. 9.

[11] Daily Courant, 19 March 1733.

merely whether if existing duties on wine and tobacco were collected by excise it would not be more advantageous to king and people.[1] By the new method the merchant would pay in proportion to his sale, when the sale was made.[2] To this it was replied that excises were ' Poll-Taxes upon the *Consumer*, raised without Distinction of Ranks, or Abilities, at an immoderate and unnecessary Expence, which levy above double the Sum upon the *People*, which They bring in to the *Government* '.[3] Far from producing the £500,000 promised, the tobacco excise would probably yield less than £30,000, and that on wine would give nothing ; or, if half a million was to be raised, a million must be taken from the people ;[4] while if for the two-shilling land-tax, which produced a million, an excise were substituted, two millions must be taken, ' which must destroy every Subject of Trade in *Britain* '.[5] It was not so cheap and easy to collect as a land-tax, and would be found to be vexatious to merchants in many ways. It would cause ' intolerable Vexations and Troubles ', and be ' the greatest Oppression upon Trade that can be conceived '.[6] One writer knew of eminent merchants prepared to sell their stock and leave off trade if the bill should pass.[7]

The greatest benefit would be stopping of smuggling and frauds in the customs. The greatness of these evils could scarcely be disputed ;[8] though Pulteney affected doubt, and certain London merchants criticized the accounts which had been circulated.[9] The report of the investigating committee showed that smugglers worked boldly and with knavery well organized.[10] In the past ten years many customs officers had been abused or murdered, great quantities of goods had been seized and condemned, and numerous vessels forfeited.[11] In addition to the actual running of goods there were glaring and flagitious frauds. Walpole asserted that the gross produce of the tobacco customs was £750,000, the net return only £160,000.[12] With the connivance of the customs officials this cheating had been reduced to a

---

[1] *Some Observations on National Treaties*, pp. 14, 15.

[2] [Walpole ?], *A Vindication of the Conduct of the Ministry*, pp. 27, 28.

[3] [Pulteney ?], *A Review of the Excise-Scheme*, p. 22.   [4] *Ibid.* p. 16.

[5] [Bolingbroke], *The Freeholder's Political Catechism*, p. 21.

[6] *Some Seasonable Animadversions on Excises*, pp. 4, 8.

[7] *Fog's Weekly Journal*, 24 March 1733.

[8] [Walpole ?], *A Vindication of the Conduct of the Ministry*, p. 15.

[9] [Pulteney], *The Budget Opened*, pp. 10, 11 ; *Daily Journal*, 31 March 1733.

[10] ' The Smugglers being grown to such a Degree of Insolence, as to carry on their wicked Practices by Force and Violence, not only in the Country and remote Parts of the Kingdom, but even in the City of *London* itself ; going in Gangs, armed with Swords, Pistols, and other Weapons, even to the Number of Forty or Fifty, by which Means they have been too strong not only for the Officers of the Revenue, but for the Civil Magistrates ' : *The Report . . . from the Committee . . . Appointed to enquire into the Frauds and Abuses in the Customs*, p. 16.

[11] *Ibid.*   [12] Coxe, i. 390.

system.[1] By this means, said Walpole, ' Every individual in the
nation must be a *sufferer* . . . while the unrighteous gains centre
in *very few* pockets, and in *very few* places ' ; [2] and he intimated
that much opposition came from those who feared that the excise
reform would interfere with their unlawful gains.[3] It was pointed
out that if all this could be brought to an end the honest trader
would be relieved of unfair competition, and the government,
actually collecting the tax on wine and tobacco, would receive
£500,000 now diverted to breakers of the law, and be able to
relieve the people of England of just so much taxation.[4] And
yet some had spoken ' as if the restraining of a few Knaves
were Matter of Oppression to all Men '.[5] It was answered that
if the customs officials were corrupt, they should be punished
by the government and the system better managed.[6] As for the
smuggling, it would continue as long as the duties were so high ;
and excise would be no prevention. Tea was excised, and not
half of it paid. ' No Goods have been so much run of late Years,
as exciseable Goods.' [7] There would be no benefit to the honest
merchant, because his goods would be made dearer : and the
enhanced price of the commodity would be shared by all consumers.[8]

Another good result would be the relief of the landed interest.
Walpole had long had this in mind.[9] Not long before this a writer
declared that ' in a Country which chiefly subsists by Trade, the
Value of Land is little regarded '.[10] In the years since 1688, it
was said, the landed men had paid to support the government
nearly £65,000,000 ; and they sometimes felt that the revolution
had been a calamity, since it had put heavy burdens upon their
estates from which they were never to be released.[11] The land-tax
was unequal because it was borne by one-twentieth of the population, while some other forms of property escaped altogether.[12]
Therefore the country gentlemen were appealed to for support
in this crisis, since with excise the government would be able to

---

[1] *The Report*, particularly the appendix ; [Walpole ?], *A Vindication of the Conduct of the Ministry*, pp. 9–12.

[2] [Walpole], *A Letter from a Member of Parliament*, p. 4.   [3] *Ibid.* p. 19.

[4] *London Journal*, 17, 24 March 1733.   [5] *An Appeal to the Landholders*, p. 5.

[6] [Pulteney], *The Budget Opened*, p. 14 ; [Pulteney ?], *A Review of the Excise-Scheme*, pp. 11, 12.

[7] [Pulteney], *The Second Part of an Argument*, p. 45 ; *Observations upon the Laws of Excise*, p. 13 ; *Fog's Weekly Journal*, 7 April 1733.

[8] [Pulteney], *The Second Part of an Argument*, pp. 18, 45.

[9] ' Of all Taxes, he rightly judged that the *Land Tax* was *the most unequal* ' : *A Letter to a Freeholder, on the Late Reduction of the Land Tax*, p. 7.

[10] *A Letter to a Member of Parliament Concerning the Reduction of Interest* (London, 1732), p. 8.

[11] *The Reply of a Member of Parliament*, p. 37 ; *Parl. Hist.* viii. 1322 ; *An Appeal to the Landholders*, pp. 6, 7, 10.

[12] *The Case of the Salt-Duty and Land-Tax*, pp. 8–17.

collect revenue of which it was now defrauded, and use this
amount to reduce the burden upon land.[1] *The Craftsman* retorted
that the benefit was doubtful, and Pulteney, following the old
argument of Locke, declared that all taxes fell ultimately upon
the land.[2]

It was said that the operation of the excise law would bring
much-needed relief to the colonial planters, now suffering under
great oppression at the hands of the tobacco factors, who controlled the import into England.[3] This was denied, for it was
said that excise would interfere with the system of credit now
prevailing, and, by enhancing the price, would lessen the consumption and so injure colonial trade.[4]

The argument of the opposition was that in general excise was
an evil thing, and they said that the present scheme was only
part of a plan to excise all commodities or most of them.[5] ' *The
Execution of* this Scheme *hath a natural and immediate Tendency
to a* GENERAL EXCISE,' said Pulteney ; [6] and in the minds of the
unreasoning this argument swept all before it. ' No such Thing
was or is intended, nor can ever be effected,' was the answer ; [7]
and ministerial writers lamented in vain the mischief which had
been unjustly done.[8]

Many things made this excise dangerous to the English people,
particularly the fact that it tended to increase the power of the
ministry and of the Crown. ' Do you in your Consciences believe
that the late *Excise-Scheme* . . . did not contain ·a *whole System
of Oppression*, and strike at the very Vitals of our *Constitution* ? '
asked Pulteney.[9] He said that the flood-gates of tyranny would
be opened, and all the evils of absolute government rush in.[10] If
the expectations of the promoters of the scheme were realized,
there would be an increase of the king's civil list, and an added
fund of £420,000 established for ever for the current service of
the year.[11] This would be paid to the Crown in lieu of a tax
annually granted.[12] Parliaments might come to have little influence if the members changed ' an *annual Tax* into a *perpetual
Excise* '.[13] ' Parliaments, who have no more to give, may be dis-

    The Landed Interest Consider'd, &c. (London, 1733) ; An Appeal to the Land-
holders, p. 24.
    [2] Craftsman, 17 February 1733 ; [Pulteney ?], A Review of the Excise-Scheme, p. 22.
    [3] The Case of the Planters of Tobacco in Virginia.
    [4] Observations upon the Laws of Excise, pp. 7, 8 ; An Answer to the Considerations,
Occasioned by the Craftsman upon Excise, pp. 12–14.
    [5] Parl. Hist. viii. 1234, 1298.   [6] The Second Part of an Argument, p. 48.
    [7] [Walpole], Some General Considerations, p. 11.
    [8] An Appeal to the Landholders, p. 15 ; The Thoughts of an Impartial Man, p. 21.
    [9] An Humble Address to the Knights, p. 30.
    [10] [Pulteney], The Late Excise Scheme Dissected, p. 6.
    [11] Ibid. p. 75.   [12] Ibid. p. 24.
    [13] [Pulteney], A Letter from a Member of Parliament, p. 17 ; Parl. Hist. viii. 1220.

appointed in the Redress of their Grievances,' said Bolingbroke.[1] Had the Crown once had such power in the days of Strafford and Laud, there would have been no parliament called and no redress of grievances, but perhaps star chamber and arbitrary power continuing.[2] In limited governments, if ever the people yielded to the executive any part of their liberty it was rarely recovered again.[3] In England absolute monarchy might be established, if not by dispensing with parliament, then by making it subservient, and this the king might do with the excise revenue in his power.[4] Moreover, the multitude of excise officers could influence elections.[5] If all this were brought to pass, parliaments would be useless, and no scourge and terror for evil ministers.[6] If the excise should yield an additional £500,000, were the English people to give up for this liberties for which they had expended two hundred millions in the past half-century, and for which they continued to expend above five millions a year?[7] There were, moreover, the objections that a person accused of violating the law was obliged to prove his innocence, and was deprived of trial by jury, and that the excise office was not unlike the inquisition.[8] Excises were inconsistent with the liberty of a free people, and would reduce Englishmen to the miserable state of the people of France, where there was horrible tyranny and arbitrary power, based upon standing armies and numerous excises, for such were *gabelles*, *aides*, and *entrées*, albeit with other names.[9] Walpole's friends had scant success in replying that no additional tax was being imposed, that the civil list was little increased, that excise revenue, though raised in perpetuity, was yet to be applied annually by parliament, and that the mode of trial was designed solely to be convenient for traders, and had been so found.[10] And they said that excises neither made nor unmade the liberties of a people, and instanced Holland.[11]

Changes were rung also upon the topics of the vast throng of officers necessary to enforce the law, the power which they would

---

[1] *The Freeholder's Political Catechism*, p. 21.
[2] [Pulteney], *A Letter from a Member*, pp. 14, 15.
[3] *Observations upon the Laws of Excise*, p. 3.
[4] [Pulteney], *The Late Excise Scheme Dissected*, pp. 7–22.
[5] *A Second Review of the Late Excise Scheme*, pp. 14, 33.
[6] *Ibid.* p. 15; *Parl. Hist.* viii. 1298.
[7] [Pulteney ?], *A Review of the Excise-Scheme*, p. 57.
[8] [Pulteney], *The Late Excise Scheme Dissected*, pp. 35, 63; *The Second Part of an Argument*, pp. 10, 58; *Craftsman*, 7 July 1733.
[9] *Observations upon the Laws of Excise*, p. 5; *A Second Review of the Late Excise Scheme*, p. 4; *Fog's Weekly Journal*, 24 November 1733; *French Excise*, pp. 1, 21, 22, 31.
[10] *London Journal*, 7 July 1733; *The Reply of a Member of Parliament*, p. 33; [Walpole ?], *A Vindication of the Conduct of the Ministry*, pp. 32–5.
[11] *Considerations Occasioned by the Craftsman upon Excises*, p. 25.

give, and the oppression which they would exert. The debts,
the taxes, and the officers of England had already given the king
a kind of power unknown in former days.[1] The excise would
increase the number of dependants whom a minister could control,
and enable him to influence elections in all parts of England.[2]
Merchants would have to deal with a larger number of officers,
and so suffer greater inconvenience.[3] It was answered that there
was to be no army of excisemen, burdensome to maintain, but
perhaps 150, or about three for each county, that they would
not meddle in the elections, and not be qualified to be elected
to parliament.[4] Was it not better to maintain this small number
at moderate charge than for the freeholders to go on paying half
a million a year for ever ? [5]

The power of the excise officers to search was played upon as
a dreadful thing. They might come when they wished, at any
hour of day or night, it was said, and enter even the rooms of
the wives and daughters.[6] ' Really,' said one writer, ' I can't
help thinking, that for a free-born *Englishman* to have his Ware-
house, Shop, and House, even to his WIFE'S BEDCHAMBER, visited
and rummaged, at all Hours of the Day or Night, by every pert
Rascal that shall think it worth his While to be troublesome . . .
is an Inconvenience, to which even the Gentleman who treats it
so mildly would not care to be subject.' [7] The reply was that
all this alarm was baseless. Everything was liable to abuse, but
at present officers visited brewers, chandlers, maltsters, soap-
makers, and tanners.[8] Excise officers had really no greater power
than officers of the customs, except that they entered the ware-
house instead of the ship ; nor could they enter a house without
first demanding admittance, and if they committed injury they
were liable to action.[9] Honest traders had nothing to dread, said
Walpole ; it was those who had to conceal iniquity who were
loud in their clamour.[10]

The controversy raged fiercely without abatement after the

[1] [Pulteney], *The Second Part of an Argument*, p. 43.

[2] [Pulteney], *The Budget Opened*, p. 30 ; *Some Seasonable Animadversions*, p. 20 ;
Parl. Hist. viii. 1324.

[3] [Pulteney], *The Late Excise Scheme Dissected*, pp. 29, 30 ; *Parl. Hist.* viii. 1302.

[4] [Walpole], *A Letter from a Member of Parliament*, p. 32 ; *The Reply of a Member
of Parliament*, pp. 31, 32 ; *Daily Courant*, 12 March 1733.

[5] *A Letter from a Member of Parliament for a Borough in the West*, pp. 12, 13.

[6] [Pulteney], *The Late Excise Scheme Dissected*, pp. 57–60 ; *The Reply of a Member
of Parliament*, p. 23.

[7] *A Second Review of the Late Excise Scheme*, pp. 26, 27.

[8] [Walpole], *A Letter from a Member of Parliament*, p. 7 ; *Reflections upon a
Pamphlet*, p. 20 ; *An Appeal to the Landholders*, p. 8.

[9] [Walpole ?], *A Vindication of the Conduct of the Ministry*, p. 32 ; *Reflections upon
a Pamphlet*, p. 19.

[10] [Walpole], *A Letter from a Member of Parliament*, pp. 28, 29.

scheme had been abandoned, because the opposition, having found
an issue with which to discredit the ministry, desired to discredit
it further, and because the government attempted to retrieve
some of what had been lost by explaining that excise was not
a bad thing. Prodigious efforts were made on both sides because
the first parliament of George II was nearly at an end, and
a general election was approaching. In September Newcastle
wrote : ' Our Affairs att home, tho I believe in no Sort of Uncertainty or danger, are farr from a State of Peace or Tranquility,
Warr as I said declared in every County, against next Election.' [1]
He added that his friends would certainly carry the parliament.
In December one of these wrote that prospects were promising,
but everywhere strong opposition.[2]

Pulteney published a pamphlet which he said was ' designed
as a New-Year's Gift, *proper* to be presented by all *honest* Candidates to their Electors '. In this he assumed that had the excise
bill been passed by parliament, the king would have spurned it
with indignation from the throne.[3] One urged electors to choose
earnest, capable representatives, not placemen or pensioners, nor
those who had ' endeavoured to entail Taxes upon you and your
Posterity, and would in Time have EXCISED even your very
Teeth '.[4] Another, beseeching men to oppose the minister at the
ensuing election, declared that children yet unborn would bless
or censure their conduct on this occasion.[5] But now that the
wild fury and unreason of the earlier contest had died down with
the abandonment of the project, the court writers obtained a
hearing with greater success. Patiently they explained all the
aspects of the plan, so that an opponent lamented that they
behaved as men whose ideas had not been refuted.[6] They said
that the scheme had been only to change the method of collecting
the duties laid on wine and tobacco, that the plan had been
proposed in good faith, and abandoned when seen to be contrary
to the wishes or best interests of the British people.[7] The present
parliament had done many excellent things, and its members
should not fail of re-election merely because they had favoured
the excise.[8] As always, support was urged for liberty, and for the
Hanoverian establishment, and for the church.[9] Through the

---

[1] Brit. Mus., Add. MS. 27732, fo. 245.   [2] *Ibid.* fo. 298.
[3] [Pulteney], *The Late Excise Scheme Dissected*, p. 18.
[4] *Advice to the Freeholders and Burghers of Great Britain*, p. 14.
[5] *A Second Review of the Late Excise Scheme*, p. 47.
[6] [Pulteney ?], *A Review of the Excise-Scheme.*
[7] [Walpole ?], *A Vindication of the Conduct of the Ministry*, pp. 6, 7 ; *The Rise
and Fall of the late Projected Excise*, p. 20 ; *Serious Reflections on the Present Condition
of Great-Britain, &c.* (London, 1733), p. 15.
[8] *Some Reasons for continuing the Present Parliament*, p. 32 ; *The Thoughts of an
Impartial Man*, p. 26.
[9] *Serious Reflections*, p. 8.

summer and autumn of 1733, on through the winter, and through the spring of the next year, Newcastle, that able and indefatigable party manager, worked for success in the elections, and ministers at length secured a safe though diminished majority.[1] Thus the episode came to an end, for the later contests with Walpole were fought out on other issues.

There were afterwards some who believed that the minister was mistaken in dropping his scheme, and that he might well have carried it.[2] But for long the hatred and odium persisted. When the removal of Walpole was debated in 1742, Lord Halifax declared that the excise was ' such an attack of our natural and constitutional rights, as was never perhaps pardoned by any nation '.[3] In later years there were pamphlets. Bolingbroke denounced it in a book which instructed princes,[4] and later it was held to scorn by a writer who condemned all prime ministers and evil favourites of the king.[5] But the judgement of posterity is better reflected in the opinion of one who stood for the cause when it failed, that ' The Thing was lost for not being generally understood ; and interested Men, supported by angry Men, prevailed, by raising false Alarms '.[6]   RAYMOND TURNER.

APPENDIX

LIST OF THE MORE IMPORTANT PAMPHLETS

In the brackets prefixed to titles are given the names of the authors, where they can be ascertained, following largely the ascription in the catalogue of the British Museum ; in the brackets appended are approximate dates of publication within the years, from advertisements in contemporary newspapers.

(a) For the excise scheme or the ministry

An Appeal to the Landholders Concerning the Reasonableness and General Benefit of an Excise upon Tobacco and Wine (London, 1733 [13 March]).

The Case of the Planters of Tobacco in Virginia, as Represented by Themselves, &c. (London, 1733 [15 March]).

The Conduct of the Ministry Compared with its Consequences : or an Impartial View of the Present State of Affairs (London, 1733).

Considerations Occasioned by the Craftsman upon Excises, &c. (London, 1733).

A Dialogue between Sir Andrew Freeport and Timothy Squat, Esquire, on the Subject of Excises, &c. (London, 1733 [10 March]).

---

[1] Basil Williams, *The Duke of Newcastle and the Election of 1734, ante*, xii. 448–88.
[2] *Parl. Hist.* ix. 262.   [3] *Ibid.* xi. 1210.
[4] *Letters. I. On the Spirit of Patriotism* (London, 1749), pp. 26, 27.
[5] *The History of Prime Ministers and Favourites, in England*, &c. (London, 1763), pp. 155–7.
[6] *A Letter from a Member of Parliament for a Borough in the West*, p. 15.

A Letter from a Member of Parliament for a Borough in the West, to a Noble Lord in his Neighbourhood there, concerning the Excise-Bill, and the Manner and Causes of losing it (London, 1733 [2 June]).

[Sir Robert Walpole], *A Letter from a Member of Parliament to His Friends in the Country, concerning the Duties on Wine and Tobacco, &c.* (London, 1733 [23 February]).

A Letter to the People of England in General (London, 1734).

A Letter to William Pulteney, Esq., concerning the Administration of Affairs in Great Britain for several Years passed, and the present State thereof, with Observations on our polemical Writers (London, 1733).

Reflections upon a Pamphlet, Entitled Observations upon the Laws of Excise, &c. (London, 1733).

The Reply of a Member of Parliament to the Mayor of His Corporation (London, 1733 [3 March]).

The Report, with the Appendix, from the Committee of the House of Commons Appointed to enquire into the Frauds and Abuses in the Customs, to the Prejudice of Trade, and Diminution of the Revenue. Published by Order of the House of Commons (London, 1733 [7 June]).

[H. Walpole and M. Concanen ?], *The Rise and Fall of the late Projected Excise, Impartially Consider'd. By a Friend to the English Constitution, &c.* (London, 1733 [6 October]).

[Sir Robert Walpole], *Some General Considerations concerning the Alteration and Improvement of Publick Revenues* (London, 1733 [14 March]).

[*Some Observations on National Treaties, &c.* (no title-page), includes] *An Impartial Enquiry into the Present Question concerning Excise; in which the Advantages arising to the King and Subject, from raising Duties by Excise, are demonstrated, and the Objections thereto obviated* [1733].

Some Observations upon a Paper, Intituled, the List. That is, of those who Voted for and against the Excise-Bill (London, 1733 [6 October]).

Some Reasons for continuing the Present Parliament, &c. (London, 1733 [27 October]).

The Thoughts of an Impartial Man upon the Present Temper of the Nation; Offer'd to the Consideration of the Freeholders of Great-Britain (London, 1733).

[Sir Robert Walpole ?], *A Vindication of the Conduct of the Ministry, in the Scheme of the Excise on Wine and Tobacco, &c.* (London, 1734).

(b) Against the excise or the ministry

Advice to the Freeholders and Burghers of Great Britain. Containing Rules and Directions for the Choice of Members to serve in Parliament, &c. (London, [1734]).

An Answer to the Considerations, Occasioned by the Craftsman upon Excise, &c. (London, 1733 [10 January]).

[Nicholas Amhurst or William Pulteney], *An Argument against Excises, in several Essays, lately published in the Craftsman, and now collected together, &c.* (London, 1733 [8 January]).

[Pulteney], *The Budget Opened. Or, an Answer to a Pamphlet Intitled, a Letter from a Member of Parliament to his Friends in the Country, &c.* (London, 1733 [13 March]).

A Collection of Letters from Several Counties, Cities and Boroughs. Containing, Instructions to their Representatives in Parliament to Oppose any Extension of the Excise Laws (London, 1733 [14 March]).

Excise Anotomiz'd, and Trade Epitomiz'd : Declaring, that unequall Imposition of Excise, to be the only cause of the ruine of Trade, and universall impoverishment of this whole Nation. By Z. G. a well wisher of the Common good, &c. (London, 1659, republished 1733 [14 February]).

Excise : Being a Collection of Letters, &c. Containing, the Sentiments and Instructions of the Merchants, Traders, Gentry, and Inhabitants of the principal Cities, Counties, Towns, and Boroughs, in England, to their Representatives in Parliament, against a New Excise, or any Extension of Excise Laws, in what Shape soever, &c. (London, 1733).

[Bolingbroke—according to the edition of 1769, Dr. Arbuthnot], *The Freeholder's Political Catechism* (London, 1733 [8 September]).

French Excise : or, a Compendious Account of the Several Excises in France, and the Oppressive Methods us'd in Collecting them. Published for the Information of the People of Great-Britain (London, [1733 ?]).

[Pulteney], *An Humble Address to the Knights, Citizens, and Burgesses, Elected to represent the Commons of Great Britain in the Ensuing Parliament,* &c. (London, 1734).

[Pulteney], *The Late Excise Scheme Dissected : or, an Exact Copy of the Late Bill,* &c. (London, 1734).

[Pulteney ?], *A Letter from a Member of Parliament to His Friend in the Country ; Giving his Reasons for opposing the farther Extension of the Excise Laws,* &c. (London, [1733]).

A Letter from a Merchant of London to a Member of Parliament, &c. (London, 1733 [14 March]).

The Most Important Transactions of the Sixth Session of the First Parliament of His Majesty King George II, &c. (London, [1733], contains a ' True Copy ' of the excise bill, revised and approved by two gentlemen who voted against it).

Observations upon the Laws of Excise : Shewing, I. That Excises must be destructive of Trade in General. II. That Excises are inconsistent with the Liberties of a Free People (London, [1733, 5 January]).

[Pulteney ?], *A Review of the Excise-Scheme ; in Answer to a Pamphlet, intitled the Rise and Fall of the late projected Excise,* &c. (London, 1733).

[Pulteney], *The Second Part of an Argument against Excises,* &c. (London, 1733 [15 January]).

A Second Review of the late Excise Scheme : Being a Full Answer to a Scurrilous Pamphlet, Entitled the Rise and Fall of the late Projected Excise, &c. (London, 1734).

Some Seasonable Animadversions on Excises : Occasion'd by a Pamphlet lately publish'd, Entituled, Considerations occasion'd by the Craftsman &c. (London, 1733 [17 January]).

Edmund Burke and the First Rocking-ham Ministry[1]

'THERE never was a season more favourable for any man who chose to enter into the career of public life.'[2] So Burke wrote of the time of his political beginnings, and with justice, as his own experience bears out. The break-down of the predominance of half a century had brought about a time of change within the solid ranks of the great whig connexion to which he belonged, and in which, always against the old traditional background, new men and policies were coming to the fore. It was in the opposition of 1762–5 and the short ministry of 1765–6 that such men as the Townshends, the younger Onslow, Dowdeswell, Meredith, and Burke himself, never before of much prominence, laid the practical foundations of that political theory which Burke was to evolve for his half-comprehending but admiring party, and gave form to the whiggism of the second half of the eighteenth century. Theory and practice grew up closely side by side. Of the former a supporter said, with simple surprise, ' Although everything seemed a kind of new political philosophy, yet it was all to the purpose ',[3] and for the reason that both theory and the actions of the men for whom it was made were being moulded by the difficulties of a new transition from government to opposition.

Nothing is more difficult than to show accurately the ' connexions ' which lay behind the names of whig and tory in the middle of the eighteenth century. Throughout the shifting of the groups, however, there is clear a more or less permanent tenure of power in the hands of the great whig connexions of Pelham and Cavendish, sometimes in alliance with those of Russell and Grenville. Round this nucleus grew up a certain solidarity and the traditions of aristocratic rule characteristic of the age. It is this group that is here called for convenience (by analogy with Disraeli's phrase) the ' High Whigs '. On Newcastle's authority, they

[1] Since this was written an article has appeared in the *American Historical Review*, vol. xxxv, p. 735, by W. T. Laprade, 'The Stamp Act in British Politics.' It uses the contemporary press to advantage, but only touches lightly on the questions treated here.
[2] *Burke Corr.* i. 67, Burke to Hely Hutchinson, n.d. (c. May 1765).
[3] *Ibid.* 103, Marriott to Burke, February 1766.

are subdivided into the ' Great Whigs '—the aristocratic leaders—
and the ' Little ' [1] or ' Young Whigs ', their followers. In contradiction to the ' High Whigs ' stand the various bands of ' Rebel
Whigs ', who broke off from time to time into the opposition which
long centred in Leicester House. From this first connexion, driven
into opposition in 1762, there grew up gradually the party of the
Rockingham whigs, who, through Burke, claimed the apostolic
succession of the whiggism of the age.[2]

Characteristically, as a man who never originated but always
idealized and intensified the thought which he found about him,
Burke assumed that the course of his career had been inevitable.
' As to myself and the part I have taken in my time', he wrote, ' I
apprehend that there was very little choice.'[3] In the same way, as
on an unavoidable hypothesis, it was on the basis of his experience
in these first years that he developed the official whig theory of the
Thoughts on the Cause of the Present Discontents, and in consequence,
it was on this experience that his party moulded their tactics.

Burke might claim that true political wisdom was ' the progressive sagacity that keeps company with times and occasions
and decides upon things in their existing conditions ',[4] but his own
methods, like his opinions, changed in reality remarkably little.
When he had once grasped the necessity of some form of party connexion for political strength, a necessity already clear in practice
to a series of oppositions, he rather consolidated and elaborated
upon the possibilities of internal solidarity of the great whig family
system as he knew it, than sought any development of the conception. Throughout all his active career he remains the man who
wrote in 1767 to the old duke of Newcastle that he had ' from
inclination and principle a strong attachment to that system of
which your Grace forms so eminent a part'.[5] In the same way for
the practical tactics of this party, for which he worked so loyally,
he had throughout his identification with it only two distinctive
principles. The first, to be applied not only to opposition but to
government, was : ' We know that all opposition is absolutely
crippled if it can obtain no kind of support out of doors ',[6] and his
context shows that he was thinking primarily of the support of
the commercial interests in the city of London. The second was
the significant suggestion, ' I never yet knew an instance of any

---

[1] Brit. Mus. Add. MS. 32967, fo. 69, Newcastle to Rockingham, 19 June 1765.

[2] When I speak of the whigs in opposition, I do not wish to suggest a newly defined
party division between tory government and whig opposition, nor to ignore the Russell
and Grenville connexions, nor the position of Pitt, the greatest of the rebels. I merely
wish to indicate that it was they who, carrying on, though in a changed form, the tradition of the old predominant groups, formed and organized the way of thinking which
was to be accepted as essentially whig.

[3] *Burke Corr.* ii. 277, Burke to Shackleton, 25 May 1776.   [4] *Ibid.* 276.

[5] Brit. Mus. Add. MS. 32985, fo. 284, 30 September 1767.

[6] *Burke Corr.* ii. 51, Burke to Rockingham, 23 August 1775.

general temper in the nation that could not have been tolerably well traced to some particular persons.'[1] The need of party in the sense in which the word was then used, the advantages to this party of a fairly widespread popular support, particularly among the trading interests of the city, where it was most vocal, some understanding of the policies most likely to obtain it, and very considerable experience in the methods whereby its existence, even in a very limited degree, might be given the most spectacular prominence : this was the practical knowledge which Burke won from observation of the first years of whig minority, and from his first taste of power as Rockingham's private secretary and prominent government supporter in the house of commons during the short ministry of 1765-6. It was a practical lesson which he was only able to learn because tactics new to the high whigs were beginning to be used by them as they turned to opposition. It was a lesson which he never learned completely, partly for personal reasons, partly because his party itself never learned it, so that he and they both tried to use rising forces without comprehending their direction.

The key-note of Burke's ideas and of the new whig tactics is struck firmly in his first important work as whig apologist, *The Short Account of a Late Short Administration*. Here Burke stressed as the chief claim to fame of the ministry of 1765-6, the policy of commercial reform which it embodied in the three linked acts— the repeal of the American Stamp Act, the American Duties Act, and the Free Port Act of the West Indies—and the close touch which it kept with a wide range of commercial interests while the policy was being evolved.[2] Though the emphasis was new and for his connexion surprising, it may be taken as a true interpretation of the actions of the Rockingham ministry, which was continually occupied with commercial matters. The trace of commercial interests can be seen even upon those of its measures which were not in themselves in any way commercial.

This emphasis is remarkable and can be attributed neither to party tradition nor to the leaders themselves in the high whig territorial group which had followed Newcastle and now turned to Rockingham. It is only necessary to examine their attitude when in uneasy alliance with Pitt, from 1757 to 1761, to see that the alliance between the high whigs and the bulk of the merchant classes of which Burke boasts, as distinct from the support of Newcastle in the treasury by the aristocracy of finance on which its business rested, was, so far as it existed, a development not dating back before their

---

[1] *Burke Corr*. ii. 49, Burke to Rockingham, 23 August 1775.

[2] *Works*, i. 183 (Bohn ed.) : ' That administration was the first which proposed and encouraged public meetings and free consultations of merchants from all parts of the kingdom ; by which means the truest lights have been received ; great benefits have been already derived to manufactures and commerce, and the most extensive prospects are opened for further improvement.'

opposition and this ministry. This new commercial policy was the
result of the first ūnmethodical attempt at adaptation made by the
connexion to general conditions themselves in a state of change.

At the beginning of their period of opposition, the whigs found
a marked development taking place in the growth of outside
influence on parliament and ministries, under stress of which the
Mercantile System was changing from a control of trade in the
interests of policy to a control of policy in the interests of organized
trade. And the rapid growth of the political influence of the export
trading interests which this implied, in particular those concerned
in American waters, was closely associated with a greater movement of opinion with its centre in the city of London, popular
radicalism. It is not possible to separate the rising clamour of the
' American Trades ' from the ferment, half social and half political,
which was leading in the city to the Wilkite disturbances, and the
early reform organizations. A particular stage of this development
caught the first whig opposition and the Rockingham ministry and
moulded its commercial policy.

The whole movement, developing through the century, had
become far more immediately serious at this time as a result, on
the one hand, of the economic consequences of the Seven Years'
war, and on the other of the political conditions caused by Pitt's
war ministry. The centre of the commercial changes lay in the
three great and closely connected trades in western waters, the
West Indian, the North American, and the African trades. The
alternating struggles and alliances of these trades obscure to some
extent their power and political importance, but everything shows
how much, in the eighteenth century, the tide of individualist commercial expansion had set to the West, and how surely these
western trades were becoming a formidable political force, and
were binding to themselves the interests of the more slowly rising
manufacturing classes who depended upon them.[1]

The Seven Years' war, the problems of the peace, and the depression which followed it made both their strength and their
anti-ministerialism clearer than had even the excise and ' Jenkins'
Ear ' agitations before. All trades were affected by the depression
after the speculative boom of the war years, but those concerned
with export in American waters suffered the most severely, for
here the problems of colonial policy entered in. The result was the
gradually rising commercial discontent which the American riots
and anti-importation agreements brought to a climax under the
Rockingham ministry of 1765–6.

---

[1] The two peaks in the rising line of their political importance were : the agitation
against Walpole's Excise Scheme, 1733 (see N. A. Brisco, *The Economic Policy of Robert
Walpole*), and the Jenkins' Ear agitation of 1739 (see H. W. V. Temperley, ' The Causes
of the War of Jenkins' Ear ', *Roy. Hist. Soc. Trans.*, ser. iii, vol. 3).

The indirect commercial results of these years were equally important and reached an equally critical situation during the Rockingham ministry, for they took the form of a series of changes in the relations of two of the component parts of the great western trade, the West Indians and the merchants trading to North America, which had the greatest effect on the history of the whig commercial alliances. The conflicts between the North American trade and the powerful, because closely interrelated, West Indian interest in England[1] have been stressed in the study of commercial conditions at this time to an extent which has excluded the recognition of the great range of interests which were common to both.[2] By the end of 1766, as will be shown, this interpretation of their relations has become definitely misleading, but even before that year it leaves out of account some important factors. Throughout the war they had been in complete agreement,[3] and the occasional antagonism of their policies only became acute when in the peace of 1762 most of the West Indians opposed territorial expansion in the interests of their sugar monopoly. It became worse when those interested in North America began to attribute their trade depression in part at least to the limitations of the Molasses Act upon the North Americans, and to enforcement of the regulations against smuggling introduced in the West Indian interest. The hostility thus begun continued to grow through 1764–5 ; but the events of 1766 under the Rockingham ministry brought a complete change. In 1764 it could be said that ' island interest ' and ' mainland interest ' were completely antagonistic.[4] In 1766, on the other hand, an observer needed to remind his correspondent that mainland and island interests were not always the same.[5] By the beginning of the war of independence West Indian planters and merchants and American merchants were working side by side.[6] The reasons for this change of attitude lay in economic considerations more fundamental than those responsible for the earlier conflict. Since the West Indies depended upon the mainland for their food-supply, it was the threat of an anti-exportation agreement in 1765 as in 1774 which aroused their alarm.

While these commercial developments were taking place,

[1] L. M. Penson, *The London West India Interest in the Eighteenth Century, ante,* xxxvi. 373.

[2] F. W. Pitman, *The Development of the British West Indies, 1700–63,* Yale Historical Publications, Studies 4 ; G. L. Beer, *British Colonial Policy, 1754–65.*

[3] They had agreed in their pressure for war with Spain, for the expansion of the African trade at the expense of the French, for the growth of the Newfoundland fisheries, and the retention of Canada in order to make this possible.

[4] Governor Bernard, quoted F. W. Pitman, *op. cit.* pp. 322–6.

[5] *Hist. MSS. Comm., IXth Report,* part 3, 24 ; Stopford-Sackville MSS., Sackville to Irwin, 25 April 1766.

[6] ' The evidence delivered on the petition presented by the West India planters and merchants to the House of Commons, as it was introduc'd at the bar, and summ'd up by Mr. Glover (1775).' Bodleian Library, Godw. P. 491(1).

moreover, Pitt's war ministry had strengthened politically the position of those very radical commercial interests to which the trade belonged. From the time of Bolingbroke and Pulteney, who first saw the strategic possibilities of eighteenth-century opposition, it had become clear that there existed this potential anti-ministerialism among the commercial classes in the city, to whom solidity and influence was given by the widely spread interests of the traders to America. That here was the basis of a ' National Opposition ' both tory leaders and rebel whigs recognized. Not, however, till the experiment of Pitt did any leader consider the possibility of retaining these allies when again in power.[1] Coming into office in abnormal circumstances, without the long-established power of Newcastle, Pitt thought he saw valuable reinforcement of his uncertain position in the combined support of the merchants and the independent country gentry which he had recently won.[2] When an alliance with the whigs became essential, Pitt, with the greatest difficulty, even reconciled the more extreme of his supporters to uneasy alliance with the hated whig oligarchy.[3]

When Pitt fell, city opinion, with increased claims to consideration and a dangerous potential leader, could never again be safely ignored. Pitt's ministry had thus opened up a problem. What was the value, not only to an opposition, but to a ministry, of support from general outside opinion and particularly from commercial interests other and wider than those of direct financial importance? It fell to a great extent to the whigs, in the transition of their first opposition and in the ministry which emphasized their fall rather than restored their strength, to reap what Pitt had sown, and to realize by experience the implications of the situation into which circumstances had led them. Among those to whom the realization was quickest, most fruitful, yet most typical in its reservations and limitations, was a new recruit of 1765, Edmund Burke.

The significance of these changes began to be clear as soon as political affairs began to settle down, after the defeat of the whigs in the struggle over the preliminaries of the peace. On the one side, it was reflected in the problems of the ministry. Though there was

[1] Their growing disillusionment within and without the house was particularly emphasized in the case of Pulteney, who was never forgiven in the city for his desertion.

[2] Cf. [R. Glover] *Memoirs of a Literary and Political Character* (1813 ed.), p. 65 *seq.*

[3] R. Glover, *op. cit.* pp. 86, 99, 105 ; Publ. Rec. Off., Chatham MSS., G. D. 8, 19, Beckford to Pitt, 20 September 1757. The uneasiness was shown by such incidents as the attack on Hardwicke and Mansfield in the city in 1758, re-echoed by Beckford in the house, and the opposition to Beckford's election as mayor (C. P. Yorke, *Life of Lord Hardwicke,* iii. 45, and Lord Lyttelton, *Memoirs,* ii. 609; Publ. Rec. Off., Chatham MSS., G. D. 8, 19, Beckford to Pitt, 15 March 1761. C. P. Yorke, *op. cit.* iii. 317).

nothing strikingly new in their commercial policy,[1] they found
themselves, as the depression grew, coping with the ever-increasing
though vaguely expressed commercial discontent, and their difficulties in the city were increased by social and economic unrest
among the mob of the Spitalfield silk weavers. It was largely in
view of the ugliness of popular opinion that they welcomed with
such enthusiasm an address from London merchants praising the
peace,[2] and that such efforts were made by a section of them for
reconciliation with Pitt.

The whig minority, however, had much more difficult readjust-
ments to make. In order to organize any form of opposition, they
had to consider a course of action in which their leaders had no
experience and to which years of office had made them averse.
As Hardwicke had said to Newcastle, they were too old easily to
go into opposition,[3] most of their links with the financial interests
and place-seekers were suddenly snapped, and moreover they
relied too much at first on an early return to power to enter
readily into the tactics which contemporaries distinguished as a
'system' of opposition. Fundamentally, moreover, they were
facing without realizing it the transition period of the whig point
of view from a governmental principle to that theory of opposition
which is implicit in the writings of Burke and overt in the
expressions of such men as Dunning and Dowdeswell in the
second half of the century. The readjustment could not be made
immediately and, though some have seen in the barrier which stood
between Pitt and the whigs in their common opposition not mere
personal interests but a conflict of principle between the old
political concept and a new one of organized party opposition,[4]
the distinction is scarcely tenable. Organized 'systems' of opposition were not new ; the rebel whigs had carried to a high pitch the
organization of 'faction', as the high whigs had called it. It was
new only to the high whigs themselves. It was they who had in
office put upon it the stigma of 'faction', which barred it to
responsible statesmen, and they no less than Pitt were restrained

[1] Even the tightening up of customs regulations in American waters which made
Grenville so unpopular, had been begun by Pitt during the war (F. W. Pitman, *op. cit.*
p. 318).

[2] *Bedford Corr.* iii. 230, George Grenville to Bedford, 19 May 1763, reports the
presentation of the address. ' The effect it has had at this conjuncture for the support
of the honour and quiet of the King's government, and for discouraging the spirit that
has been raised against it, has more than answered the most sanguine expectations.'
Bedford replied, 25 May 1763 (*Grenville Corr.* ii. 58) : ' The address of the Merchants of
the City of London gives me great satisfaction, as I think it must to every good subject
of His Majesty, as it is a strengthening in the hands of Government, and is but a just
tribute to His Majesty.'   [3] C. P. Yorke, *op. cit.* iii. 354, 10 May 1762.

[4] D. A. Winstanley, *Personal and Party Government, 1760-6.* Since this was written
Mr. Namier's *England in the Age of the American Revolution* has appeared, in which he
makes the same point as I do here with regard to the whigs in opposition in 1757
(pp. 55-8).

by their own conception. Cumberland, the king's uncle and their sole remaining support at court, Portland, Albemarle, Bessborough and Devonshire and Hardwicke, agreed with Newcastle that it was a course that would be below them, the ' Great Whigs ', though conceivably open to the ' Young Men ' and ' Little Whigs ',[1] their followers. A combination powerful enough to be immediately successful was one thing, a long series of parliamentary protests was quite another.[2] The result of these difficulties was that the whig transition to opposition was a hesitating one, and that when the movement began it was in the hands of younger and less prominent men, and it is significant that some of them, like their more important but fitful ally Charles Townshend, had known the tactics of rebel whig opposition. The movement towards opposition had in fact, until 1765, more of the nature of a half-admitted revolt than of a continuation of the high whig traditions, and the ' violence of the young men ' became the burden not only of the laments of Newcastle, but at times of the indignation of Horace Walpole,[3] and the shrewd contempt of the old country supporters.[4] The young men used as their centre their new opposition club at Wildman's, which the older leaders did not care to attend,[5] and like other oppositions earlier they quickly gained the support of the commercial sections of the party, in particular of Newcastle's old ally, Sir William Baker, who still wielded considerable power in the city.[6] But if they remained outside the effective control of the whig families, they also remained without distinctive leaders until, in the last months of the ministry, the marquis of Rockingham, encouraged by the Cavendishes, showed himself alive to their hopes and ideas, and at the same time bridged the gap which threatened to appear between them and the traditional leaders of the great whig families.

It was inevitable that this new whig opposition should follow the lines both of tactics and measures laid down earlier by the

[1] Brit. Mus. Add. MS. 32964, fo. 109. Newcastle wrote (25 November 1764) : ' As to being at the Head of such a Sort of Opposition as I am afraid This must be, his Royal Highness [the duke of Cumberland] thinks it below Him, and was pleased to say that it was below me *also*, But he will have no objection to The Young Men going on as they please.'

[2] Hardwicke told Egremont (G. Harris, *Life of Lord Chancellor Hardwicke*, 1847, iii. 351): 'He [Egremont] knew as well as any body, that in this country, there were such things as honourable connexions, which some might represent under the odious name of faction; but might really be only necessary engagements, in order to carry on and effectuate right and necessary measures.'

[3] H. Walpole, *Corr.* vi. 236, Walpole to Mann, 14 May 1765.

[4] Brit. Mus. Add. MS. 32966, fo. 79, Newcastle to Onslow, 21 March 1765, quotes the opinion of ' Stag ' Forrester.

[5] *Ibid.* 32965, fo. 127. It was only with the greatest hesitation that Newcastle agreed to attend a dinner there in the later stages of the opposition, though he was, of course, nominally a member (*History of the Late Minority* [J. Almon], 1765 List of Members).

[6] *Ibid.* 32963, fo. 375, Newcastle to Rockingham, 14 November 1764.

rebel whigs, with only such variations as circumstances made necessary, for the essence of such opposition was popularity with important sections of opinion outside the house. In tactics, therefore, they aimed more or less at the course outlined by Charles Townshend in a burst of energetic protest against the supine attitude of the old leaders. Some coalition within the house should be only supplementary to a strong movement outside :

To gain upon the minds of the people, a daily paper, upon the plan of the Prints, should be set up and circulated diligently tho' quietly, and two good pens should be employed to write from materials suggested by men of knowledge and subject to their inspection. Some leading men in each Town through the several Counties, should be admitted to confidence, and be persuaded to give their clubs and districts the tone of conversation directed from hence.

A Committee should be desired to consider and prepare heads of business for the next winter, and in one word the kingdom should be kept warm and the chiefs active and laborious during the recess. Sir W. Baker should be desired to put the City in motion, both as an example to other Counties and as the attack nearest Home.[1]

It was a programme which might have been given by Pulteney earlier or Burke later,[2] but it was the first opposition programme which had been presented to the high whig leaders, and though they received it half-heartedly, the young whigs tried with some consistency to carry it out. By their parliamentary measures, too, they sought every means to gain support from outside and particularly from city opinion.[3] Their shrewdest move was to make themselves the strongest supporters of Wilkes in the house,[4] for, wiser here than Pitt, they realized what Wilkes told Temple, that ' The trials . . . have demonstrated to me where the strength of our cause really lies; for the merchants, as I had ever the honour of submitting to Your Lordship, are firm in the cause of liberty.'[5] Their least successful side, on the other hand, was shown in their failure, especially in 1764, to take up a definite line on the question of the American trade. Correspondence preserved among the Newcastle papers suggests, however, that their failure, at least in 1764, was due more to the divergence between the West Indian and North

---

[1] Ibid. 32958, fo. 248, 30 April 1764 (also printed, from copy, in Hist. MSS. Comm. xi. 4, Townshend MSS., p. 399).

[2] Burke Corr. ii. 49, Burke to Rockingham, 23 August 1775.

[3] As early as January 1764 the opposition club at Wildman's alarmed the government, and opposition dinners became matters of political significance (H. Walpole, Letters, v. 439). Prominent members, including Townshend, wrote pamphlets, and in November 1764, Fitzherbert, Sir William Baker, and Almon, the bookseller and friend of Wilkes, tried to negotiate with the far too cautious Horace Walpole about founding a paper (Grenville Corr. ii. 457).

[4] Brit. Mus. Add. MS. 30867, fo. 243 (Wilkes Correspondence), Onslow to Wilkes, 19 December 1763 ; ibid., fo. 249 (Wilkes Correspondence), Wilkes to Cotes, 4 January 1764.

[5] Grenville Corr. ii. 71, 9 July 1763.

American interests among their supporters, than to a lack of touch
with the development of the affairs of American trade.[1] With it,
indeed, as its importance grew, their connexion was becoming ever
stronger.

Little as we know of Burke's career until he broke his connexion with ' Single Speech ' Hamilton early in 1765, there are
facts enough to suggest that at this time he gradually began to
appear politically among this younger group of the whigs. A great
deal had happened to the ambitious young Irishman since, in 1750,
he came to London, and observed that figures were more important
than eloquence in the house of commons, and that, his idea of the
aristocratic patronage of letters being exaggerated, writers swarmed
in London living only on their wits.[2] Although he had taken at
least a share in *An Account of the European Settlements in America*
in 1757,[3] and was writing the masterly annual summary of events
in the *Annual Register*, and though he was acting as private
secretary to a rising politician, Burke was still in 1761 a young man
who thought ' nothing so charming as writers and to be one ', and
who was known to Horace Walpole only as the author of the
Advantages of Natural Society.[4] But by 1765 his ambition had
turned definitely to public life. It may be no coincidence that his
obscure breach with Hamilton began in 1764, for Hamilton then
became considered a man who notoriously awaited his chance between minority and government,[5] and Burke thought his policy
became ' very reproachful to himself and extremely disgustful to
me'.[6] Among the recriminations of this quarrel he suggests that
Hamilton resented that ' others were inclined to show me more
attention than he did ', and though he takes pains to deny having
at that time any connexion with a ' Mr. T—— ' (possibly Charles
Townshend),[7] his acquaintance with Rockingham dated at least
from 1763,[8] and he appears to have been personally known to
Wilkes before his exile.[9] Moreover, a well-informed contemporary

---

[1] An opposition to the American Duties Bill was seriously discussed (Brit. Mus.
Add. MS. 32957, fos. 47, 85, 87, 230, and 235) ; Rose Fuller, a prominent West Indian
supporter, sent a letter to Newcastle strongly objecting to such a step (*ibid.*, fo. 116),
and the idea was finally given up, since unified opposition seemed impossible, Charles
Townshend, however, dividing ' in civility to Sir William Baker ' (*ibid.*, fo. 239).

[2] Burke to Smith, quoted by J. Prior, *Life of Burke* (Bohn ed., 1891), p. 33.

[3] The grounds for believing this seem satisfactorily expounded by J. Prior, *op. cit.*
p. 52. It is accepted by Burke's recent biographer, B. Newman.

[4] H. Walpole, *Letters*, v. 86, Walpole to George Montagu, 22 July 1761.

[5] *Hist. MSS. Comm. VIIIth Report, Emly MSS.* p. 190 ; *Hist. MSS. Comm. Xth
Report*, App. I, *Weston Underwood MSS.* p. 382.

[6] *Burke Corr.* i. 77, Burke to Flood, 18 May 1765.

[7] *Ibid.* i. 74, Burke to Hely Hutchinson, n.d. (*c.* May 1765). Burke was in touch
with Charles Townshend about this time (see *Corr.* i. 76, Burke to Flood, 18 May 1765).

[8] Brit. Mus. Add. MS. 35424, fo. 16 (Hardwicke MSS.), Burke to Hardwicke,
20 October 1763.

[9] This is suggested by a reference to Burke in a letter from Wilkes to Fitzherbert,
8 December 1765 (W. P. Treloar, *Wilkes and the City*, p. 46).

states that he obtained his position as private secretary to Rockingham through Fitzherbert, one of the most advanced of the young whigs of Wildman's.[1] At this same time, through the studied impartiality of his review in the *Annual Register*, his predilections began to appear.

In several ways, however, this new opposition, to which Burke was drawn like the other young whigs of his time, had met with unfavourable circumstances. They suffered partly, indeed, because they were unled, but partly for more serious reasons. Their relations with the 'Great Whigs' were unsatisfactory, without the latter allowing them to come to an open breach.[2] The old leaders looked on with distaste at the policy and alliances into which they were being forced. Hardwicke, in 1763, tried to check their enthusiastic support of Wilkes and his followers in the city. 'These are fellows', he reminded Newcastle bitterly, 'Who would have hanged Your Grace and me a few years ago, and would do so still had they the power.'[3] Newcastle and Cumberland, even while submitting, agreed that 'We must not be . . . led by Sir William Baker and some warm very well-intentioned young friends'.[4] On the other hand, their secession, which Newcastle always feared,[5] on the model of the rebel whigs before, and to which their relations with Pitt's city supporters, such as Beckford and Calvert, might have led them, was made difficult by the incalculable behaviour of Pitt. To alliance he would not commit himself, and with Pitt's formidable figure in the role which they wished, like their forerunners, to fill before the country and particularly before the restless antiministerialism of the city, the young whigs found their way towards 'popular opposition' seriously blocked. Had Pitt been a political leader of men, or had Rockingham not stepped in to bring together again the young whigs and the great families, there might never have been the practical crystallization of whig transition to which Burke gave a creed. Both factors, however, combined to leave them no choice but that intermediate political

---

[1] J. Almon, *Anecdotes of the Life of the Rt. Hon. William Pitt, Earl of Chatham*, 7th ed., 1810, i. 423. This was the kind of political information which Almon was in an excellent position to collect, particularly as at this time he had personal relations with Fitzherbert. (*Memoirs of a Late Eminent Bookseller*, 1790, p. 31.)

[2] Newcastle at least recognized that they would be forced to follow the course of the extremists (Brit. Mus. Add. MS. 32964, fo. 257): 'I said our Zealous friends, Sir William Baker etc would certainly make an opposition, and we should have to go with them, or dissolve the Whig party, for aught I know for ever. It is a Sad Dilemma To be brought to by the Behaviour of some of our Pretended Friends.'

[3] G. Harris, *Life of Lord Chancellor Hardwicke*, 1847, iii. 357, Hardwicke to Newcastle, 8 June 1763. Cf. *ibid*. iii. 344, Hardwicke to C. Yorke, 2 May 1763.

[4] Brit. Mus. Add. MS. 32963, fo. 375, Newcastle to Rockingham, 14 Nov. 1764.

[5] *Ibid*. 32965, fo. 26, Newcastle to Rockingham, 3 January 1765. He thought he saw 'a certain spirit of indifference as to persons and all parties' which suggested a plan 'To set up for Themselves without any Connection with us, or any Concern for us—or the Whig Party'.

position which made of the new whig party the compromise which was its strength in Burke's theory and its weakness in fact ; though in their last months of opposition, more or less united under Rockingham, the position was not yet clear. It is interesting, however, to note that it was not the young enthusiasts but the old leader Newcastle who encouraged Rockingham to accept the offer made through Cumberland,[1] and by making ' the most rash experiment that ever was made ',[2] to form the first whig ministry under the new conditions, which gave Burke his chance, but which came into existence without the support of Pitt, and in the teeth of the Bedfords, Grenville, and the much-feared though disputable influence of Bute.

The experiment was as unsuccessful as their most hostile critics had prophesied. The complexities of opposition were as nothing to those which they had to face on coming into power. With uncertain support at court, and a majority of placemen left over from the last two administrations, which would, as they knew ' last no longer than They find the Administration carries Every-thing clearly and roundly ',[3] and with the personal infidelities of an eighteenth-century administration enhanced by new divergencies of view among themselves, not even the most hopeful could see in their accession to power a return to the high whig *status quo*. Like Pitt before them, therefore, their chief hope lay in maintaining their prestige by the appearance of a widespread national and city support, and by keeping up contact, not only with the financial interests but with the wider bodies of opinion for whose favour they had played during their opposition. In doing so, however, they were hampered not only by their more conservative members' suspicion of ' popular ' policies, and by the lack of support from Pitt, who, as they were unpleasantly reminded by a city address on their accession,[4] retained his place in the popular affections, but by the exasperated exigence of their city supporters, whose trade remained consistently bad. One of them put with brutal frankness their attitude to politics and party. ' The Nation has lost its good Humour and unless things are set to rights, it is become a Matter of great Indifference to the Publick, and will be more so every day, " who have the places ".' The dangers before the ministry would be less parliamentary opposition than ' jealousies and disagreements among yourselves ', and, in ominous terms, ' a loss of publick Esteem by disappointing their Reasonable Expectations '.[5]

Just because of these difficulties, however, the ministry was of

---

[1] Brit. Mus., Add. MS. 32967, fo. 186, Newcastle to Portland, 1 July 1765.

[2] *Bedford Corr.* iii. 304, Sandwich to Bedford, 3 July 1765.

[3] Brit. Mus. Add. MS. 32969, fo. 392, Newcastle to Albemarle, 15 September 1765.

[4] Burke was at great pains to explain this away as representing only the less con-siderable sections of city opinion (*Annual Register*, 1765, p. 46).

[5] Brit. Mus. Add. MS. 32967, fo. 226, Colebrooke to Newcastle, 4 July 1765.

great historical importance. The adaptation of whig theory to opposition would never have taken the form it did without this fleeting experience of power, and the attempt it was forced to make to build up a compromise between the exigencies of new demands from without and old social and political conceptions still strong within. Because it had followed without system in the ways of others and played for commercial support, it was put at the mercy of a new commercial strength and organization, and the Rockingham ministry saw within a few months, what it had certainly never foreseen, the most fundamental changes of the century in British trading policy. It also saw the most definite step in the growth of the commercial men's confidence in their own political power, which among other things formed a basis for the widening claim for greater direct share in it. But, since this was rather accidental to than because of the ministry's policy, their practical experience, so far from leading them away from the traditions of the old whig rule, once again consolidated even the extremists among them in it. A disunited opposition it was before 1765, an opposition of compromise it became afterwards.

From the first this compromise was apparent. Though they succeeded, with some adroitness, in freeing themselves from obligations to Wilkes,[1] they knew on the other hand that concessions to the public's ' reasonable expectations ' were essential. A great part of their policy is to be explained as the twofold attempt, firstly, to satisfy these demands by concessions and carefully planned publicity ; and, secondly, to bring pressure to bear for this purpose on the court and the more conservative members of their party, when they fretted under this new commercial emphasis, and tended to complain, like the second Lord Hardwicke, of 'the little weight that was given to my opinion when it interfered with the plan which Lord Rockingham and his friends were previously determined to follow . . . in mercantile affairs'.[2] Their active part, therefore, in the commercial policy which Burke held forth as their chief claim to popular gratitude, consisted chiefly in seeking solutions which would be acceptable both to them and their increasingly clamorous commercial supporters, when the demands of the latter became political issues. As time went on, it consisted also in trying to minimize the conflicting interests which existed within the ranks of their commercial supporters themselves. They played on the other hand scarcely more than a passive part in the inauguration of the commercial policy, which they took up piecemeal as outside

[1] *Ibid.* 30877, fo. 51 (Wilkes Correspondence), Horne to Wilkes, 3 January 1766; J. Almon, *The Correspondence of the late John Wilkes*, vol. ii, *passim*; A. Stephens, *The Life of John Horne Tooke*, i. 231, Wilkes to Onslow, 12 December 1765. The delicate negotiation of keeping Wilkes from the scene of political action without driving him into opposition was one in which Burke took an important part.

[2] Quoted, *Rockingham Memoirs*, i. 284.

pressure was brought to bear on them. Neither Burke, as has been
rather rashly claimed for him,[1] nor any member of the ministry
could be said to have a scheme of commercial reform.

Burke was in any case of far too slight consequence to be a
deciding factor in the policy of the party, but though he can claim
no credit as a commercial reformer, in the working out of the
ministerial policy he rose from obscurity and appeared, not yet as
the prophet of the system, but instead, rather surprisingly, as one
of its most practical organizers. By the end of the ministry, in
spite of his occasional rashness he had become, together with
Dowdeswell, the chancellor of the exchequer, the most noted man
of his group. It was indeed said in the last months of the ministry
that Burke, 'not ... Lord Rockingham's right hand, but ... both his
hands', was a metaphysical visionary.[2] But his success in organiz-
ing commercial propaganda, in keeping in touch with commercial
leaders, in encouraging every sign of public support, for popularity,
he remarked, 'is current coin, or it is nothing',[3] show that
practical vigour, which, in the most fortunate periods of his
political career, was the complement of his speculative genius. It
was this which compensated in part for his lack of political finesse
and judgement, and won him his place in the Rockingham connexion, more than his much greater intellectual claims.

The evolution of the Rockingham commercial policy, which
circumstances made their only consecutive policy, falls into three
periods, which correspond also with definite stages in the growth of
Burke's influence. Each centres in an aspect of the growing
question of the claims of the American Trades.

A general but still vague feeling that something should be
done to revive the North American trade was characteristic of
commercial opinion in the earlier months of the ministry. The
new ministers were quite willing to satisfy these demands which,
unless the measures adopted should clash with the interests of the
West Indians, appeared uncontroversial. Fortunately, in so far
as any one cause of complaint had become general, it was one on
which the interests of the two trades were the same, the decline in
the smuggling of bullion from the Spanish colonies in Spanish ships
to the West Indian Islands. General commercial opinion put this
down to the activities of the authorities against them under
Grenville's new regulations.[4] The prevalent commercial bullionism
of the time laid the greatest importance on it,[5] and it would even

[1] B. Williams, *Life of William Pitt, Earl of Chatham*, ii. 183.
[2] Brit. Mus. Add. MS. 22358, fo. 35. Quoted by D. A. Winstanley, *Personal and Party
Government*, p. 243.   [3] *Burke Corr.* i. 108, Burke to Rockingham, 21 August 1766.
[4] The complaints had really begun well before the war, e.g. Pub. Rec. Off.,
Col. Off. 137/25, fo. 225. Humble Address of the Council and Assembly of Jamaica,
20 November 1752.
[5] Brit. Mus. Add. MS. 38339, fo. 225. Opinion of J. Salvador, the Jewish financier

seem that some effort at organized agitation had already been used
to crystallize demands into this form.[1] No very active measures,
however, were necessary, as the ministry almost at once set about
providing a remedy, and their deliberations resulted in the treasury
minute of 13 November 1765, which Burke later praised as so notable
a development,[2] and which was received with satisfaction by the
chief bodies of American merchants in the country.[3] From the point
of view of the ministry it was a satisfactory settlement of the
claims upon them. ' It is ', wrote Newcastle, 'as strong an Article
of Impeachment against George Grenville as can be formed ; and
it will show you have been doing something.' [4] There is some irony
in the fact that it did nothing at all ; more than a year before
Grenville, approached by the West Indian merchants, had, though
with the secrecy which relations with Spain made desirable, sent
the same orders for exempting the Spanish ships from smuggling
regulations.[5] Both ministry and merchants were to find that something more was wrong with the situation than ' those fatal orders' of
Mr. Grenville.

Even without this further experience, however, the ministry
began to find that commercial demands were not limited to one
point. Before the end of October Rockingham had discovered that
' to admit the Spanish Bullion into any Part of our Dominions in
America . . . would not quite do our Business'.[6] A very definite
breach in the Navigation Laws was suggested by the words,
which a merchant must certainly have put into Newcastle's mouth,[7]
when he hoped that ' Liberty will also be given to Spanish vessels
to return with certain Commodities . . . or otherwise the Great
Stagnation of our Trade with North America and the Exportation
of our Woollen Manufactures thither will not be put upon the
Foot it was '.[8] At this point, however, the lines of development
of commercial problems were cut across by the sudden develop-

[1] P. R. O., T. 1/443, fo. 53, Memorial of the Merchants and Principal Manufacturers
of Manchester, 5 September, 1765; and fo. 47, Memorial of the Merchants of Liverpool,
August 1765. Some organization was suspected at the time, see Brit. Mus. Add. MS.
33030, fo. 103 *seq.* Questions asked Trecothick when giving evidence in the house,
March 1766.

[2] *Works,* i. 304, ' Observations on a Late Publication '. There is a copy of the minute
in the Newcastle Papers, Brit. Mus. Add. MS. 32971, fo. 394.

[3] P. R. O., T. 1/443, fo. 50, Memorial from the Merchants of Lancaster (docketed,
read 2 December 1765); P. R. O., T. 1/447, fo. 351, Memorial from the Merchants of
Liverpool, November 1765 ; P. R. O., T. 1/451, fo. 83, Letter from the Master of the
Society of Merchants of Bristol, 21 November 1765.

[4] Brit. Mus. Add. MS. 32971, fo. 422.

[5] *Grenville Corr.* ii. 47, Jenkinson to G. Grenville, 30 April 1763. The whole transaction is described by Beeston Long, chairman of the West Indian Association, in his
evidence before the house in 1766. Brit. Mus. Add. MS. 33030, fo. 188.

[6] Brit. Mus. Add. MS. 32971, fo. 13, Newcastle to Rockingham, 22 October 1765.

[7] *Ibid.*

[8] Newcastle was consulting Sir W. Baker at the time (*ibid.*, fos. 165 and 173. Newcastle Memorandum, 27 October 1765.)

ment of the great agitation for the repeal of the Stamp Act. If events had been able to develop naturally, there were two further demands which would certainly have been raised ; and had this happened the Rockingham ministry would have had to face at once a great commercial conflict, for they were the demands on which the North American and West Indian interests were at this time fundamentally opposed. The first, the demand by the North American interests for the further reduction of the duty on foreign molasses, though it had already been made, was not at this time raised ; the second—their claim, on the analogy of the Spanish trade, for the legalization of certain forms of smuggling from the other foreign West Indies by the opening of ' free ports ', to which the West Indians were strongly opposed as threatening indirectly the effectiveness of their monopoly—was already being tentatively suggested.[1] The common danger in which the American disturbances placed them, however, interrupted this development, and threw them suddenly into alliance.

The commercial problems of the Rockingham ministry thus did not begin with the Stamp Act disturbances, though the latter completely changed their relative significance. Of Burke very little is known at this time, but he must have had opportunities, as his grip on affairs was growing, to learn lessons of the nature of the forces with which the ministry was in contact. That his influence began growing early is suggested by Lord Charlemont's story that it dated from Newcastle's attempt in the first days of the ministry to oust him in favour of another candidate by denouncing him to Rockingham as a papist and a Jacobite.[2] By the beginning of December he was certainly carrying out most confidential work,[3] and with the opening of parliament a new field was opened to him, for he was given a seat for Wendover, through the interest of Lord Verney.[4]

In the first period of the ministry commercial questions had been in considerable but not disproportionate prominence, and although the demands from without were growing under sympa-

[1] The fullest early exposition of the idea came from Lt.-Col. Campbell Dalrymple (Guadeloupe) to Lord Bute, 27 February 1763 (*Corr. of King George III*, i. 44). In P. R. O., T. 1/441, fo. 8, there is a proposal from Hughes, distributor of stamps, Philadelphia, 23 November 1765, on the same lines.

[2] Lord Charlemont, *Memoirs*, ed. F. Hardy (1810), p. 343. Charlemont did not vouch for the truth of the story. Some support is, however, given to it by the fact that Newcastle certainly had a candidate for the position, one Royer (Brit. Mus. Add. MS. 32967, fo. 346), for whom he later found another subordinate place (Brit. Mus. Add. MS. 32969, fo. 438).

[3] The buying off of Wilkes, to prevent his return. See correspondence quoted in W. P. Treloar, *Wilkes and the City*, pp. 46 *seq.*

[4] J. Prior, *Life of Burke* (Bohn ed., 1891), p. 86. His statement is supported by the List of Borough Patronage of Commoners, drawn up by Mr. L. B. Namier, *The Structure of Politics at the Accession of George III*, i. 179. Verney was also in close relations with his, at that time better-known relative, William Burke (*Grenville Corr.* ii. 49 ; *Hist. MSS. Comm., Xth Report*, App. I, *Weston-Underwood MSS.*, p. 403).

thetic treatment, there was no sign of the sudden development which was to follow. The shock to trade from the American Stamp Act disturbances, however, brought to a head tendencies which might have developed much more slowly, and by causing a rapid growth of organization, brought the ministry into relation with a new and formidable extra-parliamentary force. The second period of the ministry, covering, in the months from December to March, the agitation in England for the repeal of the Stamp Act, was its turning-point. The movement among the wide sections of commercial opinion which were affected cut across the course of commercial unrest by diverting and concentrating its needs into one political demand ; after this had been satisfied, it intensified the earlier and more general grievances, because organization and experience had given commercial opinion a confidence and knowledge of its own demands which it had not had before. It had also changed the position, however, for it had made considerable changes in the permanent relations of the West Indian and North American merchant interests.

Though the Stamp Act disturbances in America were known in England by October, and though even earlier the colonial merchants through their correspondents were sending in appeals and denunciations,[1] nothing was done until, a fortnight before the first parliamentary session of the new ministry, the first step was made in London towards a formidable commercial movement. On 4 December a meeting of London merchants trading to North America,[2] with Barlow Trecothick, who was to be the organizer of the movement, in the chair, chose a committee of twenty-eight prominent merchants to manage the business of a national commercial agitation.[3] They began their work with energy, and henceforth there was a new and incalculable factor in the relations of the ministry with the commercial opinion from which they claimed support.

The position of Rockingham and the majority of the ministry in view of this development of this active extra-parliamentary organization was a curious one, for their opponents were [4] right in accusing them of deliberately supporting the agitation. A copy of the circular which the Committee sent out to thirty trading and manufacturing towns was among the Rockingham papers, en-

---

[1] 'Letters of Dennys de Berdt, 1757–1770', ed. A. Mathews. *Publications of the Col. Soc. of Mass.*, vol. xiii, p. 431.

[2] The meeting had been publicly advertised (Brit. Mus. Add. MS. 38339, fo. 166).

[3] A copy of the names and terms of appointment of this committee is kept in the Liverpool papers (Brit. Mus. Add. MS. 38339, fo. 166). They were chosen to 'Consider of the best Method of Application for Procuring the Relief and Encouragement of the North American trade, and to apply to the Outports and to the Manufacturing Citys and Towns for their Concurrence and Assistance'. They extended their powers far beyond the wording of their appointment.

[4] Summary of the debate on the Repeal of the Stamp Act, in *Annual Register*, 1766, p. 37 : ' They represented the petitions as the result of ministerial artifice.'

dorsed by Burke, with enthusiasm ' N.B. This letter concerted between the Marquis of R. and Mr. Trecothick, the principal instrument in the happy repeal of the Stamp Act.' [1] A few weeks later an elated American agent was reporting the complete support of the ministry,[2] although Dowdeswell had definitely failed to carry his proposals for repeal in the meeting of the leaders of the connexion before Parliament opened.[3] Later, Burke himself was in direct communication with the outports on details of the agitation.[4] These facts accord ill with the generally accepted belief that the ministry made no effort to meet the situation, and that it was Pitt who forced the undecided ministry into action which conformed with public demands. Yet it is true that they did not declare themselves until well into the new year, and that even then, unlike Pitt, they compromised by laying heavy stress on the right, if not the expediency, of colonial taxation.[5] The explanation of this apparent contradiction would seem to be that with Pitt dangerous, and commercial opinion becoming organized, as it had not been since Walpole's excise, they had in reality no alternative but to support the American claims for repeal. Nevertheless, since the court and a considerable part of the non-commercial opinion from which their party was drawn took a purely political view of the colonists' riots, and were totally out of sympathy with their claims,[6] they were forced to act indirectly. There is no doubt that their intention was to force the hand both of the king and the large section of their party who thought that repeal was shortsighted cowardice, by alarming them by the ' clamour of the merchants ',[7] as a whig lord called the expression of commercial opinion, but that, to make this possible, as they made clear to their merchant supporters,[8] certain concessions must be made, on the other hand, to conservative opinion.

Under the skilful control of Trecothick, and with the knowledge of ministerial support (a condition entirely new to commercial movements of this kind, which had in the past been bitterly anti-ministerial), the organization proved the most effective of the commercial agitations up to this date, and showed at the same time how widespread were the American trading interests, yet

---

[1] *Rockingham Memoirs*, i. 319.   [2] 'Letters of D. de Berdt', p. 308.

[3] J. Adolphus, *The History of England from the Accession of George III* (1802), i. 217.

[4] *Burke Corr.* i. 99, Henderson (Glasgow merchant) to Burke, 9 February 1766.

[5] The first decision was reached in a meeting of 17 January (Brit. Mus. Add. MS. 35430, fo. 31) referred to in D. A. Winstanley, *Personal and Party Government, 1760–1766*, p. 262.

[6] The king made it clear that it was only under pressure of necessity that he agreed to the repeal on any terms (*Corr. of King George III*, i. 269. Memorandum by the king, 11 February 1766), and at one stage observers thought that the ministry would fall on the subject (*Letters of the Earl of Chesterfield* (1892 ed.), iii. 1335).

[7] Rockingham, *Memoirs*, i. 284. The expression was the second Lord Hardwicke's.

[8] 'Letters of D. de Berdt', p. 311. Reports conversations with Conway.

how surprisingly easy to bring under centralized control from London. Barlow Trecothick, in an examination before the house, showed this in a frank account of their methods.

I will give a candid account—we find America in confusion, our property in danger, our Remittances uncertain and the Trade in danger of annihilation—we were called on by the Bristol Merchants—this hastened our meeting for all the Merchants trading to North America. They met, chose a committee, they instructed that committee to write circular Letters to the manufacturing Towns requiring their Support in an application to Parliament, and to use their interest with the Members to make the interest of Great Britain the Basis of their application. . . . Many of the manufacturing Towns sent for the form of a petition which we declined particularly at Bristol—we thought it too indecent and desired them to speak for their own feelings and that none should complain but what were aggrieved.

.   .   .   .

Thirty circular letters sent for petitions to most Towns. In every Answer they were thankful for our Motions and desired copy of Petitions. In general I believe the petitions would have come though Letters had not been sent.[1]

Local bodies were formed in Liverpool, Bristol, Manchester, and Glasgow, with which the central committee kept in touch,[2] and from which at a later stage witnesses were sent to represent their grievances. Twenty-three petitions were received by the house of commons between 17 and 29 January, all expressed in terms of concerted similarity,[3] and even before they came in the first step was gained, for a parliamentary inquiry had been agreed to.

This was a valuable advance, for here there was a further opportunity to show the nature and extent of the movement, and again the ministry and merchants' organizations worked together. Rose Fuller, a West Indian and a strong supporter of the ministry, was made chairman ; witnesses of every type were called together, members of the London committee of merchants, whose powers were expanding as the agitation grew, among them Trecothick, who also sent in written notes ;[4] merchants from Glasgow, Liverpool, Manchester, and Bristol ; manufacturers from Leeds, Bradford, and Manchester. A London goldsmith gave valuable evidence on the bullion trade, a few merchants and agents from America, including Benjamin Franklin, described American conditions, and the chairman of the West Indian Association gave support [5] which showed how much the jealousies between the two trades were, at

---

[1] Brit. Mus. Add. MS. 33030, fo. 101. Cf. 'Letters of D. de Berdt', pp. 307–8, and copy of correspondence between Trecothick and the Mayor of Norwich, 6 to 27 December 1765 (Brit. Mus. Add. MS. 22358, fo. 32 *seq.* Buckingham Corr.).

[2] *Ibid.*, fo. 214 *seq.* Trecothick's notes on the Petition from the merchants of London.

[3] *Journ. of the House of Commons*, xxx. 462 *seqq.*

[4] Brit. Mus. Add. MS. 33030, fo. 214.

[5] *Ibid.*, fo. 188.

least temporarily, overborne by this new common danger.[1] Public
fervour was still further aroused by the political issues which the
colonists and their supporters in Parliament had introduced into
what seemed a commercial subject, and by the great speeches of
Pitt who was stirred from his torpor. Only less successful were the
first speeches of Burke, worked to a fever of enthusiasm by this
the first great issue of his political career.

The result was what they had hoped. Unwillingly and with
careful reservations the king and most of their supporters gave
way, the repeal was passed, and the Rockingham ministry, though
it shared the popular glory with Pitt, had passed successfully
through the crisis. Burke shared fully in this success. Not only
did he make his successful beginning in the house, but his real
power in the party had grown remarkably. His activities in keeping the ministry and the merchants in touch, during this agitation
and the parliamentary inquiry which was part of it, were probably
the most successful practical work that he ever did in power. So
active were he and Dowdeswell in establishing relations with the
merchants all over the country that he had already founded his
reputation among the general commercial interests. With Rockingham and Dowdeswell alone among the ministers, he received
before and on the fall of the ministry addresses of thanks from
several towns in terms which justify his boast that the Rockingham
administration tried to understand and satisfy the needs of every
section of commercial opinion.[2]

The third period of their office was, however, upon them. In
the crisis they had triumphed by making the demands of the
organized American trades their own, but machinery had been
set going which it was beyond their power to control. From the
beginning of the inquiry, as is plain from the fragmentary accounts
of their evidence,[3] the commercial witnesses tended to wander from
the question immediately before them to all the vague complaints
that had been only hesitatingly formed in the preceding period.
It is even possible that Trecothick and the merchant leaders, in
framing their agitation from the beginning in general terms, had
deliberately played for this object. In any case, the opportunities
for joint action, the success of their organization, and the knowledge that they were carrying the government before them, led
them, even before the repeal of the Stamp Act, to demands which

---

[1] The co-operation with the North American interests appears to have been com-
plete among the merchants in the West Indian interest, the only exception being Sir
Alexander Grant, but some of the landlords voted against the repeal; see *List of the
Minority in the House of Commons who voted against the Bill to Repeal the Stamp Act*.
Paris, 1766. (It said that it was printed in ' Paris' to avoid the possibility of unpleasant
consequences to printers and publisher.)

[2] *Burke Corr.* i. 104, 12 June 1766, address from the Merchants of Lancaster; Prior,
Life of Edmund Burke (Bohn ed., 1891), p. 90.

[3] Brit. Mus., Add. MS. 33030, fo. 78 *seqq.*

only increased with the chances of success, and removed all initiative from the Rockingham ministry. When on 21 February, after reporting the resolutions which were to form the repeal of the Stamp Act, the chairman announced that the house wished to continue sitting in committee on American trade affairs,[1] just as public opinion thought the whole matter was satisfactorily ended, the elated merchant leaders knew it had only begun.

There is yet much to be done [wrote Dennis de Berdt, member of the London Committee, and Agent for Massachusetts], The Admiralty Courts must be restrained, the exorbitant Duty on Molasses Lowerd, and the restraints on Trade removed, and this we hope to effect through the favour of the present ministry who Justly think the Interest of England and her Colonies one.[2]

With the political elements removed the purely commercial ones began to show themselves again in a truer form, but no longer an uncontroversial one. This form was the challenge by the now confident North American merchants to the West Indians, with whom they had just been in alliance, on the two points where their interests clashed most directly, and on which they had been drifting to open conflict before the interruption occurred. The remaining two of the triad of acts [3] which make up the Rockingham commercial policy are the product of this last period. It became plain, however, that the centre of activity did not lie in the ministry, whose internal difficulties were also at their height, as the dislike of the king and court party on the one hand, and the renewed activity of Pitt on the other, undermined their unity and control. It lay in the extra-parliamentary negotiations to which business in the house tended to become merely the sequel, and particularly in the relations of the committee of merchants trading to North America, and the similar committee of the West India merchants. There was considerable truth in Grenville's sneer at ' the overbearing and delegation of administration to a Club of North America merchants at the King's Arms Tavern ',[4] and the ministry could do little more than anxiously await the result.

At first it seemed as if a conflict might be avoided. The West Indians, shaken by the danger of the Stamp Act disturbance and realizing the formidable strength of the organization against them, were prepared to compromise. Rose Fuller wrote, what they would never have admitted before, that the proposed reduction of the duty on foreign molasses from 3*d.* to 1*d.* per gallon might be an

[1] *Journ. of the House of Commons*, xxx. 586.
[2] 'Letters of D. de Berdt', p. 314. Cf. p. 315.
[3] (i) Act for Repealing Certain Duties, and Encouraging, Regulating, and Securing the Trade of this Kingdom, and the British Dominions in America; (ii) Act for Opening Certain Ports in Dominica and Jamaica, &c.
[4] Brit. Mus. Add. MS. 32975, fo. 58, J. West to Newcastle, 30 April 1766. Account of Proceedings in the House of Commons.

improvement as a duty 'which will certainly be collected' and 'will also accustom the North American Colonies to obedience ',[1] and only six days after the third reading of the repeal and a fortnight before the house again resolved itself into committee, the two committees had met and come to a compromise.[2] This was reported to the ministry by a joint committee. Greatly relieved, Rockingham reported to the king that there was ' The Greatest Prospect of an Advantageous System of Commerce being Established for the Mutual and General Interest of this Country ', since ' several of the matters which might have occasioned dispute were nearly agreed between them '.[3]

Though it is unlikely that the compromise satisfied all sections of West Indian opinion, which was naturally finding some difficulty in readjusting itself to the sudden change in the relations of the American trades,[4] all would probably have gone well, had the North American merchants pressed no farther. With the two West Indian leaders, Beckford and Fuller, supporting their policy, moreover, the ministry might have maintained unbroken the united commercial support which was becoming increasingly necessary for its prestige as its position grew weaker. Early in April Horace Walpole became convinced that their only hope of maintaining themselves was by recuperation after a hasty prorogation,[5] by May Newcastle was urging the hurrying of the necessary business through the house for the same purpose. Even if this were done, he thought on the last night ' the Thoughts of our principal Friends might be known—the Sense of the City and even in some degree of the country . . . and from thence the possibility or Propriety of going on may be better judged of '.[6] It was just at this crucial point, however, that parliamentary business was held up, the opposition and malcontents given an opportunity which they were quick to take, and the ministry's prestige definitely broken, by the violent breach between the North American and West Indian interests. On 7 April there suddenly came to a head the demand among traders and manufacturers with American interests for the opening of Dominica as a free port for ships from all the foreign West Indies. Concerted petitions stressing particularly the manufacturing needs came from Bristol, Liverpool, Lancaster, and Manchester, to be followed later by a great petition from London.[7] Though it is just possible that the London Committee which was

[1] Brit. Mus. Add. MS. 32975, fo. 147, R. Fuller to Newcastle, enclosure in letter of 10 May 1766.

[2] *Ibid.* 38339, fo. 235 (copy); printed in *Gentleman's Magazine*, 1766, p. 228.

[3] *Corr. of King George III*, i. 282, 12 March 1766.

[4] See article in *Gentleman's Magazine*, 1766, p. 228.

[5] H. Walpole, *Memoirs*, ii. 232.

[6] Brit. Mus. Add. MS. 32975, fo. 72, Newcastle to Rockingham, 2 May 1766 (secret). One of his chief reasons was his well-grounded fear of the defection of Grafton.

[7] *Journ. of the House of Commons*, xxx. 708 and 750 (London Petition).

in negotiation with the West Indians had not initiated this movement, it certainly took it up with enthusiasm. The West Indians
in return, under the leadership of Beckford,[1] at once threw themselves into violent opposition, though a small section, among whom
were the Fullers, seem to have maintained their whig alliance.

The administration realized the gravity of the situation, but,
unable to check its supporters, it hastily called a cabinet
meeting to decide on a policy before the matter was brought up
in the house.[2] Their usual disunion on commercial matters was
now accentuated by even more ominous factors. While Rockingham and his group were as ever prepared to support the North
American merchants, with whom Burke and Dowdeswell were
again in close touch, Newcastle hesitated at first in face of West
Indian hostility. Others definitely opposed the suggestion with a
decision which was increased by the news which went round that
Pitt, under the combined influence of irritation with the ministry
and the pressure of his personal friend Beckford, was prepared to
support his old allies the West Indians.[3] Neither Burke nor a
deputation of London merchants,[4] moreover, could change his
attitude.

There is no space here to describe this last and greatest struggle
of the West Indian and North American merchants, which in the
dying days of a now totally discredited ministry was fought out
through rather than by ministry and opposition in the house.
Pitt indeed left the field, deserting his West Indian allies when he
discovered, what he had not before had occasion to realize, the
' ill-success to his popularity ' which a conflict with the great
North American interests brought.[5] The struggle, however, continued, and became more serious to the ministry as they realized
that the opposition, knowing their weakness, was playing for time,[6]
and that despite all their efforts their majority was melting away.
An observer remarked :

Mr. Beckford has treated the House of Commons every day this week,
and I may say until night too, with his evidence relative to the duties, free
port etc. . . . it makes but a ghastly appearance on the part of the directors

[1] P. R. O., Chatham MS. G. D. 8, 19, Beckford to Pitt, 18 April 1766.

[2] Brit. Mus. Add. MS. 32974, fo. 348, Rockingham to Newcastle, 11 April
1766.

[3] *Ibid.*, fo. 350, Newcastle to Rockingham, 11 April 1766 ; P. R. O., Chatham MS.
G. D. 8, 19, Beckford to Pitt, 18 April 1766.

[4] Brit. Mus. Add. MS. 32974, fo. 370, Rockingham to Newcastle, 13 April 1766;
ibid., fo. 389. Newcastle, rough memorandum. ' Ald. Trecothick, Mr. Barclay, Mr.
Hanbury, Merchants that went to Mr. Pitt.' Burke had seen Pitt several days earlier
when reporting the suggestion from Rockingham (*ibid.*, fo. 417).

[5] Pitt's change of attitude was first seen in the debate of 30 April (Brit. Mus. Add.
MS. 32975, fo. 58).

[6] *Ibid.*, fo. 97, West to Newcastle, 7 May 1766. *Ibid.*, fo. 98, Onslow to Newcastle,
7 May 1766.

of the political machine when in a question of such importance as that now before the House . . . only seventy members could be found to attend their dutys.[1]

Such a position could not be allowed to continue, and the ministry through Rose and Stephen Fuller, the West Indians, as well as its usual intermediaries, was trying desperately, since the opposing bodies could come to no compromise, to persuade the West Indians into agreement by the grant of new concessions to their other trade demands. Negotiations of this kind had been going on continually behind the business of opposition,[2] and on 8 May the ministry was rejoiced to hear that, through the 'infinite merit'[3] of Rose and Stephen Fuller, an agreement satisfactory to all shades of West Indian opinion had been reached. That the West Indians had good cause to be satisfied by the compensations which were made them is shown by the rough drafts and final copy of their agreement, preserved among the Newcastle papers.[4] For the ministry the success of this negotiation was the last satisfaction which they obtained, for though opposition at once collapsed, when the West Indian change of front became apparent, and the resolutions embodying their two acts for American trade were passed the same night,[5] it was too late to strengthen their cause. Fully reconciled, however, the North American and West Indian merchants continued to follow up their successes, and, laying down the main lines of the regulations for the new Free Ports,[6] concluded the commercial policy which they had forced into existence, although the ministry gave it their own name.

At this very time the exhausted ministry was falling. In July, with Burke still loyally struggling to keep up, by the example of an address from the North American and West Indian merchants, the claim of his patrons to be the favourites and benefactors of the great merchant classes with their interests in the West,[7] the first Rockingham ministry disappeared.

[1] *Chatham Corr.* ii. 417, Nuthall to Pitt, 8 May 1766.

[2] Brit. Mus. Add. MS. 33030, fo. 247. Notes on Suggested Agreement—names of West Indian witnesses, accompanied, it is stated, by a letter from S. Fuller (Agent for Jamaica) to Dowdeswell, probably that of 30 April (Add. MS. 32975, fo. 62).

[3] *Ibid.*, fos. 110, 112, 114, G. Onslow to Newcastle, 8 May 1766.

[4] *Ibid.* 33030, fo. 243. Agreement of the West Indian Committee (rough copy) docketed house of commons, 8 May 1766. Fo. 245, fair copy, with alterations. (See appendix.) That the West Indians did not consider the compromise in the light of a defeat is suggested by the wording of an invitation to Newcastle to a West Indian dinner 13 June 1766 (*ibid.* 32975, fo. 400).

[5] *Ibid.*, fo. 112, West to Newcastle, 8 May 1766.

[6] Printed. Brit. Mus. 213. i. 5(99), *Regulations for Opening the Island of Dominica as a Free Port*, approved by the Merchants of the West Indian and North American Committees in order to increase the Consumption of our Manufactures and to extend the Trade and Navigation of Great Britain. n.d. I am indebted to Miss H. Allen of Vassar College for this note. These regulations were incorporated in the statute with slight modifications.

[7] *Burke Corr.* i. 107, Burke to Rockingham, 21 August 1766; *Rockingham Memoirs*,

With it went Burke into the long opposition in which his genius was to be formed, but the lines of his career had already been laid. A year before almost unknown, he had, at a time when young and ambitious men were numerous, made a striking success in the house, and won a name in the organization of complicated commercial affairs. Friends thought that ' whatever side he engages on . . . his abilities will be conspicuous ',[1] but he had never the personal enterprise of the free-lance such as Pitt and Townshend.[2] Already his ambitions and enthusiasms were pledged to the first patrons of his political life.

Few contemporaries can have thought that the short ministry which had failed to revive the solidity of half a century's firm whig rule had in any way a permanent influence upon the political development of its time. Yet Burke saw more truly, though not for the reasons which he gave, when he saw in it great significance. In the growth of the influence of outside opinion on parliament, and in the formation of the claims of control and parliamentary reform to which this was inevitably leading up, it played, though involuntarily, a part. Further, this ministry gave its form both in practice and theory to what we consider the whig tradition of the eighteenth century. It was not the principles of the Pelhams, Cavendishes, and Russells, ruling securely as the heirs of the glorious revolution, but those which were forced out by the change from power to opposition, a compound of new needs with old loyalties. They were the principles which Burke conceived as underlying the endless personal friction, the expediencies of long opposition, and the crises of short-lived power among the band of men, for him ' far the best that probably ever were engaged in the public services of this country '.[3]   L. STUART SUTHERLAND.

ii. 9–10. Hardwicke wrote to Rockingham, 24 August 1766 : ' I was much edified by the account in the papers of your reception in Yorkshire, with the Address of the manufacturers etc., and had before read with pleasure the handsome and well-merited compliment to your Lordship by the Committee of Merchants in town upon your dismission from office. You are really beating the late Great Commoner at his own weapons.'

[1] *Hist. MSS. Comm. VIIIth Report, O'Conor MSS.*, p. 483, O'Conor to Curry, 17 November 1766.

[2] Grafton in a letter to Chatham, 17 October 1766 (*Chatham Corr.* iii. 111) gave a shrewd estimate of him. ' I cannot help saying, that I look upon it, that he is a most material man to gain, and one on whom the thoroughest dependence may be given, where an obligation is owned.'

[3] *Burke Corr.* ii. 278, Burke to Shackleton, 25 May 1776.

APPENDIX

I. *Agreement of the West Indian Committee.* Endorsed House of Commons, May 8th. 1766. (Rough Copy.) (Brit. Mus. Add. MS. 33030, fo. 243.)

(Erasures, here enclosed in brackets [ ], occur in the original. Phrases in parentheses ( ) indicate that they are in another hand.)

1. That the 18d Duty on Sugar be taken off and that 1d per Gallon be laid upon Melasses of the British Sugar Colonies imported into North America.
2. That the Time of paying the Excise on bonded Rum be prolonged (to a twelvemonth).
3. That [either] 6d per gallon be [taken off Rum and] (additional duty be) laid upon Brandy, [or that 1s. per Gallon be laid on Brandy and Rum remain as it is].
4. That Relief be given to the Spanish Trade (by a species of Free port in Jamaica for Spanish bottoms to be proposed this year).[1]
5. That the Duty on French Sugars in North America be *settled* (continued) at 5 p.c. (as it now is.)
6. That the Duty on foreign Cotton be taken off.
7. That the Duty on foreign Melasses imported into North America be reduced to 1d. per Gallon.
8. [All other Articles as Administrations think proper.]
9. That all Sugars coming from North America to Great Britain [to be warehoused and reexported] be deemed foreign.
10. (marked). [The free port of Dominica not to be carried into Execution this Year.] (The Freeport at Dominica for Goods of foreign American Growth etc. to be proposed for consideration but not absolutely determined whether to pass it or not this Session.)
11. The Consumption of foreign Sugars not to be permitted in Great Britain but upon the present high Duty.
    That the West India Committee inform the North American Committee of . . . .

II. *Fair Copy of the Above.* (Brit. Mus. Add. MS. 33030, fo. 245). This would appear to be the final form of the agreement. Here the following phrases are omitted :

4. (to be proposed this year)
10. To be proposed for consideration but not absolutely determined whether to pass it this session.

The end. That the West India Committee inform the North American Committee of . . . .

---

[1] The Jamaica free port created is to be distinguished sharply from that of Dominica (dealt with in 10). The Jamaica free port was desired by the West Indians to encourage the Spanish smuggled bullion trade. The Dominica free port was intended (like 6) to get raw cotton and other materials ' In as great a Quantity and as Cheap as possible for the benefit of our own Manufacturers at Manchester where 120,000 persons are employed therein'. The West Indians were afraid of the latter, as they saw in it a means of smuggling foreign sugar through North America. ' It is a fact very remarkable that in some years the Sugars imported from North America to this kingdom as of British Growth, exceeded considerably in Quantity what they Exported from our Colonies.' (Brit. Mus. Add. MS. 33030, fo. 247.)

III. Fo. 247 of the same manuscript consists of rough notes on the agreement point by point. Several have against them in the margin the names of three prominent West Indians, Maitland, Beeston Long, and Thomas Collett. Reference is also made to a letter from Stephen Fuller, agent for Jamaica. The notes attributed to their authority stress the bad position of the West Indian Rum trade. With regard to clause 2 it is said :

> ' The Want of this Regulation hath been most severely felt this Year, for there hath been lying in the Warehouses about 5000 Puncheons of 100 Gallons each at one time for want of a market. . . .'

So that after six months the owners had to sell it at auction to raise the Excise, and lost heavily.

With regard to clause 3

> ' If Rum should continue for many Years in the situation it is in at present, it will ruin the Proprietors of the old Sugar Plantations, and prevent the settlement of our new acquisitions, so far as relates to Sugar and Rum.'

They would have preferred the 6d to be taken off Rum, but this will do.

Lord Shelburne and the Proclamation of 1763[1]

WILLIAM PETTY, earl of Shelburne, presided over the Board of Trade from 23 April to 2 September 1763. Five weeks later a proclamation rapidly prepared by the board was no less rapidly approved and dispatched to the British colonies. This, amongst other provisions, defined the territory of three new colonies on the continent of North America, prescribed their immediate and their future forms of government, and restricted by a boundary line the westward extension of the old provinces. Its legal, constitutional, and territorial arrangements helped to determine some of the major features of imperial policy during the next ten years.

The difficulties which this proclamation caused successive ministries, the uncertainty as to the precise legal effect of some of its provisions, and the misapprehensions as to the meaning and intention of others, these form a familiar story; Lord Northington's characterization of the proclamation as a ' very silly ' document [2] has been frequently approved. The purpose of this article is not to arrive at startlingly new conclusions about the character of the royal proclamation of 7 October 1763, but rather to examine afresh the evidence upon which to base an account of its genesis. Of this the late C. W. Alvord provided an interpretation which has been in general accepted. Alvord believed that, though Shelburne had proposed the proclamation, its final form ' did not in many ways correspond ' with his intentions. ' The responsibility for the blunders which it contained must be assigned to a delay in its final preparation and to the influence of other men ' who were less informed and more conservative.[3]

---

[1] The chief manuscript sources for this note are the Shelburne Papers in the William L. Clements Library, Ann Arbor, Michigan, and the Colonial Office Papers in the Public Record Office, London. In quotations superior letters have been levelled.

[2] *Memoirs of the Marquis of Rockingham*, ed. George Thomas, Earl of Albemarle (2 vols., London, 1852), i. 353.

[3] C. W. Alvord, *The Mississippi Valley in British Politics* (Cleveland, 1917), i. 157. Cf. R. Coupland, *The Quebec Act* (Oxford, 1925), p. 30. In his *Mississippi Valley* Alvord expanded, and in some points corrected, his early essay, ' The Genesis of the Proclamation of 1763 ', Michigan *Pioneer and Historical Collections* (1907), xxxvi. 21. He discovered that in this essay he had made inferences by a process of reasoning backwards from later to earlier times which further research did not justify, *Mississippi Valley*, i. 168, n. 301. I am inclined, however, to think that he continued to make similar inferences. Cf. his assumptions upon Shelburne's views, *ibid.* i. 152, 169, 176-8.

This belief finds some warrant in contemporary opinion. The proclamation, declared Lord Thurlow during the debates on the Quebec Act, was not ' the finished composition of a very considerable and respectable person, whom I will not name, [Shelburne], but went unfinished from his hands ' : a statement which Colonel Barré, who knew Shelburne as well as it was possible to know that statesman, criticized as ' a short, but very imperfect, and for aught I know, a very incorrect, history of the proclamation '.[1] But as Thurlow also said, the proclamation met ' with nobody to avow it '. Shelburne remained ambiguously silent both as to his connexion with this document and as to his opinion of it. In 1767, to be sure, he declared :

If [by] the bounds prescribed by the proclamation of 1763 is to be understood a system of bounding not particular provinces but our American settlements in general, it seems founded on a contracted policy amounting to little less than an attempt to set limits to the encrease of our people and the extension of our dominions ; besides that, it is impracticable to prevent, along such a frontier, the taking possession of unoccupied lands.[2]

But this, as Shelburne knew, was not ' the system ' ' understood ' by the framers of the proclamation, though others might wish to understand it so ; he himself had continually asserted that, had ' a due obedience ' been paid to the proclamation, the troubles between settlers, traders, and Indians on the western frontiers of America would have been avoided.[3] Similarly, in 1766 and 1767, he was content, with the Rockinghams and with Charles Yorke, to ascribe the legal difficulties which had arisen in Canada not to the proclamation but to Governor Murray's ' misinterpretation ' of it.[4] Lord Shelburne, it would seem, did not perceive that his former colleagues had blundered in the drafting of the proclamation after his retirement from the Board of Trade.

[1] Sir Henry Cavendish, *Debates of the House of Commons in the year 1774 on the bill for making more effectual provision for the government of the province of Quebec,* ed. J. Wright (London, 1839), pp. 29, 38. The speeches of Thurlow and Barré are conveniently accessible in W. P. M. Kennedy, *Statutes, Treaties and Documents of the Canadian Constitution, 1713–1929* (2nd and revised edition, Oxford, 1930), pp. 99, 103. Barré continued his remarks by paraphrasing Thurlow, ' He says it was left in an office ; it was left a sketch, and that sketch was unfinished ', etc. A marginal note on a copy of the Law Officers' Report of 14 April 1766 in the British Museum runs : ' I am told Ld. Shelburne took this proclamation on himself, that he had left a draught of it in the office. This seems strange, but Nobody before knew [?] it. H.'. Add. MS. 35914, fo. 150. But what the second earl of Hardwicke meant by these ambiguous and awkward remarks must be left to conjecture.

[2] ' Minutes submitted to the Cabinet in the beginning of Summer 1767—relative to the System of Indian Traffick ', Shelburne Papers, 50 : 185 ; *Illinois Historical Collections,* xvi. (ed. C. W. Alvord and C. E. Carter, Springfield, 1921), p. 17.

[3] Cf. Shelburne to Colonial Governors, 13 September 1766, Shelburne Papers, 53 : 97 ; C.O. 5 : 66, p. 285. Shelburne to Johnson, 13 September 1766, *Papers of Sir William Johnson,* v. (ed. A. C. Flick, Albany, 1927), p. 374.

[4] R. A. Humphreys and S. M. Scott, ' Lord Northington and the Laws of Canada ', *Canadian Historical Review* (1933), xiv. 50.

His appointment to the board marked Shelburne's first introduction to office, after but slight experience of political life.
He took himself and his position seriously ; out of twenty-one
meetings held during his presidency he attended seventeen ;[1] and he
later averred that he tried to keep official business secret even
from the secretary of state.[2] Such unusual punctiliousness
doubtless seemed suspicious. With reason Egremont and Halifax,
the two secretaries, felt ' jealous ' and ' uneasy ' of one who in
the Grenville ministry remained the friend and representative of
Bute. Shelburne, who had aspired to Egremont's office, hoped to
increase the recently diminished powers of the board, or at least
to act as the head of an independent department.[3] Under the
Order in Council of 15 May 1761, then in force, the board had
been deprived of the power of nominating to colonial offices, and
left with the conduct of colonial correspondence alone. In effect,
even this was divided between the board and the secretary for the
southern department. But Shelburne's attempts to increase his
powers were fruitless.[4] His natural disgust [5] no doubt contributed
to the facility with which he engaged as the agent of an external
authority in an attempt to reconstitute the ministry over the
heads of the ministers. That failing, he declared the business of
the board was disagreeable, resigned, and linked his fortunes to
those of Pitt.

It would be rash hastily to ascribe these actions to a cynical
ambition or to personal jealousy. There is no doubt, however,
that Shelburne found the ministry uncongenial, and particularly
his own place in it. But this dissatisfaction arose from no disagreement on colonial policy. The story, founded on the inaccurate reporting or the inexact memory of later years, that in

[1] Board of Trade Journals, C.O. 391 : 70. Shelburne's commission is dated
23 April. He took his seat on the 26th. His last meeting was held on 30 August.
[2] Parliamentary History, xix. 509.
[3] Cf. Knox MSS., Historical MSS. Commission, Report on Various Collections,
vi. 282 ; Grenville Papers, ed. W. J. Smith (London, 1852), ii. 32 ff., 238 ; Correspondence of William Pitt, Earl of Chatham, ed. W. S. Taylor and J. H. Pringle (London,
1838), ii. 229, 235 ; Horace Walpole, Memoirs of Reign of George III, ed. Sir D. Le
Marchant (London, 1845), i. 287, 295 ; P. C. Yorke, Life and Correspondence of Philip
Yorke, Earl of Hardwicke (Cambridge, 1913), iii. 498, 514 ; Lord E. Fitzmaurice,
Life of William, Earl of Shelburne (2nd and revised edition, London, 1912), i. 169 ff.
[4] Alvord's statements that Shelburne had ' an equal weight in colonial affairs
with the secretary ', that there was a ' return to the arrangement as it was established
under Halifax ', Mississippi Valley, i. 140, 154, and the comment in C. M. Andrews,
Guide to the Materials for American History to 1783, in the Public Record Office of Great
Britain (Washington, 1912), i. 98, that on Shelburne's appointment ' the order of
1752 was renewed ', are disproved by A. H. Basye, The Lords Commissioners of Trade
and Plantations . . . (New Haven, 1925), pp. 125, 173–5 ; and there is no need to add
to that discussion. Shelburne's protest over the matter of colonial correspondence
is given in Fitzmaurice, op. cit. i. 192.
[5] Cf. Bute to Shelburne, 23 June 1763, ibid. i. 196. ' Don't be concerned at want
of information or the little paultry trappings of Ministry. If any around you whisper
you are not of sufficient importance, hear them not.'

1763 he had proposed to allow the inhabitants of the new colonies to elect their governors, but that Grenville quashed the plan, may be dismissed as apocryphal.[1] The evidence from which to glean an understanding of Shelburne's political ideas in 1763, particularly in their application to colonial problems, is comparatively scanty ;[2] but it is clear that their originality was slight, and that his acquaintance with the colonies was largely confined to the information he received after his appointment to the board.

At the age of 26, the earl of Shelburne gave little promise of that peculiar philosophic radicalism which was later to distinguish him. His temperament hardly fitted him for public life. Ambitious, sensitive, autocratic, extraordinarily suspicious, he was strangely compounded of naïveté and astuteness. The loneliness of his youth and the deficiencies of his education combined to make him abnormally self-conscious ; and his character, unfortunately, was weaker than his intellect. Already there had been sounded that note of criticism and bewilderment which the man rather than his actions inspired, and which was to swell to ever louder volume. An affinity of mind with the eighteenth-century *philosophe*, and a genuine passion for ' liberty ' was to lead him, in his aristocratic way, to patronize philosophers, and to support radical and reforming causes. But this was in the future ; and Shelburne's intellectual development was slow. He was, to be sure, already deeply interested in economics. That interest shone through his first important public speech. Some four months prior to his appointment to the Board of Trade he had been selected as Bute's apologist for the peace of Paris. He had defended the peace with ability and enthusiasm. Commerce, he declared, was now ' the great object of ambition '. The peace was a glorious opportunity as well as a diplomatic necessity. He waved aside the pamphlet war which had raged over the relative merits of Canada and Guadeloupe. Guadeloupe was a ' trifling object ' from the point of view of trade ; but North America, ' with the universal empire of that extended coast ', opened ' new fields ' for commercial development. ' The northern colonies encrease population, and of course the consumption of our manufactures, pay us for them by their trade with foreigners,

---

[1] B. Vaughan to B. Franklin, 6 March 1778, *Writings of Benjamin Franklin*, ed. A. H. Smyth (New York, 1905–7), x. 331. The document cited by Alvord, *Mississippi Valley*, i. 177, n. 315, which seems to lend colour to the truth of this alleged statement, was written not by Shelburne, but by Maurice Morgann, at the time an under-secretary of state. Shelburne Papers, 85 : 81. There seems no reason to suppose that it represented Shelburne's views. It is also extremely doubtful whether Shelburne held the opinions ascribed to him by Alvord in the following note 316.

[2] The manuscript material is mostly contained in Shelburne Papers, 48, 49, 50, 67 and 85. Partly on account of its paucity as compared with the amount available for later years, Alvord, I think, was led to read back into 1763 ideas which Shelburne may have held at considerably later periods. See *supra*, p. 241, n. 3.

and thereby giving employment to millions of inhabitants in Great Britain and Ireland.'[1]

This argument was not new ; its success depended greatly on the plausibility of dismissing Guadeloupe as a ' trifling object '. Similar pleas had been continually advanced during the last few months, and as continually replied to. Nor was an emphasis on the value of colonies as markets more than as sources of supply in itself a novelty. A balanced opinion had long embraced both aspects. Shelburne, perhaps, had listened to an exposition of free trade by Adam Smith on the occasion of a journey by stage from Edinburgh to London, but the length of the lecture had not sufficed for the novelty of the theory.[2] A dozen or more years passed before he began to advocate ' the broad principles of free trade '.[3] In short, Shelburne's imperial views, either in their political or in their economic relations, were not unconventional, and not discrepant to the broad lines of policy already laid down by the Board of Trade. He was amongst those whose imperial faith demanded an orderly and expanding empire possessed of valuable and dependent colonies.

Such was the man who in May 1763 was required by the earl of Egremont to formulate the policy of the government upon the recent acquisitions in America. For the last eighteen months Egremont had been at the southern department, at a time when colonial problems had been receiving close consideration. Now, in a long and interesting letter which showed no little appreciation of imperial responsibility, he focussed ideas which had long been considered by the board upon the new conditions in America. Two problems were fundamental : how to obtain the most considerable commercial advantages from the recent acquisitions, and how best to secure them. It was imperative to decide what new governments to establish, and what sort of governments they should be, what military protection was necessary, and in what way the colonies should contribute to contingent expenses. To preserve internal peace it was essential to conciliate the Indians ; their lands should only be acquired by fair purchase.

These major considerations, and others less comprehensive, imposed a difficult task ; and the board, Egremont conceded, might reasonably deal at once only with the more pressing of them. His letter assumed that a broad general agreement on the

[1] Speech of 9 December 1762, Shelburne Papers, 165 (unpaged) ; H. W. V. Temperley in *Cambridge History of the British Empire* (Cambridge, 1929), i. 504.

[2] J. Rae, *Life of Adam Smith* (London, 1895), pp. 153–4.

[3] Contrast Alvord, *op. cit.* i. 169. For an expression of Shelburne's mercantile views see his speech of 11 March 1766, ' Debates on the Declaratory Act and the Repeal of the Stamp Act ', *American Historical Review* (1912), xvii. 584. Not till after 1776 did Shelburne become a free-trader. The change may be partially followed in his speeches recorded in the *Parliamentary History*.

principles of policy already existed. At the same time his mind
was open ; his queries with regard to Louisiana, the Illinois, and
the navigation of the Mississippi implied a readiness to consider
questions of new settlements.[1] More fully to display his intentions and to guide the board in its decisions, Egremont enclosed a
paper of ' Hints relative to the Division and Government of the
conquered and newly acquired Countries in America '.[2] Of this
the putative author was Henry Ellis,[3] late governor of Georgia,
non-resident governor of Nova Scotia, secretary and clerk of the
council of Canada, provost-marshal of Grenada, Dominica, and
Tobago, who, according to Francis Maseres, actually drafted the
proclamation of October 1763, and who, according to William
Knox, was Egremont's right-hand man in all colonial affairs.[4] If
an accumulation of offices is any criterion, Knox's opinion may
well be believed.

This remarkable document enunciated important principles,
and, stamped with the approval of the secretary of state, its
' hints ', with two exceptions, found their way into the proclamation of October.[5] Of particular interest was its recommendation
to form the governments of the new provinces on the model of
Georgia or Nova Scotia (' the freest from a republican mixture '),
with the exception of Canada, where ' the civil government . . .
would be best administered for some time by a governor and
council only ', until the king could suitably ' indulge his new
subjects in that part of the world with representatives in general
assembly '. Seemingly new was the proposal to ' fix upon some
line for a western boundary to our ancient provinces, beyond
which our people should not at present be permitted to settle,
hence as their numbers increased, they would emigrate to Nova
Scotia, or to the provinces on the southern frontier '. The

[1] Egremont to the Lords of Trade, 5 May 1763, *Documents relating to the Constitutional History of Canada, 1759–1791*, ed. A. Shortt and A. G. Doughty (2nd and revised
edition, Ottawa, 1918), i. 127.

[2] Shelburne Papers, 48 : 543 ; C.O. 323 : 16, p. 189. Cf. C.O. 391 : 70, p. 144
and C.O. 326 : 55, p. 41. This document was discovered, identified and printed by
V. W. Crane, *Mississippi Valley Historical Review* (1922), viii. 367 ff. There he fully
proves its importance as a ' key-document ' in the sequence of documents culminating
in the proclamation of 1763, and demonstrates that most of its suggestions are therein
enshrined.

[3] The suggestion of C. W. Alvord in a footnote to the article cited above.

[4] Hist. MSS. Comm. *Rep. on Var. Coll.* vi. 282 ; *The Maseres Letters*, ed. Stewart
Wallace (University of Toronto Library, 1919), p. 62. Maseres also calls Ellis ' the
oracle of the ministry for all American matters ', *ibid.* p. 99. Ellis was granted additional leave of absence from Nova Scotia on 11 March 1763. His appointments as
secretary and clerk and provost-marshal date from 23 April. C.O. 324 : 40, fos. 219,
243, 248. See also [F. Maseres], *The Canadian Freeholder* . . . (3 vols., London,
1777, 1779), i. 361.

[5] The one exception, intentional, was the proposal to divide Canada into two.
The other was the suggestion to refer all matters cognizable by law in the proposed
Indian reservation to the civil power in the neighbouring provinces.

country to the westward of this line should be protected by ' the officers commanding at the distant posts '. But since ' many of the King's subjects ' would ' necessarily have occasion to go beyond this line for trade, and other purposes ', disputes might arise ; such disputes, indeed ' all matters cognizable by law ', should be reserved to ' the civil power in any of the neighbouring provinces '.[1]

Egremont had taken care to furnish the board not merely with the general outline of a plan, but with constructive details. He had indicated the type of government he expected the new provinces to possess. He had added to the principle of fair purchase of Indian lands that of a temporary boundary line enclosing an Indian reservation.

With these recommendations for his guidance, Shelburne spent a month in further investigation and in the preparation of his report. From the professional experience of John Pownall, permanent secretary of the board, he received invaluable assistance. He consulted extensively another, apparently Maurice Morgann. Morgann, who won some literary celebrity as the author of an *Essay on the Dramatic Character of Sir John Falstaff*, was destined to play a curious part on the colonial stage. For upwards of twenty years he served Shelburne, now in a private, now in a public capacity ; his numerous memoranda amongst Shelburne's papers have too frequently been taken as expressions of Shelburne's own opinions.[2]

The liberality of Morgann's views in 1763 may be estimated from his beliefs that colonists were ' merely factors for the purpose of trade ' ; that colonial charters should be surrendered ; and that taxes on trade should provide the means of support of government. He found himself in general agreement with the ' hints ' given to the board. To the proposal for an Indian boundary line he gave a rather sinister interpretation. The military should be increased, he wrote, and

under pretence of regulating the Indian trade a very straight line be suddenly drawn on the back of the colonies and the country beyond that line thrown, for the present, under the dominion of the Indians. The provinces being now surrounded by an army, a navy, and by hostile tribes

[1] Other suggestions were to divide Florida into two, to unite St. John's to Nova Scotia, to extend Georgia southwards to the river St. Mary's, and to annex the southern coast of Labrador to Newfoundland.

[2] Morgann's peripatetic career has left few details behind it. An inexact account is given in the *Dictionary of National Biography*, and corrected in the *Bulletin of the Institute of Historical Research*, iii. 132, x. 203. Morgann's precise connexion with Shelburne in 1763 I have been unable to discover. From the memoranda in his hand apparently of that date it seems to have been fairly close. In 1782 he wrote to Shelburne from New York, ' I have for above twenty years thrown myself upon your lordship ' (17 June 1782), Shelburne Papers, 68 : 389. Instances of his memoranda mistaken for Shelburne's opinions are cited *supra*, p. 244, n. 1. See also *Cambridge History of the British Empire*, i. 661.

of Indians . . . and being thus limited and distressed in their finances and wanting an executive for the purposes of resistance, it may be time (not to oppress or injure them in any shape) but to exact a due deference to the just and equitable regulations of a British parliament.

Interestingly enough in conjunction with views so much the reverse of radical, he seems to have favoured the creation of new governments on the Great Lakes, and near the forks of the Ohio and Illinois.[1]

Shelburne sought also, or received unasked, the advice of others ; and the opinions which he collected in general echoed the arguments of the Canada-Guadeloupe controversy of the past three years. They displayed more than one idea of policy but very little constructive detail. Nor, to be sure, was this supplementary information very extensive or very important.[2]

Upon Pownall naturally devolved the task of preparing the required report. His memoranda and drafts furnish further evidence of the consensus of opinion on the fundamentals of any North American plan. Pownall, also, substantially accepted the suggestions which had come from the office of the secretary of state. He does not seem to have approved the additional idea of forming new colonies beyond an area reserved for the Indians. By the end of May, or early in June, he had completed a ' Sketch of a Report concerning the Cessions in Africa and America at the Peace of 1763 '.[3]

This ' sketch ', possibly the first draft, formed the basis of the

[1] ' Plan for securing the Future Dependence of the Provinces on the Continent of North America ', Shelburne Papers, 67 : 107 ; ' On American Commerce and Government ', Shelburne Papers, 85 : 26. These documents, undated, appear to be written by Morgann, though 85 : 26 has a part in the middle in some one else's writing. They would seem to belong most appropriately to between May and June 1763. Morgann, it should be noted, approved of the proposals to divide Canada and Florida each into two, and agreed that Nova Scotia was the best model for any new government. I am indebted to Miss Edna Vosper of the William L. Clements Library for verifying for me these references. Morgann's approval of new western colonies (which he arrived at after much hesitation) may have been due to Amherst's support of such schemes. Cf. Amherst to Egremont, 30 November 1762, Shelburne Papers, 48 : 417.

[2] See, for example, ' Some Thoughts on Indian Affairs ', Shelburne Papers, 50 : 247, and by the same author, ' Thoughts on the Settlement and Government of our Colonies in North America, March 10, 1763 ', Shelburne Papers, 48 : 525 ; ' Hints respecting the Settlement of Florida ', Shelburne Papers, 48 : 51 ; ' Hints respecting the Settlement of our American Colonies ' and allied documents, Shelburne Papers, 48 : 475–521. Some of these papers may yet be identified, but none of them seems to possess the interest which attaches to the papers identified above and below. The sorting of these papers makes it necessary to qualify Alvord's statement that the ' advice ' which Shelburne received was ' so varied ' as almost to forbid generalization, Alvord, op. cit. i. 165.

[3] Cf. ' General Propositions. Form and Constitution of Government to be established in the new Colonies ', Shelburne Papers, 48 : 559 ; ' Mr. Pownall's Sketch of a Report concerning the Cessions in Africa and America at the Peace of 1763 ', Shelburne Papers, 49 : 333. This document is printed infra, p. 258. See also ' A Sketch of a Report with Observations on the Commission and Instructions for the Governor of Grenada ', Shelburne Papers, 49 : 293.

report which the Board of Trade was to make on 8 June. An ingenious argument has been partially evolved out of the erroneous supposition that its principles were ' quite distinct ' from those of the actual report.[1] In fact, though the report of 8 June is far more elaborate and comprehensive, there is little or no conflict of principles between the two documents. Pownall argued that ' the permitting the colonies, *for the present at least*,[2] to extend their settlements ' beyond the Appalachians was bad economics and worse policy. For the present, therefore, the land between the ' ridge of the Apalachian mountains and the river Mississippi ' should be erected into an Indian reservation under the control of the military, and with full liberty of trade ' upon some general plan and under proper regulations and restrictions '. At certain points the natural boundary line of this temporary Indian reservation would be broken to allow for Creek and Cherokee claims, for instance, on the eastern side of the mountains, and for the claims of settlers under the government of Virginia on the western.

In regard to Canada the boundaries which Pownall here roughly assigned were subsequently adopted. On the south-east, he thought, they had been clearly defined both by nature and by reason, for those ' high lands which range across the continent from Cape Rozier in the Gulf of St. Lawrence to Lake Champlain above St. Johns ' were not only ' the most convenient and certain of all natural boundaries ', but also, the ' inhabitants of the country between these high lands and the river St. Lawrence ' could not ' consistent with any rule either of reason or good policy be separated from their countrymen on the other side and taken out of a government under which they have always lived '. Hence the pretensions of certain New England colonies to extend their boundaries towards the St. Lawrence could not be admitted.[3]

Upon the form of government to be established in Canada, or in any of the new provinces Pownall expressed no opinion in this ' sketch '. Elsewhere, however, he had approved the idea that

[1] Alvord, *Mississippi Valley*, i. 171, 174. This statement has naturally been copied by other writers. Cf. Basye, *Board of Trade*, p. 129. This supposition appears to be entertained also by D. McArthur, ' The British Board of Trade and Canada, 1760–74 ; I. The Proclamation of 1763 ', Canadian Historical Association, *Annual Report*, 1932, pp. 104, 105.

[2] The italics are mine.

[3] Pownall here definitely referred to the paper of ' Hints ' sent by Egremont. ' It seems by a paper transmitted to us with the Earl of Egremont's letter to have been the idea of some person that it might be adviseable to establish two governments upon the river St. Lawrence '. This Pownall disapproved ; though he favoured the proposal to divide Florida into two. It is difficult to follow Alvord in his belief that the above remarks of Pownall in regard to Canada represented a policy of ' segregation ' of the Canadians and of closing that province to settlement. Alvord, *op. cit.* i. 174.

Nova Scotia and Georgia were the best models for any new governments, with the reservation that

at present . . . the new colonies are not, nor will they for some time, be in a capacity to receive the full impression of this free constitution to its full extent, for either they are not inhabited at all, or by such as are under a legal disability of being admitted efficient members of the community so as to act in any judicial or legislative capacity. The form of government for the present therefore must of necessity be oligarchical. . . . In respect to legislature, this rule of government may, it is conceived, be observed in all the new colonies upon the continent without exception, being equally applicable to all.

But clearly this was merely a temporary expedient.[1]

The completion of the Board of Trade report was now hurried on ; and by 8 June it was finished. Pownall's ' sketch ', generally approved, but unsuitable in form and insufficiently comprehensive, had been revised and enlarged and prefaced by a lengthy account of the advantages expected from the new acquisitions. In the work of revision it seems likely that Morgann had closely co-operated ; and to this new draft Shelburne and Pownall had both made corrections and emendations.[2] The result proved to be little more than an elaboration of those principles and suggestions which Egremont had set before the board for its examination. The scheme of a temporary Indian reservation enclosed by a boundary line was adopted. Pownall's suggested line would seem to have been approved, though its definite determination was referred to the boundaries of the new colonies and to ' strict directions ' to be given to the governors of the old. The reserved area was, as the ' hints ' of May had implied, to be open to trade under appropriate regulations. Canada, Florida, and the new West Indian Islands were specified as suitable places for settlement (the first direct intimation in regard to Canada of a policy which seems to have been implicitly accepted throughout), and its benefits urged in the case of Nova Scotia. Shelburne himself penned those phrases which recommended a conciliar form of government for Canada, and which referred the ' particular regulations and provisions to be adapted to this as well as your Majesty's other new acquisitions ' to the drafts of commissions and instruc-

---

[1] ' General Propositions. Form and Constitution of Government to be established in the new Colonies ', Shelburne Papers, 48 : 559. This paper concludes with the remark ' a great deal to be added which Mr. Pownall has not finished '. By ' oligarchical ' Pownall meant, of course, government by a governor and council.

[2] Draft of Board of Trade Report, 8 June 1763, C.O. 324 : 21, fos. 245–90 ; Board of Trade Report, 8 June 1763, C.O. 5 : 65, fo. 127, printed in Shortt and Doughty, op. cit. i. 132. A large part of the draft in C.O. 324 : 21 is in the same hand as the documents quoted supra, p. 248, n. 1. On a careful examination of the handwriting Miss Edna Vosper of the William L. Clements Library confirms my opinion that it is Morgann's.

tions for the new governors.[1]   Further details upon the laws and
constitutions of the new colonies were considered inapplicable
to this first general report.   On such points as the division of
Florida into two, the annexation of the Labrador coast to Newfoundland, the control of the Indian area, the board differed not
at all from the plan outlined for it.   In short, Shelburne had made
no new important suggestion.   The report of 8 June followed
logically from the policy outlined by Egremont and examined by
Pownall.   Its modifications are not significant.

This report was well received by Egremont.   His reply contained fresh commands : the board should prepare instructions
for the new governors ; it should inquire into the best method of
settling the new colonies.   Further, it had neglected to provide
any civil jurisdiction for the proposed Indian reservation.   The
recommendation made in May to reserve such jurisdiction to the
neighbouring provinces seems, indeed, to have escaped the notice
both of Pownall and of Shelburne.   Egremont proposed, therefore, that the whole inland area should be put under the control
of the governor of Canada.[2]   But to this new suggestion the
board saw insuperable objections ; and reverting to the idea of
military occupation, preferred to give a commission under the
Great Seal to the commander-in-chief for the government of this
territory.[3]

[1] In Shortt and Doughty, *op. cit.* i. 142, the words from ' which Objects ' to ' general
report ' are the composition of Shelburne.   The draft which Shelburne thus amended
read, following on the words ' and other new protestant settlers ', ' but these considerations together with the particular regulations and provisions adapted to their
present circumstances and situation will more properly be offered to your Majesty's
consideration in the Draught of the Commission and Instructions to that Governor,
which we shall immediately proceed to prepare against we receive your Majesty's
orders for that purpose '.   C.O. 324 : 21, fo. 273.
The omission in this report of a definite promise of representative government to
any of the new colonies can be taken neither as an important modification of principle,
nor as an exception in respect of one colony.   Contrast Alvord, *op. cit.* i. 174.
[2] Egremont to Lords of Trade, 14 July 1763, Shortt and Doughty, *op. cit.* i. 147.
[3] Lords of Trade to Egremont, 5 August 1763, *ibid.* i. 151.   On the 11th Newcastle
wrote to Devonshire : ' Our friend Mellish brought me a piece of news from London.
. . . That my Lord Shelburne, at the head of the board of trade, intends to propose
the making General Murray, who is now Governor of Canada only (as I understood it),
to be the general governor in those parts, as M. de Vaudreil the French governor was ;
and to give him all the powers, independent of assemblies, etc., which the French
governor had.'   Brit. Mus., Newcastle Papers, Add. MS. 32950, fo. 65, at fo.
82.   Newcastle, whose information about Canada was never, at the best of times,
very extensive, appears here to have got Egremont's suggestion muddled with the
declared intention to introduce a conciliar form of government in Canada.   A few
years later Newcastle was the victim of a delusion that Canada was ' without any
government whatever ; For, by the very absurd haste that there was in the then administration, upon the conclusion of the peace, his Majesty's proclamation was sent
to all the new-acquired colonies abroad, to adopt the laws of England *in toto* ; . . .
and hence these poor people have remained without any government from 1763 to
this day '.   Newcastle to Archbishop of Canterbury, 17 May 1767, Add. MS. 32982,
fo. 48.

So far the ordinary course of routine procedure had been undisturbed. It was now to be delayed and broken by a series of unexpected events, in the sequel of which the comprehensive plans of the government were to be reduced to the proportions of an emergency measure. In the first place, the alarming news had arrived of the Indian war on the American frontiers ; [1] and in the conclusion of this last report, which bore the date of 5 August, the board advocated the immediate issue of a proclamation which should quiet the Indians by prohibiting settlement in the area to be reserved to them, and which should encourage emigration to the new colonies.

On this occasion the board did not enumerate Canada amongst those colonies in which it was desirable to encourage settlement. It would be unwise to assume from this omission that the board had suddenly decided to segregate the Canadians. The primary purpose of this report had been to settle the problem of jurisdiction over the Indian lands.[2] The news of the Indian war caused the insertion of the proposal of a proclamation, with its reference to settling new colonies. This last problem, in accord with Egremont's commands, was yet under consideration. On 21 July the board had ordered its secretary to write to the governors of Canada, the Floridas, and the Islands ' for their opinion by what method, the most reasonable and frugal, the new established colonies in America may be peopled and settled with usefull, industrious inhabitants '.[3] No mention was made of Nova Scotia. On the 22nd, accordingly, Pownall wrote to Grant and Johnstone, the selected governors of the two Floridas. Those two officials were in England, and replied by the end of the month ; whereupon, on 1 August, Pownall was prompted to write to Robert Melville, who had been chosen governor of Grenada.[4] He failed to write to General James Murray, who was the selected governor for Canada, and who, indeed, was some three thousand miles away. When, four days later, the board made its report, only the letters

---

[1] Cf. Amherst to Egremont, 27 June 1763, C.O. 5 : 63 ; Johnson to Lords of Trade, 1 July 1763, *Documents relative to the Colonial History of the State of New York*, by J. R. Brodhead, ed. E. B. O'Callaghan, vii. (Albany, 1856), p. 525.

[2] Board of Trade Journals, 15 July 1763, C.O. 391: 70, p. 185. Alvord's argument, *op. cit.* i. 174, 188, 206, that the omission of Canada in the above report represented a policy of segregating the Canadians lacks corroborative evidence. It has been seen that Pownall's ' sketch ' did not suggest such a policy ; and the report of 8 June specifically advocated settlement. As to Alvord's citation of the report of 3 November 1763, *op. cit.* i. 174, n. 311, to the effect that no further provision need be made for the settlement of Canada beyond what was contained in the draft of instructions to the governor, it is notable that Murray's instructions ordered him to issue a proclamation setting forth the advantages of settlement. See Shortt and Doughty, *op. cit.* i. 198 ; also Report on Commissions for Governors, 6 October, 1763, *ibid.* i. 159.

[3] Board of Trade Journals, 21 July, C.O. 391: 70, p. 188.

[4] C.O. 326 : 55, pp. 44, 225, 233. Melville also was in England.

of Johnstone and Grant were to hand. In addition to the
Floridas it remembered the old colony of Nova Scotia ; but it
failed to mention either Canada or the Islands. Probably this
omission was unintentional ; or possibly the board felt a complete
enumeration to be unnecessary in a report primarily concerned
with another question.

However this may be, the Board of Trade now adjourned its
meetings till 30 August, and then again till 28 September. On
that day the proclamation promised a month and a half ago [1] was
ordered to be drafted. The exigencies of the summer season and
holiday time had, no doubt, contributed to delay. Moreover,
Egremont, at a most inopportune moment, had died of apoplexy ;
and Shelburne, who had been engaged in confused political
intrigues, had resigned. His room had been filled by Wills Hill,
earl of Hillsborough. Hillsborough's friend and mentor, the earl
of Halifax, took over the business of the southern department.

The domestic difficulties of the ministry having been temporarily overcome, Halifax was able to turn his attention to the
neglected colonial situation. He was quite competent, both from
his own considerable experience and from his close association
with Egremont, to continue the policy which Egremont had outlined and Shelburne had accepted. Not unnaturally, however,
he felt that, if a proclamation had to be issued, it might well
travel somewhat beyond the original suggestion. It should, for
example, declare the form of government, both for the present and
for the future, of the new colonies, define their boundaries,
proclaim a free Indian trade under appropriate regulations, and
—an important provision—empower the military to seize criminals
escaped to the reserved area and to hand them over to the civil
authorities. He agreed to the proposed commission for the
commander-in-chief for the government of this territory.[2] The
advantages expected from this extension of the purview of the
proclamation were a more speedy settlement of the new colonies
and a more effectual reconciliation with the Indians. Moreover,
it involved no departure from decisions which had already been
reached ; there was a close connexion between the original and
the additional proposals ; and there was much to be said for thus
announcing the main features of the government's policy.

These suggestions the board considered at its first meeting
under its new president on 28 September. The draft of a proclamation was at once ordered. Whatever materials Shelburne
may have left at the office, the rapidity with which the proclamation was now produced proved the absence of controversy over its

---

[1] Cf. Lords of Trade to Johnson, 5 August 1763, *New York Col. Docs.* vii. 535.
[2] Halifax to Lords of Trade, 19 September 1763, Shortt and Doughty, *op. cit.* i.
153.

details.   John Pownall, minutely acquainted with the evolution of
policy during the spring and summer, could have had no difficulty
in presenting Hillsborough with a concise account of the programme of the ministry.   Considered on the 29th and 30th, the
draft proclamation was sent to the attorney-general on 1 October.
Charles Yorke found nothing therein contrary to law.[1] He
queried once ' whether so many words are necessary ? ' and again
suggested some slight technical amendments.   A clause which
enjoined the establishment of courts of judicature in the new
colonies for determining civil and criminal cases ' according to
law and equity and agreeable to the laws and constitutions of the
mother country ' he altered to ' according to law and equity, and
as near as may be agreeable to the laws of England ', a famous
phrase.   John Pownall also went over the draft, and made a few
verbal alterations.   More important, he inserted those phrases
which stressed the temporary nature of the restrictions on the
western expansion of the colonies.   The injunction against the
granting of lands on the frontiers he qualified by the phrase ' for
the present, and until our further pleasure is known ', and to the
declaration of the intention to constitute an Indian reservation he
added ' for the present as aforesaid '.[2] Thus revised, the proclamation was presented to Halifax on the 4th, approved by the
council on the 5th, and by the king on the 7th.[3] Quite in accord
with the intentions of Halifax the board had included an ' immediate and public declaration ' of the ' intended permanent
constitution ' of the new colonies, and had resolved to insist on
the ' power of calling assemblies ' in the commissions to the new
governors.[4]

The document thus issued contained nothing new or surprising.
The novelty consisted in the form in which policies long discussed
were now announced.   Provided that the scope of the proclamation was to be extended, reasonably enough, on the lines indicated
by Halifax, there was no discrepancy between its contents and
the intentions of the ministry prior to the untoward events of
the last few weeks.   Even had there been no change in the
personnel of the ministry, it is unlikely that this ' very silly '
document would have been differently drawn.   As for this verdict
of Lord Northington, it savours more of the ill-temper of that
gouty statesman [5] than of his sense of justice.

[1] C. Yorke to Lords of Trade, 3 October 1763, C.O. 323 : 16, p. 337.

[2] Draft of proclamation, with emendations by Yorke and Pownall, C.O. 324 : 21,
fos. 321–40.   The emendations were embodied in or added to the final draft, C.O.
5 : 65, fo. 231.

[3] Board of Trade Journals, C.O. 391 : 70, pp. 213–74 ; Basye, *Board of Trade*,
p. 135.

[4] Lords of Trade to Halifax, 4 October 1763, Shortt and Doughty, *op. cit.* i. 156.
The proclamation is printed in *ibid.* i. 163.

[5] *Memoirs of the Marquis of Rockingham*, ed. George Thomas, Earl of Albemarle,
i. 353.

The proclamation, in brief, defined the territory of the new colonies, and their immediate and future forms of government ; it declared them open for settlement ; it ordered courts of justice to be erected to determine all causes ' according to law and equity, and as near as may be agreeable to the laws of England ' ; it specified a temporary Indian reservation west of the Appalachians, forbade the grant of lands in this area without express permission from the Crown, declared it open to a licensed trade under appropriate regulations, and directed that criminals therein escaped from the old colonies should be seized and returned to the provinces from which they had fled.

It failed to provide any government for the old French settlements in the Illinois country. This was the effect of ignorance. From May to October no member of the ministry appears to have been aware of the size and importance of these settlements, barely, indeed, of their existence.[1] The report of 8 June had mentioned French colonists in Florida and Eastern Louisiana, and had expressed the pious, but what was felt to be unlikely, hope that they would remain. But not until May 1767, eight months after Shelburne had again taken office, this time as a secretary of state, was the question of the need of providing some sort of government for the Illinois settlers raised in the cabinet.[2]

As the Quebec Council was later to complain, the western area was made ' subject to no civil jurisdiction whatsoever '.[3] The recommendation made in May to annex civil and criminal jurisdiction over this area to the neighbouring provinces had been consistently ignored. But this jurisdiction, according to the decisions of August and September, was to be dealt with in the proposed commission for the commander-in-chief. The misfortune was not that the proclamation omitted the matter, but that the Board of Trade later appears to have forgotten it.

The boundary line of the Indian reservation was drawn unequivocally down the Appalachian range. This natural barrier had been Pownall's suggestion. For the purposes of the proclamation it was an obvious one ; and there is no reason to suppose either that Shelburne would have drawn it differently, or that the government did not intend to make afterwards those modifications

[1] Cf. C. E. Carter, *Great Britain and the Illinois Country* (Washington, 1910), p. 15.

[2] ' Minutes of American Business ', Shelburne Papers, 85 : 89 ; printed in *Illinois Historical Collections*, xi., ed. C. W. Alvord and C. E. Carter (Springfield, 1916), p. 467. The date of these minutes appears to be on or soon after 29 May 1767, when a meeting was held at which they were the substance of discussion. See *Acts of the Privy Council, Colonial Series*, v. § 33.

[3] Council of Quebec, report of committee on Indian affairs, 8 April 1769, Quebec Legislative Council Register, C, 10 April 1769. Public Archives of Canada, Ottawa. I am indebted for this reference to Mr. S. M. Scott. Something was done for the west by the Mutiny Act of 1765. See *Calendar of Home Office Papers, 1760–65, no.* 1671 ; and cf. W. Knox's explanation in *Justice and Policy of the Late Act . . . (1774)*.

which Pownall had suggested, and which the board in June had proposed to carry through by means of governors' instructions.

Finally, the proclamation was so worded that Quebec received the same treatment as the other new provinces. To the new French subjects in Quebec little attention had yet been given. Examining the treatment accorded to these conquered colonists, Advocate General Marriott later expressed the opinion that the opening of Canada to settlement smacked of inadvertency and the ' hurry of office '.[1] But, however precipitate this procedure, it was not inadvertent. In the sequence of documents from May to October the intention seems clear, in the first place, to increase the number of protestant settlers in Canada, and, secondly, ultimately to give that province a representative form of government. Neither Shelburne nor any one else had doubts about the wisdom of this procedure. To include in the proclamation the promise of a representative assembly was to increase the allurements of settlement. Had that settlement taken place on the scale expected,[2] the problem of the laws of Canada would have become markedly changed. It was reasonable to expect that the Islands and Canada should ultimately have the same form of government as the other provinces.

What then was the legal system to be ? Charles Yorke returned the obvious reply : ' as near as may be agreeable to the laws of England '. Pownall had said much the same thing. In the new colonies, said he,

in everything that regards the general commerce of the country, the rights and liberties of the crown and people, the rules and proceedings in courts of justice, whether civil, criminal or ecclesiastical, and every other great principle of constitution relative to the important interests of the state, the laws of England shall take place and be observed with the greatest care and exactness.

There would be necessary exceptions. In the islands, for example, some ' deviation ' from this rule was essential, ' because in them are many cases arising out of the peculiar situation and circumstances, more particularly that of slavery, to which the laws of England do not apply themselves '.[3] Similarly, one of the reasons adduced by Pownall for his definition of the boundaries of Canada had been to prevent the Canadians from being put

under a variety of different governments from which they could receive no protection and to which they would consequently pay no obedience or yield any subjection to laws or constitution to them unknown and founded

---

[1] Shortt and Doughty, *op. cit.* i. 449.

[2] *Cambridge History of the British Empire*, vi. 154.

[3] ' General Propositions. Form and Constitution of Government to be established in the new Colonies ', Shelburne Papers, 48 : 559 at 562-3.

on principles the most adverse to their nature and consciences that can be imagined.[1]

Hillsborough later averred that ' it never entered into our idea to overturn the laws and customs of Canada, with regard to property',[2] and though this attempted justification came a little late, it may, on the whole, be believed. Many things had not ' entered into the idea ' of the English ministry. Very precisely it had not entered into their idea that Canada already possessed a complete legal system. But as far as they had thought about it at all, it seemed clear that ultimately English law should prevail. Exceptions, as Charles Yorke would say, were as ' may be ' ; but on this experimental question the proclamation gave no clear ruling.

On the supposition that English law had superseded French, that the ' laws, and customs, and forms of judicature ' of the Canadians had been abolished ' all at once ', Lord Mansfield early indulged in bitter comment.[3] In his later ruling in *Campbell v. Hall* he maintained that the prerogative rights of the Crown to change the laws of a conquered country could not be controverted [4] (though in this not all lawyers agreed with him) ; and Charles Yorke had earlier expressed a similar opinion.[5] But on the further question whether, in fact, the proclamation had introduced the system of English laws, Yorke and Mansfield differed. It was Yorke's belief that the proclamation had introduced only select parts of the laws of England.[6] Whatever the legal value of this opinion, it remains historically true that in practice English law was not introduced to the exclusion of French ; and theoretically Yorke's opinion was quite arguable. It is also true that between May and October 1763 no one in the English ministry had fully realized the nature of the special problem involved by the laws of Canada. As for Shelburne, his later attempts to understand the conflict of law and of opinion which arose in Canada [7] do not indicate that in 1763 he was more

[1] ' Sketch of a Report concerning the Cessions in Africa and America at the Peace of 1763.' Cf. D. McArthur, *op. cit.* p. 112.

[2] Hillsborough to Carleton, 6 March 1768, Shortt and Doughty, *op. cit.* i. 297.

[3] *Grenville Papers*, ii. 476.

[4] Shortt and Doughty, *op. cit.* i. 523 ff. There is a good discussion of this point in [F. Maseres] *The Canadian Freeholder*, ii. (London, 1779).

[5] ' The rule of law with regard to conquered countrys is that the old laws subsist till abolished by the conqueror ; and it may be done either under the *authority of the crown or that of parliament*.' ' Heads of my Brother's Speech at the Cabinet Council July the 4 . . .' [1766.] [Reported by the 2nd Earl of Hardwicke.] Add. MS. 35870, fos. 316, 317.

[6] Report of Attorney and Solicitor-General, 14 April 1766, Shortt and Doughty, *op. cit.* i. 251 ff. ; Plan of a Code of Laws . . . by Advocate General James Marriott, *ibid.* 445 at 450 ; Report of Attorney General Thurlow, *ibid.* 437 at 440–42. Thurlow admired the good sense but not the legality of Yorke's opinion. See also Thurlow in Debates on Quebec Act in Kennedy, *Statutes, Treatises and Documents*, &c., p. 100.

[7] R. A. Humphreys and S. M. Scott, ' Lord Northington and the Laws of Canada', *Canadian Historical Review* (1933), xiv. 42 ff.

farsighted in these matters than John Pownall, Charles Yorke, and the earl of Halifax. It is improbable that, had he remained at the Board of Trade, he would have avoided their ' blunders '.

' By this proclamation ', wrote Halifax to Amherst, ' you will perceive, that the propositions made by the Board of Trade in their report of the 8th of June last, have in general been adopted, with respect to the new governments to be erected, and the interior country to be reserved for the use of the Indians ; except only with regard to the first of those points, that his Majesty has thought proper to give the name of the Province of Quebec to that government which their lordships proposed to denominate the Province of Canada, and to extend the northern boundary of East Florida as far as the river St. Mary.'[1]

The provisions of the proclamation were entirely compatible with the policy outlined by Egremont in May ; the sequence of documents from May to October discloses no inconsistency. The proclamation, more or less fortuitously, represented the culmination of that policy. It was purely provisional. But what ' blunders ' it may have committed were not due to the precipitate action of ignorant and ill-advised men ; at least these men were not more ignorant than their immediate predecessors. The story of the wicked uncles ruining the more cautious policy of the young earl of Shelburne is a myth.   R. A. HUMPHREYS.

APPENDIX

TO THE KING'S MOST EXCELLENT MAJESTY [2]

May it please Your Majesty

In obedience to your Majesty's commands, signified to us by the Earl of Egremont, we have without loss of time taken into our most serious consideration those articles of the late definitive treaty of peace which relate to the cessions made to your Majesty in Africa and America by the most Christian and Catholic Kings, and also the important propositions and questions relative thereto, contained in his lordship's letter to us of the 5th instant ; We have likewise examined, with great care and attention, the papers referred to in the said letter and have as far as we have yet been able to proceed, left no means untryed of procuring every material and information which might enable us to form a judgement upon the whole matter referred to us, and to report our sentiments to your Majesty in the fullest manner ; We trust however that your Majesty will not think us inattentive to your commands, if in a matter of so great extent

---

[1] Halifax to Amherst, 11 October 1763, C.O. 5 : 214, p. 687.

[2] Shelburne Papers 49 : 333–64. There are two endorsements to this paper. One, by Shelburne, runs ' Mr. Pownall's Sketch of a Report '. The other, probably made by Dr. Priestley when cataloguing Shelburne's papers, is ' Mr. Pownal's Sketch of a Report concerning the Cessions in Africa and America at the Peace of 1763 '. I have followed modern usage in respect to capitalization. For permission to publish this document I am indebted to the courtesy of the William L. Clements Library.

and importance, comprehending such a variety of considerations and perplexed and embarrassed with such a variety of difficulties, we should not yet be ripe to submit our opinion upon every part of the reference, and that this representation should be entirely confined to the first question stated in the Earl of Egremont's letter to us, viz : ' What new governments should be established in the countries ceded to your Majesty in America ' ; for it is upon the decision of this question, that, not only the form and constitution of government, but almost every other proposition, does in some measure depend and to which they are necessarily consequential, as they must be in part provided for, and ascertained, by the commissions and instructions to the persons whom your Majesty shall appoint to the command of such new governments.

The first consideration necessary to be attended to in the formation and division of the new acquisitions upon the continent of America into separate governments, is, the true interest and policy of this kingdom, in reference to its colonies, either as that interest and policy arises from their nature and situation in general, or relatively to our commerce and political connections with the various nations and tribes of Indians now under your Majesty's dominion and protection ; both which cases do, in the present object, by a happy coincidence of circumstances, meet together in the same point, and form an exact union of system, for as in the one case the permitting the colonies, for the present at least, to extend their settlements beyond the heads and sources of those rivers and waters which do directly discharge themselves into the Atlantick Ocean or Gulph of Mexico, would probably induce a necessity for such remote settlements (out of the reach of navigation) to ingage in the production and manufacture of those articles of necessary consumption which they ought, upon every principle of true policy, to take from the mother country, and would also give rise to a separation of interests and connections, in other points, not consistent with that policy, so in the other case, such settlements would not be made or colonizing allowed without a manifest breach of our general engagements with the Indians which would naturally excite in them a jealousy and disgust that might prove of fatal consequence.

It would be both endless and unnecessary to enter into arguments to support the principles upon which this policy is founded ;—The truth of it in so far as it regards colonies in general will not, we trust, be controverted, and it has been fully proved in the case of the Indians, by the many opinions which have been reported to your Majesty and your royal predecessor by this board ; by the orders given in consequence of such reports ; by the effect of those orders ; by the stipulations of the various treaties held at Easton and Lancaster in the years 1756 and 1760 and at the Detroit in 1762, and lastly by the representation, made by Sr Will:^{m} Johnson, of what passed at these meetings, and of the present temper and disposition of the Indians in general, which reports treaties and representations have already been laid before your Majesty.

Upon this ground therefore, and upon these facts and principles, we do not hesitate to declare it to be our opinion, that, not only in the establishment of the new colonies, but in the determination of what may be proper to be done in respect to the old ones, in so far as that consideration applys itself to extension of settlements and Indian interests, the limits of their settlements and jurisdiction should not, for the present, extend beyond the sources of those rivers and waters which discharge themselves directly into the Atlantick Ocean on the one side, and the Gulph of Mexico on the other ; and that all the country lying between the ridge of the Apalachian mountains and the river Mississippi as low down to the Gulph of Mexico as the settlements and claims of the Indians extend, as also all the country lying around the Great Lakes as far as the heads of every river or water that falls into them, should be considered as lands belonging to the Indians, the dominion of which to be protected for them by forts and military establishments in proper places, and with full liberty to all your Majesty's subjects in general to trade with the said Indians upon some general plan and under proper regulation and restrictions ; the formation of which plan, as also of the military establishments makes a part of the general reference under our consideration and will be the subject of another report.

This proposition however must be considered only as a general rule admitting and requiring exceptions in some particular cases ; for as on the one hand, the Creeks, Cherokees and Catabaws have claims on this side of the mountains and the Six Nations also upon the Susquehanna, which it would be unjust to violate, so on the other hand some settlements have actually been made under the Government of Virginia ; beyond the great mountains in the forks of the Ohio, between the main branch of that river and the great Conoway river, which do not yet interfere with any claims of the Indians and which it would be equally unjust and impolitic to break up and destroy. These however are, we believe, the only cases that can be brought as an exception to the general rule and may we hope and conceive be easily provided for.

The next consideration upon the general question of format:[n] of government, is the claims and pretensions of Nova Scotia, New York and the New England colonies of New Hampshire and Massachusets Bay, in respect to the extension of their northern and western limits on the side of Canada towards the river St. Lawrence, which claims and pretensions, however necessary to be supported and maintained against the extension of Canada to the south of the river St. Lawrence whilst that province was in the possession of France, will not, nor we trust cannot, be admitted to obstruct any system that your Majesty shall think proper to establish in respect to the limits of Canada as a British colony, and which shall be founded upon reasons of sound policy and general convenience ; and therefore we would propose that the province of Canada should be bounded on the south by the high lands which range across the continent from Cape Rozier in the Gulf of St. Lawrence to Lake Champlain above St. Johns in the latitude of 45 degrees n° latitude, which high lands separate the heads of the rivers that fall into the great river St. Lawrence from the heads of those which fall the other way into the Atlantick Ocean or Bay of Fundy, and we humbly submit to your Majesty whether this boundary does not appear to be the true boundary pointed out both by nature and reason, for as on the one hand mountains and hills are the most convenient and certain of all natural boundaries, so on the other hand the circumstances of the inhabitants of the country between these high lands and the river St. Lawrence does in all respects render this boundary the most reasonable ; for these inhabitants, who are very numerous, cannot consistent with any rule either of reason or good policy be separated from their countrymen on the other side and taken out of a government under which they have always lived to be put under a variety of different governments from which they could receive no protection, and to which they would consequently pay no obedience or yield any subjection to laws or constitution to them unknown and founded on principles the most adverse to their nature and consciences that can be imagined, and therefore we hope that no claims founded upon verbal constructions of charters, to lands now occupied or possessed can be admitted to come in question upon this occasion against every principle of nature and reason : If however any embarrassment of this kind should arise on the part of the Massachusets Bay colony (and we think it can only arise from that colony as the rest are under your Majesty's immediate government) it will be in your Majesty's power to make them ample satisfaction for any such absurd claim, (if it must be admitted), by consenting to the grants they have lately made upon the Penobscot river and permitting them to extend their jurisdiction and property as far as St. Croix.

As to the extension of Canada on the north side of the river St.Lawrence, we think it should comprehend all the lands which lye upon any rivers that fall into the great river St. Lawrence from the north, and north west, extending from the river of St. Johns (the coast to n. eastward of which your Majesty has already put under the jurisdiction of the government of Newfoundland) along the said river St. Lawrence as far up as the heads of those rivers which fall into the Ottowa river from the west and southwest which we would humbly propose should be the utmost extent of the colony towards the Great Lakes on the north side St. Lawrences river and that on the south side its western extent should be restrained by a line drawn from Lake Champlain in latitude 45 due west to the said river at or near the great falls and that all the country beyond that to the west and south west and beyond the heads of the rivers which fall into the river St. Lawrence from the north and north west, should be considered as Indian lands in like manner and under the same regulations as those lying east and west of the Great Lakes and between the mountains and the Mississippi.

It seems by a paper transmitted to us with the Earl of Egremont's letter to have been the idea of some person that it might be adviseable to establish two governments upon the river St. Lawrence and its dependent territorys, and altho' we conceive that such an establishment might in some particular cases be attended with local convenience, yet as the proposition is founded upon a supposed extention of settlement and jurisdiction as far as the Great Lakes and does therefore militate against the general principle upon which all our system is founded, we cannot take upon us to recommend such a plan, the execution of which would also be attended with a very great additional expense to which the advantage resulting from it would in our opinion, independent of any other objection, bear no proportion.

There are other reasons arising out of a consideration of the embarrassments which always have and necessarily must in commercial points and in other cases attend the having two colonys established upon the same river, but as we apprehend there is not much stress laid upon this proposition we shall avoid entering into a more minute discussion of it, adhering to our opinion of having but one government and the city of Quebec to be the capital, the residence of the chief governor and the seat of justice in general and of supreme government.

Having stated to your Majesty everything that has occur'd to us with respect to the formation of a new government upon the river St. Lawrence so far as regards merely its extent and boundary and capital, the next objects of cession which present themselves to our view under this head of our report are the islands of St. John and Cape Breton, or L'isle Royale (the rest of the islands in the Gulph of St. Lawrence having been by your Majesty's direction put into the government of Newfoundland) and the only thing we have, for the present, to offer in respect to these islands is that they should be annexed to and made part of the government of Nova Scotia—in the original grant of which they were included, and from which they were separated by the treaty of Utrecht and the property vested in the crown of France.

We shall now proceed to submit to your Majesty what has occurred to us upon a considerat[n]. of that part of the definitive treaty which relates to the cession of Florida, in so far as regards the division and formation of government ; and here we cannot but lament the difficulties we are under in forming a precise judgement and idea of the nature and geography of this country, from the want of such information as may be depended upon, having very little except what we have been able to collect from the uncertain and vague accounts of writers of voyages who frequently contradict each other and in no case are entirely to be relied upon.

It is true indeed that the forming an opinion of what governments it it may be proper to establish in this country does not so materially depend upon a very precise and accurate knowledge of the nature of the country ; a general knowledge of its situation and natural boundaries may suffice for this object ; but the subsequent considerations which do materially depend upon it both in respect to commerce, military establishm[t] : and Indian regulations, are so many and important, that we thought it our duty to take this early opportunity of submitting to your Majesty whether it may not be adviseable that some able and skilful surveyors should be immediately appointed to visit examine and survey in the most accurate and particular manner the whole of this country and of that which lies between the great mountains and the Mississippi, of which there are not extant any charts or accounts that can be depended upon.

The importance of this matter led us into this digression, which we hope will not be thought unreasonable when we are speaking of a subject to which it does so immediately relate and to which we shall now return submitting it to your Majesty as our opinion, that Florida should be divided for the present into two distinct governments which may properly be distinguished by the names of East and West Floridas, the boundarys of each to be as follows Viz :

East Florida to be bounded on the east by the coast of the Atlantick Sea from the Cape of [1] Pensacola not taking more than 20 or 21 feet of water on the barr and St. Augustin not more than half that depth ; but it may be considered that they are the only permanent establishment that have hitherto been made in this wide extended country except the small port of

---

[1] *Sic.* The obvious lacuna here seems to be due to the carelessness of a clerk.

St. Marks in East Florida, and that of Mobille in West Florida, the first of which lying round the Cape of Florida is further removed from, and consequently more disadvantageously situated in respect to its commerce with, the mother country than the port of St. Augustine whilst the latter, independent of its being so embarrassed with shoals and sands as to render commerce and navigation impracticable, is situated so far to the west as to make it under any circumstances a very inconvenient seat of government.

It is possible, and we think it probable, that upon a more exact and particular survey and investigation of this country and its coasts and harbours than appears to have been hitherto taken, discoveries will be made of harbours and ports, particularly in that great promontory or tongue of land that stretches into the ocean and along the coast of West Florida, more advantageous for commerce and better adapted to navigation in all respects than those of St. Augustine and Pensacola, and therefore in forming the establishments for those two places regard must be had to this probable circumstance and no greater expence incurred in these establishments whether civil or military than will be justified upon the foot of temporary convenience.

We have now laid before your Majesty every thing that has occurred to us upon the general question of what governments it may be proper to establish, in so far as the question applies itself to the cessions in North America ; and humbly beg leave to refer your Majesty to the annexed chart of North America, on which we have marked the limits of the new colonys and what we propose should remain as Indian lands agreeable to the verbal description of them in our report, so that by comparing one with the other, your Majesty will be enabled with the greater exactness and precision to form a judgement of the several propositions we have the honour to make upon this head, and of the arrangement in general.

We come now in the next place to consider, in what manner the islands in the West Indies which have been ceded to your Majesty by the definitive treaty may be formed into one or more governments ; and upon a view of this question in every light in which it can be placed it seems reducible to the following general propositions. Viz : Either to form the whole into one general government, or to leave Dominica and Tobago as they are now under the government of Barbadoes, erecting Grenada and the Grenadilles and St. Vincents into a separate government.

The arguments in support of the first of these propositions apply themselves to the convenience, the respect and the security of the government.

It is urged that their general situation is such, as to render the communication between one and the other easy and expeditious so that the governor in chief may either personally or by his orders extend and apply his influence to the whole in every case and upon every occasion either of military service or civil government, for altho' upon a general view of the situation Dominica seems to lye at a considerable distance from the Grenad. and the communication is intercepted by the islands of St. Lucia and Martinico, yet it is so placed in respect to the winds and currents as that a ship may lay it from Grenada or at least from St. Vincents to Dominica in two days at any time, and therefore that as on the one hand the forming those islands into one government would combine together and consolidate every commercial and civil regulation forming an unity of interests operating to the benefit of the whole, both as to general security convenience and respect, so the dividing them into different governments would as necessarily create disunion of interests out of which would arise local prejudices and partialitys tending to local inconveniences to the disadvantage of the mother country, and to rendering your Majesty's Governors [and] Governments less respectable.

The same arguments of convenience and security as it arises out of situation in respect to winds and currents seems equally to apply itself to the second proposition for as Barbadoes lyes nearly an equal distance between Dominica and Tobago, so it should seem that the influence of its government might be extended to them with equal if not greater facility than it would be from Grenada.

The other considerations which appear in a general way to favour this last proposition is that Barbadoes being a well-established and well-regulated government in point of authority, jurisdiction, revenue and every other circumstance of civil establishment, it might without any difficulty communicate those advantages and regulations to the dependent isles, and therefore that there is a seeming absurdity as well as apparent injustice in taking Dominica and Tobago out of a government in such a situation to make them parts of one where everything that regards form and constitution of government is to be new created.

Specious however as this reasoning may appear, we must in our opinion conclude in favour of the first proposition for altho' we think that the constitution of Barbadoes might in some few respects be easier introduced into the other islands than a new one created, yet that it is in general such a constitution as the other islands are not capable to partake of, or if they were capable that it would not be either politick or adviseable to be introduced and established there.

It must also be considered that whatever establishments are made in Dominica and Tobago as parts of the government of Barbadoes such establishm.ts must either be absolutely independent of or totally dependent upon that of Barbadoes, because the whole constitution both judicial and legislative is confined to this island alone and therefore does not admit of such an extension of its parts and jurisdiction as would be necessary in order to form one general constitution for the whole.

And this objection appears to us to have great weight for as on the one hand an independent constitution always creates separate interests and out of that arises disunion and discord, so on the other hand a state of intire dependency upon Barbados would necessarily obstruct and prevent the improvement of the other islands because it would be for the local interests of the people of Barbadoes that they should not be improved.

Upon the whole therefore we think that the islands of Grenada, the Grenadilles, St. Vincent, Dominica and Tobago should be formed into an general government and that Grenada should be the seat of government and the residence of the Govr. Genl.

Lord Shelburne and British Colonial Policy, 1766-1768

WHEN, on 30 July 1766, Shelburne kissed hands as a secretary of state, he had already begun to acquire a mysterious reputation. Contemporaries regarded him with coolness, in part, perhaps, due to the history of his early political connexions, to the attitude of independence which he now adopted, and to his irritating talk of ' measures and not men ' ; in part to defects of character or temperament which unfitted him for public life. In private life, in his library, or on his estates, he proved himself a charming host. He became the centre of a small circle of radical and inquiring minds. At Bowood Bentham was to spend some of his happiest hours. But in public, painfully aware of his deficiencies, and no less conscious of his superiority, Shelburne shrouded himself in haughty aloofness ; he adopted poses which he dropped in private ; he was rarely natural. Previously in office he had proved himself a difficult colleague ; and by his assumptions of superior knowledge, his love of secrecy, his inordinate ambition, he was likely to do so again.

Yet if, on Chatham's ' utopian ' plan, ability was to be the test of fitness for office, Shelburne's claims could not be denied ; and now, in Chatham's ministry, he received the reward due both to his talents and to that combination of political principle and partisan devotion which had dictated his course since, not quite three years before, he had resigned from the presidency of the Board of Trade to attach himself to Pitt. His particular qualifications for the southern department were rather greater than those of his immediate predecessors, at least in so far as the southern secretary dealt with the problems of colonial administration. With some of these problems he was in part acquainted through his experience at the Board, slight as that was ; [1] in others he had long been interested ; and his opinions, so far as these were known, had gained for him the respect of the colonists, and

[1] *Ante*, xlix. 241-58.

now inspired with a renewed confidence some at least amongst those especially charged with the safeguard of colonial interests.[1]

These opinions, however, were not then sufficiently remarkable to justify any lengthy exposition now. Shelburne held prevalent views upon the nature of colonies and colonial trade. He was distinguished, perhaps, by his interest in, and the emphasis he laid upon imperial expansion. North America, ' with the universal empire of that extended coast ', he had declared as far back as 1762, offered infinite possibilities of commercial development.[2] The Romans, he said, during the debates on the repeal of the Stamp Act, planted colonies to increase their power, England to extend her commerce. He deplored the raising of a constitutional issue in the Declaratory Act. Expediency was the test of policy, expansion the end to be pursued.[3] Of constitutional issues he was impatient. While ' acknowledging the power of parliament to be supreme ',[4] Shelburne, like his friend Camden,[5] was inclined to limit the novel claims of parliamentary absolutism by some more old-fashioned, if half-realized, principle of fundamental law. ' The legislature ', wrote his friend and secretary, Maurice Morgann, ' has the power of doing many unjust and unequal things. The question is what it *ought* to do. *Right* and *right* only ought to be the measure of human power as it is said to be the limit of the divine.' [6] The rules of ' equity and justice ',[7] in short, implied the existence of some standard of political obligation which set bounds to the will of a parliamentary majority.

[1] Compare letters of Dennys de Berdt, agent for Massachusetts, of Charles Garth, agent for South Carolina, and of Richard Jackson, agent for Connecticut, under dates 19, 26 September, 8 November 1766, Publications of the Colonial Society of Massachusetts, *Transactions* (1912), xiii. 325 ; *South Carolina Historical and Genealogical Magazine* (1928), xxix. 44 ; *Pitkin Papers*, Connecticut Historical Society, *Collections*, (1921), xix. 49.

[2] *Ante*, xlix. 245.

[3] H. Hamersley to Sharpe, 20 December 1765, *Correspondence of Governor Horatio Sharpe*, iii. 243 (*Archives of Maryland*, xiv. 1895) ; *Parliamentary History of England*, xvi. 165 ; *American Historical Review* (1912), xvii. 585.

[4] Shelburne to Pitt, 21 December 1765, *Correspondence of William Pitt, Earl of Chatham*, ed. W. S. Taylor and J. H. Pringle (1838), ii. 354-5.

[5] *Parliamentary History*, xvi. 168.

[6] [Maurice Morgann, on the right and expediency of taxing America.] Shelburne Papers, William L. Clements Library, Ann Arbor, Michigan, 85/71. Morgann's view, expressed in this and other papers hereinafter cited, was that the colonies were not constituent parts of the empire, but dependencies existing for the benefit of the mother country. As such they were entitled to those rights which were the condition of their subserviency, amongst which was the right of self-taxation. C. W. Alvord, *The Mississippi Valley in British Politics* (Cleveland, 1917), i. 279-80, identifies these opinions with Shelburne's.

[7] Compare Shelburne to Moore, 11 October 1766, 18 July 1767, Public Record Office, Colonial Office Papers, 5/222, p. 7, *Documents Relative to the Colonial History of the State of New York*, ed. E. B. O'Callaghan (Albany, 1856), vii. 945 ; Shelburne to Bernard, 13 September 1766, quoted Lord E. Fitzmaurice, *Life of William, Earl of Shelburne* (2nd and revised edition, 1912), i. 301 (wrongly dated).

The new ministry began with an important reform. The
earl of Hillsborough, as a condition of again accepting the presidency of the Board of Trade, insisted, with what motives it is
not necessary to determine, that the Board should be reduced
to the position of a board of report upon reference. Even this
welcome step towards administrative order and efficiency was
not taken without an ominous quarrel, on a point of procedure,
between Shelburne and Hillsborough, little to the former's advantage ; [1] and heartily as Shelburne approved of it, it considerably
augmented the business of his already over-burdened department.
Grafton was later able to remark, with some justice, ' Were a
Solomon in the situation, I should not be of opinion that he could
go through it '. [2]   As a consequence, either now or soon after, some
reorganization seems to have taken place in Shelburne's office itself,
in regard to the allocation of duties amongst the clerks, hours of
attendance, and rules of procedure ; [3] and there was a considerable
change in its personnel.   Only one of Richmond's staff remained
with Shelburne ; and three new under-secretaries were appointed :
Richard Sutton, Lauchlin MacLeane, and Maurice Morgann.
Of these Morgann had long been connected with Shelburne, and
would now seem to have been particularly charged with colonial
business, and MacLeane, whose career is less edifying than enter-
taining, had had some experience of American life, if only as an
apothecary at Philadelphia. [4]   In this reorganized and powerful
department now centred almost the whole of colonial business.
From the reports and opinions which were therein collected,
and which (frequently regarded more as private than as public
papers) now bulk largely in the Shelburne Papers, and from
the correspondence of civil and military officials in the colonies,
Shelburne's colonial policy may be fairly accurately gauged.

A large proportion of these papers relate to the problems

---

[1] *Acts of the Privy Council, Colonial Series,* v. § 1 ; A. H. Basye, *The Lords Commissioners of Trade and Plantations . . . 1748–1782* (New Haven, 1925), pp. 157–62 ;
M. A. Thomson, *The Secretaries of State, 1681–1782* (Oxford, 1932), p. 55.

[2] Fitzmaurice, *op. cit.* i. 327.

[3] ' For the Regulation of the Secretary's Office under the Earl of Shelburne,
humbly submitted to his Lordship ', Shelburne Papers, 134/141. *Cf. Acts of Privy
Council, Colonial Series,* vi. § 727.   From a letter in Shelburne Papers, 134/137, it
would seem that in the interests of economy Shelburne had entertained the idea of
relinquishing his fees.

[4] P. M. Morin was the under-secretary continued.   J. C. Roberts remained with
Shelburne till October 1766.   *Calendar of Home Office Papers, 1766–69,* §§ 240, 290.
In Shelburne Papers, 134/141, it is observed that ' the business of the colonies cannot
be carried on properly without the assistance of three additional clerks, to be under
Mr. Morgan's immediate direction ; and that even at times the other clerks must be
called upon to help in that branch of your lordship's department '.   In September 1767
the number of clerks was increased.   For Morgann, see *ante,* xlix. 247, and for the
curious career of MacLeane, who in May 1766 had been appointed lieutenant-governor
of St. Vincent (C.O. 324/41, p. 264), see Sir C. W. Dilke, *Papers of a Critic* (London,
1875), ii. 30–46.

involved in imperial control of that vast region which stretched
from the Great Lakes to the Mississippi and to the Gulf of Mexico.
The problems of this great valley were to exercise over Shelburne's
mind a peculiar fascination, in part due to a realization of
its enormous possibilities, in part to the heavy burden of its
liabilities. As president of the Board of Trade he had himself
assisted in formulating the western policy of a government already
conscious of the need of regulating Indian trade, land speculation,
and frontier settlements. By the proclamation of 7 October 1763,
in the drafting of which Shelburne had played a part, though only
a minor part, the government had added to the principle of fair
purchase of Indian lands that of a temporary boundary line beyond
which settlement was prohibited. It had designed to supplement
the proclamation by comprehensive regulations for the control of
Indian affairs.[1] Such regulations were outlined in the Board
of Trade plan of 10 July 1764 ; but this plan, by reason of the
expense involved, was never officially accepted.[2] Of this, and
other proposals, the new secretary was aware ; but in the autumn
of 1766 he was not alive to the errors and shortcomings of the
proclamation ; he was not familiar with the disturbed and lawless
conditions in the great western area which, in 1763, had been left
void of civil jurisdiction.[3] The reports of civil and military
authorities in America were now to convince him that the old
policy of imperial administration and support had broken down.
On the one hand, the endless complaints of insufficient authority
to punish crime, to maintain order, or to prevent illicit settlements,
the reports of the activity of French traders in the Illinois country,
the tell-tale returns of the fur trade, and the gloomy prophecies
of the Indian superintendents, on the other, the angry protests of
Canadian traders against such restrictions as had been imposed
upon the trade, the land-hunger of frontiersmen, the representations of land companies, the heavy burden of expenditure, and
the pressure for economy and retrenchment, all these forced him
to devise some alternative system. A year was to elapse before
Shelburne had formulated his policy, a year in which plans were
criticized, proposals presented, and the various elements in the
problem summarized, and in which his constitutional hesitancy
was increased by the scepticism or hostility of his colleagues,
and by the extensive and contradictory advice which he received.
Not until the early summer of 1767 was Shelburne able or willing
to give full attention to these problems. But the part played

[1] *Ante*, xlix. 241–58.
[2] Plan for the Future Management of Indian Affairs, 10 July 1764, *New York Col.
Docs.* vii. 637.
[3] *Ante*, xlix. 242 ; ' Things to be considered of in North America ', Shelburne Papers,
49/17, printed in Alvord, *op. cit.* i. 277. Though not by Shelburne this document sums
up the state of information available in his office.

by the Mississippi valley in British politics, and the history and
character of Shelburne's western policy, are too familiar [1] to
warrant detailed consideration here. It is only necessary to
review some of the more significant features.

Shelburne early began to consider the possibilities of returning
to the system of provincial management of the Indian trade, and
the more novel idea of founding new inland colonies. But despite
the impatience of Charles Townshend, who, as chancellor of the
exchequer, demanded an immediate reduction in American expenses and the withdrawal of the troops from the American
frontiers, and pending a thorough investigation into the problems
of land settlement, Indian trade, civil and military expenditure,
Shelburne refused to produce a ' crude and undigested ' plan.[2]
In the meanwhile he attempted to uphold existing authorities
and to enforce existing regulations. He urged civil and military
officials to co-operate in the repression of frauds and illicit settlements, insisted that the Indian superintendents should consider
themselves under the orders of the commander-in-chief—a possible
source of unified policy—ordered a strict enforcement of the
proclamation of 1763, and approved of all measures towards
running the boundary line between white settlements and Indian
lands. Merchants and traders were assured that their complaints
would be considered ; harassed officials urged to observe the
virtues of moderation, equity, and discretion.[3] Governor John-
ston, of West Florida, Shelburne recalled in extreme disapproval
of his Indian policy.

For the Indians, indeed, Shelburne felt a real concern.

' The provinces ', he wrote, ' can never expect a lasting peace with the
Indian tribes 'till they convince them that they would rather protect
than destroy them. The traders, for selfish views, have but too much
succeeded in inculcating into the minds of these poor people, that nothing
will satisfy the colonies but their extirpation.' [4] ' Whatever resolutions
shall be taken in this matter ', he wrote to the governor of Canada in permitting to Canadian traders some relief from the restrictions imposed upon
the trade, ' it will not be the less necessary to regulate, in the strictest

[1] The most authoritative expositions are those of C. E. Carter, *Great Britain and
the Illinois Country, 1763-1774* (Washington, 1910), and of C. W. Alvord, *The Mississippi Valley in British Politics.*

[2] Shelburne to Gage, 11 December 1766, *The Correspondence of General Thomas Gage*,
ed. C. E. Carter, ii. (New Haven, 1933), 47 ; *Chatham Corr.* iii. 232 ; ' Reasons for not
Diminishing American Expence this year ', 30 March 1767, *Illinois Historical Collections*,
xi. ed. C. W. Alvord and C. E. Carter (Springfield, 1916), p. 536 ; Franklin to W.
Franklin, 27 September, 11 October 1766, *ibid.* pp. 394, 400.

[3] Shelburne to Stuart, 11 December 1766, *ibid.* p. 451 ; to Johnson 13 September,
11 December 1766, *Papers of Sir William Johnson*, ed. A. C. Flick, v. (Albany, 1927),
374, 447 ; to Colonial Governors, 13 September 1766, C.O. 5/66, fo. 285 ; to Montague,
25 October 1766, Shelburne Papers 53/201 ; to Tryon, 20 June 1767, *ibid.* 53/273 ;
to Canada Committee on Indian Trade, 30 November 1766, *ibid.* 53/9.

[4] Shelburne to Fauquier, 19 February 1767, C.O. 5/1345, fo. 307.

manner, that trade which may be carried on near the frontiers of the province, in order to prevent frauds and violences, which the traders from the prospect of impunity and a speedy refuge among the back settlers may be induced to commit. . . . It appears to me . . . that the disorders and inconveniences attending the back settlements and Indian trade have principally proceeded from the fraudulent grants and purchases of land that have been so long suffered to prevail. . . .'[1]

Shelburne was no less concerned over the decline of the fur trade. Yet the policy which he was now to advocate meant ultimately the extirpation of these poor people, and the ruin of the fur trade, consequences which it may be presumed he did not foresee, or foreseeing, knew not how to avoid.

A further explanation of this contradiction may lie in the pressure exerted upon Shelburne by financial and mercantile interests, possibly combined in unholy alliance in the pursuit of dissimilar ends. On the one hand, the Canadian fur trading organization, by way of Lieutenant-Governor Carleton, the agent of the Quebec and Montreal merchants, Fowler Walker, and their London correspondents clamoured for a free Indian trade.[2] On the other, traders in the Illinois country, in particular the Pennsylvanian firm of Baynton, Wharton, and Morgan, required protection against illegal French competition ; and the representatives of various land companies, such as the old Ohio Company, the new and powerfully supported Illinois Company, and General Phineas Lyman's Company of ' Military Adventurers ', beguiled the ears of Shelburne and his secretaries with accounts of the advantages to be expected from new inland colonies.[3] Franklin availed himself of the beginnings of a life-long friendship with Shelburne to promote the interests of the Illinois Company, of which both he and Sir William Johnson, the superintendent of Indian affairs for the northern department, were members. Lyman and Franklin jointly sought the aid of Morgann ; while the firm of Baynton, Wharton, and Morgan, partners in the Illinois scheme, and interested besides in government contracts, attempted to gain the support of Lauchlin MacLeane by means of a bribe.[4] Richard Jackson, the influential agent of Connecticut, and an

---

[1] Shelburne to Carleton, 20 June 1767, Shelburne Papers, 53/117.

[2] Compare H. A. Innis, *The Fur Trade in Canada* (New Haven, 1930), pp. 174–9 ; Carleton to Shelburne, 28 March 1767, C.O. 323/25, fo. 121 ; Carleton to Johnson, 27 March 1767, *Ill. Hist. Coll.* xi. 532.

[3] M. Savelle, *George Morgan, Colony Builder* (New York, 1932), p. 44 ; Carter, *op. cit.* pp. 111 ff. ; Alvord, *op. cit.* i. 294, 314 ff.

[4] See the letters of Franklin to W. Franklin, printed in *Ill. Hist. Coll.* xi ; MacLeane to Shelburne, January 1767, *ibid.* p. 478. It is worth note that Franklin, asked for his advice on the plan for the management of Indian affairs, criticized it briefly, and thought its regulations ' in general very good '. *Writings of Benjamin Franklin*, ed. Smyth, iv. 467. For the early interest of Morgann in western schemes, see *ante*, xlix. 248.

intimate friend of Franklin, used his ' particular friendship ' with
Shelburne, and lent the weight of his great contemporary re-
putation, in support both of these colonizing schemes and of a free
Indian trade.[1]

Shelburne's final western policy seems to have been framed,
for the most part, to accord with the desires of these business
interests. When, in September 1767, he at length submitted his
plans to his impatient colleagues, his report was based on the
advice of Franklin, of General James Amherst, who had long
favoured western settlements, and of Jackson ; and followed
Jackson's reasoning in particular.[2] Into the details of his criticisms of the policy of imperial control, and of the plan of 10 July
1764, it is unnecessary to enter. Shelburne took his stand on the
principles of *laissez-faire* and rapid expansion. On the one hand,
the Indian trade could no longer be bound ' by a variety of minute
regulations ' ; on the other, nothing was more likely to preserve
the dependency and increase the value of the colonies than ' a
facility for the rising generation to extend themselves still
further into the unsettled continent '. The ' simple system '
which he now proposed, to ' answer every intention of government, and cut off every unnecessary expence ', was to surrender
to the provinces the entire control of Indian affairs, subject to
' such general regulations as the Board of Trade should think
expedient ', to retain only the more strategic forts, and to establish two new colonies at the Detroit and on the Illinois. The
care of the less important forts, or of such of them as were retained,
would devolve upon the provinces. The expenses of the new
colonies would be defrayed by the quit rents.[3]

In October these plans were sent to the Board of Trade.
Shelburne, however, had again consulted Amherst, who wrote that
' a third seat of government on the *lower parts of the Mississippi*
should be added to those intended to be formed at the *Detroit*
and *Illinois* '. Shelburne, therefore, now suggested the establish-

---

[1] ' Remarks on the Plan for the Future Management of Indian Affairs, by Mr.
Jackson, November 1766 ', *Illinois Hist. Coll.* xi. 422. Jackson was the son of a London
merchant, a member of parliament, a barrister, standing counsel for the South Sea
Company, and, later, legal adviser to the Board of Trade.

[2] Two parallel papers in the Shelburne Papers supply the basis of this report.
These are the documents endorsed ' Plan for the Future Management of Indian Affairs
proposed when Lord Hillsborough was at the Head of the Board of Trade ' with
Shelburne's comment, ' Remarks upon which are grounded the minutes submitted
by me to Cabinet in Summer, 1767 ', Shelburne Papers, 50/357 ; and ' Observations upon a Plan for the Future Management of Indian Affairs ', *ibid.* 60/135. These
closely agree with Jackson's reasoning. General Gage, of course, was also consulted.
Cf. Carter, *op. cit.* p. 172.

[3] ' Minutes submitted to the Cabinet in the beginning of Summer, 1767, relative
to the System of Indian Traffick ', *Illinois Historical Collections*, xvi. ed. C. E. Carter
and C. W. Alvord (Springfield, 1921), 12 ; Franklin to W. Franklin, 25 November 1767,
ibid. 118 ; Shelburne to Gage, 14 November 1767, *Gage Correspondence*, ii. 53.

ment of three, rather than two, new colonies,[1] obviously bearing
a marked relation to the projects in which Amherst, Franklin,
and Lyman were interested.   The Board was required to consult
' such merchants as are most intelligent in the North American
and Indian trade ' as well as military officials acquainted with
the continent.   On the 27th, after a hurried preliminary meeting
on the part of the Canada Committee at the Tennis Court Coffee
House,[2] the merchants attended the Board, and desired further
time to consult together.   Two days later, at a meeting of the
merchants and agents, attended by Jackson, Franklin, and
Fowler Walker, they unanimously decided in favour of Shelburne's
plans.   ' The merchants ', wrote Franklin, ' to a man, disliked
the plan of regulating the trade under the superintendents ' ;
and doubtless Franklin and Jackson secured their approval of
the colonization schemes by the argument that new colonies
would greatly increase the consumption of British goods.[3]

However this may be, the winter of 1767 saw the wreck of
Shelburne's schemes.   The Board, of which Lord Clare was now
president, did not allow itself to be deceived by the specious
argument that new colonies would promote the interests of the
fur trade ; it had its doubts about provincial management of
Indian relations.   Aware of opposition, Shelburne, in a private
conversation with a member of the Board, suggested a conservative
amendment :   ' Suppose the whole management of Indians and
Indian affairs to be divided ; whatever regards the direction and
regulation of the trade to be left to the provinces, everything
regarding Indian purchases, congresses, treaties and boundaries
to remain under the particular direction of the superintendants.' [4]

But in January 1768, more perhaps for political than administrative reasons, the business of Shelburne's department was
curtailed by the creation of a third secretaryship for colonial
affairs.   Shelburne's last order in regard to western policy was
for the completion of that boundary line between white and
Indian lands, which had been an essential feature of British policy
since 1763, which would open up some land to settlement, but
which had only in part been run.[5]   In March the Board of Trade,

[1] Shelburne to Lords of Trade, 5 October 1767, *Ill. Hist. Coll.* xvi. 77 ; Amherst
to Shelburne, 22 September 1767, C.O. 5/68, fo. 303.

[2] Robert Hunter to Fowler Walker, 27 October 1767, Brit. Mus. Add. MSS.
35915, fo. 186.

[3] Board of Trade Journals, 27 October 1767, *Ill. Hist. Coll.* xvi. 101 ; Franklin to
W. Franklin, 13 November 1767, *ibid.* p. 104 ;   Barlow Trecothick to Lords of Trade,
30 October 1767, *ibid.* p. 102 ; ' Present at the Meeting of Merchants and Agents,
29 October 1767 ', C.O. 323/24, fo. 323v.

[4] ' The substance of what passed between Ld. Shelburne and Mr. Dyson about the
Superintendants, given afterwards to Ld. Clare, November 1767 ', Shelburne Papers
50/219.

[5] Shelburne to Johnson, 5 January 1768, *Ill. Hist. Coll.* xvi. 155 ; Alvord, *op. cit.*
i. 356.   The line was, of course, open to revision.

in a masterly report, swept away the more radical, but retained the more conservative features of Shelburne's programme.[1]   It is difficult not to sympathize with this report.   Shelburne's 'simple system' had ignored some of the graver problems of the west ; and there were great difficulties in the way of its adoption.[2]   It had two great merits.   Its author had grasped, fully and firmly, the inevitable destiny of the west.   His plan attempted to link mother country and colonies together in common expansion. Secondly, framed in the apparent interests of colonial speculators and colonial merchants, it gratified the desires of, and threw increased responsibility upon the colonists.   Possibly by these means Shelburne hoped to relieve the economic difficulties of the old sea-board colonies, and by diverting their attention from the strained relationships with the mother country, to capitalize in the interests of the empire as a whole that infant movement of westward expansion which was soon to dominate American life.

However this may be, it is obvious that Shelburne's western programme, to be fully appreciated, must be placed in relation to the colonial policy of the Chatham ministry as a whole.   Its significance and its shortcomings are better understood by a consideration of those problems of colonial policy and that conflict of opinion, which enabled Franklin to write, in a phrase which must not be too literally accepted, ' America . . . is now made one of the distinctions of party here '.[3]   To these other problems, and to that conflict, it is now necessary to turn.

Already in 1766 the sea-board colonies presented a scene in which provincial and continental politics, economic, social, and sectional conflicts, clashed and intertwined with imperial.   More obviously, a grave constitutional issue remained at stake.   Despite the Declaratory Act, the claims of parliamentary sovereignty were still challenged by the pretensions of provincial assemblies.

The Mutiny Act of 1765, in particular, had provided a fertile source of dispute.   Though the arrangements in force for the quartering of troops were by no means satisfactory to the commander-in-chief, who wrote irritably of his dependence on the ' temper and whim ' of colonial assemblies,[4] the act in question, by reason of the provisions which it required the colonists, at their own expense, to furnish to the troops, was regarded as a form of direct taxation, and provoked great dissatisfaction.   New York passed an act only in part complying with these requirements,[5] and similar recalcitrance was displayed later both by

[1] *Ill. Hist. Coll.* xvi. 183.

[2] For these difficulties, and the financial interests involved, see Alvord, *op. cit.* ii. 24–5.

[3] Franklin to Galloway, 8 August 1767, *Writings of Benjamin Franklin*, ed. Smyth, v. 40.   [4] *Gage Correspondence*, i. 89.

[5] Moore to Conway, 20 June 1766, *N.Y. Col. Docs.* vii. 831.

New Jersey and Georgia. ' At New York ', wrote Shelburne, ' they have made difficulties about quarters, but it appears to me . . . that it's only the remains of the storm, and wants a little good humour and firmness to finish.' [1] But a little good humour and firmness failed to finish. In a tactful letter Shelburne communicated to Governor Moore of New York the cabinet's order that the acts of the legislature of Great Britain must be obeyed ; he urged Gage to make the burden of the troops as light as possible. Gage replied that New York was far from over-burdened ; the assembly flatly refused further compliance.[2]

A second source of dispute was the parliamentary resolution for the compensation of the victims of the Stamp Act riots. With this the New York assembly, after a struggle, had complied, though it refused to compensate the lieutenant-governor, who had suffered heavily.[3] In Massachusetts, where Governor Bernard owned to having introduced the subject in ' as forcible a manner ' as possible,[4] the outcome was even less satisfactory. Again Shelburne had hoped that a little good humour and firmness would suffice. He had hinted to Bernard to pursue a ' temperate conduct ', to disdain ' narrow views, private combinations and partial attachments '. He had urged the assembly to ' finish the affair of the damages sustained ' because of the opportunity it afforded to their enemies to upbraid the administration ' for the gentle measures they adopted '.[5] But on passing an act of compensation, the assembly coupled with it an act of indemnity, thereby trespassing on the prerogative of the Crown. As for Bernard, he and the assembly continued in a course of mutual recrimination. The Mutiny Act had roused hostility ; and when Bernard, on his own responsibility, provided for a transport of troops which had been driven by storm to the refuge of Boston harbour, there was high dispute. This, remarked Bernard bitterly, will be ' worked up . . . so as to be a cause of liberty '.[6] In the action of the lieutenant-governor in taking a seat at the council, Bernard's opponents discovered a lust for power long suspected ; while Bernard considered the independent step of the assembly in appointing an agent of its own to have been grossly irregular.

[1] Shelburne to Chatham [20 ? September 1766], Public Record Office, Chatham Papers, Bundle 56.

[2] Cabinet Minute, 5 August 1766, Chatham Papers, 97 ; Shelburne to Moore, 5 August 1766, *N.Y. Col. Docs.* vii. 847 ; Moore to Shelburne, 19 December 1766, *ibid.* p. 883 ; *Gage Corr.* i. 118 ; ii. 45.

[3] C. L. Becker, *The History of Political Parties in the Province of New York, 1760–1766* (Madison, 1909), p. 53.

[4] Bernard to Shelburne, 24 December 1766, Widener Library, Harvard College, Bernard Letter Books, iv. 283.

[5] Shelburne to Bernard, 13 September 1766, Fitzmaurice, *op. cit.* i. 301 ; De Berdt to Cushing, 19 September 1766, Pubns. of Col. Soc. of Mass., *Trans.* xiii. 325.

[6] Bernard Letter Books, iv. 291.

In bitter letters he complained that the source of his, and the country's troubles, lay in the actions of one ' passionate, violent and desperate ' man, James Otis, and the ' faction ' allied with him. ' The opposition to the Stamp Act ', he declared, ' has been made . . . a stalking horse to take a better aim at the Royalty of the Government.' [1]

But apart from these ' causes of liberty ', and the graver constitutional issue, other serious grievances remained, particularly in the northern colonies. The Currency Act of 1764, prohibiting the issue of legal tender paper money, however desirable it may have been in respect to some colonies, tended to intensify the already existing currency difficulties and the persistent monetary stringency which embarrassed the debtor to creditor relationship of the colonies to England. Despite the measures of the Rocking-hams, the high price of sugar remained a serious hindrance to New England trade ; and in view of other trading restrictions which remained, the late reduction of the molasses duty had by no means completely met the difficulties of the merchants. Further, the merchants strongly objected to the powers of the vice-admiralty courts ; and in the restraints which Governor Palliser was at this time laying on the Newfoundland fisheries, the New Englanders had a particular grievance. In February 1767, Dennys de Berdt presented a memorial to Shelburne on behalf of the merchants of Boston who sent a petition on these subjects ; and about much the same time a petition from New York arrived, expressed in a manner which gave great offence. The currency question was not adumbrated in these petitions, because it was believed to be already under review.[2]

To the trading difficulties of the Bay Colony, Shelburne, so far as he understood them, was sympathetic enough. At his instigation Palliser's instructions were revised, and the affair of the fisheries satisfactorily concluded.[3] He favoured a repeal or modification of the Currency Act, probably along the lines of the plan previously suggested by Franklin to Grenville, of establishing a ' General Loan Office ', whereby paper money would be issued on loan, with safeguards against depreciation, and the interest

---

[1] Bernard to Shelburne, 22 December 1766, 7, 14, 18 February 1767, 28 March 1767, Bernard Letter Books, iv. 274; vi. 175, 199. Abstracts of these letters are in the Shelburne Papers.

[2] H. Palliser to Shelburne, 10 December 1766, Shelburne Papers, 65/45 ; de Berdt to Shelburne, February 1767, Pubns. of Col. Soc. of Mass., *Trans.* xiii. 446, 448 ; Stephen Sayre to Dartmouth, 13 December 1766, Hist. MSS. Comm., *14th Report*, App. x. 54 ; *Journals of House of Commons*, xxxi. 158 ; *N.Y. Col. Docs.* vii. 884 ; Becker, *op. cit.* pp. 65–70 ; A. M. Schlesinger, *The Colonial Merchants and the American Revolution, 1763–1776* (New York, 1918), pp. 84–9 ; C. M. Andrews, ' The Boston Merchants and the Non-Importation Movement ', Pubns. of Col. Soc. of Mass., *Trans.* (1918), xix. 168–75, 181–91.

[3] De Berdt to Boston merchants, 14 March 1767, Pubns. of Col. Soc. of Mass., *Trans.* xiii. 451 ; to Cushing 14 February 1767, *ibid.* p. 450 ; Schlesinger, *op. cit.* p. 87.

appropriated to ' the American Service ', a plan which Franklin
and others now distrusted and disliked.[1]   But for an impartial
review of these economic grievances the times were hardly pro-
pitious. While Chatham was in retirement, after his ' fatal
journey ' to Bath, Townshend had been holding ' very strong
language ' about American taxation, and disclaiming ' almost
every word of Lord Chatham's language on the subject ' ; [2] and
now the coincidence of the New York petition with the reports
of the Massachusetts Indemnity Act and the continued disobedi-
ence of New York to the Mutiny Act gave general offence. Was
this the requital for the repeal of the Stamp Act, the modification
of the Sugar Act, the Free Port Bill ? ' New York ', wrote
Chatham, ' has drunk deepest of the baneful cup of infatuation,
but none seem to be quite sober.' [3] Shelburne himself was
' very much disgusted '.[4] ' The infatuated conduct of the assembly ', he wrote, ' in refusing even present obedience to the
act, precludes, I am afraid, all considerations of the merits or
principles of it.' . . . ' As things stand in America, there are so
many considerations cross upon each other, that all the difficulties
of the situation are scarce within the compass to be stated.'
A vigorous policy was essential ; yet New York was not America ;
the Mutiny Act was ill-drawn and doubtful in principle ; and
at all costs no precedent should be established ' which may hereafter be turned to purposes of oppression '.[5]

Two papers drawn up by Morgann reflect opinions in Shelburne's circle.

' When the grievance of a Stamp Act was removed ', wrote Morgann,
' a sound politician would not have left behind so irritable a thing as a
compensation for sufferers, considered as criminals by those who were to
compensate them. . . . But the demand of compensation would at most
but irritate for a time. The Mutiny Act may inflame. It is wonderful
that the legislature of Great Britain should commit its dignity by that act
to the petulance of provincial assemblies. There is no bottom to the im-
propriety of *enacting* that those assemblies should *enact* and accompanying
that act by a requisition from the throne.'

[1] Franklin to Galloway, 11 October 1766, William L. Clements Library ; Garth
to Committee of Correspondence, 6 June 1767, *South Carolina Historical and Genealogical Mag.* (1928), xxix. 295 ; same to same, 31 January 1767, *ibid.* p. 128 ; Franklin
to Galloway, 13 June 1767 ; to W. Franklin, 28 August, 1767, *Writings of Benjamin
Franklin*, ed. Smyth, v. 25, 45. This plan was discussed both in 1766 and 1767.
No action was taken.
    [2] Grenville to Buckinghamshire, 27 January 1767, *Lothian MSS.*, *Hist. MSS.
Comm. 16th Report*, p. 274.
    [3] Chatham to Shelburne, 7 February 1767, *Chatham Corr.* iii. 193. ' The devil
has possessed the minds of the Americans.' Beckford to Chatham, 12 February
1767, *ibid.* p. 203.
    [4] Johnson to Pitkin, 12 February 1767, Mass. Hist. Soc., *Coll.* (5th Series), ix. 216.
    [5] Shelburne to Chatham, 6, 16 February 1767, *Chatham Corr.* iii. 191, 206 ; English
practice in quartering troops, Shelburne Papers, 58/129 ; Queries concerning the Bill
of Indemnity and Oblivion, *ibid.* 58/243.

In fact the Mutiny Act was 'wholly impolitic and most unhappily timed'. Further, by repealing the Stamp Act yet passing the Declaratory Act, the government had merely suggested that 'the timidity of the British Parliament kept pace with its ill dispositions'. Additional misfortunes had arisen from the stupidity of provincial governors, and of Governor Bernard in particular, who preferred a 'good argument' to a 'wise measure' and 'retired to his closet to vent his chagrin in womanish complaints'. The time had arrived when 'America for want of proper treatment may be lost. She has been too much tampered with already.' A firm, yet convincingly just, policy was essential; and that policy was clearly marked out. The Mutiny Act should be repealed, the principles of the late acts declared erroneous, and an example made 'of *one province only* and *of one man*'. 'Fortunately for this purpose' there was 'an offence committed in a more special manner by one province, and in that province, more particularly, by one factious, guilty demagogue'. In Massachusetts, wrote Morgann, the laws of trade and navigation, those essential ties, had been grossly infringed, particularly by James Otis. The charter of that province, therefore, should be declared void, and Otis brought to England to be impeached by the commons. Massachusetts might then be given a more liberal charter. Such conduct, 'so manifestly just' that it could not be 'converted into a common cause', would plainly prove that Great Britain was 'not to be trifled with in essentials'.[1]

These proposals, it must be admitted, did more credit to Morgann's heart than to his head. Shelburne can hardly have considered them very seriously. At the outset the ministry agreed that the Massachusetts Indemnity Act should be disallowed. This procedure was both normal and inevitable. New York presented a more difficult problem. Four proposals were made to the cabinet. The governor of the province could be given 'power to billet' the troops as he pleased. All regarded this as 'highly exceptionable'. Shelburne's co-secretary, Conway, favoured the imposition of a 'local extraordinary Port Duty',[2] which everyone else regarded as absurd. A third suggestion was to appropriate some of the provincial revenue to the service of the troops. Townshend insisted that the Crown should be addressed to 'assent to no law whatever, till the Mutiny Act was fully obeyed'. Lord President Northington regarded this as so severe an interdiction that it could only be done by act of parliament;

---

[1] Remarks on the present state of America, April 1767, from Mr. Morgann, Shelburne Papers, 49/711; Observations on British policy towards North America, *ibid.* 85/81. Part of this last paper is transcribed in Fitzmaurice, *op. cit.* i. 315.

[2] Compare Johnson to Pitkin, 17 May 1767, on Conway's attitude to the Mutiny Act, Mass. Hist. Soc., *Coll.* (5th Series), ix. 228 ff.

and this was the policy agreed upon. With the exception of
Conway, the cabinet was united.[1] Shelburne, however, assented
reluctantly, possibly ' oblig'd to swim with the stream ',[2] possibly
not altogether averse to a drastic stroke aimed at one province
only. Much at a loss, he had toyed with the idea of passing
an act reciting the Declaratory Act, granting a general pardon
and oblivion for all past offences, and declaring that future dis-
obedience to acts of parliament should be regarded as high
treason. Offenders, he suggested to Chatham, could be tried
' either *within the Colonies* or *sent over to Great Britain* '.[3]

Such an emphasis on the Declaratory Act was little likely to
be popular ; but a further expedient suggested itself to Shelburne.
Governor Bernard, for whom Shelburne was beginning to feel a
hearty dislike, had long wished to exchange Massachusetts for
some more peaceful and more lucrative province ; he had long
contended that he should be summoned home to lay the state of
his government before the ministers. He had repeatedly solicited
both his friend and relative, the secretary at war, Lord Barrington,
and Richard Jackson, who had been associated in the agency of
the province, to secure this end.[4] It was with indignation that
Bernard learnt, in the summer of 1767, that his removal had been
considered on account of his disagreement with the people of
Massachusetts.[5] ' If you want to lose your Colonies, you should
begin with the Governors ', Shelburne remarked oracularly in
later days ;[6] and now, in May and June 1767, he contemplated
recalling both Bernard and Moore. Draft letters were prepared
for this purpose. A new governor was to be sent out to New
York. Bernard was to be given a year's leave of absence, during
which time his duties would devolve upon the lieutenant-governor.[7]

It is idle to speculate as to why such letters were never sent,
and tempting, though dangerous, to conclude that Shelburne failed
to get the consent of his colleagues. It is certain that by now

[1] For the attitude of Grafton and of Lord Chancellor Camden see *Autobiography
and Political Correspondence of Augustus Henry, Third Duke of Grafton*, ed. Sir William
R. Anson (1898), p. 126 ; Horace Walpole, *Memoirs of the Reign of King George III*
(G. F. Russell Barker, 1894), ii. 318.

[2] De Berdt to Cary, 3 January 1769, Pubns. of Col. Soc. of Mass., *Trans.* xiii.
353.

[3] Shelburne to Chatham [26 ? April 1767], Chatham Papers, Bundle 56. Cf.
Chatham Corr. iii. 231, 232.

[4] *The Barrington-Bernard Correspondence*, ed. E. Channing and A. C. Coolidge
(1912), pp. 106, 112, 121, 199.

[5] Bernard to Jackson, 29 July 1767, Bernard Letter Books, vi. 30.

[6] Fitzmaurice, *op. cit.* i. 466. For Shelburne's dislike of Bernard see de Berdt to
Cushing, 4 January 1770, Pubns. of Col. Soc. of Mass., *Trans.* xiii. 393 ; Franklin to
W. Franklin, 25 November 1767, *Writings of Benjamin Franklin*, ed. Smyth, v. 65 ;
Parl. Hist. xvi. 477.

[7] The tenor of these letters I communicated in a brief note to the *American Historical
Review* (1932), xxxvii. 269. To the letters there cited should be added ' Draft to Lieut.
Gov. Colden, June 1767 ', Shelburne Papers, 85/140.

Shelburne's influence in the cabinet was small. Moreover, the
initiative in colonial affairs was slipping from his hands. In
January Charles Townshend had ' pledged himself ' to find a
revenue in the colonies ; and from ' general conversation ' the
secretary of state had learnt with surprise that the chancellor
of the exchequer proposed to establish a board of customs in
America and to secure a revenue by means of import duties.[1]
After this startling announcement, Grenville in the house had
moved for a reduction of American expenses, and for the withdrawal of the troops from the frontiers in America, contrary to
the government's plan of scattering them in the outlying areas ;
and Townshend had ' harangued most inimitably on both sides
of the question '.[2] The opposition united to secure a sudden and
factious victory in reducing the land tax. In March affairs came
to a head, with a battle royal between Townshend and Shelburne.
As chancellor of the exchequer Townshend needed to present
a clear-cut financial policy to the commons. Shelburne's vague
plans and academic hesitancy he regarded with contempt. He
now threatened to withhold the budget unless immediate provision
were made for the reduction of American expenses and for the
disposition of the western territory. Shelburne with acerbity
refused to produce a ' crude and undigested plan '.[3] On this point
the immediate victory was his ; but disgusted with this vacillation,
this perpetual postponement of a vital issue, Townshend proceeded
to go his own way. What the secretary of state could not do,
the chancellor of the exchequer would. Henceforward the direction in colonial affairs ceased to come from the secretary's reorganized office. Henceforward, Shelburne devoted himself almost
exclusively to the details of his western programme, of which
Northington, indeed, implies that he had got the ' mastery ' by
June ; [4] and from now on Shelburne, thus preoccupied, stood more
and more aloof from his colleagues. ' Never cordial ', he was now
accused of ' great coldness ', amounting almost to hostility ; and
it is probable that in the trying circumstances of this early summer
of 1767 his worst faults displayed themselves.[5] Chatham, it is
true, had arrived in town, only to fail to remove Townshend, to
collapse, and to retire to solitude at Hampstead. ' Here, in fact,
was the end of his administration.' [6] With Chatham prostrate

[1] *Chatham Corr.* iii. 184–5.

[2] Cf. *Gage Correspondence*, ii. 49 ; *Correspondence of King George III*, ed. Sir John
Fortescue, i. 453 ; *Chatham Corr.* iii. 211, note.

[3] *Ibid.* 232–3 ; *supra*, p. 261, n. 2.

[4] Grafton, *Autobiography*, p. 175.

[5] *Ibid.* pp. 154, 213 ; *Correspondence of George III*, i. 480 ; *Chatham Corr.* iii.
241, note. The statement that Shelburne now ceased to attend cabinet meetings
[D. A. Winstanley, *Lord Chatham and the Whig Opposition* (Cambridge, 1912), p. 119],
is incorrect.

[6] Grafton, *Autobiography*, p. 124.

with gout and fevers, deaf to all appeals for help, with the lord president paying the price of a life-long devotion to port by a complication of distempers which made business irksome, the unhappy Grafton stood at the head of a ministry of which the great officers were more and more divided. Conway was anxious to resign. Townshend's career was unchecked.[1]

In April the privy council had disallowed the New York Barrack Act ; on 13 May it disallowed the Massachusetts Indemnity Act. On the same day the bill for the suspension of the legislative powers of the New York assembly came before the commons ; and on that day Townshend announced his intention of establishing the board of customs, and proposed fresh revenue duties by way of indirect taxes, ' contrary to the known decision of every member of the Cabinet '.[2] The customs' board, however, the cabinet had approved ; and very probably Shelburne had acquiesced in that decision.[3] By the end of the session, on 2 July, the restraining Act, Townshend's Revenue Act, and the Act for establishing a board of customs had been passed. It must be admitted that the opposition had consistently made the position of the ministry most difficult by its eagerness to secure strategic victories. ' The current ', wrote Franklin in April, was ' strong against America in general, which our friends in the ministry are obliged a little to give way to.' [4] A great ' rage against America ', he complained, had been ' artfully worked up by the Grenville faction ' ; [5] and the conduct of the opposition lent countenance to the charge that it was, in fact, playing politics with the American question.[6] No member of the ministry had defended the Massachusetts Indemnity Act ; yet before it was disallowed in a normal course of procedure, and after it was known that the privy council had not prejudiced the question as to whether it was null and void *ab initio*, repeated motions in the lords and commons displayed the desire of the opposition to obtain tactical advantages and to embarrass the ministry ; while the conduct of the various sections of the opposition on the restraining Act did credit to their ingenuity, but to little else.[7]

Hardly had that act been passed—to come into force in

---

[1] ' Mr. Charles Townshend comes every day in the House to talk with Mr. Grenville, and to abuse Lord Chatham, and laugh at the Administration ; and speaking in relation to what would be proper to be done in America, he said Mr. Conway was upon that subject below low-water mark.' Grenville's Diary, 1 April 1767, *The Grenville Papers*, ed. W. J. Smith, iv. 222 ; cf. *ibid.* 225.

[2] Grafton, *Autobiog.* p. 137.

[3] *Ibid.* p. 127. Compare two papers of opinions in Shelburne Papers, 58/235, 243.

[4] Franklin to Galloway, 14 April 1767, William L. Clements Library.

[5] *Ibid.* 20 May 1767, William L. Clements Library.

[6] Johnson to Pitkin, 11 April 1767, Mass. Hist. Soc., *Coll.* (5th Series), ix. 222 ff.

[7] For a sympathetic account of these manoeuvres, see Winstanley, *op. cit.* pp. 133–6, 139.

October—when the news arrived that New York had already made
sufficient provision for the troops.[1] It was with ' real pleasure ',
in transmitting the act, that Shelburne wrote that he considered
its provisions to be unnecessary.[2] At the same time he inquired
into the many complaints of Governor Bernard. The attorney-
general reported that the lieutenant-governor had no right to a
seat in the council, though his presence there was not unconstitutional ; and that the governor had the right—only to be used
with discretion, but which Bernard had freely exercised—of
negativing the election of councillors. These decisions Shelburne
communicated to Bernard in an official letter of approval of his
conduct. He added, in a phrase peculiarly trite, ' Extremes,
even of legal right . . . though sometimes necessary, are always
inconvenient '.[3]

' I was very happy ', Shelburne told Grafton two months later,
' that no real evil had happened to the King's affairs or to the
public, while I had the care of that quarter of the world [America],
but that it had been reduced in the main to some degree of order
and obedience to parliamentary authority, from a very different
state in which I found it.' [4] Much may be allowed for the trying
nature of this particular conversation ; but Shelburne, apparently,
was not ill pleased with the work of the late parliamentary session,
except in regard to Townshend's revenue duties. Despite his
rather vague belief in natural law, he could yet employ what he
later termed the ' specious language of the supremacy of the
British Legislature ' ; [5] and he, the ardent free-trader of later
days, still invested the laws of trade and navigation with a sacro-
sanct character. He probably approved of the board of customs
set up to prevent infraction of these laws ; he was present at
a meeting of the cabinet when it was decided to increase the
number of vice-admiralty judges.[6] Though unpopular, these
measures, it is true, were not dangerously so.[7] But it could not
be said that Shelburne had shown a very keen appreciation of the
economic difficulties of the colonies ; and while he had opposed
Townshend on the question of an immediate reduction of American

---

[1] See *Acts of Privy Council, Colonial Series*, v. § 66.

[2] Shelburne to Moore, 18 July 1767, *N.Y. Col. Docs.* vii. 945. At the same time
Shelburne wrote to the Governors of New Jersey and Georgia ordering obedience to
the Mutiny Act.

[3] Report of de Grey, 25 August 1767, Shelburne Papers, 61/701 ; Shelburne to
Bernard, 17 September 1767, A. Bradford, *Speeches of the Governors of Massachusetts,
&c.* (Boston, 1818), p. 117. The Massachusetts Assembly complained in regard to
this letter that Bernard had misrepresented the state of the province to Shelburne.
On 4 February 1768, the Board of Trade, on Shelburne's reference, reported that the
house had no right to choose an agent on its sole authority. C.O. 325/1.

[4] *Chatham Corr.* iii. 296 ; cf. *ibid.* iv. 324–5.

[5] 20 January 1775, *Parl. Hist.* xviii. 162.

[6] 19 August 1767, Shelburne Papers, 161.   [7] Cf. Andrews, *op. cit.* pp. 178–9.

expenses and over fresh revenue duties, his own plans to meet those expenses which, even before the reduction of the land tax, and yet more after, ' alarmed and astonished ' the treasury,[1] were far from impeccable.   Townshend's attitude was not un-justifiable.

Shelburne's plans for this purpose may be comprised under the two heads of economy and reform.   His western policy was economical throughout, always provided that his rather vague designs of securing a sufficient revenue for his new inland colonies from quit rents were sound, a point on which there were grave doubts.[2]   On the quit rents in the old colonies and for future grants of lands he placed extravagant hopes.   ' A wild project ', wrote a late secretary to the treasury in October 1766, ' is talked of for paying off the Civil List debt, and providing an American revenue both together.   It is only supposing that the quit rents in the colonies, if properly collected, will be sufficient to support the military establishment there.'[3]   Rumour doubtless exaggerated, but it had its basis in fact.   On 11 December Shelburne circularized the colonial governors demanding an ' exact estimate ' of the annual expenses of the ' entire establishment ' of each colony and its available revenue, and an account of the manner of imposing quit rents and granting lands.[4]   On the same day he expounded to General Gage the purpose of this inquiry.

' The forming an American fund to support the exigencies of government [he wrote] in the same manner as is done in Ireland, is what is so highly reasonable that it must take place sooner or later.   The most obvious manner of laying the foundation for such a fund seems to be by taking proper care of the Quit Rents and by turning the grants of land to real benefit, and which might tend to encrease rather than diminish the powers of government in so distant a country.'[5]

To utilize the American quit rents—a legally, if not politically unchallengeable source of revenue—was no new idea ; and for some time the method of granting lands had been felt to need ' particular attention '.[6]   On this last point Shelburne's intention was clear.   He did not wish to exact the payment of arrears of rents long overdue.   On the other hand, nothing could be ' more reasonable than that the proprietors of large tracts of land ', bought for speculative purposes, ' should either pay their quit rents punctually ' or ' relinquish their grants ' in favour of those

---

[1] Franklin to W. Franklin, 11 October 1766, *Ill. Hist. Coll.* xi. 400.
[2] See Alvord, *op. cit.* i. 348, for a discussion of this point.
[3] Whately to Grenville, 20 October 1766, *Grenville Papers*, iii. 334.
[4] Shelburne to Colonial Governors, 11 December 1766, *N.Y. Col. Docs.* vii. 880. See also *ibid.* 889.
[5] Shelburne to Gage, 11 December, 1766, *Gage Corr.* ii. 50.
[6] Board of Trade Report, 6 June 1765, *Acts of Privy Council, Colonial Series*, vi. § 646.

who would. He was convinced that a reform in the system of
granting lands would avoid ' future suits at law, and in great
measure prevent the Indian disturbances ' ; and though he was
able to take no definite step in this direction, to the last he maintained his purpose.[1]   What this step would have been can only
be hazarded, but from a memorandum on the revenue of South
Carolina, endorsed by Shelburne ' Extream good observations ',
it is probable that it would have been the establishment of proper
quit rent rolls.[2]   At the same time Shelburne believed that the
quit rents, once the general system had been reformed, would be
politically and financially very valuable, sufficient at any rate to
' encrease . . . the powers of government '.[3]

Doubtless with this in mind, Shelburne, in April, pursued his
inquiry by demanding from the Boards of Trade and Admiralty
an account of the civil establishment of the governors, judges,
and other officers concerned with the administration of justice in
the colonies, and of that of the officers of the admiralty courts.[4]
' All the salaries allowed in this government are very low ',
Governor Franklin of New Jersey had written to him in February ;
and amongst less vigorous letters from other governors, one from
Bernard in March denouncing the ' illiberality of low minds priding
themselves in the dependence which their superiors are obliged to
have upon them '.[5]   In reply to this requisition the Board of
Trade detailed the sources of the salaries, except in the cases of
Maryland and Pennsylvania, in which colonies the Board reported
it was ignorant whence the salaries came.   Only in Virginia and the
Carolinas, the Board affirmed, were the salaries of civil officials
supplemented by the quit rents.[6]   But if Shelburne had thoughts
of increasing the utility of these feudal survivals, the reports
which now came from the governors, while no doubt finally convincing him of the need for reform, should have caused him to
hesitate.   In the New England colonies such rents did not exist ;
from New Jersey, Pennsylvania, and Maryland the Crown received
nothing ; in the Floridas none had yet been collected.   But in
the other colonies the reports, for the most part, disclosed a chaotic
state of land management and land granting, and of the auditing

[1] *Gage Corr.* ii. 50 ; Shelburne to Chatham, 1 February 1767, *Chatham Corr.* iii.
185 ; Shelburne to Gage, 14 November 1767, *Gage Corr.* ii. 54.

[2] ' Memorandum from Mr. Tomson . . . ' dated 15 February 1762, Shelburne
Papers, 49/165.   See also B. W. Bond, *The Quit Rent System in the American Colonies*
(New Haven, 1919), p. 434.

[3] *Gage Corr.* ii. 50 ; *Chatham Corr.* iii. 185.

[4] Shelburne to Lords of Trade, 9 April 1767 ; to Lords of Admiralty, 28 April 1767,
Cal. Home Office Papers, 1766-9, §§ 461, 476.

[5] W. Franklin to Shelburne,. 21 February 1767 ; Bernard to Shelburne, 2 March
1767, Shelburne Papers, 51/793, 540.

[6] Report of Board of Trade on Establishment of Salaries, &c., 16 April 1767,
C.O. 324/18, p. 148.

and collection of rents. The income was usually diminutive ; the rents were usually in arrears. The report from Virginia was the most encouraging ; but even here the deputy auditor wrote that the arrears were considerable, and that all methods of avoiding payment were employed.[1]

' The Proprietary and Charter Colonies paying a mere acknowledgment only to the Crown, and the unchartered provinces little more till within these few years ', wrote Gage, summing up the matter, ' tho' more will be gained than usual by a greater care in the collection of the Quit Rents, yet it does not appear, that any very great and considerable sum will accrue to the Crown therefrom for many years to come.' [2]

Meanwhile the battle had occurred between Shelburne and Townshend over the question of an immediate reduction of American expenses. Driven to give his own views of the appropriate sources for that ' fund for American expenses ' which everyone agreed was highly proper, Shelburne detailed three : a ' better management ' of the quit rents and of the future grants of land, such aids ' as may be beneficial to the colonies, at the same time as they lessen the burthen of the Mother Country ', thirdly and ' chiefly ', requisitions to be granted annually by colonial assemblies.[3] Yet the requisition system could not, by its warmest friends, have been called highly successful. As for the quit rents, which Shelburne here relegated to a comparatively minor position, the criticism which must be directed against Shelburne's anxiety to increase their value is not, first and foremost, that no large revenue could be expected from these dues for some time, if at all ; nor that, while the colonists manifested little objection to the principle of the rents, they did object to their collection.[4] It is that Shelburne's design was political in nature. It is hard to escape the conclusion that from a reorganized system of the rents Shelburne hoped to secure a revenue which would have fulfilled Townshend's schemes in another way. ' Governors INDEPENDENT ! ' said Samuel Adams. ' What a sound is this ! It is a discord in the ear of a Briton. A power without a check ! What a solecism in a free government ! ' [5]

Whatever Shelburne's intention, his policy failed of completion, as his western policy, to which he now gave all the energy he could spare for colonial problems, was to fail of adoption. Already he was almost completely isolated from his colleagues. In July rumours pervaded the town that he was to be dismissed, or at

[1] These reports are in Shelburne Papers, 55 and 56, duplicated in British Museum, Kings MSS. 206. See Bond, *op. cit.* p. 433 ; Alvord, *op. cit.* i. 283.

[2] Gage to Shelburne, 5 April 1767, *Gage Corr.* i. 131.

[3] ' Reasons for not Diminishing American Expence this year ', *Ill. Hist. Coll.* xi. 536.

[4] Bond, *op. cit.* pp. 457-8.

[5] R. V. Harlow, *Samuel Adams*, p. 101, quoting *Boston Gazette*, 10 August 1767.

least removed from the control of colonial affairs.[1] 'The confusion among our great men', wrote Franklin in August, 'still continues as much as ever' ;[2] and the domestic scene was crowded with intricate negotiations in which the king and Grafton sought the aid of sections of the opposition, and to which Shelburne remained a 'total stranger'.[3] Not, however, till December was an alliance concluded between Grafton and the Bedfords, of which one condition was a division of Shelburne's office. Shelburne consented with reluctance to this arrangement. To Grafton's argument that 'a horse, my Lord, could not go through the business of your office properly', he even contended that on the contrary the business of the colonies had been very well managed.[4] In January 1768 the division took place. At last there was a third secretary of state for the colonies. But whether through pique, weariness, or good sense, Shelburne refused the new office.[5] Allegiance to Chatham alone kept him in a ministry whose colonial, foreign, and domestic policy he more and more deplored. Continually more obstructive and continually more distrusted, anxious to retire and yet unwilling to go, he remained in the cabinet till October, when he resigned, and entered into immediate opposition.

From that fatal battle in March 1767 Shelburne had lost the initiative in colonial affairs ; and the ground thus lost was never recovered. He had been unable to supply the concrete programme required. His position is clear. It is Townshend, too lightly dismissed as 'brilliant' but 'erratic', who needs to be better understood.

R. A. HUMPHREYS.

[1] Sedgwick to Weston, 8 July 1767, *Underwood MSS., Hist. MSS. Comm. 10th Report*, Part i. p. 407 ; *Grenville Papers*, iv. 28 ; J. H. Burton, *Life and Correspondence of David Hume*, ii. 406.

[2] Franklin to Galloway, 8 August 1767, *Writings of Benjamin Franklin*, ed. Smyth, v. 40.

[3] *Chatham Corr.* iii. 294.   [4] *Ibid.* p. 296 ; Fitzmaurice, *op. cit.* i. 328, 329.

[5] *Ibid.* i. 329, 330.

Wood's Halfpence

THE heated and prolonged controversy over William Wood's patent to coin halfpence and farthings for Ireland, which between 1722 and 1725 seemed likely to wreck the ministry of Walpole and to throw into the melting-pot the whole question of the political status of Ireland, still awaits a satisfactory elucidation.[1] The present paper does not attempt to reconstruct the ' secret history ' of the somewhat discreditable negotiations which preceded the grant of the patent,[2] nor does it challenge the accepted accounts of Lecky,[3] Froude,[4] or Leslie Stephen,[5] in so far at least as the mere narrative of the dispute is concerned. Its purpose is to examine afresh the real nature of the Irish opposition to Wood's patent and to reassess the significance of the crisis in the history of Anglo-Irish relations.

Several considerations justify the investigation. The first is that existing accounts do not seem to have made full use of the first-hand evidence which is available : they have drawn upon the Coxe and Southwell manuscript collections at the British Museum,[6] and, to a lesser extent, upon the Irish State Papers in the Public Record Office,[7] but have tended to neglect the manuscript letters of Archbishop King in the Library of Trinity College, Dublin.[8] Secondly, it is a fact that the dispute over Wood's patent has hitherto attracted attention mainly as the indispensable line of approach to the study of Swift's *Drapier's Letters*. This preoccupation with the political activities of

---

[1] Sir Henry Craik in his life of Swift (ii. 313, 2nd ed.) suggested that any attempt at a complete explanation ' would be ' a hopeless task '.

[2] See Coxe, *Walpole*, i. 218 *seqq*.

[3] *Leaders of Irish Public Opinion*, pp. 41–8 ; *Ireland in the Eighteenth Century*, i. 449–55.

[4] *English in Ireland in the Eighteenth Century*.

[5] *Swift*, in the English Men of Letters series.

[6] Used by Coxe and Ballantyne (*Carteret*).

[7] The latest edition of Swift's *Drapier's Letters*, by H. J. Davis (1935), contains a useful narrative account of the dispute based upon this evidence, but the King correspondence has not been utilized. The Irish State Papers covering the dispute are State Papers 63, vols. 380–5. They have not yet been calendared or indexed.

[8] This consists of two series, one contained in King's Letter Book, used to some extent by W. M. Mason in his *History and Antiquities of the Collegiate and Cathedral Church of St. Patrick*, and the other is the so-called Lyons' Collection, which has not received proper attention.

Swift during the crisis has, from the historical point of view, been unfortunate. It has, for example, led historians to suppose that Swift's faulty and exaggerated economic reasoning is conclusive evidence of the essential unreality of Irish economic complaints against the coinage ; it has tended to obscure the effective part in the rejection of the patent taken by such men as Archbishop King,[1] Lord Midleton,[2] and William Conolly ; [3] and it has secured general acceptance for the conclusion that the dispute is important as ' the first grand struggle for the independence of Ireland '.[4] It will be suggested in the course of the present argument that the Irish did in fact develop a cogent if not entirely conclusive case against the halfpence on economic grounds ; that the Irish Lords Justices and Irish privy council did hardly less than Swift himself to make the ultimate surrender of the patent inevitable ; and that it is erroneous to hold that the Irish leaders, apart from Swift, sought to win from England legislative independence. Thirdly, it may be urged that existing accounts have over-stressed the constitutional significance of the struggle and have under-estimated its considerable political consequences in the history of the Irish question during the eighteenth century.

During the course of the controversy every conceivable economic argument against the coinage was pressed into service by the Irish pamphleteers.[5] Some of the contentions were patently absurd, others more reasonable. It is plain, however, that Walpole and his colleagues steadily refused to admit that the Irish had advanced a single valid plea against the currency of Wood's coin. Most historians who have dealt with the topic seem to agree with Coxe that the ' whole clamour rested on partial or ignorant representations '.[6]

It is true, of course, that at a time when zeal against Wood and all his works was a short cut to popular favour in Dublin,

[1] William King (1650–1729), archbishop of Dublin, 1703, member of the Irish privy council.

[2] Alan Brodrick, Lord Midleton (1660–1728). Entered Irish parliament in 1629 as member for the city of Cork. Chosen Speaker, September 1703. June 1707, attorney-general. October 1714, appointed lord chancellor of Ireland. April 1715, raised to peerage as Baron Brodrick of Midleton. August 1717, Viscount Midleton. Resigned office as lord chancellor, 25 May 1725.

[3] William Conolly (?–1729). Elected Speaker of the Irish house of commons, 12 November 1715. He held this office till his death. He was, at the time of the dispute, a member of the Irish privy council, Chief Commissioner of Irish Revenues, and one of the three Lords Justices (the others being Midleton and Shannon) appointed to govern Ireland in the interval between the departure of Grafton (May 1724) and the arrival of Carteret (22 October 1724).

[4] W. M. Mason, *History of St. Patrick's*, p. 347.

[5] The most complete list of the prose pamphlets and broadsides on Wood's coinage is given by Davis, *Drapier's Letters*, pp. 352–73.

[6] Coxe, *Walpole*, i. 217.

there were many besides Swift himself who did not disdain to
rest their case against the patent upon the very crudest appeals
to partisan spirit.   Again, few of the pamphlets contained any
respectable economic analysis.   That, however, was only to be
expected.   The writers, even if we assume that they were capable
of the feat, would have been defeating their own purposes
by offering theoretical arguments for popular assimilation.   So
much may be admitted, but it should be recognized at the same
time, that the Irish did have several sound reasons for rejecting
the patent on economic grounds.

The criticism which was passed on the patent, immediately
the details of the grant were available in Ireland, was that the
intrinsic value of the coinage was too low.[1]   According to the
terms of the grant, one avoirdupois pound weight of copper was
not to be converted into more farthings and halfpence than would
make 30d. by tale.   On the Irish estimate the cost of the pound's
weight of copper was one shilling.   These ' facts ' were used to
formulate the wildest and most improbable calculations as to the
immediate profits of coining.   On 23 September 1723 it was resolved by the Irish house of commons ' that the loss to the nation
by the uttering of this coin would amount to 150 per cent.' [2]   The
author of *Ireland's Consternation* tried to prove that the country
would stand to lose £200,000 by the patent, though Wood had
been given permission to coin only £100,800 worth of copper ! [3]
A more ' scientific ' estimate was that of one Maples in his *Remarks
on the Copper Coin Intended for the Use of Ireland*, 1723, which
gave the ' loss to the public ' as between £57,674 8s. 0d. and
£82,168 16s. 0d., according to the weight of the various issues
coined by Wood.[4]

Estimates of this order could not claim much consideration from
a man of Walpole's financial ability.   Even the most reasonable
of them made no allowance for Wood's costs of production.   As
Walpole pointed out copper prepared for coinage was always
valued at eighteenpence and not at one shilling per pound at the
London Mint.[5]   In addition Wood had to meet the charges for
coining and a long list of miscellaneous costs—for management,
transport, douceurs to Irish agents, and the fees of the comptroller—as well as presumably to recoup himself for the £10,000
which he is said to have paid for the patent to the duchess of

[1] The patent is dated 12 July 1722.   Publ. Rec. Off., Patent Roll, 8 Geo. I, pt. v.
no. 5.   Details were not available in Ireland till the beginning of August 1722.

[2] *Commons' Journals*, iii. 323.

[3] Publ. Rec. Off., St. Pap. 63, 381, fo. 801.   Walpole's comment on this sheet was
' the most errant Grub-Street paper I ever read in my life '.

[4] Maples' calculations were those used rather unscrupulously by Swift in his third
Drapier's Letter.

[5] P.R.O., St. Pap. 63, 381, fo. 801.

Kendal, to whom the original grant had been made. One need have no hesitation, therefore, in condemning the Irish complaints as to the inordinate profits which Wood was supposed to be making.

Two other considerations, associated with the Irish contention that the intrinsic value of the coinage was too low, were, however, more reasonable. The Irish were apparently convinced that the difference between the nominal and intrinsic value of the coin would greatly aggravate two evils from which Ireland had suffered acutely : the practice of counterfeiting, and the tendency of gold and silver to leave the country. Ireland had suffered a great deal in the past from the activities of counterfeiters, and it is not surprising that opponents of the coinage should have attached considerable weight to this argument. The precise danger is indicated in a letter from Archbishop King to Hopkins, secretary to Grafton, dated 21 July 1722.[1]

' It is not easy,' he says, ' to counterfit old coin for tho' they can give the same stamp, yet they can hardly give the old look, hence it is that every new Coinage gives great opportunity to counterfiting, as we experienced in the time of King William when all the Species were new, a Swarm of false coiners then arose and great numbers were hanged, whereas now the Practise is much abated ; we must therefore Expect new Brass Pieces, every town will have shops set up for that mystery.' He also adds significantly, ' I know not what may be the penalty by law for counterfeiting such Coin, but I doubt much whatever the penaltie whether Juries will be prevailed on to find the forger guilty, perhaps they will believe that the poor man had as good a right and as great a necessity on him to cheat the publick as the Patentee.'

King's fears were more than justified once the conflict had got well under way, as can be seen from a letter of Carteret to Newcastle of 14 November 1724. Emphasizing the popular aversion to the halfpence he pointed out that

' the Copper Coyn now current in this Kingdom (the worst that ever was seen) is by them (i.e. the Irish) admitted to be much less in value than what has been coined by Wood. To this last indisputable fact, which I have insisted upon to several persons, they reply that the Kingdom is already overstocked with Copper Money, and therefore would be ruined should they receive any additional summe : and it is notorious that a great quantity of this bad copper money which before lay dead, and was a load to the Owners has now attained a currency—for no other reason but that those who received it might be furnished with an argument against Wood's Patent.' [2]

By that time what might be called a forgers' paradise had already come into existence.

[1] *Proceedings of Royal Irish Academy*, iv. 66. I have fixed the date by consulting King's Letter Book, N. 3. 7.   [2] Brit. Mus. Add. MS. 9243, fo. 46.

Fears were also entertained that the halfpence would drive gold and silver out of the country, just at the time when other forces had reduced the stock of such coinage to a minimum. Ireland had been recently drained of foreign currency (such as ducatoons, plate pieces, and dollars) as a result of the premium offered for it by the English East India Company, which was prohibited by law from exporting English coin.[1] The stock of English silver coins circulating in Ireland had been reduced by the existing disparity in the exchange rates between gold and silver in England and Ireland.[2] The normal balance of payments on trading account between the two countries necessitated the transfer of gold from Ireland, and as foreign gold coins were not current in England, Irish reserves of English gold coin had been depleted. It was only natural, in these circumstances, for Irish pamphleteers to predict that by raising Irish internal prices, the new coin would lead to an adverse trade balance, an unfavourable foreign exchange rate, and a further loss of the precious metals.[3] Ireland was peculiarly anxious on this score, and panic fear would probably of itself have soon produced the danger in which every Irish pamphleteer believed. Convertibility of the halfpence into legal tender coin would have imposed some check on the depreciation of the coin, but Wood's patent, unlike former grants, contained no guarantee in this respect. Irish fears of a recrudescence of counterfeiting and of a drain of gold can hardly therefore be pronounced either frivolous or fantastic.

An entirely different Irish objection to the coinage, that the safeguards contained in the patent against the enforced currency of the halfpence were illusory, seems, at first sight, more difficult to sustain. According to the patent the coins were ' to pass and to be received as current money, by such as shall or will, voluntarily and willingly and not otherwise, receive the same within the same kingdom of Ireland and not elsewhere '. This clause alone might appear to establish the justice of Walpole's defence that the English ministry had never contemplated forcing the currency on an unwilling people. The home government remained consistently irresponsive to Wood's suggestions that the halfpence should be made even limited legal tender, and the above provision did, in fact, make possible the boycott of the coin and

---

[1] King to Southwell, 9 June 1724. King's Letter Book, T.C.D. fo. 110.

[2] *Ibid.* ' Tis farther to be observed that 21 shill[s] (*i.e.* in silver) which is the value of a guiney in England makes in Ireland 22 shill[s] and ninepence, whereas a Guiney Passes for 23 shill[s] with us, therefore he who sends Silver into England gains threepence mor by it y[n] if he sent Guineys, this advantage tho' it may seem little yet in a manner has intirely drained us of our English money which was given us in Lieu of foreign Silver.'

[3] E.g. *A Defence of the Conduct of the People of Ireland in their Unanimous Refusal of Mr. Wood's Copper Money*, Dublin, 1724, pp. 29, 31.

the successful resistance to the patent.[1] Nevertheless, as the Irish were quick to note, the clause did not debar the government from making indirect but none the less strenuous efforts to introduce the halfpence. The Irish leaders had never disputed the legality of the patent. As King wrote to the Irish Secretary, Southwell, on 23 March 172^3/$_4$,

' it was not on the illegality of the Patent, nor chiefly on the abuse of it by the Patentee (which was not so much as mentioned by the Lords) that Parliament insisted, but on the unavoidable mischief and destruction it would bring on the Kingdom, and on its being obtained by most false and notorious misinformation of his Majestie '.[2]

It was hard work, also, preventing the popular resistance to the patent from flagging, and but for Swift's whirlwind campaign in the *Drapier's Letters*, Walpole's persistence might have triumphed.[3] Quite early in the dispute the prime minister had informed Grafton that, in his opinion, the patent was ' very well to be supported ' and from that position he never deviated.[4] The method adopted to force the currency was to bring pressure to bear on the Irish Commissioners of the Revenue to accept the coin. The money collected in this way would be used to pay the Irish army, and through that channel it was hoped it would pass into circulation among the smaller traders and retailers.[5] The Irish parliament was not unaware of this chink in its protective armour and accordingly petitioned the king on 17 December 1723 that he

' be graciously pleased to give Directions to the several officers entrusted in the receipt of Your Majesty's Revenue that they do not, on any pretence whatever, receive or utter such $\frac{1}{2}$d. or $\frac{1}{4}$d., as the most effectual means to prevent their Currency and satisfy the minds of your people '.[6]

This petition was politely ignored. The determination of the English ministry to keep this device as a weapon in reserve for the enforcement of the patent was demonstrated later, when it was suspected that the Irish Commissioners of the Revenue had anticipated permission and had given their subordinate

---

[1] The article on Swift in Palgrave's *Dictionary of Political Economy* (iii. 504–6) argues rather unconvincingly that the intention of the government was in fact to give the coin legal tender status. The facts, however, are all against the supposition.

[2] King's Letter Book (henceforward cited as K.L.B.), fo. 90.

[3] King to Gorge, 12 December 1724 : ' You commend the Spirit that this poor Kingdom has shewed and owne that it has hitherto prevented the Currence of them (the coin) but you shou'd consider, that spirit was due and has been kept up by the pamphlets published on this occasion, particularly that condemned in the proclamation ' (the fourth *Drapier's Letter*), *ibid.* fo. 195.

[4] Walpole to Grafton, 24 September 1723. P.R.O., St. Pap. 63, 381, fo. 808.

[5] Coghill to Southwell, 18 August 1724 : ' if the officers of the revenue receive them, they must go from them to the soldiers and the soldiers must passe them '. Brit. Mus. Add. MS. 21,122, fo. 15.

[6] *Journals of the Irish House of Commons*, iii. 368.

officials instructions not to receive the coin. In fact, no such orders had been given, but Walpole's instructions were explicit : that if the suspicion proved to be correct the Irish Lords Justices were immediately to countermand the Commissioners' regulations.[1] It is clear that, notwithstanding anything contained in the protecting clause in the patent, Walpole was convinced that a way might be opened for the halfpence by means of this manoeuvre.

Yet another criticism urged against Wood's patent by the Irish was that it provided no adequate system of regulation for the control of the currency. It has already been shown that the more moderate opponents of the halfpence throughout contented themselves with an attack on the terms of the patent itself, but there were not lacking those who complained that Wood had profited by his comparative freedom from effective supervision to abuse his contract.

There can be little doubt that the control of the coinage was lax. Wood's patent compared unfavourably with former grants in so far as it did not oblige him or his agents to convert the coin on demand into legal tender currency.[2] This in itself might have been sufficient temptation to the patentee to debase the halfpence. The Comptroller appointed to inspect and assay the coins was paid by Wood and would, for that reason alone, have been more manageable and compliant than an independent official.[3] Further scope for irregularities was afforded by the permission granted to Wood to manufacture the coins, not at the Tower of London under Treasury supervision, but at Bristol. It is known that Sir Isaac Newton, as Master of the Mint, strongly disapproved of this clause of the patent.[4]

This lack of a strict regulation made the restrictions on the amount to be coined by Wood very largely inoperative and freed him from any close observance of the terms of his grant. That Wood did actually avail himself of the opportunities presented to him may be easily proved. One of the facts brought to light at the time of the official inquiry into the coinage was that no less than four different sorts of halfpence and farthings had been coined by Wood and dispatched to Ireland.[5] The four varieties differed considerably in size, weight, and fineness, and according to Swift three of them were debased.[6] It also appears that Wood's copper, the currency of which was limited by the

[1] Orders in Council dated 6 August 1724. Brit. Mus. Add. MS. 9243, fo. 34.
[2] *A Defence of the Conduct of the People of Ireland in their Unanimous Refusal of Mr. Wood's Copper Money*, Dublin, 1724, pp. 21, 24.
[3] W. M. Mason, *History of St. Patrick's Cathedral*, p. 326, n. v.
[4] Newton to the Lords of the Treasury, 29 January 172^2/$_3$, *8th Report of the Hist. MSS. Commission*, Appendix, Pt. I, p. 79.
[5] King to Southwell, 9 June 1724, K.L.B. fo. 110.
[6] *Prose Works*, ed. Temple Scott, vi. 68.

patent to Ireland, obtained circulation in London and Bristol.[1] There are no conclusive proofs of Wood's actual dishonesty, but these facts are sufficient to give point to the Irish contention that a stricter system of supervision should have been established. Where the possibility of fraud being perpetrated was thus never in doubt, it was not surprising that suspicion attached to the halfpence from the beginning.

Lastly, there was the plea that the amount to be coined under the patent was excessive. It is extremely difficult, in fact, to be certain of the exact monetary requirements of Ireland in 1722. According to King the Irish had a sufficient stock of copper coinage already, the true need being for fresh supplies of small silver currency for retail purposes.

' As to our wanting halfpence for Change,' he wrote to Gorge on 17 October 1724, ' it is most false. We have more halfpence than we need. Already it is true, we want change, but it is of Sixpences, Shillings, half Crowns and Crowns, our Silver and our Guineys being almost all gone, and the General Current Coin of the Kingdom is now Moydors which are Thirty Shillings a piece.' [2]

The same is implied by Monck–Mason, who pointed out that the patent itself did not directly assert the shortage of copper money in Ireland. It merely stated that ' His Majesty had received information that there was a great want of small money for making small payments '.[3] Nevertheless, there is little reason to doubt that some new copper coins were urgently needed. Swift himself did not dispute this, and the coinages of 1737, 1741, 1750, 1760, 1766, and 1769 establish the point beyond argument.[4]

The Irish were on stronger ground when they maintained that an issue of £100,800 [5] would have been obviously excessive at a time when the total currency of Ireland was reckoned to be about £400,000.[6] Even the reduction of the amount to be coined to £40,000 failed to quiet Irish fears on this head.[7] According to the newly appointed Primate, Hugh Boulter, the addition of

[1] Dr. Hawkshaw to King, 23 September 1724. T.C.D. Lyons' Correspondence.
[2] K.L.B., Letters at end of volume cc.
[3] W. M. Mason, *History of St. Patrick's*, p. 331 n.   [4] *Boulter's Letters*, ii *passim*.
[5] This figure is sometimes incorrectly cited as £108,000, *e.g.* Lecky, *History of Ireland in the Eighteenth Century*, i. 452.
[6] *Boulter's Letters*, i. 10. The author of the *Defence of the Conduct of the People of Ireland*, however, estimates (p. 40) that Ireland had at least £30,000 of copper in a total circulation of £500,000. On these figures an additional £40,000 would have left the proportion of copper as 12·96 per cent. instead of 12·5 per cent. as above.
[7] King to Southwell, 6 February 172⁴/₅. ' . . . This instead of satisfying them (the people of Ireland) has continued as much to put them out of humour as the Patent it Self, for they look on it as Treating them as fools and Children who cou'd not see that admitting 40 Thousand p^ds. of Brass was to make way to what Quantity Woods pleased for who cou'd Stint or controul him if he had Sent in 200^d Thousand pounds.' K.L.B. fo. 212.

this amount to the copper already in circulation in Ireland would
have meant that one-eighth of the whole currency would have
been copper.[1] This would give £15,000 as the amount of copper
in circulation in 1722, when Wood's patent was granted, or 3·75
per cent. of the total cash. The proposal in its amended form was,
therefore, to raise the proportion of copper from 3·75 per cent. to
12·5 per cent. Even Boulter agreed that this would have been
excessive, and suggested that a more reasonable figure would
have been £10,000.[2] As this amount occurs repeatedly in the
Irish petitions for fresh coinages after 1725, it may be taken as
probably a fair estimate. If this is so, then the original licence
to issue £100,800 of copper, even though it was to be spread over
a number of years, could with justice be condemned as completely
out of relation to Irish monetary requirements. Despite the
frequent issues of the next fifty years no more than 340 tons of
copper in all were coined over the whole period.[3]

In the face of these objections, which appeal to the unbiassed
observer as far from fancied, the question remains whether the
attitude of the English government was dictated by an unreasoning determination to enforce the patent despite all opposition,
or whether its action was governed by other considerations. At
the time, the conduct of the English ministers appeared to be
inspired by the customary casual disregard of Irish susceptibilities and totally deficient in fair-minded statemanship. To
some extent, this view may be sustained. Walpole in particular
petulantly condemned the Irish economic objections to the coinage as wrong-headed and frivolous. Unable or unwilling to
understand the resistance to the patent, he accused the Irish
leaders of treason, the Irish people of defiant disloyalty to the
Crown, and the Irish executive officers of complicity in the popular
tumults. On the strength of an official inquiry, at which no
Irish witnesses were heard, he tried every available means of
enforcing the currency of the halfpence, and it was only when
the stability of his own ministry and the connexion between the
two countries appeared to him to be endangered, that he submitted.

On the other hand, it is essential, in judging Walpole's handling of the dispute, not to ignore or underrate the difficulties
with which he had to contend. He had to sustain a project which
was not his own and to shoulder the responsibility for its unsavoury
associations. There is nothing to indicate that he did not believe the currency scheme would benefit Ireland. In fact, the
persistent efforts which he made to ensure its success were due

[1] Boulter to Newcastle, 19 January 172⁴/₅. *Letters*, i. 10.
[2] *Ibid.*
[3] W. M. Mason, *History of St. Patrick's*, n. c, section II, p. xcvi.

only partly to his concern for the royal prerogative : partly
they were due also to his conviction that a sound economic
proposal was being wrecked by interested politicians and fana-
tical demagogues.[1] It is not too much to say that, if he had been
more ably supported in Ireland by the Lord Lieutenant in the
early stages of the dispute, if he had been less solicitous for the
preservation of the royal prerogative, and if he had shown a
greater willingness to compromise, there is no reason to suppose
that he would have been unable to effect an amicable settlement
with the Irish. Walpole has often been accused of being ' more
tenacious of office than of principle ', and some have even doubted
his political courage. His eventual surrender to the Irish is
sometimes quoted as an example of his weakness in this respect.
More properly, however, attention should be directed to his long
and stubborn struggle to fight what he considered popular fanati-
cism at the risk of his own fortunes.[2] Walpole's conduct may
not have been impeccable, but it was certainly not weak.

The defence of Walpole's Irish policy between 1722 and 1725
depends largely upon several considerations which have not
hitherto been adequately considered. Walpole was prevented
from dealing effectively with the crisis at the outset by the incompetence and procrastination of Grafton as Lord Lieutenant.
His efforts to promote an impartial inquiry into the coinage were
frustrated by the Irish refusal to send over to England the
necessary evidence. His decision to deal firmly with the in-
stigators of the boycott of the coin was turned by the recalcitrancy of the Irish Lords Justices and the Irish privy council.
These difficulties were not of his own making, and yet they were
decisive in ensuring the final breakdown of his policy.

Whether or not Walpole had any real grounds for the suspicion
that Grafton had actually betrayed the ministry is uncertain.[3]
He was, however, justified in regarding the Lord Lieutenant as
primarily to blame for the actual development of a crisis in Anglo-

---

[1] Walpole to Grafton, 24 September 1723. P.R.O., St. Pap. 63, 381, fo. 808 : ' All
attempts of this kind have always secret springs and supports as this, I believe, has
from both sides of the water '. Walpole is here alluding to the supposed intrigues
of Carteret with the Brodricks for the rejection of the patent.

[2] Walpole to Grafton, 3 October 1723. P.R.O., St. Pap. 63, 381, fo. 818. Referring to the Resolutions of the Irish Parliament against the coinage, Walpole says :
' I know very well what these things mean in an English Parliament, but I suppose
you talk another language in Ireland. But let this pass. I have weathered great
storms before now, and I hope I shall not be lost at last in an Irish hurricane.'

[3] Walpole to Grafton, 24 September 1723. P.R.O., St. Pap. 63, 381, fo. 808. Letter
marked ' private '. ' Forgive me my Lord ', wrote Walpole, ' if I tell you I do not
wonder at all, th[t] nobody appears in defence of the King's patent, when you think it
advisable to write and express yourself in the manner you do in your publick letter.
If you think it proper to disclaim it and the principal of his Maj's servants cannot be
diverted from taking notice of it in a parl[y] way, I shall wonder at nothing that shall
happen upon this occasion.'

Irish relations. No one could pretend that Grafton had acted with the requisite firmness or promptitude. Procrastination was, apparently, his besetting sin, and, in the situation, procrastination was sufficient to allow the smouldering Irish discontent to assume unmanageable proportions. His naive acceptance of the case against the patent as canvassed in the popular prints, his omission to inform Walpole of Irish objections to the coinage until the Irish parliament had come to their Resolutions on the subject,[1] and his total inability to suggest any method of dealing with the agitation,[2] justifiably incurred Walpole's severest censure.

From the first he acted in a completely unbusiness-like fashion, and undoubtedly ranged Irish sentiment against himself and the English ministry by his refusal to treat Irish protests as they deserved. He ignored the early letters criticizing the project from Archbishop King and from the Irish Commissioners of the Revenue.[3] He did nothing to allay the exaggerated fears of the Irish or to acquaint Walpole with the way in which the antagonism to the patent was developing. He placed no obstacles in the way of the more violent members of the Irish house of commons,[4] and seemed oblivious of the fact that his own as well as Walpole's credit was at stake. The only piece of positive advice which he tendered to the English ministry was that a soft answer should be returned to the Addresses of the Irish parliament against the halfpence.[5] It may be inaccurate to suggest that he was intimidated, but he can be criticized for having only inadequately appreciated the real strength of his own position. He may have felt some personal embarrassment at having to correspond with Carteret, with whom his relations were strained,[6] but whenever differences of opinion between the two were at all serious, he was repeatedly assured by Walpole and Townshend that he could depend upon their support as against the secretary of state.[7] The contrast

---

[1] P.R.O., St. Pap. 63, 381, fo. 808.

[2] Grafton to Walpole, 20 October 1723. *Ibid.* fo. 824.

[3] The letter from King was dated 10 July 1722. K.L.B. N. 3, 7 ; that from the Revenue Commissioners to Hopkins, Grafton's Secretary, was of the 7 August 1722. P.R.O., St. Pap. 63, 380. Grafton's suggestion that the letters had only been sent several months after the patent had been passed is therefore untrue. P.R.O., St. Pap. 63, 381, fo. 800.

[4] Grafton to Walpole, 24 September 1723. *Ibid.* fo. 809.

[5] *Ibid.*, 20 October 1723. ' All that I would presume to advise is that such an answer might be obtained as will not irritate a country where there is such a visible coolness of affections, nay so much ill blood stirring, as may sometime prove very hurtful to His M's service and interest here.' P.R.O., St. Pap. 63, 381, fo. 824.

[6] Grafton to Townshend, 20 November 1723. He refers to Carteret as ' a minister to correspond with by the duty of my office in whom I can have no confidence and from whom (to say no more) I am to expect no support, nor to desire it from him either in this country or in another place '. P.R.O., St. Pap. 63, 382, fo. 845.

[7] Townshend to Grafton, 17 March 172³/₄. P.R.O., St. Pap. 63, 383, fo. 891.

between Grafton's mismanagement of the early stages of the Irish rupture and Carteret's own masterly handling of the issues after his appointment as Lord Lieutenant is well marked, and affords a striking commentary on the respective abilities of the two men. Walpole was clearly dissatisfied with Grafton's bungling, and showed his disapproval by the manner in which he recalled him to England.[1]

The complaint is still made in some quarters that Walpole never gave the Irish case a fair hearing. It should be remembered, however, that he did his utmost to promote an impartial inquiry into Wood's alleged abuses of his patent, and that the blame for the failure of the Irish to appear in London as witnesses against Wood in fact rests partly with Grafton and partly with the Irish themselves.

In his reply to the Addresses of the Irish houses of parliament,[2] the king had promised that he would give the necessary orders for inquiring into and punishing any abuses which might have been committed by the patentee, and that ' he would do everything in his Power for the satisfaction of his People '.[3] Orders for an official inquiry had accordingly been given in March 1724, and on the 10th of that month Carteret, as secretary of state, had commanded Grafton ' to give directions for sending over such Papers and witnesses as shall be thought proper to support the objections made against the Patent, and against the Patentee, in the execution of the Powers given him by the said Patent '.[4]

Grafton's efforts to carry out these instructions, however, failed to break down the steady refusal of the Irish privy council to co-operate. In his reply to Carteret of 20 March, Grafton gave his reasons for his inability to send over the witnesses. He had, he said, been advised by the Irish attorney-general that he had no executive power of his own to send over persons thought subject to a criminal prosecution in Great Britain. Lacking compulsory powers, Grafton was not the sort of man who was capable of achieving his ends by persuasive methods. The witnesses against the patent who had appeared before the Irish parliament had mainly been ' traders and men of business of a middle rank ', and Grafton soon decided that the task of inducing them to undertake an expensive journey for an unspecified period was an impossible one. The Lord Lieutenant clearly found his commission both inconvenient and uncongenial.[5]

---

[1] Grafton to Newcastle, 14 April 1724. *Ibid.* fo. 915.

[2] The commons presented their Address on the 27 September 1723 (*Commons' Journals*, iii. 325) and the Lords on the following day (*Lords' Journals*, ii. 750).

[3] P.R.O., St. Pap. 63, 382, fos. 836–7. The King's Letter was dated from Göhre, 2 November (N.S.) 1723.

[4] *Ibid.* 383, fo. 889.   [5] *Ibid.* fo. 894.

Further efforts to secure evidence encountered fresh obstacles. By 24 March, when he next wrote to Carteret, Grafton had become convinced that it would be hopeless to try to secure the witnesses, as these had now revealed themselves as Wood's own correspondents. Nor could the documentary evidence be supplied, for the Resolutions against the patent had not been framed on any special reports to which recourse might be had for information, but upon the evidence taken before a committee of the whole House. All the original papers used on that occasion were still in the possession of the house of commons and the Lord Lieutenant had no authority to requisition them.[1]

It was thus that the committee of the English privy council which met at the Cockpit on 9 April 1724 to consider the representations of the Irish parliament against the coinage was unable to proceed with the inquiry for lack of material. Wood was heard in his own defence, and it was apparently at his request that orders were given for an assay of the coins to be made by the officers of the Mint.[2] As Newcastle, the new secretary of state, wrote to Grafton on 14 April,[3] the neglect to provide evidence had put the king in a difficulty : his majesty had therefore been obliged to proceed 'according to the known rules and maxims of Law and Justice'. It was hoped that, as a result of the assay, his majesty would 'be enabled to judge of the Patentee's behaviour and to redress whatever may have been done amiss in this affair'. Clearly revealed in the same letter is Newcastle's own conviction that the Lord Lieutenant might very well have been more resourceful in dealing with the Irish. The objection that the witnesses were Wood's own correspondents he considered irrelevant, since 'the same zeal that induced them to appear before the two Houses might reasonably engage them to do this further service to their country, as they apprehend it, without which one cannot see but what they have already done must prove ineffectual'. He threw out the obvious suggestion that Grafton should try guaranteeing the witnesses their expenses.

Even this letter failed to produce any effect on Grafton, who had now been informed that he was to be superseded by Carteret.[4] He merely explained that Newcastle was wrong in thinking that the witnesses had testified out of patriotic fervour, since they had only been compelled to do so by parliament. He also pointed out, more reasonably, that the witnesses were afraid that 'any defect or failure of their evidence in England would expose them to the resentment of the people and of the two Houses of Parliament here, whom they all look upon to be the Prosecutors'.[5]

---

[1] P.R.O., St. Pap. 63, 382, fo. 902.   [2] *Daily Courant*, 10 April 1724.
[3] P.R.O., St. Pap. 63, 383, fo. 914.   [4] *Daily Courant*, 6 April 1724.
[5] Grafton to Newcastle, 23 April 1724 ; P.R.O., St. Pap. 63, 383, fo. 920.

In view of these fruitless attempts to secure papers and witnesses, there is small wonder that the English ministry, convinced of the legality of the patent, and fully persuaded of Ireland's need of a fresh copper coinage, should have come to the conclusion, even before Newton's report on the assay, that the Irish objection to Wood's currency was unfounded and factious. Every effort had been made by Walpole to ascertain the real grounds of dissatisfaction with the patent, but Grafton's incompetence and Irish recalcitrancy had combined to prevent the Irish case being stated in London. The impression that the Irish were being merely obstructive was only heightened by Sir Isaac Newton's report on the assay, which was dated 27 April 1724. This was entirely favourable to Wood,[1] and must have confirmed Walpole's view of the inability of the Irish to prove their case. It is hard to see what more Walpole could have done.

The question nevertheless remains : why did the Irish refuse to send over the requisite papers and witnesses ? The most satisfactory explanation is to be found in a letter of Archbishop King to Edward Southwell of 23 March 172³/₄. The demand for information had arrived at a very inconvenient moment, since the Irish parliament had been prorogued in December 1723. As King pointed out,

' If this letter [Carteret's to Grafton of 10 March 1724] had come while the Parlement was sitting and had been communicated to the Houses, they wou'd have appointed certain persons to have acted for them and raised a fund to support them . . . but for any without Such Authority to make himself a party for the Legislature and People of Ireland wou'd be a bold undertaking and perhaps dangerous, for if such undertaker or undertakers shou'd fail in producing all evidences that may be had or any of the Papers necessary to make the case evident, they must expect to be severely handled by the next Parlement for their officiousness, and bare the blame for the miscarriage of the cause . . . '

It was this difficulty which prevented the Irish privy council from intervening.

King also regarded the request for written evidence as unpractical. The original papers could not, as has been seen, be removed from the possession of the officials of the house of commons, and copies of them would not be legally satisfactory. As

---

[1] Although King, Swift, and the other Irish leaders never cast doubt on the integrity or veracity of Newton, they steadily refused to acknowledge the findings of the report on the ground (a) that Wood and his comptroller had themselves carefully selected the coins submitted for assay ; (b) that the report dealt only with the coins struck off between March 1723 and March 1724, none of which had been imported into Ireland, the coins complained of being of the 1722 issue ; (c) that the pieces assayed all bore the same impression, whereas no less than four different sorts had been circulated in Ireland ; (d) that all the evidence given was one sided and that no Irish witnesses were heard. For Irish criticism of the report see particularly *A Defence of the Conduct of the People of Ireland in their Unanimous Refusal of Mr. Wood's Copper Money*, Dublin, 1724.

for the witnesses, the Lord Lieutenant had not even the means
of discovering who the persons actually were who had testified
before the Irish parliament.

Finally, it was generally felt in Ireland that the production
of the evidence was not necessary to substantiate the Irish contentions. Objection had been taken not so much to Wood's abuse
of his grant as to the patent itself, ' which had been obtained
by most false and notorious misinformation of his Majestie '. A
licence to coin £100,000 worth of copper for Ireland carried with
it its own condemnation.[1]

The most that can be said on the whole question of the Irish
failure to produce papers and witnesses is that the practical
difficulties outlined by King prevented the Irish from complying with Carteret's instructions, and that, as Grafton never
defended himself as strongly as he might have done, Walpole was
left with the conviction that the Irish were unwilling to submit
their grievances to an English tribunal.

The main difficulty with which Walpole had to cope after the
publication of Newton's report, however, was the resistance of
the Irish executive officers. Throughout the critical period of
the dispute, the Irish Lords Justices and privy council, from whom
Walpole expected, if not active support, at least helpful advice,
showed a fixed determination to resist all attempts to introduce
the halfpence. It was this particular form of opposition which,
in a very real sense, was the decisive element in the struggle.

The English ministry had been disconcerted but not greatly
perturbed by the Resolutions and Addresses of the Irish parliament. It had no reason, at any rate before the publication of
the fourth *Drapier's Letter*, to fear the consequences of the in-
cipient pamphlet warfare in Ireland. Even the popular ' associations ' to boycott the coins might not have been necessarily
fatal to the success of Wood's enterprise. The failure to convert
or to constrain the chief Irish executive officers, on the other
hand, completely undermined the efforts made to uphold the
patent. The desertion of the Lords Justices and privy council
meant that the English government in Ireland was paralysed.
Walpole's only resource was the dispatch of Carteret to bring the
Irish executive to a sense of its responsibilities. By that time,
however, Swift had united the Irish people behind the privy
council, and nothing but surrender on the part of the English
ministry offered the least probability of a settlement. It is not
an exaggeration to say that, if the Lord Justices and privy councillors had been compliant, not even the ' fierce indignation ' of
the Drapier would have sufficed to wreck Wood's patent.

[1] K.L.B. fos. 88–92. Quoted in part by W. M. Mason, *History of St. Patrick's*,
p. lxxxvii, and by H. J. Davis, *Drapier's Letters*, pp. 229–31.

The first manifestation of independence was the refusal of the Irish privy council to facilitate the official inquiry by sending over papers and witnesses. The reason for this step has already been indicated. This was followed up on 20 May by an address of the Lords Justices and privy council against the coinage. All the arguments used in the Resolutions and Addresses of the Irish parliament were reiterated, and a petition was made against the introduction of the copper through the instrumentality of the Commissioners of the Revenue.[1] It is perhaps significant that the manifesto was signed on the very day that the new Lords Justices were sworn.[2] Midleton, Shannon, and Conolly, it may be conjectured, wished to leave no doubt about their attitude to the halfpence from the very outset. The address was, in fact, a challenge which heralded the new source of difficulty for the home government. It was probably meant not so much as an encouragement to popular opposition as a warning to the English ministers.

More serious was the attitude assumed by the Lords Justices towards the Orders in Council issued on 6 August 1724,[3] consequent upon the report of the committee of the English privy council dated 24 July. The Lords Justices were to be requested by one of the principal secretaries of state ' immediately to order His Majesty's Commissioners of the Revenue, and all his other officers in Ireland, that in case they or any of them have given any orders, directions, significations, or intimations whatsoever to hinder or obstruct the receiving or altering the Copper Money, they do revoke the same '. It was also directed that the amount of Wood's copper already coined (£17,000) and a further £23,000 worth [4] be ' suffered and permitted, pursuant to the terms of the Patent, without any Lett, suit, trouble, molestation, or denial of any of His Majesty's officers and Ministers whatsoever to pass and be received as current money, by such as shall be willing to receive the same '. These orders confirmed the fears, which had been entertained for some time past in Ireland, that Walpole intended to make use of the Commissioners of the Revenue to effect his purpose. As a matter of fact, as Conolly wrote to Newcastle on 15 August, no orders to refuse the coin had been given.[5] There could, however, be no mistaking the English ministry's intention to introduce the coin in this indirect manner.

Preliminary accounts of the findings of the English privy council had reached Ireland on 30 July,[6] and it had been con-

---

[1] P.R.O., St. Pap. 63, 383, fo. 938.   Full text given in Davis, *Drapier's Letters*, p. 211.
[2] P.R.O., St. Pap. 63, 383, fo. 940.   [3] Brit. Mus. Add. MS. 9243, fo. 34.
[4] The amount of Wood's coin had been reduced from £100,800 to £40,000 by the Committee.   [5] P.R.O., St. Pap. 63, 384, fo. 128.
[6] Coghill to Southwell, 1 August 1724.   Brit. Mus. Add. MS. 21, 122, fo. 13.

jectured by Coghill, at least, that orders for the acceptance of
the coins would probably follow. It was not, however, till
14 August that the official report and the Orders in Council
became available across St. George's Channel.[1] A meeting of
the Irish privy council was called, but it broke up without coming
to any resolutions on Newcastle's instructions, and without
offering any advice.[2] This action amounted to a plain refusal
to come into line with the ministry. The stand was supported
by the Irish Commissioners of the Revenue, who had been given
more explicit instructions to receive the coin by the English
Treasury officials.[3]

Patriotic feelings were probably not alone in influencing
the Irish officers to adopt this spirited attitude : the Lords
Justices and the Commissioners were now obviously afraid, on
their own account, to commit themselves to any line of action
which might have the effect of burdening Ireland with the hated
coinage. Of the Lords Justices, Midleton was speaker of the
Irish house of lords and Conolly occupied the corresponding
position in the commons. Both were placed in a very embarrassing position. Neither could expect to avoid serious trouble when
the Irish parliament reassembled, if they lent themselves to the
very ministerial manoeuvre against which both the commons and
the privy council had so recently petitioned. Shannon, the other
Lord Justice, was hardly less vulnerable as commander of the
Irish forces, since it was generally anticipated that the army
would also be used as a means of putting the coins into circulation. He would have to bear the main share of the unpopularity
which would undoubtedly be the lot of the soldiers when they
came to spend their wages among the Irish tradespeople. For
the Commissioners of the Revenue, compliance would involve
a breach of their obligation only to receive legal tender.[4]
They, therefore, declined to accept the instructions from
the Treasury as sufficient warrant for the 'dereliction of duty
involved.[5]

It was this behaviour of the Lords Justices and the Commissioners, and not the resolve to enforce the coinage at all costs,
which prompted Walpole to despatch Carteret to Ireland before
the time when he would normally have been expected to take up

[1] Coghill to Southwell, 18 August 1724.   Brit. Mus. Add. MS. 21, 122, fo. 15.
[2] Conolly to Newcastle, 20 August 1724.   P.R.O., St. Pap. 63, 384, fo. 130.
[3] Coghill to Southwell, 7 September 1724.   Brit. Mus. Add. MS. 21, 122, fo. 15.
[4] King to Southwell, 10 September 1724.   K.L.B., fo. 163.   King points out in
this letter that the Irish lawyers considered that it would be ' unsafe for the Commissioners to obey those instructions without a positive and express command from
his Majestie '.   Such a proceeding would have involved a resort to the dispensing
power, which was constitutionally suspect.
[5] Coghill to Southwell, 7 September 1724.   Brit. Mus. Add. MS. 21, 122, fo. 17.

his official duties as Lord Lieutenant,[1] Walpole felt that it
would be equally dangerous either to allow the Lords Justices to
continue in office after this defiance or to remove them specifically for their conduct at a time when popular opinion in Ireland
had become so enflamed. The only ' expedient ' which remained
was for their period of office to be terminated by sending over
the viceroy.

Carteret did not, however, arrive in Dublin till 22 October,[2]
and in the interval, the Lords Justices were enabled to make
a final demonstration of their independence. On 3 October,
Newcastle felt compelled to write at length to the insubordinate
deputies partly in justification of the past conduct of the ministry
in dealing with Irish discontent, but mainly with a view to recalling the Lords Justices to a proper sense of their duty. He
suggested that they should in future ' use their best endeavours
to pacify a mistaken people ' and, as a contribution to this end,
recommended that they should give greater publicity to the two
vital facts which seemed hitherto to have escaped the Irish :
namely that ' His Majesty never intended by any compulsory
orders to enforce the currency of this copper money ' and that
' its quantity in the patent had been reduced by $\frac{3}{5}$ '. Enclosed
with the letter was a copy of a proposal of Wood's, dated 29
September 1724, in which the patentee announced his willingness
' to forbear coining, importing into, or uttering in Ireland any
of this coinage, untill such time as his Majesty's Officers and
Ministers of Ireland shall have considered and propos'd any
further regulations and restrictions, that may effectually prevent
my exceeding the quantity now agreed to '. Newcastle concluded
his letter with the advice that the Justices should not lay themselves open to the charge of having countenanced seditious and
audacious libels.[3]

This protest evoked from the Lords Justices a strenuous
defence of their past conduct. They were at pains to make clear
that the riots and disturbances which they were accused of
fomenting had in any case been grossly exaggerated in England.
They admitted that there had been local unrest and disturbances
at Cork and Dublin, but at neither place had any serious rioting

[1] Walpole to Newcastle, 1 September 1724. P.R.O., St. Pap. 63, 384. ' The popular frenzy and aversion to the taking this money I am afraid is now carried to such a
degree, that it will scarce be prudent to attempt forcing their inclinations, especially
when they are Supported and countenanced in their obstinacy by their Governours and
those that are in authority under His Majesty, for how is it possible that the King's
pleasure should be known, much lesse that it should be obey'd, by the People, when
the L^{ds} Justices refuse to signifie His Majesty's pleasure to the people and the Councell
breaks up without coming to any resolutions, when the King's orders are under their
consideration. This makes it impracticable to hope to change the minds of the people.'

[2] Ibid. Ballantyne and other authorities give 23 October. Carteret, p. 116. This
seems incorrect.   [3] P.R.O., St. Pap. 63, 384 (folio numbered).

occurred. Late in August a mob had prevented a cargo of the
coinage being landed at Cork, but the rioters had been induced to
desist from their original idea of burning the ship. At Dublin,
on 7 September, Wood's effigy with a halter round its neck had
been paraded round the city by a crowd of about a hundred
people, and a few days later a second and larger mob had repeated
the demonstration. On both occasions, however, the Lord
Mayor had had no difficulty in dispersing the mob or in securing the effigy. The leaders of the latter disturbance had been
committed to Newgate. These demonstrations, the Justices explained, could be put down not to the activity of local agitators
but to the universal dread of the enforcement of the coinage.
Part of the trouble had been that the report of the English privy
council of 24 July had been dispersed in print among the people
before it had come to the hands of the Irish executive, and had
caused a violent spirit of popular opposition. Rumours had also
been circulating that Wood was on the point of shipping over
great quantities of coin without waiting for the government to
consider his own proposals, and that, within the restriction
recently imposed, he intended to enforce the currency of his coin.
In conclusion, the Lords Justices gave it as their opinion that
their studied moderation in action, so far from aiding the malcontents, had been the decisive factor in the restoration of
public order. They were convinced that, if they had ' used any
extraordinary act of power to quell the ferment of the people or
the licences of the press at that time, greater trouble would have
been provoked. Whereas for the past few weeks both Dublin
and the rest of the country had been in a state of perfect tranquillity.' [1]

Having defended their past conduct in these terms, the
Lords Justices apparently decided to make at least some demonstration to Newcastle of their goodwill. On 12 October, two
days after the receipt of Newcastle's letter, they convened a
meeting of the Lord Mayor, sheriffs, and magistrates of Dublin,
and recommended them to suppress all riots and tumults and to
prosecute the authors and printers of seditious libels. Beyond
this, however, the Justices were unwilling to go. On 15 October
they submitted their difficulties to the Irish privy council. The
result was completely disappointing. The suggestion that the
Commissioners of the Revenue had issued orders forbidding the
receipt of the halfpence was repudiated, Newcastle's advice
about the desirability of giving greater prominence to the findings of the English privy council was contemptuously rejected,
and once again it was declared that no advice could be tendered.[2]

[1] Lords Justices to Newcastle, 17 October 1724. P.R.O., St. Pap. 63, 384.
[2] *Ibid.*

It was quite evident, by this time, that the Lords Justices were relying on passive resistance to combat Walpole's attempts to coerce Ireland, and that even when Carteret did arrive at Dublin he would find in the privy council a determined centre of opposition to the patent. There are good grounds for believing that Carteret's later decision to recommend the surrender of the patent may be ascribed, in part at least, to the difficulty of dealing with this official resistance.

It has not, hitherto, been noticed by historians that during the course of the quarrel over Wood's halfpence the English ministry and the Irish leaders were really arguing at cross purposes with each other. This source of mutual misunderstanding may be ascribed to a change of attitude, on both sides, with regard to the relative importance of the ' economic ' and ' constitutional ' issues involved in the dispute. Originally the English ministry had consented to promote the patent for economic reasons, in so far as it was designed to supply an obvious lack of copper money in Ireland. The Irish leaders, on the other hand, had opposed the scheme, in the first case, very largely because the Irish executive had not been consulted. That is to say, resistance had been offered, initially, to what was regarded as a ' constitutional ' innovation. Later, as the rift became wider, both sides reversed their positions. The Irish discovered that the currency scheme not only raised a constitutional difficulty but also threatened to ruin the country economically. It is probably safe to say that, when the contest was at its height, Irish public opinion was far more concerned about the injury which native pamphleteers prophesied would be done to Irish trade and commerce than about the larger political question which preoccupied Swift. A corresponding change of front occurred on the English side. From the point of view of Walpole, Townshend, and Newcastle, Irish resistance to the coinage raised issues of the highest constitutional significance. Failure to promote the patent meant for them far more than a check to their own political credit. It would, on their view, have thrown doubt on the king's prerogative rights and have brought in question the status of Ireland as a ' depending kingdom '. Hence their reluctance to withdraw the patent until circumstances compelled them.

This two-sided change of attitude rendered reconciliation doubly difficult. It meant that both English and Irish misconstrued the true position adopted by their opponents, and it meant also that each side not unnaturally accused the other of deception. To mutual misunderstanding there was thus added mistrust. The Irish leaders were fully persuaded that the question of the prerogative and of Irish ' independency ' had been raised by the English ministry to confuse the issues and to delay concessions, while Walpole and Townshend, in their turn, both considered that Irish economic objections to the patent, groundless as they considered them, were being used as a cloak for more sinister designs in the way of legislative independence.

This change of front, however, was not the result of duplicity on either side, but lay implicit in the circumstances and in the way in which the contest evolved. It is perhaps worth while trying to explain how it occurred.

Take the Irish resistance first. There are several reasons why Archbishop King and other Irish leaders should have opposed Wood's scheme in 1722, mainly on the score of non-consultation. The memory of their defeat over the question of the appellate jurisdiction of the Irish house of lords was still fresh in their minds. The Declaratory Act of 1719 and the omission to consult the Irish executive officers in the matter of the patent were undoubtedly construed as marking the fixed determination of the English to disregard Irish constitutional liberties. Ireland was peculiarly sensitive on this point at the time, and it is easily intelligible, therefore, why attention was initially concentrated on this aspect of the dispute. Again, granted that the country did need a further stock of small change, a carefully drafted patent to supply a new copper currency would have seemed unobjectionable from the economic standpoint. Until the amount of the coinage and the conditions of its issue were known, the immediate necessity seemed to be that the Irish executive should be duly consulted. The economic danger of an excessive or unregulated grant was definitely foreseen, but emphasis tended to fall at this time on the ' constitutional ' aspect of the project. This is clear from King's letter to Grafton of 10 July 1722.

' I hear ', King said, ' there is a design to coin brass money for Ireland, this is in my opinion a matter of vast consequence both to his Majestie and his subjects for if it be not managed with the utmost caution, it will drain the Kingdom of the little gold and silver y^t is left in it & compleat the general misery wch is already intolerable . . . I hope therefore your Grace will consider well of this before you let it pass and I am humbly of opinion, y^t if it be resolved such a design shou'd be prosecuted, the people here shou'd be consulted before this be imposed on y^m & y^t the mint shou'd be set up by his Majesty here and only he have the benefit of the coinage.' [1]

It is noticeable that King in this early letter did not assert that the country had no need of a new copper issue : that was a discovery which he made later when the emphasis shifted to the economic defects of the patent.

This change was probably due to tactical considerations.

[1] K.L.B. N. 3, 7.

It soon became apparent that the most effective as well as the simplest plan to resist the coinage would be not to contest its legal validity or to raise the question of 'independency' but simply to boycott the halfpence on economic grounds. This was the burden of the first three *Drapier's Letters :* but the idea had occurred to King as early as September 1722.[1] Then, too, no one could overlook the superior popular appeal of the economic argument. This is well illustrated by the difficulties which Swift, in the person of the Drapier, pretended to find in threading his way through the complicated legal and constitutional problems involved in the question of the prerogative.[2] Lastly, after the effective reply made by Walpole in the Privy council report of 24 July 1724 to the charge of non-consultation,[3] this grievance was allowed to drop into the background.

As far as the English ministry was concerned, its ultimate insistence upon the constitutional aspect of the dispute followed logically from its refusal to admit the force of the Irish claim that the patent would have harmful economic consequences. Walpole and Townshend were confirmed in this line of thought by the stubborn Irish antagonism, which seemed to them to have assumed proportions completely unwarranted by any simple desire to prevent the circulation of the halfpence. In these circumstances, it was only natural that the English ministers should have come to view Irish resistance as an attack both upon the royal prerogative and upon the principle of the political subordination of Ireland.[4]

It was indeed the concern felt for the royal prerogative which was one of the main obstacles in the way of a settlement, in so far as it made Walpole reluctant to grant the one concession which would have calmed Ireland : the withdrawal of the patent.

' This is so tender a point ', as Townshend wrote to Grafton on 14/25 October 1723, ' and must always be so well guarded, that t'is the highest

---

[1] K.L.B. N. 3, 7. King to Annesley, 3 September 1722: 'We have only one remedy, and that is not to receive these in payments ; the Patent oblidges none but such as are willing of themselves, if therefore Landlords, or but a few of them refuse to take their rents in brass, I am of opinion it will break the neck of the Project '.

[2] H. J. Davis, *Drapier's Letters*, pp. 11–14.

[3] P.R.O., St. Pap. 63, 384, fo. 113. Text quoted by Davis, pp. 213–25.

[4] A letter from Wood to Molyneux, his brother-in-law, and one of his agents in Ireland, is interesting in this connexion. It is dated 10 August 1723 : ' Dear Bro,— In order to remove the difficulties attending my Irish coinage I waited upon the Lord Lieut. and made a representation to him of the whole affair, as also I did to Mr. Walpole, and I hope entirely to the satisfaction of them both, and tho' any one at sight may be satisfied of the goodness of the copper, yet to put it out of all dispute I desired the Lords of the Treasury to order the Comptroller of the Mint to make his Report, which accordingly was done and entirely in my favour as to every part of the coinage. This wholely justifieth me, so that if any complaint or remonstrance in Parl. (which I have heard of) should be made, it can be in effect no other than against his Majesty and Ministry for making the grant.' P.R.O., St. Pap. 63, 381, fo. 788.

folly in any one to attack it, unless there is the most manifest evidence of some misapplication, whereas you will find in this case, that all the steps were taken with the utmost caution to avoid any just imputation.' [1]

Throughout the struggle everything was done to prevent the prerogative from suffering any injury. Grafton, for example, had particularly exerted himself to stop any parliamentary Resolution ' which may be indecent with regard to the Prerogative '. It was thought necessary by Walpole to incorporate in the privy council report of 24 July 1724, along with the defence of the methods used to procure the patent, a special vindication of the king's prerogative rights of coining. It is quite certain also that the hesitation of Newcastle to adopt Carteret's recommendation for the withdrawal of the patent,[2] and the long delay in effecting the final surrender, were due entirely to the difficulties connected with the preservation of the royal prerogative.[3]

It is also interesting to note that long before the publication of the fourth *Drapier's Letter*, the English government had come to the conclusion that the Irish parliament, seizing on the resentment caused by Wood's patent, was engaged in an attack on the Act of 6 George I. This is clear from the official correspondence of both Townshend and Newcastle. On 23 January 172^3/$_4$ Townshend wrote to Grafton :

' It has appeared very evidently that the spirit in Ireland, which has been at the bottom of all the noise for some time past, has been an earnest desire of Independency, and of setting up themselves for the direction of matters in all respects as a parliament of England.' He continued : ' It is not to be doubted but the meaning of the Irish Parliament is to grasp at more authority and lessen their subjection to England ', and finally drew the Viceroy's attention to ' these dangerous attempts, which are destructive of the Dependency that Ireland ought to be under '. [4]

The same note was sounded by Newcastle in a letter to Conolly of September 1724 :

' You may believe ', he said, ' that this affair is not considered now as what effects the personal interest of the King or his Ministers much less any Regard had in it to Mr. Wood ; but it is plainly a National Concern ; it is a renewal of attempts ill-founded in themselves, very ill timed (for I am sure it shows no skill to chuse to attack a Government and a Nation in full Prosperity and vigour) attempts that every Man in England of howsoever different principles on other things will unite to oppose and which should they succeed must end in the Ruin of Ireland.' [5]

---

[1] P.R.O., St. Pap. 63, 381, fo. 819.

[2] Newcastle to Carteret, 29 December 1724. P.R.O., St. Pap. 63, 384.

[3] Carteret had given his opinion that the patent would have to be surrendered on 16 December 1724 (Brit. Mus. Add. MS. 9243, fo. 55), yet the exemplification of the surrender was dated 14 August 1725 (W. Mason, *St. Patrick's*, p. 346, n.s.).

[4] P.R.O., St. Pap. 63, 383, fo. 881.   [5] *Ibid.*, 384, fo. 183.

There is little room for doubt that the home government regarded the sentiments expressed by Swift in the fourth *Drapier's Letter* as the logical conclusion of the controversy and, moreover, was firmly convinced that the other Irish leaders were of one mind with the dean.

It is in this respect that the focussing of attention upon the propagandist activities of Swift during the crisis has led historians astray. The evidence suggests, however, that the English ministers profoundly misunderstood the real nature of the Irish revolt, and that the advanced political ideas canvassed by Swift were totally unrepresentative of Irish feeling at the time.

The mass of the uneducated Irish were undoubtedly little moved by the constitutional debate. What united them behind the Drapier was the fear of the depreciation of Wood's coin if ever it obtained circulation. The merchants and public corporations, with their ' associations ' to refuse the coin, also thought almost exclusively in terms of the probable economic consequences of the patent. The landed and propertied class, according to Boulter, had the sense to see that their interests would in no sense coincide with the prosecution of a campaign for legislative independence.[1] The country, as a whole, was sincerely loyal to the Hanoverian dynasty, and although there were some Irish Jacobites [2] their activities gave no ground for serious concern. In their Addresses and Resolutions against the patent, the Irish houses of parliament consistently urged their complete and unwavering attachment to the Crown. As has already been emphasized, no effort was made by the Irish parliament to cast doubt upon the legality of the patent or upon the prerogative rights involved. The considerations which actuated the politicians were primarily the sense of injury due to the Irish executive not having been consulted and a feeling that the patent ought to have been promoted in Ireland, the coins struck in Ireland, and the profit devoted to the public service.

As for the views of the Irish leaders, there is plenty of evidence to show that they were not all interested in the question of ' Independency ' as a practical policy. Most of them disapproved of the notion strongly. It is true, of course, that Archbishop King acted in very close collaboration with Swift in the boycotting of the coin,[3] and that he was regarded by Midleton, the lord chancellor, as being jointly responsible with Swift for the promotion of ' independency '.[4] King's own letters, however, are far more guarded and cautious in tone than one might have expected if the archbishop had identified himself completely with

[1] Boulter to Newcastle, 19 January 1724–5. *Letters*, i. 9.   [2] *Ibid.* p. 8.
[3] See Davis, *Drapier's Letters*, Introduction, pp. xliii–xlviii.
[4] Coxe, *Walpole*, iii. 402.

the position adopted by the Drapier. The terms in which, for example, he refers to Swift's more inflammatory pamphlets are not consistent with that supposition.[1] The reason why King refused to sign the Proclamation issued by Carteret against the author of the *Letter to the Whole People of Ireland* was not that he agreed with the political opinions vented in the pamphlet but simply because he wished to sustain the spirit of opposition to the coinage, which he considered would be damped by immediate compliance on the part of the privy councillors with the Lord Lieutenant's action.[2] King was an enemy of Wood's patent and an ardent champion of the appellate jurisdiction of the Irish house of lords, but it would be erroneous to contend that he was in favour of Irish legislative independence.

Lord Midleton was uncompromising in his antagonism to Wood's project, but he had no sympathy with the extremist views of Swift. The lord chancellor was, in fact, greatly concerned at the prospect of English public opinion being misinformed on the real objectives of the Irish as a result of the publication of Swift's fourth letter. Writing to Thomas Brodrick on 17 November 1724, he termed the *Advice to the Whole People* 'that hot-headed libel' and went on to conjecture that

'it will probably raise such resentment as may turn to the prejudice of the kingdome, if care be not taken to have it understood, that the kingdome is in no sort of the mind of the author or his patron . . .[3] The kingdome', he continued, 'hath received and probably may receive more damage by the politics and wrangling of those two men, than it would have been in the power of its worst enemys to have brought upon it, without the assistance of indiscreet and seditious pamphleteers ; but sure their follyes and crimes are not to be placed to the nation's account.'[4]

Nor was it individuals alone who reacted unfavourably to the Drapier's fourth Letter, as may be seen from Carteret's report upon the meeting of the Irish privy council, which he summoned on 27 October 1724 with the object of proceeding against its author, and of discovering 'the real temper and disposition' of the councillors. On that occasion Carteret defended the legality of the patent, and attacked the pamphlet as treasonable. He then made two practical proposals. The first of these—that the author, printer, and publisher should be prosecuted by due course of law—was carried 'after some debate'. The second—that

[1] King to Southwell, 26 November 1724. K.L.B. fo. 191. He refers to the fourth *Drapier's Letter* as 'ludicrous and satyrically writ' and to Swift's *Seasonable Advice* as 'foolish enuff, and impertinent'.

[2] King to Gorge, 12 December 1724. *Ibid.* fo. 195. King says definitely in this letter that he and those who also refused to sign the Proclamation (the bishop of Elphin, Dr. Coghill, and Lord Allen) 'did by no means approve of several things in it' (i.e. the fourth Letter).

[3] Swift's patron was, of course, King.   [4] Coxe, *Walpole*, iii. 402.

a Proclamation should be issued offering £300 reward for the
discovery of the author—was resisted only by the archbishop of
Dublin, the bishop of Elphin, and two others. These were
afraid that the Proclamation would be generally interpreted,
' as an oblique way of forcing the Halfpence ', and that it would
be likely, for that reason, to increase the danger of public disorder.
Carteret also failed in his endeavour to induce the council to
condemn the whole of the fourth Letter as treasonable, with the
result that the Proclamation was issued only against ' several
Seditious and Scandalous Paragraphs highly reflecting upon His
Majesty and His Ministers, tending to Alienate the Affections of
His good Subjects of *England* and *Ireland* from each other, and
to promote Sedition among the People '.[1] It is significant, as
King pointed out, that the Proclamation made no mention
of the halfpence whatsoever.[2] A ' considerable number of the
Council ' were, indeed, of the opinion that, as an alternative to
the specification of the offending paragraphs by the Attorney-
General, ' something might be inserted in the Proclamation to
satisfy the people that the Author was not prosecuted for what
he writ against the halfpence '.[3] The council was, therefore, explicit in its condemnation of Wood's coinage. It was, however,
no less emphatic, as Carteret reported, in its repudiation of the
idea of independence.

' I think it my duty to acquaint Your Grace ', he wrote to Newcastle,
' that all who spoke upon this occasion, which was the greatest part of those
that were present, expressed the utmost duty for His Majesty, and an
abhorrence and detestation of the notion of Independency, upon which
Mr. Conolly particularly exerted himself.' [4]

The conclusion is inescapable that the privy council as a body
supported Swift's attack on Wood's currency proposals, but dis-
sociated itself entirely from his championship of Irish legislative
independence.

    One final piece of evidence, this time of the way in which
popular opinion reacted to the idea of Irish legislative autonomy,
may be derived from Carteret's account of the proceedings taken
against Swift's pamphlet *Seasonable Advice*. This had been
addressed to the grand jury before whom Harding, the printer
of the fourth *Drapier's Letter*, was to appear. On 21 November
1724, despite all the efforts of the attorney-general and solicitor-
general, the grand jury, by a majority of one, decided not to
make the presentation. For this they were discharged by the
Chief Justice, Whitshead. A fresh grand jury was returned on

---

[1] Carteret to Newcastle, 28 October 1724.   Brit. Mus. Add. MS. 9243, fos. 39–41.
[2] King to Gorge, 12 December 1724.   K.L.B., fo. 196.
[3] Carteret to Newcastle, 28 October 1724.   Brit. Mus. Add. MS. 9243, fo. 41.
[4] Carteret to Newcastle, 28 October 1724.   *Ibid.*

the 23rd, and again the attempt to obtain a presentation had to be abandoned.   According to Carteret, ' My Lord Chief Justice, in his Charge to them, enlarged so much upon the absurdity of the notion of Independency, that some impertinent people, who stood by, were heard to say by way of criticizing upon this conduct, *He need not have gone out of his way to discourse upon that subject* '.[1]   It is clear from this that the general view in Ireland was that the constitutional problem of Ireland's ' dependent ' status was not merely secondary but also irrelevant to the main issue in dispute : the attempt to force acceptance of Wood's coinage.   It is true enough that Swift's third paragraph in his *Seasonable Advice* had been a defence of what he had said in the fourth *Drapier's Letter* regarding ' independency '.   The paragraph which, however, must ·have appealed most strongly to the jurors was the fourth, in which Swift had asked them to consider ' what influence their finding the *Bill* may have upon the Kingdom . . . '   ' The people in general ', he had reminded them, ' will conclude it is done in Favour of Wood's Coin, they will think we of this Town have chang'd our minds, and intend to take those Halfpence, and therefore that it will be in vain for them to stand out.'   It had been thus that King had reasoned when he refused to sign the Proclamation in the privy council, and there can be small doubt that the grand jury refused to find the bill against Harding for this particular reason, and not because they had been converted to Swift's plea for ' independency '.

    If the contentions advanced in this paper are correct, accepted views of the Anglo-Irish dispute over Wood's halfpence stand in some need of revision.   So far English historians have without much question accepted Coxe's view that Townshend and Walpole were justified in their condemnation of Irish opposition to the coinage as merely factious.   The evidence which has been presented in this paper may be said to make such an assumption extremely doubtful.   Irish fears of the economic consequences of Wood's currency scheme were founded on something more than either fanaticism or separatism, and they were, allowing for the exaggeration of some pamphleteers, on the whole reasonable.   On the other hand, it is equally true that Irish historians have not done justice to the attempts made by the English ministry to discover a satisfactory solution for Anglo-Irish differences.   It may be conceded that Walpole profoundly misjudged the actual scope and purpose of the Irish resistance to the patent, but it cannot be maintained that his policy, given his mistaken hypothesis, was blatantly prejudiced or obviously unstatesmanlike.   A good deal of the responsibility for the failure to promote

[1] Carteret to Newcastle, 24 November 1724.   Brit. Mus. Add. MS. 9243, fo. 51.

Wood's scheme which is usually borne by Walpole would more properly be placed upon Grafton. Two other points seem worthy of emphasis : first, that it is a mistake to concentrate attention exclusively on the part played by Swift in the rejection of the halfpence, and second, that it is a mistake also to view the dispute ' as the first grand struggle for the independence of Ireland '.

It may also be urged in conclusion, that the ultimate significance of the crisis in the history of Anglo-Irish relations has not always been fully appreciated. Lecky saw in the surrender of the patent the first triumph won by Irish public opinion.[1] It was more than that. The main importance of the rejection of the halfpence was that, in the course of the struggle, the Irish were welded together in a spontaneous unity which they had never achieved before. It was a unity of feeling which cut clean across both political and social differences, and which was noted equally by the Irish leaders and by the representatives of the English interest. As Boulter wrote to Newcastle soon after his arrival in Ireland, ' the people of every religion, country, and party here, are alike set against Wood's halfpence, and their agreement in this has had a very unhappy influence on the state of this nation, by bringing on intimacies between Papists and Jacobites, and the Whigs, who before had no correspondence with them.' [2] Archbishop King in June 1724 had drawn the attention of the Irish secretary to the same phenomenon. ' I conceive ', he had written, ' that if no further assistance or encouragement be given Woods he will make little of the Patent, for I never saw the Kingdom so universally averse to anything as they are to these halfpence *from the herb Women to the Nobles.*' [3] Swift, perhaps, said the final word when he summed up what had happened in his fourth *Drapier's Letter*. ' Money ', he concluded, ' the great *Divider* of the world, hath by a strange Revolution, been the great *Uniter* of a most *Divided* people.' [4]

The dispute also taught both sides a lesson. It made England conscious of the Irish problem for the rest of the century, and led immediately to the administration of Ireland by the ' Undertakers '. It taught Ireland the virtues of ' agitation ' long before the advent of O'Connell, and made it inevitable that the new tactics should be employed on many future occasions as the surest means of extorting concessions.

A. Goodwin.

---

[1] *Leaders of Public Opinion in Ireland*, p. 48.
[2] Boulter to Newcastle, 19 January 1724–5. *Letters*, i. 8.
[3] King to Southwell, 9 June 1724. K.L.B., fo. 110.
[4] H. J. Davis, *Drapier's Letters*, p. 77.

The Duke of Newcastle as Ecclesiastical Minister

'YOU are in so good a way of thinking as to our bishops and have done so right with them ', observed the duke of New-castle to Sir Robert Walpole approvingly in August 1723, 'that I, though an ecclesiastical politician, shall not presume to give you any more advice.'[1] The ambition to become 'an ecclesiastical politician', avowed thus early when the duke was yet only an officer of the royal household, remained one of the strongest and most constant interests of his protracted public career. With the advancement to office of state his claim to be 'the ecclesiastical minister' was recognized ; and he rejoiced in the title, as also in such testimonies as that of his brother, Henry Pelham, in 1752 that 'it was notorious to all the world that he was the only person in the administration that had spoken to the king upon those points of business for many years '.[2] However highly or meanly historians may rank his preoccupation with bishop-making, there can be little doubt that it furnished him with as much pleasure—and at least as many embarrassments—as his conduct of civil affairs. In view of his own predilections, more-over, it cannot be without value in illustration both of his personal character and of his public policy to essay an estimate of his achievement as ecclesiastical minister.

Posterity, thanks to the preservation of his voluminous correspondence, is not denied at least a spectator's share of the satisfaction so evidently derived by himself from the complicated moves in the game of preferment, by which obscure divines became royal chaplains, chaplains were advanced to royal prebends, prebendaries were installed in deaneries, deans waived their modest *nolo episcopari* in deference to the wishes of their energetic patron, and prelates of the little bishoprics were trans-lated finally to the solace of lucrative sees or to the metropolitical thrones of Canterbury and York. The name of Newcastle's clerical dependents was indeed legion ; and therefrom sprang his prime

[1] Newcastle to Walpole, 25 Aug. 1723, Add. MSS. 32686, fo. 316.
[2] Newcastle to H. Pelham, 27 July/7 Aug. 1750, vol. 32721, fo. 471 ; H. Pelham to Newcastle, 19 Oct. 1752, vol. 32730, fo. 142.

source of embarrassment, since the number of disappointed
divines even in the gross total of his episcopal recommendations
was considerably in excess of the clients duly rewarded for
fidelity and ability.   In truth, the duke as ecclesiastical minister
in no wise differed from himself as civil minister in respect of his
inability to limit promises within the practical possibilities of
fulfilment.   Dr. Thomas Newton, a divine who had repeated
experience of the gulf which divided assurance from performance,
would have subscribed no doubt to Mr. Namier's searing exposure
of his Grace's defects of character, though himself using kinder
words of censure.   'The truth is, the duke was a good-natured
man ; he had not the courage to say No, to anyone ; he was
willing to oblige everyone, at the time perhaps seriously intended
it ; and consequently promised more than he was ever able to
perform '.[1]   The results of his hesitation and equivocations were
visited upon his head in the form of sharp and angry remonstrances from clerics smarting under the disappointment of
apparent betrayal ; and from their complaints has been drawn
much of the opprobrium heaped upon a generation of worldly
and self-seeking clergy who were at little pains to conceal either
their solicitation of favours or their resentment at denial.   Few,
indeed, of his clients equalled the gracious and elegant reply
penned by Dr. James Johnson, one of his chaplains, on being
informed of the probability of the miscarriage of plans for his
episcopal preferment :

> 'Quam pro me curam geris, oh! precor optime pro me
> deponas,'

'an answer', as the duke boasted, 'which he believed no
parson belonging either to his grace of Canterbury or to the lord
chancellor would ever have made to either of them '.[2]

In other respects besides prodigality of promises Newcastle
reproduced in his ecclesiastical negotiations the traits which
marked his conduct of civil business.   Despite a pride in the
position of sole ecclesiastical minister, he must needs confide
details of every candidate, every interview with the king, every
whisper of criticism or opposition, to his brother, to Hardwicke,
to Stone, to the primate, and to a variety of other episcopal and
political friends ; and his inquiries were accompanied by requests
for advice, desire to escape the responsibility of decision, and
complaints of the hardships of his position when each appointment
involved the discomfiture of many.   On two occasions, in 1748
and 1752, when a series of important episcopal nominations were

---

[1] 'Some Account of the Life of Dr. Thomas Newton, Bishop of Bristol, by Himself ',
in The Lives of E. Pocock, Z. Pearce, T. Newton, and P. Skelton, ii. 100 (2 vols. 1816) ;
cf. L. B. Namier, England in the Age of the American Revolution, pp. 77–8.

[2] Newcastle to H. Pelham, 27 July/7 Aug. 1752, Add. MSS. 32728, fo. 400.

to be made, the duke was away in Hanover in attendance upon the king ; so that the entire process of negotiation from beginning to end was transacted through the cumbrous and indirect medium of correspondence, to the great confusion of issues and distraction of persons.

Not the least of the hardships of his situation as seen by himself were the vagaries of George II in ecclesiastical preferments. It would be unveracious indeed to ascribe to that monarch either the esoteric theological interests of his consort Queen Caroline or the zealous devotion to the established church of his grandson and successor George III ; but lack of these qualities by no means implied absence of stubbornness and prejudice in determining nominations to the episcopate and minor offices. It may be suspected, indeed, that His Majesty, apart from personal friendships and predilections for individual divines, was moved less by concern for the reputation of the bench than by a delight in teasing his ecclesiastical minister. He seems to have taken the measure of Newcastle, and to have enjoyed the duke's display of anxiety, apprehension, and alarm whenever any of his recommendations was met with disapproval or refusal. Thus, though George II generally gave way in the end to the assault of ministerial pressure, he knew well how to present an appearance of resolute intransigeance, protesting vigorously that his ministers ' were always in haste and that he would take a little time ' to think over their proposals. In 1752, when the see of Durham was vacant, and Newcastle was particularly eager for the translation of Bishop Trevor of St. David's, the king at first replied, ' No ! not the bishop of St. David's ; he is a high-church fellow, a stiff, formal fellow, and nothing else ; there are a great many better than he '.[1] His protracted obstinacy on this occasion drove his minister to despair ; ' I will put my shoulders to the work, but I doubt the success. . . . I work hard, I do my best, and we may all be whispered out of our characters.' [2] Having given way so many times, George II evidently enjoyed to the full a personal exercise of the royal prerogative in 1757, when Archbishop Herring's death vacated the primacy during the brief period of the Devonshire-Pitt administration ; and His Majesty made so skilful use of his power as to procure three episcopal translations and one nomination in accordance with his wishes. Upon occasion he could prove wholly obdurate, as his ecclesiastical minister discovered in his iterated requests for further preferment for Dean Ashburnham of Chichester ; for the effect upon the royal conscience of repeated pictures of ' a numerous family of Ashburnhams and Pelhams in the straitest circumstances and no

[1] Newcastle to H. Pelham, 18/29 June 1752, Add. MSS. 32728, fo. 19.
[2] Newcastle to W. Murray, *ibid*. fo. 23.

prospect of being better ', and with ' little to keep them but high blood ' was to make him refuse all save the bishopric of Chichester, tardily bestowed in 1754.

But if George II had chastised Newcastle with whips, George III used scorpions ; and the duke on his side showed neither readiness nor pliancy to adapt himself to the circumstances of a new reign. ' As to ecclesiastical affairs ', observed Warburton sardonically to Hurd in March 1761, ' the duke of Newcastle seems to be on the point of shutting-up shop. What a number of bankruptcies it will make in your dear Cambridge.' [1] To shut up shop was in effect the advice given to Newcastle by many of his friends, especially Hardwicke ; but its execution was impossible to one of the duke's character. Instead, he clung to the shadow of a position, the substance of which slipped steadily from him ; and his correspondence became an ascending threnody of lamentation. ' Pray, pity me and advise me ; never was poor minister so used or got into such a scrape ', he wrote to Hardwicke [2] ; whilst to Devonshire he confessed with truth, ' if my declaring for anybody is the only reason against him, I am sure I am a fool to remain where I am '.[3] The story of Newcastle's relations with George III and his advisers constitutes, however, too considerable a part of the record of his ecclesiastical administration to receive an anticipatory verdict.

Next to cordial relationship with the ruling king, the ease of the ecclesiastical minister depended chiefly upon the degree of confidence established with the archbishop of Canterbury ; and in this regard Newcastle's period of office coincided virtually with the primacies of Herring from 1747–57, and of Secker from 1758–68. His relations with the two archbishops presented remarkable features of contrast, for whereas with Herring he began and continued in uncertainty and semi-confidence, with Secker his friendship was sincere and his agreement close. In part his difficulties with Herring sprang from similarity of temperament, for the archbishop was diffident, timid, and fearful of conflict, yet capable like the duke of a determined obstinacy upon occasion. Thomas Herring, indeed, had striven earnestly to escape the responsibility of translation from York to Canterbury ; he loved the garden of Bishopthorpe and his bowls ; the offer of Canterbury almost threw him into a fever through mental agony ; and, deferring to the persuasion of his political friends, he came to Lambeth overwhelmed with a sense of his incompetence and inadequacy to its dignity. ' I leave your lordship to consider ', he wrote to Hardwicke, ' what a thing of nothing I am like to

---

[1] *Letters of a late Eminent Prelate* (Warburton to Hurd), Letter cli, p. 327.
[2] Newcastle to Hardwicke, Add. MSS. 32925, fo. 155.
[3] Newcastle to Devonshire, vol. 32926, fo. 382.

become by removing into a station where I shall find, and everyone else that observed would find, that I had neither learning to support a proper credit, nor discernment and spirits to go through the proper business.' [1] To the establishment of cordial relations between primate and ecclesiastical minister there was raised an almost immediate barrier by Newcastle's successful pressure upon Thomas Sherlock of Sarum to accept translation to London in succession to Gibson in 1748. The history of past relations between Fulham and Lambeth, particularly whilst Gibson had lived at Fulham and Wake at Lambeth, was sufficiently discouraging to a man of Herring's apprehensive temperament ; and to this tradition of rivalry there was added the stubborn fact that Sherlock, before accepting London, had refused the primacy. The archbishop could not fathom the reasons which had led Sherlock, after declining both York and Canterbury, to remove to Fulham ; but his suspicion that the removal boded ill for his own peace was to be abundantly justified. At least it seemed to indicate that Newcastle, whose sole responsibility for the offer of London to Sherlock was well known, would look to that quarter for counsel rather than to Lambeth. 'I don't suspect his friendship ', Herring assured Hardwicke of the duke, ' and I think I may build upon his firmness, but I see his attachments plain enough and I cannot love and trust him as I do your lordship.' [2]

With such ' a very insignificant and pusillanimous man ' (as the archbishop styled himself) as primate, it was little surprising that the ecclesiastical minister believed that he could ignore archiepiscopal wishes and assume an independent attitude in ecclesiastical appointments. Within a year of Herring's establishment at Lambeth, Henry Pelham was protesting against his brother's quiet contempt for the archbishop. ' I wonder you take no notice of the archbishop in these vacancies ', he observed ; ' it makes him look little, and since you have placed him at the head, I think you should not yourself show you think him insignificant '.[3] In similar terms Hardwicke voiced the same complaint. ' I submit it to your consideration ', he wrote to Newcastle, ' whether in such a number of ecclesiastical preferments as come now to be disposed of at once, it will not have a wrong appearance not to show some regard to an archbishop of Canterbury so lately made and so entirely attached to you.' [4] The divergence thus clearly evidenced was not lessened when archbishop and minister became involved in conflict, both upon

[1] Herring to Hardwicke, 17 Oct. 1747, Add. MSS. 35598, fo. 283.
[2] Same to same, 21 Jan. 1748/9, *ibid.* fo. 393.
[3] H. Pelham to Newcastle, 30 Sept. 1748, vol. 32716, fo. 395.
[4] Hardwicke to Newcastle, 8 Nov. 1748, vol. 32717, fo. 294.

grounds of political and of personal policy in relation to episcopal appointments. At times Herring was capable of rigid firmness, as his attitude towards Dr. James Johnson and Dr. Thomas Hayter was to show. The primate, indeed, was a church-whig of the school of Gibson, surviving into an age when its shibboleths were no longer relevant to the political situation ; but he stood firmly upon the principles of his upbringing and found himself inevitably at variance with the duke.

Newcastle's profession of political fidelity in his capacity as ecclesiastical minister was made to Bishop Hoadly of Winchester in 1760, when that prelate was almost the sole relict of the heroic age of party polemic.

> ' The rule which I have laid down to myself in all recommendations which I have ever made to the crown, has been, first to recommend none whom I did not think most sincerely well-affected to his majesty and his government, and to the principles upon which it is founded ; and in this I believe I have been as seldom mistaken as ever anybody was in such a course of years.' [1]

Translation of precept into practice, however, was exceedingly difficult during the period from 1748 to 1760, when the duke was in control of episcopal preferment. After the collapse of the Jacobite rebellion in 1746, the traditional strategy of Newcastle by which the opposition was accused of Jacobitism was no longer available. Instead, he had to prepare, especially after the unexpected death of Frederick, prince of Wales, in 1751, for a political future in which, as Mr. Romney Sedgwick has observed, ' the actuarial value of the king's life-interest and the successor's reversion ' had been rudely shaken.[2] In such circumstances he pursued a line of conduct designed to attract support from new quarters with the object of securing his own position and in the hope that his own continuance in office might be ensured.

To such a course of compromise Herring was entirely antipathetic, as might have been predicted of the hero of the Yorkshire association for the defence of civil and religious liberties in 1745. In 1747, before his removal to Canterbury, he had criticized the preferment by Newcastle to the deanery of Ripon of Mr. John Fountayne, nephew of Bishop Sherlock, and of tory antecedents.

> ' How that promotion would be relished by some of our ecclesiastics here in the cathedral who have been active whigs I can't say ', he confided to Hardwicke. ' I doubt but ill ' ; . . . ' for to speak plainly of Mr. Fountayne, my lord, though he is a worthy gentleman and has a good estate here, yet as he is the first whig of a very tory family, I doubt his distinction here would go down very ill with the old whig gentlemen.' [3]

[1] Newcastle to Hoadly, 31 May 1760, Add. MSS. 32906, fo. 387.
[2] R. Sedgwick, *Letters from George III to Lord Bute*, introduction, p. xii.
[3] Herring to Hardwicke, 11 July 1747, Add. MSS. 35598, fo. 269.

After his translation to Canterbury, Herring carried his scruples so far in this connexion as to oppose the candidature of a cleric of the high church and tory school for election as prolocutor of the lower house of Canterbury Convocation, although there was no intention to lay any business before the assembly.

> ' But in good truth ', his Grace assured Hardwicke, ' I know many of the old whigs are almost peevish upon the countenance shewn to a certain set of men, who, however clear they may appear in the duke's eye, will never obtain the good opinion of the old whigs ; and for my own part, not only from my old dispositions but out of friendship to the duke whom I love, I would keep as clear as possible from all connections with them or anybody like them.   I am confident if the duke should ever insist upon an attachment to this sort of people as an evidence of his old friends' affection to him, he would create himself great uneasiness.' [1]

In view of this enunciation of principle, it could have been foreseen that all the points of difference between Herring and Newcastle should centre around the persons and preferment of Dr. James Johnson and Dr. Thomas Hayter.   The stage had been set for conflict by events in the household of the young prince of Wales, wherein, upon the death of Frederick in 1751, a new appointment of officers had been made in order to ensure whig control of the education of the heir-apparent.   Lord Harcourt was appointed governor, Dr. Thomas Hayter, bishop of Norwich, preceptor, Andrew Stone was created sub-governor, and George Lewis Scott sub-preceptor.   Mr. Sedgwick has traced the detailed story of the accusations preferred by Harcourt and Hayter of Jacobitism against Stone and Scott, and has demonstrated the inadequacy of the foundations for such charges.[2] Notwithstanding, the controversy proved the occasion of a sharp conflict between Herring and Newcastle when the death of Bishop Butler of Durham in 1752 opened the way for the creation of a series of episcopal vacancies.   Newcastle desired to advance his friend Bishop Trevor of St. David's to Durham, but George II refused him as ' a high-church fellow, a stiff, formal fellow and nothing else ' ; whereupon Herring pressed the claims of Hayter, ' their royal highness ' preceptor, because of the very eminent distinction with which the king has been pleased to honour him ', and intimated that if Hayter should fail of Durham, he would propose his translation to London whenever that see were vacant.[3] To Newcastle this recommendation seemed ' very ignorant ',

---

[1] Herring to Hardwicke, 22 June 1754, Add. MSS. 35599, fo. 199.

[2] R. Sedgwick, *Letters from George III to Lord Bute*, introduction, pp. xxi *seqq.* Unfortunately Mr. Sedgwick takes an unjustifiably adverse view of Herring and Hayter, even repeating the *canard* of the latter's illegitimacy, which was disproved in the *Quarterly Review* of April 1822 (xxvii. 186–7).

[3] Herring to Newcastle, 19 June 1752, Add. MSS. 32728, fo. 46.

and ' wrote (poor man) as if nothing had happened to make such recommendation at present extraordinary '.[1] If the duke could not succeed for Trevor, he hoped to secure the promotion of his protégé, Dr. James Johnson, who had been introduced into his household by Stone, had been made a royal chaplain, and thrice dispatched on Hanover journeys, and whose elevation seemed, therefore, a natural consequence. The archbishop associated Johnson with Stone as a Jacobite, and in replying to the duke contrived the remarkable feat of leaving Johnson unmentioned throughout his letter. To Hardwicke he explained that he could not insert

> ' in any light the name of Johnson. It is utterly against my stomach and my good conscience to do it. I protest to your lordship, it would seem to me abusing our good master, and there is on political accounts a greater abhorrence of the man among the whigs, the great whigs, than ever I met with of any man ; and to endeavour to cram him down at this juncture is to me the strongest piece òf enthusiasm I will call it, that I can conceive '.[2]

So great was Herring's indignation that Hardwicke and Henry Pelham wrote to Hanover urging Newcastle not to press his favourite, which his grace agreed very reluctantly to do, hoping that in return the archbishop upon the next occasion would give ' a strong recommendation ' for Johnson.[3] Unfortunately this ' next occasion ' occurred immediately by the vacancy of the see of Gloucester, when the primate rather than recommend Johnson asked to be excused from suggesting further names. In the end Newcastle obtained his way ; Trevor was translated to Durham, Johnson nominated to Gloucester, and as a sop to the archbishop, one of his friends, Dr. Ellis, sent to St. David's. The episode was followed by a formal, if uncordial, reconciliation between primate and duke, and between Herring and Johnson, who shook hands.[4] The agreement did not prevent further differences arising upon future vacancies, but with the subsidence of the *cause célèbre* of Jacobitism in respect of Johnson and Stone, no important conflict arose before the death of Herring in 1757.

The primacy of Matthew Hutton (contrived by George II's personal intervention) from 1757–8 was too short in duration for any relationship to be established between him and the duke ; but with the elevation of Thomas Secker to the see of Canterbury, Newcastle embarked upon a period of complete cordiality and confidence with the new primate. The ecclesiastical career of

[1] Newcastle to H. Pelham, 26 June/7 July 1752, Add. MSS. 32728, fo. 105.
[2] Herring to Hardwicke, 15 July, vol. 35599, fo. 57.
[3] Newcastle to Herring, 26 Aug./6 Sept., vol. 32729, fo. 188.
[4] Herring to Hardwicke, 21 Nov., vol. 35599, fo. 83.

Secker, alike in its success and its eclipse, illustrated with singular
fidelity the varying political tempests of the Hanoverian church.
He was raised to the bench as bishop of Bristol in 1734, and translated to the see of Oxford three years later ; there had been added
to these poor bishoprics no wealthy deanery *in commendam*, but
instead Secker had been compelled to retain the onerous parish
of St. James, Westminster. His political conduct in the house
of lords had given umbrage both to the administration and to the
court. In common with all his episcopal brethren he had opposed
the ministerial bill in February 1742/3 to reduce the duties on
spirituous liquors, having spoken against it and signed the protest
against its passing.[1] In 1748 he had spoken against the bill to
disallow from Michaelmas of that year all Letters of Orders to
Scottish episcopal clergy not granted by a bishop of the Church
of England or Ireland, and had joined with his brethren in a solid
episcopal vote of twenty voices against its acceptance.[2] Worse
still, after the debate on the Convention of El Pardo on 1 March
1738/9, he and Benson of Gloucester (known in parliament as
' the two brothers '), together with the bishops of Lincoln and
Lichfield, had voted against the administration ; and on 28
January 1741 during that very difficult session for the Walpole
ministry, Secker and Benson had voted with the ' formed opposition ' in favour of the appointment of a select committee to
inquire into the conduct of the war, especially in relation to the
alleged insufficiency of reinforcements to Admiral Vernon's
expedition to the West Indies.[3]

For the enormity of his juncture with a ' formed opposition '
at a most critical moment, the court could not forgive Secker ;
and to the scandal of his public conduct there had been added
the private offence of the attendance of the prince of Wales at
St. James's Church (in which parish Norfolk House was situated),
the baptism of several of the prince's children by Secker, and the
failure of an eirenic mission entrusted to the bishop as intermediary between George II and his eldest son.[4] Accordingly, in
1750, when Herring and Hardwicke wished to secure for their
friend the rich deanery of St. Paul's (resigned by Butler on his
translation from Bristol to Durham), the way was not easy.
Hardwicke assured Newcastle that ecclesiastically Secker was a
most suitable candidate, and with regard to ' his conduct in

[1] Cobbett, *Parliamentary History*, xii. 1300–1 ; B. Porteous, *Life of Secker*, prefixed to Secker's *Works*, i. p. xvi.

[2] Porteous, *Secker*, p. xix ; Newcastle to Hardwicke, 8 May 1748, Add. MSS. 32715,
fo. 32.

[3] Cobbett, *Parliamentary History* (Notes from Secker MSS.), xi. 1015 ; Hare MSS.
p. 244 (*H.M.C. 14th Report ;* Appendix, part ix) ; L. B. Namier, *England in the Age
of the American Revolution*, pp. 55–8, for ' formed oppositions '.

[4] Porteous, *Secker*, pp. xv-xvi.

parliament some years ago ' he ' had long since declared himself entirely convinced of the mischievous tendency of formed oppositions and had expressed his resolution in the rightest manner on that subject '.[1]   George II replied to these solicitations . ' that it was not necessary to dispose of it immediately, that he would take a little time ' ; but finally, as was usual with him, he gave way.

> ' When I told him how the bishop of Oxford had renounced opposition ', reported the duke of Newcastle of his interview with the king, ' the king answered, "I know, Benson has.   He has acted like a gentleman, and I know, has declared it to the opposition themselves.   He has told my Lord Limerick that he would never be for a secret committee again as long as he lived." ' [2]

Restored now to royal favour, Secker was warmly pressed by Hardwicke and Newcastle for the primacy when the sudden death of Hutton (the result of a chill caught by faithful obedience to the desire of the administration for his personal attendance at debates in the house of lords on 16 and 17 March 1758 on the Navy Bill) caused its vacancy.

> ' I think it will be most advisable for your grace to name the bishop of Oxford singly to his majesty ', observed Hardwicke to Newcastle on the morrow of Hutton's death, ' not by way of nomination, but by the way of suggestion, as the fittest man ; and if the king objects, or hesitates, to name nobody else to-day.   I, who love communication and am apt to blame the want of it in others, cannot help thinking it will be proper for your grace to speak to Mr. Pitt on this subject.' [3]

George II received the suggestion so favourably that Newcastle felt ' he had just reason to hope the king would make the choice recommended to him ' ; [4] and Secker was duly translated.   Some of Newcastle's whig friends criticized the appointment, despite the part Secker had played in support of the duke of Marlborough in the famous Oxfordshire election of 1754.

> ' He is attached to nobody but myself and my friend Lord Hardwicke ', reported Newcastle of the new primate to one such critic, Mr. J. White, M.P. for Retford, adding : ' I sent early to him with relation to his conduct towards the Dissenters.   He has explained himself wholly to my satisfaction and what I am persuaded will be to theirs.   He has assured me that he is well with Dr. Avery and Dr. Chandler.   I shall speak to both of them upon the new archbishop's subject, and I shall talk to Dr. Lawrence and to some who are of a different party among the Dissenters ; and you may assure them all that I will answer for the new archbishop so far as relates to them.' [5]

[1] Hardwicke to Newcastle, 20 July 1750, Add. MSS. 32721, fo. 418.
[2] Newcastle to H. Pelham, 23 Aug./3 Sept., vol. 32722, fo. 223.
[3] Hardwicke to Newcastle, 20 March 1758, vol. 32878, fo. 276.
[4] Newcastle to Secker, 20 March, *ibid*. fo. 278.
[5] Newcastle to J. White, 1 April 1758, vol. 32879, fo. 5.

The grounds of these suspicions on the part of the Dissenters were set forth in the reply of the duke's correspondent.

> ' Your grace undoubtedly knows that the archbishop has always had a strong connection with the Bishop of London, and was a strong advocate (though I think not a very argumentative one) for the introduction of bishops into America. I mention this . . . with some doubt how far weight should be given him in the closet during the life at least of the Bishop of London." [1]

The junction of Sherlock of London and Secker at an earlier date to advocate the establishment of Anglican bishops in the Plantations had been a source of extreme embarrassment to Newcastle and to Archbishop Herring. But the new primate had learned ecclesiastical as well as political wisdom, and during his primacy, without abandoning his conviction of the utility of an American episcopate, he acted with singular caution and moderation in this matter, whilst preserving a friendly correspondence with the leading Dissenters in England. [2]

Having secured Secker's elevation, Newcastle was loud in professions of their unanimity. The archbishop requested the ecclesiastical minister to ' favour him on all occasions with his direction and counsel, and believe that giving it in the plainest and freest manner would be esteemed by him the highest obligation ' ; and the duke in the year following praised the conduct of the primate who ' acted with great clearness and uprightness with him in everything '. [3] As they enjoyed prosperity together, so they were joined in adversity when George III became king. Newcastle complained to Secker of the attitude of Bute, which must become more friendly ' if it is not determined that *we* should have nothing to do in ecclesiastical preferments ' ; and the archbishop replied by assuring the duke that he ' knew nothing at all from any other quarter ' of ecclesiastical matters. [4] The nomination of a score of new royal chaplains without consulting the primate was sufficient evidence of the truth of his statement, and during Newcastle's intermission of office between 1762 and 1765, Secker was little consulted. Accordingly, when the duke returned in 1765 he invited the archbishop's co-operation in the business of church preferment. At last Newcastle had made an archbishop entirely after his own heart.

Unfortunately, when his ecclesiastical ally was so satisfactory his political colleagues were not. In particular William Pitt,

---

[1] J. White to Newcastle, 5 April 1758, Add. MSS. 32879, fo. 74.

[2] A. L. Cross, *The Anglican Episcopate and the American Colonies*, cc. iv-vii; Porteous, *Secker*, pp. xxxii-xxxvi.

[3] Secker to Newcastle, 25 March 1758, Add. MSS. 32878, fo. 360 ; Newcastle to Trevor, 3 Oct. 1759, vol. 32896, fo. 243.

[4] Newcastle to Secker, and Secker to Newcastle, 8 and 9 Aug., vol. 32926, fos. 306, 328.

though professing, like Carteret, that ' the creating deans, bishops, and every placeman besides was quite out of his line, and he would willingly relinquish them to the duke of Newcastle ',[1] did not wish this declaration to be taken too literally. Newcastle, following the advice of Hardwicke, communicated to Pitt on 24 March 1758 the recommendations which he had made to the king, and then reported to his friend ' the great uneasiness in talking to him upon any subject which does not quite square with his own views and inclinations '.[2] On March 29 the Great Commoner made his first move in the game of ecclesiastical preferments, by requesting a prebend for Mr. Ballard, chaplain to the House of Commons, whom Speaker Onslow was anxious to promote.

> ' I, knowing my entire inability to do this mighty matter ', he wrote to Newcastle, ' beg leave to rest it with your grace upon the justice and decency of the pretension. As I have not had one word to say concerning hierarchies and powers, I would fain hope that I might be indulged an humble prebend in the name of the commons of England.' [3]

The indulgence was speedily granted, and Mr. Ballard became a prebendary of Westminster.

Appetite being thus whetted, in the year following Pitt ventured to say his word concerning hierarchies and powers. In September 1759 the see of Worcester being vacant, Newcastle contrived the translation thither of his friend Johnson of Gloucester.

> ' I own it gave me great pleasure ', his grace observed to Trevor of Durham : ' I asked it and pressed it without ever having had an application from the Bishop. My friendship to him has long made me determined to do it, if I could. I have often found that those who have from accident waited some time have been sufficiently recompensed afterwards. . . . I have always put poor Johnson with regard to myself upon a different footing from everybody and there I must and do leave it.' [4]

A last echo of the charge of Jacobitism against the bishop was found in Newcastle's express assurance to the earl of Coventry that in political matters ' in everything that concerned the whig interest in the county or town of Worcester ', Johnson would act ' in such a manner that if you will only tell me what you would have him to do, and what public or private declarations he should make, I am sure of his compliance '.[5] Upon the vacant see of Gloucester Pitt had set his eye ; and he was determined to make

[1] B. Williams, *Life of Chatham*, i. 320–1.
[2] Newcastle to Hardwicke, 27 March 1758, Add. MSS. 32878, fo. 388.
[3] Pitt to Newcastle, 29 March, *ibid.* fo. 420.
[4] Newcastle to Trevor, 3 Oct. 1759, vol. 32896, fo. 243.
[5] Newcastle to Johnson, 2 Oct. ; and to Coventry, 3 Oct. *ibid.* fos. 214, 246.

either a bishop or a placeman ; either William Warburton, dean of Bristol, must be made bishop of Gloucester, or Mr. Robert Nugent, M.P. for Bristol, and a lord of the treasury, must be made vice-treasurer of Ireland. Newcastle's situation was sufficiently difficult without this intervention. He had promised the marquis of Granby to bring his tutor, Dr. John Ewer, on the bench, for the marquis's own rapid rise in the profession of arms seemed to him to demand a corresponding advancement of his tutor in the church militant. Hardwicke was anxious to see the dean of Lincoln, Dr. John Green, raised to the episcopate, and George II was eager to advance one of his own chaplains. Newcastle's dilemma was illustrated by his memorandum of ' heads of Mr. Pitt's conversation ' ; in which he set down that, whilst Pitt allowed that the duke ' was known to be the channel of preferments and answerable for the right disposition of them ', and affirmed that ' he would not be disposing minister if he could ', yet ' he wished *one* bishop, one time or other, Dr. Warburton for the sake of Mr. Allen. He wished also for the dean of Exeter [Dr. Charles Lyttleton]. He was not pressing.' [1] A short time before, the ecclesiastical minister had observed to Bishop Sherlock of London that ' in the present state of the administration, ecclesiastical as well as civil applications are such that when they are made in favour of deserving men, they cannot be resisted without risking inconveniences which might be at this time of consequence to that unity and unanimity which seem to attend the public measures now carrying on '.[2] Accordingly, Newcastle informed Lord Granby that his claims must be waived in favour of Pitt. ' If I am to continue in this most disagreeable situation, I must have proper support in the treasury, and I must keep well with Mr. Pitt, two things pretty difficult to bring about.' [3] Warburton, therefore, became bishop of Gloucester ; and the unity of the administration was preserved. ' It now facilitates all our arrangements in the house of commons ', commented the duke, with the consoling addendum : ' Mr. Pitt is in a good humour ; all goes well this session '.[4] ' We must both yield to necessity ', he wrote again to Granby, ' especially when by so doing we promote or rather secure the great point of union and harmony amongst those who are to carry on the king's service. . . . Mr. Pitt and myself were never so well together or so likely to continue so as we are at present.' [5] Pitt had good reason to be contented, for he had gained both points. Warburton was

---

[1] ' Heads of Mr. Pitt's Conversation ', Add. MSS. 32897, fo. 173.
[2] Newcastle to Sherlock, 22 Aug. 1759, vol. 32894, fo. 374.
[3] Newcastle to Granby, 30 Nov., vol. 32899, fo. 196.
[4] *Ibid.* fos. 282, 308, 401.
[5] Newcastle to Granby, 13 Dec., vol. 32900, fo. 20.

a bishop, and on 7 January 1760 Nugent became vice-treasurer of Ireland.

The optimistic promise of future peace was rudely shattered by the death of George II on 26 October 1760, within a year of the mounting of this hurdle. The duke's friends were divided in advice whether he should resign on the accession of George III or accept the new king's invitation to remain in office in association with Bute. Unable to make up his mind, he remained ; and in a paper of ' heads for my conference with Lord Bute ', dated 14 December, he inserted an item concerning ecclesiastical preferments : ' to whom should applications be made ? should they be communicated by the duke of Newcastle to Lord Bute before being laid before the king ? . . . should Pitt be acquainted with all recommendations ? ' [1] On the advice of Hardwicke this topic was omitted, because

> ' it is truly said to be a delicate point, and may be construed, or a handle be taken to represent it, as aiming to seize the whole administration. Besides I would not advise the proposing to acquaint Lord Bute first with all applications before the king is spoke to about them. That might prove very inconvenient in future and be subject to complaints of breach of faith. I think that should be left to execution and the natural progression of things. Neither should I like the naming of Mr. Pitt on this particular point.' [2]

During 1761 the soundness of this counsel was put to the test, for four sees were vacated by death that year, including three of the most important, York, London, and Winchester. When the first of these vacancies occurred on 16 January at St. David's, Hardwicke advised his friend to proceed cautiously yet firmly.

> ' It will be called hard and overbearing upon the king to dispute with his majesty about the first bishopric which has fallen in his reign. . . . Your grace concludes very truly that one single instance is not the point ; but are all employments ecclesiastical and civil to be given away *by application to one man ?* That must not continue. All I can say is, get your parliament through as well as you can, and then bring it to a decision.' [3]

Newcastle soon had the mortification of seeing his former clients, lay and clerical, making haste to curry favour with the new court. Granby and the duke of Rutland approached George III in behalf of Dr. Ewer ; and when the see of London was expected to be vacant at the beginning of February, Bishop Drummond of St. Asaph, who had been raised to the bench by Newcastle's influence, and had been designated by his Grace for translation either to York or London as occasion occurred, called upon Bute,

[1] Add. MSS. 32916, fo. 51.
[2] Hardwicke's comments, *ibid.* fo. 79.
[3] Hardwicke to Newcastle, 19 January, 1761, *ibid.* fo. 398.

who assured him that he ' was very desirous to promote everything in his favour and he would talk to his Grace about it '.[1]
Before London was actually vacant, however, by the death of
Sherlock on 18 July, Winchester had become vacant by the death
of Hoadly on 17 April. Newcastle sent numerous letters in
favour of his friends ; and in all respects save one, the resultant
shuffle was not unwelcome to his wishes. St. David's was given
to Dr. Samuel Squire who, in addition to having been university
chaplain and secretary to Newcastle, had been clerk of the closet
to George III when prince of Wales. Bishop Thomas of Sarum
was translated to Winchester, and Drummond of St. Asaph to
Sarum, Newcombe of Llandaff was removed to St. Asaph, and
Ewer nominated to Llandaff. The great exception was London ;
and Newcastle was horrified to learn that Hayter was being
mentioned in this connexion :

> ' The report that the bishop of Norwich is to be bishop of London, a
> man so disagreeable to the whole bench, and who has acted so un-
> gratefully to me, who made him everything that he ever was, shews
> such a disregard to me, and to my situation, and to what I owe to
> myself, that I own it is with difficulty I swallow it, *even at present.*' [2]

The duke's friends could afford him no comfort. Hardwicke,
though uncertain whether the *contretemps* could ' proceed from
design or from want of sufficient opportunities of seeing one
another and conferring together ' between the duke and Bute,
insisted that he had ' always feared some disagreeable incidents
of this kind would happen from the loose uncertain manner in
which his Grace's bargain was clapt up upon the king's accession '.[3]
Newcastle spun schemes, for the translation of Drummond,
scarcely in possession of Sarum, to York, vacant by Gilbert's
death on 9 August, and for the removal of the bishop of Lincoln
to London ; but the reply of Bute was brief to the point of rude-
ness.

> ' The very dangerous state the bishop of London has been in for some
> time past has given his majesty ample time to consider of a proper
> subject for filling that important see. I should suppose therefore in
> the event of the present bishop's death, the king has some proper
> person in his thoughts, unless your Grace's recommendation should
> make some alteration.' [4]

The duke found this letter shocking. ' Is this the way to engage
me to undertake the carrying on an impracticable war continued
by our own fault, ambition, and obstinacy ? . . . Never was poor

---

[1] Drummond to Newcastle, 4 Feb., Add. MSS. 32918, fo. 263.
[2] Newcastle to Devonshire, 11 July, vol. 32925, fo. 9.
[3] Hardwicke to Newcastle, 12 July, *ibid.* fo. 26.
[4] Bute to Newcastle, 17 July, *ibid.* fo. 133.

minister so used or got into such a scrape.'[1]   Still he continued
to spin schemes ; that Drummond should even go from Sarum
to London, *en route* for the anticipated translation to York, and
Hayter to Sarum ; and he even proposed this shuffle to Bute,
only to be met with the frigid reply : ' Must not the king make
one bishop ?   By this your Grace will have a friend or creature
of your own at London.'[2]   From the interview Newcastle
retreated crestfallen, since Bute ' had not the civility to express
any concern or to make any excuse or to propose any reparation
for this in the subsequent promotions '.   His Grace was trying to
decide whether ' to swallow it and thereby make the most con-
temptible figure that ever man did, or to resign his employment,
in which case Lord Bute was ready and desirous to undertake it ',
when after an interval of three days the ubiquitous intermediary,
Count de Viry, the Sardinian minister, called upon him to express
Bute's regret that he should be so disturbed ' for a bishop of
London ', especially since ' it was not . . . Bute's doing '.[3]   Newcastle therefore remained at his post, resolved, as he assured his
friends, to make the case of Drummond the *articulus stantis aut
cadentis* of the church.   ' If my Lord Bute wishes to keep up
decencies with us, he will lose no time in settling this vacancy
. . . for our friend the bishop of Salisbury.'[4]   Hardwicke agreed
' that the promotion of the bishop of Norwich to the see of London
. . . would not be thought a sufficient justification by the public
or by the whig party ' for the duke's resignation.[5]   But Hardwicke
was wiser than Newcastle, and saw that the latter's fondness for
producing schemes to deal with all possible vacancies ' might be
represented as cramming a long list down his Majesty's throat '.[6]
Bute indeed made precisely this criticism.

> ' He complained greatly of me ', reported Newcastle, ' that I would
> recommend to everything and particularly to every ecclesiastical
> preferment that fell . . . that first I would have a bishop of London,
> then I would make an archbishop of York, and my Lord Hardwicke
> would recommend the new bishop.   That this had offended the king,
> and that though he loved and esteemed the bishop of Salisbury more
> than any one bishop upon the bench, he did not know what the king
> would do.   His Majesty was so offended with the duke of Newcastle
> for recommending to *everything*. . . . I beg therefore that this one
> single instance may be seen in its true light.   The best, the most
> proper person in the opinion of my Lord Bute to be made archbishop
> of York is not to be made, singly because the duke of Newcastle at

---

[1] Newcastle to Hardwicke, 18 July, Add. MSS. 32925, fo. 155.
[2] Newcastle to Devonshire, 5 Aug., 32926, fo. 187.
[3] Newcastle to Hardwicke, 7 Aug., *ibid.* fo. 284 ; cf. *Grenville Papers*, i. 384
[4] Newcastle to Devonshire, 8 Aug. 1761, Add. MSS. 32926, fo. 302.
[5] Hardwicke to Newcastle, 8 Aug., *ibid.* fo. 302.
[6] Same to same, 11 Aug., *ibid.* fo. 368.

the head of the treasury, etc., has presumed to recommend him.   I
believe no history can parallel this single circumstance, and no man
of common sense can think it is done with any view but either to
force me out immediately or to show me upon what mean terms, if
any, I should be permitted to stay in.' [1]

At last it appeared as if resignation was seriously contemplated.   On 5 October 1761, however, Pitt resigned from the
administration, and in such circumstances even the unlikely
hazard of the voluntary self-effacement of Newcastle could not
wisely be risked.   'To bring him into temper' the duke was
offered his pleasure in all the church promotions save one :
Drummond was translated to York, Thomas of Lincoln to Sarum,
Yonge of Bristol to Norwich, the dean of Lincoln, Dr. Green,
raised to that see, Dr. Thomas Newton (who had waited so often
and patiently upon Newcastle's favours) nominated to Bristol,
and Dr. James Yorke, son of Lord Hardwicke, made dean of
Lincoln.   Only the translation of Hayter to London represented
the ability of Bute to defeat his rivals if he had the will.   'His
lordship', wrote Newcastle of Bute, 'was so civil and obliging
to me that except in one instance he joined with me in the
recommendation to all the vacant bishoprics and deaneries.' [2]
Providence intervened to make Bute's triumph short-lived, for
in January 1762 Hayter died ; and Newcastle, though professing
to Archbishop Secker his resolve 'to wait and to say nothing
upon the vacancy till he was spoke to ', inquired whether the
primate would approve his thoughts on the matter.[3]   Finally,
the king advanced Bishop Osbaldeston of Carlisle to London, and
Dr. Lyttleton, dean of Exeter, who had enjoyed the former
support of Pitt and now had that of Grenville, was made bishop
of Carlisle in recognition of his services to the whigs in Exeter,
where 'whiggism durst not hold up its head ' when he first came,
but before his departing there was ' a respectable body of gentlemen both of the city and county at large ' whom the dean had
formed ' into a society whose avowed principles were the support
of the king and the government .' [4]

On 26 May 1762 the resignation of Newcastle at last was
forced.   Thereupon Bute entered into the heritage which he had
coveted so long.   'There is no part of my situation arising from
the king's partiality to me ', he acknowledged to Grenville, 'that
I prize more than ecclesiastical patronage, not for the sake of
making friends or forming a party, but from conviction that a
proper choice of the clergy, especially of those in the higher

[1] Newcastle to Hardwicke, 17 Aug., Add. MSS. 32927, fo. 68.
[2] Newcastle to the earl of Scarborough, 1 Oct., vol 32929, fo 7.
[3] Newcastle to Secker, 9 Jan. 1762, vol. 32933, fo. 150.
[4] Dr. C. Lyttleton to Newcastle, 17 Feb. 1755, vol. 32852, fo. 513.

11

preferments, is rendering to my king and country a most essential service.'[1]   These were indeed impeccable sentiments ; and the same divines who had thronged Newcastle's antechambers found their way to Bute's headquarters, confident that they possessed the qualities necessary for preferment under his régime.

> Old Pelham retiring was leveed by friends
> Whom oft he had helped to accomplish their ends,
> Peers, commoners, ribbands, blue, red (but no green),
> All, crowding around the old statesman were seen.
>
> But Wagstaff observing on looking around
> That no grateful prelate was there to be found,
> Cried out : What ! none of the black and white Order
> From our warm Land's End to cold Caledon's border.
>
> I know that your Grace many of them has made.
> True : but vile ingratitude sticks to their trade.
> For none are so famous (see Wolsey in Baker)
> As these reverend dons for neglecting their maker.[2]

With such a plenitude of candidates and such high-principled sentiments, it was unfortunate that the administration of Bute was so short-lived, for the only major preferment which fell to his lot before he was succeeded in turn by the Grenville administration in April 1763 was the see of Exeter, vacant by the death of Bishop Lavington on 13 September 1762.   To this dignity Dr. Frederick Keppel was nominated ; having been pressed upon the attention of Newcastle for some years by his brother, the earl of Albemarle (whose capture of Havana synchronized aptly with the elevation of Frederick to the bench), and having been re-commended also by his father-in-law, Sir Edward Walpole, to Pitt for episcopal preferment in 1761.   His elevation at this juncture was interpreted rightly, not only as ' a bit of reward or compliment to Lord Albemarle ', but also as a sign of the interest of Bute, from whom indeed the new bishop believed he could have secured a promise of translation to Sarum when that see should become vacant, if he had taken advantage of the claims of his family to the royal gratitude.[3]   The single bishop made by Bute afforded little gratification to his admitted desire to adorn the bench with proper and creditable figures.

To Grenville fortune was but little kinder, for though she presented him with the opportunity of recommendation to the important see of London in 1764, upon the death of Osbaldeston,

---

[1] *Grenville Papers*, i. 419.   [2] Add. MSS. 32942, fo. 302.
[3] *Chatham Correspondence*, ii. 134–5 ; Hardwicke to Newcastle, 17 Oct. 1762, Add. MSS. 32943, fo. 261 ; 'earl of Albemarle to Newcastle, 1 Aug. 1765, vol. 32968, fo. 399.

this preferment, together with the consequent appointment to Peterborough, constituted his sole occasion of episcopal promotion during his tenure of office.   As aspirants to the bishopric of London there appeared the bishop of Hereford, whose brother Lord Vere solicited Grenville, as he had done Newcastle, for the translation of the senior prelate on the bench, whose eighteen years without a removal was deemed ' a glaring slight ' upon his family (unless, indeed, ' his being a gentleman ' might have been an objection !) ; [1] and Warburton of Gloucester, who employed no other hand than his own to remind the minister of his pretensions, albeit he had nothing wherewith to commend them save ' an unfeigned zeal for the service of religion and of his royal master '.[2]   Unfortunately the royal master had already fixed on the translation of Bishop Terrick of Peterborough, who had been in his mind ' even so early as when the present bishop of London was appointed to it ' ; [3] and to Peterborough Dr. Robert Lamb, dean of that cathedral, was nominated, who had been brought often to Newcastle's notice by his brother, Sir Matthew Lamb, grandfather of Lord Melbourne.   In the circle of Newcastle and his friends the incident was regarded as convincing proof ' where the sole power is ', namely, in Bute though out of office.

In July 1765, however, Grenville likewise found himself out of office, and the task of constructing a new ministry was discharged by the duke of Cumberland, with the help of Newcastle himself.   Accordingly, the marquis of Rockingham became head of the administration, and Newcastle was appointed lord privy seal with (what was singularly to his taste) the office of church minister.   Once again his Grace's correspondence glowed with epithets of graciousness towards the throne and lively anticipation towards his clerical friends.   It seemed in truth as if the Lord had blessed Job more in his end than in his beginning.   At once the duke insisted upon Secker's being joined with himself as counsellor in church preferments in reparation for his recent exclusion.   ' His majesty was pleased to tell the archbishop of Canterbury, my coadjutor of my own naming ; " My lord archbishop, I depend upon you to take care of the university of Oxford.   The duke of Newcastle will take sufficient care of Cambridge." ' [4]   Newcastle wrote several letters to define exactly the mode of procedure in recommendations, so that the secretaries of state should not sign any warrant without previous notification from himself of the royal pleasure ; and then he set to work to compile lists of deserving divines.

[1] Vere to Grenville, 3 May 1764, Grenville Papers, ii. 311.
[2] Warburton to Grenville, 5 May, ibid. 313 ; 11 May, ibid. 316.
[3] Grenville to Warburton, 8 May, ibid. 314.
[4] Newcastle to Dr. Powell, 18 July 1765, Add. MSS. 32968, fo. 66.

In intention the duke's programme was strictly correct and honest ; and it was not his fault, though it was his grievous misfortune, that circumstances played him a sorry trick in removing prelates whom he would fain have seen to enjoy good days and preserving those whose decline would have contributed to the relief of his embarrassments.

> ' Upon the first framing of a plan of administration and in the first paper I had the honour to present to the duke [of Cumberland] upon that occasion and in all the subsequent papers I constantly mentioned my humble request : that Dr. Cornwallis, bishop of Lichfield, might succeed to Ely when vacant ; the bishop of Oxford [Hume] to Salisbury, and the bishop of Chichester Dr. Ashburnham to the deanery of St. Paul's. They have all three been many years bishops, have never once varied in their principles or conduct through the whole course of their lives, and are very meritorious, reputable men in all respects. The two last have a great number of children and very little to maintain them with.' [1]

Of these three prelates John Hume had an especial claim to the duke's favour, having entered his household as tutor to Lord Lincoln, earned the warm regard of the duchess of Newcastle, acted as his Grace's spiritual counsellor, and having been preferred to a residentiaryship of St. Paul's in 1748, to the see of Bristol in 1756, and to that of Oxford in 1758, holding *in commendam* with this bishopric the deanery of St. Paul's since 1758. A further complication arose from the ambitions of Bishop Keppel of Exeter, to whom Newcastle in vain pointed out his youth and consequent expectation of a sufficiently long life to see London, Durham, or Winchester again in the market.

> ' Though you wish that I could point out anything in the church that would be as agreeable to me as Salisbury ', observed the bishop to his brother Albemarle, ' for the accommodation of the duke of Newcastle and his friends, I can't help saying that that bishopric is my great object and preferable to any other on the bench, Durham and Winchester excepted, where I think there is no great probability of an opening soon. And the present bishop of Salisbury is not only old and infirm, but in a very bad state of health ; and if I should succeed to him, it would make me extremely happy, if I was even sure of never being removed from it. I therefore hope you will press the duke of Newcastle in the strongest terms and procure me a promise from him of the bishopric of Sarum.' [2]

Both Keppel and his brother were insistent, because they believed they could have obtained a definite promise of this translation if they had pressed their case at the time when Bute enjoyed royal

---

[1] Memorandum relating to the bishops, 21 July 1765, Add. MSS. 32968, fo. 138.
[2] Bishop Keppel to Albemarle, 29 July 1765, *ibid*. fo. 333.

favour. In September 1765 the deanery of Windsor became vacant, and Keppel consented to exchange his uncertain hopes of Sarum for an additional £950 a year with the added advantage of Windsor's situation in relation to the court ; ' a very fine preferment for a man of quality who has a bishopric at a distance ' and who, moreover, was the ' youngest bishop but one on the bench ' commented Newcastle.[1] Even this arrangement had only been possible through the magnanimous surrender by Lord Barrington, in order to relieve the duke of a promise made by Grenville in the king's name of the deanery when vacant to Shute Barrington.

Nothing had been done to assuage the wounded family pride of the Ashburnhams, for though the bishop of Chichester had declared ' he would choose rather to be set quite aside as altogether unworthy of his Grace's notice ' than to be promised the deanery of St. Paul's *in commendam* if Hume went to Sarum, he was understood not to be so positive in regard to Windsor. Moreover, why should he be passed over for Hume, who ' though his junior on the bench was . . . to have his inclinations consulted, and to be preferred and put over his head, to which preference he was not entitled from any consideration whatever, either public or private, either as a churchman or as a gentleman acting zealously with a party in parliament '.[2] Such was Newcastle's embarrassment that he forwarded this letter to Hume, only to receive a startlingly simple reply. ' I will only observe that the bishop of Chichester is his [Lord Ashburnham's] friend, and I am properly *yours*. Will Lord Ashburnham consent to weigh our merits in this scale ? If not, he asks more of your Grace than he would grant you himself.' [3]

In such circumstances the duke could only remark to Albemarle, ' I hope to God the old bishop of Salisbury will live ', and to Secker, ' I hope the poor bishop of Salisbury is rather getting better than otherwise. I shall for my own particular be under the greatest uneasiness if it should happen.' [4] The venerable prelate at Sarum did linger long, almost long enough to save the face of the ecclesiastical minister, if that indeed were the real desire of Newcastle rather than his wish to see Hume at Salisbury. The bishop died on 20 July 1766 when the administration was tottering to its fall, the king had already seen Pitt, and by the end of the month the new ministry was announced. The duke could have left the filling of the see to Pitt, but this would have

[1] Newcastle to Secker, 3 Oct., and to Albemarle, 7 and 9 Oct., Add. MSS. 32970, fos. 167, 213, 240.

[2] Lord Ashburnham to Newcastle, 23 Sept., vol. 32970, fo. 23.

[3] Bishop Hume to Newcastle, 26 Sept., *ibid.* fo. 72.

[4] Newcastle to Albemarle, 24 Sept., *ibid.* fo. 39 ; to Secker, 23 Dec., vol. 32972, fo. 320.

frustrated his scheme for Hume, upon which his heart was set though his courage was unequal to its consequences.

Behind the stage-thunder of the mendicant Ashburnhams there was the more formidable figure of Bishop Frederick Cornwallis of Lichfield, whose claims were inconveniently supported by Rockingham, the head of the declining administration, on the morrow of the death of the bishop of Sarum.

> ' Your Grace ', he observed with the utmost delicacy of sentiment and expression, ' must be under difficulties, and though . . . I would not wish to add to them, yet I should feel that I did not act kindly by your Grace if I did not suggest to you my thought at this time.   Indeed I am in some degree obliged in honour to Bishop Cornwallis to say something in his behalf.   Your Grace is so well acquainted with the merit, integrity, and worth of Bishop Cornwallis—the kind, uniform, and firm part which he has acted, and the very high light and favour in which he stands with the whole whig party—that I am sure your Grace must feel that both from his constant personal attachment to your Grace, and also from the coincidence of his principles with your Grace's sentiments, that he in the general judgment will be looked on as the properest person to be promoted.'

Rockingham acknowledged indeed Hume's claim on the basis of Newcastle's private favour and sentiments towards him, and admitted that ' it was a severe dilemma '.   ' Your Grace ', he added, ' has lived as a public man and must have made many private sacrifices to public considerations.   If your Grace can do this, I must say that I am clear in opinion that Cornwallis' promotion will be the most to your public honour.' [1]   The only reply possible to such a declaration was an admission on the part of the duke that private obligations must take precedence of public considerations.

> ' A very unadvised promise of many months and often repeated ', he related to the sympathetic ear of Secker, ' cannot be broke through, if I am not released from it, which I shall not be.   And when I consider the stress that is laid upon it by the poor duchess of Newcastle, who is the greatest comfort of my life, and almost my only companion at home, I scarce wish to be released from it.' [2]

The affair was doubly a woman's bishopric, for in addition to the duchess, the influence of Lady Mary Hume was brought to bear to insist upon the fulfilment of the promise made to her husband ; [3] and accordingly his Grace placed the name of the bishop of Oxford before George III, where, however, an unexpected hitch occurred.   The king, as Newcastle reported, ' in a most cruel

---

[1] Rockingham to Newcastle, 21 July, Add. MSS. 32976, fo. 199.
[2] Newcastle to Secker, 21 July, vol. 32976, fo. 203.
[3] Newcastle to Lord Kinnoul, 10 Sept., vol. 32977, fo. 62.

manner, hesitated and almost refused to carry into execution a proposal of his own for removing the good bishop of Oxford, at the duke's most earnest request, to Salisbury ' ;[1] so that the primate's aid was invoked to second the recommendation, to whom his Majesty confided that ' as he was going to have a new administration, he thought he could not do this without previously acquainting Mr. Pitt with it, and that was the reason he had said that he must consider of it '.[2] Upon receipt of this news, Hume made haste to placate the new minister : and ' knowing that his friend Lord Lincoln was Mr. Pitt's first favourite, asked leave to desire the assistance of Lord Lincoln in it, with Mr. Pitt '.[3] Whereupon George III, having secured the assent of his new adviser, sent for his old servant to assure him ' that he was extremely glad to do what he had done for the bishop of Oxford, as it pleased the duke. But he owned he had another inducement to it, and that was that he knew it would be agreeable to the duchess of Newcastle, and desired his Grace to tell her so from him '.[4]

As a consolation to Cornwallis of Lichfield, the deanery of St. Paul's, vacated by Hume's translation, was offered to him *in commendam*, to the great chagrin of Ashburnham of Chichester, who repeated his mistake in regard to Windsor by announcing too late his willingness to suffer such a sop to be accorded for the relief of his anger. It would have been the part of wisdom in the duke to have preserved silence towards Bishop Cornwallis until such time as the immediate smart of disappointment had been assuaged. Instead, he sent a characteristically embarrassed and fawning letter, which provoked from that prelate a rejoinder more correspondent with the temper of his Grace's missive than consonant, perhaps, with the humility of a Christian bishop.

> ' I own ', wrote his Grace, ' I have scarce courage to write to your lordship upon this subject. I have, I am afraid, disobliged many by my preference of the bishop of Oxford to the bishopric of Salisbury. But it is your lordship, and your lordship only, who have just reason to complain of me. It is of you I ask pardon ; and I will hope from your superior merit (which from most unfortunate incidents I have not been able to pay that regard to which I ought), and from your generous way of thinking and acting, that I may have your forgiveness, and by a continuance of the same most valuable friendship which I have had now for so many years, be made in some degree, easy in an affair which has, and will ever give me, so much concern.' [5]

[1] Newcastle to Portland, 24 July, Add. MSS. 32976, fos. 221 ; 82.
[2] Newcastle to Rockingham, 26 July, *ibid.* fos. 255 ; 89.
[3] ' A Narrative of what has passed in relation to the present change in the Administration,' *ibid.* fo. 89.
[4] *Ibid.* fo. 92.
[5] Newcastle to Bishop Cornwallis, 12 Aug. 1766, Add. MSS. 32976, fo. 406.

Much more followed in the same strain of abasement and appeal ; and in reply Cornwallis did not mince words, nor seek to disguise his chagrin.

> ' I was honoured ', he allowed, ' with your Grace's letter, but am sorry to say it gave me little comfort or satisfaction. You congratulate me indeed, and say you are much rejoiced at my having accepted the deanery of St. Paul's. For what reason I know not. As to myself, I have no joy in it. I am not fond of expedients. And had the recommendation to it come from your Grace, I should have rejected the deanery. For your Grace must be sensible, after the hard treatment I had met with from you, that I could not with honour have accepted it. Nor was I desirous of accepting it at all. But when I was well informed in what manner and through whose kind and generous interposition his majesty had been graciously pleased to make me the offer of it, I then did not think myself at liberty to decline it. Though it is by no means a preferment either suitable or agreeable to me, and of course it cannot be expected that I should be delighted with it.'

After an allusion to the promise to Hume, which had been represented to himself as an engagement the duke ' had still some hopes of being released from ', the bishop of Lichfield referred to the former occasion when also, in relation to the translation of bishop Johnson from Gloucester to Worcester, public respects had been made to yield to private importunity.

> ' I am unwilling ', he continued, ' to say more upon this disagreeable subject ; but as your Grace has thought fit to mention that this is the *only instance* in which you have given cause of discontent to any of my family, your Grace must excuse me if I remind you of one other, pretty similar to this, which happened somewhat less than seven years ago. The reasons then assigned why you could not serve me, were your Grace's long and intimate connection and friendship with the bishop of Gloucester, his thorough attachment to you and his attendance upon you. Surely my lord, the disregard then shewed to me, may be allowed to have given just cause of some dissatisfaction at least, not only to me, but to my family and friends. It certainly did. And your Grace was then pleased to say it went to your heart that you could not serve me, and hoped for my forgiveness. It was immediately granted, and the hardship forgotten ; and so it would have remained, had not the late unfortunate transaction brought it back to my mind with an additional pungency. I assure you that I do not mean to reproach your Grace or add to your concern by anything I have said. On the contrary, I beg that you will give yourself no further uneasiness about this matter. I thought, in justice to myself, I could not avoid stating the case as it appears to me. Having done that, give me leave to add that I will not only forgive you, but heartily compassionate your distress. I am persuaded others have been more to blame in this affair than yourself. Nothing can destroy the regard

and esteem I have always had and still do retain, for your Grace or efface that friendship you have so long honoured me with.'[1]

Despite its eirenic conclusion, Cornwallis' letter was a model of directness, vigour, and cogency. Although much censured as self-seeking, Cornwallis was not unjustified in his estimate of Newcastle's fidelity to promises. In August 1768 the see of Canterbury was to be vacant again, by the death of Secker, and the duke, though out of office, could not forbear to write many letters concerning the succession. To Drummond of York he wrote that ' he was the only person who could fully supply the vacancy in every respect with ability, dignity, and what was most material, independence '.[2] No approach was made to Drummond, however ; and instead, after Thomas of Winchester had declined translation, the duke of Grafton recommended, and George III nominated, Cornwallis. Whereupon Newcastle assured the new primate that he approved the appointment cordially. ' My sentiments and wishes upon this subject were known to my friends before there was any talk or surmise about it. I don't mean by this to take any merit to myself, for God knows I have none.'[3] Similarly, he declared to Rockingham : ' I much approve this measure ; for I not only flung it out to the archbishop of York before there was any notion about it ; but it is what I have declared I myself would have done, had I been in the station where I once was.'[4] It is therefore surprising to read his private avowal to Hume : ' I think it ought to have been offered to the archbishop of York. I think he had a right to expect it. But as I always knew he would not accept it, I was very clear to declare my opinion that the present archbishop would be the properest man.'[5] It is difficult to feel any confidence that if the duke had been church minister in August 1768, Cornwallis would not have suffered another bitter disappointment. His elevation enabled a full reconciliation between the duke and himself before Newcastle died in the November following.

The duke of Newcastle's bishops have passed into history with the opprobrium of time-servers. Yet the bench of his nomination deserves a milder estimate. Some were munificent in building, as Trevor at Durham, Drummond at York, Johnson at Worcester, and Keene at Chester. Learning and piety were not lacking representatives in Secker, Hume, Lowth, and Warburton. If many of the bishops were mediocre men, they were typical of too many of their brethren in every age, and mediocrity, though

[1] Bishop Cornwallis to Newcastle, 25 Aug., Add. MSS. 32976, fo. 458.
[2] Newcastle to Drummond, 4 Aug. 1768, vol. 32988, fo. 380.
[3] Newcastle to Cornwallis, 12 Aug., ibid. fo. 410.
[4] Newcastle to Rockingham, 17 Aug., ibid. fo. 449.
[5] Newcastle to Hume, 27 Aug., vol. 32991, fo. 41.

not a virtue, can hardly be accounted a vice.   It is the reputation
of Newcastle himself rather than of the episcopate which suffers
from a critical survey of his period of office as ecclesiastical
minister.   He described himself as

> ' one who had never designedly done any injury to any one man in
> the world ; who during the course of half a century had had oppor-
> tunities to have served many, and to have shewed the greatest marks
> of attention and affection to all his own relations who by their be-
> haviour had suffered him to do it ; and who flattered himself he had
> for above half a century held an irreproachable conduct, if not a very
> meritorious one, towards his country and the present royal family '.

So far as motive and intention were concerned, this was a truthful
description.   Moreover, the duke was a good churchman according to the standards of his age, as his correspondence with Hume
upon purely spiritual matters proves, and his interest in the church
was sincere.   Nobody desired more than he to fill the bench with
good prelates.   The fault lay in his methods of procedure and
execution.   No ecclesiastical minister could please all clients or
reward all talents.   A great number and variety of interests, both
public and private, had to be considered.   Newcastle admittedly
was prodigal of promises.   In cases where the stubborn pressure
of circumstances compelled disappointment of some, silence was
the only part of prudence for an ecclesiastical minister.   But
silence was impossible to the duke.   In a crisis his correspondence
rose through a crescendo of embarrassment and lament to a
diminuendo of self-abasement and humility.   It might have been
supposed that he was the suppliant and his clients the patrons.
He learned little wisdom in this regard from his protracted career
as an ecclesiastical politician.   At the root of all his tortuous
expedients and excuses lay the fear which compassed him around.
The duke could not endure to disappoint anyone, and must needs
try to win back the esteem and regard of the unfortunate by
excuses, justifications, appeals, and cajolery.   His fear of
criticism and unpopularity was his fundamental undoing.
Throughout his public career he suffered the agonies of those
whom terrors take hold on as waters and tempests steal away
in the night.

NORMAN SYKES.

The Waning of 'The Influence of the Crown'

'THE crown has so many offices at its disposal', wrote David Hume in 1741, 'that, when assisted by the honest and disinterested part of the house, it will always command the resolutions of the whole so far, at least, as to preserve the antient constitution from danger. We may, therefore, give to this influence what name we please ; we may call it by the invidious appellations of *corruption* and *dependence ;* but some degree and some kind of it are inseparable from the very nature of the constitution, and necessary to the preservation of our mixed government.'[1]

The influence of the crown did, in the eighteenth century and long after, receive many 'invidious appellations'. Members in opposition cried out against the use of places, pensions, and peerages to make and maintain parliamentary majorities. Exponents of the theory of a free legislature deplored the 'subjection' of parliament to court influence, and even Blackstone displayed some concern over the power of this 'influence most amazingly extensive'.[2] But Hume was not alone in his belief in the necessity of 'corruption'. Without exception the ministries of the eighteenth century employed court favours to maintain themselves in office, and practical politicians saw no way to 'get the King's business done' in parliament without the use of influence. Loud as were the protests of the Rockingham whigs against the methods of George III and Lord North, Dunning's resolution in 1780 stated only that the influence of the crown 'ought to be diminished', not destroyed. Toward the end of the century there was doubtless much truth in the assertion of the pamphleteer, William Knox, that since there was 'an absolute necessity of vesting in the executive a *certain degree* of influence . . . the only question for reasonable men to discuss is what that degree ought to be '.[3]

---

[1] *Essays Moral, Political and Literary* (ed. Green and Grose, London, 1875), i. 120–1.

[2] Blackstone, *Commentaries*, i. 336.

[3] [William Knox], *Considerations on the Present State of the Nation* (London, 1789), p. x.

Yet in the reign of Queen Victoria the influence of the crown, known to be an undeniable fact and believed to be a constitutional necessity in the reigns of the first three Georges, no longer existed. Melbourne, Peel, Russell and Palmerston possessed no such electioneering machinery as had Walpole, Newcastle, North, and the younger Pitt. The crown's ' fund of influence with which nobody else could compete ' [1] did not provide the basis for Victorian parliamentary majorities, and while some like Bagehot looked back on the old system without lament, others like the third Earl Grey cast a wistful eye on methods that appeared to have produced governments more stable than those of the 1850's. [2]

The disappearance of the ' corrupt ' influence of the crown, it is now recognised, effected a vital change in the British constitution. The court's inability to make and control majorities by means of the 'king's interest ' reduced the sovereign's personal influence and lessened his control over the personnel of the ministry. At the same time, the way was cleared for the development of the cabinet and the two-party system in modern form. But, though the significance of the disappearance of crown influence is well understood, there is a considerable disagreement as to the time and manner in which it occurred. Perhaps the most common assumption is that the Reform Act of 1832 destroyed at a single stroke, or at least rendered largely impotent, the old system. [3] The very nature of crown influence, so closely bound up with the ancient electoral order, makes its survival beyond even a limited extension of the franchise a strong improbability. The ministers of William IV and Victoria could not manage elections and majorities in the same manner as the servants of the first three Georges, and this fact suggests that the Reform Act was the agency of destruction. The other most widely accepted opinion

---

[1] Holdsworth, *History of English Law*, x. 580.

[2] See W. Bagehot, *Essays on Parliamentary Reform* (London, 1883), pp. 151–69 ; Earl Grey, *Parliamentary Government* (London, 1858), pp. 40, 98–9.

[3] Such was the opinion expressed by Bagehot and Lord Grey in the passages cited above. It was common to most nineteenth-century constitutional writers. See J. B. Bernard, *Theory of the Constitution* (London, 1834), pp. 217–19, 434 ; W. E. Hearn, *The Government of England* (London, 1867), pp. 373–9 ; T. E. May, *The Constitutional History of England since the Accession of George III* (2 vols., London, 1861), i. 115. Taswell-Langmead at one point appears to confuse the influence of the crown with the personal influence of the sovereign, but at another he seems to imply that the great Reform Act destroyed the royal powers of corruption. See his *English Constitutional History* (London 1875), pp. 654–7, 673–8. The sense of these passages remains unchanged in A. L. Poole's ninth edition of Taswell-Langmead (London, 1929), pp. 665–9, 700–4. See also F. C. Montague, *Elements of English Constitutional History* (first published 1894, new ed. London, 1936), p. 207 ; D. J. Medley, *Student's Manual of English Constitutional History* (2nd edn., London, 1898), pp. 215–20 ; Jesse Macy, *The English Constitution* (New York, 1897), pp. 409, 434–6. Among more recent writers, D. L. Keir believes that the Reform Act of 1832 diminished but did not wholly destroy the old system of crown influence : *The Constitutional History of Modern Britain, 1485–1937* (London, 1938), p. 405.

is that, for a variety of reasons, the old system came to an end about 1782. George III's failure to establish 'personal government ',[1] the salutary effect of exclusion acts,[2] and the economical reforms of the Rockingham ministry [3] have all been alleged as the reason for its destruction. According to these views, the younger Pitt ruled without employing 'corruption', and thereafter the use of influence was largely confined to private boroughmongers.

Now, on the one hand, it is clearly established that the influence of the crown was not destroyed in 1782. The myth concerning George III's loss of power during Pitt's ministries has been dispelled,[4] and no legislation prevented the most effective use of crown influence to secure a government majority in the election of 1784.[5] Moreover, the economical reforms of the Rockinghamites, though they achieved a moderate diminution of the 'king's interest ', fell far short of the goal, and the reforms were so imperfectly conceived that much further legislation was required.[6]

On the other hand, there is considerable evidence which indicates that the old system of making and controlling majorities had been broken before 1832. Though parliament remained unreformed during the regency and reign of George IV, Lord Liverpool did not command such a fund of influence nor did he exercise so great a measure of control over parliament as had the first ministers of an earlier day. During most of his regime the ministry retained a precarious control over the house of commons by the sufferance of independent members ; patronage resources were comparatively meagre ; and the government did not make the efforts characteristic of Newcastle or Henry Fox to extract the utmost political advantage from favours, pensions, and appointments.[7] As early as 1809, Thomas Grenville pointed out that 'the influence of what they call corruption is, for practical purposes, too small rather than too great ',[8] though he added

---

[1] G. B. Adams, *Constitutional History of England* (New York, 1921), pp. 404–5.

[2] Porritt, *The Unreformed House of Commons* (Cambridge, 1903), i. 221–2.

[3] W. E. H. Lecky, *History of England in the Eighteenth Century* (New York, 1891), v. 24–5.

[4] D. G. Barnes, *George III and William Pitt, 1783–1806* (Stanford, 1939), *passim*.

[5] C. E. Fryer, 'The General Election of 1784 ' in *History*, ix. 221–3 ; Mrs. Eric George, 'Fox's Martyrs : the General Election of 1784 ' in *Transactions of the Royal Historical Society*, 4th Ser., xxi. 133–68.

[6] D. L. Keir, 'Economical Reform, 1779–1787 ' in *Law Quarterly Review*, l. 368–85.

[7] See K. G. Feiling, *The Second Tory Party, 1714–1832* (London, 1938), pp. 281–2 and ff. See also W. R. Brock, *Lord Liverpool and Liberal Toryism, 1820 to 1827* (Cambridge, 1941), pp. 85-105. It is impossible to agree with Mr. Brock that ' nothing save a salaried office could insure the votes of a member ' (p. 98), and his work is open to other objections (cf. *ante*, lviii. 125–6). But the general tenor of his argument concerning the patronage system and the stability of Liverpool's majorities is in accord with the bulk of contemporary evidence.

[8] *H. M. C., Dropmore MSS*. ix. 296.

that this could not be said in public. In the same year Pitt's old patronage secretary, George Rose, delivered a detailed speech, which he later expanded into a pamphlet, on the decline of crown influence. Henry Brougham subjected it to jocosely savage criticism in the *Edinburgh Review*, but Rose's arguments were not without weight : the government at this time was unquestionably denied the use of numerous types of influence employed by previous ministries.[1]

The administration itself does not appear to have become seriously concerned about the decline of its influence until after the general election of 1818. From then on the printed manuscripts and memoirs of the time display numerous references to the decreased influence of the crown, and political transactions point continually to the weakening control of ministers over their followers. In May 1819 Lord Liverpool corresponded with the Regent concerning a means ' of recovering that weight and influence which ought to belong to every government ' considering ' the evil temper and disposition which has been so apparent in some of the late proceedings of the house of commons ' ; [2] and William Lamb openly taunted the government on the floor of the house at ' the failure of those means of patronage by which they were enabled to attach adherents '.[3] That the resources of influence were by no means exhausted is witnessed by the purchase of the Grenville connection at the price of a dukedom and several offices in 1821–2.[4] But when Henry Brougham tried to revive the clamour against the influence of the crown, his efforts fell woefully flat.[5] Moreover, the patronage secretaries

[1] George Rose, *Observations respecting the Public Expenditure and the Influence of the Crown* (London, 1810) ; *Edinburgh Review*, xvi. 187–213.

[2] A. Aspinall, ed. *The Letters of King George IV, 1812–1830* (3 vols., Cambridge 1938), ii. 289–92. It is interesting to observe that at this critical moment in the fortunes of the Liverpool government, there is no evidence that the ministry made any effort to purchase support by a distribution of favours. The cabinet simply decided to make the revival of the malt-tax a stand-or-fall issue, and the opposition unwittingly saved them the trouble by proposing what amounted to a vote of nc confidence.

[3] Hansard, 1st ser., xl. 506.

[4] See *Memoirs of the Court of George IV*, i. 255–6 and ff. This transaction evoked some of the most delightfully malicious comment of the period and apparently provoked a duel between the dukes of Buckingham and Bedford : *Journal of the Rt. Hon. Henry Edward Fox*, pp. 101, 115.

[5] On 24 June 1822 Brougham moved a resolution ' that the influence now possessed by the crown is unnecessary for maintaining its constitutional prerogatives, destructive of the independence of parliament, and inconsistent with the well government of the realm ' ; Hansard, 2nd Ser., vii. 1265–1319. The resolution was defeated, 216 to 101, and though Castlereagh took pains to answer Brougham in detail, few other members spoke on either side. The impression is that, in strong contrast to Dunning's resolution of 42 years earlier, interest in the whole issue was languid, and despite the fact that more than 300 members were present in a sitting that did not conclude until after midnight, the debate was almost totally ignored in the printed letters and memoirs of the day. After this occasion the issue of the influence of the crown was never again debated by the unreformed parliament.

of the period occasionally revealed their worries over their diminishing resources. Charles Arbuthnot circulated a 'treasury
note' in 1822 in which he complained that if 'the just and
necessary influence of the crown' were further reduced, 'it will
be quite impossible for any set of men to conduct the government
of this country'.[1] In the ministerial crisis of March 1827 Stephen
Lushington thought that 'considering how much the crown's
powers of grace and favour have been diminished in latter years,
it would be of great benefit that its first minister, who is to dispense the small residue of these favours, should be in the house of
commons'.[2] John Wilson Croker showed Canning in April
how tenuous was the ministry's hold upon the great tory borough-
owners, and his conclusions indicated that the Liverpool ministry
had been considerably in their debt.[3] When Wellington became
prime minister he was forcibly struck by the lack of patronage
at his disposal for 'the king's service in parliament'. He wrote
to Sir Herbert Taylor in 1830, 'Yet I must say that no government can go on without some means of rewarding services. I
have absolutely none!'[4] The duke could be disingenuous, and
his statement is an obvious exaggeration, even if considered only
in its context. But the opposition stalwart, Henry Brougham,
wrote in the same year of 'the diminished patronage of the crown'.[5]
Though radicals and the opposition still tried to make political
capital out of the supposedly evil power of ministerial corruption,
politicians in the days of George IV perceived that the old system
of influence was breaking up.

It appears, then, that there existed before 1832 a considerable
amount of opinion to the effect that the power of royal influence
had greatly declined. How far was this opinion correct ? Since
knowing men often misjudge political factors in their own time,
can we accept the conclusion suggested by their evidence ? An
examination of the actual resources of crown influence may provide the answer.

The chief resources employed about the middle of the eighteenth
century may be grouped under four headings : money, patronage,
honours, and 'imperceptible influence'.[6] Government funds

[1] Hansard, 2nd ser., vi. 1174.

[2] C. S. Parker, *Sir Robert Peel* (3 vols., London, 1847), i. 454–5 ; cf. *Letters of King George IV*, iii. 207–10.

[3] L. J. Jennings, ed., *The Croker Papers* (3 vols., London, 1884), i. 370–2.

[4] *Despatches, Correspondence, and Memoranda of Field-Marshal Arthur, Duke of Wellington*, 3rd ser., vii. 286–7.

[5] *Ibid.* vii. 173–4. There are numerous other statements of this sort. In 1823, for instance, Wellesley wrote to George IV of 'the limited and reduced condition of the lord lieutenant's patronage ' : *Letters of King George IV*, ii. 553. Space precludes a lengthier catalogue of such opinions.

[6] For a description of the operation of government influence in the middle of the eighteenth century, the work of Professor L. B. Namier is unsurpassed. See his *The Structure of Politics at the Accession of George III* (2 vols., London, 1929) ; and

were used to subsidize the ministerial press, to provide pensions, to purchase close boroughs, and to carry on such electioneering devices as parades, free beer for electors, and the patronising of local tradesmen. Patronage provided jobs for electors, employment for parliamentary placemen, and positions for the friends, relatives, and dependents of those who could supply the government with votes in parliament and the constituencies. Honours attracted the 'many who cannot be caught by the bait of covetousness [but] are caught by the bait of vanity'.[1] 'Imperceptible influence', in the form of favours which government could distribute by means of contract awards, loan issues, and leases of crown lands, played an important part in securing the support of both mercantile and landed interests. An analysis of these resources will demonstrate the extent of the political influence to be derived from them during the regency and reign of George IV.

The government funds which had been employed for political purposes in the middle of the eighteenth century came from four main sources. First were the monies from the civil list which were charged against secret service, pensions, and the privy purse. From 1714 to 1780 annual disbursement for secret service averaged £57,106.[2] Of this sum, £6000 was always divided equally between the two secretaries of state, who may or may not have devoted it to political purposes.[3] Another portion of the secret service fund was issued 'without imprest, account, or other charge' to the secretaries of the treasury, who employed a large share of it to maintain ministerial majorities.[4] In the reigns of the first two Georges another part of secret service money was handled by the disburser of 'the king's money', a fund employed for charity, spies, and the government press.[5]

England in the Age of the American Revolution (London, 1930). The term 'imperceptible influence' was employed (perhaps coined) by Pitt's patronage secretary, Rose : *Observations respecting the Public Expenditure*, p. 57.

[1] Lord John Russell, *An Essay on the History of the English Government and Constitution* (London, 1823), p. 422.

[2] This figure is an average (minus shillings and pence) of the sums recorded as disbursed for secret service in *Parliamentary Papers*, 1868–9, No. 366, I. 51–183. In *Structure of Politics*, i. 242, Namier prints from the Liverpool papers a list of secret service funds for the years 1728–60 which differ slightly from those given in *Parliamentary Papers*. The general trends in the two sets of figures are roughly the same, however, and the differences may be accounted for by the fact that, whereas the figures in *Parliamentary Papers* are based on a financial year ending 10 October, the financial year for the figures in the Liverpool papers ends on 5 July.

[3] Namier, *Structure of Politics*, i. 238.

[4] There is no indication in government records of how the secretaries of the treasury spent their secret service money (see *Calendar of Treasury Books and Papers*, iii. pp. iii-iv) ; but ample evidence is provided by the private accounts of John Roberts printed by Namier in *Structure of Politics*, ii. 519–78 ; and by *The Parliamentary Papers of John Robinson*, ed. W. T. Laprade, pp. 164 ff.

[5] From 1714 to 1740 the disburser of 'the king's money' was Thomas Lowther, who left eight folio volumes of his accounts in the exchequer. His accounts are not

The pension list, which usually contained some members of parliament and their dependents, averaged £95,447 from 1721 to 1780.[1] The privy purse did not provide funds for political purposes until November 1777, when George III decided to devote £12,000 a year from that source to financing elections.[2]

A second source of money was the collection of the crown's hereditary revenues from the excise and the post office, the duchies of Lancaster and Cornwall, fines from the alienation and wine offices, the 4½ per cent. duties in the Leeward Islands and the Barbadoes, and numerous droits, escheats, quit-rents, and forfeitures at home and in the colonies.[3] Some of the funds from these sources (apparently charged on the civil list as 'special service')[4] were turned over to the secretaries of the treasury for election purposes. Owing to the nature of these revenues, the amount varied greatly. In the years 1761–8 the sum averaged £50,835.[5]

Scotland and Ireland provided the two remaining sources of a ministry's political funds. The Irish pension list, which had grown to more than £122,000 by 1777, was international in composition and included Frenchmen, Dutchmen, Germans, Scots, and English members of parliament.[6] The Scottish government provided the crown with an annual surplus, disposable at the absolute discretion of the crown as an hereditary revenue, which

calendared, but for his position and operations, see *Calendar of Treasury Books and Papers*, i. pp. vi-ix; ii. 210, 220, 243, 528; iii. pp. xi, xxvi-lxxx, 3, 6, 9, 19, 37, 43, 159, 160. After 1740 official records concerning ' the king's money ' are not available.

[1] Pensions employable for political purposes were paid in two ways. First, there were those paid out of the exchequer by regular order or warrant; and second, those paid by the paymaster of pensions from a lump sum issued by way of imprest, to a special list in his possession. The figure given above is an average of those paid in both fashions as recorded in *Parliamentary Papers*, 1868–9, No. 366, I, 51–183.

[2] Namier, *Structure of Politics*, i. 233; cf. *Parliamentary Papers of John Robinson*, pp. 55 ff. The account of sums charged to the privy purse thus rose from £48,000 to £60,000 in the fiscal year 1778.

[3] For a general description of these petty revenues, see *Parliamentary Papers*, 1868–9, No. 366, II, appendix, pp. 455 ff.

[4] The compiler of public accounts in *Parliamentary Papers*, 1868–9, No. 366, assumes that ' special service ' was a separate and casual civil list expense. But in the *Parliamentary Papers of John Robinson* it appears that whenever a sum is set down under special service, that figure can be established, with four exceptions, by adding up the sums which he received from the hereditary revenues. One exception is apparently a typesetter's error (pp. 158–9), and another shows only a slight discrepancy. In the two remaining cases the special service funds were taken from the civil list. For the years which Robinson's papers cover, the public expenditure accounts indicate only two special service items (1771 and 1772), and in each case the same sum appears in Robinson's papers as drawn from the hereditary revenues. It would thus appear that the sums disbursed for special service were drawn from the hereditary revenues, supplemented perhaps when necessary from the parliamentary grant for the civil list.

[5] *Parliamentary Papers of John Robinson*, p. 138.

[6] Sums paid out for Irish pension list are recorded in *Parliamentary Papers*, 1868–9, No. 366, I. 253–357. For an interesting commentary, see *Thoughts, English and Irish, on the Pension List of Ireland* (London, 1770).

approached £10,000 toward the end of the century,[1] and Scotland's small pension list included Scottish peers and the wives and widows of prominent politicians in the northern kingdom.[2]

It was possible for ministries to employ monies from these four sources for political purposes because there was as yet no clear-cut distinction between public property and the private property of the king, and because parliament possessed practically no control over expenditure.[3] The ministry did not have to account for disbursements; and payments for secret service, pensions, and the like were kept secret. After 1780 the gradual modernization of the British financial system so greatly altered these conditions that it is doubtful if the income of the state could any longer be employed for ' corruption '.

In 1780 the house of commons resolved ' that it is competent to this house to examine into and to correct abuses in the expenditure of the civil list revenues, as well as in every other branch of the public revenue, whenever it shall seem expedient to the wisdom of this house to do so '.[4] Parliament in the same session passed an act appointing a commission of public accounts, the first since the Hanoverian succession, with full power to inquire into the entire financial system and to recommend reorganization.[5] The fifteen reports of this commission laid the basis for a series of reforms which followed. In 1785 were established five commissioners for auditing the public accounts. Thereafter their powers were continually broadened, and under their supervision audited expense accounts were laid annually before parliament.[6] The first reform of the civil list took place in 1782. Burke's Act[7] of that year divided all charges on the civil list into eight classes, to each of which was allotted a departmental budget. The responsibility for the maintenance of each was fixed on a designated royal official. The privy purse alone remained the sovereign's private fund; in all other departments accounts of expenditure were required. Although this measure did not

[1] *Parliamentary Papers*, 1868–9, No. 366, II. appendix, 360–1. Cf. Hansard, 2nd ser. i. 46.

[2] Thirtieth Report of the Select Committee on Finance, 1798 (*Reports from Committees, 1798–1803*, XIII), 458–9, 475.

[3] During the reigns of William III and Anne parliament had annually ordered commissions to present accounts of public income and expenditure, but at the Hanoverian succession this practice stopped abruptly. After 1714 dispensers of public money were subject to no check but that of the auditors of the imprest, whose powers were strictly limited and whose offices became sinecures. See *Parliamentary Papers*, 1868–9, No. 366, II. 326 ff. Occasionally the commons requested an account, but those presented gave little real indication of how the money was spent. See *Commons Journals*, xx, 512–20, 523–40 ; xxv. 205–8 ; xxxii. 466–603.

[4] *Parliamentary History*, xxi. 367.   [5] 20 George III c. 54.

[6] The commissioners were established by 25 George III c. 52. The most important amending acts were passed in 1794, 1799, 1801, 1805, and 1806.

[7] 22 George III c. 82.

prove immediately effectual, continued investigation and regulation gradually pared away the crown's independence in finance
until, by 1830, the king had lost the last moiety of discretion over
civil list expenditure.[1]

The particular rivulets from which political funds had flowed
were also dammed by reforms. Burke's Act limited disbursements from the civil list for home secret service and special service
to £10,000 a year, and accounts of this expenditure were ordered
to be kept and presented to parliament if called for.[2] This
reduction did not go into effect until after Pitt's election of 1784,
but in 1785 home secret service expenditure dropped to £7364,
and thereafter the fund was kept within the £10,000 limit.[3]
English civil list pensions were likewise restricted. The sum was
not greatly curtailed, but Burke's Act required pensions to be
paid publicly at the exchequer and the list to be presented annually to parliament. These practices prevented further cir-
cumvention of the old laws prohibiting pensioners from sitting
in the commons. The first lord of the treasury was allowed to
grant a secret pension only if he registered an oath that it was not
given for a political reason, or to any member of parliament.[4]
In 1793 the Irish and in 1810 the Scottish pension funds were also
reduced and the publication of lists required.[5] The sums devoted
to pensions declined further during the reign of George IV,[6]
and by the first civil list act of William IV the total amount which
the king could devote to pensions from any source was limited
to £75,000.[7] The hereditary revenues, too, came gradually
under control. During the latter years of George III's reign
these revenues were subjected to an increasing number of en-
cumbrances, and under George IV they were applied to regular
government charges.[8]

[1] *Parliamentary Papers*, 1868–9, No. 366, II. appendix 604–5. Civil list reorganization was complicated by the establishment of the regency in 1812 and the union
of Irish and English exchequers in 1817, but regulations narrowed royal control over
the larger sums which resulted.

[2] 22 George III c. 82, arts. 24–9. An unlimited sum was allowed for foreign secret
service, but accounts thereof were to be presented if called for.

[3] *Parliamentary Papers*, 1868–9, No. 366, I. 193. The three branches of home and
foreign secret service and special service were consolidated and limited to a lump sum
of £23,200 in 1830 ; *ibid*. II. appendix, p. 605.

[4] 22 George III c. 82, arts. 17–23. The law placed restrictions upon the granting
of pensions until the total yearly grant from the English civil list should be reduced
to £90,000. Thereafter the limit was to be £95,000, which suggests that the legis-
lators based their figure on the average for the years preceding the act.

[5] See *Parliamentary Papers*, 1868–9, No. 366, II. appendix, 601–5 ; Kiernan,
History of the Financial Administration of Ireland, pp. 283–4. The act curtailing the
Scottish pension list was 50 George III c. 111.

[6] *Parliamentary Papers*, 1868–9, No. 366, II. appendix, 617.

[7] 1 William IV c. 25.

[8] *Parliamentary Papers*, 1868–9, No. 366, II. appendix, 604–5. William IV gave
up all the hereditary revenues except those from Lancaster and Cornwall.

These reforms, which began in 1780, gradually dried up the sources from which the ministerial party could draw public funds for political purposes. Moreover, Curwen's Bribery Act of 1809 [1] laid down regulations so stringent that Lord Liverpool declared it had ' put an end to all money transactions between government and the supposed proprietors of boroughs '.[2] When Henry Brougham attacked the influence of the crown in 1822, he not once accused the government of diverting the income of the state to any ' corrupt ' uses.[3] There is, then, evidence to support the conclusion that the money influence of the crown, which had played a part in maintaining ministerial majorities in the middle of the eighteenth century, had been largely destroyed by the early years of the nineteenth. Conclusive proof that the Liverpool government never used public funds to acquire support is lacking. Peel seems to have used some in Ireland in the election of 1812, though his resources were admittedly meagre.[4] But if the ministry could still tap the state treasury, reform had made it impossible for Arbuthnot or Planta to dispose of sums comparable to those available to Roberts or Robinson.

In contrast to the decline of money resources, the use of honours appears to have increased. While there seems to have been no increase in the bestowal of political baronetcies,[5] the Thistle and order of St. Patrick remained political rewards.[6] The peerage and the order of the Garter underwent considerable expansion, and George III adopted expedients to expand the order in 1786 and 1805 for obviously political reasons.[7] Pitt's

[1] 49 George III c. 118. This act, as is well known, had little or no effect in preventing corrupt practices by private members.

[2] Yonge, *Life of Liverpool*, i. 444. Liverpool gave unequivocal instructions to Peel, his Irish secretary, to observe strictly the provisions of the act in conducting the Irish elections of 1812, and Peel wrote to Croker, ' I am placed in a delicate situation enough here, bound to secure the government interests, if possible, from dilapidation, but still more bound to faint with horror at the mention of money transactions, to threaten the unfortunate culprits with impeachment if they hint at an impure return, and yet to prevent those strongholds Cashel, Mallow, and Tralee from surrendering to the enemies who besiege them ' : Parker, *Peel*, i. 38, 47.

[3] Hansard, 2nd ser., vii. 1265–99.   [4] Parker, *Peel*, i. 49–50.

[5] Whereas the first two Georges created a total of some 90 baronets, George III made well over 200 in the first forty years of his reign. (Creations listed in volume v. of G.E.C., *Complete Baronetage*). The high rate of creations appears to have continued after 1800, among which were to be found wealthy men of business with a parliamentary interest, like Peel and Lopez. But many of the augmented number of creations were given to doctors, lawyers, and service officers, and others were gazetted in order to revive the honour in a family in which the direct line of succession had been broken. Contemporary documents, moreover, do not evince the concern, as in the case of peerages, that baronetcies were being abused to augment the influence of the crown.

[6] See the lists of those knighted during these years in Burke's *Orders of Knighthood*.

[7] In 1786 the Duke of Rutland, ruthless dispenser of crown patronage in Ireland, wrote heatedly that ' no necessity of political management should have broken into an institution of 400 years' standing ' : H.M.C., *Rutland MSS.*, iii. 308. But there was considerable justification for George III's moves, in that the increased number of princes of the blood who must have Garters cut down the number of Garters which

ninety-two peerage creations are notorious, and in 1797 Burke, observing the trend, is said to have accepted some of the blame ‘ for so disproportionate an increase of honours, by having deprived the crown and the minister of so many other sources of recompense or reward, which were extinguished by my bill of reform ’.[1] Burke may have overestimated the effect of his Act, but the high rate of peerage creations both during and after Pitt’s time appears to confirm the general import of his assertion ; namely, that honours were being used to compensate in part for the loss of other forms of patronage. Nevertheless, ministers continued to show considerable restraint in recommending creations. They expressed concern at the increase in peers, even as they made them, and yet applications far outnumbered their recommendations.[2] In 1812 Peel and Liverpool agreed that it would be wrong to promise two peerages in return for seven votes in the commons.[3] The dukedom which bought Lord Buckingham in 1821–2 appears to have been granted with reluctance.[4] Toward the close of Liverpool’s regime the crown was bestowing peerages upon royal favourites and as rewards to faithful followers in the fashion accepted in later periods which boasted their freedom from the ‘ corruption ’ attributed to the unreformed parliament.[5]

Imperceptible influence, by its very nature, is extremely difficult to gauge. The position of the crown as a great landed and financial corporation and as the repository of a mass of minor discretionary powers provided the ministry with many means to oblige private citizens. There was seemingly no limit to the ways in which small favours could be employed to aid the ministerial ‘ interest ’. Criminals were paroled to secure electoral votes, naval vessels were paid off in government constituencies, and scores of other favours which only government could bestow served as powerful inducements in securing political support. The use of many of these means continued long after the great

could be given to the nobility. (See G. F. Beltz, *Memorials of the Order of the Garter*, London, 1841, pp. cxxix-cxxxvi). George IV did not bestow Garters solely with an eye to political profit. The Marquis of Buckingham entered the order in 1820, though he was then manoeuvring in opposition, and a dukedom was required to buy his support two years later. In 1826 the ministry gave way to the king's wish to confer the Garter on Devonshire, who was in opposition : *Correspondence of Charles Arbuthnot*, ed. A. Aspinall (London, 1941), p. 85. Arbuthnot was rightfully sure in 1828, however, that Wellington would ‘ not agree to letting any of the opposition have a blue ribband ’ : *H.M.C.*, *Bathurst MSS.*, pp. 657–8.

[1] N. W. Wraxall, *Historical Memoirs of his Own Time* (4 vols., London, 1836), p. 53. The general correctness of Burke's statement is accepted by Professor A. S. Turberville (*History*, xxi. 353–4, 356), who shows that Pitt's successors carried on the policy of using peerages as political currency, though he believes an expansion of the peerage was inevitable as a result of the economic and social changes of the nineteenth century.

[2] *History*, xxi. 356–7.   [3] Parker, *Peel*, i. 42–3.
[4] *Letters of King George IV*, ii. 489.   [5] Yonge, *Liverpool*, iii. 379–80.

Reform Act, and the research of a lifetime would be required to ferret out the whole extent of the use of such favours. But the record of what George Rose singled out as three important forms of ' imperceptible influence '—government contracts, loans, and leases of crown lands—will explain much of the story.[1]

Government contracts, Rose observed, provided ministers with ' great as well as unobserved influence '.[2] In the middle of the eighteenth century there existed no regulated form of competitive bidding. Many of the most profitable contracts were under the management of the treasury, the headquarters for the distribution of government patronage, and the treasury's practice was to award contracts largely on the basis of political ' recommendations '.[3] Namier has estimated that of the fifty-one or fifty-two merchants in the parliament of 1761, thirty-seven ' can be proved to have had extensive business dealings with the government ',[4] and patronage secretaries listed contractors as placemen whose votes would generally be given for the ministry of the day.[5] In 1782 an Act introduced by the Rockingham ministry disqualified government contractors for seats in the commons and required in every contract a clause to the effect that no member of parliament was to receive any benefit thereby.[6] Pitt later introduced open bidding and put an end to the system of letting out contracts for military stores with an eye to political interest. At the outbreak of the war with France he transferred the purchasing of army provisions to the victualling commissioners, who had formerly handled naval provisions alone, and the transport board was established to provide all other types of military stores.[7] Then, as now, interested parties could find ways to frustrate the intent of such laws and regulations, and Pitt's reforms certainly did not put an end to peculation in government contracts. But after this time opposition protests against ' corrupt ' contracting died away, and if the ministry continued to derive any appreciable ' interest ' therefrom, it was far less than in the days when contracts were awarded ' by favour ' to merchants who sat in the house.

Before Pitt's time government loans were handled in much the same manner as contracts. The general practice was ' for the minister to settle, with a few select friends in the city, the terms on which they should be made ; and then to give these, lists of

---

[1] To these three Rose adds the freedom of government officials from account for public money and unlimited home secret service money, which we have considered above : *Observations respecting the Public Expenditure*, pp. 57–8.

[2] *Ibid.* p. 29.   [3] Namier, *Structure of Politics*, i. 61, n. 1.   [4] *Ibid.* i. 61.

[5] *Parliamentary Papers of John Robinson*, pp. 14–17 ; Rose, *Observations respecting the Public Expenditure*, p. 40.   [6] 22 George III c. 45.

[7] Rose also estimated that these regulations effected a considerable saving to government : *Observations respecting the Public Expenditure*, pp. 30–32.

more private friends, intended to be favoured, with specific sums
for each '.[1]   Financiers sought seats in parliament, and when
government credit was sound, they eagerly applied for a ' slice '
of government loans.[2]   In the course of his financial reforms Pitt
did away with this system.   Public notice of an intended loan
was given through the Bank of England, and the treasury encouraged loans from all reputable firms.[3]   When competition
did not exist, Pitt apparently tried to stir up rivalry among the
great banking houses.   In 1793 when money was scarce, he told
the commons that in arranging for a loan ' he had done everything in his power to excite a competition among the monied
men, but without effect ; for it so happened that he had not
received two offers on the occasion '.[4]   Pitt's impartial system
received encomiums even from Fox.[5]   His new policy was so
widely accepted by 1795 that mere suspicion of partiality in
negotiating a loan in that year brought on a parliamentary inquiry and a pamphleteer's bitter protest.[6]   No Act ever excluded
financiers from parliament, but Pitt's reforms destroyed the influence to be derived from the floating of government loans.

The leasing of the crown lands in Walpole's time was one of
the treasury board's special prerogatives.[7]   Every lessee became
directly dependent upon the treasury for his renewal, which must
occur within thirty-one years, but at any intermediate date the
treasury could renew a lease upon terms more favourable to the
applicant.   The influence involved in the control of crown leases
becomes apparent when it is realized that in 1787 (the year of the
first printed survey) more than eighty members of lords and
commons rented royal property.[8]   Efforts made to curtail this
influence had only a limited effect.   The *Nullum Tempus* Act of
1768 was designed to prevent the treasury from revoking royal
grants for political reasons,[9] but it failed to weaken ministerial
control of crown leases.   Over the protests of several landed
magnates, a royal commission was appointed to investigate the
management of crown property in 1786.[10]   Upon the basis of its

[1] *Observations respecting the Public Expenditure*, p. 26.

[2] Namier, *Structure of Politics*, i. 67–72.

[3] William Newmarch, *On the Loans Raised by Mr. Pitt during the First French
War, 1793–1801* (London, 1855), pp. 8 ff. ; J. H. Rose, *William Pitt and the National
Revival* (London, 1911), p. 181.

[4] Debrett's *Parliamentary Register*, xxxv. 157.   [5] *Ibid.* xxxvii. 315.

[6] See *A Letter to the Right Honourable William Pitt, Chancellor of the Exchequer,
on his Conduct with respect to the Loan* (London, 1796).

[7] *H.M.C.*, *Egmont Diary*, iii. 253.

[8] See *Reports of the Commissioners appointed to enquire into the State and Condition
of the Woods, Forest, and Land Revenues of the Crown* (2 vols., London, 1797), pp. 1–59,
where is given a complete list of all crown leases.

[9] A. S. Turberville, *A History of Welbeck Abbey and its Owners* (2 vols., London,
1938–9), ii. 103–24.

[10] *Parliamentary History*, xxvi. 208–10 ; 26 George III c. 87 ; *Commons Journals*,
xlv. 549.   Commission extended by 30 George III c. 50.

report Pitt introduced a bill to reorganize crown leases, but it proved ineffective.[1] Further reorganization took place in 1810 and 1814,[2] and several investigations were ordered in the 1820's. Their reports indicated that management remained inefficient and liable to political influence.[3] Daniel Harvey's plaint in 1830 that the crown lands, as managed by the government, were ' quite sufficient to corrupt both houses of parliament ' was no doubt an exaggeration.[4] But when evidence even after 1832 indicates that the influence of crown leases was still effective in electoral contests,[5] one must conclude that inquiries and legislation had not removed crown lands from the sphere of politics in the unreformed parliament.

Three of the four important forms of ' imperceptible influence ' had thus been partially curtailed before the great Reform Act. Other forms continued in use. The Liverpool government, for example, dispensed taxation remittances through local supporters in the period after Waterloo,[6] but the tendency of administrative and financial reforms was to reduce the old fund of special favours by which government could attach adherents.

The most important element in the influence of the crown in the eighteenth century was probably the system of patronage. Hume and Blackstone both stressed the influence derived from the large number of offices at the disposal of the government. So generally recognized was the power of patronage that from 1675 onward fairly persistent efforts had been made to prevent the government's use of ' placemen ' to make majorities.[7] Such endeavours were guided in two directions : to disfranchise placemen and to exclude placemen from seats in parliament. Before 1780 some success was achieved in both ways. Under Queen Anne postmasters were disfranchised,[8] and a series of Place Acts from 1693 to 1742 excluded several categories of officers from the house of commons.[9] Had certain provisions of the Act of Settlement gone into effect, all placemen, including cabinet ministers, would have been ineligible to sit in the commons, but ' West's expedient ' in 1705 softened the exclusion clauses and established the system of re-election upon acceptance of ' an office or a place of profit under the king '.[10] The other Place Acts of the period were strictly limited in character, and numerous

---

[1] 34 George III c. 75.   [2] 50 George III c. 65 ; 54 George III c. 157.

[3] *Parliamentary Papers*, 1823, No. 110 ; 1826, No. 368 ; 1829, No. 317.

[4] Hansard, 2nd ser., xxiii. 1067.

[5] G. Kitson Clark, for example, points out that the election at Hastings in 1834–5 ' turned on the renewal of leases for some crown lands in the neighbourhood ' : *Peel and the Conservative Party*, p. 219.

[6] Feiling, *Second Tory Party*, p. 282.

[7] Porritt, *Unreformed House of Commons*, i. 204 ff.

[8] *Ibid*. i. 300.   [9] *Ibid*. i. 206–17.

[10] 4 Anne c. 8.   Re-enacted by 6 Anne c. 7 art. 25.

exclusion bills brought in by the opposition were usually defeated.
Lord Egmont explained the rejection of the bill of 1734 in this
manner : [1]

> I found by discourse with the two Mr. Towers that they yesterday
> purposely avoided being at the House because they were in their
> judgments for the bill to limit the number of officers in Parliament,
> but yet were not willing to disoblige the ministry who warmly pressed
> the rejecting that Bill. Mr. Moore also told me he would not be there,
> because though he liked the Bill, he did not know if the passing it at
> this time might not embarrass the King's affairs as we are going into
> a war, when it will be necessary the next Parliament should consist
> of members that will concur in the Court measures as Placemen will be
> sure to do. Mr. Page told me he left the House as the question was
> going to be put, because he could not oppose so reasonable and popular
> a Bill.
>
> My brother Parker did the same, and I was informed that of those
> present at the debate, there were counted twenty friends of the Court
> who left the House, for the eyes of men are very searching on such
> occasions. I own I avoided being there because I really think it is
> inconsistent with our Constitution and dangerous to our liberties ;
> that so many Placemen should have seats among us . . . yet I ap-
> prehended some danger might arise from passing it, because parties
> are now so high and envenomed against each other, that were the new
> Parliament almost entirely independent of the Crown, I know not how
> violently they may behave against the public measures next year . . .
> especially considering the characters of Sir William Wyndham, Mr.
> Pulteney, Shippen and others who are the promoters of this Bill, some
> of whose principles are suspected to tend to a Commonwealth and others
> more than suspected to be Jacobites.

With such opinion prevalent at Westminster, it is easy to see
why Place Acts were rarely passed. Furthermore, there is little
evidence that those in the statute book had any real effect in
curtailing the influence of the crown. A large majority of government officials could vote if otherwise qualified, and there remained
a considerable number of places tenable with a seat in parliament.
John Robinson made a list of them in 1774 which reveals that
there were in England 425 offices and categories of offices, in
Scotland 24, and in Ireland 14, which could be held with a seat
in lords or commons.[2] The total of 463, however, omits army
officers and various petty officials in Ireland, who were also
eligible and accounted placemen in the house. At no time during
the eighteenth century did every eligible placeman occupy a seat
in the commons, but the most cautious estimates indicate well

---

[1] H.M.C., *Egmont Diary*, ii. 37–8.
[2] *Parliamentary Papers of John Robinson*, pp. 9–11.

over 100 placemen in each parliament from the days of Walpole through those of North.[1]

After 1780, however, legislation and administrative reorganization inexorably broke up the old system of patronage. Here the same forces were at work which effected a reduction in both ' imperceptible influence ' and the pecuniary influence of the crown, and a changing attitude toward the employment of patronage worked in the same direction. A comparison of the situation in the disposal of patronage in several of the most important fields before and after 1780 will indicate the nature of the great alterations which took place.

Sinecure offices, once termed by Castlereagh ' more likely than any others to secure parliamentary influence ',[2] had played a considerable part before 1780 in attaching ministerial adherents. Though many sinecurists were not removable at pleasure, the desirability of a well paid job with little or no labour made sinecures valuable rewards for political service. There was a sizeable cluster of functionless offices in the royal household, the duchies of Lancaster and Cornwall, the county palatine of Lancaster, and the earldom of Chester.[3] Another group existed in the exchequer and in the offices of the pipe, the pells, and the first fruits.[4] There were roughly 200 sinecures in the customs.[5] Although no move was made to weed out such functionless offices until the second Rockingham ministry, in 1782 there commenced a constant and unremitting attack upon sinecures. Burke's Act abolished 134 offices in household and ministry.[6] Treasury regulations under Shelburne did away with 144 sinecures in the customs,[7] and the Exchequer Act of 1783 condemned a large

---

[1] Estimates of placemen in parliament vary considerably because compilers made different inclusions, some including and others omitting military officers, officials not removable at pleasure, and lords lieutenant. See *Parliamentary Papers*, 1823, No. 529; *Parliamentary Papers of John Robinson*, pp. 14–17; Namier, *Structure of Politics*, i. 266, n. 2; Rose, *Observations respecting the Public Expenditure*, pp. 41–3.

[2] Hansard, 2nd ser., vii. 1304. The award of many sinecures, however, often had little to do with political influence Many were private ' jobs ', or were assigned to provide salaries for effective offices to which no emoluments were attached, or were given as a form of pension to reward meritorious service, or to provide for the dependents of those who had died for their country. When reform had abolished many sinecures in 1817, parliament empowered the crown to ' grant pensions as rewards for official services in lieu of those sinecures which were formerly applied to a certain extent for such purposes '; *Parliamentary Papers*, 1834, No. 519, p. 10.

[3] More than 30 officers of this group were commons placemen in 1774: *Parliamentary Papers of John Robinson*, pp. 14–17.

[4] See *Commons Journals*, xxxviii. 705–12.

[5] A. L. Cross, ed., *Eighteenth Century Documents relating to the Royal Forests, the Sheriffs, and Smuggling* (New York, 1928), pp. 248–88. In these papers Commissioner Musgrave complains that there is too much private jobbery and not enough political influence in appointments to customs sinecures.

[6] 22 George III c. 82. Of these officers, 22 were commons placemen, and 9 sat in the lords. See also the *Fourth Report of the Select Committee on Finance*, 1797, pp. 68–72.   [7] Rose, *Observations respecting the Public Expenditure*, p. 5.

number of exchequer sinecures to extinction upon the death of their incumbents.[1] George Rose estimated that Pitt's reforms abolished 765 needless revenue offices in 1789 and another 196 in 1798.[2] Legislation in the early nineteenth century weeded out still more useless offices,[3] many of which had been converted into sinecures by administrative reform. A select committee of the commons, appointed to investigate sinecures from 1810 to 1812, found that many of the 342 sinecures still existing were to be abolished upon the death of their holders.[4] Another investigation in 1817 resulted in the abolition or ' regulation ' of 313 other useless offices.[5] In 1822 Castlereagh boasted that since 1815 more than 2000 civil offices rendered useless by the close of the war had been abolished.[6] Finally, in 1834, another select committee found that of 108 offices alleged still to be useless, 8 were not sinecures, 2 had already been abolished, and 43 had been ' regulated '. The remaining 55 were condemned, and the committee wrote the epitaph of the sinecure by announcing the establishment of the principle ' that anything in the nature of a sinecure office, with emoluments attached to it at the public charge, is alike indefensible in principle, pernicious as a means of influence, and grievous as an undue addition to the general burthen of the nation '.[7] The progress of reform since 1782 makes it clear that the epitaph of 1834 was inscribed over a body long moribund if not altogether defunct as a means of political influence.

The destruction of the sinecure accompanied that of the old method of granting offices in reversion. When demands for patronage were greater than the supply, the government had sometimes promised offices upon the death or removal of the incumbent. Thus in 1762 Lord Henley, desirous of holding posts then occupied, asked ' two reversions for signing the peace ',[8] and patronage was thereby mortgaged to pay for present support in the future. But acts regulating sinecures commonly prohibited grants in reversion, and an Act of 1808 [9] which temporarily suspended the power to grant any office in this way was later

---

[1] 23 George III c. 82.

[2] Rose, *Observations respecting the Public Expenditure*, pp. 10–11.

[3] 47 George III sess. 1, c. 12 ; 48 George III c. 9 ; 51 George III c. 71. The reform movement did not extend to Ireland until after the union. When Rutland became lord lieutenant in 1784, he laid down as a principle of administration ' to create offices which may increase its patronage and extend its powers '. He actually did create several sinecures : *H.M.C., Rutland MSS.*, iii. 82, 94, 127.

[4] Findings summarized in *Parliamentary Papers*, 1834, No. 519, pp. 9–10.

[5] *Parliamentary Papers*, 1817, Nos. 405, 406, 407. Hansard, 2nd ser., vii. 1304–6.

[6] Hansard, 2nd ser., vii. 1306.

[7] *Parliamentary Papers*, 1834, No. 519, pp. 3–5. For further information on the abolition of sinecures, see *ibid.*, 1830, No. 451 ; *ibid.* 1833, No. 650 ; *ibid.* 1835, No. 507.

[8] Earl of Ilchester, ed., *Letters to Henry Fox, Lord Holland* (London, 1915), p. 156.

[9] 48 George III c. 50.

extended through 1814.[1] Thereafter the use of reversions as a means of influence fell into desuetude.

Another great change in the system of patronage occurred in the revenue departments. Before 1780 the treasury had engrossed all appointments in customs and excise,[2] and the numerous revenue officers had been turned into borough voters and electioneers for the ministry of the day.[3] Reformers in Shelburne's administration complained that these officers were ' appointed from country fox-hunters, bankrupt merchants, and officers of the army and navy ' with ' much more attention being paid to their interest as votes than to their abilities and education for the duty of their offices '. [4] The revenue officer, more than any other factor, produced the ' treasury boroughs ' of the eighteenth century. In 1782, however, Crewe's Act disfranchised the majority of revenue officers.[5] John Robinson's calculations for the election of 1784 show how serious a blow this was to the old system of influence. Speaking of Hastings, he observed that ' the disfranchising bill has made great alterations in this and other boroughs ' ; and of Winchilsea he wrote, ' . . . the revenue officers having been struck off leaves scarce a good voter '.[6] After the union with Ireland, disfranchisement was extended to Irish revenue officers,[7] and henceforward the placeman-voter ceased to exist as a widespread institution.[8] The development of preliminary qualifications for civil servants from 1787 onwards also worked to remove political influence from revenue appointments.[9]

In other spheres the patronage system was weakened not by legislation but by custom. Earlier in the century, Walpole and the Pelhams had unhesitatingly dismissed army officers who voted against the ministry in parliament. Cobham, Bolton, Pitt, Erskine, and Conway had lost their commissions in notorious

---

[1] 50 George III c. 88 ; 52 George III c. 40.

[2] E. E. Hoon, *The Organization of the English Customs System, 1696–1786* (New York, 1938), pp. 197–201 ; E. Hughes, *Studies in Administration and Finance, 1558–1825* (Manchester, 1934), pp. 266–316.

[3] Contemporary estimates of 40,000 to 60,000 revenue officers (*Parliamentary History*, xxii, 1342–4) have been adopted by Hunt, Lecky, and other historians. Existing data indicate that they are far too high. An examination of *Reports of the Select Committee on Finance* from 1791 to 1797 shows that 15,000 is a much more likely figure.

[4] A. L. Cross, *Eighteenth Century Documents*, pp. 246, 250.

[5] 22 George III c. 41. Only those holding office by letters patent, the higher posts and sinecures, still retained the vote. The act was extended to the lowest rank of voters in the complicated system of Scottish elections by 37 George III c. 138.

[6] *Parliamentary Papers of John Robinson*, pp. 80–1.

[7] 43 George III c. 25.

[8] Dockyard workers in parliamentary constituencies were not removed from the sphere of election politics until 1847, and were never disfranchised : see *Parliamentary Papers*, 1852–3, No. 511, pp. iii-iv, xiii-xiv.

[9] See Hoon, *The Organization of the English Customs System*, pp. 204–7 ; Hansard, 2nd ser., vii. 1301–2.

political cases, and Walpole once roundly declared that if any officer should ' even show aversion to a minister, that minister would be the most wretched of creatures if he did not cashier him, and he left the practice as a legacy to his successors '.[1] George Grenville, accepting the legacy, insisted that ' the king canot trust his army in the hands of those who are 'against his measures '.[2] Lords lieutenant were treated in the same fashion. Throughout the eighteenth century they were accounted place-men to be appointed and dismissed for political reasons, and even the Rockingham whigs removed lords lieutenant in opposition to replace them with friends.[3] Early in the nineteenth century this practice came to an end. The celebrated dismissals during the regency and reign of George IV—Sir Robert Wilson from the army and Lord Fitzwilliam from the lieutenancy of Yorkshire—were based on allegations of sedition rather than political op-position. In 1821 Lord Palmerston, then secretary at war, asserted that during his period in office ' no officer had ever been dismissed the service for his conduct in parliament '. Such a practice he declared ' a pitiful principle ' based on ' mean and miserable feelings of resentment '.[4] Even in the most severe political crises the Liverpool government permitted army officers to vote against them with impunity.[5] Lords lieutenant were appointed when in opposition, as was Buckingham in 1813 and Morpeth in 1824, and Liverpool retained Devonshire, Darlington, and Portland in lieutenancies despite their consistent voting against him. The ministry still possessed the unquestioned right to cashier such opponents, but declined to continue political patronage in the army and county government.

There are evidences of similar if less emphatic trends in ap-pointments to the church, the law, and the colonies. While private jobbery and charity had played a great part in such appointments before 1780, political influence had often been a major factor. Bishop Gibson and the duke of Newcastle erected complex systems of clerical patronage,[6] and George III once

---

[1] Basil Williams, The Life of William Pitt, Earl of Chatham (2 vols., London, 1913), i. 67. The same sentiments in practically the same words are attributed to Henry Pelham in Parliamentary History, ix. 1351.

[2] Toynbee, ed., Letters of Horace Walpole, vi. 69. See also W. J. Smith, ed., The Grenville Papers (4 vols., London, 1852), ii. 166, 321.

[3] See O. Browning, ed., The Political Memoranda of Francis, Fifth Duke of Leeds, Camden Society, N.S., xxxv. 22–3, 65.   [4] Hansard, 2nd ser., vi. 311–12, 321.

[5] Probably the most critical issue Liverpool's government ever faced was Tierney's motion of the state of the nation of 18 May 1819. On that occasion 19 army officers voted against the ministry, and Colonel Ponsonby, aide-de-camp to the prince regent, paired off for the opposition. Not one dismissal resulted.

[6] See Norman Sykes, Edmund Gibson (Oxford, 1926), pp. 83 ff., and Church and State in England in the XVIIIth Century (Cambridge, 1934), pp. 41–91. There is a malicious and amusing description of Newcastle's methods in Memoirs of a Royal Chaplain, 1729–1763 (Hartshorne, ed., London, 1905), p. 218.

seriously considered Lord Mansfield's proposal 'that I should pitch on some bishop to recommend to me in ecclesiastical affairs, that I might keep that great engine of power in my own hands instead of in the ministry '.[1] The magnitude of 'that great engine of power ' in the middle of the eighteenth century was measured by the ministry's right to control a large number of the appointments to 2 archbishoprics, 24 bishoprics, and 851 minor church appointments in England and Wales. In Ireland there were 8 archbishoprics, 35 bishoprics, and about 200 livings ; and over 250 ministers in Scotland.[2] Scores of legal appointments were also made with an eye to political interest, especially high-ranking law officers of the crown, Welsh judges, and judges in the admiralty court, all of whom were accounted placemen under ministerial influence. Colonial officials were part of government patronage, and during the century the ministry constantly encroached upon the patronage of the East India Company. It cannot be said that the practice in these appointments was reversed as it was in the case of lords lieutenant or army officers, but there are indications of moves in the same direction. The crown had surrendered all its patronage in the church of Scotland by 1829.[3] Wellington maintained that his church appointments during the ministry of 1828–30 were strictly non-political,[4] and a savage critic of the method of church preferment, writing in *Blackwood's* in 1831, admitted that ' of late years ' the government had filled many clerical offices ' with the most disinterested views '.[5] As early as 1811 Francis Horner thought that the appointment of judges without regard to political interest had become ' established morality '.[6] The American revolution diminished the number of colonial appointments, and reforms in 1782 and 1814 abolished practices which had made many overseas posts desirable political rewards.[7] Castlereagh assured the commons in 1822 that the colonial service was no longer a source of influence and pointed out that seven-eighths of colonial appointments were in the hands of local officers.[8] Pitt's endeavour ' to give the crown the power of guiding the politics of India

[1] Sedgwick, ed., *Letters of George III to Bute*, p. 212.
[2] These figures are based on *Court and City Kalendar*, 1755, pp. 110–11 ; *Parliamentary Papers*, 1833, No. 762, pp. 6–7 ; and Bentham's *Church of Englandism and its Catechism Examined* (London, 1817–18), p. 383. They differ slightly from those given in Sykes, *Edmund Gibson*, p. 109 ; and *Church and State*, p. 149.
[3] Parker, *Peel*, ii. 99.   [4] *Wellington Despatches*, 3rd ser., vii. 361–4.
[5] *Blackwood's Edinburgh Magazine*, xxxi. 191. After the Reform Act, the Ecclesiastical Commission Acts did away with many clerical sinecures and put an end to much jobbery and influence in church appointments : see W. L. Mathieson, *English Church Reform, 1815–1840* (London, 1923), pp. 111 ff.
[6] *Memoirs of Francis Horner*, ii. 92–3.
[7] 22 George III c. 75 ; 54 George III c. 61.
[8] Hansard, 2nd ser., vii. 1300–1.

with as little means of corrupt influence as possible '[1] was hardly attended with success, but the number of posts in India at the disposal of the government depended so much on the relationships between ministers and company directors that Indian patronage never became the source of influence that many feared.[2] Wellington called on the board of control to provide him with some appointments for political purposes in 1828, though the president became concerned with a plan in which he ' considered it to be a settled point that the patronage of India should be separated from the government '.[3]

The effect of reform and voluntary surrender of ministerial discipline over placemen was a distinct diminution, though not a total destruction, of the eighteenth-century system of patronage. In 1826 the treasury still possessed ten seats to which it could nominate supporters.[4] An investigation in 1821 revealed that there were still 89 placemen in the commons ;[5] but of these, 19 were not removable by the ministry, 13 were not directly removable, and a half-dozen were then in opposition. Castle-reagh pointed out that only 47 or 48 of them held offices ' in a sense to which influence could be fairly attached ',[6] and the majority of these were members of the ministry.

This evidence of a decline in the resources of crown influence lends considerable weight to the plaints of politicians in the reign of George IV that the old system of government ' corruption' was then breaking up. Whereas Walpole had been confident in 1734 that the crown could always out-spend the gentry in elec-tions,[7] the Liverpool administration employed little or none of the public funds for political purposes. Honours have continued to be political rewards down to the present day, but some of the sources of ' imperceptible influence' were extinguished in Pitt's time. The Irish union gave the ministry a strong hold on the 100 new members, but Irish Exclusion Acts weakened their grip,[8] and Catholic emancipation pretty effectively destroyed govern-ment control in most Irish constituencies. The general trend of legislative reform and administrative reorganization supports Feiling's contention that in the early years of the Liverpool

---

[1] *Parliamentary History*, xxiv. 408.

[2] See *Cambridge History of India*, v. 314–15 ; C. H. Philips, *The East India Com-pany, 1784–1834* (Manchester 1940), pp. 251–4. Brougham asserted in 1822 that by agreement the government was ' allowed to dispose of 1/14 of the whole patronage of India ' : Hansard, 2nd ser., vii. 1273–4.

[3] Colchester, ed., *A Political Diary, 1828–1830, by Edward Law, Lord Ellenborough* (2 vols., London, 1881), i. 215–221 ; ii. 72, 92.

[4] Feiling, *Second Tory Party*, p. 343.

[5] *Parliamentary Papers*, 1822, No. 542.

[6] Hansard, 2nd ser., vii. 1302–3.   [7] *H.M.C., Egmont Diary*, ii. 39.

[8] 41 George III (U.K.), c. 52. This act was slightly modified in 1813 by 54 George III c. 16. Irish judges were excluded by 1 and 2 George IV c. 44.

government the ' old cement of patronage was more than half gone '.[1]

Most convincing of all arguments is the plain fact that Wellington lost the election of 1830. Never since the Hanoverian succession had the ministry of the day, backed by the influence of the crown, been defeated at the polls.[2] Walpole had emerged triumphant in 1734 despite the overwhelming unpopularity of his late excise bill. The younger Pitt, with the crown on his side, had been able to defy parliament and the whig grandees in 1784. Yet Wellington, professing himself satisfied with the backing of William IV,[3] found that he could not elect a parliament to support his ministry. Lord Ellenborough thought the elections had ' not been attended to in time ', though the *Edinburgh Review* asserted that the treasury had estimated the government would gain ninety-three seats in the election.[4] So poor were treasury calculations, however, that even after the election disasters Wellington thought he had sufficient support, and not until he met parliament did he realize the true weakness of his position.[5] The duke had complained of the paucity of his patronage, and the election demonstrated how greatly the influence of the crown had diminished since Dunning's celebrated resolution.

A particular moment in time when the influence of the crown became insufficient to control parliament cannot be definitely determined. The process of diminution was gradual, not cataclysmic. Stemming from the Rockinghamite reform movement in 1780 was a steady flow of reforms which had a cumulative effect in reducing the ' king's interest '. Halévy's assertion that by 1815 the tories ' were pledged to the defence of all the abuses employed by the eighteenth-century whigs to secure their power ' [6] must be rejected, for the progress of reform continued unabated. Liverpool wrote to Bathurst in 1818 that ministers were going to cram reform down the regent's throat because ' economy and reduction are the passions of the day, and . . . if he wishes to

---

[1] Feiling, *Second Tory Party*, p. 282.

[2] Feiling states (*ibid.* p. 3) that ' Before 1831 there is no example of ministers, if supported by the crown, being beaten at the polls ' ; and D. L. Keir (*Law Quarterly Review*, l. 370) asserts that ' it continued to be true right up to 1832 that no ministry was ever defeated on a dissolution '. These statements are obviously slips of the pen. Wellington certainly lost the election of 1830. How little the influence of the crown counted in subsequent elections is shown by the failure in 1834–5 of William IV and Peel to repeat the success achieved by George III and Pitt in 1783–4, and by Victoria's failure to retain her beloved Melbourne in 1841.

[3] *Wellington Despatches*, 3rd ser., vii. 240.

[4] *Political Diary . . . by Ellenborough*, ii. 305 ; *Edinburgh Review*, cii. 263–4. Wellington wrote confidently to Peel in June ' that after the general election we should have numbers ' : *Wellington Despatches*, 3rd ser., vii. 106–8.

[5] *Ibid.* vii. 240 : *Political Diary . . . by Ellenborough*, ii. 380–1.

[6] Halévy, *History of the English People in 1815*, p. 18.

preserve his government, he must allow them to manage the questions of establishments of all descriptions in such a way as to give no pretext to our friends to vote against us '.[1] Hardly a pledge to maintain abuses ! Liverpool's statement points to two other factors in the process of gradual diminution : the change in attitude toward the use of ' corruption ' and the growing force of public opinion. Men in parliament no longer abstained from voting on place bills for fear of the ministry or the security of the state. Ministers no longer cashiered army officers and lords lieutenant in opposition, or carried out wholesale purges in the civil service for political reasons. At the same time, the development of the press and education had increased the weight of what contemporaries called ' the popular element of the constitution '.[2] There was much greater concern for ' opinion out-of-doors ', and the effect of that opinion was certainly vital in the election of 1830. These factors lead to the conclusion that the gradual process of diminution probably began to have serious effects upon the ministry's control of parliament toward the end of the Napoleonic wars, the very time when Rose and Grenville voiced doubts about the strength of the powers of ' corruption '. How serious were these effects is impossible to estimate, for the ministry continued to hold its own with the support of independent members, though there is room for considerable doubt whether Liverpool would have weathered the elections of 1818, 1820, and 1826, had the state of public opinion been different. But clearly by 1830 the process of diminution had weakened the effectiveness of the influence of the crown so far as to destroy its power to maintain a parliamentary majority.

The traditional versions expounded in the standard constitutional histories must therefore be revised. The destruction of the influence of the crown occurred, not in the 1780's nor in 1832, but in the period lying between. It was effected, not by any enactment or group of enactments, but by a long train of legislation, administrative reform, and changed attitudes in public life. The forces motivating these alterations were the constant pressure of opposition parties striving to reduce ministerial power, the need for economy and retrenchment after the American revolution and during and after the wars of the French revolution, and

[1] H.M.C. Bathurst MSS. p. 456. In 1822 every department of civil government except the customs was under investigation, and Castlereagh emphatically announced to the commons that the ministry was proceeding ' on the principle of restraining within due bounds the whole influence of the crown as far as it had any tendency to be employed for corrupt purposes ' : Hansard, 2nd ser., vii. 1303–4.

[2] ' In the five years ending in 1789, 880 petitions were presented ; in the five years ending in 1831, 24,942 ' : C. S. Emden, The People and the Constitution (Oxford, 1933), p. 77. See Lord John Russell's estimate of the power of public opinion in 1823 : Essay on the English Government, pp. 429–30.

13

the social and economic changes in British life as reflected in the growth of the power of public opinion through a cheaper and more influential press.   In its last years, ministers had managed the unreformed parliament without the whole system of influence thought so indispensable in the eighteenth century, and one vital obstacle to the development of cabinet government and the two-party system in modern form had already been removed.

ARCHIBALD S. FOORD.

Crewe's Act, 1782[1]

THE bill to disqualify revenue officers from voting in parliamentary elections, which received the royal assent on 19 June 1782, had a longer history and a more radical purpose than the rest of the Economical Reform legislation.

Dislike of revenue officers, of whom 90 per cent. were employees of the boards of customs and excise, was as old as their establishment. At the beginning of the eighteenth century customs and excise officials were excluded from parliament[2] and customs, excise and post office officials were forbidden to take part in elections.[3] In 1733 Walpole's excise bill was opposed on the ground that it would 'extend the influence of the Crown' from the sea-ports, 'already . . . in a manner taken prisoner by the Officers of the Crown . . . over all the inland towns and corporations in England'.[4] When, therefore, in 1770,[5] Dowdeswell moved for a bill to disfranchise the majority of revenue officers his motion seemed 'well calculated to catch many persons'. Nevertheless it was rejected 'by a very handsome majority'[6]—263 to 188. Ten years later the Rockingham whigs revived Dowdeswell's project and, as Crewe's bill, made it an important part of their programme. It was the most revolutionary part, for it alone was directed against the influence of the Crown without doors.[7] This object was expected to make it

---

[1] 22 Geo. III c. 41. 'An Act for better securing the Freedom of Elections of Members to serve in Parliament, by disabling certain Officers, employed in the Collection or Management of his Majesty's Revenues, from giving their votes at such Elections.' The officers concerned were those employed (unless appointed by letters patent) by the following revenue departments: customs, excise, stamps, salt, windows, and houses, and post office, including foreign mail service.

[2] 11 Will. III c. 2 (Excise); 12 and 13 Will. III c. 10 (Customs).

[3] 3 Will. and Mary c. 1.

[4] Pulteney, 12 March 1733, Parliamentary History, viii. 1325.

[5] In debate on State of Nation, 12 February 1770, Parliamentary History, xvi. 834-40; Cavendish Debates, i. 444-57.

[6] George III to North, 12 February 1770, Correspondence of George III (ed. Fortescue), ii. 754.

[7] This, Crewe stated in the debate on the second reading of the bill on 13 April 1780, 'ought to be their aim as much as endeavouring to restrain that influence within doors, or the work of reformation would only be done by halves'. (Parl. Hist. xxi. 404.)

palatable to the allies of the Rockingham whigs outside parliament, who were invited to regard it as a measure of parliamentary reform. But it seems to have alienated some of those inside parliament who had voted for Dunning's resolution but were not willing to deprive the king of influence at the price of depriving Englishmen of votes.[1] The bill was twice defeated in the house of commons—in April 1780 and again in March 1781.[2] It was introduced for the third time in April 1782, thirteen days after Rockingham succeeded North as first lord of the treasury, and passed both Houses. The purpose of this note is to suggest that the Act was not 'a telling blow at governmental corruption of the constituencies '[3] and therefore does not deserve to rank as one of the reasons for the shrinkage in Crown influence which took place in the half century between 1780 and 1830.[4] This was so less because Crewe's Act was ineffective than because it was incapable of achieving its object.

It is not possible to state accurately how many revenue officers were disfranchised by Crewe's Act. But at least it is possible to discount those contemporary and later estimates which exceed the total number employed in the revenue departments affected. In the house of commons, for example, Earl Nugent claimed that the Act would disfranchise nearly 40,000,[5] and Mr. Vyner and Sir Watkyn Lewes that it would disfranchise 60,000.[6] Rockingham's estimate is more moderate but still startling. He is reported to have stated that ' the Custom House alone . . . had 5000 persons belonging to it, besides about 2500 more of extra tides-men &c., and the Excise at least 4000 more, who were voters '.[7] None of these estimates can

---

[1] Dunning's amended resolution ' That it is necessary to declare that the Influence of the Crown has increased, is increasing, and ought to be diminished ' passed the house of commons on 6 April by 233 votes to 215. In the debate on Crewe's bill Sir Thomas Clavering and Sir Matthew White Ridley, who had both supported Dunning's resolution, maintained that this did not bind them to support Crewe's bill. (*Morning Chronicle*, 14 April 1780.)

[2] By 224 to 195 on 13 April 1780 (on the debate on the second reading) and by 133 to 86 on 21 March 1781 (on the debate on the Order of the Day for the second reading). (*Parl. Hist.* xxi. 403–414, 1396–9.)

[3] Grant Robertson, *Select Statutes Cases and Documents*, p. 248.

[4] D. L. Keir, (Economical Reform 1779–87) in *Law Quarterly Review*, l. 368–85 states that all the Economical Reform legislation of 1782–3 worked either badly or not at all. He does not prove his case for Crewe's Act.

[5] 16 April 1782, *Parl. Hist.* xxii. 1337; *Parliamentary Register*, vii. 50.

[6] 25 April 1782, *Parl. Hist.* xxii. 1342, 1344; *Parl. Register*, vii. 78, 79. Earl Nugent and Mr. Vyner opposed the bill. Sir Watkyn Lewes supported it because it would disfranchise a fifth of the electorate ' who were under influence '.

[7] 3 June 1782, *Parl. Hist.* xxiii. 101. This report of Rockingham's speech tallies with that given in the *Parliamentary Register* (viii. 339), the *Morning Chronicle* (4 June 1782) and the *Political Magazine* (1782, p. 577). But the *London Chronicle* reports Rockingham as saying that ' 23,000 different voters were influenced by the revenue, and one-fifth of these under orders of the first Lord of the Treasury '. (*London Chronicle*, 1782, p. 534.)

be accepted.[1] A return published in 1828 shows that in 1797 the customs and excise departments employed a staff of about 12,500 and the smaller revenue departments about 1500.[2] The figures compiled by the select committee on finance, 1797, show that the total revenue establishment for 1782 was between 500 and 1000 less than in 1797: that is, in 1782 it was about 14,000.[3] Clearly the figures of 40,000 and 60,000 are wild exaggerations; to accept even Rockingham's figures would mean that in 1782 more than nine-tenths of the total customs and excise employees enjoyed the franchise and that one-tenth of the total electorate were revenue officers. This is so unlikely that it is difficult not to suspect that his figures represent the total number of employees: that is, the number of those disqualified from voting, not the number of those who were actually deprived of a vote.[4]

Since ' freedom of election ' was the avowed object of Crewe's Act the first and greatest test of its efficacy was the general election of March 1784. The king and Pitt were then blamed not only for having ' sentenced, condemned and executed '[5] a parliament that was less than three and a half years old but also for their folly, ' considering the present diminished state of royal patronage '[6] as a result of Crewe's Act, in imagining that a general election would give them a more favourable house of commons.[7] This was not the official government view. The election was managed by George Rose, Pitt's secretary to the treasury, under the supervision of John Robinson, who had been North's secretary to the treasury.

[1] They have, however, all been accepted. Lecky, combining them, says that 'It was stated in the debate that no less than 12,000 of these officers had been created under the late Government, and that they altogether numbered in England, according to some account, 40,000, according to others 60,000 '. (History of England in the Eighteenth century, v. 143.) Erskine May refers to Rockingham's statement only (Constitutional History of England, i. 368.) Grant Robertson repeats Lecky's hybrid statement that 12,000 revenue officers had been created by North's administration (Select Statutes, p 248) and D. L. Keir takes it from Grant Robertson. (Constitutional History of Modern Britain, p. 328.)

[2] Public Offices Establishments. A Return of the Number of Persons Employed and Pay and Salaries Granted in all Public Offices or Departments in the years 1797, 1805, 1810, 1815, 1819 and 1827. Parliamentary Papers, 1828, xvi.

[3] Select Committee on Finance, 1797, appendix to 4th Report, 5th and 6th Reports, Appendices to 7th, 8th, 9th, 10th, 11th and 23rd Reports, Reports from Committees of House of Commons, 1803, xii and xiii. The increases in establishments between 1782 and 1797, due to increased business, were largely offset by decreases due to the abolition of sinecures and reorganization of the collections.

[4] Rockingham died on 1 July 1782. This was his last appearance in the house of lords. All the reports emphasize that he was ill and spoke with difficulty. It seems likely either that he himself did not clearly distinguish between disqualification and disfranchisement or that he was wrongly reported.

[5] Burke, 14 June 1782, Parl. Hist. xxii. 944.

[6] Vulgar Errors Political, 1784, p. 18.

[7] Windham believed, wrongly, that one of the reasons why parliament was not dissolved during the Fox-North coalition was that ' the power of the Crown in general, for those purposes (the creation of a new parliament), has been so abridged by Crewe's Bill that the same hope cannot be entertained from that measure as formerly '. (Windham to the Earl of Northington, 17 July 1783, Winham Papers, i. 38.)

Robinson certainly did not regard Crewe's Act as a fatal blow at
the 'ministerial influence in all the sea-port boroughs '.[1] His nearest
approach to anxiety is his comment on the situation at Hastings.
' The disfranchising bill ' he noted ' has made great alterations in
this and other boroughs, yet it is hoped that this borough with great
attention may as formerly be got to return two friends '.[2] Robinson's confidence was justified: the government did not lose seats in
1784 as a result of Crewe's Act, and naturally did not do so later,
when its purpose was even more easily frustrated.

The disfranchisement of customs officers was potentially more
dangerous than the disfranchisement of excise officers because the
customs establishments varied much more widely in size from
borough to borough. For the same reason the effect of disfranchisement is more obvious in customs boroughs. I have therefore
given the Act the benefit of the doubt by taking customs boroughs as
evidence of its effect. At the end of the eighteenth century customs
officers were employed in about seventy-five boroughs in England
and Wales.[3] In each borough the effect of the Act depended less on
the number of revenue officers than on the size and composition of
the electorate.[4] In boroughs where the electorate was large the Act
could make little difference because even the total number of revenue
officers (who could hardly all have been voters) was not a considerable proportion of the electorate.[5] But in a few boroughs with a
small electorate, consisting nearly always only of corporation or of
freemen, the total number of revenue officers was as large or larger
than the number of electors.[6] In this group of perhaps fifteen

[1] *Vulgar Errors*, p. 18.
[2] *Parliamentary Papers of John Robinson* (ed. W. T. Laprade), p. 18. The first part
of this sentence is quoted by A. S. Foord (' The Waning of the Influence of the Crown ',
ante, lxii (1947), 501) as evidence of Robinson's apprehension; the whole sentence
suggests confidence rather than apprehension.
[3] Appendices to 4th and 5th Reports of Select Committee on Finance, 1797, *Reports
from Committees*, 1803, xii; Public Offices, *Parliamentary Papers*, 1822, xvii (2).
[4] For example, most of the boroughs with a large customs establishment had a very
much larger electorate. Therefore even if all the customs employees had been voters
their disfranchisement would only have affected a small proportion of the electorate.
These boroughs were: Bristol (175 customs officers: 6000 electors); Hull (165: 1182);
Liverpool (336: 2300); Southampton (80: 600); Yarmouth (111: 781). The
exceptions were: Plymouth (129: 160); Portsmouth (129: 110); Rochester (245:
630). The figures in this and the next two footnotes are taken from *Reports from Committees*, 1803, xii, *Parliamentary Papers*, 1822, xvii (2) and T. H. B. Oldfield, *History
of the Boroughs of Great Britain*, 1792.
[5] For example: Bristol (175 customs officers: 6000 electors); Cardigan (12: 1200);
Colchester (16: 1400); Dover (62: 1200); Exeter (46: 1200); Gloucester (13: 3000);
Lancaster (42: 1800); Liverpool (336: 2300); Newcastle (96: 2500); Shoreham
(23: 1200).
[6] They were: Beaumaris (65 customs officers: 24 electors); Dartmouth (35: 20);
Fowey (49: 63); Harwich (26: 32); Hastings (31: 12); Lyme Regis (20: 31); New
Romney (30: 8); Newport (7: 24); Rye (61: 6); Scarborough (14: 38); Winchelsea
(9: 6).
Of these, Harwich, Hastings, Rye, Scarborough and Winchelsea are noted both by

boroughs, where a large proportion of the electorate held or could have held revenue offices, Crewe's Act had its greatest effect. Many of them were old and no longer active sea-ports. Their inactivity and their small electorate probably provided adequate safeguards against Crewe's Act. The Act reduced the electorate in all the boroughs that it affected, and in these boroughs it was reduced to a handful. In some cases this was probably a help rather than a hindrance to corruption.[1] Moreover, the fact that voters were now debarred from revenue office did not mean that they were excluded from influence. For their relatives and friends might be given office, or they themselves might be turned into government beneficiaries by being given a share in the income of some of the disfranchised placemen. At Hastings and Rye, for example, new voters were billeted upon the disfranchised revenue officers to whose votes they had succeeded.[2] At Harwich, as late as 1803, certain voters were found to be in receipt of annuities from revenue officers and an attempt to invalidate their votes on this ground failed.[3]

It is therefore not surprising to find that, while the number of government boroughs did decline towards the end of the eighteenth century, the list of lost boroughs bears little relation to the list of boroughs seriously affected by Crewe's Act, many of which were among the safest of government boroughs in the early nineteenth century.[4] Even the one or two boroughs which appear on both lists—for example, Harwich and Portsmouth—cannot be said to have been lost as a result of Crewe's Act, and Harwich was only lost

Robinson and by Oldfield as affected by Crewe's Act. Oldfield also notes that Dartmouth, New Romney and Newport were affected. In some cases Oldfield gives the numbers disfranchised: Dartmouth, 20; Hastings, 31; New Romney, 30; Newport, 36; Rye, 25; Scarborough, 8; Winchelsea, 9. He adds figures for several Cornish boroughs: Bossiney (10 disfranchised out of an electorate of 11); Newport (36 out of 60); West Looe (10 out of 60); Helston (34 out of 70); Saint Germains (30 out of 50).

Of the boroughs listed above, nine were corporation boroughs (Beaumaris, Dartmouth, Harwich, Hastings, Lyme Regis, Newport (Isle of Wight), Scarborough, West Looe, and Helston). In three (New Romsey, Rye, Saint Germains) the franchise belonged to the freemen; in two (Winchelsea and Bossiney) it belonged to freemen and freeholders; Newport (Cornwall) was a burgage borough and Fowey an open borough. (Halévy, *Histoire du Peuple Anglais au XIXe siecle,* i. 121–36; Oldfield, *History of the Boroughs, passim.*)

[1] We should expect this. But I have only found one contemporary criticism of the bill on the grounds that it would make smaller an electorate which was already only a small proportion of the population. This was made by Mr. Fitzgibbon and Sir Lucius O'Brien in the Irish house of commons. (*Parliamentary Debates of Ireland* (1784), i. 401.)

[2] Oldfield, *History of the Boroughs,* iii. 30, 73.

[3] R. H. Peckwell, *Cases of Controverted Elections in the second Parliament of the United Kingdom,* 1802 (1805), i. 397–400.

[4] In 1761 there were about thirty-two seats ' under more or less immediate government influence ' (Namier, *Structure of Politics at the Accession of George III,* i. 170–5); in 1792 about twenty-six (Report on the State of Representation, 1792, compiled by the Society of the Friends of the People, printed in *Annual Register,* 1793, pp. 94–7; Oldfield, *History of the Boroughs, passim*) ; in 1810 about fourteen (Oldfield, *Representative History of Great Britain,* 1817, iv. 416; *The Englishman's Mirror,* 1800.)

temporarily.   This I think provides the confirmation of my suggestion that Crewe's Act did not achieve its object.   Far from being
' the most telling blow ever administered to government influence at
elections ',[1] it affected few boroughs and even those it does not seem
to have freed from government influence.   On the contrary, there
is every reason to endorse Oldfield's verdict that the Act did not
strike ' at the evil . . . which it was meant to remedy '.[2]

BETTY KEMP.

[1] Lecky, *History of England in the Eighteenth Century*, v. 143.
[2] Oldfield, *History of the Boroughs*, iii. 262.

Some Eighteenth Century Civil Servants: The English Revenue Commissioners, 1754-98

DESPITE all the research of the last twenty years into British administration in the eighteenth century very little attention has yet been given to the personnel of the senior offices on whom, then as now, much depended. Until the end of the century the formal structure and duties of the revenue boards changed little, yet between 1700 and 1800 not only their efficiency and attitude to work but also their role in the constitutional mechanism altered greatly. This paper seeks to discuss some of these changes in the light of the personnel of the boards, whose importance was increased by the absence of administrative policy on the part of the Government. The Scottish and Irish boards have been excluded, as they were subject to special local influences. With the accession of the duke of Newcastle as First Lord of the Treasury in 1754 the administrative traditions of the age of Godolphin which, though much attenuated, had survived under Walpole and Henry Pelham, seemed to be submerged. The year 1798 which saw the Tax Office reorganized to deal with the new income tax, the Salt Board abolished, and many lesser changes brought about under pressure from the Select Committee on Finance of 1797, offers a convenient vantage point for summarizing the changes made since economical reform became a live issue. These, therefore, are the terminal dates of the study. Two English revenue boards have been excluded from the survey, the Wine Licence Office which, being abolished in 1757, hardly belongs to this period, and the Hawkers and Pedlars Office since, unlike the others, it was not a patent office, and in any case was less like a working revenue board than a sinecure. In 1724 the Treasury Lords were scandalized at ' the loose and unaccountable doings of the Commissioners for . . . Hawkers and Pedlars who have suffered the income thereof for at least two years together to be wholly embezzled '.[1] In 1763 the commissioners were ' meeting but at one season of the year, about midsummer ', they all resided far from London, and left the work of

---

[1] P[ublic] R[ecord] O[ffice], T. 27/23, fo. 451.

the office to the solicitor, Mr. Cracherode, an old schoolfellow of Bute and Dashwood.[1] In 1797 the commissioners' attendance still consisted mainly of daily meetings in June, and was dismissed by the Select Committee as 'very inconsiderable'.[2]

The official duties of most of the boards, the Customs,[3] Excise, Salt,[4] Taxes,[5] Stamps,[6] have been previously studied; the business of the Hackney Coach Office was 'to regulate and license Hackney Coaches and Chairs, within the Cities of London and Westminster, Suburbs of the same, and the parishes comprised within the weekly Bills of Mortality'.[7] It was therefore an office which not only raised a revenue in 1777 exceeding £13,000 per annum [8] and in 1797 exceeding £26,000,[9] but exercised a police power over hackney coachmen,[10] and to safeguard its revenue sought to protect its licensees from competition.[11]

In the middle of the eighteenth century there were few public issues on which politicians could take a stand in advance, and men entered politics mainly for private purposes. By 1754 a comparable situation obtained in the revenue administration. Because the Government was able to borrow so freely, and the whole cost of war was not immediately borne by the taxes, the fiscal structure haphazardly created at the end of the seventeenth, endured till the end of the eighteenth century. In the fiscal administration, therefore, the tendencies of the system of influence to discourage politicians from pursuing an active policy were strengthened by the ease and cheapness of public borrowing. As it was, new taxes could be contentious enough, and successive Governments were glad to postpone any fundamental alterations in the revenue system. Much of the annual revenue, moreover, went to service the national debt, and since the public creditors were a normally contented body, there was by 1754 little inducement to secure the maximum efficiency in tax collection.[12] As therefore neither fiscal nor administrative policy was of much account in the middle of the century, private purposes had full sway.

[1] British Museum, Add. MSS. 38335, fo. 60.

[2] *10th Report of the Select Committee on Finance 1797*, reprinted in *Reports from Committees of the House of Commons* (London, 1803) (cited *infra* as *Commons Reports*), xii. 257, 259.

[3] E. E. Hoon, *The Organisation of the English Customs System 1696-1786* (New York, 1938).

[4] E. Hughes, *Studies in Administration and Finance 1558-1825* (Manchester, 1934).

[5] W. R. Ward, 'The Office for Taxes 1666-1798', *Bulletin of the Institute of Historical Research*, 1952.

[6] E. Hughes, 'The English Stamp Duties 1664-1764', *ante*, lvi. 234-64.

[7] *Commons Reports*, xii. 261.

[8] C[ommons] J[ournals], xxxviii. 154.

[9] *Commons Reports*, xii. 263.

[10] *Ibid.* 63, 261-2.   [11] C[alendar of] T[reasury] B[ooks and] P[apers], i. 24-5, 35.

[12] For the Government's attitude to the land tax, which was a tax free for the service of the year, see my book, *The English Land Tax in the Eighteenth Century* (London, 1953).

The Government had three chief interests of a ' private ' nature in the revenue administration. Firstly, since the revenue commissionerships were incompatible with a seat in parliament, to appoint sitting members to them was a useful, if expensive, means of securing a vacancy in the House. In 1756, for example, James West considered that ' probably Mr. [Henry] Bankes would give the nomination for Corfe Castle ' for a vacancy in the office of the Second Justice of Chester,[1] but by 1762 Bankes had bargained successfully for a lucrative place on the Customs Board, partly through the influence of Charles Jenkinson to whom he was distantly related.[2] Again in 1780 the king and Lord North determined to move Charles Garth to the Excise Board, for it would be ' useful to have his seat vacated '.[3] The Government also sought to use its patronage to gain political support, sometimes as part of a bargain with a faction leader, occasionally more directly, as when in 1781, by the influence of Lord North, the £300 pension which had been given to Richard Tickell in 1779 to write against ' the Opposition at home, chiefly the Shelburnites ', was exchanged for a place at the Stamp Board.[4] Then thirdly, in the revenue administration as in the church, provision must be made for members of the political nation who were alleged to be in need. Wardel George Westby, for example, had to sell the Ravenfield property in Yorkshire which his family had held for generations, and take refuge on the Customs Board in 1731; the plight of Henry Poole and his father, two of Newcastle's relations who were ' starving ' after the loss of their Minorca place in the Seven Years' War, is well known. Poole's distress was alleviated first by a pension and the sinecure place of Paymaster of Exchequer Bills,[5] then by a seat at the Excise Board.[6] But the need for effective administrators was never quite overlooked. Even in the jobbery of his last appointments, Newcastle appointed Henry Reade[7] to the Taxes Board, though he might not have done so had not Reade been tutor to Lord Lincoln's children.[8]

Both George III and the aristocracy had an interest in the revenue administration. Several commissioners were royal servants;[9] more

[1] L. B. Namier, *The Structure of Politics at the Accession of George III* (London, 1929), i. 55.

[2] Brit. Mus. Add. MSS. 38200, fo. 123: N. S. Jucker, *Jenkinson Papers* (London 1949), p. 64.

[3] J. Fortescue, *Corr[espondence of King] Geo[rge] III* (London, 1927–8), v. 154.

[4] Windsor Castle Archives: Secret Service Accounts, January to April, 1779, p. 16; J. H. Jesse, *George Selwyn and his Contemporaries* (London, 1843–4), iv. 162; *Journal and Correspondence of Lord Auckland* (London, 1861–2), iii. 159, 164.

[5] P.R.O. T. 54/37, fos. 70-1.

[6] Namier, *Structure*, i. 269, 272–3, 286–7; ii. 548; Brit. Mus. Add. MSS. 32884, fo. 308: 32886, fo. 356: 32909, fos. 382, 391–2.

[7] On whom see my article on ' The administration of the window and assessed taxes 1696–1798 ', *ante*, lxvii. 532.

[8] Brit. Mus. Add. MSS. 33067, fo. 126.   [9] See Table IV. below.

were sons of peers, such as John and Henry Fane, sons of the 8th earl of Westmorland (in the Tax and Salt Offices), John Byng, second son of the 3rd Viscount Torrington (in the Stamp Office), or Augustus Phipps, fourth son of the 1st Baron Mulgrave (in the Excise Office), not to mention a host of more distant relatives. Peers and leading politicians also sought provision for other dependents, and especially amanuenses and men of business. Thus Joah Bates, Lord Sandwich's old tutor, later his private secretary, and a well known conductor of music, was installed at the Victualling and Customs Boards;[1] Thomas Nuthall, the elder Pitt's solicitor and confidant,[2] and later Maurice Morgann, secretary to Lord Shelburne, came into the Hackney Coach Office, and Thomas Allan, North's private secretary and adviser on Irish matters, was made a Customs Commissioner.[3] Political friends of peers had also to be accommodated, such as Henry Vernon, M.P., a friend of Gower and relative of Bedford,[4] and Marmaduke Gwynne, the brother of Howell Gwynne, M.P. for Co. Radnor, who was supported by Lord Powis.[5] Perhaps the most extraordinary appointment in this class (and one which aroused curiosity at the time) [6] was that of Henry Grenville who was made a Customs Commissioner by his brother George, as this ' would oblige him to vacate his seat in Parliament, [and] . . . exempt him from involving himself in the unhappy differences in his own family '.[7]

Lower in the social scale, the legal profession and the gentry were also interested in the commissionerships. Firstly, they, and particularly the lawyers, desired a secure income which, apart from official stipends, was not acquired as easily then as a century later. As late as 1813 Augustus Cavendish Bradshaw applied for a place at the Customs Board, confessing ' a situation of that kind wd. be a provision for me for life ',[8] and at least two prominent politicians of limited means, Jenkinson [9] and Burke,[10] almost entered the revenue boards in their early days. Revenue commissionerships were applied for on a number of occasions as a marriage provision. Beaumont Hotham, the second son of Sir Charles Hotham, whose promising career in the firm of Chitty of Amsterdam ended when

[1] *Hist. MSS. Comm. Rutland MSS.* iii. 232.

[2] Brit. Mus. Add. MSS. 38335, fo. 62.

[3] *Beresford Correspondence*, ed. W. Beresford (London, 1854), i. pp. vii, x. 97–8, 118–19; *Corr. Geo. III*, iii. 33, 386.

[4] *Bedford Correspondence*, ed. Lord John Russell (London, 1842–6), ii. 222, 230–4; iii. 358–60; Brit. Mus. Add. MSS. 32930, fo. 37; P. C. Yorke, *Life and Correspondence of Lord Hardwicke* (Cambridge, 1913), iii. 440.

[5] Brit. Mus. Add. MSS. 32861, fos. 312, 316.

[6] *Hist. MSS. Comm. 10th Report App. pt. i (Weston Underwood MSS.)*, p. 388.

[7] *Grenville Papers*, ed. W. J. Smith (London, 1852–3), iii. 117–18, 191–2.

[8] *A. Aspinall, Corr[espondence of King] Geo[rge] IV* (Cambridge, 1938), i. 233.

[9] *Grenville Papers*, i. 277.

[10] *Diary and Correspondence of Lord Colchester* (London, 1861), i. 38.

the company collapsed in the South Sea Bubble, sought and obtained a Customs Commissionership first in Scotland and then in England to enable him to marry.[1]   Barne Barne in 1788 applied for a place for the same purpose, and being kept waiting lived out his days a bachelor.[2]   But perhaps the majority resembled the anonymous applicant to Newcastle for a Commissionership of Taxes who was ' desirous of having some genteel employ in this county '.[3] ' Genteel employ ' was a powerful bait to both squire and lawyer.

Finally there were the professional civil servants themselves. Their main interest was naturally in permanence of tenure, but the more important officials such as under-secretaries of state regarded places on the boards as retirement pensions.   William Knox, indeed, complained bitterly that he ' was denied common justice ' by being refused when other under-secretaries such as John Pownall, Stanier Porten, and Claudius Amyand, besides diplomats such as William Cayley and Sir Alexander Munro, were appointed to revenue boards.[4]   Nor were civil servants alone in regarding these places as an insurance against infirmity.[5]

In the middle of the eighteenth century there were few checks upon this play of private interest.   No formal qualifications for appointment were demanded, and only momentary indignation because ' Sussex people are too fond of *sinecures* ' caused Newcastle to see that Henry Poole received some instruction on his appointment in 1760.[6]   There were informal age limits in the more lucrative offices, and William Mellish hesitated in applying to pass his excise place on to his son of ' between 22 & 23 years . . . which I own is very young '.[7]   But even this limitation did not apply to less valuable places at the Hackney Coach Board where young men of this age were often appointed.   The main limitation on the First Lord of the Treasury in disposing of these places was the king.   George II was furious when in 1758 Newcastle presented the prince of Wales's demand for the preferment of George Lewis Scott his sub-preceptor (though he finally agreed)[8] and both Newcastle and Grenville took it as a sure sign of loss of royal confidence when George III deferred dealing with revenue appointments, saying ' he would think of it '.[9]   North also informed the king fully of all the circumstances before seeking his consent to new appointments.[10]

[1] A. M. W. Stirling, *The Hothams* (London, 1918), pp. 281-8; *C.T.B.P.* v. 77.
[2] P.R.O. 30/8/111.   [3] Brit. Mus. Add. MSS. 32928, fo. 340.
[4] *Hist. MSS. Comm. Various MSS.* vi. 183, 197.   [5] Namier, *Structure*, i. 27-8.
[6] Brit. Mus. Add. MSS. 32911, fo. 441; 32912, fos. 191, 233, 279.
[7] Brit. Mus. Add. MSS. 32900, fo. 309.
[8] Brit. Mus. Add. MSS. 32877, fo. 350.
[9] Brit. Mus. Add. MSS. 32938, fo. 365; R. Sedgwick, *Correspondence of George III and Lord Bute* (London, 1939), p. 107; *Grenville Papers*, iii. 205, 207.
[10] Brit. Mus. Add. MSS. 37833, fo. 67.

Such then were the motives which led men to influence revenue appointments. The outcome of this wire-pulling is illustrated in the following tables. Classifications of this kind add precision to a purely impressionistic account of the personnel, but it is notoriously difficult to adopt useful categories and at the same time justify every individual classification under them. Thus the majority of commissioners owed appointment to their family interest, or to introduction by influential patrons. Many of the former had rendered some political service in return for their appointment, but the latter were normally quite unpolitical, and benefited from a compliment paid to the patron. This large class may usefully be subdivided, though in some cases this second qualification is difficult. There is a clear distinction between the members or connexions of the great political clans such as the Cavendishes, Grenvilles, and Pelhams, and families which profited from local electoral strength in parliamentary boroughs, such as the Bullers and Bonds. But the distinction is not so easy to establish in other cases. Thus Sir Joseph Pennington has been included in the former group by virtue of his intimate connexion with the Lowther family who at the time of his appointment connected themselves by marriage with Bute, then at the height of his power. On the other hand, although George Whitmore owed his appointment largely to the pressure of Lord Powis, who had made himself into a political figure of consequence, he is classified with the latter group on the ground that the enduring political strength of his family lay in their influence at Bridgenorth. Thus the sub-divisions of Table I cannot be regarded as completely exclusive.

TABLE I. FAMILY INTEREST AND INFLUENTIAL INTRODUCTION

A. Members or connexions of aristocratic and important political families

Commissioner	Board Customs	Connexions
Welbore Ellis Agar	1776–1805	Apptd. through his uncle Welbore Ellis, later Lord Mendip.[1]
Richard Cavendish	1737–61	Married the niece of the 1st duke of Devonshire.
Henry Grenville	1765–6	Apptd. through his brother George Grenville.
James Jeffreys	1766–86	Apptd. through his stepson the duke of Grafton.[2]
Sir Wm. Musgrave	1763–85	Son of 4th Bt. of Haytor Castle; managed the electoral interest of his stepson Lord Carlisle.[3]
Henry Pelham	1765–88	Apptd. through his 'near relation' Newcastle.
Sir Jo. Pennington	1763–9	Family connexions with the Lowthers.

[1] Brit. Mus. Add. MSS. 37833, fos. 67, 71.
[2] Brit. Mus. Add. MSS. 32915, fo. 43; 32934, fos. 299, 365.
[3] *Hist. MSS. Comm. Carlisle MSS.* pp. 213–43.

TABLE I (*Contd.*)

Commissioner	Board Excise	Connexions
Thomas Bowlby	1762–6	Apptd. through the Brudenell family with whom he was connected by his marriage with daughter of 3rd earl of Cardigan.
Timothy Caswell	1789–1802	Former deputy Paymaster to Rigby; later a parliamentary supporter of Pitt.
George Jas. Cholmondeley	1782–1801	Grandson of 3rd earl of Cholmondeley; great nephew of Horace Walpole.
Thomas Farrington	1756–8	Uncle of 2nd Viscount Townshend; supported by Thomas Townshend, M.P.
Heneage Legge	1776–82	Apptd. through his cousin the 2nd earl of Dartmouth.[1]
Anthony Lucas	1767–89	Political connexion of Calcraft and Rutland.
John Luttrell Olmius, 3rd earl of Carhampton	1785–1825	A parliamentary supporter of Fox who concluded a bargain with Pitt.
David Papillon, jnr.	1754–90	Succeeded his father by influence of Hardwicke, with whose family he was long intimate.[2]
Augustus Phipps	1792–1826	Son of 1st Baron Mulgrave.
Sir Henry Poole	1760–3, 1765–7	Related through his mother to the Pelham family.
Henry Vernon	1763–5	Related to Bedford, a friend of Gower.[3]
James Vernon	1710–26, 1728–56	By influence of his father, the secretary of state, with Shrewsbury.[4]

Stamps

John Byng	1781–99	2nd son of 3rd Visct. Torrington; he died 5th Visct.
George Jas. Cholmondeley	1781–2	*Vide supra.*
Marmaduke Gwynne	1763–5	Through his brother Howell Gwynne, M.P. and Powis.
Charles Mellish	1793–6	A political connexion of the 2nd duke of Newcastle.[5]
Richard Shelley	1729–55	Nephew of 1st duke of Newcastle.
William R. Spencer	1797–1826	Grandson of 2nd, nephew of 3rd, duke of Marlborough.

Taxes

John Fane	1756–63	Eldest son of 8th earl of Westmorland.
Thomas Windham	1762–77	By influence of his uncle, Lord Melcombe.[6]

Salt

W. A. S. Boscawen	1792–8	Junior branch of the Boscawens, Lords Falmouth.
Henry Fane	1763–71	2nd son of 8th earl of Westmorland.[7]
Sir Richard Gamon	1784	Previously secretary to the Board; marriage connexions with Grafton, Southampton, Chandos, and Jeffreys *supra*.
John Milbanke	1753–66	' Put in by the D. of N. at the request of Mr. Tho. Pelham whose tutor he was abroad ';[8] brother-in-law of Rockingham.

[1] Brit. Mus. Add. MSS. 37833, fos. 67, 71.   [2] Brit. Mus. Add. MSS. 38335, fo. 49.
[3] Yorke, *Hardwicke*, iii. 440.   [4] Brit. Mus. Add. MSS. 40794, fo. 3.
[5] W. T. Laprade, *Parliamentary Papers of John Robinson* (Camden Soc. 1922), p. 43
[6] Brit. Mus. Add. MSS. 32924, fo. 51.   [7] Brit. Mus. Add. MSS. 34713, fo. 122.
[8] Brit. Mus. Add. MSS. 38335, fo. 53.

TABLE I (*Contd.*)

Commissioner	Board	Connexions
	Salt	
Denzil Onslow	1756–65	Apptd. through his cousin the Speaker.[1]
Henry Talbot	1733–84	Younger brother of Lord Chancellor Talbot.
	Hackney Coaches	
Jacob Reynardson	1775–1811	Son-in-law of Speaker Cust; brother-in-law of Baron Brownlow.

B. Consolation prizes to M.P.s who lost their seats

	Customs	
John Frederick	1761–82	A parliamentary supporter of Newcastle, defeated at West Looe, 1761.
	Excise	
William Burton	1737–82	Former parliamentary supporter of Walpole.
John Orlebar	1738–65	Lost his seat contesting co. Beds. on behalf of Bedford and Walpole.[2]

C. Members of families important for local political influence

	Customs	
John Buller	1797–1823	Of the Bullers of Looe.
Sir John Evelyn	1721–63	Family influence in Surrey; marriage connexions with the Boscawen and Godolphin families.
Beaumont Hotham	1728–63	Son of Sir Charles Hotham, Bt.
William Levinz	1747–63	Apptd. through the duke of Leeds;[3] also supported Newcastle in parliament and Notts.
Francis F. Luttrell	1793–1819	Family influence at Minehead.
Gwyn Vaughan	1728–41, 1744–58	Son of William Gwyn Vaughan, M.P.
	Excise	
John Buller	1790–3	Of the Bullers of Looe; also supported by his uncle, Lord Bathurst. [4]
William Burrell	1774–90	Son of Peter Burrell; son-in-law of Sir Charles Raymond.
Frederick Frankland	1753–63	Family influence at Thirsk; his daughter married Thomas Pelham of Stanmer.
Richard (Bagot) Howard	1765–74	Apptd. through his father, Sir Walter Wagstaffe Bagot, M.P.[5]
Robert Nicholas	1790–1822	Son-in-law of Sir Thomas Frankland of Thirsk.
Charles Polhill	1726–55	Brother of David Polhill, M.P. who married the sister of Newcastle and Henry Pelham.
John Plumptre	1739–54	Influence in Notts. where his father was a great friend of Newcastle.
Edward Tucker	1763–4	Family influence at Weymouth.
George Whitmore	1755–63, 1765–75	Supported by Powis; influence at Bridge-north.

[1] *Hist. MSS. Comm. 9th Report App. pt. xiv (Onslow MSS.)* p. 503.
[2] F. St. J. Orlebar, *Orlebar Chronicles* (London, 1930), p. 320.
[3] Brit. Mus. Add MSS. 32711, fo. 258.
[4] *Hist. MSS. Comm. Abergavenny MSS.* p. 51.   [5] Cf. Jucker, *op. cit.*, p. 97.

TABLE I (*Contd.*)

Commissioner	Board	Connexions
	Taxes	
Barne Barne	1791–1820	Family influence at Dunwich.
John Bromfield	1724–55	Brother-in-law of George Trenchard, M.P. who controlled a seat at Poole.
Charles Deering	1769–98	Apptd. through his brother Sir Edward Deering, M.P.[1]
John Eames	1773–95	Political influence in the Isle of Wight.
Richard Frankland	1749–61	Family influence at Thirsk.
Francis F. Luttrell	1783–93	*Vide supra.*
Alexander Popham	1783–4	A parliamentary supporter of Fox.
John Trenchard	1755–98	Apptd. for giving Sir Richard Lyttelton the family interest at Poole.[2]
Edward Tucker	1767–9	*Vide supra.*
	Salt	
Edward Astley	1722–63	Grandson of Sir Jacob Astley, M.P.
Joshua Churchill	1742–73	Nephew of Awnsham Churchill, M.P. and Joseph Damer, M.P.
Sir John Gresham	1763–85	Son-in-law of Sir Kenrick Clayton, M.P.
	Hackney Coaches	
Thomas Bond	1741–62	Family influence at Corfe Castle.
Nathaniel Templeman	1762–74	By purchase from Thomas Bond;[3] family influence in Dorchester.

D. Men with no political influence appointed by influential introduction

	Customs	
Wardel George Westby	1731–56	Apptd. by the interest of the duke of Norfolk.[4]
John Windham Bowyer	1750–80	Apptd. through the duke of Cumberland, to whom his brother was Paymaster in 1745.[5]
Augustine Earle	1740–62	A Norfolk connexion of the Walpoles.[6]
William Lowndes	1772–1808	Through his father Charles Lowndes, M.P.[7]
Martin Whish	1781–1818	Tutor at King's College, Cambridge, to Lord John Clinton.
	Stamps	
James Bindley	1764–1818	Negotiated by his brother John on retiring from Excise Board.
Sir James Calder	1763–4	At Groningen with Bute.[8]
Everard Fawkener	1783–1803	Through his brother William and Lord Carlisle.
John Kenrick	1762–3, 1765–81	Through Nathaniel Ryder, M.P.[9]

[1] Brit. Mus. Add. MSS. 34713, fo. 117.
[2] Brit. Mus. Add. MSS. 32737, fo. 55; 38335, fo. 55.
[3] Brit. Mus. Add. MSS. 38335, fo. 62.   [4] *Genealogist*, n.s. xiii. 263.
[5] *C.T.B.P.* v. 830; Brit. Mus. Add. MSS. 38335, fo. 49. John Windham took the name of Bowyer after his marriage with his cousin Mary Windham, the great-granddaughter of Sir Edmund Bowyer, Kt.
[6] Brit. Mus. Add. MSS. 32737, fo. 212; 32854, fos. 72, 74.
[7] *Hist. MSS. Comm. 10th Report App. pt. i* (*Weston Underwood MSS.*), p. 407; *Correspondence of Edmund Burke*, ed. Earl Fitzwilliam and Sir Richard Bourke (London, 1844), i. 137.
[8] Brit. Mus. Add. MSS. 32967, fo. 456.   [9] Brit. Mus. Add. MSS. 38335, fo. 58.

TABLE I (*Contd.*)

Commissioner	Board	Connexions
	Stamps	
Matthew Kenrick	1737–62	
Robert Thompson	1754–65	By influence of Sir Kenrick Clayton, M.P.[1]
Richard Tickell	1781–93	A government scribbler put in by Lord North.
William Waller	1775–86	Attorney to Warren Hastings.[2]
Martin Whish	1778–81	*Vide supra.*
	Taxes	
John Farnaby	1789–98	3rd son of Sir Thomas Farnaby, Bt.; brother-in-law of Charles Deering *supra.*
George Heathcote	1778–98	Son of Sir Thomas Heathcote, Bt.
Christopher Rigby	1744–63, 1765–83	' By the interest of Mr. Medlicott his predecessor with . . . Lord Halifax.'[3]
	Salt	
Thomas Sutton	1741–56	At Westminster School with Newcastle.[4]
Oliver Tilson	1766–88	Probably connected with Christopher Tilson, the Treasury clerk.
	Hackney Coaches	
William Douglas	1782–1817	A charitable return for the requisitioning of his Portsmouth estate for fortification.[5]
William Gallop	1756–8	Appointed through Sir Jacob Downing, M.P.[6]
John Philpot	1728–56	Possibly a professional connexion of Jas. West.[7]
William Morton Pleydell	1777–82	An old friend of Lord North.[8]
Thomas Sutton	1725–41	*Vide supra.*

Group A contains many of the names of the great political clans of the eighteenth century and their connexions. Thus Richard Cavendish was the son of Edward Chandler, a bishop of Durham notorious for his nepotism. He married Elizabeth, daughter of Lord James Cavendish, and his sister married Elizabeth's brother Richard. In 1752 he took the name of Cavendish, and in 1761 the duke of Devonshire who had brought him into the Customs Office, now secured his election to parliament and demanded a large pension for him.[9] David Papillon, junior, succeeded his father at the Excise Board by the influence of Lord Hardwicke, who had been on intimate terms with 'old Pap' since their schooldays,[10] an intimacy which warrants Papillon's inclusion in group A rather than group D. Most of these appointments were of a charitable nature, and Cholmondeley, Legge, Boscawen, and Spencer who

[1] Brit. Mus. Add. MSS. 38335, fo. 58.
[2] Brit. Mus. Add. MSS. 29133–4; 29136; 29140–6 *passim.*
[3] Brit. Mus. Add. MSS. 38335, fo. 55.   [4] Brit. Mus. Add. MSS. 32861, fo. 387.
[5] *Corr. Geo. III*, v. 414.   [6] Brit. Mus. Add. MSS. 32865, fo. 118.
[7] Brit. Mus. Add. MSS. 34733, fo. 170.   [8] *Corr. Geo. III.* v. 414.
[9] Namier, *Structure*, i. 269, 272, 273; ii. 574. Devonshire as First Lord had granted him the reversion of the office of Auditor of Excise in 1757.
[10] Brit. Mus. Add. MSS. 38335, fo. 49.

suffered from ' a natural, constitutional indolence [which] governed him with irresistible sway ',[1] all represented the impoverished junior branches of wealthy families. Timothy Caswell, however, had been hunting places even before he entered parliament in 1761,[2] and after acting as deputy Paymaster of the Forces to the notorious Rigby 1768–82, he approved himself to the younger Pitt by steadily voting for the Government; Anthony Lucas managed Calcraft's interest at Wareham in the 'eighties,[3] and was on good terms with the elder Calcraft's patron, the duke of Rutland and his family, who expected him to mollify John Mortlock at Cambridge by favours at the Excise Board.[4] It is not surprising that the most highly paid boards were much sought after by aristocratic families, and there were examples of shameless jobbery. Thomas Farrington, for example, an uncle of the second Lord Townshend, entered the Excise Board after a quarrel over patronage between Henry Fox and the Townshend clan in 1755–6.[5] Denzil Onslow followed two relatives as Receiver General of the Post Office (1727–40),[6] then moved into the family seat at Guildford (1740–7), being later prosecuted by the Attorney General for not completing his accounts;[7] he was next provided for as Paymaster of the Board of Works (1743), and finally made a Salt Commissioner solely because the Paymastership was required for another.[8] Moreover, of the whole group only two commissioners, Sir William Musgrave and Thomas Bowlby, revealed any evidence of administrative ability; Bowlby had a good record at the Excise Board, was later the first Comptroller of Army Accounts for generations to try to put his office in order,[9] and although in 1780 the Commons defeated North's determined attempt to appoint him, a placeman, to the commission for examining the public accounts, he was well spoken of all round the House.[10]

Besides the three members of parliament of Group B who were compensated for the loss of their seats, and the eight of Table II, twenty-five former M.P.s were appointed to the Boards in this period, mostly classified in groups A and C. In the latter group were represented many families with a well entrenched local electoral interest. There were the two John Bullers of the celebrated electioneering family of Looe; there was Thomas Bond whose brother sat for Corfe Castle for many years, and whose family controlled one seat there. Edward Tucker's family was influential

[1] *Annual Biography and Obituary*, xix. 457.

[2] Brit. Mus. Add. MSS. 32912, fo. 387; 32914, fo. 56.

[3] Laprade, *Parliamentary Papers of John Robinson*, p. 86.

[4] *Hist. MSS. Comm. Rutland MSS.* iii. 13, 115.

[5] Brit. Mus. Add. MSS. 32861, fos. 96, 477; 32862, fo. 181; 32863, fos. 203, 263, 384.

[6] *Hist. MSS. Comm. 9th Report App. pt. xiv (Onslow MSS.)*, p. 503.

[7] *C.T.B.P.* v. 73. [8] Brit. Mus. Add. MSS. 38335, fo. 53.

[9] P.R.O. 30/8/231. [10] W. Cobbett, *Parliamentary History*, xxi. 554.

at Weymouth, which borough his uncle John represented 1735–47 and 1754–78,[1] and it was to placate disputes between John Tucker and Lord Melcombe at Weymouth, that Edward was appointed Stamp Commissioner.[2] The two Franklands with their connexion Nicholas, represented the family which controlled Thirsk, and between 1747 and the abolition of the seat in 1832, there were few years in which Dunwich was not represented by some member of the Barne family of Sotterly. Again, although Burrell and Eames were barristers of some note, the administrative record of this group is totally mediocre.

Group D is composed partly of men such as Westby and Calder [3] who had proved financially unable to sustain a political interest, but mainly of men who could never offer political services in return for a stipend, and profited by some connexion with the influential. Thus Martin Whish had been tutor to Lord John Clinton at Cambridge, and Thomas Sutton was a school-friend of Newcastle. John Farnaby, the third son of a Kent baronet, entered the Tax Office after his regiment had been disbanded in 1787. Group D, like the whole of Table I, consisted mainly of charitable appointments, but even in Newcastle's time charity could not be dispensed entirely regardless of the public interest; even Henry Poole was uncomfortable, but hoped ' our case is so singularly unfortunate that it could not be taken ill by anybody '.[4] The limits to charity were drawn tighter as time proceeded, and even in the middle of the century some officers with a good reputation were appointed in this table, such as Robert Thompson, who spent all his life in office, and James Bindley, a celebrated collector of books, prints, and medals. He assisted Malone in correcting the *Life of Johnson* after the death of his friend Boswell,[5] helped Nichols with his *Illustrations*, and Bray with the publication of Evelyn's *Diary*. Bindley had a name for hard work,[6] and produced a *Collection of the statutes now in force relating to the stamp duties* in 1775.

The next group of commissioners consists of those members of parliament appointed solely or mainly with a view to vacating their seats.

Most of these members moved out to enable the Government to bring in a friend (as Edward Hooper took office ' to vacate a seat for Sir Thomas Robinson '), but Mortlock's appointment was probably to get rid of a nuisance. He was reprimanded by the House in 1786 for altering the names in a bill appointing land tax commissioners while it was in the Ingrossing Office, to keep his

---

[1] Brit. Mus. Add. MSS. 38335, fo. 60; 32909. fo. 88.
[2] *Grenville Papers*, i. 448–9.   [3] Brit. Mus. Add. MSS. 32917, fos. 294–7.
[4] Brit. Mus. Add. MSS. 32877, fo. 128.
[5] J. Nichols, *Illustrations of the Literary History of the XVIIIth Century* (London, 1817–58), v. 457; Brit. Mus. Add. MSS. 34567, fo. 396.
[6] *Gent[leman's] Mag[azine]*, 1818, ii. 280.

TABLE II. APPOINTMENTS MADE TO VACATE PARLIAMENTARY SEATS

Commissioner	Board	Connexions
	Customs	
Henry Bankes	1762–76	His family controlled one seat at Corfe Castle.
William Hey	1776–97	Introduced by the Yorkes.
Edward Hooper	1748–93	A well known adherent of Lord Granville.[1]
	Excise	
Charles Garth	1780–4	A parliamentary supporter of North as his father had been of Newcastle.[2]
William Mellish	1751–60	A supporter of Pelham and Newcastle in Nottinghamshire and parliament.
David Papillon, snr.	1742–54	At Morland's School, Bethnal Green, with Hardwicke.[3]
	Taxes	
Daniel Bull	1763–91	Apptd. to give Shelburne vacant possession of the borough of Calne.
	Salt	
John Mortlock	1789–98	Personal influence at Cambridge; supported by Rutland.

opponents off the commission; Pitt had him censured and would have had him expelled at once had not Mortlock and Rutland rallied sufficient voting strength. But Mortlock was an ally beyond Rutland's control, and it may well have been the promise of the first vacant commissionership (to which he was appointed in the following year) that persuaded him to resign from parliament in 1788.[4] Daniel Bull [5] and William Hey were concerned only to oblige the Government by keeping a seat warm till the Government obliged them with a place; the latter indeed ' strenuously pressed for one of the Commissioners of Excise or Customs ',[6] and proved probably the most slothful commissioner of the whole century. William Mellish withdrew from parliament to provide a seat for Newcastle's kinsman, John Shelley, and during the Seven Years' War regularly advised the duke on matters of administration and finance. From 1758 he was shrinking from being made Secretary of the Treasury, an office he endured for a few weeks in 1765, but despite this timidity was probably the ablest of the group.

Very important in eighteenth century politics were the men of business, and they too received their reward on the revenue boards.

[1] *Letters of Horace Walpole*, ed. Mrs. P. Toynbee (Oxford, 1903–18), ii. 65, 355.

[2] For a full account of his career see L. B. Namier, ' Charles Garth and his connexions ', *ante*, liv. 443–70, 632–52.

[3] Yorke, *Hardwicke*, i. 51.

[4] *C.J.* xli. 827; *Hist. MSS. Comm. Rutland MSS.* iii. 306. On Mortlock see H. M. Cam in *Cambridge Antiquarian Soc. Proc.* vol. xl and my *Land Tax*, pp. 173–4.

[5] On whom see Namier, ' Thomas Duckett and Daniel Bull . . .', *Wiltshire Archaeological Magazine*, xliv. 106–10.

[6] Brit. Mus. Add. MSS. 37833, fos. 67, 71.

TABLE III.   MEN OF BUSINESS AND AMANUENSES

Commissioner	Board	Connexions
	Customs	
Thomas Allan	1778–85	Lord North's private secretary.
Joah Bates	1785–99	Tutor at King's College, Cambridge, and later secretary to the earl of Sandwich.
	Excise	
John Bindley	1763–5	Previously secretary to Board; political agent to Charles Townshend.
George Quarme	1766–75	Travelling tutor and friend to Rockingham.
Richard Stonehewer	1767–72	Tutor at Peterhouse, later under-secretary and confidant, to Grafton.
	Taxes	
Thomas Bradshaw	1763–7	Adviser to Grafton, to whom he became Secretary of the Treasury.
George Quarme	1761–3	Vide supra.
	Hackney Coaches	
Maurice Morgann	1783–1802	Shelburne's private secretary.[1]
Thomas Nuthall	1756–75	Man of business to the elder Pitt.[2]

Here, George Quarme, Rockingham's old tutor, would accept nothing less than a revenue place;[3] he was turned out of the Tax Office in 1763, and Rockingham appointed him to the Excise Board in 1766.   Stonehewer was tutor at Peterhouse to Grafton, with whom he lived in lifelong intimacy,[4] and when he became his pupil's under-secretary in 1765, it was 'his Grace's intention that Mr. Stonehewer *only* should attend his person and receive his commands'.[5]   There are the more politically minded men of business, Thomas Allan, Thomas Nuthall, and Bradshaw, Grafton's adviser, 'couleur de crème'.   John Bindley was a strange and unlovable character, the son of a Smithfield distiller, who began a political career in the Excise Office, and sought the attention of every First Lord by abominable persistence in thinking out new revenues.   About October 1761[6] he was appointed secretary to the Excise Board, and soon began to dun his old schoolfellow Jenkinson for promotion to the Board itself,[7] which he gained in 1763.[8]   In the next two years Bindley maintained connexions with Newcastle, Bute and Grenville,[9] but his importance derived from his association with Charles Townshend who, he declared,

[1] C. Symmons, *Life of Milton* (London, 1806), pp. 81–4.
[2] Brit. Mus. Add. MSS. 38335, fo. 62.   Nuthall figures prominently in both the *Chatham Correspondence*, ed. W. S. Taylor and J. M. Pringle (London, 1838–40) and the *Grenville Papers*.
[3] Brit. Mus. Add. MSS. 38335, fo. 55; 32873, fos. 244, 480; 32924, fo. 52.
[4] *Autobiography and Correspondence of the Duke of Grafton*, ed. Sir W. R. Anson (London, 1898), p. 3.
[5] *Hist. MSS. Comm. 10th Report App. pt. i (Weston Underwood MSS.)*, pp. 392–3.
[6] P.R.O. T. 54/38, fos. 242, 398.
[7] Jucker, *op. cit.* p. 29; Brit. Mus. Add. MSS. 38210, fo. 62.
[8] Brit. Mus. Add. MSS. 32946, fo. 143; Jucker, *op. cit.* p. 40.
[9] Jucker *op. cit.* pp. 29, 85, 135, 141, 155; Brit. Mus. Add. MSS. 38203, fos. 33, 325.

' loves me '.[1]   Bindley was the agent through whom the negotiations passed to regain Townshend for the Grenville Ministry;[2] his self-importance thrived on this negotiation, and he began to demand election to parliament for one seat after another.[3]   But not till late in 1766 did he come in for Dover, and he withdrew from politics at the next election.   By this time his patron was dead, and Bindley's mixture of fawning and aggressiveness hindered his making other friends.   Even worse, while in office Bindley had fallen into the clutches of Alexander Fordyce, and leaving his business in the care of one of Fordyce's friends, had met disaster.[4]   By persistent effrontery, however, Bindley developed a new market for wines among his old political acquaintances,[5] and extracted various sums, and finally a pension of £1,000 per annum from Lord North.[6] In this group there were several men of fair ability, but usually their main interest was not in administration; Morgann, for example, a man who notoriously fished for compliments, sought them mainly in the world of literature, and is remembered for starting a famous red herring in Shakespearian criticism.

The next group consisted of personal attendants and friends of the royal family.

TABLE IV.   ROYAL SERVANTS

Commissioner	Board	Connexions
	Excise	
Henry Reveley	1784–97	Household servant to both king and queen.
George Lewis Scott	1758–80	Sub-preceptor to Prince George, 1750.
	Stamps	
John Barnard	1742–73	Deputy Surveyor of Woods, 1742; probably connected with Leicester House; page of the backstairs to George III.
	Salt	
John Hillersdon	1773–98	Perhaps apptd. through his mother, a god-daughter of George II.[7]
Sir Richard Reynell	1784–98	Secretary to the Lord Steward of the Household.
Edwin F. Stanhope	1785–98	Gentleman usher 1762–84, and equerry 1784–1807, to queen.

[1] Jucker, op. cit. p. 155.

[2] Ibid. pp. 140, 301–3; Brit. Mus. Add. MSS. 38203, fo. 159; Grenville MSS. (John Murray), 28 August 1764 (I am indebted to Sir John Murray and the History of Parliament Trust for permission to examine these papers); Grenville Papers, ii. 465, 482.

[3] Jucker, op. cit. p. 193; Brit. Mus. Add. MSS. 38202, fo. 208; 38204, fo. 3; 38304, fos. 93, 110, 129; 38458, fo. 69.

[4] I am indebted for this information to Miss L. S. Sutherland.

[5] Brit. Mus. Add. MSS. 38215, fo. 77: 38470, fos. 256, 294, 298, 308.

[6] Windsor Castle Archives: Secret Service Accounts, 1779–82 passim; Corr. Geo. III, v. 468–9.

[7] Gent. Mag. 1798, p. 538.

This group is associated with George III rather than with his grandfather, for Barnard was appointed with the triumph of the Leicester House Opposition in 1742, and was later page of the backstairs to George III.[1] The future tone was set in 1758 when Bute peremptorily demanded preferment for Scott, the prince of Wales's sub-preceptor, 'the Prince . . . thinking [it] derogatory to his dignity to suffer a person to remain unprovided for who once had the honour to be concerned in his education';[2] Newcastle's

TABLE V. ADMINISTRATORS

Commissioner	Board	Career
	Customs	
Richard Frewin	1786–1813	For many years an able Customs House official.
Samuel Mead	1742–76	Previously commander of a Customs vessel.
Corbyn Morris	1763–78	Secretary 1751–61, and Commissioner 1761–3 of Customs in Scotland.
William Roe	1788–1819	Commissioner on the public accounts, 1780.
William Stiles	1783–1807	Previously secretary to the Board.
	Excise	
Stamp Brooksbank	1775–92	Previously secretary to the Board.
William Jackson	1793–1809	Clerk in the office 1780–93.
	Stamps	
William Blair	1737–61, 1765–78	Clerk in the secretary of state's office; clerk of the Privy Council; Clerk of the Signet.
	Taxes	
William Blair	1761–5	Vide supra.
George T. Good-enough	1798–1802	Treasury clerk 1767–82; secretary to Board, 1782–98.
Henry Kelsall	1735–62	Chief Clerk of the Treasury under Walpole.
William Lowndes	1798–1823	Previously employed by Pitt to draft parliamentary bills for the Treasury.
Henry Reade	1762	Previously Examiner of Surveyors' Books.
Joseph Richardson	1738–56	Previously Commissioner in Alienations Office.[3]
Edward Young	1720–73	Surveyor-General of Woods and Forests 1716–20.
	Salt	
Edward Bishop	1782–92	A Treasury clerk.
Milward Rowe	1771–82	Chief clerk of the Treasury.
	Hackney Coaches	
Francis Capper	1722–59	
Richard Capper	1759–1801	Negotiated by his father on resigning.[4]
John Cookson	1732–83	
John Soley	1749–1814	

[1] Gent. Mag. 1773, p. 360.
[2] Brit. Mus. Add. MSS. 32877, fos. 350, 382, 408; H. Walpole, Memoirs of the last ten Years of the Reign of George II (London, 1822), ii. 284–5.
[3] C.T.B.P. iii. 147.   [4] Brit. Mus. Add. MSS. 38335, fo. 62.

relative, Henry Pelham, had already been accepted by the king, but had to stand down.   It is interesting to note that no less than three household officials were rapidly appointed after the king's triumph in establishing the Government of the younger Pitt.

Despite all the claims of the aristocratic and political world, however, a considerable number of commissioners were in effect professional civil servants to whom administration provided the career of a lifetime.

The majority of these commissioners had risen to the boards from the ranks, and at the least represented the hard core of experience in the revenue departments of this period.   Some of the earlier appointments may not have been very able men, for during the long reign of Newcastle many of the duke's acquaintances with no special talents were kept in office for great periods.   Henry Kelsall's long service at the Treasury, or Blair's decades as clerk in the Secretary of State's Office, and Clerk of the Privy Council, do not prove their ability (though ability they may have had), and Samuel Mead, a seaman, was probably not fitted for the Customs Board by commanding a Customs ship.[1]   But among the appointments of the middle of the century, Corbyn Morris was an ingenious economist, though confessing that he wrote all his books for the sake of their dedications;[2] Brooksbank had been secretary to the Commissioners for Forfeited Estates 1755–62, and to the Customs Commissioners 1761–3, in Scotland, where he complained ' how hot the water is I live in ',[3] and in England his ' conduct as Commissioner [was] . . . tinctured with a spice of reform '.[4]   Morris's promotion was aided by a political interest at Bishop's Castle,[5] and Stamp Brooksbank was launched by his father, a director of the Bank,[6] but they had laboured hard before rising to the Board. Many of the other former clerks and secretaries brought to the board by the younger Pitt, men such as Frewin (who was probably the son of a Customs officer of the same name), Goodenough and Stiles, represented the ablest type of civil servant upon the boards at this time, and showed that it was possible at the end of the eighteenth century as at the beginning, for men with few advantages besides ability, to rise from the bottom to the top of a Government department.   It is notable too that at the highest level the revenue departments were not entirely self-contained, and there was some

---

[1] *C.T.B.P.* i. 362.   He applied for promotion as an admiral in 1745.   *Bedford Corr.* i. 41–2.

[2] J. H. Burton, *Life and Correspondence of D. Hume* (Edinburgh, 1846), ii. 147; cf. Brit. Mus. Add. MSS. 32877, fo. 448.

[3] Brit. Mus. Add. MSS. 35636, fos. 196–7.

[4] A. L. Cross, *Eighteenth Century Documents relating to Royal Forests, etc.* (New York, 1928), pp. 289–96.

[5] Brit. Mus. Add. MSS. 35634, fo. 379; Grenville MSS. (John Murray), Corbyn Morris to George Grenville 28 August 1753, 11 September 1753.

[6] Brit. Mus. Add. MSS. 32852, fo. 331.

interchange of personnel between the boards; in particular into the revenue boards as well as the land tax receiverships at the end of the century, there was a filtering of officials from the Treasury which probably even then contained some of the ablest men at the Government's disposal. Bishop, one of the Treasury clerks, was also an opulent army agent. Thus the class of capable officials which declined greatly in number after about 1710, never quite disappeared, and was notably reinforced towards the end of the century. Finally there was the curious group of Hackney Coach Commissioners. The two Cappers, father and son, Cookson and Soley, were all barristers and were all appointed abnormally young, and all rose to senior offices in their Inns of Court. It seems that the Hackney Coach Office was insufficiently lucrative to tempt the political world, and so was filled by young barristers whose fortunes were not yet made; certainly the legal profession predominated.

Lastly there was another group of officials who regarded the commissionerships as a retirement pension.

TABLE VI. OFFICIALS VIRTUALLY IN RETIREMENT

Commissioner	Board	Career
	Customs	
Claudius Amyand	1756–65	Under-secretary of state 1751–6.
Thomas Boone	1769–1805	Brother of Charles Boone, M.P.; governor of New Jersey 1760; South Carolina 1761–4.
Sir Alexander Munro	1786–1810	Consul at Madrid 1766–86.
Sir Stanier Porten	1782–6	Apptd. through Lord Rochford to whom he was under-secretary of state.[1]
John Pownall	1785–8	*Vide infra.*
	Excise	
William Cayley	1755–67	Envoy to Portugal 1723–5; Consul at Cadiz 1726–46.
John Pownall	1776–85	Apptmt. a convalescent benefit on his retirement as under-secretary of state.[2]

The most interesting member of this group to which brief reference has already been made, is Claudius Amyand, who sprang from a Huguenot family which advanced remarkably by mutual assistance, and who always looked to Newcastle as his patron. Indeed as under-secretary of state to Lord Holdernesse (1751–6), Amyand did not scruple to communicate unofficial letters to Newcastle even against his chief's commands.[3] The son of one of George II's surgeons, Amyand was a placeman all his life, and finally retired from the Customs Board in 1765 when he displaced the City Chamberlain as land tax receiver for London, Westminster and Middlesex, an office the Chamberlains had held almost continuously

---

[1] *Corr. Geo. III*, iii. 279.
[2] J. Nichols, *Literary Anecdotes of the Eighteenth Century* (London, 1812–15),viii. 66.
[3] Brit. Mus. Add. MSS. 32730, fo. 56; cf. 32728, fo. 53.

since the introduction of the tax.[1]   Thomas Boone was driven into retreat by the angry assembly of South Carolina; [2] William Cayley had built up a small West India fortune as Consul at Cadiz,[3] and entered parliament for Dover till he could be provided for. Although this group of commissioners regarded their careers as finished, some at least were worth their stipend.   Before John Pownall, for example, came into the revenue administration, the impulse had gone out of his career.   He spoke of ' living in total ignorance and oppressed with infirmity ',[4] of his inability to write reports,[5] and of constant playing truant from work,[6] but his opinions were valued by the Government whether on the Eden Treaty,[7] or navigation policy,[8] or Turkish trade.[9]

A few remaining commissioners cannot be classified for lack of information.   The picture of the revenue personnel drawn above would probably not be greatly altered by fresh information about them, but in one respect they are not a random sample.   Apart from Tash and Blount, all were appointed late in the period when economical reform was on foot, and Spiller, Jenkins, Hayes and Meadows might all belong to the class of able administrators whom Pitt brought to office, and whose origins were nearly always obscure.

TABLE VII.   UNCLASSIFIED

Customs	Excise	Stamps	Taxes
Thomas Tash	Richard Spiller	Lewis Jenkins	George Blount 1763–98
1752–62	1797–1807	1792–1806	Horace Hayes 1795–1806
			Edward Meadows 1793–1810

On the whole, the personnel varied little in social composition from board to board.   The best paid boards, the Customs and Excise, attracted more men of social and political consequence, and the Hackney Coach Office was a backwater; but otherwise there was little fundamental difference.   There was, however, a marked change in the character of appointments between the beginning and the end of the period.   Of the 38 commissioners sitting in 1754, no less than 29 were from Table I; and although in the younger Pitt's time M.P.s still took their toll of revenue places, of the 29 appointments he made after 1784 (4 of which are unclassified), only 12 came from Table I, for there was a sharp decline in the number of places given to borough-mongering families, and to patrons whose favours are classified in group D.   Moreover,

[1] See my Land Tax, pp. 112–13.
[2] L. B. Namier, ' Charles Garth and his connexions ', ante, liv. 462 seqq.
[3] Brit. Mus. Add. MSS. 32691, fos. 405–6.
[4] Hist. MSS. Comm. Various MSS. vi. 110.   [5] Ibid. 111.
[6] Ibid. 114.   [7] Brit. Mus. MSS. 34420, fo. 255.
[8] Brit. Mus. Add. MSS. 38219, fos. 46, 48, 131.
[9] Brit. Mus. Add. MSS. 38221, fos. 1, 3.

whereas professional civil servants sitting in 1754 were veterans of uncertain capacity installed by Walpole, those appointed by Pitt included some of the best officials of the whole century. Thus the increased efficiency of the revenue administration at the end of the eighteenth century was called out by financial strain, compelled by outside pressure, and especially by the reforming commissions of enquiry, guided by the revival of policy in the Treasury, and also assisted by the appointment of a better type of commissioner. Pitt's reign of virtue was by no means unspotted,[1] but it had solid achievements to its credit.

Nothing is known of the education of some 40 of the 139 commissioners, but of the rest 62 had been at universities (24 at Oxford, 36 at Cambridge, 3 in the Netherlands), 53 had been at Inns of Court, and 48 had attended leading schools, of whom 24 had been at Eton and 18 at Westminster.[2] But in educational background the commissioners are not readily to be compared with their modern fellows, for many of the feeblest had the best educational pedigrees, while some of the serious men of business acquired their education outside the academic resorts of the wealthy. In the later eighteenth as in the nineteenth century several commissioners acquired a literary reputation in their spare time, quite apart from those like Tickell and Morgann who were primarily men of letters. The writer of the obituary of William Robert Spencer, indeed, considered his poetry would be remembered when his family was forgotten. As regards age, the haphazard system of the eighteenth century produced much the same result, allowing for the shorter expectation of life, as the modern ladder of promotion. The ages of thirty-five commissioners are not known, or cannot be estimated within a narrow margin; the average age of the rest on first appointment was:

Customs	Excise	Stamps	Taxes	Salt	Hackney Coaches	All Boards
45	40	36	44	40	36	41

With the increasing number of men of business appointed by Pitt 1784–98, the average age of new appointments rose to 45, but this was still no higher than the average for the senior board, the Customs. Thus it was normal to appoint men of mature age, but still with a capacity for useful work.

[1] John Luttrell Olmius who was deprived of a promised appointment as a Post Captain by the fall of Fox's ministry, was appointed by Pitt to a vacancy created by his purchasing Thomas Allan's place at the Customs Board for £2,000 down and £400 per annum for his life out of the salary. (*Gent. Mag.* 1829, i. 368; Brit. Mus. Add. MSS. 38293, fo. 233.) Allan's retirement was compelled by blindness.

[2] There is an interesting contemporary comment on the ' old school tie ' in a letter from John Jeffreys to Claudius Amyand, 10 March 1753, referring to the charges against Andrew Stone: ' I look upon it as a general attack upon Westminster and Christ Church ' (Leominster MSS. quoted in Manchester M.A. thesis by L. Scott on ' The undersecretaries of state 1755–75 ').

Socially the commissioners came mostly from the landed classes and the legal profession, but there were also a few from the merchant class, a few sons of clergymen, and at least one doctor's son. Geographically the commissioners were well spread over the whole of England, with a few from Wales, Scotland, and Ireland as well, though inevitably there was a concentration in London and the Home Counties, and especially Kent, a great home of professional and administrative families for centuries past. Since the patronage of these places belonged to the Treasury, the great political connexions were represented in the Administration as in the house of commons. Earle and Astley were two of Walpole's Norfolk connexions, and Kelsall one of his protégés at the Treasury. Poole, Shelley, and Pelham represented the Sussex, and Plumptre, Mellish, and Levinz, the Nottinghamshire, spheres of Newcastle's influence. Successive generations of the Yorke family promoted numerous political and professional friends, including the two Papillons (the elder having influence at Dover),[1] Brooksbank and William Hey, the lethargic deputy recorder of Dover [2] and Chief Justice of Quebec.[3] The newer connexions included those of Grafton (with Bradshaw, Stonehewer, James Jeffreys, and perhaps Richard Gamon), Powis (with Gwynne and Whitmore) and Rutland (with Lucas and Mortlock), but as in the house of commons the majority were not connected with the great political packs.

Perhaps the most curious collection of commissioners came from Dorset. Here the families of Bankes and Bond who shared the electoral control of Corfe Castle were both represented on the revenue boards, and Bond disposed of his place by sale to Nathaniel Templeton, whose father was a Dorchester attorney, and whose uncle's electoral interest in Dorchester was much sought after by Newcastle.[4] William Morton Pleydell, who succeeded Templeman, was presumably the son or grandson of Edmund Morton Pleydell of Milbourne St. Andrew, who had been returned in 1722 for Dorchester with Joseph Damer, the uncle by marriage of Joshua Churchill the Salt Commissioner, only to be turned out by the House on petition; however, he represented the county 1727–47. Joshua Churchill belonged to another family with political influence in Dorchester, who were landowners in Dorset, and important booksellers in London and Dorchester.[5] Another political family in Dorset was represented by John Trenchard, who entered the Tax Office 'in the room of his uncle [John] Bromfield [a Hampshire man] by the interest of Sir Richard Littleton . . .

[1] Brit. Mus. Add. MSS. 38335, fo. 49.
[2] Brit. Mus. Add. MSS. 35597, fo. 353; 35636, fos. 443, 445; 35637, fo. 29.
[3] Brit. Mus. Add. MSS. 35915 passim.
[4] Brit. Mus. Add. MSS. 32734, fos. 19, 361, 363.
[5] Nicholas, Literary Anecdotes, i. 149–50.

in consideration of giving him the Trenchard interest in the borough of Poole '.[1] (The daughter of Martin Whish who later entered the Excise Board on the interest of the duke of Newcastle married his great nephew.)[2] Edward Tucker came in on the strength of his uncle John's interest in Weymouth,[3] and it was while M.P. for Weymouth that Welbore Ellis secured the succession of his kinsman Welbore Ellis Agar to the Dorsetshireman Bankes at the Customs Board.[4] Dorset was also represented by John and Henry Fane, sons of the 8th earl of Westmorland, who both sat for Lyme Regis and by Anthony Lucas, Calcraft's manager at Wareham. Thus by means of mutual assistance a group of comparatively unimportant families secured for Dorset more revenue commissionerships than any other county.

The attraction of the revenue boards in this period lay partly in the security of tenure. William Mellish of the excise wrote in 1758 that ' the post I now enjoy I look upon as an employment for life, unless I should misbehave in it ',[5] and in 1797 the Stamp Commissioners confessed that though none of their places were granted for life, ' nevertheless they have always been understood so to be held, unless in cases of misconduct '.[6] In 1754 Hardwicke requested that Papillon might resign his place to his son, commenting (as if Newcastle had forgotten) that ' the King may turn out the son as easily as the father. Indeed, my dear Lord, the doing of it will give me a great deal of ease. '[7] The commissioners' confidence in their security was well founded for, except during the 'sixties, changes in the commissions not known to be due to death, resignation, or transfer to another office were very unusual. There were none in the Hackney Coach Office, below the political level, and except in the 'sixties none in the Tax Office and only one in the Stamp Office; and they were very uncommon elsewhere.

Not unnaturally therefore the changes of the 'sixties caused great outcry, for they conflicted with a well established tradition. Rigby, who was throughout in favour of ' a general *déroute* ',[8] confidently justified the upheaval: [9]

> These turned-out gentlemen are surprised that all the world is not
> as angry at their removal as themselves, whereas the truth is, nobody
> cares a farthing for them . . . the Commissioners of all the Boards
> inferior and subordinate to the Treasury, such as the Customs,
> Excise, Salt, Duties, Taxes &c. had possessed themselves with a

[1] Brit. Mus. Add. MSS. 38335, fo. 55.
[2] J. Hutchins, *History of Dorset* (Westminster, 1873), iii. 327.
[3] Brit. Mus. Add. MSS. 32909, fo. 88; *Grenville Papers*, i. 448–9.
[4] Brit. Mus. Add. MSS. 37833, fos. 67, 71.
[5] Brit. Mus. Add. MSS. 32878, fo. 126.
[6] *6th Report of Select Committee on Finance 1797, Commons Reports*, xii. 155.
[7] Brit. Mus. Add. MSS. 32735, fo. 18.
[8] *Bedford Corr.* iii. 169–71.   [9] *Ibid.* 185–8.

notion that Lord Bute could not maintain his ground, and that they should soon return under their old master. In consequence of this idea, they very foolishly and unjustifiably neglected not only even that civility which the First Lord of the Treasury had a right to expect from them, and they had been long enough used to pay, but also, in their official acts demurred in their obedience to Treasury orders. . . .

Furthermore, according to Rigby, Bute offered to continue in their offices all who would ask it as a favour, but on Newcastle's advice they refused and were turned out. By Rigby's account, therefore, the revenue commissioners now suffered from the dilemma of the ' king's friend', whose inclination and interest were towards permanence of office and loyalty to the king, but who might be tempted in a crisis to seek the shelter of a faction leader. If Rigby's story is true, Newcastle's complaints that ' my heart is almost broke for the cruelties with which they are treating poor innocent men ',[1] are wide of the mark, and there are two pieces of evidence for it. In the first place the commissions were normally overhauled at the beginning of a reign,[2] and in 1760 at least Beaumont Hotham had trembled in his shoes.[3] When George II's days were plainly numbered Newcastle had found ' the behaviour of the Commrs. of the Customs *difficult*', especially naming Amyand, the most success-ful placeman of them all.[4] If the prospect of a change of king made the commissioners ' difficult ', a change of king and First Lord was worse. Then secondly, among the apparently predestined victims in 1763 was Henry Pelham, the last of Newcastle's relatives to be promoted. Newcastle was certain of his fate.[5] In fact Pelham was interviewed by Bute and Fox, and assured by the former that the only reason for the removals was Newcastle's misconduct, and that he was only sorry for those who depended on their stipends. Pelham, while not disguising his political affections, promised ' to do his duty *in his office*, Lord Bute said that was all he desired of him, *To do his duty in his office* '.[6] This interview staggered Newcastle and Hardwicke,[7] but Pelham kept his place, and soon H. V. Jones was reporting that even Ferdy Poole might be reprieved.[8]

Rigby also contended that ' when some of the persons removed have been found to be real objects of compassion, even of the very Duke of Newcastle's particular friends, Sir Francis Poole's son for one, . . . Lord Bute has given them places equal in value to those they were turned out of '. Poole indeed was made Receiver General of Excise, and Newcastle got the duke of Devonshire to

[1] Yorke, *Hardwicke*, iii. 440.
[2] Brit. Mus. Add. MSS. 32916, fo. 347; 33040, fos. 89–107; P.R.O. T. 29/26, fo. 36.
[3] Brit. Mus. Add. MSS. 32916, fo. 373.   [4] Brit. Mus. Add. MSS. 32907, fo. 88.
[5] Yorke, *Hardwicke*, iii. 442.   [6] Brit. Mus. Add. MSS. 32945, fos. 435–7.
[7] Brit. Mus. Add. MSS. 32946, fos. 3–5, 43.   [8] *Ibid.* fo. 29.

act as surety for him.[1] Besides Poole, nine commissioners of
Customs, Excise, Stamps, and Taxes were displaced in 1763. But
of them John Fane resigned to become M.P. for Lyme Regis, and
ample provision was found for all but three of the rest, even for
Frederick Frankland, who intended to resign in any case on account
of health.[2] Of the three who went uncompensated, Whitmore and
Quarme had been beneficiaries of shameless jobbery, while Beaumont
Hotham was an old man who was fortunate not to have been
displaced when the reign began. In short, so far as the revenue
commissioners were concerned, this was a very kid-gloved revolution, and most of those who lost their places suffered more in prestige
than income.

The old corps, however, determined to restore the *status quo
ante*; in 1765 Poole, Rigby, Whitmore, Kenrick and Blair returned
to their old places, and in 1766 Quarme was placed in the Excise
Office by Rockingham. In the course of this reshuffle Sir James
Calder, Edward Tucker, and Marmaduke Gwynne were ejected
from the Stamp Office. Edward Tucker had sufficient political
interest to climb back in 1767, this time to the Tax Office. The
other two, however, together with Henry Grenville who was
sacrificed in 1766 to Grafton's stepfather Jeffreys, were the only
commissioners displaced as the political pendulum swung back,
for reasons other than death, resignation or transfer to another
lucrative office. No doubt the tenderness shown by both sides to
the commissioners removed was due partly to respect for their
connexions, but seems also to have arisen from a sense that they
had a life interest in their places and were entitled to compensation
if they were deprived.

This security of tenure was illustrated also in various retirement bargains based on the assumption that office was a negotiable
asset. David Papillon, Francis Capper, Matthew Kenrick, and
William Roe resigned their places to a son, William Mellish declared
his willingness to do,[3] and Edward Hooper tried to bargain his
resignation against a promise of preferment for his godson Nathaniel
Gundry.[4] Proposals for quartering outsiders upon revenue commissioners had been known since Walpole's time,[5] and while
Wraxall grossly exaggerated their significance,[6] they were not
uncommon. Commissioners would negotiate to resign their
places to anyone who would pay them part of the salary;[7] Joseph
Richardson, who survived four years after his retirement in 1756,
extracted the entire salary from John Fane,[8] and Christopher Rigby

[1] Brit. Mus. Add. MSS. 32946, fos. 173, 323.   [2] *Ibid.* fos. 212–13.
[3] Brit. Mus. Add. MSS. 32900, fo. 309.
[4] P.R.O. 30/8/146.   [5] *Hist. MSS. Comm. Egmont Diary*, i. 287.
[6] *Historical Memoirs of his own Time* (London, 1836), iv. 460–2.
[7] For unsuccessful proposals of this kind see Brit. Mus. Add. MSS. 32878, fo. 81;
38200, fos. 116–17.   [8] Brit. Mus. Add. MSS. 32913, fo. 65.

had to pay a consideration annually to his predecessor Thomas Medlicott.[1] But North early proclaimed his complete opposition to such practices,[2] and they were probably not as common on the revenue boards as elsewhere.[3] Richard Frewin was himself quartered on a minor official to compensate him for leaving the Long Room for the Customs Board.[4] From quartering it was only a step to outright purchase, as Templeman purchased from Bond.[5] This was rare on the revenue boards but not uncommon in lesser offices.[6] The extraordinary bargain made by John Luttrell Olmius with Thomas Allan in 1785, purchasing his place in the Customs (which was filled by John Pownall) for £2,000 down and £400 per annum for life from the excise place which Olmius took over from Pownall has already been mentioned. Even apart from such arrangements commissioners gained a certain influence from their places; thus Christopher Rigby gained a Commissionership of Hawkers and Pedlars for his natural son Humbo. Francis Fownes Luttrell obtained a Treasury place for his son,[7] while Stamp Brooksbank founded a dynasty of Treasury officers. Bargains of this sort were not stopped even by the introduction of compulsory pensioned retirement early in the nineteenth century.

The question of the patronage exercised by the revenue commissioners is a complex one, and is unlikely to be cleared up until the history of each department has been thoroughly studied. Although Tax Office patronage was from the beginning in Treasury hands,[8] it is certainly erroneous to accept as universally valid for other boards statements such as that of Woodcock the Excise Commissioner in 1736 that ' though they used to have the appointing their own officers, yet upon the renewing the commission the Treasury would nominate them all '.[9] In the second half of the eighteenth century many appointments were filled by the excise commissioners in turn.[10] In 1758 the Customs Board were filling Cornish vacancies without the Treasury's knowledge;[11] individual commissioners had rights of presentation[12] and sometimes balloted for a vacancy.[13] There were also limitations upon patronage by either Treasury or Board. Officials who bore financial responsibility for their subordinates commonly exercised the patronage

[1] Brit. Mus. Add. MSS. 38335, fo. 55.
[2] Hist. MSS. Comm. 13th Report App. pt. vii (Lonsdale MSS.), pp. 132-3.
[3] E.g. Brit. Mus. Add. MSS. 32873, fos. 244, 480; 32909, fos. 391-2.
[4] Brit. Mus. Add. MSS. 38278, fo. 241.   [5] Brit. Mus. Add. MSS. 38335, fo. 62.
[6] Brit. Mus. Add. MSS. 32885, fo. 308; 32918, fo. 33.
[7] Brit. Mus. Add. MSS. 38274, fos. 47, 339, 351, 357.
[8] See my Land Tax, ch. v.   [9] Hist. MSS. Comm. Carlisle MSS., p. 163.
[10] Brit. Mus. MSS. 32965, fo. 384; 35637, fo. 365; 35639, fo. 99; cf. 35641, fo. 148; 38204, fo. 356; 38206, fo. 166.
[11] Brit. Mus. Add. MSS. 32877, fo. 382.
[12] Brit. Mus. Add. MSS. 35597, fo. 132; 35624, fo. 206; 35625, fo. 1; 38203, fo. 270.
[13] Brit. Mus. Add. MSS. 38204, fo. 156.

themselves,[1] and boards were reluctant to waive rules governing their appointments for either Treasury or private patrons.[2]   The Customs Board in 1759 successfully maintained against the Treasury its right to nominate to places ' not . . . upon the establishment '.[3] Although it has been suggested that the Salt Board lost its independent patronage in the 'thirties,[4] Charles Jenkinson knew cases when ' the whole power of the Treasury [was] made use of to induce them to give way & they would not ',[5] and when the Customs Board would not yield in 1762, Hooper told Jenkinson to ' applaud this sturdy adherence to what as managers of this Revenue is our duty '.[6]   Yet although certain boards showed independence at certain times, extensive patronage to the lesser revenue offices was exercised by the Treasury.   At present no separate spheres of influence belonging to the Treasury and boards are apparent, and the balance between them probably shifted according to the circumstances of policy and the play of personality.

The main work of the revenue boards did not of course consist in appointing and being appointed, though in the absence of fiscal or administrative policy matters of patronage were bound to loom large.   The revenue offices have been regarded by some modern students as complete backwaters,[7] almost sinecures, but this was not the contemporary view.   One of Walpole's Excise Commissioners was ' convinced there's not £1000 a year in the King's gift so dearly earned.   We meet every day of the year (Sundays and holidays excepted) at nine in the morn, and have full employment at the Board till twelve.'[8]   Gibbon at Lausanne in 1784–5 abhorred the thought of coming home to the Customs or excise, having been assured that he ' need not work above five days in the week ',[9] and while one applicant would ' rather be a Commissioner of Customs in London, than King of Poland, if I were obliged to spend my life at Warsaw ',[10] such places were known to be ' attended with considerable labor '.[11]   A paper compiled in the middle of the century, however, concluded that while the Customs Board worked hard to despatch current letters queries and disputes, it did not give sufficient consideration to broader matters of policy, and there was insufficient check upon the attendance of slack commissioners.[12]   This was probably the situation then in all the chief

[1] Brit. Mus. Add. MSS. 32878, fo. 96.
[2] Brit. Mus. Add. MSS. 32886, fos. 500, 502, 503 ; 39201, fo. 319.
[3] Brit. Mus. Add. MSS. 32887, fo. 485.   [4] E. Hughes, op. cit. pp. 306-7.
[5] Brit. Mus. Add. MSS. 38205, fo. 136.   For an example of their obstinacy see Brit. Mus. Add. MSS. 38304, fo. 67.
[6] Brit. Mus. Add. MSS. 38198, fo. 102.
[7] A. Hope-Jones, Income Tax in the Napoleonic Wars (Cambridge, 1939), pp. 34-5.
[8] Hist. MSS. Comm. Carlisle MSS. pp. 157-8.
[9] Private Letters of Edward Gibbon, ed. R. E. Prothero (London, 1896), ii. 130.
[10] Jesse, Selwyn, iv. 142.   [11] Aspinall, Corr. Geo. IV, i. 233.
[12] Brit. Mus. Add. MSS. 18903, fos. 78 seqq.

boards, but as business increased and fiscal and administrative reform set in, the strain on some of the commissioners became quite modern in its intensity. Pownall complained in 1786 that ' my time in official concerns was so fully engaged that I have not for many months past enjoyed an interval of a Sunday, Custom ho. holiday, or a single evening '.[1] But the lesser boards were always quieter, and in 1753 John Milbanke spoke satirically of the Salt Commissioners: [2]

> My fellow labourers at the Board hang their heads, not through weight of business but periwig, and knit their brows not upon any knotty point, but to hold on their spectacles. This is high treason and they are all staring at me, but if I am any judge of their optics they cant reach me. . . .

Individual commissioners such as Pennington [3] and Rigby [4] were notorious for their poor attendance, and others overstayed the vacations which the commissioners took in turns in the summer months.[5]

Even in 1780 the Taxes and Stamp Commissioners were attending only three times a week, the Salt Commissioners twice, the Commissioners for Hackney Coaches and Hawkers and Pedlars once. The Commissioners on the public accounts therefore recommended that these boards should be amalgamated.[6] In 1781 the Treasury took up the cause enthusiastically,[7] but nothing was done immediately, and in 1785 Pitt declared himself opposed to such a merger on the grounds that the Excise Board ' was already overloaded ', and that the duties on hackney coaches and hawkers and pedlars would in any case soon be abolished.[8] However, the hostility of shopkeepers to the hawkers and pedlars was sufficient to keep those duties alive,[9] and by 1798 the situation had changed materially. The duties administered by the Stamp and Tax Offices had enormously increased, the latter was working much harder,[10] and soon could hardly cope with its business by meeting daily,[11] and the former was meeting every day except on holidays.[12] The Salt, Hackney Coach and Hawkers and Pedlars Offices were still quiet, however, and the select committee revived the demand for amalgamation; [13] this time Pitt transferred the salt duties to the Excise Office. He hesitated whether to combine the duties on hawkers and pedlars and hackney coaches under a new Board of Police revenue,[14] thought of placing the hawkers and pedlars duties

[1] Brit. Mus. Add. MSS. 38219, fo. 181.   [2] Brit. Mus. Add. MSS. 33094, fo. 68.
[3] Brit. Mus. Add. MSS. 38206, fo. 170.   [4] Brit. Mus. Add. MSS. 38335, fo. 55.
[5] Brit. Mus. Add. MSS. 33095, fo. 69.   [6] C.J. xxxviii. 142-3.
[7] P.R.O. T. 29/50, fos. 77, 169, 216.   [8] Cobbett, *Parliamentary History*, xxv. 307.
[9] *Ibid.* 554 *seqq.*; xxvi. 5 *seqq.*   [10] See my article, *ante*, lxvii. 532.
[11] Brit. Mus. Add. MSS. 38364, fo. 79.
[12] *6th Report of Select Committee on Finance 1797*, *Commons Reports*, xii. 159.
[13] *Ibid.* 242, 257, 261.   [14] *Colchester Diary*, ii. 134-5, 136.

under the Tax Office,[1] and finally did nothing. (The former course was adopted in 1810.)[2] A generation later, when the income tax had lapsed, the Stamp and Tax Offices were amalgamated, and the fiscal administration had attained almost its modern form. Thus in the second half of the eighteenth century, the question of the work of the revenue boards was settled in principle; those which were of real significance to the national revenues were loaded more and more heavily, those which were not were already threatened with abolition.

Of much greater interest than the amount of work which the revenue commissioners did, is the question whether they exercised any influence upon policy and legislation. In the eighteenth century as today the influence of civil servants in these fields was dependent upon circumstances and personalities, but it was significant at times and increased towards the end of the century when administrative reform was much agitated, and the character of appointments to the boards was changing. Of course the boards periodically sought new clauses to assist their administration, as did the Stamp Office in 1765,[3] but during the Seven Years' War, Henry Reade of the Tax Office recommended and secured important additions to the window duties as a matter of fiscal policy.[4] At the same time Mellish was Newcastle's constant counsellor on taxation and borrowing, but whether he swayed policy further than to secure increases in the ale and beer duties instead of a shop tax is not clear.[5] Morris's ideas were also more effervescent than efficacious, and it is uncertain whether William Blair made any difference to the drafting of the great Stamp Act;[6] but Bindley in the early 'eighties was 'annually employed in forming the taxes' and impressed Grey Cooper and North with a 'high opinion of his services'.[7] Later the influence of commissioners is more clearly discernible. When in 1784 Pitt introduced the Commutation Tax, designed to check smuggling by exchanging most of the tea duties for an extra window tax, 'there was no debate but " who was the real inventor of Pitt's plan " '.[8] The answer to this is still obscure, but the plan had certainly been going the rounds in the administration before he came into office, and had been championed by John Pownall.[9] When Shelburne wished to undertake reform in the revenue boards, he entrusted an investigation to two commissioners, Musgrave and Brooksbank, a future commissioner, William Stiles, and George

[1] P.R.O. T. 22/9, fo. 385.　　　　　　[2] 50 Geo. III c. 41.
[3] Brit. Mus. Add. MSS. 38339, fo. 28.　　[4] *Ante*, lxvii. 527.
[5] Brit. Mus. Add. MSS. 32887, fos. 177, 322; 32894, fos. 55 *seqq.*; 32900, fos. 206, 308; 32913, fo. 430; 32914, fos. 11, 317, 432-3, 425.
[6] E. Hughes, *ante*, lvi. 257-8.　　[7] P.R.O. 30/8/229.
[8] *Hist. MSS. Comm. Rutland MSS.*, iii. 113
[9] A. L. Cross, *18th Century Documents*, pp. 296 *seqq.*, 299 *seqq.*

Rose;[1] Musgrave's reports on the Customs [2] passed to the younger Pitt,[3] and formed the basis of his policy of letting sinecures fall in.[4]

Another of Pitt's parliamentary triumphs, the consolidation of the Customs duties,[5] originated in a proposal of the Customs Board as far back as 1777.   In 1781 the Treasury took up the idea enthusiastically,[6] and Grey Cooper later said in parliament that 'the scheme had made considerable progress' in the course of correspondence between North and 'a very intelligent Commissioner of the Customs' now serving elsewhere,[7] Sir William Musgrave (noted for his forthright advice on tariff questions).[8] The main lines of the plan were thus ready for Pitt to promulgate; the success of the scheme turned upon the efficient execution of the laborious work of revision and consolidation, and this was the task of William Stiles,[9] who had been made secretary to the Customs Board by Shelburne, and another long-service Customs official, Richard Frewin.   These two also made up the statutory commission on fees taken by Customs officers in 1789,[10] securing a bill based on their report;[11] both were rewarded by places on the Customs Board and both, and especially Frewin, regularly advised the Government on tariff policy and cognate matters.[12]   Stiles died in 1807, but Frewin's career continued; in 1813 he was brought into the Treasury;[13] in 1820 he was advising on the Navigation laws, and was complimented in the House for designing the Navigation Act of 1822. He was also said to have been engaged not only in the consolidation of the Customs duties of 1787, but 'in every subsequent revisal of that complicated system of our laws, including [that of] 1819'.[14]

The career of William Lowndes (one of the numerous great-grandsons of the prolific Secretary of the Treasury) in some ways resembled that of Frewin.   He was introduced to the public service by Gibbs Crawford, Solicitor to the Stamp Office, who employed him to draft legislation.   By 1787 he was doing the same for Pitt,[15] the drafting of whose bills had occasioned sharp criticism,[16] and in whose favour he became permanently entrenched by the speed with which he mastered the income tax plan.   It was Lowndes who

[1] Lord Fitzmaurice, *Life of William, Earl of Shelburne* (London, 1912), ii. 227.
[2] Cross, *op. cit.*, pp. 250, 268, 281.   [3] P.R.O. 30/8/285.
[4] *4th Report of Select Committee on Finance 1797*, *Commons Reports*, xii. 57–8.
[5] *Hist. MSS. Comm. Rutland MSS.* iii. 375, 376.   [6] P.R.O. T. 29/50, fos. 169, 216.
[7] Cobbett, *Parl. Hist.* xxvi. 634.
[8] Brit. Mus. Add. MSS. 34419, fos. 120, 133; 34420, fo. 24.
[9] Brit. Mus. Add. MSS. 38222, fo. 155.
[10] *4th Report of Select Committee on Finance 1797*, *Commons Reports*, xii. 79.
[11] P.R.O. 30/8/285.
[12] Brit. Mus. Add. MSS. 38219, fos. 86, 97; 38236, fos. 6–7, 173–4; 38248, fo. 260; 38253, fos. 265, 266; 38271, fo. 220.   Frewin later received a large gratuity for his services.
[13] Aspinall, *Corr. Geo. IV*, i. 233.   [14] *Gent. Mag.* 1822, ii. 568.
[15] P.R.O. 30/8/153.   [16] *Hist. MSS. Comm. Rutland MSS.*, ii. 224.

drafted the Act, and who was made chairman of the reorganized Taxes Board to carry it out.[1]   (At the same time Goodenough, who had built up the inspectorate supervising the levying of the assessed taxes was also made a commissioner.)   Lowndes not only took over the organization of land tax redemption, drafted many scores of public acts relating to taxes, and undertook the consolidation of the duties managed by the office,[2] but is said to have conceived the fundamental alterations in the income tax so successfully introduced by Addington, for whom the credit has been claimed.[3] Certainly he received £1,000 gratuity for his work on this occasion.[4] Lowndes appears to have enjoyed the fullest confidence of Pitt's successors, and was pressed by Vansittart not to retire.   When health compelled Lowndes's retirement in 1823, the Treasury marked the occasion by a special minute praising his ' zeal and ability ' and ' very important services ', and gave him a special retirement allowance above the rate now fixed by Act.[5]   Thus at the end of the eighteenth century older traditions of work and efficiency had revived in the English civil service, and they bore fruit from time to time in policy and legislation.

W. R. WARD.

[1] P.R.O. T. 22/10, fos. 16, 480.   I am indebted for some of the following references to Dr. A. Farnsworth.

[2] P.R.O. T. 29/79, 29 June 1802.

[3] A. Farnsworth, *Addington, Author of the Modern Income Tax* (London, 1951).

[4] P.R.O. T. 22/10, fo. 252; cf. T. 29/81 fo. 501.

[5] *Gent. Mag.* 1828, i. 283; *Annual Biography and Obit.* xiii. 99.

Henry Fox as Paymaster General of the Forces

TO be unmistakably identified as the 'Public Defaulter of unaccounted millions'—and in an address presented to the sovereign by a Lord Mayor of London on behalf of the Livery of the City—is not a common experience for an ex-minister of the Crown; but in 1769 it befell the unpopular Henry Fox,[1] who had been Paymaster General of the Forces from 1757 to 1765. It was, indeed, not the first time that he had been attacked on the financial conduct of his office. In 1763, in a debate opened by Sir John Phillips (a prominent tory country gentleman), William Aislabie had raised much the same issue in the house of commons, where it was received with 'loud marks of approbation';[2] but on this occasion little public attention was aroused, and 1769 was the first time that it was taken up with vigour, and outside parliament. The City's address, like a Middlesex petition of the previous month, echoed charges made in the house of commons when Alderman Beckford, the mouthpiece of many popular causes, had asserted that more than forty millions of public money remained unaccounted for in the army Pay Office, and that legal process in regard to this had been issued from the exchequer, but had been suspended by the king's sign manual warrant. Beckford had called upon members of the Treasury Board then present to correct him if he had been misinformed, but not a word had been uttered.[3]

These charges were ultimately dropped, but merit examination, an examination that must be based on some understanding of the nature of Henry Fox's office, and of the procedures relating to army finance and to contemporary law. The office of Paymaster of the

[1] Earl of Ilchester, *Henry Fox, first Lord Holland*, 1920, ii. 332. Fox was raised to the baronage in 1763. For the documents and an account of Beckford's speech, see the *Gentleman's Magazine*, 1769, pp. 290, 329 *seqq.*, and 363.

[2] Horace Walpole, *Memoirs of the Reign of George III*, ed. D. le Marchant, 1845, i. 243. William Aislabie was one of the two joint Auditors of the Imprests, to whose office Fox's accounts were to be rendered. As will be seen below, there were sufficient reasons for Fox's accounts not being in the Auditors' hands as early as 1763, and Aislabie ought to have known this.

[3] The date of this is uncertain, but is not unlikely to have been during the debate on the Budget of 1769. The occasion for the attack would seem to be the active part taken by Stephen and Charles James Fox against Wilkes in the Middlesex election. (Ilchester, *op. cit.* ii. 329.)

Forces had a continuous history from 1662, when Henry Fox's own father, Sir Stephen Fox, had been the first tenant. Before his time it had been the custom to appoint Treasurers at War, *ad hoc*, for this or that campaign; the practice of the Protectorate Government foreshadowing, however, a permanent office. Within a generation of the Restoration the status of the Paymastership began to change. In 1692 the then Paymaster, the earl of Ranelagh, was sworn of the privy council; and thereafter every Paymaster, or when there were two Paymasters at least one of them, was sworn of the council if not already a member. From the accession of Queen Anne the Paymaster tended to change with the Ministry, and eighteenth century appointments must be considered as made not upon merit alone, but by merit and political affiliation, the office becoming a political prize and perhaps potentially the most lucrative that a parliamentary career had to offer.

The duty of the Paymaster was to act as sole domestic banker of the army. He received, mainly from the exchequer, the sums voted by parliament for military expenditure, and from other quarters he received fortuitous sums such as those realized by the sale of old stores. He disbursed these sums, by his own hands or by Deputy Paymasters; such disbursements being made under the authority of sign manual warrants as far as related to the ordinary expenses of the army, and under Treasury warrants in the case of the extraordinaries, that is to say the expenses unforeseen and unprovided for by parliament. During the whole time in which public money was in his hands, from the day of receipt until the issue of his final discharge, the *Quietus* of the Pipe Office, his private estate was liable for the money in his hands; and failing the *Quietus* this liability remained without limit of time, passing on his death to his legal representatives. *Nullum tempus occurrit regi.*

A necessary preliminary to the issue of a *Quietus* was the audit of accounts by the Auditors of the Imprests in the exchequer. This audit was subject to protracted delay. Since it happened that in 1769 not even Fox's first year's account was as yet finally audited and declared, those who were unacquainted with the working of the administrative machine—or sought to play upon the ignorance of others—could plausibly stigmatize Fox as a ' defaulter '. But it must be said that for such delay there were sufficient explanations, a few of which may be summarized. To begin with, the Pay Office was plagued with excessively complicated book-keeping. In part this was due to the system of statutory appropriation, which not only earmarked the total voted for a given year, confining it to the services incurred in that year, but also analysed the appropriation in some detail according to different heads of service.[1] In part it

---

[1] See the annual Appropriation Acts.

was due to the fact that, especially in war, more or less heavy calls
were made on account of the extra-ordinaries, which required
distinct accounting.   Other causes of complication were services
which, although of regular annual occurrence, were nevertheless
unprovided for by parliament in the latter's votes and appropriations.   Such services were Chelsea Hospital, financed by deducting
one day's pay in the year from most military personnel; widows'
pensions, found by increasing the establishment of every company
by two fictitious men; and administrative expenses, a fund for which
was formed by deducting a poundage of 5 per cent. from most of
the Paymaster's issues.   These matters may be studied in detail in
the reports of the commissioners for examining the public accounts,
1780–7,[1] and elsewhere.[2]   A most superficial reading carries conviction as to the inevitability of great delay in the Pay Office, especially when it is recollected that eighteenth-century campaigns were
conducted overseas, often at great distances, with slow and uncertain
communications.   It seems that the Pay Office did relatively well
in delivering Fox's final accounts to the Auditors only seven years
after his resignation, for the accounts of his three peace-time
successors were not ready until eleven or twelve years after resignation.[3]

Great delay arose in the Audit Office itself, after the submission
of a Paymaster's accounts.   This was to a considerable extent
beyond the power of the Auditors of the Imprests to remedy, for
it was caused by the exacting requirements of the law.   By law
these two joint Auditors were the sole officers entitled and empowered to examine a Paymaster's accounts, and by law they must
be satisfied not only that every disbursement had actually been
made, but also that it was duly authorized.[4]   In consequence,
whatever previous examination might have taken place, the Audit
Office had again to compare the accounts with the establishments,
warrants, and the like; they were bound to require the production
of acquittances vouching every disbursement, and they had to
check all arithmetical calculations.   If proper documents were
wanting, a Paymaster's account could not be closed until the defect
had been made good by the issue of a sign manual warrant em-
powering the Auditors to pass the unvouched items.[5]   In the haste
and confusion of campaigning, a failure to obtain vouchers, or

---

[1] Reports Nos. 4–7, 9, and 10.   These are printed in vols. 38 and 39 of the *Journals
of the House of Commons*.

[2] For instance, Public Record Office, Chatham Papers, P.R.O. 30/8, bundle 231,
booklet entitled ' Business done at the Treasury '.

[3] *Commissioners for Examining the Public Accounts*, Rep. 4.

[4] Except in the matter of army contracts.   The Comptrollers of Army Accounts
were responsible for certifying that the terms of these contracts were complied with
before the contractors were paid.

[5] See for instance, P.R.O., T. 29/38, Treasury minute of 10 June 1766.

their subsequent loss, was inevitably not infrequent. It must be borne in mind that by the time the Auditors came to do their work many accountable individuals and many of the meaner recipients were dead, or lost sight of; and some, in any case, were foreigners who were not and never had been amenable to English law.

In addition to such inevitable causes of delay, there were others which were within the power of the Auditors to remedy; amongst them what appears to have been a departmental regulation that the accounts of one Paymaster should not be passed until those of his predecessor were completed. It also seems that the exacting demands made by war and its aftermath upon the personnel of the Audit Office were not matched by an adequate increase in staff. This was certainly so in the contemporary navy Pay Office; but, on the other hand, it must be admitted that on at least one occasion (as noticed below), the Treasury Board was satisfied that untrained labour would not be of assistance in the Audit Office. In fairness to the Auditors of the Imprests it should be mentioned that the speed of the Audit Office was not greatly increased by the placing of the joint Auditorships in commission; for the five commissioners, even when urged on by Pitt, did not succeed in overtaking arrears. They failed, for instance, to have Fox's final account ready for declaration until 1788; and the Paymasters' accounts for the period of the American War were being declared, on an average, about ten years after the period to which they related.[1] So far as Fox is concerned we have both the statement that Fox wrote repeatedly to successive Secretaries at War urging haste, (presumably in clearing regimental accounts),[2] and also his executor's testimony that Fox had requested two of his Deputy Paymasters to submit their accounts direct to the Audit Office, to avoid the delay which would have occurred had they been sent to the Pay Office for consolidation there with his own account.[3] Fox was not a defaulter, if that implies that he had retarded the submission of his accounts and vouchers to the Auditors; and if subsequent delays in passing the accounts could have been diminished, the blame (if any) appears to rest rather upon the Audit Office, or the Treasury.

The view that Fox was not blameworthy derives some further support from an investigation of Beckford's charge that legal process had been suspended by 'the King's Sign Manual'. On 19 May 1768 the Treasury Board received a memorial from Lord Holland, as Fox then was, praying to be allowed further time to make up his accounts as late Paymaster. His reasons appeared sufficient, and the Board forthwith directed the preparation of a

---

[1] See the Declared Accounts in question: P.R.O., A.O. 1, bundles 84–93, Rolls 113–16 and 118–23.

[2] Ilchester, *op. cit.* ii. 335.

[3] *Commissioners for Examining the Public Accounts*, Rep. 4, app. 3.

warrant for stay of process for one year.[1] It does not appear that this was other than a normal Treasury warrant, nor is it clear why (supposing that Beckford had his facts correct, or was correctly reported), a sign manual should have been requisite. So far from conniving at delay, the Board at the same time directed John Powell of the Pay Office to appear before them and explain the cause of the delay. He gave as reasons 'the extent and nature of the services, the bulk of the accounts, and the unusual hurry that was unavoidable in his office during the late war'. He added that the accounts of the years 1757 and 1758 were then before the Auditors, and that those of 1759 would be delivered in a few weeks. He also stated that in preparing the accounts of subsequent years difficulty might arise 'from several Regiments not being cleared', and delivered an account detailing them. The Board at once ordered a letter to be written to the Secretary at War requesting the latter to hasten the clearance of the regimental accounts.[2] The Board's wish and intention to speed up the completion of Fox's accounts was further emphasized a year later when the Deputy Auditors attended, Powell being summoned again. Solely to avoid delay, the Board sanctioned a certain technical procedure which they disliked and ruled as not permissible in future, and they questioned the Deputy Auditors as to progress in their office, suggesting to them an increase in staff. The Deputies succeeded in satisfying the Board that new and untrained staff would be of no assistance, and were dismissed after being recommended in the strongest manner to exercise all possible despatch.[3] The Treasury appear to be cleared of Beckford's imputation of 'going slow'. The latter seems to have understood the circumstances only imperfectly, and the episode illustrates how true was the observation made many years later by George Rose, one of Pitt's joint Secretaries of the Treasury, that formerly it had been almost impossible for a true judgement to be formed on matters connected with public finance, except by those who had the conduct of them.[4] If there was blame for delay, it probably rested mainly on the Audit Office, for it is doubtful whether at that period [5] the Treasury Board had legal power to compel an increase of Audit Office staff, should the Auditors not agree to such a course.

[1] P.R.O., T. 29/39. Treasury minute of 19 May 1768, and warrant of the same date, T. 54/40 p. 441. Ilchester, *op. cit.* ii. 335, states that a six months' stay of process had already been granted, but this appears to have left no trace in the Treasury minute and warrant books.

[2] P.R.O., T. 29/39. Treasury minute of 2 June 1768.

[3] P.R.O., T. 29/40. Treasury minute of 22 June 1769. This was upon an application by the Deputy Auditors of the Imprests, and appears to have arisen in the ordinary course of business.

[4] *A brief examination into the increase of the revenue during Pitt's administration,* 2nd edn., 1806, p. 1.

[5] I.e. before 25 Geo. III, c. 52, which instituted the Audit Commission in 1785.

In spite of these facts, which go some way towards the exculpation of those concerned, it is not, however, to be denied that at the time of the Address in 1769 Fox continued to retain very large balances of public money; and, as will later be indicated, the uses to which some of these balances were put were of a nature to lay the Governments of the day under some obligation to him.[1] For the retention of these large balances there were, nevertheless, various grounds of justification. It was necessary for him to continue to hold public money because his responsibility for paying services incurred during his period of office continued, whether the demands presented themselves before or after his retirement. It might even be necessary for him, after retirement, to apply for further issues from the exchequer.[2] This appears to have been bound up with legal considerations, for, when in 1782 it was decided to obtain power in future to vest a retiring Paymaster's balance in his successor, to enable the latter to carry on the retiring Paymaster's services and to avoid money lying idle, it was thought necessary to resort to statutory[3] and not administrative action.[4] But when all delayed charges appeared to have been presented, when the practical ground for retaining balances after retirement was no longer of force, the law did not forbid, and custom permitted, their retention, and there were no prompt and convenient sanctions for enforcing their delivery. Before recourse could be had to the Court of Exchequer for this purpose, it was first necessary to ascertain what was the sum of money to be claimed, and, as already indicated, it was a very long time before the exact amount could be known. Further, although it was the practice to issue a writ of distraint for the purpose of enforcing prompt delivery of complete accounts to the Auditors,[5] it was the sensible practice not to issue process for the recovery of balances upon each separate year's account, but to carry forward the balance from one year to the next, until the final account. There does not appear to have been power to enforce payments 'on account', and when such payments were made they seem to have been made under the authority of a statute, as in 1769.[6] When in 1781 a number of public accountants were to be required to pay in specified balances under an indemnity, a special Act was necessary.[7] Thus it is abundantly clear that the law sanctioned and practice required the retention.

[1] See below, pp. 246-7.

[2] See, for instance, P.R.O., T. 29/38. Treasury minute of 13 February 1767, and other similar minutes.

[3] See 22 Geo. III, c. 81, which is printed in Danby Pickering's edition of *Statutes at Large*, though not in Ruffhead's edition.

[4] I.e. not by Order in Council, Privy Seal, sign manual, or Treasury warrant.

[5] As, for instance, in Fox's case referred to above.

[6] See 10 Geo. III, c. 52.

[7] See 21 Geo. III, c. 48.

The magnitude of the Paymaster's balances raises other considerations, which were of equal force before and after retirement. The public money in the Paymaster's hands was not legally a consolidated fund, any part of which could be drawn on for any purpose. The money voted and issued on account of any year was not available for the service of any other year ; and likewise, the detailed appropriations of the vote of any year were not available for any other head of service than that prescribed in the Appropriation or other Act. Consequently, when a Paymaster had exhausted his receipt on some particular head of service, no matter how much money he might have in hand in respect of other heads, he was compelled to apply for more money on the exhausted head, thus increasing yet further the balances in his hands.[1] Another factor tending to increase the balances was the circumstance that a Paymaster was also *ipso facto* Paymaster of Chelsea Hospital, the establishment having the care of disabled and aged soldiers, both as in-patients within its walls and as out-patients resident all over Great Britain. Money for the out-patients was voted annually by parliament,[2] and funds for the hospital itself were, as already noted, furnished by deducting one day's pay from most active members of the military forces, supplemented also by drawing on the fund of poundage deducted from the Paymaster's issues. But all these revenues were in practice inadequate. The declared accounts of Paymasters of Chelsea Hospital show considerable sums owing to them by the public, and there seems to be no other explanation of the manner in which Paymasters of Chelsea Hospital contrived to pay out far more than they received, than by supposing that they raided for this purpose the balances of the Paymasters of the Forces. This fact has been obscured because the commissioners for examining the public accounts were directed to enquire into the balances of the Paymasters of the Forces, but not into those of the Paymasters of Chelsea Hospital; and the circumstance seems to have escaped their notice, or at least their publicity. When in January 1783 the Treasury Board, on the authority of the Act of 1781, set about demanding repayment of Fox's balance of £288,529, they were informed that his estate was actually owed £220,521 on account of the hospital, so that the net claim was reduced to £68,008.[3] Thus to finance his deficit on the hospital the Paymaster had, in his capacity as Paymaster of the Forces, to hold larger balances than he need otherwise have done, whilst the nominal amount of his balances represented a fictitious inflation of the sums actually in his hands.

[1] For Lord North on this subject, see William Cobbett's *Parliamentary History*, xxii. col. 211. He was speaking in the debate on the first four reports of the commissioners for Examining the public accounts, 10 May 1781.

[2] See the annual Appropriation Acts, *passim*.

[3] P.R.O., T. 29/53. Treasury minute of 14 January 1783.

Yet another factor confusing the true state of the balances was the practice of issuing subsistence in advance, the period varying between one month for the forces at home and twelve months for those in India; and issuing pay for garrisons and staff (and certain other services) from two to eighteen months in arrear— the arrears much exceeding the advances. These withheld arrears were employed as temporary finance for the army extra- ordinaries until such time as parliament voted the amount of the latter, and thus enabled the Treasury to carry out the withheld payments, the money for which had been otherwise applied for the time being.[1]

Although there were all these proper grounds for the holding of large balances, nevertheless, so far as it is possible to judge, the balances which successive Paymasters actually held appear to have been too great to be justified by necessity. The system of manage- ment was open to abuse, for while law and custom permitted the employment of balances for the Paymaster's private enrichment, neither law nor custom limited the extent to which this might be practised; provided always that when needed the money was forth- coming. There was, moreover, a sinister distinction between the situation of the Paymaster of the Forces and that of certain other public accountants such as the Treasurers of the Navy and of the Ordnance. With the exception of some relatively small sums re- quired for paying exchequer and Treasury fees on passing accounts, &c., the two latter officers applied to the Treasury for money merely as the mouthpieces of Boards of Commissioners. The Navy, Victual- ling, Sick and Hurt, and Ordnance Boards had no personal incentive to apply for larger sums than were really necessary, for they were not personally the custodians of the cash. It was otherwise with the Paymaster of the Forces, for he not only kept the cash but was the sole authority for deciding when to apply for money and how much to apply for. This was a situation of some delicacy, and it is not difficult to believe that the temptation to apply for more than was really necessary continually presented itself to Fox and his successors, up until the time of the regulation of the Paymaster's office in 1782.[2] The Treasury Board acceded to all such applica- tions, having no information by which to judge their propriety, nor, apparently, any legal power to demand it. That the resulting situa- tion was more satisfactory for the holder of the Paymastership than for the public may be inferred from the zeal with which the Pay- mastership was sought by those politicians who looked to places

[1] For this see especially P.R.O. 30/8, bundle 231, booklet entitled ' Business done at the Treasury '.

[2] Before 1759 it had been the custom to apply every four months for about one- third of the year's vote, but after that period to apply as and when demands for payment were approaching (*Commissioners for Examining the Public Accounts*, Rep. 5).

of profit rather than of power or honour. Richard Rigby, for instance, Paymaster from 1768 to 1782, was said to have made the Paymastership the avowed goal of his ambition. Fox's father-in-law, the duke of Richmond, told the duke of Newcastle in 1747 that, while welcoming the proposal to make Fox Secretary of State, 'we still wish him the Paymaster's place, as it is less precarious and a better thing, for his family's sake'; [1] and when Fox achieved it ten years later, it was '. . . the very thing he wished'.[2]

The means by which the great gains might be made require explanation. The Paymaster's letters patent provided for a salary of £3,000 as Paymaster of the Forces, another £365 as Paymaster of Chelsea Hospital, and a third salary, also of £365, as one upon the establishment of General and Staff officers. In addition, he received an allowance of £600 for the contingencies of his office, and a further allowance for paying the salaries of his under-officers and clerks. Fox's allowance under the latter head is uncertain, but is not likely to have fallen below the £1,500 allowed to Pitt, nor to have exceeded the £1,760 allowed to Rigby. This gross receipt was reduced by departmental poundage, already referred to, by taxes,[3] and by the sums necessary to defray the clerical payroll and contingent expenses. Comparable calculations based upon a document in the Chatham Papers [4] and upon figures in the sixth report of the commissioners for examining the public accounts, suggest that after all deductions are taken into account the clear profit of office was about £2,940 in the first case, and about £2,964 in the second. It is probably not wide of the mark to suggest that Fox's clear official profit did not greatly exceed £3,000 on the average. It was, however, the contemporary practice, established beyond the memory of man, for a Paymaster to supplement his official emoluments by profitably employing a part of the balances in his hands and taking that profit to his own use. This was one of the accepted perquisites of office; nor (despite the applause which the elder Pitt received for his alleged refusal as Paymaster to profit by these balances) [5] was there anything approaching public

[1] Brit. Mus. Add. MSS. 32,714, fo. 219, quoted by Ilchester, op. cit. i. 145.
[2] J. Calcraft to Lord Charles Hay, 9 July 1757, Brit. Mus. Add. MSS. 17,493, fo. 78.
[3] Land Tax, the 1s. in the £ 'Pension Duty', and the 6d. in the £ Civil List Duty, were all payable in respect of Pay Office emoluments, though not every member of the staff was burdened with all three. It does not seem possible to determine how much of the gross sum paid for all taxes actually relates to the Paymaster's salaries.
[4] P.R.O. 30/8, bundle 76.
[5] The English Pericles, p. 32. This is an anonymous pamphlet apparently written about the spring of 1759. See also John Almon, Anecdotes of the Life of the Rt. Hon. William Pitt, Earl of Chatham, &c., (6th edn.,) 1797, i. 243, for the statement that when Pitt retired from the Paymastership, the balances belonging to his office were found intact in the Bank. See also B. Williams, The Life of William Pitt, Earl of Chatham (1915), i. 154-5.

condemnation of the practice until another generation had arisen and until after the great and fruitless expenditure of the American War.[1]

Although it has always been known that the tenure of the Paymastership was, by reason of the magnitude of the sums passing through a Paymaster's hands, a very paying proposition, the actual amount of profit that could be made has hitherto been quite unknown. A corner of the veil is now lifted. Sir Lewis Namier recently drew attention to a set of Henry Fox's private ledgers containing, *inter alia*, accounts relating to his private transactions with public money in his hands, preserved amongst the Bunbury Papers in the Bury St. Edmunds and West Suffolk Record Office.[2] A similar ledger for the short term of office of Fox's successor, Charles Townshend, has been preserved with them and provides useful supplementary information.[3] Fox's ledgers, mostly for a period of twelve months each, cover the years 1758 to 1773 ; that is to say, they begin a few months after he had taken office, and they continue long after his retirement—indeed to within a few months of his death. The first ledger of the set is unhappily missing, and for lack of the journals and vouchers much in the surviving books is obscure ; but their general tenor is informative enough, and, sur-prisingly, they show that what is termed Fox's ' Private Account ' (as distinguished from his ' Office Account '), was actually made up in the Pay Office itself. The fortuitous survival of the ledger for Charles Townshend's ' Private Account ' suggests that this was the normal practice of the period.

Each ledger contains what is described as an ' Inventory ', which is in effect a balance sheet setting out the commencing balances on those various accounts which constitute the ledger proper. These accounts display the transactions of the year, or other accounting period, which followed after the date of the inventory ; the inventory itself revealing the state of affairs at the day on which the ledger opens. On the debtor side of the inventory appear the sums in respect of which Fox was a debtor to the Pay Office or other source of money ; and on the creditor side appears the disposition of Fox's indebtedness, the sums advanced to sundry persons (of whom Fox was thus a creditor), the sums invested in public or other securities, and that resting in the form of cash. It

---

[1] Another source of profit which, according to Edmund Burke, his predecessor as Paymaster General (Richard Rigby) had enjoyed, arose upon the contract for clothing the pensioners belonging to Chelsea Hospital. Burke stated the profit, which pre-sumably was annual, at £700. (See John Debrett's *Parliamentary Register*, vii. 277.) No such profit is identifiable in Fox's private ledgers, but this does not necessarily prove that it was not taken. There is no evidence of Fox's having taken a commission on foreign subsidies. For this alleged practice see B. Williams, *op. cit*. i. 155.

[2] Referenced as in boxes E. 18/853(1) and E. 18/853(2). The books would appear to have come into the family's possession through the marriage of a daughter of General Henry Edward Fox, Henry Fox's youngest son, who ultimately took on the duties of administrator of his father's final account.   [3] See Appendix.

is to be noted that the figures brought into the inventory are not always those appearing at the close of the accounts in the previous ledger; investments are sometimes adjusted to their current market value before being entered in the inventory, a process that might involve either ' writing up ' or ' writing down '. Thus the balance on the inventories, which in most cases represents an excess of advances by Fox over and above his indebtedness to the public, is explicable as profits taken credit for in the books but not yet realized by being turned into cash. An exception is the closing balance, which reveals that Fox's indebtedness exceeded the assets available for discharging it, and appears to be connected with the payment of Charles James Fox's debts.

From the inventories have been compiled Tables 1 and 2,

TABLE 1

STATEMENT OF HENRY FOX'S INDEBTEDNESS TO THE PUBLIC, &C.

(Extracted from the inventories in his private ledgers.)

Date	On Pay Office Account &c.	On Crown Land Revenue Account & to Private Persons	Total
	£	£	£
5 Jan. 1759	133,969	7,956	141,925
5 Jan. 1760	188,867	8,356	197,223
5 Jan. 1761	413,087	8,537	421,624
5 Jan. 1762	628,154	8,822	636,976
5 Jan. 1763	800,620	9,177	809,797
18 Jan. 1764	306,080	9,505	315,585
1 Jan. 1765	159,374	5,010	164,384
1 Jan. 1766	289,364	5,452	294,816
1 Jan. 1767	398,937	5,009	403,946
29 Sep. 1767	426,937	5,810	432,747
29 Sep. 1768	498,937	7,985	506,922
29 Sep. 1769	519,465	6,549	526,014
29 Sep. 1770	489,799	6,249	496,048
29 Sep. 1771	484,799	6,409	491,208
25 Dec. 1772	464,974	7,346	472,320
25 Dec. 1773 *	464,397	75,441	539,838

* Built up from the balances carried forward at the close of the last surviving ledger.

which show respectively the money with which Fox was operating and the manner in which it was disposed. The figures of indebtedness on Pay Office account require little comment. Much of the money was drawn out of an account at the Bank of England where, by custom and for convenience, Paymasters were wont to keep army cash, though they were not yet positively required by statute to do so. Smaller sums came through Hoare's Bank, with which Fox had already been banking as a young man.[1] These latter

[1] Ilchester, op. cit. i. 25.

16

represent the proceeds of sales of stores, of repayments by sub-accountants, and remittances in respect of Irish troops employed. In 1760 and 1761 considerable sums were taken in the form of Exchequer Bills which, at that difficult time, were perhaps issued to the Paymaster in lieu of cash. It should always be remembered, however, that the ledgers only deal with money employed by Fox privately, and so represent only a part of the public balances in his hands, the remainder lying at the Bank of England or elsewhere for the current needs of military expenditure. Before passing on from the first Table it may be remarked that the great increase in indebtedness to private persons arising in 1773 is due to a large borrowing from John Powell, and is almost certainly connected with the payment of Charles James Fox's debts.[1]

TABLE 2

ANALYSIS OF HENRY FOX'S ADVANCES, INVESTMENTS, &C.

(Extracted from the inventories in his private ledgers.)

Date	On Mortgage	On Bonds	In Stocks	In Cash	Sundries	Total
	£	£	£	£	£	£
5 Jan. 1759	62,000	42,110	24,960	11,702	3,415	144,187
5 Jan. 1760	63,395	54,540	63,128	15,108	4,812	200,983
5 Jan. 1761	62,000	62,485	302,581	2,581	4,162	433,809
5 Jan. 1762	86,950	36,024	380,990	145,399	4,597	653,960
5 Jan. 1763	100,250	56,140	313,323	367,714	3,157	840,584
18 Jan. 1764	110,950	23,498	249,220	72,220	5,884	461,772
1 Jan. 1765	131,250	30,052	140,055	17,544	5,731	324,632
1 Jan. 1766	132,793	26,750	248,829	34,101	5,334	447,807
1 Jan. 1767	145,451	38,900	320,656	81,899	5,234	592,140
29 Sep. 1767	222,784	29,795·	346,495	4,883	20,678	624,635
29 Sep. 1768	260,284	27,937	376,830	10	20,794	685,855
29 Sep. 1769	265,784	34,137	356,204	10	35,116	691,251
29 Sep. 1770	256,784	42,839	295,017	7,186	38,269	640,095
29 Sep. 1771	178,084	41,255	388,166	5,706	38,689	651,900
25 Dec. 1772	148,321	41,967	390,995	—	38,009	619,292
25 Dec. 1773*	150,460	53,405	266,961	—	38,629	509,455

* Built up from the balances carried forward at the close of the last surviving ledger.

Regarding the second Table, a few notes may explain the principal variations. The increase in mortgages in 1767 is accounted for by seven fresh advances; and the fall in 1770–1 by the repayment of a single large one (£53,000) advanced to Sir Blake Delaval and his brothers. The rise in the holding of public funds from 1761 reflects speculations with the loans of that and the following year, a residuum being retained for the interest it brought in, and further purchases and sales being made from time to time. Fox was not a man to leave money long lying idle.[2] As far back

[1] For this, see below, pp. 252–3.
[2] A significant exception is to be found during the acute financial crisis of 1759, when between 16 and 19 April he acquired £10,500 in gold specie. This he kept in a chest until 3 November of the same year, when he paid it into Hoare's Bank.

as 1735 he had written : ' I don't see why any more of my money
than is necessary for the election should lie dead at Mr. Hoare's '.[1]
Consequently, except when Fox has just been speculating on a
grand scale (as in 1761 to 1763), or was still varying his investments
considerably (as in the following four years), little is lying idle in
the form of cash bringing him no return.   The increase in the
sundries in 1767 and 1768–9 is largely accounted for by advances
to his extravagant elder son Stephen, and to his natural son Charles
Cooper.

A study of the ledgers indicates that the bulk of Fox's gains
was derived from interest on mortgages, bonds, and public investments, though two spectacularly successful *coups* which greatly
increased his capital must be described later.   The individuals
favoured with loans on mortgage or bond fall into various categories.   A number of them were personal friends, though other
loans were clearly business transactions, sometimes concealed
under the name of a nominee such as his nephew, Lord Digby.
The mortgages were in nearly all cases for considerable sums,
advanced to persons of large landed estate, such as Earl Ferrers,
Sir Blake Delaval and his brothers, the earl of Oxford, &c.   Interest
at the normal mortgage rate of 4 per cent. was payable on the bulk
of these, but the advances made in the hard times of 1761 and 1762
were at the higher rate of 5 per cent.   The recipients of advances
on bond were more various, and considerable loans, at rates of
from $3\frac{1}{2}$ per cent. to 5 per cent., were made to such relatives as the
duke of Richmond,[2] and the marquis of Kildare ;[3] to his one time
patron the duke of Cumberland (an interest-free loan in 1761, and
another at 4 per cent. contracted in 1762 and repaid with accumu-
lated interest after their estrangement at the end of that year) ;[4]
and to such friends as that man-about-town George Selwyn,[5] who
failed to pay up his interest, and Sir George Macartney.[6]   Such
loans included, no doubt, both investments and the fruits of Fox's
generosity to those he held in affection.   Some of the smaller loans
can clearly not be classed as investments.   Such was the loan of
£500, on bond at 5 per cent., to William and Edmund Burke, made
in 1766 when William Burke had common interests with Fox in
East India speculations, on which neither interest nor capital had
been paid at Fox's death, and for which the executor was still

[1] Ilchester, *op. cit.* i. 25.   [2] His wife's brother.
[3] The husband of his wife's sister.
[4] Ilchester, *op. cit.* ii. 176.   The amount of the first loan was a thousand guineas,
and of the second loan, £8,000.
[5] Selwyn's loan was of £2,000.   Interest owed but unpaid at December 1773 may
be computed at almost £1,200.
[6] The amount of the loan varied at different times between the limits of £2,000
and £7,000.   Interest was paid only intermittently, and £1,120 appears to have been
outstanding in December, 1773.

struggling to get satisfaction in 1780 ; [1] or the loan of £1,050 made in 1773 to Edward Moore, Receiver and Register for the Office of Hackney Coaches and Chairs, and Index Maker to the house of commons, who, when pressed for payment pointed out firstly that he was owed money by Fox's estate both on Fox's account and on Charles James's, and secondly that ' I formerly was qualified by holding Lord Holland's stock to vote in the India House. When the law was altered Lord Holland lent me the £1,050 towards purchasing an East India qualification, and I did so principally to oblige his Lordship, who lent it me at 4 per cent. for that purpose '.[2]

Of particular interest are the large loans which Fox made from time to time, either directly or through an intermediary, to jobbers and brokers on the London market, on the security of stock or scrip, sometimes for a year, or more often for a shorter period, a practice that throws some light on the embryonic London Stock Exchange. Thus in 1758, by an intermediary Mr. Tucker, he lent £25,000 to the broking and jobbing firm of Lejay and Chamier,[3] and in March 1759 he lent £20,000 for one year at 5 per cent., soon after increased by a further £12,000. Renewed in 1760, the loan of £20,000 was not paid off until April 1761. In 1760, during the subscription to the government loan of that year, he lent to unspecified persons £12,000 on the security of stock, and £20,000 on the security of lottery tickets, for three months at the same rate.[4] In 1765 he lent a total of £21,760 at 5 per cent. to Nathan Modigliani of Old Bethlem, a Jewish broker and jobber very active in East India speculation, and £1,500 to Samuel Gardiner of Change Alley, broker, to carry them over to the next ' Rescounter ', or quarterly settlement day. In 1766 Modigliani received a loan of £30,000 between ' Rescounters ' (of which £20,000 was renewed), and one Dawes received the sum of £10,000 for the same purpose.

[1] Executor's Letter Book, p. 73, Bury St. Edmunds &c. Record Office E.18/360/5.

[2] Executor's Letter Book, p. 70. Moore held a contingent promissory note of Fox's, liability for which the executor would not admit. The note related to Charles James's affairs. The ground of the direct debt is significant of Fox's unpopularity. Fox had asked Moore to make extracts from the house of commons journals of every entry relating to public accountants ' for the last hundred years ', and had never paid for the work. Moore's tender of what he considered to be his net legal debt appears to have been refused.

[3] Anthony Chamier, a successful stockbroker of Huguenot descent. ' He acquired such a fortune as enabled him, though young, to quit business and become, what indeed he seemed by nature intended for, a gentleman.' (Sir John Hawkins, *The Works of Samuel Johnson, LL.D., together with his Life*, &c. (1787) i. 423.) He later held minor office, and was a friend of Dr. Johnson.

[4] Charles Townshend's ledger shows him making such loans out of his balances in the same way, though necessarily on a smaller scale. Loans from the Bank of England on the security of scrip were recognized to be essential to the success of a subscription, and it seems probable that merchant banks were increasingly rendering the same service to their clients ; but the whole subject of the finance of the stock market at this period remains obscure.

In 1770 he lent to ' a friend of Mr. Fisher's ',[1] the sum of £30,500 on the security of £20,000 Bank Stock, and a further £11,000 on the security of £5,000 East India Stock.

Fox employed the services of a number of agents in the transaction of his financial concerns. Until their breach in 1763 [2] John Calcraft, a close friend and associate of many years' standing and the richest of the army commissaries of the day, was clearly working closely with him; Samuel Touchet, a merchant who crashed in a spectacular manner in 1763,[3] did a good deal for him in later years, and a number of lesser men carried out minor operations on his behalf. But his chief man of business throughout the period was John Powell, accountant (and later cashier) of the Pay Office, in whose hands these ledgers show the bulk of Fox's idle cash to have lain. Powell was later to be the only one of Fox's three named executors who consented to act, was himself to become extremely wealthy, and was destined to end his career in disgrace and suicide in 1782, despite the ill-judged attempts of Edmund Burke, Paymaster at the time, to shelter him.[4] Transactions between Fox and Powell, as shown in the ledgers, are extraordinarily numerous and complicated. In the absence of other information they are indeed impossible to unravel, but everything suggests that Powell was fully informed of Fox's proceedings, being perhaps the only man who ever has been or will be.

The sundries in the accounts embrace a miscellaneous variety of transactions such as shares in turnpikes, in a privateer, in an Indiaman (called ' Lord Holland '), and advances to members of his own family.

The two speculative *coups* already referred to demand particular attention for the large capital profits which they brought, for the part they played in causing Fox's intense unpopularity, and for their significance in the financial history of the time. They arose in connexion with the raising of the government loans during the Seven Years' War; and after them must be mentioned lengthy operations connected with speculation in East India stock and the development of political ' management ' in the East India Company from 1763 onward.

The ledgers show, though not always in full detail, Fox's part in the raising of the government loans of 1759, 1760, 1761, and 1762. In 1759, when the duke of Newcastle's attempt to raise the then almost unprecedented sum of £6,600,000 [5]—coinciding with

---

[1] William Fisher of Change Alley, one of the biggest dealers of the day.

[2] The circumstances of their estrangement have never become altogether clear, but Calcraft threw in his lot with Lord Shelburne, and Fox considered him guilty of the blackest treachery and ingratitude.

[3] For him see Alfred P. Wadsworth and J. de L. Mann, *The Cotton Trade and Industrial Lancashire, 1600–1780* (Manchester) 1931, pp. 243 *seq.*

[4] Sir Philip M. Magnus, *Edmund Burke* (1939) pp. 121–3.

[5] Of earlier loans only that of 1748 (£6,930,000), appears to have been greater.

a payments crisis arising from the needs of wartime remittances—nearly led to disaster in the City,[1] Fox made his first payment on a subscription of £117,700.   He did little to help the Treasury in its hour of need, however, as he sold out all but £17,700 before the second payment became due, and by early May had parted with the whole, estimating his loss at £644 18s. 3d.   A letter of 27 April to his broker, which came into the hands of the duke of Newcastle, ordering the broker to sell all that Fox held, as '. . . I have no opinion of the Subscription ; I don't think it will grow much better ; the Duke of Newcastle consults too many people about it '.[2]   Fox formed a somewhat more favourable impression of the prospects of the 1760 subscription, making a first payment on £260,000, a second payment on £145,700, a third payment on £130,700, and a fourth payment on £87,700.   But though he dealt a good deal in the loan throughout the year, he closed the account in 1761 with an estimated loss of £182 18s. 5d.

So far his dealings had not proved profitable.   Those in the loans of 1761 and 1762 had, however, a very different result.   In 1761 Fox put his name down for £300,000 out of the £12,000,000 to be raised, and he paid the first instalment of 15 per cent. on his subscription.   He then took to purchasing in the market, and in the first four months of that year paid out, either in his own name or in the name of others, the enormous total of £773,936—all public money.   The loan was constituted of three parts : perpetual 3 per cent. stock, long annuities (for 99 years) at £1 2s. 6d. per cent., and lottery tickets.   Fox participated in all three.   He began his sales in March, almost two months before he ceased purchasing, which suggests that the market quotations of the three parts were rising unequally, as buyers preferred and demanded one rather than another.   By the end of 1761 he had divested himself of all proprietorship in the loan save for long annuities worth £10,000 a year, and a few lottery tickets.   The reason for his initial subscription may have been creditable ; as a member of the Ministry it may have seemed proper to assist at a time when Pitt's vehement conduct of the war was making unprecedented demands upon the public purse and the money market.   But his subsequent market purchases cannot be regarded as anything but speculative ; they did nothing to assist Government (the subscription list being already filled), and tended merely to force up the market quotations. His sales prove his true object, and his memoir suggests that these transactions were somewhat on his mind, as the stir in the house of commons about his balances at that time gave good cause.

[1] L. S. Sutherland, ' Samson Gideon, Eighteenth Century Financier ', *Transactions of the Jewish Historical Society of England*, xvii. 86–7.

[2] Brit. Mus. Add. MSS. 32,890, fo. 343, quoted by L. S. Sutherland, *loc. cit.* pp. 86–7.

The sudden and great rise of the stocks (so he writes) has made me richer than I ever intended or desired to be . . . The Government borrows money at 20 % discount. I am not consulted or concerned in making the bargain. I have, as Paymaster, great sums in my hands which, not applicable to any present use, must either lie dead in the Bank or be employed by me. I lend this to the Government in 1761. A peace is thought certain. I am not in the least consulted, but my very bad opinion of Mr. Pitt makes me think it will not be concluded. I sell out and gain greatly.[1]

It seems not unfair to observe that the amount he lent directly to Government was very small. The outside world was certainly optimistic about a speedy peace—hence the rise in the stocks and the speculative fever. But it is difficult indeed to believe, as Fox would apparently have us do, that in his position he had no inside information as to the progress of negotiations.[2] When the outside world's mistake became evident the market broke, and at the end of the year the market value of Fox's retained long annuities was below their cost to him. But this represented only a temporary recession, and by the end of 1763 he had taken credit for realized and book profits in the neighbourhood of £103,000—little of which, if any, appears to have been lost afterwards.

Success again attended his participation in the loan of 1762. His memoir continues:

In 1762 I lend again; a peace comes, in which again I am not consulted, and I again gain greatly. If anybody should say that I advised a peace, let it be considered that that was in November last. I had no money in the Funds then, and indeed thought that my advice would not be taken, nor was it, but on the contrary a declaration of war with Spain followed.

Readers may wonder at his statement that he had no money in the Funds at this period, since his private ledgers show that he held a large block of long annuities, and never less than £60,000 of the four-per-cents. of 1762, not to mention a great holding of navy bills.[3] However, there is no ground for casting suspicion on his exactitude when he admits to having gained greatly, for by the end of 1764 his ledgers show an actually realized profit on this loan amounting to upwards of £56,000.

[1] Henry Fox's 'Memoir', written in 1763, is printed in the *Life and Letters of Lady Sarah Lennox*, by the countess of Ilchester and Lord Stavordale (1902), i. 3–79. This, with the subsequent passage quoted, appears on p. 72.

[2] It has already been seen that at this period Fox had a close financial association with the stockbroker Anthony Chamier. These great capital gains of Fox's were made at the same period as was Chamier's fortune. Of the latter, Sir John Hawkins, writing in 1787 (*op. cit.* i. 423), stated that it arose by Chamier's ' dealings in the funds, and, it was supposed, with the advantage of intelligence which, previous to the conclusion of the peace before last, he had obtained '.

[3] It may be true that Fox had none of his *private* resources in the Funds, but in view of the use to which the public balances was put, the passage quoted has a certain air of the disingenuous.

Fox's operations in East India stock were more complex, and in the long run less rewarding. Their course is known to us in outline from other sources,[1] and the ledgers serve to fill in some, though not all, of the gaps. In the ten years between 1763 and 1773, when his active concern in East India affairs ceases, he was pursuing in his dealings in the stock two main purposes, sometimes both at the same time. He was furthering the political interests of a series of Governments in obtaining a control over the election of the directors of the great political organization which the East India Company had become, and he was seeking on his own account opportunities of gain in the speculative boom which swept over the Company between 1766 and 1769, as a result of Clive's successes in India. The political interests of Governments necessitated the provision of funds to create votes at the Company's elections, pledged to support candidates favoured by the Administration. The course of these great so-called 'splitting' campaigns can best be traced from the stock ledgers of the East India Company itself. Neither the Company's stock-ledgers nor these Pay Office private account ledgers give a full picture of Fox's part in the campaigns, since the management of the funds he provided was in the hands of such men as John Calcraft (at first), John Powell and others. The private account ledgers make, however, occasional references to the payment of fees for numerous stock transfers (e.g. thirty-six in the 1764 campaign), and they give more information on Fox's holdings than do the Company's stock ledgers, since they include stock evidently held by him in the names of others. Thus the Company's ledgers show Fox as purchasing £500 on 3 March 1763 (to qualify him as a voter in the first annual election of directors in which Government actively intervened), and as purchasing another £500 later in the year. Before the next election he disposed of this holding in such a way as to create two votes, but does not re-appear as a holder of stock himself until June 1767. In his own ledgers he is shown as buying not £500 but £11,000 on 3 March 1763, and retaining £10,500 of it through 1764, and purchasing much greater holdings in the next two years.

Fox's political activities in the Company fall into two periods, 1763–4 and 1768–73. In the first period his activities require little explanation. His nominees voted, it is true, for the candidates of Laurence Sulivan's party in the election of 1763, and for the candidates of the rival party under Lord Clive in 1764, but this was because Fox was Paymaster both under the Bute Administration and under that of George Grenville, and the two ministers supported different sides in the Company's conflicts. After he relinquished

[1] For the course of East India affairs and the evidence of Fox's participation in them, see L. S. Sutherland, *The East India Company in Eighteenth Century Politics* (Oxford), 1952, chaps. vi and vii.

the Paymastership in 1765, however, it might have been expected that Fox's assistance to Government in East India matters would cease. In fact it did so until the autumn of 1768, but at that time he began once again to place some of his balances at the disposal of the Grafton Administration for the same purpose. Men concerned with East India affairs spoke of £25,000 stock administered for this purpose in the contested Company election of 1769; his ledgers suggest that probably at least £30,000 more was being used for this purpose.[1] Though we have no explanation of this renewed employment of his balances on Government's behalf, it may be noted that it coincides with the entry of his two elder sons, Stephen and Charles James, into parliament as active young Government supporters, and with the renewal of his own earlier pressure for an earldom. He continued to provide this assistance until the end of 1772 when, after all the dispositions had been made for the Company election of 1773, his ledgers confirm the evidence of those of the Company that he unexpectedly sold out, thus depriving his nominees of any right to vote—no doubt to the embarrassment of Government. Whether his action was due to the pressure of his sons' debts (soon to reach a crisis), to some disagreement with the Ministry, or to alarm at the fall in the price of East India stock which was badly affected at this time by the financial crisis which hit the London market in 1772, and by the particular difficulties of the Company which led to Lord North's East India regulation next year, no evidence is at present available.

Of Fox's purely speculative activities in the stock, which took place between 1766 and 1769, the ledgers are more informative, though here, too, incidental references in them show that much was done by nominees whose affairs only enter accidentally into these accounts. The great boom in East India stock began when the news reached England that Clive had taken over the Diwani, or financial control, of Bengal. Clive's agent, John Walsh, who was purchasing largely on his principal's instructions, advised Fox to do likewise; and those informed in East India affairs were soon aware that he had made considerable purchases, and was prominent amongst the group of speculators who were 'bulling' the stock. The Company ledgers, however, retain no trace of these purchases apart from one of £40,000 stock by John Powell on 29 April 1766. Fox's ledgers, on the other hand, show that between 23 and 25 April he added £50,000 (purchased at prices varying between 174 and 181) to a holding of £20,000; that between 14 and 23 May he added £30,000 more (purchased at much the same prices); and that by 16 July he held £115,000. Of this he sold £65,000 between 11 and 12 September, at prices ranging between 207 and 210, and

[1] See below, p. 248.

at the end of the year he calculated his gains (realized, and estimated on the current value of his holdings of stock), at £41,958.

The rise in the price of stock which lies behind these gains, considerable though it was, was not so great as the ' bulls ' had hoped, and was partly at least the result of organized pressure from them (pressure exerted with all the technique of the ' splitting ' of votes learned in recent contests), for an increase in the Company's dividend. It is known that Fox put his holdings at the disposal of the organizers of this pressure group, and it has been estimated that at least 300 votes were created by this group for the Company's quarterly Court on 26 September 1766. These ledgers throw a striking light on the part Fox's holdings played in this campaign, for on 13 September 1766 there is an entry of payment for forty-three transfers of East India stock, and on 25 September another for no fewer than 118 transfers explicitly stated to be for ' raising the dividend '.

Throughout the vicissitudes of the negotiations of 1767 between Chatham's Administration and the Company, which resulted in the first parliamentary intervention of the century in the Company's affairs, Fox continued to buy and sell on a large scale, and in 1767 and 1768 his speculations continued to be very profitable. But 1769, the year in which the break came in the inflated stock prices and many speculators crashed, brought to him, too, a reversal of fortune. At the end of September 1768 his holding stood at £80,000 valued at 274. At the end of September 1769 he still held £61,000, but he valued it at 225 ; and on the twelve months' operations he wrote off a loss of £17,857 5s. Part of this loss was no doubt incurred for political reasons. A purchase of £25,000 stock in February 1769 in joint ownership with John Powell and Clotworthy Upton, and the loan to them of money to purchase another £15,000 each to be held on the same terms, is probably connected with his responsibilities in the creation of votes in support of the Ministry's supporters in the Company elections of that year, and an insurance fund created to guarantee voters against a fall in the value of their stock.[1] Some of the loss was incurred not by him but by his son Stephen, who had been concerned disastrously in dealing in futures on the inflated market,[2] and whose liabilities he took over; but it ended the days of his great profits from

---

[1] Cf. L. S. Sutherland, *The East India Company in Eighteenth Century Politics*, p. 188.

[2] A well-informed contemporary said in August 1769 (I. Barré to Lord Shelburne, *ibid*. p. 192), that Fox had to pay the ' difference ' on £50,000 stock for the jobbing operations of his son Stephen. Fox's ledgers show that he had paid out well over £15,000 to clear Stephen of his speculative engagements. He paid £7,810 to the Jewish firm of Fatio & Co., the balance of Stephen's account with the brokers Delafontaine & Brymer, who crashed at this time ; and paid another well-known Jewish jobber, Isaac Ximenes, £4,510 as the difference on £11,000 stock between 267½ and the ruling price of 226½, besides taking over the stock at the current rate. He later paid Ximenes a further £2,732 15s. 7d. in full settlement of Stephen's account.

dealing in India stock; and his interest in it henceforth, though still considerable, appears to have been confined to that of salvaging the remains of his speculative interests and carrying out his political obligations. Thus although in the years 1766–8 he took credit for realized or book capital profits of over £68,000, when he finally divested himself of his stock in 1773, less than £15,000 remained as a capital gain.

The manner in which Fox invested his capital gains and that part of the profits derived from the employment of his balances which was not required for his current consumption is interesting. Landed property was not only in the nature of a gilt-edged investment but was also a sound foundation for social position. One might not make a fortune from possessing it, but by it one might conserve a fortune or position already made. The ledgers show Fox steadily spending on real estate, into which he put (after allowing for a few small sales credited in the ledgers), a sum which at the end of 1773 aggregated £193,000. The famous Holland House, first leased and afterwards purchased by him, seems mainly to have been bought out of his private means, for no more than £4,000 appears in the books on this account. But Kingsgate, on the north-east coast coast of Kent—a small property which his ageing fancy turned into a costly folly—appears for a total of £14,615. It may be mentioned that he left Kingsgate to his son Charles James who was, inevitably, compelled to sell it, and that the purchaser was the same John Powell whose fortunes were so closely linked with his own. Another purchase was a town house in Piccadilly, formerly Lord Monson's, and bought for £16,000. When sold in 1771 the consideration money did not come back into these ledgers, and it is of course possible that other properties bought with public money were sold and accounted for elsewhere than in the Paymaster's ' private account '. The remaining purchases, some large, some quite small, were scattered about the southern counties, and occasionally they took the form of a purchase of quit rents.[1]

It was not to be expected that with such resources Fox should not live on a correspondingly lavish scale. In addition to anything that may have been paid out of his private income, these ledgers stand charged under the head of ' house-keeping ' with a sum that averages, from 1758 to 1773, almost exactly £6,000 a year. At the contemporary purchasing power of money, this indeed seems living like a grandee.[2] It is matched by the scale of his disbursements

[1] A fixed perpetual rent, often nominal, in return for which a tenant went free and quit from all other rents and services. It may be contrasted with a rack rent, or full economic annual worth of a property (which was therefore capable of improvement).

[2] In 1784 the household and miscellaneous expenses of the duke of Portland stood at £4,000 p.a. H. J. Habakkuk, in *The European Nobility in the Eighteenth Century* (1953), p. 10.

when travelling on the Continent as an English Milord. Expenses incurred in France during the years 1763 to 1765 totalled £20,620; and in 1768 and 1769 a further £10,466. It is hard to resist the suspicion that these sums include payment of his sons' foreign debts, but if this is so it must be pointed out that the youths are shown as receiving still more money in other distinct parts of the ledgers. Minor embellishments for Fox's residences are represented by paintings. In 1762 he paid twenty guineas apiece to Hogarth and Ramsay 'for my picture', and next year he paid a further bill of Hogarth's for £34 2s. 6d. Ramsay provided another canvas in 1766, by which time the price had risen to twenty-five guineas, but the subject is not indicated. Reynolds was, however, the artist most patronized, no less than £341 being paid for paintings in 1765. Of less interest is the fact that the public balances provided thirty guineas for six places at the coronation of George III, together with 1,000 guineas for cash lost at Lord Harrington's, with other small losses of a similar nature.

It is natural to examine the ledgers to see whether they impinge upon parliamentary life. They do not suggest any unusually heavy expenditure on electioneering. There is a reference in 1759 under 'Promiscuous Payments' to a sum of £25 for an old election debt at Windsor, dating, no doubt, from Fox's heavily contested election there in 1757.[1] In 1762 there was also a payment to Sir Jacob Downing of £91 4s. 3d. 'for re-election', which must be connected with Downing's interest in the borough of Dunwich, for which Fox was elected in 1761.[2] Apart from these minor matters, however, the balances seem to have been drawn on only for advancing the elections of his sons (and perhaps his nephew), and in connexion with the borough of Malmesbury.

Fox had been elected High Steward of Malmesbury in 1751 and held the position for some years,[3] apparently until the earl of Suffolk was elected to the office in 1763.[4] It was an office of importance solely for electoral purposes. The ruling body of this borough was described in 1833 as 'self-elected, irresponsible to the inhabitants of the town, and composed chiefly of labourers without education and of the least instructed class of retail tradesmen'. It was also a body 'which has long ceased to exercise any municipal function but that of returning to Parliament the nominees of the patron of the borough'.[5] The High Steward, who was elected

---

[1] *Official Return of Members of Parliament* (House of Commons Sessional Paper of 1878 No. 69–1, vol. 72). See also J. Calcraft to the earl of Loudoun, 8 July 1757, Brit. Mus. Add. MSS. 17,493, fo. 73ᵛ.   [2] *Official Return of Members of Parliament.*

[3] Ilchester, *op. cit.* i. 171. Sir L. B. Namier, *The Structure of Politics at the Accession of George III,* (1929), i. 538, n. 2. See also *Correspondence of John, 4th Duke of Bedford,* ii. 243–4.   [4] G. E. C., *Peerage.*

[5] *1st Report of the Commissioners appointed to enquire into the Municipal Corporations of England and Wales* (House of Commons Sessional Paper of 1835, No. 116, vol. 23, app.. part 1, p. 75.

annually, was normally a man of importance and exercised a strong influence over the creation of burgesses and the exercise of their votes. In the general election of 1761 the burgesses had evidently given Fox some trouble, as he drafted a scheme for their control which he hoped would 'put an end to those cabals and strugglings in the choice of new Burgesses, which have given Mr. Earle so much trouble and through which he has with great Difficulty, by his honesty, spirit, ability and attention carry'd through this election '.[1] In the same scheme, which he submitted to the earl of Suffolk, who had a strong local family influence, he offered ' to go hand in hand with his Lordship in the choice of Burgesses and Members for that place and hopes his son may have the Honour to do so after him ', but no one connected with him sat there again till 1774 when his son Charles James was elected for the borough.

The Malmesbury account is active during 1759 to 1761, and again from 1769 to 1773. Fox's expenditure in the former period totals about £5,677, but this sum was recouped in its entirety by cash payments of £2,000 from Sir Robert Long, and the balance from Mr. Conolly. Sir Robert Long was brother-in-law of John Tylney, elected for Malmesbury at the general election of 1761 ; Thomas Conolly (brother-in-law to Lady Holland), was elected at a by-election in 1759,[2] and again at the general election of 1761. The disbursements include many items entered as ' loans ', some of which are described as being made to so-and-so, ' a new burgess '. The nature of some other and larger payments is not specified, but notice may be taken of £25 14s. for ' small expenses paid on account of next election ' (which might refer to a parliamentary, a High Steward's, but more probably a burgess's election), and of a disbursement of £100 described as ' Secret Service '. It is tempting to connect this with assistance which, on at least one occasion, Fox obtained from Government to secure the High Stewardship at an annual election, but the connexion with the ledger entry is doubtful.[3] When the

[1] Wilts County Record Office, Trowbridge, No. 88 (Suffolk and Berks MSS.). The manuscript is endorsed ' Paper delivered to Lord Suffolk by Mr. Fox in 1760 '. ' Mr. Earle ' is William Rawlinson Earle of Condwell, Wilts, M.P. for Malmesbury, 1727–47, and subsequently for Cricklade. We are indebted to Miss M. Ransome for a transcript of the document and for this information.

[2] It would appear that in Conolly's absence—perhaps in Ireland—his mother, Lady Anne Conolly, had received from Fox a contingent offer of the seat for her son. ' It strikes me ', wrote Fox, when reporting his action to the duke of Devonshire, ' that Conolly would be very glad to find himself a Member of Parlt., at his arrival '. (4 March 1759, Devonshire MSS. 330, 229.)

[3] See Namier, loc. cit. A document on elections amongst the duke of Newcastle's papers, endorsed 12 December 1760, contains a note of ' £1,000 given to elect Mr. Fox High Steward ' of Malmesbury, and continues : ' Q. Whether the £1,000 was the King's money. To speak to Mr. Fox about it.' The document then refers to the members elected for Malmesbury in 1754 (Brit. Mus. Add. MSS. 32,999, fo. 119). The conjunction of this with a repayment by Fox of £356 18s. 6d. for ' remainder

Malmesbury Account is reopened in 1769, it is with a disbursement of £1,100 for bank bills remitted to ' Mr. [Charles] Fox ', who over the years 1769 to 1773 received a further £1,460. The only other item is £620 for ' cash paid Mr. Collins draft '. When the last ledger closes the total debit is £3,180 and no recoupment has been received from any quarter. Yet the nature of these transactions becomes fairly clear when it is found that Charles James Fox was elected a member at the next general election, in 1774; his fellow member being William Strahan.

Fox first had occasion to provide for the election of his two elder sons in the general election of 1768. Stephen might, it seems, have secured a safe seat at Stockbridge, and some preparations to this end were made from September 1766,[1] but finally New Sarum was chosen—a borough for which his uncle and grandfather had sat in former years. His election there cost £2,600. Charles James was returned for Midhurst, £3,000 being paid to Lord Montague on this account. It appears that Fox hired this borough jointly with his brother Lord Ilchester, the other elected member being the latter's son, Lord Stavordale.[2]

The expenditure incurred in bringing Fox's elder sons into parliament was the least of the burdens they laid on him, for their extravagance was notorious. The researches of Lord Ilchester have shown the extent of the drain on him.[3] The ledgers give only part of the story, but they show Stephen as receiving over £67,000 in all from the public balances, of which, however, some £50,000 was treated as a debt on which he began to pay interest in 1773.[4] Charles James is shown as costing the still greater sum of £118,718 of which £100,000 was the amount placed in the hands

from Malmesbury ' on 24 April 1754 (Brit. Mus. Add. MSS. 33,044, fo. 27), suggests that the assistance was concerned rather with the general election of 1754 than of 1760, and that the repayment closed the account. In must, in any case, be emphasized that the £100 entered in Fox's ledger is a disbursement, not a receipt, and that the whole receipt came to him through the hands of Long and Conolly.

---

[1] In 1756 Fox had, according to Lord Ilchester (*op. cit.* ii. 13–14), leased Sir Robert Henley's interest in this borough for ten years. The account in the ledgers, which dates from after the end of this period, does not mention Sir Robert Henley but is entitled ' Sir George Macartney on account of Stockbridge Election '. Macartney's name does not otherwise appear in the account. £3,600 was advanced directly to Stephen, and £500 previously advanced to a Mr. Harmood was transferred to this account, making in all £4,100. Of this, Harmood refunded £300, and Stephen cleared his £3,600 either by bills to a certain Mr. Moore, or by cash paid by Moore on his behalf. This was possibly the same Moore who has been mentioned above, p. 242. The balance of £200, which would appear to have been part of the advance to Harmood, was written off as a loss.

[2] Ilchester, *op. cit.* ii. 325.   [3] Ilchester, *op. cit.* ii. 351 *seqq.*

[4] The sum also includes some small sums paid in early days to the tutor who was travelling on the Continent with him.

of John Powell to buy off the annuitants [1] (shown in the ledgers to include a high proportion of the more speculative dealers, Jewish and Christian, on the London market) who had been speculating on his chance of succeeding to the family fortunes. In contrast to this disheartening picture the third son Henry Edward cost much less. His father cared for him—and therefore spoiled him—less than his brothers, and he was made of different stuff, for he avoided notoriety and pursued a creditable military career. The public balances helped to start him off, carrying him as far as a lieutenancy of Dragoons for no more than £2,687. Of this, the initial cornetcy cost £1,000, and was sold for just over £1,100. The lieutenancy itself cost £1,365. This son was later to take upon his shoulders voluntarily the task of acting as 'administrator' of his father's final account as Paymaster. Of Fox's three named executors his son, Charles James, and his nephew, Lord Digby, had declined to act, leaving John Powell to do all the work. After Powell's suicide the house of commons was treated to the spectacle of an attorney-general thirsting for a prosecution in regard to the late Paymaster's balances, but baulked of his prey for lack of any legal representative to prosecute.[2] It was in these circumstances that Henry Edward consented to act as administrator, and it was something like twenty-three years before he was freed from his responsibilities.[3]

If Fox was generous to his legitimate children, he did not forget his natural ones. A son, Charles Cooper, received all told over £11,000, of which £3,000 purchased a colonelcy, and £5,500 was treated as a loan. A daughter, Alicia, was less handsomely treated; but she received £100 for wedding clothes when she was married to Edward Young, who shortly afterwards became bishop of Dromore (and was thence translated to Ferns), in which capacities he enjoyed a moderate accommodation by way of loan on bond. Fox also stood by the widow of John Ayliff, who had been his agent as Receiver General of the Crown Land Revenue for the South Wales district. This agent forged Fox's signature and was hanged for it.[4] The £969 he owed Fox remained in the ledgers, never called in, until they close; and a small annuity helped to rescue Mrs. Ayliff from privation.

[1] Ilchester, *op. cit.* ii. 354. Over £73,000 of this sum was in fact borrowed from Powell (cf. p. 240). It would be interesting to know the source from which a man in Powell's position could have supplied so large a sum. Richard Rigby, the Paymaster at the time, does not appear to have been on very good terms with Fox, but possibly the money came from his balances through Powell. Powell's whole career suggests that he was also able to play with Pay Office money on his own account.

[2] William Cobbett, *Parliamentary History*, xxiv. col. 673, 23 February 1784.

[3] His final payment on account of his father's balances, by which at last Henry Edward became 'Quit', was made on 1 December 1807, forty-two years after Fox's retirement, and a third of a century after his death. See the last folio of Fox's final Declared Account, P.R.O., A.O. 1, 76, roll 100.

[4] Ilchester, *op. cit.* ii. 112.

The story unfolded by these ledgers is an astonishing one, even though contemporary comment has prepared us for it.   A man of medium fortune took a public office the net worth of which, so far as official emolument is concerned, appears to have been not more than £3,000 a year.   After eight years' tenure he retired; yet as the result of his tenure he continued until the end of his life to receive an income vastly greater than his official profit when he was in office.   The annual average ' unofficial ' profit from within a few months of Fox's taking office until within a few months of his death was £23,657—or more than seven and a half times the net salary.[1]   In a single year, 1766, his profit of £54,851 was over eighteen times the net salary; and altogether he laid out in landed property alone £193,366, or almost sixty-five times the value of the net annual salary.   Further, he was able to save his family from disgrace, and, almost certainly, ruin, by having the means with which to pay his sons' debts without realizing all that he had of his private estate.   Yet there was nothing illegal in what he did, nor, according to the customs and notions of his age anything grossly improper.

Opinion as to the propriety of such gains was, nevertheless, changing.   A beginning in reform was made, in 1782, with the Regulating Act [2] implementing there commendations of the commissioners for examining the public accounts and passed by the Rockingham Administration.   Amongst other things this Act required the Paymaster's cash to be remitted from the exchequer to an official account at the Bank of England, drawings upon that account to be made by warrants stating the service for which the money was required.   A continuation of reform was made shortly afterwards, when Henry Dundas was responsible for a similar Act [3] regulating his office of Treasurer of the Navy, which was another recommendation of the commissioners.   The latter's recommendation that the office of Treasurer of the Ordnance should be similarly regulated was not, however, heeded until after Pitt's death.   How quick was the change in outlook and how far these measures effected their ends is, however, uncertain.   The regulation of the Paymaster's office may have been effectual, but that of the other two offices was not.   Although Dundas, as Lord Melville, was acquitted of his impeachment for alleged irregularities, the impression given by a reading of the evidence at the impeachment is that the condemned self-enrichment had merely been transferred from the Treasurer to a subordinate; and a Treasurer of the Ordnance was detected in improper conduct in the years immediately after the regulation of

<hr>

[1] The *Gentleman's Magazine* printed an obituary notice on Richard Rigby (vol. 58, pp. 369–70), in which the Paymastership, at the time of Rigby's appointment in 1768, is referred to as ' a place, by the lowest computation, then valued at £16,000 p.a. '.

[2] 22 Geo. III, c. 81.   [3] 25 Geo. III, c. 31.

his office.[1] With a civil service tradition as well established as this, and with effective public condemnation so slowly developing, it is not to be expected that in a previous generation public officers should act according to a high standard of conduct unnatural to the age in which they lived.

Nevertheless, the fact remains that Fox was, at least from the sixties onward, acutely unpopular. Various explanations can be adduced for this fact. Some stress has been laid on the contrast presented between his career and that of the elder Pitt. It is likely that contempt for him for his decision to drop out of the struggle for power with Pitt in 1757, and to accept a position of profit rather than of honour, has been more keenly felt by subsequent historians than by his contemporaries; certainly it caused little if any surprise at the time. More important in this connexion probably, as drawing public disfavour on Fox, was the ill-judged pamphleteering carried on on his behalf (and, no doubt, with his connivance) by Dr. Francis in the *Test* against Pitt, the popular hero, during his short-lived Ministry of 1756; and the contrast between the two men was too striking to ignore. But the form taken by the various attacks on Fox makes it plain that the feeling against him arose largely from his Paymaster's balances and the use he made of them. This was partly due to circumstance. To make outstanding gains from the office a Paymaster must hold it for some time and under the conditions of war. Though the profits made under such circumstances by Sir Stephen Fox and Lord Chandos had become legendary, no Paymaster in recent times had both had the chances which were open to Fox and taken advantage of them. Only two men among his more recent precedessors had held it under these conditions, Henry Pelham from 1730–43 and the elder Pitt from 1746–55. The latter, as has already been said, was understood to have refused to employ his balances at all, and the former was known to have died a comparatively poor man. Among his immediate successors Charles Townshend (1765 to 1766), clearly had no such scruples, but he held the office in time of peace and for too short a tenure to make great profits; and the same applied to Lord North and George Cooke, who jointly succeeded Townshend. It was not until the Paymastership of Richard Rigby, during the American War of Independence, that Fox's gains were rivalled. At the time of the attacks on him Fox thus stood in unenviable isolation.

Moreover, the dates at which the two attacks on him were launched, 1763 and 1769, have some relevance when the method by which he made some of his biggest capital gains is considered.

---

[1] *Commissioners of Military Enquiry* 1806–12, Rep. 12. *House of Commons Sessional Paper of 1810*, no. 81, vol. 9. The Regulating Act was 46 Geo. III, c. 45 (1806).

The attack of 1763 followed his great speculative gains in connexion with the Peace, and that of 1769 followed his participation in jobbing and corruption within the East India Company, which had just resulted in a series of painful scandals when the crash in the stock came. Though the political morality of the eighteenth century was in many ways low, leading politicians, ever since the South Sea scandals, had been careful not to incur the stigma of using their position to speculate on the stock market, and discredit attached to a major political figure who was known to have engaged in the ' infamous practice of stock jobbing '. The greatness of Fox's balances during the course of the Seven Years' war, his success in employing them to increase his wealth, the evidence of this wealth displayed in his own way of life and that of his family, but above all the means he employed to increase his capital were probably the main causes of his sustained unpopularity. As Fox himself remarked : ' Obloquy generally attends money so got.' [1]

LUCY S. SUTHERLAND.
J. BINNEY.

APPENDIX

CHARLES TOWNSHEND'S LEDGER

The ledger containing the ' Private Account ' of Charles Townshend who, as Fox's successor, was Paymaster General of the Forces from June 1765 to August 1766,[2] is smaller than those of Henry Fox, is less elaborately bound and less fairly written. It contains entries up to 27 July 1769, almost two years after Townshend's death,[3] and then the ledger appears to have been laid aside without any attempt to balance and close the accounts.

Corresponding to the inventories in Fox's ledgers, there are three ' General States ', taken at 11 June 1766, 25 December 1766, and 12 September 1767. These ' General States ' show that indebtedness was to the Pay Office alone, and that by June 1766 Townshend was already operating with £99,500 of public money, a figure which had risen to £150,784 at the end of his life. As in Fox's case, some of this money arose out of remittances for the pay of Irish troops, and some by direct drawing on the Bank of England, which in Townshend's case appears to have been by draft in favour of John Powell. The bulk arose out of taking Exchequer Bills (probably issued to the Paymaster in lieu of cash), on which Townshend pocketed the accrued interest.

[1] Henry Fox's ' Memoir ', countess of Ilchester and Lord Stavordale, *op. cit.* i. 72.
[2] In accordance with the usual contemporary practice, Townshend remained Accountant to the Crown in respect of the Pay Office until the close of the current half year in December 1766.
[3] 4 September 1767.

The disposition of the indebtedness shows no advances specifically stated to be on mortgage, but Townshend made sundry advances upon bond; for example, £500 to his brother, the fourth Viscount Townshend, and £1,000 to Chase Price, M.P., both being at 5 per cent., and a further £6,000 to Sir George Yonge, at 4 per cent. Two large advances made on unspecified security were £10,500 to Edward M. D. Howarth (the cash being paid to 'Mr. Woodhouse'), and £20,300 to the duke of Buccleugh (of which the initial £2,300 was 'cash paid to sundry persons'). There is clear evidence of the purchase of real estate in the £3,000 paid for 'Mr. Allenson's estate in Hertfordshire'.

Like his predecessor, Townshend used his balances to speculate on the stock market. In June 1766 he held in Government stocks £66,000 valued at £66,859, and in India stock £5,500 valued at £9,900. He was constantly switching, and at Christmas his Government stocks were down to £45,000 worth £46,013, and his India stocks were up to £17,000 worth £37,400. At his death he had jettisoned all his India stock save the minimum holding of £500 qualifying for a vote; he held £9,000 Bank stock worth £13,320; and his Government stocks were now worth £81,115. The latter included a participation in the Loan of 1767, but as the holding is described as Scrip and not as Omnium, it is probable that he bought it in the market and was not an original subscriber.[1]

City names already familiar in Fox's ledgers appear again in Townshend's as receiving accommodation. Modigliani was lent £10,000 'to Rescounter in May next' (a period of three months), and loans on the security of stock were made, as for instance £5,000 to G. Shergold on Bank stock 'to opening', and the same sum to Modigliani on India stock. Like Fox, Townshend had £1,000 invested in an Indiaman, and like Fox he placed his surplus cash in John Powell's hands, the amount at Townshend's death being £13,628. It may also be noted that his speculation in East India stock occurred at a time when, as chancellor of the exchequer, he was actively concerned in the Chatham Administration's intervention in the Company's affairs.[2]

Owing to the less detailed manner in which the ledger is written up, and the imperfect state in which it was abandoned, it is impossible to calculate Townshend's gains as exactly as it is possible to calculate Fox's. It can, however, be stated that by April 1767 gains of £8,259 were recorded, of which £7,071 arose out of successful East India speculation.

It is clear from this ledger that Townshend employed his balances in the same way as Fox had, and it appears highly probable that, as in Fox's case, Powell of the Pay Office was closely connected with his new chief's operations, and was an important agent in the private profit making of both Paymasters.

[1] The Loan of 1767 consisted of 3 per cent. stock, of which part was issued in accordance with the subscription list, and the remainder was divided amongst the proprietors as determined by a lottery. The united interest was known as the Omnium, and the separate interests as Scrip. Original subscriptions were for Omnium.

[2] L. S. Sutherland, *op. cit.* pp. 151 *seqq.*

Britain and the Alliance of Hanover,
April 1725-February 1726

ON 30 April and 1 May 1725 Spain and the Emperor signed treaties of peace, commerce, and alliance at Vienna, thus settling between themselves differences which Britain, France, and the United Provinces had been unable to settle in nearly a decade of negotiating.[1] Spain made remarkable concessions.[2] In the treaty of peace she not only held herself strictly to the letter of the Quadruple alliance, but also guaranteed the Pragmatic Sanction. In the treaty of commerce she placed the subjects of the Emperor on an equality with those of Britain and granted permission to the Imperial Ostend East India Company to trade with any part of the Spanish dominions, excepting Spanish America.[3] The treaty of alliance was purely defensive, the Emperor promising merely his good offices, and if these failed his mediation, on behalf of Spanish claims to Gibraltar. The settlement caused considerable apprehension in the rest of Europe, and on 3 September 1725 Britain, France and Prussia signed a counter-alliance at Hanover.[4] In article 2 the contracting parties guaranteed each other's territories and rights, inside and outside Europe; commercial rights were mentioned particularly. On 17 February O.S. 1726 parliament approved unanimously of the alliance of Hanover and strongly condemned the treaty of commerce.[5]

The purpose of this article is to examine the reasons which made British ministers so anxious to form the alliance of Hanover,

---

[1] For accounts of the negotiations leading immediately to the treaties, see principally: E. Armstrong, *Elisabeth Farnese* (1892), pp. 169-87; A. Arneth, *Prinz Eugen von Savoyen* (Wien, 1858), iii. 170-81; G. Syveton, *Une cour et un aventurier*; *le Baron de Ripperda* (Paris, 1896), pp. 52-115; A. Baudrillart, *Phillippe V et la cour de France* (Paris, 1890-1901), iii. 130-91; J. Dureng, *Le duc de Bourbon et l'Angleterre, 1723-1726* (Paris, 1911), pp. 235-79.

[2] For the texts of the treaties see, J. de M. Rousset, *Recueil historique d'actes, négotiations, mémoires, et traités, depuis la paix d'Utrecht . . . (Jusqu'à celle d'Aix-la-Chapelle)*. (The Hague, 1728-55), ii. 110-86. There were two treaties of peace binding the Emperor as head of the Habsburg dominions and as head of the Empire.

[3] Perhaps this was what the Emperor most desired. See M. Braubach, *Versailles und Wien von Ludwig XIV bis Kaunitz* (Bonn, 1952), pp. 148-9.

[4] For the text of the treaty, see Rousset, *op. cit.* ii. 189-99.

[5] *Journals of House of Commons*, xx. 582; *Journals of House of Lords*, xxii. 597-8. (Hereafter abbreviated H.C.J. and H.L.J. respectively.)

and the process by which the alliance came to be accepted by parliament. Some excuse is obviously necessary for re-opening discussion on the first of these questions in view of the monumental study by J. F. Chance of British diplomacy during the period between April 1725 and August 1726, and of a good deal more besides.[1] Chance reconstructed with great accuracy and in massive detail the day-to-day development of the negotiations. He did not, however, go beyond establishing the record of events; he came to no general conclusions about the exact order of priorities governing British foreign policy during this period and, indeed, deliberately refrained from making them, for he regarded himself as a sort of professional researcher whose job was to amass the facts.[2] What he failed to do himself, others failed to do for him. His work in no way modified the existing interpretation of events, which was based on a number of studies, good within their fields, but approaching the alliance of Hanover from a non-British or a not exclusively British angle. Of these the most influential was that of the Belgian historian, Huisman, which traced the fortunes of the Ostend Company from its inception to its destruction.[3] Huisman's work, although over fifty years old, has not been superseded within its terms of reference.[4] It is important, however, to realize what those terms of reference were. Huisman did not set out to write a diplomatic history of the period; he was concerned with only one aspect of it and, by isolating one factor among several, tended to get the picture somewhat out of focus; moreover, it was precisely the British angle which he covered least adequately, for he made no use of British archives. If, so far as the diplomatic aspect of the alliance of Hanover is concerned, a new interpretation depends upon making better use of what is already in print rather than on added documentation, the reverse is true in regard to the second of the problems, that of describing the reaction of British public opinion to the treaties of Vienna. There has been no detailed treatment of this question, and the decisive work has been an article, written fifty years ago, by G. B. Hertz, entitled ' England and the Ostend Company '.[5] This is unsatisfactory for a number of reasons. In the first place it is concerned with a different problem, that of tracing the development of British hostility towards the Ostend Company during the whole of the Company's active life, a task which necessarily reduced the amount

---

[1] J. F. Chance, *The alliance of Hanover* (1923).

[2] Chance, *op. cit.* p. v.

[3] M. Huisman, *La Belgique commerciale sous l'Empereur Charles VI* (Brussels, 1902).

[4] Most of the work done on the Ostend Company since Huisman has been concerned with more detailed treatment of episodes to which he gave only passing mention. For an account of this, see F. Prims 'Voor de geschiedenis van de Oostendse Compagnie', *Mededelingen van de Academie van Marine van Belgie*, vii (1953), 131-6.

[5] *Ante*, xxii (1907), 255-79.

of attention which could be given to any episode in it.   The
disadvantage of tackling such a long period can be clearly seen in
the account given of the period between the treaties of Vienna
and final parliamentary approval of the alliance of Hanover.   The
reading is restricted largely to pamphlets and to parliamentary
debates as derived from Cobbett;   no use is made of the reports
of foreign ambassadors in London, French and Dutch, whose
dispatches contain much that is of value for British parliamentary
history and provide invaluable material for a detailed account of
the fluctuations of public opinion.   Moreover the whole account
is so telescoped as to be positively misleading.   Thus the sketch
of public opinion on the eve of the parliamentary session of 1726
is derived almost wholly from pamphlets of a later date, written
either near the end of the session or during the following two years.
In addition rather tendentious selections are made from the documents;   this is the case with the accounts which Hertz gives of
Charles Forman's ' Letter to Pulteney ', which is misdated, and
of the speech from the throne of January 1726.   Finally, the
validity of Hertz's account is reduced still further by the careless
transposition of a speech from a Commons' debate of January
1727 into a discussion of the debate of January and February
1726.[1]   It may be said then that the existing account of the British
attitude to the alliance of Hanover requires correction since it is
based on works concerned for the most part with particular aspects
of the problem.

The prevailing view of the alliance of Hanover over the past
fifty years has been that in a situation of admitted complexity the
most serious consideration for Britain was the need to defeat the
challenge to her economic and commercial superiority represented
by the concessions made to the Ostend Company in the treaty of
commerce;   that although other considerations existed, such as
the threat to Gibraltar and the potential dangers to the European
balance of power and the Protestant interest in Europe involved
in a supposed Austro-Spanish marriage alliance, they were of less
importance;[2] and finally, that British ministers were encouraged,

---

[1] *Ante*, zzii (1907), pp. 266-8.

[2] The most extreme form of this view is to be found in E. Bourgeois, *Manuel
historique de la politique étrangère* (Paris, 1906, 4th edn.), i. 302, in which the alliance
is attributed to commercial jealousy alone.   Huisman, *op. cit.* 314, 332-3, 354, was
very close to this point of view, for he suspected that talk of a marriage alliance was
used by Britain and France as a means of enlisting European allies;   M. Immich,
Geschichte des Europäischen Staatensystems von 1660 bis 1789 (Munich and Berlin, 1905),
pp. 257-60, hinted at the same possibility.   The following admit that other factors,
though less important, genuinely disturbed British ministers—B. Williams, ' The
foreign policy of Robert Walpole 1721-1731 ' (*ante*, xv (1900), 666-9, 671-2) and again
in *The Whig Supremacy, 1714-1760* (Oxford, 1939), p. 187;   J. Dureng, *op. cit.* pp. 331-
2;   A. Goslinga, *Slingelandt's Efforts towards European Peace* (The Hague, 1915), pp. 83-5;
J. F. Chance, *op. cit.* pp. 38-9, 65-6;   W. Michael, *Englische Geschichte im achtzehnten*

if not compelled, to make the alliance by a violent and spontaneous
outburst of public indignation, aroused principally by the spectre
of commercial rivalry.[1]   If this is so, then a dramatic change
occurred in the British attitude to the Ostend Company as a result
of the treaties of Vienna, for before 1725 neither the administration
nor public opinion had shown any inclination to take decisive
action against the trade from Ostend.   Official British opposition
had been restricted almost entirely to the making of representations
to the Emperor against the recruitment of British seamen and the
use of British capital, and to ineffectual attempts by legislation to
deter British subjects from engaging directly or indirectly in the
activities of the Company.[2]   And even here the objection had
been to some extent political as well as commercial, for the establishment of the Company had been attributed to Jacobite exiles, whose
activities seemed designed to undermine the stability of the Protestant
succession.[3]   Only on one occasion before 1725 did Britain go
beyond diplomatic protests and economic retaliation—in 1723,
when she associated herself with the Dutch in a joint declaration
to the Emperor stating that the Ostend trade constituted a *casus
foederis* to which the engagements made under the triple alliance
of 1717 were applicable.[4]   And even this was not the serious threat
that it seemed at first sight.   Its real purpose was to exacerbate
Dutch-Imperial relations so that the United Provinces would be
brought round to the view that their differences with the Emperor
could best be settled by accession to the quadruple alliance, a move
which Britain desired for the effect it might have in facilitating
the solution of the vexed problem of the Italian investitures still
outstanding between Charles VI and the king of Spain.[5]   That

Jahrhundert (Leipzig, 1896-1945), iii. 410-25, 435-6; P. Geyl, *Geschiedenis van de nederlandse
stam* (Amsterdam, 1937), iii 232-3; P. Muret, *La prépondérance anglaise, 1715-1763*
(Paris, 1949), pp. 162, 164-6. Only Miss Sutherland, in an aside, has denied the
supremacy of the commercial issue, attributing more importance to the threat to
Gibraltar; L. S. Sutherland, *The East India Company in Eighteenth Century Politics*
(Oxford, 1952), p. 27.) This is more true of the situation in 1727 than in either
1725 or 1726.

    [1] G. B. Hertz, 'England and the Ostend Company', (*ante*, xxii (1907), 264-5,
268, 271); C. Grant-Robertson, *England under the Hanoverians* (16th edn., 1949), pp. 48-9;
J. H. Plumb, *England in the Eighteenth Century* (1950), pp. 64-5.

    [2] For the representations see Huisman, *op. cit.* pp. 121-2; W. Michael, *op. cit.*
iii. 383-4, 388. The inadequacy of legislation is demonstrated by three Acts, in 1719,
1721, and 1723, each imposing heavier penalties than the last on British subjects
engaged in the Ostend trade (*Statutes at Large*, v. 230-1, 348-53, and 466-8).   In
1724 parliament tried another tack and reduced duties on coffee, tea, and chocolate
(*Statutes at Large*, v. 482-95). It was not easy to catch smugglers from Ostend, for
ships leaving there at night could be in England before news of their departure had
been received (N. Laude, *La compagnie d'Ostende et son activité coloniale au Bengale 1725-
1730* (Brussels, 1944), pp. 71-2).

    [3] Sutherland, *op. cit.* p. 27; Geyl, *op. cit.* iii. 222-5.

    [4] H. J. Tiele, *De zending van Pesters naar Hannover, Augustus—December 1723*
('s Gravenhage, 1921), p. 15.

    [5] Tiele, *op. cit.* pp. 28-55.

Britain was only going through the motions of co-operating with the Dutch in order to get their support for other purposes is clear from her attitude to the subsequent Dutch attempt to secure French accession to the declaration. The British ambassador at Paris was instructed not to press the matter in the face of French opposition, but merely to do what was necessary to save appearances.[1] When the French refused, Britain dropped the matter. A little later in 1724, Britain rejected a proposal originating with the United Provinces to secure discussion of the Company's status at the congress of Cambrai, again through a determination not to act without the concurrence of France.[2] So unsympathetic indeed did the Government's attitude seem that even in 1725 it was rumoured that Walpole had been bribed by the Company to keep things quiet.[3] Balked in their attempt to secure joint diplomatic action and too timid to take the initiative themselves, the Dutch did what they could to impede the Company's progress by imposing severe penalties on Netherlanders serving in or financing Ostend ships, denying Ostenders insurance facilities in the United Provinces, and forbidding the provisioning of Ostend ships in Dutch ports in the East Indies.[4] They made sure too that the issues involved in the Company's continued activities were brought to the attention of the European public. In a number of learned pamphlets Dutch writers alleged that the establishment of the Ostend Company was a flagrant violation of the treaties of Munster and the Barrier.[5] These pamphlets were sometimes translated into English and

[1] Townshend to H. Walpole, 29 January 1723/4 (Brit. Mus., Add. MSS. 48981 (Townshend papers)).

[2] Goslinga, op. cit. pp. 74-9.

[3] Rev. R. Wodrow, Analecta or Materials for a History of Remarkable Providences mostly relating to Scotch Ministers and Christians (Edinburgh 1843), iii. 233-4.

[4] C. M. Blankenheijm, Geschiedenis van de compagnie van Ostende (Leiden, 1861), pp. 54-5; J. de Hullu, 'Over den Chinaschen handel der Oost-Indische Compagnie in de eerste dertig jaar van de achtiennde eeuw', Bijdragen tot de Taal-land-en-Volkenkunde van Nederlandsch-Indie, 'n Gravenhage, Deel 73 (1917), pp. 50-6.

[5] Dissertation où l'on prouve le droit exclusif de la compagnie orientale des Provinces Unies au commerce et à la navigation des Indes Orientales, contre les prétensions des habitants des Pais Bas espagnols ou autrichiens, traduite du Latin (A la Haye. Chez T. Johnson, 1724, pp. 22). According to W. P. C. Knuttel, Catalogus van de pampfletten—verzameling berustende im de koninklijke bibliotheek ('s Gravenhage, 1889-1916), iv. 57, the original, in Latin, was probably written by A. Westerveen, secretary of the Dutch East India Company. A second Dissertation concerning the Right of the Dutch East India Company to Trade and Navigation against the Inhabitants of the Spanish, now Austrian Netherlands. In Answer to the Objections of Mr. P. Macneny. Written by Order of the Dutch East India Company by Abraham Westerveen, Advocat, Counsellor, and Secretary to the said Company. Done into English with some notes by J. J. Hague. Printed for T. Johnson, 1724, pp. 63. There was also a Dutch translation from the Latin original (see Knuttel iv 60-61). Défense du droit de la compagnie hollandoise contre les nouvelles pretensions des habitants des Pays Bas autrichiens et les raisons ou objections des avocats de la compagnie d'Ostende. Par Jean Barbeyrac, professeur en droit à Groningue et membre de la société royale des sciences à Berlin (A la Haye. Chez T. Johnson, 1725, pp. 131). These pamphlets are among the Lansdowne collection at University College, London. I thank the Librarian of University College for permission to use the collection.

distributed to M.P.s.[1] Hardly any contribution to the argument, however, was made by British writers, except as a commentary on Dutch writers. The only independent contribution on the British side significantly thought it necessary to argue that Britain ought to consider the destruction of the Ostend Company not merely as an obligation to which she was bound as a guarantee of the Barrier treaty, but as a defence of her own interests.[2]

To a considerable extent this pattern persisted even after the treaty of commerce. The concessions made to the Ostend Company in 1725 undoubtedly increased the dangers to British interests; not only was the threat to the East India Company greater, but an entirely new threat arose to the more influential interests of West Indian and Spanish merchants. It was not merely that the treaty of commerce extended most favoured nation treatment to the Emperor's ships, though this was bad enough and endangered the market for British manufacturers in Spain and Portugal.[3] Articles 2 and 3 of the treaty, by permitting merchant ships and men-of-war of both contracting parties to provision in any port belonging to either, made possible, it was argued, direct and unrestricted trade by the Emperor's subjects with the Spanish colonies.[4] And British merchants were well-fitted to appreciate the value of such a concession for their own restricted trade had been subject to persistent interruptions.[5] Nor did the dangers end there. Soon after the treaty was concluded Spain threatened to repudiate altogether British trading privileges in Spain and the Indies unless Gibraltar was restored immediately.[6] Yet these dangers, although clear, considerable, and immediate, were not

[1] In addition to *A second dissertation* . . . the remonstrance of the Dutch East India Company (L'Hermitage, 14 May 1723; Brit. Mus., Add. MSS. 17677 KKK5 (Dutch transcripts)). The Emperor's argument was also available in English in the *Réfutation des arguments avancées de la part de Mess. les Directeurs des Compagnies d'Orient et d'Occident des Provinces Unies contre la liberté du commerce des habitants des Pais Bas sujets de Sa Majesté impériale et Catholique dans les climats éloignés à prétexte des articles 5 et 6 du traité de Munster* (A la Haye, 1723, Selon la copie à Bruxelles, Chez Eugene Henry Fricz, Imprimateur de Sa Majesté Impériale et Catholique, 1723, pp. 71), which was translated and distributed to M.P.s (Michael, *op. cit.* iii. 396). An abstract appeared in A. Boyer, *The Political State of Great Britain*, xxvii. 1-54.

[2] Boyer, *op. cit.* xxvii. 217-25.

[3] Chammorel, 24 September 1725 (Archives Étrangères—Correspondance d'Angleterre, t. 325). Hereinafter abbreviated, ' Corr. d'Angl.'.

[4] ' Remarques sur le t te de Vienne, Communiqué par H. Walpole dans les lers jours d'Octobre ' (Corr. d'Angl., t. 353). Probably Horace Walpole derived his arguments from the remonstrance of the Dutch West India Company. (Rousset, *op. cit.* ii. 203-14.) None of these fears materialized, for the treaty was never put into operation (J. Lefèvre, *Étude sur le commerce de la Belgique avec L'Espagne au XVIII*e *siècle* (Brussels, 1921), p. 29).

[5] E. Donnan, ' The Early Days of the South Sea Company, 1711-1718 ', *Journal of Business and Economic History*, ii (1929/30), 419-50. Boyer printed a list of forty-seven ships, taken or plundered by Spaniards in the West Indies since 1712. (Boyer, *op. cit.* xxxi. 229-58.)

[6] Stanhope to Townshend, 6 August 1725 (Brit. Mus., Add. MSS. 32, 744).

the main consideration of British ministers in making the alliance of Hanover. Their main consideration was the far-reaching dangers which seemed to proceed from the treaty of peace and the supposed Austro-Spanish marriage alliance. In the public presentation of their case, however, ministers laid emphasis upon the Ostend trade for two reasons; firstly, because it provided a means of enlisting the support of the Dutch, whose accession to the alliance was desired, as it had been to the quadruple alliance, in order to assure parliament that in the event of a war involving Britain, the Dutch would be involved too, and thus disabled from advancing their commerce at Britain's expense; and secondly, because it constituted such evidence of clear and present danger as would help to persuade parliament to accept the alliance and grant supplies. Even in parliament the Ostend trade did not dominate discussion; as much concern was expressed there about another present danger, the religious crisis in northern Europe. Nor did the Ostend trade arouse the degree of fury traditionally ascribed to it; the mood in which parliament addressed itself to the problem of trade was one of reluctant acceptance of the possibility of war rather than enthusiastic bellicosity at the exhilarating prospect of a commercial crusade.

Two questions are thus involved so far as British policy is concerned: what was the reaction of ministers to the situation created by the treaties of Vienna; what was the reaction of public opinion? The two questions are not entirely separate, for what ministers did was necessarily affected by what they supposed public opinion wanted, or at least was willing to accept. Nevertheless the distinction is a useful one.

The first of the treaties of Vienna to be disclosed officially to the British and French courts was the treaty of peace whose contents became known to them in the middle of May; although signed on the following day, 1 May, the treaty of commerce was not officially published at Vienna until 30 June, by which date the negotiations which were to culminate in the alliance of Hanover had already begun. The official news of the conclusion of a treaty of peace between the Emperor and the king of Spain did not come as a complete surprise to British ministers in London. From time to time since January 1725, Saint-Saphorin, the British representative at Vienna, had reported talks between Spanish and Imperial representatives concerning a marriage alliance between one or more of the Spanish Infants and one or more of the Austrian archduchesses.[1] Then, however, the reports had been either discounted on the grounds that Spain would not be so foolish

[1] Saint-Saphorin to Townshend, 18 February, 19 February, 14 March 1725 (P.R.O., S.P. 80/54).

as to throw away Anglo-French friendship and place herself at the mercy of the Emperor, or else characterized as a mere diplomatic manoeuvre designed by Spain to force Britain into more active support for Spanish demands at the congress of Cambrai.[1] In May, when the existence of serious negotiations at Vienna was no longer denied, there remained still a certain reluctance to face the facts, which took the form of suggesting that a rapprochement between the Emperor and the king of Spain ought to be welcomed as a release from the difficulties incurred in mediation on Spain's behalf at Cambrai.[2] This, however, was little more than a pose, and collapsed as soon as official news was received of the conclusion of the treaty of peace and of its contents. The treaty aroused apprehension on a number of grounds. The more immediate danger was argued to spring from a disturbance in the balance of power. In the British view the real enemy was the Emperor, the king of Spain being lost in infatuation for his wife, Elizabeth Farnese, a wild, ambitious woman from whose inconstancy little was to be feared or hoped. It was suspected that the Emperor, having effectively destroyed the system of collective security established by the treaty of quadruple alliance, would use his newly acquired strength and prestige to make himself arbiter of European affairs.[3] Saint-Saphorin, an intelligent observer with wide diplomatic experience, whose opinions came to be received with great respect by Townshend, gave warning early in May in massive detail that the Emperor's tactics henceforth would be to incite differences on all sides in the hope of keeping ' une boutique ouverte de mediations ', and that unless Britain and France stood firm the Emperor would make all Europe his clients.[4] Moreover the Emperor might now consider himself in a position to settle certain religious problems outstanding in the Empire and in Poland in a manner highly injurious to the Protestant interest in Europe. In Germany, particularly in the Rhineland, Catholicism had made considerable advances since 1713. A large number of converts had been claimed, including the Elector Palatine and the electoral prince of Saxony, who thus followed his father's example.[5] In 1719 a succession of anti-Protestant measures had occurred in Western Germany and provoked a series of reprisals upon Catholic

[1] Broglie, 5, 12 April 1725 (Corr. d'Angl., t. 350).

[2] Chammorel, 14 May 1725 (Corr. d'Angl. t. 351).

[3] Broglie, 3 May 1725 (Corr. d'Angl., t. 350); Saint-Saphorin to Townshend, 1 May 1725 (S.P. 80/54); Townshend to Stanhope, 20 June 1725 (quoted in Chance, op. cit. p. 41).

[4] Saint-Saphorin to Townshend, 11 May 1725 (S.P. 80/55). For Saint-Saphorin's earlier diplomatic career, see S. Stelling-Michaud, Saint-Saphorin et la politique de la Suisse pendant la guerre de succession d'Espagne, 1700-1710 (Villette-les-Cully, 1935).

[5] E. Preclin and E. Jarry, Les luttes politiques et doctrinales aux XVII* et XVIII* siècles (Histoire de l'Eglise depuis les origines jusqu'à nos jours (Paris, 1955), t. 19, pp. 366, 374-5).

communities in Prussia, Hanover, and Hesse-Cassel.[1] These disturbances had made a considerable impression in Britain, where
both houses of parliament had pledged their support for any
measures which the king might consider necessary to secure redress
for the Protestants in the Palatinate.[2] For a time indeed a religious
conflict had been feared. The intervention of the Emperor,
however, under pressure from Britain and Prussia, had averted a
war and brought reprisals to an end; but the Protestant communities
had not been restored to their privileges. Britain and Prussia
held the Emperor responsible for this failure to secure redress in
Germany, arguing that a perpetuation of religious differences
offered him an opportunity of enhancing his authority there.
The religious situation became inflamed again as a result of an
incident in Thorn in July 1724. The exact sequence of events in
the so-called blood bath of Thorn in December 1724 is submerged
beneath the contradictory reports of zealous partisans, but the
important facts are not in doubt.[3] In July a quarrel broke out
between the students of the Jesuit college and the Protestant
townsfolk which resulted in the siege and desecration of the Jesuit
college. The military restored order, and a commission of inquiry
was instituted which in November presented a report favourable
to the Jesuits. In December ten Protestants were executed for
their part in the disturbances. In addition the town was ordered
to give compensation to the college and Protestants were deprived
of their remaining school and church and forced to share the
magistracy with Catholics. The incident was small in itself, but
served as a focus for the religous fears and political ambitions of
a number of Powers. To the Protestant States, and to Britain
and Prussia in particular as guarantors of the treaty of Oliva, the
judgment was a matter of considerable concern, for it was argued
that failure to obtain reparation for the Protestants at Thorn would
further weaken and perhaps destroy the solidarity of the Protestant
interest in Germany. Britain and Prussia suspected the Elector of
Saxony, whose leadership of the *Corpus Evangelicorum* they strongly
resented, of having deliberately inflamed the situation in Thorn in
order to justify the introduction of Saxon troops into Poland,

[1] M. Naumann, *Oesterreich, England und das Reich, 1719-1732* (Berlin, 1936), pp. 31-50;
Michael, *op. cit.* iii. pp. 151-9; G. Pariset, *L'état et les églises en Prusse sous Frédéric-
Guillaume Ier, 1713-1740* (Paris, 1897), pp. 745-76. There is also a good account in
Recueil des Instructions, xviii. *Diète Germanique*, ed. B. Auerbach (Paris, 1912), pp. 127-46.
[2] *H.L.J.* xxi. 345-6. Considerable attention was given to the matter by Boyer,
op. cit. xviii. 127-8, 196-203, 221-3, 301-3, 310-12, 382-4, 384-7; xix. 600-40.
[3] R. Frydrychowicz, 'Die Vorgänge zu Thorn im Jahre 1724', *Zeitschrift des
Westpreussischen Geschichtsvereins* (Danzig, 1884), xi. 73-97; F. Jacobi, 'Neuere
Forschungen über das Thorner Blutgericht 1724', *ibid.* xxxv (1896), pp. 19-34;
G. Rhode, 'England und das Thorner Blutgericht 1724', *Historische Zeitschrift*, v.
164, pp. 496-528; *Recueil des Instructions*; *Pologne*, ed. Louis Farges (Paris, 1888), i
304-8.

and to advance his aim of securing the Polish throne for his son.[1] Both had made unsuccessful representations at Dresden and at Warsaw. The situation was highly dangerous, for though Britain intended to go no further than making representations the king of Prussia had reached the limits of his patience and seemed likely to abandon diplomatic pressure in favour of " extravagant measures " which might precipitate a religious war.[2] The treaty of peace made at Vienna, the union of two great Catholic Powers, as Saint-Saphorin was quick to point out, brought this contingency much nearer, for, in Townshend's opinion, it would at once encourage the king of Poland to persist in his refusal to make reparation for what had happened at Thorn and make the Emperor much less susceptible, if not openly hostile, to the suggestions of Britain and Prussia that he should bring pressure to bear upon Augustus II to satisfy their demands. So far as German affairs were concerned the treaty of peace seemed likely to encourage the Emperor to adopt a more authoritarian attitude towards the Protestant princes.[3]

Even more alarming possibilities, however, were read into the treaty of peace. The fact that it had been secretly negotiated, between parties whose antagonism had defied the combined diplomatic strivings of Britain, France and the United Provinces for a decade, and on terms entirely favourable to one of those parties, inevitably made it suspect. It did not require much scepticism to doubt that Spain would have conceded so much for so little, and to find, mistakenly, the explanation in a secret treaty, concluded at the same time as the public treaty, in which Spain had received recompense for her liberality. Confirmation or at least support came from those best qualified to judge. On 1 May 1725 Saint-Saphorin declared that he was entirely convinced that the basis of the published treaty was a formal marriage-contract between Maria Theresa and Don Carlos.[4] On 16 June he wrote that it was impossible to explain the abandonment by Spain of the securities previously demanded for Don Carlos in Italy, other than by supposing a marriage alliance.[5] Similar reports came from Dubourg, the French representative at Vienna, who on 11 May asserted confidently to Morville, the French foreign minister, that the betrothal of Maria Theresa and Don Carlos would be

[1] *Recueil des instructions*, xviii. 136-46. There may have been some basis for their suspicions: see dispatch of Flemming, Saxon minister, of 7 February 1725, quoted by Frydrychowicz, *loc. cit.* pp. 96-7.
[2] Chance, *op. cit.* pp. 22-55; J. G. Droysen, *Geschichte der Preussischen Politik* (Leipzig, 1869), iv, pt. 2, 368-9.
[3] Saint-Saphorin to Townshend, 19 February, 31 March, 11 April 1725 (S.P. 80/54), Saint-Saphorin to Townshend, 11 May 1725 (S.P. 80/55); Townshend to Saint-Saphorin, 22 June/3 July 1725 (S.P. 80/55).
[4] Saint-Saphorin to Townshend, 1 May 1725 (S.P. 80/54).
[5] Saint-Saphorin to Townshend, 16 June 1725 (S.P. 80/55).

announced soon.[1] Morville informed Broglie, the French ambassador in London, that it was difficult to believe that there was not a secret article giving satisfaction to Spain, although he admitted there was no certain information.[2] In London, according to Broglie, the opinion was that a triple marriage alliance was on the point of being signed at Vienna, and that certain territorial arrangements would accompany it; thus the prince of Asturias would marry Maria Theresa, who would receive the kingdoms of Naples and Sicily as a marriage dowry, and Don Carlos would marry the Emperor's second daughter and receive the duchies of Tuscany and Parma; in the event of the Emperor's death without male heirs, the prince of Asturias would become Emperor, Don Carlos king of Spain, Naples and Sicily, and Don Philip duke of Tuscany and Parma.[3] Three weeks later details had changed; Don Carlos would marry Maria Theresa and receive Tuscany and Parma which he would then exchange for the Low Countries.[4] Finally, on 22 June 1725 Stanhope, the British ambassador at Madrid, declared that a secret treaty had been concluded at Vienna at the same time as the public treaty, in which, among other things, a marriage had been arranged between Don Carlos and the Emperor's second daughter.[5]

All this was conjecture, uncertain and contradictory, and based, as Stanhope had been the first to admit, on hints and insinuations. Nevertheless it was the best opinion available and, in the light of Spanish concessions, readily accepted. The various discrepancies in these reports about the character of the marriage alliance, whether it was single, double or triple, an article or a treaty, were much less important than the fact that the reports all agreed that some such alliance had been concluded. This being so, thought Townshend, a scheme was unfolded ' more vast and extensive, and more full of pernicious prospects than any that has hitherto been formed '.[6] He set forth his reasons for these fears in a letter to Newcastle on 24 August 1725. The letter faithfully reproduced a line of speculation begun by Saint-Saphorin early in May.[7] Townshend wrote:

---

[1] Syveton, *op. cit.* p. 121.

[2] Morville, 13 May 1725 (Corr. d'Angl., t. 351).

[3] Broglie, 10 May 1725 (Corr. d'Angl., t. 351).

[4] Broglie, 31 May 1725 (Corr. d'Angl., t. 351). These various reports were distorted echoes of the unfulfilled proposals for a redistribution of the Habsburg dominions which Ripperda had taken to Vienna in November 1724 as a complement to the proposed marriage alliance.

[5] Stanhope to Newcastle, 22 June 1725 (Brit. Mus., Add. MSS. 32,743). Further afield both Saxony and Bavaria suspected a secret marriage engagement and the Emperor's assurance that there was ' wenig Sicheres ' in their suspicions only confirmed their doubts. (A. Philipp, *August der Starke und die pragmatische Sanktion*, Leipziger Historische Abhandlungen, iv. p. 33.)

[6] Townshend to Newcastle, 13/24 August 1725 (S.P. 43/6).

[7] ' Relation commune de Monsieur Dubourg et de Moy. St. Saphorin ', 11 May 1725 (S.P. 80/55).

You know how weak in health king Philip is and not likely to be
long lived, and the prince of Asturias is in a hectical and consumptive
way, so that in all probability Don Carlos will come to be king of
Spain by the time the intended marriage takes place, and being
sent to Vienna to be bred up there and having the Austrian dominions
joyned to the vast territories of Spain may become more formidable
to the rest of Europe than ever Charles Vth. was, by reason of his
relation to the crown of France.   The life of the present Christian
king is the only direct obstacle to his laying in his claims to that
kingdom; if he should dye without heirs, as his state of health is
far from being strong or much to be depended on, it is easy to
see what resistance the duke of Orleans and his party will be able
to make to the power of Spain and the Austrian territories.[1]

What Townshend envisaged, therefore, was the possibility that
Don Carlos might be at once ruler of the Habsburg dominions,
king of Spain, and king of France. It is easy to underestimate
the force of such reasoning, for none of the conditions which
Townshend postulated was achieved; the prince of Asturias out-
lived Philip V, who did not die until 1746, Don Carlos did not
marry Maria Theresa, and the young Louis XV lived until 1774
and left an heir. And even if the conditions had been achieved
their conclusion might yet have been different if the Emperor had
had a son.[2] There is something in the view of the *Craftsman* that
the chance of Don Carlos becoming the greatest prince on earth
was about as great as a Welsh lady, who, if an uncle, three brothers,
and two sons happen to die, may be left a considerable fortune.[3]
Yet such a succession of deaths was not without a recent precedent:
little more than a decade earlier the main branch of the French
royal family had been almost destroyed in less than a year.
Admittedly deaths on this scale did not occur often and weakly
children lived far longer than contemporaries and rivals expected
or hoped, but the contingency of an early death had to be faced.
Charles II of Spain is an obvious case in point: he took a terrible
time to die, but even before his accession to the throne, when he was
only three, the discussion had already begun on what was to happen
when he died and continued for the next thirty years.   Townshend's
preoccupation with the dangers of mortality, therefore, was not
the manifestation of a morbid imagination, but the legitimate
speculation, acknowledged by his colleagues to be such, of a statesman accustomed to the existence of failing and disputed successions.[4]

[1] Townshend to Newcastle, 13/24 August 1725 (S.P. 43/6).
[2] The Empress was reported pregnant in 1727 and the *Craftsman* advertised a
forthcoming consolatory epistle to Don Carlos. (*Craftsman*, 24/25 February O.S.
1727: Burney collection).
[3] *Craftsman*, 16/20 January O.S. 1727 (Burney).
[4] ' Notes of domestic and foreign affairs during the last years of the reign of George I
and the early part of the reign of George II ', in Lord Peter King, *Life of John Locke*
(1830), ii, Appendix, pp. 14-15, 17, 25-6.

The treaty of peace, thus interpreted, threatened not only the balance of power and the security of the Protestant religion, but even the political independence of the rest of Europe.

It was these considerations, the existence of a potentially very dangerous situation, which set in motion the negotiations for a counter-alliance at Hanover on 29 June and dominated them thereafter. The treaty of commerce which was in Townshend's hands early in July did not basically alter the situation. It was important, however, for two reasons: firstly, it strengthened the case for counter-measures, not only because it constituted a serious and immediate threat to British commerce, and a more remote threat to British naval supremacy, but also because its concessions to the Emperor gave further support for already existing suspicions of a secret marriage alliance; secondly, it provided an opportunity of enlisting the support of the Dutch in such measures. The character of these measures needs to be emphasized. The Emperor seemed to be the person to watch, for his ambition was thought to have inspired the rapprochement with Spain and to constitute the main dangers arising out of it; if he could be ' brought to sense ' then Spain would be forced to follow suit. Townshend was convinced that this could be done by forming an Anglo-French alliance sufficiently broadly based to enable the northern Powers, the German States, both Protestant and Catholic, and the United Provinces to accede to it.[1] He was aware of the difficulties involved in trying to bring together Powers whose interests and ambitions not only differed greatly, but sometimes, as in the case of the United Provinces and Prussia, openly conflicted.[2] Such difficulties, indeed, were an insuperable obstacle to any step beyond the making of a mere diplomatic demonstration. Townshend, however, at this stage aimed at nothing more; he was confident that the Emperor would abandon his plans in the face of a determined show of opposition from the rest of Europe.[3] In this demand for the creation of a position of strength and in the underlying assumption that the Emperor could be ' terrified into reason by well-concerted alliances ' he enjoyed the full support of the rest of the Cabinet; the differences which emerged later sprang from his impatience to hasten the process of persuasion by making further gestures, such as a proposal to partition the Austrian Netherlands, which seemed unlikely to prove acceptable either to Britain's

---

[1] Townshend to Newcastle, 16/27 November 1725 (S.P. 43/8); Chance, op. cit. pp. 63, 102-3.

[2] Goslinga, op. cit. pp. 92-3. For an account of earlier Dutch-Prussian differences, see G. J. Rive, Schets der staatkundige betrekkingen tusschen de Republiek der Vereenigde Nederlanden en het koningrijk Pruissen, 1701-1767 (Amsterdam, 1873), pp. 1-105.

[3] Townshend to H. Walpole, 16/27 August 1725 (Original in Brit. Mus., Add. MSS. 48981; copies in Brit. Mus., Add. MSS. 9154, 9156 (Coxe Transcripts)).

allies or to British public opinion, and liable to stiffen rather than weaken the Emperor's resolution.[1]

The achievement of at least temporary Prussian support proved a relatively easy matter. Frederick William I arrived at Hanover on 27 July to discuss certain matters unrelated to the impending alliance. On the same day he was presented with a draft of the projected treaty, which with minor changes he accepted on 7 August. A month later the definitive treaty was signed. ' The chief bait ' that drew Frederick William I into the alliance was the promise by Britain and France in a secret and separate article of the treaty to support Prussian claims to the duchies of Julich and Berg; other inducements were promises to uphold the liberties of the Empire and to restore the Protestants of Poland to their former privileges.[2] Where the king of Prussia had serious misgivings, however, which led to his defection from the alliance in August 1726, was in regard to article 2 which specifically engaged the contracting parties to maintain each other in their commercial rights, as well as in other rights and possessions inside and outside Europe. This could be held to support Prussia's claims to the duchies of Julich and Berg, but in the estimation of Frederick William I it also indubitably involved Prussia in opposition to the Ostend Company; and he was determined at all costs to avoid a war to enable ' Messieurs les Hollandais ' to sell ' le thé, caffé, et fromage, porcelaines etc. plus cher '.[3] His suspicions were well founded, although he exaggerated Dutch militancy. Townshend admitted on a number of occasions that the article had been designed specifically to attract the Dutch.[4] Even with this inducement, however, the Dutch were not to be hustled into accession. The importance of the concessions made to the Ostend Company was fully appreciated in the United Provinces. In September it was reported from the Hague by the Dutch regent, Ittersum, that opinion in Amsterdam was united in the fear that the treaty of commerce would make a second Amsterdam of Ostend.[5] Nevertheless the Dutch—the States of Holland as well as the non-maritime provinces of the republic which were more vulnerable to Imperial retaliations— were reluctant to take any action which might involve them in a war against the Emperor, at least until the British parliament had placed itself firmly behind the policy of its Government.[6]

[1] H. Walpole to Townshend, 30 August/10 September 1725 (Brit. Mus., Add. MSS. 48981).   [2] Chance, op. cit. pp. 63-73; Droysen, iv. 2, 378-81.

[3] A. Waddington, Histoire de Prusse (Paris 1923), ii. 404-11; Chance, op. cit. pp. 106-7, 116-20.

[4] Chance, op. cit. pp. 65-6; Broglie (Hanover), 27 July 1725 (Corr. d'Angl., t. 351). Townshend to H. Walpole, 8/19 October 1725 (S.P. 43/7).

[5] ' Letters and papers from Mons. d'Ittersum at the Hague to the Secretaries of State', 25 September 1725 (S.P. 84/284).

[6] Ittersum 25 September 1725, 25 February 1726 (S. P. 84/284); Finch to Townshend, 16 October 1725 (S.P. 84/286); Th. Bussemaker, ' Een memorie over de

The fate of the alliance indeed depended upon vigorous parliamentary approval of the Government's action. Townshend was well aware of this,[1] and of the fact that the reasons which had led to his forming the alliance would be unlikely to recommend it to the British public. He turned to the task of formulating a case which parliament could accept with enthusiasm. This was not an easy business, even in London, for it depended upon an accurate appreciation of the state of public opinion; it was much more difficult for someone in Hanover who lacked direct contact with British opinion and was by temperament rather hasty. These difficulties are well illustrated in the two attempts which Townshend made in November and December 1725 to draft a speech from the throne.[2] The proposed king's speech began with a reference to the distressed condition of Protestants in Europe and continued with a reference to the threat to British trade. The main justification of the alliance of Hanover, however, was sought in an imminent Jacobite invasion, encouraged and assisted by Spain and the Emperor. There was no reference, either implicit or explicit, to the supposed marriage alliance. The whole was couched in very militant language and read like a declaration of war. The manner in which Townshend approached the question of enlisting parliamentary support was sensible enough. Walpole admitted that arguments based on dangers to trade and particularly to religion stood much more chance of acceptance than those based on suspicions and speculations of the sort represented by the supposed marriage alliance.[3] What he could not accept was the underlying assumption in Townshend's drafts that opinion in parliament would be sufficiently bellicose to swallow the reference to the Pretender, which attributed much more certainty to the possibility of a Jacobite invasion than properly belonged to it. There can be no doubt that in this instance Walpole was a better judge than Townshend both of parliament's capacity for credulity and of its readiness for war.

republiek uit 1728 ', *Bijdragen en Mededelingen van het historisch genootschap*, Deel 30, 1909, pp. 122-30.

[1] Townshend to Newcastle, 16/27 November 1725 (S.P. 43/8). Townshend to R. Walpole, 7/18 December 1725 (quoted in W. Coxe, *Memoirs of the Life and Administration of Sir Robert Walpole* (1798), ii. 494-5).

[2] The first draft was included in a letter to Newcastle of 16/27 November 1725. The original is in S.P. 43/8. It has been printed by Michael, *op. cit.* iii, Appendix iv, pp. 595-6. The second was included in a letter to Newcastle of 30 November/11 December 1725, the original of which is in S.P. 43/8. This has not been printed. A third draft, undated and unsigned, but probably drawn up by Robert Walpole, has been printed by Coxe, *op. cit.* ii. 493-4. It stands much nearer the final speech than either of Townshend's drafts. C. B. Realey, in his ' The early opposition to Sir Robert Walpole 1726-1727' (*Bulletin of the University of Kansas*, Kansas, 1931, Humanistic Studies, iv, Nos. 2-3, p. 187), mistook this last for the original.

[3] R. Walpole to Townshend, 2/13 October 1725 (Coxe, *op. cit.* ii. 485-6), and so did Horace Walpole (H. Walpole to Townshend, 30 August/10 September 1725 (Brit. Mus., Add. MSS. 48981)).

In May 1725 the French ambassador in London had reported to Paris that most of the people with whom he had spoken—and they were principally members of parliament—wanted peace and would make war only if it could be shown to be an absolute necessity.[1] The same mood of caution seems to have been dominant at the end of the year. In December 1725 Chammorel, the French Resident in London, noticed that although the destruction of the Ostend Company and the redress of the grievances of Polish Protestants were matters of great concern, there was a general hope that peace would not be disturbed.[2] Feeling certainly ran high on the matter of trade. The treaty of peace, printed in May in Abel Boyer's monthly *Political State,* had suggested at once a secret treaty, or secret articles, with concessions to the Ostend Company.[3] In June 1725 a pamphlet had appeared, entitled, *Mr. Forman's letter to the Rt. Hon. William Pulteney, showing how pernicious the Imperial Company of commerce and navigation, lately established in the Austrian Netherlands, is likely to prove to Great Britain as well as to Holland.*[4] Forman, an Irishman, a Jacobite, and a former first clerk in the secretary-at-war's office when Pulteney had held that office, wrote to protest at what he considered the indifferent opposition of British ministers to the threat from Ostend, and to appeal for united action by Britain and the United Provinces to suppress the Company and completely prohibit private adventurers trading to the Indies.[5] It is significant, however, not only that

[1] Broglie, 14 May 1725 (quoted by Dureng, p. 347).
[2] Chammorel, 24 December 1725 (Corr. d'Angl., t. 353).
[3] Boyer, *op. cit.* xxix. 408-17; xxx, 88.
[4] The pamphlet is in the Lansdowne Tracts and bears the date and place of publication, Rotterdam, 20 June.
[5] Charles Forman, or Charles Forman McMahon as he sometimes called himself, left England in 1715 in order to escape the consequences of having deliberately delayed instructions to General Wills during the rebellion. He went to France, with his wife and two daughters, leaving three sons in Ireland to be taken care of by relations, and made contact immediately with the Jacobite Court from which in 1717 he succeeded in obtaining a pension. Still short of cash, however, early in 1718 he considered taking up military service in Spain. The projected trip never seems to have come off. Early in 1719 Forman is said to have attempted to secure the support of John Law, Controller-General of French finances, for a mad-cap plan for a partition of the British Isles. In December 1720, with Law now in disgrace, Forman is said to have made an unsuccessful attempt to recover his plan. What happened immediately afterwards is not clear, but Forman probably left France at once, and found no fixed home. In October 1724 he was in Amsterdam where he wrote the *Letter to Pulteney.* In the following year he was living in Rotterdam. The publication of his pamphlet provoked Finch, the British envoy at the Hague, to ask for his removal. Whether in fact he was moved on I do not know, but Finch was assured that Forman had been told to shut up or get out. He died on 28 April 1739. In addition to his *Letter to Pulteney* he was author of the *Defence of the Irish* and ' of several political pieces and letters signed Camillus '. (Rev. R. Wodrow, *Analecta* . . . 1843, iii. 233; Forman's *Letter to Pulteney* . . . pp. 2, 39; *H. M. C. Stuart Papers,* ii (1904), 321; iii (1907), 2; iv (1910), 265, 275; vi (1916), 172, 297-8; W. Finch to Tilson, 4 August 1725, W. Finch to Townshend, 6 October 1725 (S.P. 84/286); J. Daridan, *John Law. Père de l'inflation* (Paris, 1938, pp. 44-8).) There is an obituary notice in A. Boyer, *Political*

he should have considered it necessary to argue that the destruction of the Ostend trade was in the British interest, and that this could be accomplished without war, but also that he should have given as a reason the danger to the Protestant cause involved in allowing the transfer of the commerce and riches of the East Indies to a Catholic State.[1] A large abstract from the pamphlet, together with the remonstrances of the Dutch West and East India Companies, appeared in the August number of the *Political State*.[2] In the same month Starhemberg, the Imperial ambassador at London, reported a conversation with an M.P. who complained that in attacking British commerce the Emperor was ' jumping in the eyes of the English nation '.[3] In September the treaty of commerce, with the treaty of peace and the alliance of Hanover, was officially published.[4] There is no doubt that it aroused considerable indignation. Chammorel wrote in September that a nation as dependent upon trade as Britain must inevitably wish for the destruction of the Ostend Company. Its goods were cheaper than those of the English East India Company and, no matter what the precautions, would always by virtue of their cheapness find a ready market in Britain.[5] Certainly the English East India Company was beginning to feel the pinch of competition. In October and November its sales of tea were considerably affected by the influx of smuggled tea from Ostend.[6] The Company looked to the Government for advice and assistance. In an assessment of the situation made at the end of October, the governor of the Company, Harrison, complained that unless action was taken immediately it would be impossible to root out the Ostend trade without a great deal of trouble. The Company, he argued, already had powers under acts of parliament, presumably 5 Geo. I. c. 21 and 9 Geo. I. c. 26, to seize in Indian waters all British subjects engaged in

---

State, lvii. 457-8. It is stated there that Forman became a secretary to Law, but I have been unable to find evidence of it. [1] *Mr. Forman's letter* . . . , p. 39.

[2] Boyer, *op. cit.* xxx. 105-56, 303-8, 517-27. [3] Syveton, *op. cit.* p. 120.

[4] *The Treaties of Vienna, Friendship and Commerce. The Treaty of Hanover*, printed by S. Buckley, 1725, pp. 65. In parallel columns of Latin and English.

[5] Chammorel, 24 September 1725 (Corr. d'Angl., t. 352).

[6] L'Hermitage, 30 October and 13 November 1725, Brit. Mus., Add. MSS. 17677 KKK (7). A complaint of the introduction of contraband tea into Ireland was made by the Company in November (Dureng, *op. cit.* p. 288 n.2). It is not possible, of course, to give detailed figures about smuggling, but it was estimated at Ostend that about three-quarters of the merchandise sold by the Company was bought by British and Dutch merchants (Laude, *op. cit.* p. 72, n. 1). The cargo of two of the Company's ships which arrived at Ostend in August 1725 contained 493,237 pounds of tea (S.P. 77/72 (Flanders) fos, 229-30). Some interesting, and occasionally quite graphic details on smuggling from Ostend are provided in the information volunteered by one, H. Macleane, who was then living there and hoped that his industry would secure him some small sinecure. In three letters of 6, 11, 29 May 1725 he listed some fifteen ships so engaged, giving in each case their tonnage, captains, and ports of origin and for eight of the ships, estimates of the amount of tea on board (H. Macleane to Secretary Tilson, 6, 11, 29 May 1725; S.P. 77/72).

trade on their own account or under foreign commissions; it now requested either some further authority from the king to execute its powers, or the interception of Ostend ships by ' His Majesty's ships in our seas '.[1] Harrison was not very hopeful of the acceptance of the latter course of action, and with very good reason. There was a great deal of difference between interception by the Company in Indian waters, and interception by ' His Majesty's ships in our seas '; the first could be repudiated by the Government or overlooked by the Emperor, and in any case would be difficult to establish; the second would be tantamount to an act of war and would constitute a challenge which the Emperor could not ignore.[2] At this stage the Government did not wish to throw down such a challenge, although it anticipated that matters would come to a head with the accession of the Dutch, who would insist on joint measures for stopping the Ostend trade.[3] The Company, therefore, had to be content with private action, and in November and December it ordered its agents in Bengal to refuse all help and pilotage to Ostenders and to seize all Englishmen found aboard them.[4] It was thought unlikely that the Company would go beyond this and commit itself to retaliatory measures in association with the Dutch Companies until parliament had given its approval of the treaty of Hanover.[5] To at least one well-informed observer, Dr. William Stratford, writing in December, the issue was plain—' We must lose our trade or engage in a war. Many think we shall choose the former.' [6]

In fact the issue was not seen simply as war or trade. Peace seemed threatened from other directions, perhaps more dangerously. The possibility of an attempted Jacobite restoration could never be discounted at a time of European crisis, but the evidence for thinking such an attempt likely at the end of 1725 was slight and confused, altogether too meagre to stand up to common inspection.[7] Outside the circle of ministers there is no evidence that at this stage a Jacobite threat was seriously feared.[8] A religious war

---

[1] ' An assessment by E. Harrison 31 October 1725 of the Ostend East India Company '), S.P. 35/58).

[2] R. Daniel to C. Delafaye, Brussels, 9 January N.S. 1725/6 (S.P. 77/72).

[3] Chance, *op. cit.* pp. 102-3; Dr. William Stratford, 29 January/9 February 1725/6. *H.M.C. Portland MSS.* vii (1901), 418.   [4] Dureng, *op. cit.* p. 347.

[5] Chance, *op. cit.* pp. 102-3.   [6] *H.M.C. Portland MSS.* vii. 407.

[7] In 1725 there was nothing more solid to point to than the activities of Wharton in Vienna and the movement of Russian ships off the Irish coast. For a description of these scares see Chance, *op. cit.* pp. 132-50. The Emperor and Philip seem to have given more thought to the possibility of a Jacobite restoration in 1726 and 1727, but even then the undertaking was to follow the actual declaration of war. (' Project du duc de Wharton pour rétablir le Prétendant ' in Stanhope to Newcastle, 19/30 July 1726 (Brit. Mus., Add. MSS. 32,747); Arneth, *op. cit.* iii. 222-3, 556, n. 8). M. J. Carpio, *España y los ultimos estuardos* (Madrid, 1952), pp. 253-5.

[8] For opinions of ministers, see Newcastle to H. Walpole, 19/30 November 1725 (Brit. Mus., Add. MSS. 32,744); Townshend to Newcastle, 4 October 1725 in Coxe, *op. cit.* ii. 480-4.

in the north, however, was regarded as a much more serious possibility by the British public. The affair at Thorn had aroused considerable interest and indignation in Britain, and still overshadowed all other considerations even at the beginning of 1726.[1] Almost every issue of Boyer's *Political State* throughout 1725 contained references to it, and the impression is conveyed that in providing such ample information the editor was guided by the wishes of his readers: thus, Boyer published the letters and representations of the kings of Prussia, Sweden, Denmark and Britain, and Catholic and Protestant accounts of the incident itself, whilst on one occasion nearly an entire issue was devoted to the publication of the treaty of Oliva in order to show the specific grounds on which Britain laid claim to the redress of Protestant grievances in Poland.[2] In addition, a number of pamphlets couched in very violent language, and unmistakably Protestant in character, related the incident to earlier oppressions in Germany, and called upon Protestants of all denominations to forget their differences and unite against the common enemy who held in jeopardy the Reformation itself.[3] In September and October, Chammorel and l'Hermitage, the Dutch Resident in London, agreed that a war was commonly expected in the spring, in which the Emperor, sustained by Spain, would inevitably intervene on the side of the king of Poland.[4] At the same time Boyer argued that the treaty of Hanover had been made primarily to meet this threat and to redress the grievances of the oppressed Protestants

---

[1] Boyer, *op. cit.* ; xxxi. 1-15. Even fifty years later the bloody executions at Thorn were still sufficiently well-remembered to be used during the public debate on Catholic emancipation in Ireland as evidence of the indelible malignancy of Catholics; then they were coupled with the burning of Huss. (R. B. McDowell, *Irish Public opinion 1750-1800* (1944), p. 72).

[2] Boyer, *op. cit.* xxix. 1-36, 41-3, 62-8, 95-6, 218-55; xxx. 85-8, 193-5, 288-93, 374-87, 508-10, 523-58, 592-4.

[3] *An Alarm to Protestant Princes and People who are all struck at in the Popish Cruelties at Thorn, and other Barbarous Executions abroad,* London, printed for Eman Matthews, at the Bible in Pater-noster Row. 1725; *Remarks on the Speech of the Reverend Father the Advocate for the Jesuits of Thorn ; delivered before the Assessorial Tribunal of the Great Chancellor of Poland: insolently, heathenishly, and ridiculously demanding Sentence against the Protestants of the said City. In a letter to Britannicus.* By Philopatris. London, printed and re-printed in Dublin, by R. Dickson and E. Needham, at the Cheshire-Cheese in Crane-Lane 1725; *A Faithful and Exact Narrative of the horrid Tragedy lately acted at Thorn, in Polish Prussia: by the Contrivances and Instigation of the Jesuits,* London. Printed and sold by J. Roberts, in Warwick Lane. 1725. This was reproduced in full by Boyer, *op. cit.* xxix. 1-37; *The Source of all the Sufferings the Protestants in Thorn, in Great Britain etc. have undergone from Popish Princes, being a Collection of some Principles in the Church of Rome, strictly engaging 'em to persecute their Protestant Subjects. With some Observations and Advices thereupon.* London. Printed for James and John Knapton, at the Crown in St. Paul's Church-yard: and sold by J. Roberts in Warwick Lane, 1726. The incident was given a good airing by Dutch pamphleteers; Knuttel lists 12 pamphlets as having appeared on Thorn in 1725 (Knuttel, *op. cit.* pp. 64-6.)

[4] Chammorel, 8 and 15 October 1725 (Corr. d'Angl., t. 353). L'Hermitage, 5 October 1725 (Brit. Mus. Add. MSS. 17677 KKK (7)).

of Poland.[1] This opinion was shared by Dr. Richard Hill, a former diplomat of considerable experience.[2] To Hill, as to Dr. William Stratford, the issue appeared as a simple choice between two alternatives; either ' with England, France, and the king of Prussia in defence of Luther, or with the Emperor, Spaign, the Zarina etc in defence of king Augustus '.[3] Both Boyer and Hill grossly over simplified the European situation and British policy, for to argue as if Britain had been the unyielding champion of Protestant rights in Poland and as if the security of the Protestant religion was the only thing at stake was very far from the truth. It was, however, an impression which the Government was very anxious to convey, for it regarded a call to religion as an essential element in any appeal to parliament to part with peace and tranquillity.[4]

Anxieties about trade and the religious situation in the north dominated but did not exhaust political speculation in the last months of 1725. Some concern was also aroused by Spanish statements in regard to Gibraltar. In July, in the first flush of belligerency after the ratifications of the treaties of Vienna, Spain had demanded immediate action along the lines set forth in George I's letter to the king of Spain of May 1721, namely a special assembly of parliament to consider the immediate restitution of the fortress, upon a threat of withdrawing British commercial privileges.[5] By September she had modified her ardour somewhat and proposed that the question be put to parliament upon the return of George I to London.[6] British ministers had no intention of giving up Gibraltar or even of putting the question to parliament and, Townshend apart, attached little importance to the Spanish threats of reprisals.[7] Nevertheless the threats could not simply be ignored. Parliament had convinced views about the importance of Gibraltar and steps, therefore, had to be taken to make sure that it was left in no doubt about the king's determination never to abandon it.[8] Accordingly, in July 1725 men and provisions were sent there, not from fear of attack, but because ' these precautions would

[1] Boyer, op. cit. xxx. 192, 559.
[2] For details see D. B. Horn, British Diplomatic Representatives 1689-1789 (Camden, 3rd ser.), vol. xlvi, 1932.
[3] Dr. [R.] Hill to Sir T. Hanmer, M.P., 30 November 1725. H.M.C. Laing MSS. ii. 218-19.
[4] R. Walpole to Townshend, 2/13 October 1725 (quoted in Coxe, op. cit. ii. 485-6).
[5] Stanhope to Townshend, 14 July 1725 (Brit. Mus., Add. MSS. 32,743).
[6] Dureng, op. cit. p. 349.
[7] Chance, op. cit. p. 124. For differences of opinion between British ministers in 1725 on Spanish threats see Coxe, op. cit. ii. 474-9; King, op. cit. pp. 24-26, and ' An account of what passed at Sir Robert Walpole's ' (Brit. Mus., Add. MSS. 32,687, fos. 155-60).
[8] For the earlier development of these views see S. Conn, Gibraltar in British Diplomacy in the Eighteenth Century (New Haven, 1942, pp. 28-72).

convince the City of London and all England, that it was never the
king's intention to give it up '.[1] For similar reasons Townshend
urged in December that the king of Spain should be informed that
Britain would not yield the fortress on any terms.[2] Finally, on
the eve of the parliamentary session, perhaps as a result of a report
that the duke of Wharton had returned from Vienna with a copy
of George I's letter to the king of Spain, which he had received
from Ripperda and intended to place before the house of lords,
members of parliament were reminded once more, in an anonymous
pamphlet, of the commercial and strategic reasons for retaining
Gibraltar, a bulwark of Great Britain.[3]

It seems clear that in January 1726 a majority of opinion,
although pessimistic about the chances of preserving peace,
particularly because of the situation in northern Europe, did not
want to precipitate a war.[4] In February, although opinion was
still disinclined to war, it seemed that it might be brought to
accept it as a last resort. This change was attributed to the good
effects of the king's speech and the addresses of both houses.[5]
The speech from the throne of 31 January which emerged from
the attentions of Townshend and Walpole was a cautious, just,
but shrewd appraisal of the motives which had led to the alliance
of Hanover, combining a statement of the immediate dangers to
British interests with speculation about the wider implications of
the treaties of Vienna for the balance of Europe.[6] It began:

> The distressed condition of some of our protestant brethren abroad,
> and the negotiations and engagements entered into by some foreign
> powers which seem to have laid the foundations of new troubles
> and disturbances in Europe and to threaten my subjects with the
> loss of several of the most advantageous branches of their trade,
> obliged me, without any loss of time, to concert with other powers
> such measures as might give a check to the ambitious views of
> those who are endeavouring to render themselves formidable,
> and put a stop to the farther progress of such dangerous designs;
> for these ends I have entered into a defensive alliance with the most
> Christian king and the king of Prussia, to which several other powers,
> and particularly the States General have been invited to accede:
> and I have not the least reason to doubt of their concurrence.

The only statement open to exception perhaps was the reference

---

[1] Townshend to Newcastle, 6/17 July 1725 (S.P. 43/6).

[2] Townshend to Newcastle, 3/14 December 1725 (S.P. 43/8).

[3] Newcastle to H. Walpole, 19/30 November 1725 (Brit. Mus., Add. MSS. 32,744).
An abstract of *Gibraltar, a Bulwark of Great Britain. In a Letter to a Member of Parliament
containing some Considerations of that Place, in respect of our Trade in general, particularly
with regard to Barbary, Spain, France, etc.*, appeared in Boyer, *op. cit.* xxxi. 33-57.

[4] Chammorel, 10 January 1726 (corr. d'Angl., t. 354); Broderick to Middleton, 10/21
February 1726 (Coxe, *op. cit.* ii. 496).

[5] L'Hermitage, 22 February 1726 (Brit. Mus., Add MSS. 17677 KKK (8)).

[6] *H.C.J.* xx. 544-5.

to the accession of the United Provinces, which concealed the
fact that serious difficulties, threatening protracted negotiations,
still stood in the way of an early success.[1]   Yet some such assurance
was regarded as necessary if parliament was readily to give its
approval to the Administration's proposals.[2]   The reference to
the Pretender, which followed, carefully avoided Townshend's
direct accusation that Spain and the Emperor were giving a
sympathetic hearing to his overtures, and alluded only in general
terms to the encouragement which the unsettled European situation
must undoubtedly give to the Jacobites, whose instruments and
emissaries, it continued, were already engaged in soliciting support
in ' those courts whose measures seem most to favour their purposes '.
This reflected Walpole's determination to avoid provocation as
well as his feeling for what parliament would accept.   The same
scrupulous attention to parliamentary susceptibilities inspired the
reference to military requirements.   Much was made of the fact
that the king did not intend to increase the army which would
have been an unpopular step under any circumstances in the
eighteenth century, certain to release a flood of cant about the dangers
to the traditional liberties of the free-born Englishman, but to
strengthen the navy.[3]   The speech concluded with an appeal for
vigorous support for the measures already taken and proposed, as
the only effective deterrent to would-be aggressors.   Essentially
the demand was for the establishment of a position of negotiation
from strength.

There is little information available on the debates on the
speech, but from the meagre reports which have survived, it seems
that only two criticisms were made, both by inveterate opponents
of the Administration.   In the Commons Shippen went through
his inevitable motions, and this time attacked the Administration
for having sacrificed British to Hanoverian interests.[4]   In the
circumstances of 1726 this was a curious thesis; the opposite
could have been argued with much greater force.   But such was
British sensitivity to the accusation of Hanoverian dominance,

[1] The Dutch had refused to be associated with the secret clause of the treaty relating
to Julich and Berg, demanded British and French participation in a war against the
pirates of Algiers and Morocco and, as a precaution against precipitancy, insisted on
the introduction of a clause into the treaty whereby all action against the Ostend
Company should be determined by common consent of all the contracting parties to
the alliance (Chance, *op. cit.* pp. 104-22, 290-3; Goslinga, pp. 95-6).

[2] Chance, *op. cit.* p. 292.

[3] The intention here was to deprive the Emperor and Spain of the capacity for
making mischief by denying them access to the treasures of the Spanish galleon and
flota fleets by means of a naval blockade.   As a piece of military strategy it was most
ill-conceived, for, as Defoe remarked, the sea was a big place.   The Spanish fleets
escaped from the Indies and by-passed the squadron stationed off the coast of Spain
to reach home safely and intact.

[4] *Wentworth Papers, 1705-1739,* ed. James J. Cartwright (1883), pp. 456-8; Dureng,
op. cit. p. 347-49.

and such was the coherence of the case which had been presented
to parliament that the main attack on the Administration's negotiations was subsequently conducted along these lines.   In the Lords,
Bathurst took exception even to the reasonable assessment of the
activities of the Pretender made in the king's speech, dubbing it
as a deliberate attempt to inflame opinion.[1]   The ' bugbear of the
Pretender ' was to become a familiar theme with the Opposition
as it assumed greater significance in the arguments of the Administration.   On the whole, however, there was general agreement in
parliament that the measures of the Administration deserved
support, so that it was rumoured in London that William Pulteney,
who had gone into opposition in April 1725, had come to an arrangement with Walpole.[2]   Both houses carried unanimous addresses
which answered all the points made in the king's speech and pledged
the utmost support.[3]

The major discussion, however, of the Administration's foreign
policy awaited more detailed information.   On 10 February O.S.,
both houses were presented with copies of the treaty of Hanover,
excluding the secret article relating to Julich and Berg, and of the
treaties of peace and commerce concluded at Vienna in April
and May 1725.[4]   The latter were laid before the Commons in
answer to an address originating with the Opposition which had
seemed to portend some resolution about commerce.[5]   A week's
delay was allowed in order that members might become thoroughly
familiar with the contents of the treaties, copies of which were
made available to each of them in Latin and English.[6]   The debates
began in both houses on 17 February O.S., and were well attended.
In the Commons in a large house of about 420, the Administration's
case was opened in a set speech which lasted over an hour and a
half by Horace Walpole, who had been recalled from his embassy
at Paris in order to present it.[7]   The practice, thus adopted in 1726,
of giving the responsibility for the exposition of foreign affairs to
one who had been intimately connected with its every development,

---

[1] *Wentworth Papers*, pp. 456-8.   Another speech in the same vein was made by
Lord Falmouth.   It is uncertain whether Chance is referring to this or later debates
when he declares that many of the speeches are contained in Brit. Mus., Add. MSS.
33033.   In either event, however, the statement is inaccurate, for the volume in
question contains accounts of the proceedings of both Houses only.

[2] *Wentworth Papers*, pp. 456-8.

[3] *H.C.J.* xx. 548; *H.L.J.* xxii. 576.

[4] *H.C.J.* xx. 567; *H.L.J.* xxii. 590; 10 February O.S. 1726, House of Lords MSS.
Documents in this depository are arranged according to the date of presentation.
I have to thank Mr. Bond of the Manuscript Room of the House of Lords for permission
to use them.

[5] L'Hermitage, 12 February 1726 (Brit. Mus., Add. MSS. 17677 KKK (8)).

[6] L'Hermitage, 22 February 1726 (Brit. Mus., Add. MSS. 17677 KKK (8)).   The
treaties appeared in the February edition of Boyer.   (Boyer, *op. cit.* xxxi. 112-52).

[7] Boyer, *op. cit.* xxxi. 196-207; W. Coxe, *Memoirs of Horatio, Lord Walpole*, 2v.
(1820), i. 198-201.

is a clear indication of the importance which the Government attached to the presentation of a well-informed argument to parliament, for the withdrawal of Horace Walpole from Paris was a serious inconvenience from a diplomatic point of view; such a move, however, was more or less a political necessity, for with Townshend and Newcastle in the Lords, and in view of Robert Walpole's self-confessed aversion to speaking on European affairs, the Government lacked a recognized spokesman on foreign affairs in the Commons.[1] Horace Walpole prefaced his speech in 1726 with a characteristically long-winded account of the progress of events in Europe since 1713. When he came at last to examine the significance of the treaties of Vienna he contributed little that was new to the argument. He underlined the commercial danger and the importance of Protestant solidarity, noticed the Thorn affair and in somewhat disingenuous terms applauded the pressure which Britain had brought to bear on the king of Poland, and referred optimistically to the resolution of the States of Holland to accede to the alliance of Hanover, without mentioning the conditions of accession upon which they still insisted. The only new point which he raised was that which the Administration had most at heart, namely the supposition that the treaties of Vienna were to be cemented by the marriage of Maria Theresa and Don Carlos. The alliance of Hanover, he insisted finally, was a purely defensive arrangement intended to preserve for its members possession of their existing territories and rights in the face of these threats. In the debate that followed the main argument did not pursue any of the points which Walpole had raised. At first sight it seems surprising that the Opposition ignored the opportunity of testing the validity of Walpole's speculation about a secret marriage alliance. The fact that they did not challenge him on the marriage alliance was due principally to the cautious way in which he had referred to it, as a possibility which might reasonably be inferred from the concessions made by Spain, and to the care which he had taken to place greater emphasis on more immediate dangers which were not disputed at this stage. It was only in 1727, when the Administration declared the alliance to be a fact and opened its mind on the dangers which might follow from it, that the Opposition awakened to the opportunity there provided of discrediting the whole concept of the alliance of Hanover; for the fact turned out to be the confessions of Ripperda, whose extravagances were notorious, and made a rather uncertain beginning to an argument which involved the acceptance of several other uncertainties.

[1] Horace Walpole was recalled again, for the same reason, in 1727 and 1728. See Newcastle to H. Walpole, 10 November 1726 (Brit. Mus., Add. MSS. 32,748); and Newcastle to H. Walpole, 4 January 1727/8 (Brit. Mus., Add. MSS. 32,754). For Robert Walpole's views on foreign affairs see a very interesting letter from him to Newcastle of ? December 1725 in S.P. Domestic 35/60.

The Opposition of 1727 was capable of extracting the maximum profit from such an opening; it enjoyed good parliamentary leadership in the Commons and by means of the *Craftsman* exercised influence far in excess of that which mere numbers in parliament could command; moreover it had a definite objective in the destruction of Robert Walpole. The Opposition of 1726, however, was a very different thing: although numerically not very different from its successor, it was completely disorganized, a number of isolated voices in both houses and nothing more, whose attentions were concentrated upon the Hanoverian aspect of the alliance of Hanover. Shippen and others alleged that the treaty would involve the country in a war for the defence of the king's German territories.[1] There were several answers to this. The first, made by Pelham, secretary-at-war, was that the restraining clause of the Act of Settlement had never been intended to deprive the king of assistance in the event of an attack on his German territories, but had merely made such assistance conditional on the prior consent of parliament.[2] The second, made by Robert Walpole, avoided all constitutional niceties; in existing circumstances, he argued, it was more likely that Hanover would be dragged into a war in defence of British interests, for opposition to the Ostend Company involved the possibility at least of reprisals upon the king's German territories.[3] George I himself seems to have suffered some apprehension on this score.[4] The debate thus anticipated the later and larger controversy between Lord Chesterfield and Horace Walpole.[5] In the Lords the debate followed much the same course, except that the commercial issue achieved greater prominence. The Opposition, perhaps persuaded by private affirmations of good faith from the Spanish ambassador, denied that Spain intended to harm British commerce.[6] Newcastle successfully countered this attack by quoting from a recent letter of Stanhope's reporting a conversation with Ripperda in which the latter had reported the existence of a secret treaty engaging Spain to give full support

[1] Boyer, *op. cit.* xxxi. 204; Chammorel, 4 March 1726, Corr. d'Angl., t. 354.

[2] Boyer, *op. cit.* xxxi. 204.

[3] Chammorel, 4 March 1726, Corr. d'Angl., t. 354; R. Marini, *La politica sabauda alla corte Inglese dopo il trattato d'Hanover 1725-1730 nella relazione dell ambasciatore piemontese a Londra* (Chambéry, 1918), p. 28.

[4] Marini, *op. cit.* p. 25; A. W. Ward, *Great Britain and Hanover* (Oxford, 1899), p. 127.

[5] In *The Case of the Hanover Forces in the Pay of Great Britain, impartially and truly examined; with some seasonable Reflections on the present Conjuncture of Affairs.* London. Printed for T. Cooper at the Globe in Pater Noster Row. 1743 and *The Interest of Great Britain steadily pursued. In Answer to a Pamphlet entitled, the Case of the Hanover Forces etc.,* part i. London. Printed for J. Roberts in Warwick Lane—1743.

[6] For reports of the debate, see Boyer, *op. cit.* xxxi. 209-12; L'Hermitage, 1 March 1726 (Brit. Mus., Add. MSS. 17677 KKK (8)); *H.M.C. Portland* vii. 424. For Spanish connections with the Opposition, see Syveton, *op. cit.* p. 177. Pulteney was also in contact with the Imperial resident in London (Coxe, *Memoirs, etc. of Sir Robert Walpole* ii. 492).

to the Ostend Company, and the Emperor to give military support in operations against Gibraltar.   When motions to lay addresses of thanks before the king, expressing support for the Administration's measures, were put, they were carried by large majorities in both houses.[1]   The addresses, drawn up in almost identical terms in both houses, gave the Administration all that it desired in the way of parliamentary support; they expressed gratitude for the alliance of Hanover, pledged the support of parliament against any attacks made on the king's Hanoverian dominions as a result of the alliance, and strongly condemned the treaty of commerce.[2]

The Ostend trade, coupled now with the potentially more explosive issue of Spanish depredations, had thus been acknowledged as a national concern.[3]   The discussion of the question had moved away from the academic problem of the legality of the Ostend trade under the treaty of Munster to a consideration of the practical measures which could be taken against it.   In March or April a pamphlet had appeared, entitled *The importance of the Ostend company considered*, which suggested that the British and Dutch East India Companies concert policy to destroy Ostend ships wherever they were met.[4]   It is significant, however, that it was still considered necessary to devote considerable space to arguing the common interest of Britain and the United Provinces in destroying ' this cockatrice whilst young ', and even to arguing that the trade of both countries was reciprocally advantageous.   Apparently, it was still felt by some that the Ostend Company was a Dutch rather than a British concern.   In December 1728 indeed when the problem facing the Administration was that of explaining its inability to overcome a condition of ' broken peace and undeclared war ', a Government-inspired writer argued that this had always been the case and that the grand quarrel had always been between Britain and Spain.[5]   Undoubtedly, this was a piece of special pleading, but as applied to the period from 1727 onwards it had some validity, for the Ostend question then tended to become overshadowed by the rapid deterioration in Anglo-Spanish relations resulting from the seige of Gibraltar and the West Indian blockade.   Even in 1726 it is doubtful whether British opposition to the Ostend Company was as widespread, violent, and spontaneous as has been suggested.   The February debates, according to

---

[1] In the Commons by 285 votes against 107 (*H.C.J.* xx. 582); in the Lords by 94 votes against 15 (Boyer, *op. cit.* xxxi. 212).

[2] *H.C.J.* xx. 582; *H.L.J.* xxi. 597-8.

[3] Boyer published in March 1726 an abstract of a pamphlet, addressed to M.P.s, giving a detailed account of forty-seven ships alleged to have been taken or plundered by Spanish guarda costas since 1712 (Boyer, *op. cit.* xxxi. 229-58).

[4] This is in the Lansdowne Tracts.   An abstract appeared in Boyer, *op. cit.* xxxi. 355-77.   A French translation appeared at the Hague.

[5] *London Journal*, Saturday, 21 December O.S. 1728 (Burney collection).

Dr. Stratford, had convinced ' men of all sides that these things must end in a war ', but the prospect was reluctantly admitted rather than gladly accepted.[1]   Opinion was still susceptible to quick and considerable fluctuations, and in April 1726 the French Resident reported that conversations led him to believe that many people thought a rupture could still be avoided, provided that the Emperor could be given a means of making an honourable retreat.[2]   The Administration, too, acted on the assumption that there was no enthusiasm for war.   Townshend remained convinced that a little firmness and vigour would defeat the Emperor's bluff, and favoured a naval blockade of Ostend, yet dared not attempt it because of the risks of being involved in a war without the Dutch.[3]   Even after their accession to the alliance of Hanover it was deemed necessary to advise the East India Company to make a direct and well detailed appeal for royal authority to make reprisals on Ostenders; ' thus will the load be taken off of the king himself '.[4] By this time, however, such considerations were both too late and too early, for Britain had committed herself, under Fleury's persuasions, to attempt a negotiated settlement.

The Administration's position had not been an easy one.   It had detected a number of dangers in the treaties of Vienna, some immediate, some distant but potentially of much greater significance. Since parliament was liable to respond more readily to clear and present dangers these had been given prominence: one of them had been the Ostend trade, whose denunciation would make possible the accession of the United Provinces to the alliance of Hanover, a step which the Administration much desired, not so much because of the positive addition of strength which this would bring, as because of the guarantee which it would give against the possibility of the Dutch making commercial profit out of neutrality; parliament had responded in the manner intended. There was no question, however, of the nation having been roused to a fever pitch of militancy.   By dint of careful management it had been brought to accept the idea of war, but only as a last resort, and even then under conditions which in practice could never be satisfied.

G. C. GIBBS

---

[1] *H.M.C. Portland*, vii. 424: letters of Dr. William Stratford, 19 February O.S. 1726.
[2] Chammorel, 15 April 1726 (Corr. d'Angl., t. 355).
[3] Townshend to Finch, 18 March 1725/6, 29 March 1726 (S.P. 84/289).
[4] Chance, *op. cit.* p. 381.

The Beginning of Parliamentary Reporting in Newspapers, 1768-1774

NEWSPAPERS entered the field of parliamentary reporting late.[1] The traditional veil of secrecy over parliamentary news, long enforced by Standing Orders, had earlier often been defied or evaded. During the seventeenth century occasional reports of debates appeared in newsletters and pamphlets. In the first half of the eighteenth century these were supplemented and superseded by more regular reporting in monthly magazines. Abel Boyer printed debates in *The Political State of Great Britain* from 1711 until his death in 1729, and the magazine continued to publish accounts until 1737. The *Gentleman's Magazine* began reports in 1731, and the *London Magazine* in 1732: at first both copied from the *Political State*, but they came increasingly to print their own versions. These periodicals all confined publication to the parliamentary recess, purporting to take advantage of an apparent loophole in the prohibition on reporting: this was expressly closed by a resolution of the house of commons on 13 April 1738. The magazines thenceforth resorted to the transparent subterfuge of mythical assemblies, but they were not called to account until April 1747, when the house of lords took action concerning reports of the treason trial of Lord Lovat. The two printers were reprimanded, and released only on promise to avoid future offence. The *Gentleman's Magazine* at once stopped reports. The *London Magazine* ceased to attribute speeches to individual members, but continued general summaries of debates until lack of public interest caused their suspension in 1757.[2]

London newspapers thus far had apparently made no attempts to print reports of debates; in the few cases where the house of commons had acted the offending publications had all been pamphlets or provincial papers.[3] The century, however, had seen the growth of a metropolitan press.[4] By 1757 there were in existence

---

[1] This paper is confined to the reporting of debates in the house of commons, and omits any study of the publication of division-lists.

[2] Surveys of this phase of Parliamentary reporting may be found in B. B. Hoover, *Samuel Johnson's Parliamentary Reporting* (Los Angeles, 1953), pp. 1-32; and in F. S. Siebert, *Freedom of the Press in England, 1476-1776* (Urbana, 1952), pp. 346-52.

[3] *Journals of the House of Commons* (henceforth *C.J.*), xix. 30, 43, 53; xx. 143; xxi. 8,5 104, 108, 115, 227, 238, 249; xxii. 703, 707, 713; xxiv. 230, 232, 798, 854.

[4] This study is based on the newspaper collections in the British Museum and the Guildhall, supplemented by information from the *Times Tercentenary Handlist of English and Welsh Newspapers, 1620-1920*.

at least three daily newspapers, the *Public Advertiser*, the *Gazetteer* and the *Daily Advertiser*, while triweekly papers included the *London Evening Post*, the *General Evening Post*, and the *Whitehall Evening Post*. In that year a period of rapid expansion was stimulated by an oversight in the drafting of a new Stamp Act, which made publications of six or more pages liable to a tax of only 3s. per edition, instead of a halfpenny or penny per copy.[1] New triweekly papers founded were the *London Chronicle* and *Lloyd's Evening Post* in 1757, and the *St. James' Chronicle* in 1761. The daily *Public Ledger* was established in 1760. Among the flood of weekly periodicals that made an appearance, often short-lived, were the *North Briton* and the *Weekly London Journal*,[2] both launched in 1762.

Competition drove the newspapers to venture into the forbidden pastures of parliamentary reporting. On 1 February 1760 complaint was made in the Commons that four newspapers, the *London Chronicle* of January 31 and the *Gazetteer*, the *Public Advertiser* and the *Daily Advertiser* of 1 February, all contained 'printed Accounts of the Proceedings of this House, in contempt of the Order, and in Breach of the Privilege of this House'. The printers were ordered to attend at the Bar of the House.[3] The offending issue of the *London Chronicle* in fact contained only the formal vote of thanks by the Speaker, on behalf of the House, to Admiral Hawke for his naval services, and Hawke's reply.[4] On 4 February the printers attended, confessed their offence, and were resolved guilty of breach of privilege. They were released after a reprimand from the Speaker.[5] Two years later, on 20 January 1762, a copy of the *London Chronicle* was again a cause of complaint. The issue included nothing more than a formal speech made by the Speaker on 2 December 1761, but the printer, on his attendance at the House, was ordered into the custody of the Serjeant at Arms.[6] This severity achieved its purpose. Although the newspapers were full of political items, no further attempt to publish the proceedings of parliament was made until the excitement over the Middlesex election of 1768.

The heightened political interest led then to a further expansion of the London press. The *North Briton*, extinct since 1763, was revived on 10 May 1768. William Beckford and other City Radicals founded the *Middlesex Journal or Chronicle of Liberty*, a triweekly newspaper whose first number was published on 4 April 1769.[7]

---

[1] Siebert, *op. cit.* pp. 354–5.

[2] This was later *Baldwin's Weekly Journal*.

[3] *C.J.* xxviii. 741.

[4] No copies of the other newspapers appear to survive, but they probably copied this item.

[5] *C.J.* xxviii. 745.

[6] *C.J.* xxix. 109, 120.

[7] H. R. Fox Bourne, *English Newspapers: Chapters in the History of Journalism* (1887), i. 198.

Soon afterwards, on 28 June 1769, the daily *Morning Chronicle*, printed by William Woodfall, made its first appearance.[1] In October of the same year another triweekly paper, the *London Packet*, was launched.[2] Three new weekly papers, two of ephemeral existence, were also started during this period. The *Parliamentary Spy* lasted only from 21 November 1769 to 25 May 1770. The *Whisperer*, founded on 11 February 1770, survived until 11 January 1772. *Bingley's Journal*, started on 9 June 1770, proved of stronger vitality, and on 11 May 1771 the *North Briton* was merged with it.[3] In the middle of 1770 there were being published in London at least five daily, eight triweekly and four weekly papers, all carrying political news.

By that time the publication of debates was already well advanced. A tentative lead had been given by John Almon, the printer and political journalist, who in his later memoirs claimed the sole initiative in the matter.

> When the spirit of the nation was raised high by the massacre in St. George's Fields,[4] the unjust decision upon the Middlesex election, etc., Mr. Almon resolved to make the nation acquainted with the proceedings of Parliament: for this purpose he employed himself sedulously in obtaining from different gentlemen, by conversation at his own house and sometimes at their houses, sufficient information to write a sketch of every day's debate, on the most important and interesting questions; which he printed three times a week regularly in the *London Evening Post*. . . . During two sessions, this practice of printing sketches of the debates continued, without any notice being taken; and Mr. Almon furnished them constantly, from the best information he could obtain. Though they were short they were in general pretty accurate, and their accuracy was perhaps the cause of the printer's security.[5]

Unfortunately no copies of the *London Evening Post* survive for the years 1768 and 1769. Indirect confirmation of Almon's statement, however, is provided by the increasingly frequent appearance, in his later collection of *Debates*, of short reports from the beginning in November 1768 of the second session

[1] A. Andrews, *History of British Journalism* (1859), i. 194.

[2] The date is obtained by calculation from the earliest surviving copy, no. 384, printed on 3 April 1772.

[3] Horace Walpole, *Memoirs of the Reign of King George the Third*, ed. G. F. Russell Barker, 4 vols. (1894), iii. 200 n. The paper later appeared as *Bingley's Weekly Journal*, *Bingley's Journal*, and *Bingley's London Journal*.

[4] This 'massacre' was the suppression on 10 May 1768 of a riot outside the King's Bench prison, where Wilkes was confined; some five or six persons were killed by soldiers sent to maintain order.

[5] *Memoirs of John Almon, Bookseller, of Piccadilly* (1790), p. 119. In his edition of Wilkes's correspondence, *The Correspondence of the late John Wilkes with his Friends, etc.* (1805), Almon stated, v. 52, ' On the meeting of the new parliament in the year 1769, some occasional sketches of the proceedings of the house of commons were printed in the London Evening Post '.

of the parliament elected earlier in that year.[1] These accounts developed during 1769 from brief summaries in reported speech, with few references to individual members, into longer narratives giving some indication of the course of debate and even a few supposedly verbatim extracts from speeches.   Rival periodicals displayed more prudence.   The other newspapers and the magazines did not venture beyond general sketches of the arguments used in the main debates on Wilkes, supplemented by a few division-figures and lists of speakers.

First to throw caution aside and print what purported to be full-length reports were not the newspapers but the monthly magazines, ambitious to resume their traditional role.   This step came with the opening of the third session in January 1770.   John Almon himself apparently believed that the future of reporting lay with the magazines.   On 1 January he founded the *London Museum*, a new monthly political review whose advertised purpose was to print ' an accurate Journal of the Proceedings and Debates of the Present Parliament '. The second number, which appeared on 27 January, included a number of speeches, and the magazine continued to publish debates until its demise in the following year.[2]   At the end of January, too, the *London Magazine* printed a full report of the debate of 9 January on the Address, given under the guise of ' Proceedings of a Political Club '.[3]   The account was at once copied by the *Parliamentary Spy* in its issues of 30 January and 6 February.   In the next month the magazine announced the resumption of regular reporting,[4] and henceforth every number contained reports of debates in one or both Houses.   The example of these two competitors was at once followed by the *Gentleman's Magazine*.   From February it published similar long reports under the title ' The Debates is a newly-established Society ', ostensibly a debating club for young gentlemen modelled on parliament.   Many of these accounts were promptly copied by *Lloyd's Evening Post* within a few days of their appearance in the magazine.

The initiative remained with the magazines only until the opening of the next session in November 1770.   Most of the daily, triweekly and weekly newspapers, which apart from the *London Evening Post* had hitherto not advanced beyond the general arguments of debates and occasional lists of speakers, then began to publish full reports. The debate on the Address on 13 November was given at great

[1] J. Almon, *The Debates and Proceedings of the British House of Commons from 1743 to 1774* (1766–75), vol. viii.

[2] No copies of the magazine survive, and this information was derived from advertisements in the *London Evening Post* for 27 January 1770 and 9 March 1771, and the *Middlesex Journal* for 6 April 1771.   Cobbett's *Parliamentary History* acknowledges a dozen reports between 16 February 1770 and 7 February 1771.   (xvi. 807, 874, 902, 904, 907, 923, 943, 1055, 1119, 1322, 1341, 1355).

[3] *London Magazine*, 1770, pp. 32–7.   [4] *London Magazine*, 1770, p. 65.

length during the next two or three weeks in William Woodfall's *Morning Chronicle*: this account was probably ' Memory ' Woodfall's first essay at Parliamentary reporting. The narrative was copied, either wholly or in part, by the *General Evening Post,* the *Gazetteer,* the *London Evening Post,* the *Middlesex Journal,* the *London Chronicle* and the *North Briton*.[1] Even the *London Museum* seems to have adopted this report,[2] and the only alternative published account of the debate was that in the first three numbers of the *Gentleman's Magazine* for the next year. Most newspapers were still printing speeches from this debate in early December. Space could be found for only a few important debates in such detail. The next debate reported at great length by Woodfall was that of 27 November, on a motion relative to proceedings in the Court of King's Bench. His account in the *Morning Chronicle*, over 17,000 words long, was again copied during the next few weeks by the *General Evening Post,* the *Gazetteer,* the *Middlesex Journal,* the *London Chronicle* and the *North Briton*.[3] John Almon produced his own version of this debate, and presumably published it in the *London Museum*.[4] The *Gentleman's Magazine* printed a different account from April to August 1771, so three reports of the debate were eventually in circulation.

The third important debate before the Christmas recess took place on 6 December, over a motion concerning the administration of justice in Westminster Hall. It would seem that the *Morning Chronicle* once more produced a long account, and that this was the report copied over the period from 25 December to 26 January by the *General Evening Post,* the *London Chronicle* and the *Gazetteer*;[5] certainly William Woodfall on 7 February 1771 published an expanded version of this account, together with his report of the debate of 27 November, in the pamphlet *Vox Senatus*. A shortened form of this report appeared months later in both the *Gentleman's Magazine* and the *London Magazine*. The *Middlesex Journal* published from 20 December 1770 to 22 January 1771 its own full account of the debate under the heading ' Extract of a Letter from a Gentleman in London to his friend at Leeds in Yorkshire '. This narrative was reprinted by the *North Briton* from 12 January to 2 February. During December, too, the *London Evening Post* also printed its own versions of a number of speeches from this debate. The same pattern continued after the Christmas recess. A few important

---

[1] The *Morning Chronicle* does not survive for the period, but all the extant identical reports appeared simultaneously with or after those in the *General Evening Post*, which acknowledged the *Morning Chronicle* as the source.

[2] The account in the *Parliamentary History*, xvi. 1055–79, ' from the *London Museum* ', is identical with that in the *General Evening Post*.

[3] As before, only the *General Evening Post* acknowledged the source.

[4] The account in Almon's *Debates*, ix. 19–28, did not appear in the *London Evening Post*, and is different from that in the newspapers.

[5] The *General Evening Post* only makes an acknowledgment for one speech to the *Morning Chronicle*.

debates were reported at length, but most accounts were still brief or covered only a few speeches. No clear picture of this phase of parliamentary reporting can be drawn, because insufficient evidence has survived to make it possible either to establish how many newspapers were publishing debates, or to determine which of the reports were original compositions.

Eight newspapers were prosecuted by the house of commons during February and March 1771. Complaint was made by Colonel Onslow on 8 February of certain abusive reports in the *Middlesex Journal* and the *Gazetteer*. After the ground had become more general, Colonel Onslow on 12 March instigated proceedings against six other papers. These were the *St. James' Chronicle*, the *General Evening Post*, the *London Evening Post*, the *Whitehall Evening Post*, the *Morning Chronicle*, and the *London Packet*.[1] The list was not comprehensive, for the *London Chronicle*, *Lloyd's Evening Post*, several weekly papers and some monthly magazines were printing reports at this time.[2] No further attempt to do so, however, was yet made by two of the four newspapers which had given offence in 1760, the *Public Advertiser* and the *Daily Advertiser*. The *Public Advertiser*, printed by Henry Sampson Woodfall, was bold enough to publish the Junius letters, but it contained no debates for this period.[3]

Some newspapers produced their own reports and only copied from their competitors to supplement them: other papers relied solely on pirating accounts. Since the newspaper files are often missing or incomplete, it is impossible to identify the sources of many reports. Accounts in one paper that subsequently appeared in other periodicals, however, were almost certainly original compositions: if they had been published earlier elsewhere, all the rival printers would have copied them at the same time. The foremost reporter was John Almon, who published frequent accounts in the *London Museum* and the *London Evening Post*. The *Morning Chronicle*, the *Middlesex Journal* and the *Gazetteer* also sometimes printed their own versions, but usually copied from each other and from the *London Evening Post*. Both the *General Evening Post* and the *London Chronicle* apparently published only pirated reports, and the *General Evening Post* even printed two or three different accounts of many speeches and debates. Selective or systematic reporting had not yet begun. Newspapers published only such narratives and speeches as they found convenient: sometimes reports were left unfinished; sometimes individual speeches were added to supplement earlier accounts. The same periodicals varied their methods for

[1] *Parliamentary History*, xvii. 58–71, 75–83.

[2] The *Public Ledger* and other newspapers for which no files survive may also have been publishing debates.

[3] Complete files of the *Public Advertiser* exist for the period 1768–74. No copies of the *Daily Advertiser* have survived for the years 1768–71, but complete files for 1772–4 contain no reports of debates.

different debates. No paper attempted a comprehensive coverage even of the major political debates.

From the time the newspapers began full reports, the monthly magazines found themselves at a disadvantage. Their accounts were now forestalled. This competition may well have been the reason why John Almon soon stopped publication of the *London Museum* and concentrated his attention on the *London Evening Post*. Both the *London Magazine* and the *Gentleman's Magazine* reserved only a few pages each month for parliamentary reports. Gradually they abandoned any attempts to provide their own versions, and based their parliamentary sections on the reports already printed in the newspapers. Although the magazines summarized these accounts drastically, they fell far behind. They must have persevered with their reports only because of the appeal to a wider public outside London. Debates were not printed openly as such: only the *London Evening Post* sometimes made no pretence of concealing either debates or speakers. The other newspapers and the magazines always gave some such headings to their reports as ' Robinhood Society' or ' A Great Assembly' or ' A Common Assembly'. Except in the *Middlesex Journal*, too, the names of the speakers were put in skeleton form or some other disguise. The caution of the newspapers on this point proved unnecessary. No heed was paid as to whether reports had been thinly veiled when in 1771 the house of commons finally acted to stop their publication.

Complaints by Colonel Onslow of the practice of parliamentary reporting led to the summoning of the printers of eight newspapers before the Bar of the House. Some attended, on 14 March, but three took refuge in the City of London, which claimed an exclusive right of arrest within its own boundaries. A crisis was provoked by the calculated refusal of a few city officials to allow messengers from the house of commons to apprehend the defiant printers. Fifty days after Colonel Onslow had first raised the subject, the quarrel culminated in the House sending two City officials to the Tower, Alderman Oliver on 25 March and the Lord Mayor on 27 March. The reaction of the press to the measures of the House varied considerably. *Lloyd's Evening Post* and the *London Chronicle* at once stopped the publication of debates after Colonel Onslow on 5 February had drawn attention to the standing orders of the House. The *London Evening Post*, the *Middlesex Journal* and the *Gazetteer* all continued to print debates throughout the period of crisis: these were the papers of the three printers who were defying arrest. The printers of the *St. James' Chronicle* and the *General Evening Post* promised to stop publishing reports when they attended the House on 14 March.[1] The *St. James' Chronicle*, which had begun reporting

[1] For the proceedings of that day see the manuscript Parliamentary Diary of Matthew Brickdale (Bristol University Library), iv. 13–37.

only on 9 March, did stop, but the *General Evening Post* was printing debates again within a week.[1]   Both the *London Chronicle* and *Lloyd's Evening Post* resumed reporting early in April.

The house of commons had signally failed to stamp out the reporting of its debates.   The nominal triumph of imprisoning two City magistrates had produced no practical result, and the House lacked the authority to detain them after the end of the session. The three defiant printers had continued to publish reports, and by the Easter recess even those who had been intimidated or had submitted to the House were also in the field again.   The attitude of the City officials made it clear that if the Commons insisted on enforcing a prohibition of reporting the task would be faced afresh each session.   The House therefore contented itself with the token vindication of its authority, and accepted the situation.   The victory of the newspapers was not complete, for the Commons retained and often exercised the power of excluding strangers.   In 1772 the House cleared the gallery for the debates on the Royal Family Marriage Bill.   This step defeated every reporter except John Almon; only the *London Evening Post* contrived to publish a few belated accounts of these debates.   The other newspapers contained little or nothing about the proceedings on the bill, and for a time fell back upon the debates of the Irish house of commons, and even those of seventeenth-century parliaments![2]   In 1774, too, the House was always cleared for the legislation on America,[3] and the measure effectively prevented any full accounts of the debates in the newspapers.   For the debate of 22 April the *General Evening Post* could follow a long report of proceedings on a copyright bill only with the statement, ' At four o'clock the order for the second reading of the bill for regulating the government of Massachusetts Bay came on, which produced a warm debate that continued to almost seven o'clock '.[4]

Although from 1771 there was no effective ban on parliamentary reporting, the printers were slow both to appreciate the reality of their new freedom and to reap full advantage from it.   Only gradually were the disguised headings and skeleton names abandoned. The more cautious newspapers, such as the *General Evening Post*, the *London Chronicle*, and *Lloyd's Evening Post*, were still using skeleton names in 1774, and sometimes even such headings as ' Debates in a

[1] No files exist for the three other papers prosecuted, the *Morning Chronicle*, the *London Packet* and the *Whitehall Evening Post*.

[2] The only definite statement found on the closing of the gallery concerns the debate of 9 March 1772 (*Parliamentary History*, xvii. 399 n.), but it can be inferred from the almost complete failure of the newspapers to produce any reports on such a controversial subject.

[3] The statement in the *Parliamentary History*, xvii. 1295 n., is confirmed by the newspapers: see, for example, the *General Evening Post* for 15, 17, 26, 29 March, 23, 26, 30 April, 4 May.

[4] *General Evening Post*, 23 April 1774.

Great Assembly '. Nor did any rapid development of reporting take place.

For some years John Almon remained the leading reporter. In 1772 the *London Evening Post* adopted a regular system, every Tuesday publishing reports of the debates during the previous week. Within a year, however, Almon dropped this weekly column and thenceforth reported debates in the next issue. He covered almost every debate of importance, but his accounts were generally short, with a few conspicuous exceptions: that for the debate of 21 May 1773 on Lord Clive ran from 22 May to 1 June, to a length of over 10,000 words. Apart from the *London Evening Post*, only the *Gazetteer* is known to have been printing frequent original reports in 1772 and 1773. The usual practice of the other newspapers was to give very brief summaries as soon as possible, and subsequently to copy the reports in the *London Evening Post* or the *Gazetteer*. The *General Evening Post*, the *Middlesex Journal*, the *London Chronicle*, *Lloyd's Evening Post*, the *Morning Chronicle*, and the *St. James' Chronicle* all followed this method.[1] The two weekly political papers, *Bingley's London Journal* and *Baldwin's London Weekly Journal*, also copied the newspaper reports. Many individual speeches were also printed in newspapers separately from the reports. Most accounts and speeches were short, and many of the longer reports were cut when copied by the *Middlesex Journal* and other papers. Every periodical, too, omitted debates through carelessness or lack of space. Parliamentary reporting was still in its infancy: about a dozen London papers contained debates, but rarely were more than two different versions of the same debate in circulation.

The year 1774 saw a marked advance. Most newspapers began to publish at least occasional reports of their own composition. William Woodfall gave long accounts of a few selected debates in the *Morning Chronicle*, but avoided subjects of political controversy. The *Morning Post* and the *St. James' Chronicle*, which carried in every issue a ' Diary of the Proceedings of the House of Commons ', both produced regular original accounts. The *Middlesex Journal* embarked on the publication of its own full reports; from 1 February the paper was enlarged in size ' in order to give a circumstantial account of the debates in both Houses of Parliament '. The *Public Ledger*, too, was printing long accounts immediately after the debates, and these were copied by the *General Evening Post*, the *London Chronicle*, and sometimes other papers. The *Gazetteer* took advantage of its position as a daily newspaper to print short reports on the day after each debate, but now began to stop the publication of fuller accounts. The *London Evening Post* concentrated on the main political topics.

---

[1] No files survive for the *London Packet*, the *Public Ledger*, the *Whitehall Evening Post* or for the *Morning Post*, which was founded on 2 November 1772. The files of other newspapers are often incomplete.

When the gallery was shut for the debates on the American legislation, this newspaper repeated its performance of two years before in the similar circumstance of the Royal Family Marriage Bill, being the only paper to produce reports of the debates.

The other daily and triweekly papers, and the weekly periodicals of Baldwin and Bingley, continued as before to pirate accounts from their more enterprising rivals. Also still copying these newspaper reports, in drastically shortened form, were the monthly magazines. By this time the *Gentleman's Magazine* did not publish a parliamentary section every month, but the *London Magazine* attempted a wide coverage in an unbroken series of reports, and fell far behind; a year afterwards it was belatedly printing the debates of June 1774.

By the dissolution of the parliament in 1774, reporting had already developed far from the outlines of arguments and lists of speakers which had been bold innovations soon after the general election of 1768. Reporting was now expected of newspapers. The evidence of the printers before the house of commons on 14 March 1771 had shown that even then newspapers omitting debates received complaints from their readers and suffered a drop in circulation. In 1774 over a dozen papers were reporting debates, and although each at times still copied from a rival, at least seven were producing their own versions of debates. ' The unreported Parliament ' had seen the birth of parliamentary reporting in its modern form.[1]

Competition had produced fullness, variety and promptness. Accuracy could come only with the employment of shorthand writers; certainly it is not to be expected in the circumstances of the time. Often no admittance into the house of commons was allowed during important debates. Reporters when under this handicap were obliged to fall back upon sources of dubious authenticity. John Almon's remarks in his memoirs show that hearsay from conversations in the lobby of the House or gossip in coffee houses formed the basis of many early reports.[2] Access to the gallery, however, does appear to have been possible during most debates, although this privilege might involve some arrangement with the door-keepers.[3] Even then the reporter's task was a hard one. The position of the gallery made it difficult to hear and impossible to see many members. No notes were allowed before 1783.[4] The proprietors of the newspapers sent agents to memorize the debates

---

[1] The phrase, ' the unreported Parliament ' appears to have been coined by John Wright in his edition of *Sir Henry Cavendish's Debates of the House of Commons during the Thirteenth Parliament of Great Britain*, 2 vols., 1841–3.

[2] J. Almon, *Memoirs*, p. 119.

[3] Paul Mantoux, *Notes Sur Les Comptes Rendu Des Séances Du Parliament Anglais au XVIIIe Siècle conservés aux Archives du Ministère Des Affaires Etrangères* (Paris, 1906), p. 68.

[4] A. Aspinall, ' The Reporting and Publishing of the House of Commons' Debates 1771–1834 ', in *Essays presented to Sir Lewis Namier*, ed. R. Pares and A. J. P. Taylor, London 1956, pp. 230–9.

as best they could, and the details learnt were used as the basis of reports which owed more to imagination than information. The *General Evening Post* of 27 December 1770, indeed, after having given two-thirds of a column to a speech by Alderman Oliver, conscientiously added, ' N.B. The argument here displayed consisted only of a few words in the mouth of the Alderman.'

Besides those engaged for the purpose by the printers, there were in operation a number of independent writers paid for each contribution.[1] Gradually, however, each newspaper came to have a specialist reporter. Some of the problems such men faced at the time are conveyed in this description by James Stephen, who reported for the *Morning Post* during the closing years of the North ministry.

> No man was allowed to take a note for the purpose.—We were obliged therefore to depend on memory alone and had no assistance in the work, one Reporter for each House being all that any Paper employed.—We were obliged to sit in the Gallery from the sitting of the House till its adjournment, and afterwards, however late, to begin and finish our work before we retired to rest. The Papers consequently went late to press after an important debate; but this being a great disadvantage to them, both in their advertising interests and their sale, the poor weary reporter was always importuned for the utmost possible dispatch, and quickness of composition was not less in request than strength of memory and correctness of stile.[2]

Even after newspapers had ceased to copy reports verbatim from their rivals, and prided themselves on printing original accounts, it was natural for reporters to remedy the defects of their memory by making use of the information garnered by those of their competitors who went to press beforehand. ' Memory ' William Woodfall himself owed much of the fame for the fullness and accuracy of his reports to this practice.[3] Hearsay and memory were imperfect sources, and newspaper proprietors endeavoured to supplement them by more direct methods. There was an ancient tradition that members who wished could make their views known to their constituents. Newspapers accordingly invited members to publish their own speeches, in order to avoid misrepresentation. Typical was this advertisement in the *London Evening Post* for 11 December 1770.

> The Members of either House, who would choose to avoid any disagreeable Imputation by having their Speeches spuriously given to the Public, may, by enclosing them to A.B. at the Printers, have them faithfully conveyed to the Public through a most respectable Composition. The Manuscripts, immediately after composition, will be destroyed.

---

[1] P. Mantoux, *op. cit.* pp. 68–9.
[2] *The Memoirs of James Stephen written by himself for the Use of his Children*, ed. Merle M. Bevington, 1954, p. 291.   [3] *Memoirs of James Stephen*, p. 293.

Some members undoubtedly did supply information, but only a few of the many individual speeches printed in the newspapers were genuine. There is no safe guide to determine their authenticity. Two speeches by Alderman Sawbridge on shorter parliaments were circulated to the newspapers: yet while the one for 26 April 1771 was spurious, that for 4 March 1772 was certainly the actual speech made in the House.[1] Although Lord Clive's long speech of 30 March 1772 that appeared in the newspapers was an accurate version of the original speech, the simultaneously published report of Governor Johnstone's reply on the same day was fictitious.[2]

Diverse as the origins of newspaper reports were, members of the house of commons appeared unanimous in criticism of their misleading and inaccurate character. Alexander Wedderburn, when asked if a speech attributed to him in a newspaper was correct, is reputed to have made this reply. 'Why, to be sure, there are in that report a few things which I did say, but many things which I am glad I did not say, and some things which I wish I could have said.'[3] Edmund Burke complained to the House on 8 February 1771, 'I have been made to express sentiments of the constitution, I have been made to express sentiments of America, directly contrary to those I have expressed'.[4] During a debate of 14 February 1774 on Horne's libel other members gave their opinions. The younger Thomas Townshend said: 'I have sometimes borrowed a paper to hear what I said myself, sometimes very much surprised at it.' Lord North declared more bluntly: 'I have often read the report of our debate as stated in the newspapers. I am sorry that the people of this country, that our constituents are so grossly imposed upon, when those debates are conveyed to them as the real sentiments of the gentlemen in this House.'[5] The reports, of course, did vary in quality, according to such factors as the possibility of access to the House, the memory and ability of the writers, and the amount of space allocated for the accounts. Political bias in their compilation was rare, despite the charge against its rivals made by the *Morning Chronicle* on 19 February 1774. 'We flatter ourselves a dispassionate relation of facts will be highly acceptable to our readers, especially where the spirit of misrepresentation is unfortunately too prevalent.' Newspapers like the *London Evening Post* and the *Middlesex Journal*

---

[1] Compare the report in the *General Evening Post* for 2 May 1771 with Brit. Mus. Egerton MS. 230, pp. 220–7: and that in the *Gazetteer* for 10 March 1772 with Brit. Mus. Egerton MS. 234, pp. 238–46. These volumes in the Egerton MSS. form part of the Parliamentary Diary of Henry Cavendish, for which see below.

[2] Compare Clive in the *General Evening Post* for 2 and 4 April 1772, with Brit. Mus. Egerton MS. 239, pp. 197–233: and Johnstone in the *General Evening Post* 4 to 11 April 1772, with Brit. Mus. Egerton MS. 239, pp. 233–43.

[3] Quoted, under the date of 1771, in John Lord Campbell, *The Lives of the Lord Chancellors* . . . (8 vols. 1845–69), v. 93.

[4] Brit. Mus. Egerton MS. 224, p. 170.

[5] Brit. Mus. Egerton MS. 251, pp. 211–13.

were opposition in sympathy, and often inserted partisan comments in their reports. Nevertheless, there was not likely to be much deliberate suppression so long as any information on debates possessed a scarcity value.[1] Newspapers usually copied, without comment or alteration, reports even from rivals of differing political views.

The value of newspaper reports in this period can be assessed by comparison with the manuscript parliamentary diary of Henry Cavendish, which contains almost verbatim accounts based on shorthand notes taken down in the house of commons by Cavendish himself.[2] The reports did maintain a certain minimum standard of accuracy. With very rare exceptions, all the members named in any account as speaking in a particular debate had actually done so, and the side they had taken was correctly indicated. Many speeches, however, were completely omitted.[3] Most of the early reports were short, not more than brief summaries. They were generally accurate in the scanty information they gave, but the longer reports that became increasingly frequent do not stand up to critical examination.

The first of such reports that appeared were full of mistakes. That in the *London Magazine* for the debate of 9 January 1770 omitted some speeches and placed others in the wrong order. Points made by one member were attributed to another: thus it was the younger Thomas Townshend who complained of Lord Botetourt's conduct, and not Colonel Barré as given in the magazine. Over half the whole account was concerned with Edmund Burke's speech. The report of the same debate in the *Gentleman's Magazine* contained speeches by three members, Lord George Sackville, Charles Jenkinson and Charles James Fox, none of whom are mentioned in the Cavendish Diary or in any other account of the debate: they are almost certainly fictitious. All the full reports for the year in the *Gentleman's Magazine* suffer from marked defects.[4] A number of speeches are given at even greater length than in the Cavendish Diary, and much of the substance of the speeches, including many references to persons and events, cannot be traced at all in the Diary. William Woodfall's early reports face the same charge.[5] Their very length should render them suspect: indeed, the account of Serjeant Glynn's second speech on 6 December 1770 is over thirty times as long as the version in the Cavendish Diary. Despite the fame of

[1] *Memoirs of James Stephen*, pp. 291–3.

[2] Brit. Mus. Egerton MSS. 215–63, 3711.

[3] Comparison with the Cavendish Diary has been made for the names of the speakers in all the newspaper reports, from 1768 to 1774, and for the wording of many long accounts.

[4] The reports examined are those for the debates of 9, 22, 24, 25, 31 January, 12 February and 27 November 1770.

[5] Those for 13 and 27 November, and 6 December 1770 have been examined.

Woodfall's memory, the reports are not characterised by the retention of the actual phrases used by the speakers. At best only the
general patterns of the speeches are the same: the wording is entirely
different. John Almon was forthright in his condemnation of
Woodfall's account for 27 November 1770. 'It is proper to inform
the reader that the series of speeches which has been published,
purporting to be the speeches of this night's debate, are not authentic, that they are in many parts false, and almost everywhere a misrepresentation.'[1]

Little improvement had occurred in the standard of reporting by
1774. The accounts in such other newspapers as the *Gazetteer* and
the *Middlesex Journal* suffered from the same defects of an inaccuracy
that often merged into fiction. The most favourable verdict on
contemporary reporting was perhaps that given by William Woodfall
himself in the *Morning Chronicle* of 26 March 1774. After having
printed a five-column account of a debate, he inserted the following
notice.

> The public are requested to read the above not as an exact account
> of the debate on the subject, but as a mere skeleton of the arguments
> urged upon the occasion; the writer is conscious of the impossibility
> of an auditor's carrying away the arrangement of the arguments, or
> the exact phraseology used by the speakers; he submits it to his
> readers as the substance of the debate, but he does not venture like
> his brethren, to call it a perfect report of what was said on the
> occasion.

The value of newspaper reports is therefore limited to names and
general arguments. Points made by speakers were usually marshalled in the wrong order, and sometimes even ascribed to other
members : never has the exact wording been captured. Nothing
better, indeed, can be expected from contemporary conditions.
Only in the next decade, when reporters were allowed to take down
notes, was any marked improvement in standard possible. The
parliamentary columns of the newspapers before that time are best
regarded as the creation of imaginative artists, who often worked
with scanty materials. Their impressions varied from brief sketches
by Almon to the masterpieces of Woodfall.

University of Glasgow   PETER D. G. THOMAS

[1] J. Almon, *Debates,* ix. 20.

Edmund Burke and the County Movement, 1779-1780

THE fame of Edmund Burke has long been disputed ground. His biographers have ceased to be malicious, and though varying in candour are now united in admiration ; and the historians of political thought, rediscovering in him an upholder of natural law, have become more, rather than less, enthusiastic. But as the nature of English eighteenth-century politics has come to be more fully understood, he has suffered at the hands of the general historians, whose aspersions lose nothing in effect from being casual. A fame that rested on words of public wisdom and acts of private benevolence was bound to lose lustre when historians began to reassemble the sober, workaday political context, and when the orator once more had to compete against the coughing and shuffling of lesser, and less vulnerable, men in the House. It was particularly damaging that he should have been detected at the source of what some historians believed to be a long-standing imposture, the ' Whig interpretation ' of the early years of George III's reign. The battle recently joined on this subject [1] may open a new phase in the adventures of a reputation. It is more likely that a reassessment will be entailed by the newly available papers of Burke, Rockingham and Portland at Sheffield and Nottingham ;[2] and it is possible that the historians and biographers will be reconciled. But until the new material is academically processed,[3] only limited studies are useful. The intention of this paper is to examine Burke's association with the county petitioning movement of 1779–80, a crucial episode in his political career.

[1] An attempt to trace the genesis of the ' Whig interpretation ' of George III and to expose Burke's *Thoughts on the Cause of the Present Discontents* as an Opposition fiction was made by Romney Sedgwick in the introduction to his edition of *Letters from George III to Lord Bute, 1756–1766* (London, 1939). The latest phase in the dispute has been provoked by Herbert Butterfield, *George III and the Historians* (London, 1957).

[2] For permission to quote from the Wentworth Woodhouse Muniments, deposited in the Central Library, Sheffield, I am indebted to the earl Fitzwilliam and the Trustees of the Wentworth Woodhouse Estates ; and for the Portland MSS., deposited in the Library of the University of Nottingham, to the Librarian, and to the duke of Portland.

[3] I refer, of course, to the edition of the Burke correspondence now in progress under the general direction of Professor Thomas W. Copeland. An early by-product is Thomas W. Copeland and Milton Shumway Smith, *A Checklist of the Correspondence of Edmund Burke* (Cambridge, 1955).

In late 1779 the Administration of Lord North seemed about to founder.[1]   Its incapacity, disorder and debility were unusual even in an age when government was often weak and unsystematic and before the machine had habituated men to the idea and practice of efficiency. The war with the American colonists and the Bourbon Powers which came to their aid had brought military and naval humiliation, economic distress and, with the rise of the volunteer movement, an explosive Irish problem.   North, dilatory and indecisive, was no man to lead a war-time Ministry ; and only the narrow-minded resoluteness of the king and the faithful labours of the ' men of business ', Jenkinson and Robinson, gave it a semblance of co-herence.[2]   Opposition was gathering momentum.   The Rocking-ham group had behind them a long course of disappointment. The *Present Discontents*, the manifesto which Burke had written ten years before, had impressed its slogans and ways of thought upon them in a remarkable manner ; but it had not pointed out the high road to power.   They had learned only too well not to accept office save on their own terms as to men and measures—a self-restraint vexing to ambitious newcomers like Charles James Fox, who sat looser to doctrines of party and who was prepared to enter a coalition, even with ministers, in the hope of permeating it and winning a gradual ascendancy.[3]   Burke himself was beginning to wonder whether his aristocratic associates were of the stuff to ' storm the closet ' effectively.

> Ill success, ill health, minds too delicate for the rough and toilsome business of our time, a want of the stimulus of ambition, a degeneracy of the Nation, which they are not lofty enough to despise, nor skilful enough to cure, have, all together, I am afraid contributed very much to weaken the spring of Characters, whose fault it never was to be too electrick and too firmly braced.

He confessed himself for the first time at a loss to know what line the party should follow.[4]

---

[1] ' Every day seems more and more to confirm the probability of Lord North's downfall. '   Batt, Q.C., to James Harris, M.P., 22 Nov. 1779.   *A Series of Letters of the First Earl of Malmesbury, His Family and Friends from 1745 to 1820* (ed. earl of Malmes-bury, London, 1870), i. 442.

[2] For the problems of the North Ministry and its internal disorder, see H. Butterfield, *George III, Lord North, and the People, 1779–1780* (London, 1949), chaps. ii–iv ; and for an analysis of its membership, Ian R. Christie, *The End of North's Ministry, 1780–1782* (London, 1958), pp. 3–9.

[3] Fox to Burke, 24 Jan. [1779], W[entworth] W[oodhouse] M[uniments] B1–758 ; Fox to Rockingham, 24 Jan. 1779, *The Memorials and Correspondence of Charles James Fox* (ed. Lord John Russell, London, 1853), i. 206–10.

[4] Burke to William Baker, 12 Oct. 1777, Hertfordshire Record Office, Baker Letters, No. 58. Cf. Fox to Burke, 8 Sept. 1777, *Works* (Rivington, London, 1852), i. 349 : ' I have been living here [at Chatsworth] some time, with very pleasant and very amiable people ; but altogether as unfit to storm a citadel, as they would be proper for the defence of it.'

As its tactician, he had been a failure. The importunities of an ardent nature had beaten in vain against the bland indolence of old families who were hard to draw from the hunting field or New-market, the care of an estate or the importance of local magistracy. One by one he exhausted the devices of opposition. An attempt at a secession from parliament broke down from half-heartedness ; attacks on the conduct of naval and military operations or war finance involved the Rockinghams in the ambiguities that are the bane of every wartime opposition ; and they deepened the suspicion of factiousness by patronizing disgruntled admirals and generals (a Keppel, a Howe, a Burgoyne) and by coldness or open hostility towards the patriotic subscriptions.

In the autumn of 1779 Burke returned ' full of care and chagrine ' [1] from camp, where he had been discussing ' the sad state of politics ' with the Cavendishes and the duke of Grafton.[2] With Grafton he had revolved the idea of an impeachment of ministers, a measure that would require, he said, ' considerable concurrence without doors '.[3] How to collect support without doors was indeed the problem of the Opposition. Burke did not suspect that within the next few weeks events were to proffer a solution.

The county movement of 1779–80 had a particular content of grievance and aspiration, and it was a particular method of political action. We may examine its content and method before considering its progress. It was, in the first place, a simple demand for order and economy in administration. Sinecures, exorbitant emoluments, pensions and the accumulation of debts on the Civil List (which parliament had already twice in the reign had to discharge) sorted ill with what the Yorkshire petitioners were to call ' a rapid decline of the trade, manufactures, and land-rents of the kingdom '.[4] The initiators of the Yorkshire petition, the Rev. Christopher Wyvill and his North Riding friends, certainly had it in mind to combat any additional land tax ; [5] and Yorkshire had everything to lose from an equalization of the tax which, now standing at 4s. in the £, was so assessed as to fall with special severity on the Home Counties.[6] Ordinary human parsimony, without any partisan afterthought,

---

[1] William Burke to Portland [before 22 Sept. 1779], Portland MSS.

[2] Burke to Portland, 24 Sept. 1779, *ibid.*

[3] Burke to Lady Rockingham, 3 Oct. 1779, W.W.M. R140–36.

[4] The Rev. Christopher Wyvill, *Political Papers* (York, n.d.) i. 7.

[5] Wyvill, iii. 114, 116, 131, 151. See also H. Butterfield, ' The Yorkshire Association and the Crisis of 1779–80 ', *Transactions of the Royal Historical Society*, Ser. 4, xxix (1947), 77, n. 3 ; and W. R. Ward, *The English Land Tax in the Eighteenth Century* (London, 1953), p. 125.

[6] For example, in 1777 Essex (with 26,375 houses and cottages) paid the net sum of £86,992 0s. 2½d., while Lancashire (with 43,092 houses and cottages) paid only £20,273 8s. 10d. *Parliamentary Papers, General Collection*, lx, Accounts and Papers, ii, 1780 and 1781, Nos. 12, 17 and 19. ' A Stock Holder ' in the *Public Advertiser* of 8 Jan. 1780, arguing for an equal land tax, said that in the two northern counties the tax was not more than 4d. in the £.

must be reckoned as among the strongest incentives to the signing of the petitions and the voting for them in the House. There were also a few professed economists with a genuine interest in administrative and fiscal reform, such as Shelburne, the leader of the Chathamite wing of Opposition, and his kindergarten or brains trust, which included Dr. Richard Price.

The county movement must be seen again as one of the periodic revulsions of the ' outs ' against the ' ins '. So long as a spoils system operated, the contest of Court and Country was a recurrent theme of English history. The one factor most nearly common to the supporters of this movement was their exclusion from office in the royal household and central administration,[1] and much of its strength derived from country gentlemen who, so far from wanting office, gloried in their independence. When the marquess of Carmarthen wished to vote in parliament for economical reform, he thought it his duty first to resign his office as vice-chamberlain to the queen.[2] Dislike of placemen, pensioners and contractors was the very badge of the country member ; [3] he could hardly resist a programme which promised not only the exclusion of contractors from the House and of revenue officers from the franchise but also, in Burke's Civil Establishment Bill, the limitation of pensions and the place hunt of the century.[4] Well might Wyvill, writing to Sir George Savile, the paragon of independence, trust that ' there is still sufficient vigour and public spirit left in this Kingdom to form a Country Party able to cope with the Crown, and to save the Constitution '.[5] But if the Country origins of the county movement helped to impart impetus, equally they circumscribed the range of its success. Precisely because they were independent and locally minded, many of the country gentlemen who signed the petitions despised and distrusted the organization that alone could make them effective. To submit to control from London was to deliver oneself over to the Court.

The non-partisan motives of economy and antipathy to the Court gave the movement a great head of steam. This the politicians, within parliament and without, hoped to harness to turn wheels of their own. The first great group of politicians with ulterior designs was that of the parliamentary Opposition, the

[1] But this exclusion was not complete, and Court writers in the newspapers liked to publish inventories of offices of profit held by the ' patriots ' : e.g. *Public Advertiser*, 9 Feb. 1780.

[2] P[*arliamentary*] H[*istory*], xx. 1339–40.

[3] ' Public economy meets the ideas of most of them, who have any thing of the old feelings of country gentlemen left. They have a natural antipathy to inordinate gain in any body and they are more disposed to the censure of abuses among trading people, than of those among any other description of men.' Burke to Joseph Harford, 4 Apr. 1780, *Works*, i. 426.

[4] For the terms of Burke's Bill see *P.H.* xxi. 111–35.

[5] Wyvill to Savile, 18 Dec. 1779, Wyvill, iii. 159.

Rockinghams, and for most purposes, the less numerous Chathamites. It is natural to suppose that after fourteen years in the wilderness the Rockinghams were aiming at office ; but their immediate and ostensible purpose was the reduction of the influence of the Crown. ' Influence ' had long been a Rockingham shibboleth. Burke and the aristocrats whose thinking he tried to do for them had certainly come to believe their own propaganda. The weakness in the Rockingham position, which the county movement was to expose cruelly, was that they could not be whole-hearted in attacking influence. The influence of the Crown was one thing, the influence of the aristocracy was another ; and even the influence of the Crown was a less baneful thing if it was exercised by the Rockinghams themselves. The statement in the Yorkshire petition that ' the crown has acquired a great and unconstitutional influence, which, if not check'd, may soon prove fatal to the liberties of this country ',[1] was therefore no bolt from the blue. To go no further back than 3 November 1779, Rockingham is found writing to Burke:

> It matters not whether it has *as yet* been declared at the market cross in every town in England, that the *system* of *government has misled* and that *the corrupt influence of the Crown* has enabled the Ministers to carry into execution the Measures by which this Country has been ruin'd—I *now believe* that the above is the general predominant opinion of the Nation and I think the means of power, and the means of corrupt influence in the Crown must soon submit to be *shorn*. N.B. I much prefer the shears to the Hatchets.[2]

So the pupil gave his instructions to the tutor, and soon the shears were being sharpened. Resolutions which Burke drew up in December for presentation to the great county meeting at York blamed governmental neglect and mismanagement on ' the excessive and dangerous influence of the Crown ',[3] and when on 11 February 1780 he introduced his plan of economical reform to the house of commons he did not scruple to avow his real motive. ' . . . what, I confess, was uppermost with me, what I bent the whole force of my mind to, was the reduction of that corrupt influence, which is itself the perennial spring of all prodigality, and of all disorder. . . .'[4]

To the second group of politicians bent on exploiting the county movement, mere economical reform was too timid a measure. ' Moving the People of England to carry so small a Reform ', wrote Dr. John Jebb, ' would be tempesting the ocean to drown a fly.' [5] The claim for a more equal representation and for annual parliaments had been coming alive in numerous pamphlets in the seventeen-seventies and it was beginning to be translated into terms of political

---

[1] Wyvill, i. 8.   [2] Rockingham to Burke, [3 Nov. 1779] W.W.M. R140–9.
[3] *Ibid.* R138–1.   [4] *P.H.* xxi. 2.
[5] Jebb to Wyvill, 19 Dec. 1780, Wyvill, iv. 500.

action by radicals in London and as far afield as Yorkshire.[1]   It had even made some headway in the Rockingham camp.   At an inn one night late in 1779 the duke of Richmond entertained Burke's friend Walker King [2] to ' a dish of politics ' that his guest found unpalatable : it was a scheme of annual elections by manhood suffrage in equal constituencies.[3]   Certainly, Wyvill and his friends (among them Walpole's correspondent the poet Mason) had their eyes fixed on radical courses ; but while support was being marshalled their secondary intentions were discreetly muted.   They are innocently disguised in the resolutions prepared for the great York meeting and in Wyvill's canvassing letters as measures ' to restore the Freedom of Parliament ',[4] and the petition itself is silent on the subject. But once the movement was launched, the true objective stood revealed.[5]   The battle was then joined between Burke's mild remedies and the speculative propositions of the Rev. Orator Wyvill.

As an example of political method, the county movement combined three modes of action : it employed petitions, it established committees of correspondence and association culminating in a national reunion, and it made use of the county organization. Vindicated at the Revolution, the right of petitioning was dear to every whig heart ; in fact, it was ' the first principle of the Constitution '.[6]   Petitioning and instruction to M.P.s were the only constitutional means whereby electors might express opinions on emergent issues.   Instructions had been struck out of the Rockingham canon by Burke at Bristol in 1774.   Yet by 1779, as Burke himself confessed more than once,[7] petitioning had fallen into discredit from its fruitlessness.   Experience with the Yorkshire petition in 1769 had shown the need for a committee not only to promote the signing but also to follow up the business after the petition had been presented.[8]

From the appointment of committees it was a short step to correspondence between them, and thence to a national association. There was, as Professor Butterfield has pointed out,[9] a literature of association, but for those who did not study it there was the example at home of the Jews and nonconformists and abroad of the Americans,

[1] G. S. Veitch, *The Genesis of Parliamentary Reform* (London,1913), chap. ii.

[2] Walker King, later bishop of Rochester, had been appointed tutor to the duke of Richmond's son on Burke's recommendation, he succeeded Burke as private secretary to Rockingham and he was one of Burke's executors.

[3] Walker King to Burke, 5 Nov. 1779, W.W.M. B1–825.

[4] Wyvill, i. 5 and iii. 117.

[5] On 21 Jan. 1780, the Yorkshire Committee began to speak of an association to promote shorter Parliaments and a more equal representation.   *Ibid.* i. 66–7.

[6] Sir Anthony Abdy to Rockingham [after 7 Sept. 1769], W.W.M. R10–5.

[7] Burke to Richard Champion, 9 Oct. 1778, *Works*, i. 378 ; Burke to unknown duke, 2 Dec. 1779, Maggs Catalogue 317 (Nov.-Dec. 1913) Lot 3304.   I owe the second reference to Professor Copeland.

[8] J. Dixon to Rockingham, 7 Oct. 1769, W.W.M. R10–9.

[9] *George III, Lord North and the People*, pp. 255–63.

for if Dungannon yet lay in the future, Philadelphia had been an incorrigible fact. Richmond had proposed to use associations throughout the country to promote his plan of parliamentary reform.[1] A year before, Burke had urged that if there were to be petitions at all, they ought to be prosecuted ' even as far as legally they may go ', [2] and now, early in December 1779, when he saw the possibility of making trouble for the Government over a by-election in Hampshire, he advised friends there, after petitioning, to ' appoint a committee to report to a future meeting the success of their application as well as to correspond with such other Counties, Cities and Boroughs as may be disposed to the same legal mode of address '.[3] Petitioning was to be made part of a system. It was said of the second resolution, establishing a committee to correspond and to form a plan of association, that it was studiously held back and smuggled through the great York meeting of 30 December amidst the clamour ; [4] but the ideas it embodied at least had the respectability of a long pedigree, and Burke himself applauded as the wind was sown.[5]

Of the forty-one petitions for economy presented to the house of commons between February and April 1780, twenty-six came from English counties and three from Welsh ; and of the non-county petitioners, only the cities of Westminster and London were of much importance.[6] The historic county was still in 1780 a natural organ of political action. With its high sheriff and grand jury, its petty and quarter sessions, it was an administrative and judicial unit ; with its lord lieutenant and militia, a military unit ; with its differentiated land-tax assessment, a fiscal unit ; with its race meeting (in thirty-five English counties out of forty),[7] its county town, its county families, a sporting and social unit ; and it was given a political being by its two members of parliament, who had to be publicly nominated and occasionally voted for by the forty-shilling freeholders, and by the institution of the county meeting.[8] The counties' proud name for independence had historic warrant. The personal government of Charles I, we are told, broke ' on the rock of the county organization '.[9] George Lawson, the mid-seventeenth century constitutionalist, who seems to have influenced

---

[1] Walker King to Burke, 5 Nov. 1779, W.W.M. B1–825.

[2] Burke to Champion, 9 Oct. 1778, *Works*, i. 378.

[3] Burke to unknown duke, 2 Dec. 1779, Maggs Catalogue 317 (Nov.–Dec. 1913) Lot 3304.

[4] Johnson to William Eden, 1 Jan. 1780, Brit. Mus. Add. MS. 34,417, fos. 1–2.

[5] ' I admire their measure of the Choice of a Committee. Without this they would have done nothing. All is well—very well.' Burke to Lady Rockingham, 2 Jan. 1780, W.W.M. R140–10.   [6] *Journals of the House of Commons*, 8 Feb.–12 Apr. 1780.

[7] James Weatherby, *Racing Calendar*, viii (1780), ii–iv.

[8] See B. Keith-Lucas, ' County Meetings ' in *Law Quarterly Review*, lxx (1954), 109–14.

[9] Quoted by J. R. Tanner, *English Constitutional Conflicts of the Seventeenth Century* (Cambridge, 1948), p. 78.

Locke, traced the 'supreme power civil' to the forty counties.[1]
And looking back to the fourteenth century, the Yorkshire radicals
declared that 'various were the occasions in those times, when the
Commons gave for an answer, to any new propositions of magnitude,
that they dared not agree without conference with their countries '.[2]
It was the counties that rallied against the Young Pretender in '45
and in favour of Wilkes in '69. And now, late in '79, the Opposition was talking freely of calling them out again.

The idea was encouraged by the refusal of some of them during
the summer to raise voluntary subscriptions for defence,[3] a refusal
to be interpreted as a snub to Government. It was also encouraged
by the efforts of William Burke, Edmund's raffish 'cousin', to
breathe some energy into the 'snug chaste corps' of the Rockinghams,[4] who, if they were to regain their lost lead, would have to
choose new ground to fight on. The notion of using the counties as
a focus for discontent gradually insinuated itself. In Essex, for
example, some 'hot-headed and heavy men' of the Tory breed seemed
willing to move against Government. 'Ned', wrote Will Burke,
'had rather encouraged the idea of leaving such people to stirr and
bustle, in the hopes that when they had gathered the people together
and warmed their imaginations, they might be taught wisdom and
discretion by solemn men.'[5] Here then was the precise formula
for action : malcontents of respectability, having roused a popular
expectancy, were to be 'led and seduced into reason' by the
Rockinghams. Within this same month of October cousin Will
was already collecting support. Hampshire, according to one
friend, was 'ready for anything, to instruct, to remonstrate or what
not, without reserve against Ministers ', while another hoped to do
the same for Gloucestershire. The plan was 'that the thing being
concerted by the party, advertisements just at the same time, should
be in all the Countys, where there are any friends of the Constitution. . . . County A is always more ready to stirr, when they see
County B in motion.'[6]

To these intimations of an Opposition plot, one is entitled to
add certain demonstrations made possible by election disputes in
two of the counties, Middlesex and Hampshire, where electors
were plainly spoiling for a fight with Government. In both counties
the lord lieutenant was accused of interfering in the ministerial

---

[1] John Bowle, *Hobbes and His Critics* (London, 1951), pp. 91, 94.

[2] Memorial of the meeting of deputies in London, Mar. 1780, Wyvill, i. 434.

[3] See, for example, William Burke to Portland, 12 Aug. 1779 (Portland MSS.), in
which Burke remarks : ' The conduct of Dorsetshire and Hertfordshire seems to
imply that the Whig Spirit is not dead, but sleepeth here. . . .'

[4] Same to same [before 22 Sept. 1779], *ibid.* Quoted by A. S. Turberville, *A History
of Welbeck Abbey and Its Owners* (London, 1938–9), ii. 144 as ' a smug chaste corps '.

[5] Same to same, 9 Oct. 1779, *ibid.*

[6] Same to same [before 30 Oct. 1779], *ibid.*

interest.[1]   In Middlesex, North's refusal of the Chiltern Hundreds to George Byng, already a member of parliament, frustrated the Rockinghams' plans to have their nominee elected as Wilkes's colleague, and led to a petition, intended, as Professor Butterfield thinks,[2] to work up another *cause célèbre* on a Middlesex election issue. In Hampshire, the issue of influence was freely ventilated thanks to the king's provocative decision to bestow the white wand of comptroller of the household on the ministerial candidate shortly before the election began.[3]   In a third county by-election about this time, in Devonshire, there was ' a sturdy opposition to the Court candidate ',[4] and Opposition used the occasion to obtain a request to the sheriff for a county meeting to consider a petition.[5]

One other faint premonition of the Rockingham plan of campaign was the appearance on 25 November, the opening day of the parliamentary session, of the first issue of the *London Courant*.   This new morning daily, which was to be the principal organ of the county movement,[6] was published ' At the Solicitation of many Persons of high Rank and Abilities ' by John Almon, already a veteran in the Opposition cause.   The decision to establish it had been taken at least as early as 6 November,[7] and before it was launched one of Rockingham's henchmen seems to have been invited to act as its York correspondent.[8]

In all great movements, the elements of organization and spontaneity are hard to disengage ; and at this point when the momentum of the argument seems to demand the inference that the Yorkshire movement took its rise from a Rockingham conspiracy, we are stopped short by the contrary testimony of all the chief actors.[9]   According to Wyvill's own account, the plan of a county

[1] George Byng to Portland, 7 Nov. 1779, *ibid.*; *P.H.* xx. 1270-2, 1315-18.

[2] *George III, Lord North and the People*, pp. 184-96.

[3] The king to Robinson, 1 Dec. 1779, Add. MS. 37,835, fo. 53 ; the king to North, 1 Dec. 1779, *Correspondence of King George III* (ed. Sir John Fortescue, London, 1928), iv. 506.   Although the Opposition candidate in Hampshire, Jervoise Clark Jervoise, was not a strict Rockinghamite, he had been joined with the dukes of Bolton, Portland and Manchester, all Rockinghamites, in an Association for supporting Public Liberty established in Hampshire some years before (*General Advertiser*, 3 Jan. 1780), and he was feted at the county meeting at Winchester on 3 Jan. 1780, when the Yorkshire petition was adopted.   At this meeting, the petition was moved by Sir Thomas Miller, M.P. for Lewes, who had been William Burke's informant about the readiness of the county for action.   *Public Advertiser*, 8 Jan. 1780.

[4] Horace Walpole to William Mason, 11 Dec. 1779, *Letters of Horace Walpole* (ed. Peter Cunningham, London, 1906), vii. 292.

[5] *Public Advertiser*, 12 Jan. 1780.

[6] See, for example, R. M. Trench Chiswell to Almon, 25 Jan. 1780, Add. MS. 20,733, fo. 14.

[7] The date of the advertisement on the back cover of one of Almon's pamphlets, *A Letter from Lieutenant-General Burgoyne to his Constituents* (1779).

[8] ' I fear can't do Almon the service could wish his being a daily paper and we have only the post three times a week.'   Stephen Croft, sen. to Rockingham, 28 Nov. 1779, W.W.M. R136-17.

[9] Wyvill, i. 9, 35 ; iii. 113n ; *P.H.* xx. 1301, 1350 ; W. Mason to Walpole, *Letters*, vii. 288, n. 1.

meeting originated in conversations he had with three other gentlemen of the North Riding on 23 November, no doubt from the mixed
motives already suggested ; thereupon, about the time parliament
was being opened, he visited or wrote to other friends and set in
motion the summons to the York meeting. There is no reason to
doubt this accepted story. We may agree with Burke when, in
introducing his plan of economical reform, he remarked : '. . . I
cannot indeed take upon me to say I have the honour to *follow* the
sense of the people. The truth is, *I met it on the way*, while I was
pursuing their interest according to my own ideas.' [1] It remains to
consider how the Rockinghams met the Yorkshire initiative on the
way, tried to take it firmly by the hand and found it a refractory ward
with ideas of its own.

Wyvill's enterprise offered the politicians of the Rockingham
group an opportunity and a challenge—an opportunity because the
stirring of the great county of York gave them a far more effective
purchase, so to speak, against the Ministry than the rather anaemic
by-election disputes in the Home Counties or even the troubles in
Ireland ; and a challenge because they sensed at once the *arrière pensée*
in the none-too-inscrutable mind of its prime mover. In the days
that followed, therefore, they set themselves two objects. On the
one hand, they tried to diffuse the movement in the country and to
take parallel action in parliament. On the other, they tried to contain it within safe limits, notably in Yorkshire itself, which, having
assumed the lead, might be expected to fix the pace and direction.
This second and more difficult task depended, as they fully understood, on how successfully a party of aristocrats could play a popular
game.

The first problem was to guide the proposed meeting in Yorkshire, Rockingham's home county, where his political influence had
been pervasive for twenty years or more.[2] Rockingham's first
news of Wyvill's plan reached him in London about the end of
November. His informant was a friend, Stephen Croft, sen., of
York, whom Wyvill had invited to sign the advertisement calling
the meeting.[3] Croft was to prove a faithful agent of the marquess
in the inner councils of the movement. He did his best to damp
down the jealousies of aristocratic leadership and the suspicions that
it was all a ' tempest of Rebellion from the *Mandate of Grosvenor
Square* '.[4] He reported Wyvill's opinionated flirtation with ' perplexed questions ' and passed on to his fellow agitators in York

---

[1] *P.H.* xxi. 14.

[2] ' Hitherto I have been elected in Lord Rockingham's dining-room ', said Sir
George Savile in 1780. R. I. and S. Wilberforce, *Life of Wilberforce* (London, 1838),
i. 56–7. See also Cedric Collyer, ' The Rockinghams and Yorkshire Politics, 1742–61 '
in *Publications of the Thoresby Society*, xli, pt. 4, pp. 352–82.

[3] Croft to Rockingham, 28 Nov. 1779, W.W.M. R136–17.

[4] Same to same, 17 Dec. 1779, *ibid.* R136–4.

Rockingham's desires, hopes and misgivings. For Rockingham left no room for doubt as to the kind of meeting he intended. It must be ' very numerous and very respectable ' ; the propositions there laid down should be ' grave serious and well considered ' ; the petition should be ' confined to stating the ruined situation of this once great Country, . . . a reprobation of the measures by which it has been brought into such peril and weakness, . . . the propriety of inquiry into the causes and . . . loudly calling for a reduction of the power and influence of the Crown'. Such speculative propositions as short parliaments, more county members and manhood suffrage ought to be avoided as crude, incalculable in effect and certain to lead to wrangles. He recommended, however, a demand for legislation to disfranchise revenue officers and to disqualify contractors from sitting in parliament.[1]

Advice was followed by more practical guidance. John Lee, a Yorkshire lawyer and later Rockingham's Attorney-General, not only wrote to Wyvill deprecating short parliaments[2] but drafted a petition for adoption by the meeting. Though Burke later assured the House that he ' neither interfered directly nor indirectly in the county association of York ',[3] as Rockingham's trusted tactician he was almost inevitably active. Among the Rockingham papers at Sheffield there is one document[4] in which Burke has written the answers to a questionnaire by Croft on the proper mode of conducting the York meeting ; and another,[5] certainly in Burke's hand and almost as certainly of his authorship, containing draft resolutions plainly intended to be presented to the same meeting. Before Christmas Lee's petition and Burke's resolutions made the journey north, and on 28 December in a conclave at York of the promoters of the county meeting they were introduced as coming from a local commoner, so as to dissemble their true origin.[6] Lee's petition it has not been possible to trace ; but it seemed to Wyvill too long and directed to too many objects.[7] Burke's resolutions differed from those first drafted by Wyvill on four essential points : they proposed a petition to the Lords as well as to the Commons ; the suggested committee, though it was to correspond with similar bodies, was not to be instructed to form a plan of association ; ' the dangerous and excessive influence of the Crown ' was emphasized ; and, finally, Burke's resolutions were free from any hint of ulterior aims. Wyvill was too wary a politician to need Walpole's warning that ' the great Barons . . . are coming to put their sickle into the

---

[1] Rockingham to Croft, 12 Dec. 1779 (copy), *ibid*. R1–1040.
[2] Lee to Wyvill, 14 Dec. 1779 (copy), *ibid*. R1–1041.
[3] *P.H.* xx. 1382.
[4] W.W.M. R1–1045.
[5] *Ibid*. R138–1.
[6] Croft to Rockingham, 26 Dec. 1779, *ibid*. R136–6.
[7] Same to same, 28 Dec. 1779, *ibid*. R136–7.

fruits of your plough ',[1] and he was adroit enough to get his own petition and resolutions adopted by the previous meeting. He permitted himself one inexpensive gesture of appeasement by accepting into his petition a reference to the ' great and unconstitutional influence ' of the Crown at the instance of ' one of the Poachers '.[2]

The great county meeting in the Assembly Rooms at York on 30 December did its work well. It adopted, with hardly a dissentient, the petition and resolutions adopted by the preliminary meetings ; sixty-one gentlemen were appointed a committee to supervise the signing of the petition, to correspond and to draft a plan of association for submission to a later meeting. Though the Rockinghams had suffered a reverse they could console themselves with the hope that there was yet time to control or frustrate Wyvill's extravagant fancy. Meanwhile in numbers and respectability the meeting had been worthy of England's first county. Property of an annual value of £800,000 had been represented there, said Rockingham ;[3] and efforts to exclude peers and members of parliament had miscarried, ' not the first time ', added his lady, who could never resist a pun, ' not the first time that a *miscarriage* may have turn'd out a fortunate Event '.[4]

In the meantime, the Rockingham politicians had been working not only to manage the York meeting but also to spread the movement out of doors and to provide a legislative counterpoint within parliament. At the beginning of December, within a day or so of the receipt in London of the news of intentions in York, Burke is found urging the development of like action out of the by-election in Hampshire.[5] Hampshire proved, indeed, to be the second county to petition.[6] On 20 December, the Middlesex electors who had gathered to further their election protest decided to switch to the more profitable line opened up by Yorkshire,[7] and theirs was the third county to petition. About the same time a petition for economical reform was being shown about in Cheshire in the Rockingham interest,[8] and at Christmas Rockingham's sister was planning to rally Northamptonshire to the cause.[9] The requisition to the Sheriff of Sussex for a county meeting was dated from Goodwood, Richmond's home, on 29 December, and signed by three

[1] Walpole to Mason, 25 Dec. 1779, *Letters*, vii. 297.
[2] Mason to Walpole, 31 Dec. 1779, *ibid*. p. 298n.
[3] *P.H.* xx. 1350.
[4] Lady Rockingham to Burke, 2 Jan. 1780, W.W.M. R140–10.
[5] Burke to unknown duke, 2 Dec. 1779, Maggs Catalogue 317 (Nov.-Dec. 1913) Lot 3304.
[6] *Public Advertiser*, 8 Jan. 1780.
[7] Butterfield, *George III, Lord North and the People*, p. 194.
[8] Earl of Stamford to Portland, 25 Dec. 1779, Portland MSS.
[9] Lady Charlotte Wentworth to Lady Rockingham (endorsed ' Christmas 1779 '), W.W.M. R140–42.

Rockingham peers.[1] In short, the Opposition had prepared the
ground far and wide even before the success in York came to fertilize
it. Every effort was made to capitalize on the Yorkshire example ;
and the means used afford an instructive glimpse into the working
of an aristocratic political machine in the days before popular
parties.

Late on the night of 1 January the diligence from York brought
Rockingham's groom to his London house in Grosvenor Square.
To the mistress of the house he delivered a letter from the marquess
and five printed copies of the petition adopted at York two days
before. Lady Rockingham, a woman of intelligence and some
political insight, at once wrote to Portland, at Burlington House,
enclosing two copies and asking him to send one to George Byng.
The duke by midnight had the other in the press, presumably that
of Almon, whose office was only a few yards away, on the opposite
side of Piccadilly. The three remaining copies Lady Rockingham
sent to Shelburne, Burke and Admiral Keppel ; and a fourth, which
she clipped from the York newspaper, was soon in the Bath coach
on its way to John Lee. Left without a copy herself, she begged
Portland to let her have some of those to be printed in London, so
that she might give them wider circulation and have news for
' some friends who may call tomorrow for information '.[2] Portland,
always a diligent political middleman, helped to stir Hertfordshire
by letters to two friends there enclosing copies of the petition ;
and his letter to Byng was passed on to Lord Ossory who, as lord
lieutenant, proceeded to summon Bedfordshire.[3] So one might go
on tracing out the filaments of the Rockingham connection. Soon
Lady Rockingham was to be justified in writing that ' It now seems
to be quite an *Influenza* that spreads fast '.[4]

In January, seventeen petitions, most of them on the York model,
were adopted at county meetings, and one county,[5] in lieu of a
petition, instructed its members to support economy in parliament.
There was then a lull until the end of February, when the movement
had a new lease of life, with eight further county petitions. In all,
including cities and boroughs, forty-one petitions were sent to the
house of commons. They had various origins. The usual procedure was for a sufficient number of men of substance to sign a
requisition to the sheriff, asking him to call a meeting. Frequently
the sheriff, who was a royal appointee, would decline the request.

---

[1] *General Evening Post*, 8–11 Jan. 1780.

[2] Lady Rockingham to Portland (endorsed ' R. at half-past ten, 1 January 1780 '),
Portland MSS. ; same to same (endorsed ' January 1, 1780. R. near 12 o'clock '), *ibid.*

[3] William Baker to Portland [2 Jan. 1780], Portland MSS. ; William Plumer to
Portland, 2 and 5 Jan. 1780, *ibid.*; Earl of Upper Ossory to Portland, 4 Jan. 1780, *ibid.*;
Kentish Gazette, 19–22 Jan. 1780.

[4] Lady Rockingham to Portland, 17 Jan. 1780, Portland MSS.

[5] Northamptonshire.

Thereupon in some counties [1] the lord lieutenant would call the meeting. In others,[2] the signatories to the requisition when rebuffed would issue a summons of their own, trusting to their local consequence to underwrite what was strictly an irregularity. Some meetings [3] originated in a request by the Grand Jury at the assizes or by the assembled justices at quarter sessions. Two of the later meetings [4] were called in the name of the ' yeomen and free-holders ' in default of action by the nobility and gentry, the 100 requisitioners in each case making up in numbers what they lacked in individual weight. The underlying thought is that the county can be called out only by a respectable accumulation of property, just as it is held that none but freeholders ought to attend and vote.

It would be as naïve to detect the hand of the Rockingham Opposition in the origin of all these meetings as to suppose that they were the spontaneous uprising of an outraged people. But though the obscurity of the subject forbids firm conclusions, it is possible to make a fairly well informed guess at the extent of the Rockingham influence. The evidence suggests that of the twenty-seven county meetings, twelve were directly inspired by Rocking-ham connections. This does not necessarily mean that the Rocking-hams were the sole initiators or that without their lead the meetings would never have been held—but only that they, sometimes with others, are to be discovered at the fount. They actively assisted and possibly initiated the movement in six other counties. They gave general support, by attendance and in other ways, to meetings started by others in seven counties. Only in two counties has no evidence appeared of their participation.

Like nearly all of its kind, the movement was carried along by a small minority. As an estimate of the total membership of the committees of the English counties and of London and Westminster, the figure of 1,000 would not be far amiss. To most members election signified not a duty but a mark of esteem. Many of the counties, especially those remote from London, filled their commit-tees, where they bothered to choose them at all, almost entirely with local worthies. Places like Cumberland, Cheshire, Northampton-shire and Somersetshire were making the ritual protest against the improvidence of London and the Court, though a local magnate with a cousin or brother in the great world of politics might be persuaded to load the affair with a party bias. Nearer London, it was a more serious, more professional business. Government scribblers began to notice the recurrence of familiar faces at the different meetings. There were complaints of the ' Importation of London Eloquence ' into Norfolk,[5] and in the *Public Advertiser* a correspondent took pity on

---

[1] *E.g.* Bedfordshire and Sussex.   [2] *E.g.* Kent and Gloucestershire.
[3] *E.g.* Dorsetshire, Essex, Derbyshire.   [4] Buckinghamshire and Cambridgeshire.
[5] *Public Advertiser*, 24 Feb. 1780, letter signed ' E. F., a Gentleman in Norfolk '.

those *itinerant* Patriots, who move about through the different Counties, begging and praying for Petitions to give a fillip to their present deplorable political Despondency. . . . Though they are a Species of Vagrants in every County, they presume to call themselves the People of each County through which they pass ; and endeavour to impose their own stale Complaints upon the World, as the Voice of the People.[1]

But before soaring away on the wings of the literary evidence, it is safer to stop and count. Calculation shows that there were thirteen men who belonged to four or more committees. All but one were members of parliament. Seven of them [2] are easily identifiable as members of the Rockingham set. Two [3] are independents who frequently voted with Opposition. Two others are what it would be convenient to call metropolitan ' radicals ', one of them Wilkes himself.[4] An examination of the twenty-five or so who had three committees to their credit reveals the same pattern : the active men were either of the aristocratic opposition or radical parliamentary reformers. Though an occasional progressive peer, such as Courtenay in Devonshire or Mahon in Kent, might steer his county committee into radical courses, the real strength of the radicals lay particularly in Middlesex, Surrey and Essex. The chairmen of the Surrey and Essex committees were brothers-in-law,[5] and Yorkshire was linked up by the person of Wyvill, who had in recent years been the active, and was now the absentee, incumbent of an Essex parish.[6] The struggle in Yorkshire between the two groups of politicians was thus a microcosm of the struggle in the country as a whole.

While the Rockingham campaign out of doors was enjoying an equivocal success, the campaign in parliament was developing only with rubs and hindrances. The discovery of what was afoot in Yorkshire caused a sudden revision of Opposition tactics. When parliament met on 25 November, the Opposition amendment to the address of thanks in both Houses demanded ' new councils and new counsellors ',[7] and it soon became apparent that the weight of the Opposition assault would fall on the conduct of the war in America and at sea, the mismanagement of home defence and the disturbances in Ireland. There were already signs—for example, parallel motions on Ireland in the two Houses—that the followers of

---

[1] *Public Advertiser*, 13 Jan. 1780.

[2] Viscount Althorp, George Byng, William Baker, Lord G. H. Cavendish, Sir Robert Clayton, Lord Spencer, William Plumer.

[3] Humphrey Sturt, Sir William Wake.

[4] The limits of Wilkes's own ' radicalism' are clearly indicated by Miss Lucy S. Sutherland in her Creighton Lecture for 1958, *The City of London and the Opposition to Government, 1768–1774* (London, 1959), pp. 12–15.

[5] Sir Francis Vincent and Sir Robert Smyth respectively.

[6] *Dictionary of National Biography*, *sub* Wyvill.

[7] *P.H.* xx. 1033, 1098.

Rockingham and Shelburne were acting in concert.   On 6 December, an observant member would have noted a shift in the emphasis of their disgust.   They were dwelling on a fresh grievance and making it an article of union.   ' The first men of rank, fortune, and character, in both houses ', said Fox in the midst of a debate on Ireland, ' had firmly and virtuously resolved to set their faces against this increasing, this alarming influence of the crown. . . . The sense of danger had brought about this coalition.' [1]   Again on the 8th and 9th, Fox reverted to the ' enlarged ' and ' fatal ' influence of the Crown.[2]   Meanwhile in the Lords Richmond on the 7th moved ' an unexpected motion ' [3] calling on the king to make economies in the Civil List, whereupon Rockingham elaborated on the evils of royal influence, a topic on which he had been silent in a long, discursive speech twelve days earlier.[4]   On 15 December Burke in the Commons and Shelburne in the Lords gave notice of their intention to move measures of economical reform after the Christmas recess.   Opposition had found a cause which they hoped to bring home to the business and bosoms of the independent country gentlemen.

It was Burke who, in the critical few months between December and April, bore the heat and burden of the day for his party.   While others were raising the counties by the exertions of connection Burke was labouring, as he told a friend, at ' " whereas," and " nevertheless " and " made and provided " and " anything to the contrary notwithstanding ", . . . drawing sketches of Acts of Parliament, of a very disagreeable kind . . . for the mercy of saving the life by cutting off the limb has the aspect of cruelty in the *operation*.'[5] The mind which a few years later was to cause astonishment by its mastery of the Indian administration now played powerfully upon the Treasury and Exchequer, the Ordnance and the Board of Trade and the paymaster's office, his Majesty's stables, the clerkship of the pells, the Board of Green Cloth, the Jewel Office and the whole rank growth of the central government and royal household; and beyond that to the Duchies of Lancaster and Cornwall and the County Palatine of Chester.   Sketches of the plan passed from hand to hand among the Rockinghams.   By 11 February, a bare two months after the first rumours had blown down from York, the drafting was all but done, and the battle was opened in parliament.

Burke had a clear idea of the tactics he wanted to pursue: it was to leap *in medias res*, exploiting support in the country to hustle

[1] *P.H.* xx. 1225.

[2] *Ibid.* cols., 1249, 1253.

[3] *Annual Register*, 1780, p. 72.   *Cf.* Duke to Duchess of Rutland, 8 Dec. 1779 : ' The Duke of Richmond made a motion. . . . There was no communication.   Nobody knew what it was, so it was ill attended.' H[istorical] M[anuscripts] C[ommission] 14th Report, Appendix I (Rutland III), p. 22.

[4] *P.H.* xx. 1255 ff.

[5] Burke to Lady Rockingham, 16 Jan. 1780, W.W.M. R140–6.

through Bills whose very intricacy exposed them to defeat in detail.

> . . . I see no hope of doing good but by the rapidity and decision of
> our proceeding [he wrote to Portland].   Our strength is without,
> and not within the house ; and whatever may tend to abate the
> spirit of reformation now abroad, would . . . be very ill compen-
> sated by the gain of some parliamentary advantages in the Course
> of a slow methodical parliamentary proceeding. . . . We have
> already cut deep into the Session—Little more time remains for us.
> It will not be borne by the people, who are hungering and thirsting
> after substantial reformation, that we should balk their appetite
> with a long Grace, or with a formal laying on the dishes.   We must
> let them instantly fall to.[1]

The plan of legislation under duress began in February.   On the
8th, Savile, a fragile, revered figure, introduced the Yorkshire
petition with its 8,000 and more signatures, throwing his bundle of
sheepskins vehemently on to the table of the house of commons.
At half-past one on the morning of the 22nd, in the first of a historic
series of divisions, Savile lost his motion for an account of pensions
by a mere two votes in a large house—a result, however disappointing to Opposition, which showed that a solid block of
independents was veering in the wind of popular impatience.[2]   The
Civil Establishment Bill, the centrepiece of Burke's scheme, was
introduced on the 23rd and given a second reading on 2 March,
but the real test came when the House descended from generous
principles which all could approve to prickly particulars which for
some carried a sting.   In committee on the 8th the first clause,
abolishing the office of third secretary of state, was lost by 201 to
208.

It was at about this point that the whole movement came to a
crisis.   There was a problem of how to proceed in parliament now
that North's tactics of assent in gross and opposition in detail
were made obvious; and there was the problem of how to prevent
the movement from fraying out at the edges into the merely faddish
and eccentric or from breaking down under the strain of internal
dissension.   Even from the outset the Opposition appeal to the
country had met responses of varying warmth.   Several counties
had not thought fit even to meet.   One, having met, declined to
petition.   Two or three petitioned but refused to elect committees.
Some were offended by the modes adopted to secure signatures.
Others objected to being made use of by ' the regular *faculty* of
profess'd politicians '.

---

[1] Burke to Portland, 16 Jan. 1780, Portland MSS.

[2] Actually, the decisive division (188–186) was taken on North's amendment to
confine the published list of pensions to those paid at the exchequer, thus excluding
those on the Civil List.   The debate is in *P.H.* xxi. 85–104.

[3] Burke to Lady Rockingham [before 14 Jan. 1780], W.W.M. R140–9.

Many Persons, who were at first struck with a political *Mania* about
public Economy begin . . . to secede from the petitioning Party,
who disturb the Repose of His Majesty's good Subjects. This
Desertion proceeds not more from a clearer View they have got of
the Subject, than from the Indignity of its having been the Measure
of a mere Adventurer from the Banks of the Liffey; a Man, who
having neither Right to, or Hopes of, a Place himself, has out of
mere Resentment, inflamed the feeble Mind of his Patron, and
induced him to become a strolling Beggar of Subscriptions in various
Corners of the Kingdom.[1]

Each new move of the managers to the left brought a corresponding defection on the right. And Wyvill was now moving
rapidly to the left. Before the end of January he had introduced
into the Yorkshire Committee the plan of an association to support
only such parliamentary candidates as would take a test to uphold
economical reform, shorter parliaments and a more equal representation.[2] Having sown these seeds, he departed for London, where
he negotiated with the chairmen of other committees for a general
meeting of deputies from the petitioning counties. This proposal
frightened more counties out of the movement. Fox had to caution
the indiscreet Essex chairman, who had spoken about 'delegates',
'to avoid every word that has been used in the commotions in
America' in favour of the innocuous terms 'deputies' or 'agents';[3]
and all the blandishments of Shelburne and his fellow peer the earl
of Radnor failed to convince the Wiltshire Committee that it ought
to be represented in London.[4]

It is apparent that while the Shelburnites and a few of the
Rockinghams like Fox and Richmond welcomed the meeting as a
useful spur to parliament during a critical stage in the progress of the
economical reform legislation, Rockingham and his more cautious
associates looked askance at their new allies, an 'anti-Parliament'[5]
nosing the accredited body 'in the very seat of its authority'.[6] It
was to resolve this difference as well as to decide on the conduct
of the parliamentary campaign that Shelburne and Richmond waited
on Rockingham at Grosvenor Square on 10 March, the eve of the
deputies' first meeting.

The decision on parliamentary tactics was probably the easier.
On the rejection of Burke's next proposition, the Opposition was

[1] *Public Advertiser*, 31 Jan. 1780.
[2] Wyvill, i. 67–8.
[3] Fox to Sir Robert Smyth, 11 Feb. 1780, Essex Record Office, Smyth Archives,
D/D Fg Z1, printed in A. F. J. Brown, *English History from Essex Sources, 1750–1900*
(Chelmsford, 1952), pp. 189–90.
[4] Correspondence of Shelburne and Radnor with John Awdry, chairman of the
Wiltshire Committee, in Wiltshire Record Office, Awdry Archives, 109/809.
[5] A common description used not only by enemies but even by friends such as
Savile (Wyvill, iii. 204).
[6] Burke in *A Letter to a Noble Lord, Works*, v. 220.

to move resolutions in both Houses asserting the right of parliament
to control the Civil List.   On the rejection of these, Opposition
would secede and (here was the element of compromise) if the
committees after discussion did not press at once the questions of
short parliaments and electoral reform, Opposition would associate
on the basis of economical reform.[1]   The significance of the compromise was that it committed much to the deputies, for the note
they sounded might be expected to set the tune for the counties
still within the movement at their adjourned meetings in late March
or April.

Seventeen committees were finally represented when the deputies
assembled in London.   In six meetings extending over ten days
they set the seal of their assumed authority on the radical programme
of economical reform, 100 new county members and tests for
parliamentary candidates, and they approved a rationale of association for these purposes in a memorial to be circulated to the counties.[2]
The great men of the parliamentary Opposition watched the proceedings in the Great Room in King Street with differing emotions.
They saw their compromise rejected, and all three points recommended as fit to be articles of association.   Wyvill indeed softened
the blow towards the end of proceedings by drafting an accompanying letter to the counties which tactfully hinted that the proposal
for shorter parliaments might be deferred by some committees.
But outright defeat was the fate of a last-minute bid by Rockingham
to emasculate the work of the deputations.   On the 19th a further
conference at Grosvenor Square resolved ' That the question of
shortening the duration of Parliaments and of alteration in the
representation be *not recommended* to be made articles of association
but only recommended to the Counties as objects greatly deserving
consideration and to know the general sense of the Kingdom. . . . ' [3]
Resolutions based almost verbatim on this were introduced into a
last meeting of the deputies on the 20th.   Nothing could show
more clearly than the result of the voting how the initiative had
slipped out of the grasp of the professional politicians.   The motions
were lost respectively by twelve deputations to five and eleven to
six.[4]   It is probable that both wings of Opposition at Grosvenor
Square had covered ways to friends in King Street ;   but all one can

[1] W.W.M. R162–7–1.
[2] Wyvill, i. 116–29, 426–38.
[3] There is something symbolic in the fact that the document at Sheffield (W.W.M.
R162–7–2) recording the result of this conference is written in Rockingham's hand as
far as the word ' made ', and thereafter in the hand of Richmond, who continues :
' It is understood that if generally wished by the petitioning counties the shortening
the duration of Parliaments in a considerable degree will be adopted and supported, as
well as the principle of a considerable addition or substitution of members more
independently chosen than the present, carried into execution with equity in the different parts of England.'
[4] Wyvill, i. 127–8.

say with certainty is that the members of parliament among the deputies were strongly concentrated in the minority.

What Rockingham had lost in London he yet hoped to recover at York. He wasted no time in entreating two of his friends in the Yorkshire Committee to urge adherence to the ' plain and direct objects ' of the petition, in particular to oppose the idea of annual parliaments on the ground that ' in general it is by no *means relished* ' and to show other committeemen the letters in which he uttered these cautions.[1] His friends did their best in the committee but ' found that the doctrine of *annual* Parliaments had been so power-fully *preached up* [both Wyvill and Mason were clergymen] and had got such full possession of the minds of many well-meaning persons that it was of some moment to be able to obtain the alteration of a *single word* '.[2] The ' single word ' was the substitution of triennial for annual parliaments ; and with this amendment alone the ad-journed county meeting at York on 28 March adopted the resolves of the London meeting of deputies as the basis of their association. Yorkshire had led twenty-five counties to petition ; it remained to be seen how many would follow her in the bolder step of association.

Much would depend on the struggle in parliament. By the end of March the time seemed ripe for acting on the decision of the first Grosvenor Square conference. Since then, it is true, the expectation that the House would reject ' Mr. Burke's next proposition ' had been agreeably disappointed : the Commons had voted by 207 to 199 to abolish the Board of Trade.[3] But the pinch came when, as the Bill progressed, the House was asked to abolish offices in the royal household. The tug-of-war between loyalty and parsimony that threatened to dismember many a country gentleman was won by loyalty often enough to restore the Government's majority. ' . . . we went on with some tolerable success in my bill ', wrote Burke in retrospect, ' until we came to the gates of St. James's. We lost fifty in our attempt to storm that strong post.' [4] On failing to carry the abolition of treasurer of the chamber, Burke all but resigned the contest, declaring his indifference to what became of the rest of the Bill.[5]

Nothing now stood between Opposition and their plan to move a resolution asserting parliament's right to control the Civil List. It had been known for three or four weeks, ever since Government had declined a challenge on the issue,[6] that some such general proposition might well be successful ; and if successful, and coupled with a denunciation of royal influence, it would expose to

[1] Rockingham to Croft, 23 Mar. 1780, W.W.M. R1–1052.
[2] Rev. H. Zouch to Rockingham, 28 Mar. 1780, *ibid.* R140–75.
[3] *P.H.* xxi. 278.
[4] Burke to Joseph Harford, 4 Apr. 1780, *Works*, i. 426.
[5] *P.H.* xxi. 309.
[6] *Ibid.* cols. 178–93.

ridicule a House that refused to implement it. So Opposition seem
to have reasoned. It remained to find a form of words that would
ring true, strike hard and yet give no offence to the independents
(this Dunning did), to keep the intention a secret and to choose an
occasion. The choice fell on 6 April, the day when the House was
to take the petitions into consideration, the day also of the adjourned
meeting of Westminster freeholders. Government looked to the
day with some apprehension, and strengthened guards were posted
about Westminster Hall, where a great gathering listened to a
harangue by Fox and agreed to associate on the Yorkshire terms.
Yet later in the day, when Dunning rose in the House to move
'that the influence of the Crown has increased, is increasing and
ought to be diminished', the Ministry was surprised and its ranks
were thrown into confusion. At midnight the House divided,
233 for, 215 against ; and went on to pass without division motions
asserting its control over the Civil List and its duty to redress the
abuses complained of in the petitions.[1]

This success, the climax of the whole campaign, caused jubilation
among some members of Opposition[2] but only among the unrealistic,
for the victory was fortuitous with no roots in the facts. Resolves,
as Savile said,[3] 'declaratory and theoretic, and not going directly
to any effect', gathered in many who would stickle at the reform of
particular abuses. While Opposition had rallied its supporters,
Government had been caught with many of its troops dispersed and
out of action. Fears of an early dissolution may have caused some
to subscribe to a harmless aphorism[4] and the not inconsiderable
number who always voted on the merits of a case may have been
impressed by the constitutional argument of Dunning, by the pal-
pable dismay on the treasury benches and even by North's impolitic
and unaccustomed loss of temper. By the 24th, however, the
House was back to normal. On that day, Ministry defeated by
the comfortable margin of 254 votes to 203 Dunning's motion for
an address to the king against a dissolution or prorogation until
royal influence had been diminished and other abuses mentioned in
the petitions had been removed. The *volte-face* is to be attributed in
part to the nature of the motion itself. Some members objected to

[1] *P.H.* xxi. pp. 340–74.
[2] *Cf.* Rockingham to Shelburne, 9 Apr. 1780, (copy) W.W.M. R166–23 ; 'The
event of that day [6 Apr.] confirms me *more* and *more* that *much* is in *our hands* at
present....'
[3] Savile to Wyvill, 24 Aug. 1781, Wyvill, iii. 328.
[4] *Cf.* Shelburne to Lord Mahon, 7 Apr. 1780, quoted by Lord Fitzmaurice, *Life
of Shelburne* (London, 1876); iii. 74–5 : 'It is acknowledged, that the approaching
Election has a very great influence on the divisions now taking place in the House of
Commons in favour of Reform and redress of grievances. The county members have
very generally voted on the public side; except a few who are likely to lose their seats
by not doing so.' Also Fox in *P.H.* xxi. 526; and Hans Sloane to Earl of Buckinghamshire, 12 Mar. 1780 (H. M. C. Lothian).

21

the implied encroachment on the royal prerogative ; [1] many, especially as the militia camps were beginning to assemble,[2] can have had no love for what one newspaper called ' Mr. Dunning's Motion for the House to sit all the Summer ' ; [3] and perhaps there were those who felt that, having voted with Dunning on the 6th, they had made a sufficient gesture to popularity.[4]   The net swing of sixteen independent votes from Opposition to Ministry was alone enough to have turned the tables ; but the relative merits of the two motions were perhaps less important in reversing the result than the relative efficiency of the Whips.   North owed his reprieve primarily to the greater success of Administration in holding its supporters at Westminster and bringing up reinforcements, some from as far away as Ireland.[5]   In the following weeks Burke's Bill was slowly stabbed to death, and in late June it was discharged from the order paper.   The great offensive had failed in parliament.

By that time it had failed also in the counties.   Only ten of them [6] together with London, Westminster, and Newcastle could be induced to associate.   Several, using the pretext of partial success in parliament, deferred the measure,[7] and Cheshire dissolved its committee.[8]   Adjournment *sine die* is written large across the history of the movement in many parts of England.

Lord George Gordon had been in a humiliating minority of one in opposing the introduction into the House of Burke's Establishment Bill ; [9] but he lived to take a strange revenge.   After the Gordon riots, the Protestant Association seemed to the mass of the respectable (who have always ruled England) a *reductio ad absurdum* of popular politics, and all associations, save those for military defence, irreparably lost caste.   The Opposition was grievously split between economical and parliamentary reformers, with Rockingham upbraiding those who had brought the great enterprise to ruin by embracing speculative propositions [10] and Shelburne retorting on him for ' obstinately stopping the free course of

[1] *E.g.* Lord George Germain in *P.H.* xxi. 522.   *Cf.* the comment of the historian the Rev. W. Coxe in a letter to Lord Herbert, 10 May 1780.   Lord Herbert (ed.), *Henry, Elizabeth and George* (London, 1939), p. 475.   A motion similar to Dunning's had been defeated 142–70 on 15 June 1779.   *P.H.* xx. 854–76.

[2] *Gazetteer*, 18 Apr. 1780.

[3] *Public Advertiser*, 27 Apr. 1780.

[4] It was this ' treachery ' that Fox singled out for special blame when he spoke in the House after the announcement of the division.   He found the origin of the defeat in the county members ; but in fact only five county members swung from Opposition on the 6th to Administration on the 24th.

[5] *P.H.* xxi. 498.

[6] Yorkshire, Essex, Somersetshire, Surrey, Buckinghamshire, Devonshire, Middlesex, Huntingdonshire, Hertfordshire, Dorsetshire.

[7] Berkshire, Cambridgeshire, Gloucestershire, Suffolk, Sussex.

[8] *Northampton Mercury*, 24 Apr. 1780.

[9] *P.H.* xxi. 73.

[10] *E.g.* Rockingham to Croft, 18 May 1780, W.W.M. R1–1062, partly printed in *Memoirs of the Marquis of Rockingham and his Contemporaries* (ed. earl of Albemarle, London, 1852), ii. 409.

popular spirit, which alone can ever oppose the Court '.[1] Outside parliament, the radicals of Yorkshire and the metropolis, to whom the events of 1780 had imparted a brisk rotation, shot off at a tangent into the unexplored vacuities of parliamentary reform. North, with the king behind him, was left as *tertius gaudens*, until the country gentlemen should find the American war no longer supportable. As a sound political tradesman who understood the conditions of his time, North had feared much less from the movement than Burke and the Rockinghams had hoped from it. Government thought so little of the threat that the sheriffs it appointed in February 1780 showed themselves more and not less accommodating than their predecessors in complying with requisitions for county meetings.[2] North's fate, as he and the king realized, depended not on petitions and associations in the counties but on divisions in the House.

Long afterwards, in 1796, his apprehensive imagination stirred by a real revolution, Burke painted ' the portentous crisis ' of these years in high colours. ' Such was the distemper of the public mind', he wrote, ' that there was no madman, in his maddest ideas, and maddest projects, who might not count upon numbers to support his principles and execute his designs.' [3] Yet at the time it was the sluggishness of his supporters that most impressed him ; and his disappointment at the want of systematic perseverance underlies his evasive replies to the requests of the Devonshire and Yorkshire committees to renew his efforts.[4] The general election later in the same year only confirmed his estimate of the public torpor.[5]

Yet if for England 1780 was no revolution *manqué*, the failure of the petitioning movement did effect a genuine disturbance in the affairs of the Rockingham group, and especially of the party manager. In trying to spread their sails to the breeze of popular favour, they had raised it to a storm and had had to run ignominiously for shelter. After all their efforts, they were thrown back upon the dreary,

---

[1] Shelburne to Barré, Dec. 1780, Fitzmaurice, iii. 106–7.

[2] The sheriffs whose term of office expired at the end of January 1780 had divided about equally between those who did and those who did not comply with the requisitions. Eight counties held their first meetings after the new sheriffs had been appointed and in the six cases about which I have information the sheriff complied in four. Moreover, among the new sheriffs were Sir G. Onesiphorous Paul, who had taken the chair at the Gloucestershire meeting and was a member of the committee, and John Grant, who was a member of the Berkshire committee.

[3] *Works*, v. 219–22 (*A Letter to a Noble Lord*).

[4] Burke to Viscount Courtenay, 24 July 1780 (copy), W.W.M. B1–918 and *Works*, i. 439–41 ; Burke to Wyvill, 14 Aug. 1780, Wyvill, i. 290–1.

[5] Though Christie concludes (*op. cit.* p. 156) that ' Political partisanship played no small part in the elections of 1780 ', there is little evidence that economical reform was much debated. At York itself Lord John Cavendish was not greatly troubled by his refusal to subscribe to the association. During the election he wrote to Rockingham : ' We have today canvassed Walmgate, the Shambles and all the dirtiest part of the town, with hardly a negative. One of your best friends refused me a vote on account of my not signing, and two refused C. Turner [the other Rockingham candidate] because he had signed and we heard no more about it.' W.W.M. R141–14. See also Christie, pp. 112–13.

despairing round of opposition within doors, with nothing to hope but from national misfortune. A wider gulf had opened between them and the followers of Shelburne, and it was never to be securely closed. Even within their own ranks, there was a new tension between the old guard of Rockingham, Portland and Burke and the more zealous reformers Fox and Richmond.

For Burke the movement of 1780 was a bitter awakening to his own wisdom. Intellectually, he knew what to expect from the ambiguous game on which he had led the Rockinghams, but the reality, when it came, was not the less painful for that. As to the initiative in the country, he understood the dangers of a purely managed stirring among the people. ' . . . the want of a real concurrence in opinion may possibly be concealed ', he told a friend, ' but the chief part of the delusion will be on ourselves, because we may be led to count upon a strength which may fail us when we have most reason to call for it '.[1] As to the movement in parliament, he was fully awake to the obstructive power of particular interests ; he well knew that ' the cold commendation of a public advantage never was, and never will be, a match for the quick sensibility of a private loss '.[2] Once the movement had been launched in the counties, Burke left it to his friends with connections. He himself was a member of only two committees and an inactive member at that. His work was in and for parliament ; and here he had to stomach not only defeat but also an emulous rivalry and ingratitude. Beside his own, the labours of Savile, Clerke, Dunning, Thomas Pitt and Crewe were derisory ; and to confound them all in undiscriminating votes of thanks [3] was an insult that would have rankled with men less sensitive than Burke. Such brief holiday of popularity as he enjoyed came to a sudden end when he denounced the Yorkshire demands to the Buckinghamshire meeting [4] and when he offered a stony resistance in the House to Sawbridge's motion for annual parliaments.[5] Long before this, however, he had all but abandoned his Establishment Bill. His despondency was due not merely or even mainly to personal pique; it was due rather to a flaw in his character as a politician. Though he warned against crying for the moon, Burke was the perfectionist who would take nothing if he could not have all. He was of too stiff a fibre for the hundred little acquiescences, the dilutions of principle, the connivances at rough justice that the practice of government must tolerate. He was a man of consummate political wisdom, but of little political aptitude. When wounded, as he now was, in the rough-and-tumble, he was apt to sink into a querulous self-pity, which was the least attractive side of a disposition for the most part lovable.

The county movement came for Burke in the middle of his parliamentary career. Hitherto, he had been the man of party.

---

[1] Burke to Champion, 24 Jan. 1780, *Works*, i. 415.   [2] *P.H.* xxi. 4.
[3] *E.g.* that of Dorsetshire (Wyvill, i. 205).   [4] *Works*, v. 609–12.   [5] *P.H.* xxi. 603–15.

Now the disappointment of high hopes set him on another course. Economical reform has an epilogue in the general election of 1780 ; and taken together they caused displacements in the Rockingham group. While the former made Fox the darling, it made Burke the ogre, of the radicals ; and while the latter advanced Fox from Malmesbury to the City of Westminster, it relegated Burke from Bristol to Rockingham's borough of Malton. The loss of Bristol was for Burke the final sad commentary on popular constancy. He had serious thoughts of quitting a field of 'vain contention', and his retirement from public affairs was widely believed to be imminent.[1]

> If there were any two objects upon which the people of England had *seemed* to set their hearts for some time past [he wrote to Lady Rockingham] they were the reduction of the influence of the Crown, and the shortening the duration of Parliaments. Mr. Sawbridge moved the latter and I the former. We are both cast out of Parliament in the two principal cities, and most popular elections in the kingdom. There is no standing against the inference to be drawn from this extraordinary fact. If I were to come into Parliament by any of the little posterns and sally ports of the constitution my moving such Bills as I formerly did . . . would be a piece of buffoonery to which I am little inclined to submit.[2]

Return Burke did through the little postern of Malton. He offered his Bill again in 1781 and went down to an even more decisive defeat. When at last in the spring of 1782 Rockingham was called to office, Burke readily consented to ' lie by ', having, as he admitted, second-rate pretensions,[3] and the pay office without a seat in the Cabinet was as much as he expected. The economical reform of 1782 was a much abated thing, and the early death of Rockingham deprived its author of his patron and of his source of influence in the counsels of the party. Portland was no substitute, and Fox, whom he followed rather than led into the coalition, was a not very competent politician, who could give Burke friendship but could not tether him to the party as the frail marquess had done.

By 1784, when hopes of ousting Pitt had ebbed, Burke's transition was complete. Henceforth, he would be less prompt to the party call ; there would be a certain recklessness in his behaviour. From the same Will Burke who had set his feet on the path of the county movement, he had acquired a new and all-devouring interest—India. There was to be one last convulsion of party violence in the regency crisis of 1788–9, but for the rest the prophet of party had given himself up to causes that transcended it. At last mankind might claim its own.

University of Canterbury, Christchurch   N. C. PHILLIPS

[1] *E.g.* Samuel Romilly to the Rev. John Roget, 27 Oct. 1780, *Memoirs of Sir Samuel Romilly* (London, 1840), i. 135.

[2] Burke to Lady Rockingham [27–8 Sept. 1780], W.W.M. R140–4.

[3] *Ibid.* B23, document in Burke's hand headed ' Memoranda for Consideration ', endorsed on cover ' 1782 (March) '.

Parliament and Foreign Policy in the Age of Stanhope and Walpole

ONE of the most important results of much recent work on parliament has been to make clear the precise part played by patronage in eighteenth-century government. The belief that eighteenth-century parliaments were infinitely corruptible and eighteenth-century governments infinitely corrupting, which even so distinguished a scholar as Sir Richard Lodge appears to have held,[1] has, like the King's Friends and the tyranny of George III, joined the growing collection of historical myths. Scholars of all schools and none are agreed nowadays that pensions and places, while indispensable to government, were not enough in themselves to establish and maintain harmonious and effective relations between king and parliament in the eighteenth century. The studies of Miss Betty Kemp, Professor Robert Walcott, Dr. Owen, Mr. John Brooke and Mr. Ian Christie, to mention only the more recent detailed accounts, have demonstrated beyond dispute that no government in that period had enough pensions and places to manage parliament by these means alone, that those who enjoyed them differed, for various reasons, in the closeness and consistency of their attachment to government and, most important of all, that there was a substantial element in every parliament which was uncommitted and insensitive to all offers of loaves and fishes.[2] They are also agreed that no administration which wished to last for long could afford to dispense with able parliamentary leadership, capable of defending on the floor of each house all aspects of government policy, and having policies that could be so defended.[3] Yet, despite the fact that the importance of leadership and argument in managing parliament in the eighteenth century is undeniable and undenied, indeed perhaps partly for that reason, they have received scant attention

---

[1] Sir R. Lodge, *Great Britain and Prussia in the eighteenth century* (Oxford, 1923), p. 129, where, in an aside, the more revealing for being an aside, he refers, in connection with parliament's acceptance of the Peace Preliminaries of Paris in 1762, to the ' fascinating simplicity of political corruption in the eighteenth century '.

[2] Betty Kemp, *King and Commons, 1660–1832* (1957) ; Robert Walcott, *English politics in the early eighteenth century* (Oxford, 1956) ; J. B. Owen, *The rise of the Pelhams* (1957) ; John Brooke, *The Chatham administration, 1766–1768* (1956) ; I. Christie, *The end of Lord North's ministry, 1780–1782* (1958).

[3] Kemp, pp. 100–2 ; Owen, pp. 34–8, 56–7 ; Brooke, p. 10 ; Christie, p. 233.

from most scholars of parliamentary history in recent years, and, in practice, parliamentary management, even on occasion politics itself, has been reduced to jobbery. The modern student of eighteenth-century parliamentary history, indeed, like Lord Chesterfield, and with more genuine weariness than he affected to feel on withdrawing from public life in 1748, may well claim : ' I have been behind the scenes both of pleasure and of business. I have seen all the coarse pulleys and dirty ropes which exhibit and move all the gaudy machines, and I have seen and smelt the tallow candles which illuminate the whole decoration to the astonishment and admiration of the ignorant multitude '.[1] If, as is generally agreed, contemporary parliamentary management involved more than the manipulation of spoils, then it must also be admitted that its present treatment is greatly un-balanced. Important questions such as the need which govern-ments felt to argue for their policies, particularly for their foreign policies, by speech and writings, their anxiety to formulate a case which parliament could accept, and to make, adjust, and even on occasion surrender, policies according to the known or assumed prejudices of parliament, cannot be tucked away in a few perfunctory sentences, and deserve to be treated as seriously as other, more familiar, aspects of eighteenth-century government.[2]

The purpose of this study is to examine the various ways in which such questions were tackled during a specimen period, roughly the age of Stanhope and Walpole, and in so far as they were concerned with foreign policy during that period.[3] The choice of period is purely arbitrary, except in so far as it is dictated by the writer's knowledge, and doubtless a similar approach could be made to other periods. The decision to restrict further the scope of the investigation to parliament's concern with foreign affairs, where it is not again just a matter of the writer's competence, can be defended on more positive grounds, for foreign policy was a large part of eighteenth-century government and political controversy.[4]

Nowhere, indeed, was parliamentary leadership, the need to have and to be able to express a convincing argument, more necessary than in the field of foreign affairs, nowhere was its absence felt more acutely or followed so quickly and so surely by disastrous results. The major political controversies of the period, it is worth recalling,

---

[1] *The letters of Philip Dormer Stanhope, 4th Earl of Chesterfield,* ed. by Bonamy Dobrée (1932), 6 vols., iii. 1109, Chesterfield to Solomon Dayrolles, 23 February 1748.

[2] The notable exceptions amongst those already mentioned are Owen and Christie. There is a great deal that is relevant to this aspect of parliamentary management during Anne's reign in Dr. D. Coombs, *The Conduct of the Dutch : British opinion and the Dutch alliance during the war of the Spanish Succession* (The Hague, 1958).

[3] I should like to thank Professor Mark A. Thomson for many kindnesses and, in par-ticular, for having read this article in typescript and for giving me much helpful advice.

[4] For some authoritative remarks on the substance of politics in the eighteenth century, with particular reference to foreign affairs, see R. Pares, *King George III and the politicians* (Oxford, 1953), pp. 2–5.

or at any rate the majority of them—those of 1701, 1711/12, 1717, 1739–43, 1762, 1780–2 and 1791—largely concerned foreign affairs. Yet in constitutional theory, which has changed little, either in substance or in language, on these matters since the seventeenth-century, foreign policy lay unambiguously in the king.   To quote one typical pronouncement, made by a critic of government, John Snell, in a debate on the Septennial Bill in the Commons on 24 April 1716, O.S., ' by the known and standing law of the land, the right of making peace and war, treaties and alliances, are undeniably the King's prerogative ; and his Majesty may exercise that right, as to him seems best ; and most for the good and benefit of his people, without application to Parliament, either to approve or confirm '.[1] Even in practice the executive enjoyed and was conceded greater freedom and more independence in foreign affairs than in other matters.   For all that, however, there was a considerable difference between what was permissible in theory and what was tolerated in practice.   William III had attempted and for a time succeeded in conducting foreign affairs according to the letter of the constitution, acting as his own foreign minister, a role to which he was inclined by temperament and which experience rendered him better equipped to perform than any of his ministers, and conducting foreign policy without reference to parliament, save to disclose what was absolutely necessary to secure supply, which was precious little.[2]   Parliament tolerated the ignorance in which it was held as long as foreign policy appeared to follow aims consistent with British interests, and, as long as such harmony persisted, ignorance suited the king well.   A very different situation, however, arose when the king sensed dangers of which parliament seemed oblivious or when it appeared to parliament that British interests were being disregarded.   Then ignorance proved at best inconvenient, at worst crippling.   Such a situation arose during the period 1698–1701 when William III was made to see very clearly the serious disadvantages attached to policies inspired and conducted without regard to parliament, and complained, seemingly unaware of his own responsibility in the matter, that indifference and parochialism were so general that it was ' as if no other country existed but this island and that it need not concern itself with what happened anywhere else in the world '.[3]

[1] A. Boyer, Political state of Great Britain (1711–40), 60 vols., xi. 653. For some illustrations of parliament's attitude to the crown's control over foreign policy since the eighteenth century, see C. S. Emden, Selected speeches on the constitution (Oxford, 1939), 2 vols., i. 231–58.

[2] Mark A. Thomson, ' Parliament and foreign policy, 1689–1714 ', History, xxviii (1953), 234–9 ; G. Davies, ' The control of British foreign policy by William III ', in Essays on the later Stuarts (1958), pp. 91–122. There are some interesting remarks on the lack of diplomatic experience of William III's secretaries of state in D. B. Horn, ' The diplomatic experience of secretaries of state, 1660–1852, History, xli (1956), 90–3.

[3] F. J. L. Krämer, Archives de la maison d' Orange-Nassau (3rd ser., 3 vols., Leiden, 1907–9), ii. 51, William III to Heinsius, 15–25, Feb. 1698.

William III overcame the crisis of 1701, and the methods which he adopted need not detain us here, for they have been well described elsewhere.[1] It is enough to say that the principal lesson drawn from the affair, and one which it may be supposed was not lost upon Robert Walpole, who began his parliamentary career in that year, was that parliament could not be ignored in foreign affairs, and that it was safer in some measure to take parliament into the king's confidence rather than to allow a situation to develop in which the best laid plans might be wrecked or could be saved only by hastily contrived measures, potentially dangerous to the crown itself. At any rate—and one must note the existence of other factors having the same tendency, such as the inexperience of Anne and a growing interest in and knowledge of Europe, which the lapsing of the Licensing Act and war itself encouraged—parliament received more, and more regular, information about foreign affairs after 1701 than it had done before, in speeches from the throne, which invariably contained some statement about foreign policy, from ministers expounding policy to the houses, and in treaties and papers laid before the houses at their request or upon the initiative of the crown.[2]

This system, in operation in Anne's reign, with some refinements and with changes from time to time according to the personalities of ministers and the importance of foreign affairs themselves, was continued under the Hanoverians. Indeed, if some such system as has been outlined above had not been in existence in 1715, the Hanoverians would have needed to invent it. In addition to financial necessity and political convenience, the fact that the Hanoverians were, by a clause of the Act of Settlement, obliged to secure parliament's consent before engaging in war for the defence of Hanover, necessarily involved giving parliament a good deal of information about foreign affairs, for it was held in parliament that policies touching upon Hanover, above all others, deserved parliament's close and constant attention.[3] Parliament, indeed, was as sensitive to the possibility that British interests were being subordinated to those of Hanover as the government was to the possibility of European action in favour of the Stuarts, and with as much and at times as little cause. Certainly the elector wished, and on occasion was able, to use his position as king of England to advance and protect Hanoverian interests to the injury of specifically British interests, though the occasions were not as numerous as opposition leaders made them out to be, and of course

[1] Mark A. Thomson, *ubi supra,* 235–9.
[2] Mark A. Thomson, *ubi supra,* 239–43.
[3] *Journals of House of Lords,* xxi. 606, where in a protest it is stated, ' All treaties therefore with Princes of the North should, above all others be made in the plainest, and most unexceptionable terms ; or, if the way of wording such treaties shall occasion any doubt, no method of clearing it should be neglected or avoided '.

he kept as quiet about them as he possibly could.[1]   However, complete silence was out of the question, and to practise deceit involved imparting some information, involved trying to make out a case on British grounds for what had been done, which was more often one-sided than altogether false, more often challenged than passively accepted.   At any rate the new reign persisted with the now established conventions.

The speech from the throne continued to contain a regular statement about foreign affairs, varying in length according to the state of foreign affairs themselves.   During the years 1715–20 when foreign policy was a major concern of parliament a paragraph or two was common ; in the years 1726–31 when foreign policy was perhaps the major public business of parliament the greater part of the speech was devoted to it.   Very properly, government attached considerable importance to the speech, which was written and often rewritten by the king's ministers.   Parliament required a lead ; as Henry Pelham observed of parliament in 1746, ' composed of as true Whigs, and friends to this government, as any since the Revolution . . . but they are not servants, they are friends ; they must therefore be treated as such ; they must see the interest of their country is pursued ; they may be led, but they cannot be drove '.[2] The speech from the throne provided such a lead, for every detail of it was required to be answered in the addresses of thanks of both houses, or could only be left unanswered at the charge of committing a discourtesy to the king, which parliament could rarely bring itself to perform.[3]   It is true that in theory, as the government insisted and the opposition admitted, and even in practice, the customary compliments of thanks in the addresses did not preclude subsequent parliamentary examination and censure of policy. These was certainly a good deal of cussedness in the frequent complaints of the opposition that an address was ' too particular ', and of make-believe in their nostalgia for a golden period in the past

---

[1] There were occasions, in 1725–6, for example, when the defence of specifically British interests could be held to have endangered the interests of Hanover.

[2] W. Coxe, *Memoirs of Horatio, Lord Walpole* (1820), 2 vols., ii. 195–6, Henry Pelham to Horace Walpole, 30 July 1747.

[3] Professor Walcott, p. 142, notes that at the beginning of the 1708 session the Lords took the unprecedented step of refusing to answer the queen's speech.   In the period 1715–31 I have found only one other instance, recorded as follows in ' Sir Edward Knatchbull's *Parliamentary Diary* ', 23 Jan. 1727 ; ' Memorandum.   'Tis observable in the King's speech when he desires the same confidence may be reposed in him as last year viz. the unlimited vote of credit, there was no notice taken of it at all in the address, but only to desire the King to put the nation in a posture of defence and the House would grant such supplies as the exigency of affairs required.   I believe it the first instance in many years when the speech was not answered in every particular.' I should like to thank Dr. Newman of the University of Leicester for having drawn my attention to this valuable diary which he is editing for the Royal Historical Society and for having allowed me to use his transcripts which are deposited with the History of Parliament at the Institute of Historical Research.

when parliament had ' kept to generals upon such occasions '.[1] As
a government spokesman said in reply to such criticisms in 1735:

> At this rate, Sir, the gentlemen who have the honour to serve the
> crown must have a very hard task : if they or their friends propose
> a long and particular address, they are then accused of endeavouring
> to impose upon the honour and dignity of this House, and if they
> propose a short address, and expressed in the most general terms,
> insinuations are then made, that their modesty proceeds from a con-
> sciousness of guilt ; so that let them chuse which way they will, it
> is impossible for them to avoid censure.[2]

But there was more to it than faction. The speech from the throne
and the addresses of thanks were published in the Votes which
recorded parliament's daily proceedings. Thus in seeking to keep
down the addresses of thanks to mere expressions of affection for
the king and zeal for his service, the opposition hoped ' to avoid
giving the impression without doors, to people who were not
perfectly acquainted with our methods of proceeding, which is the
greatest part of mankind, that the Address of this House was the
real sense of the House, with respect to every particular measure
mentioned in the Address '.[3] And there is this much to be said
for the argument, that it was precisely this interpretation of the
addresses that English diplomatic representatives in Europe were
instructed to underline. A further practical objection to the long
and detailed speeches from the throne and addresses of thanks
characteristic of the period after 1726 was perhaps that it was not
always easy to remember every word as it was said. The opposition, Shippen complained, hearing the speech and the motion read
only once, were ' obliged in some manner to shoot flying '.[4] And
although not entirely true, for the Commons heard the speech read
twice, first by the lord chancellor in joint assembly with the Lords
in the Lords' chamber, and then by the speaker in their own
chamber, it was certainly the case that the opposition was less
fortunately situated than government supporters and well-wishers
who had commonly received a preliminary hearing of the speech
and of the proposed address at a meeting specially convened for
the purpose at the Cockpit or the London house of a minister some
days before the opening of parliament.[5]

[1] W. Cobbett, *Parliamentary history of England* (1806–20), 36 vols., ix. 646–7, a report
of a debate in the Commons on the address of thanks of January 1735, and typical of
many such debates.

[2] Cobbett, ix. 678.   [3] Cobbett, ix. 646–7.   [4] Cobbett, ix. 189.

[5] The king's speech of November 1718, together with the text of the addresses, was
shown to some of the government's friends in both houses the day before parliament
opened : W. Michael, *England under George I. The Quadruple Alliance* (1939, English
trans.), p. 75. Egmont records having rejected four invitations to such meetings in
1730, 1732, 1733 and 1734, in terms which suggest that by then it was a firmly established convention : *Historical Manuscripts Commission, 16th Report. Manuscripts of the
Earl of Egmont. Diary of Viscount Perceval* (1920–3), 3 vols., i. 2, 214, 365–6 ; ii. 7.

Considerable care was undoubtedly given to the preparation of the king's speech, at least by those ministers who had some sense of parliamentary management, though Carteret, characteristically, was inclined to regard it as a small matter. ' Two days will do for that ', he is reported as having said to George II in November 1744.[1] For a speech to go through several drafts, from a number of hands, appears to have been fairly usual, and the alterations were by no means always so frivolously semantic as Hervey suggests them to have been.[2] The construction of one speech from the throne can be followed in detail. The speech from the throne opening parliament in January 1726, for example, was the result of the joint efforts of the duke of Newcastle, Robert Walpole and Lord Townshend, and reached its final form after three preliminary drafts.[3] It is a good illustration of the difficulties that frequently arose when there was a gap to bridge between what government would have liked parliament to believe, which of course often differed from what government itself believed, and what parliament could be expected to believe. Parliament was not usually irresponsible, but, as Robert Walpole observed, it was more easily impressed by immediate, concrete, and easily comprehended dangers, particularly to the protestant religion, than by those less easily defined anxieties which often formed the real motive force of diplomatic action.[4] Yet if the protestant card was a good one to play, worthy of inclusion in the ' hereditary speech ' which Hervey professed to observe during the twenties,[5] it could not be played indiscriminately.

For a discussion of preliminary meetings in the post-Walpole period, see L. B. Namier, ' The Circular Letters ; An eighteenth century Whip to Members of Parliament ', *ante*, xliv. (1929), 588–611.

[1] Coxe, ii. 95 ; a quotation from a letter from the duke of Newcastle to Lord Hardwicke of 3 Nov. 1744.

[2] Apart from the king's speech opening parliament in 1726, which I consider in the text, see *Some materials towards Memoirs of the Reign of George II by John, Lord Hervey*, ed. by Romney Sedgwick (1931), 3 vols., iii. 928, which refers to alterations in a king's speech concluding the parliamentary session of 1740. Hervey notes being called upon to draw up another speech at the end of the 1733 session, and that then his draft was modified by Robert Walpole : i. 200–4. Two other examples of combined drafting, in 1718 and 1744, are mentioned in Michael, p. 75 and Coxe, ii. 97.

[3] For the various drafts, see P[ublic] R[ecord] O[ffice], S.P. 43/8 (Regencies-Hanover), Townshend to Newcastle, 16/17 Nov. 1725, printed in W. Michael *Englische Geschichte im Achtzehnten Jahrhundert* (Leipzig and Basle 1896–1955), 5 vols., iii, Appendix IV, 595–6 ; Townshend to Newcastle, 30 Nov./11 Dec. 1725 ; W. Coxe, *Memoirs of the Life and Administration of Sir Robert Walpole* (1798), 3 vols., ii. 493–4. For the speech itself, see *Journals of House of Commons*, xx. 544–5.

[4] Coxe, *Memoirs...of Sir Robert Walpole,* ii. 486, Robert Walpole to Townshend, 2/13 October 1725. Horace Walpole was of the same opinion (Brit.[ish] Mus.[eum] Add. MS. 48981 (Townshend Papers), H. Walpole to Townshend, 30 Aug. 1725).

[5] ' The King was forced to meet his Parliament with a sort of hereditary speech, for it was just in the same strain with the last half-dozen of his father's, the topics of which were the uncertain state of Europe, the intricacy of affairs, the natural protraction of treaties, the hopes of a happy conclusion being at hand, and the dependence he had in the loyalty and goodwill of his Parliament for supporting him with money and troops.' Sedgwick, i. 75.

There was a limit to parliament's capacity for credulity, even in those matters that it held most important.   In 1726 it was Walpole and Newcastle in London, more cautious by nature, but also nearer and more attentive to public opinion, who made a better assessment of what was acceptable to parliament than Townshend, who was by nature more impulsive and, in Hanover, was cut off from direct contact with that opinion and subject to that peculiar diplomatic light-headedness which a short period of stay in Hanover frequently induced in British ministers.   Foreign policy, indeed, frequently looked different to ministers in Hanover than it did to ministers in London.   But, if the air of Hanover had its dangers, so had the air of London.   Ministers in London tended at times to be quite hag-ridden by public opinion.   In 1729, for example, European problems, despite three years of intense diplomatic activity, still remained unsettled, fixed, as the *Craftsman* observed, in a sort of earthly purgatory in which Britain bore most of the inconveniences of war and enjoyed none of its advantages.   Townshend, in Hanover again, counselled caution and urged patience, and so did his under-secretary, Tilson, who in his best bedside manner, gently reproved his colleague, Delafaye, in London, for being too hasty.   'This', he wrote, and the analogy which followed was appropriate in a correspondence so much of which was made up of reports of his own and Delafaye's state of health, ' is not a juncture to bully.   Soothing and anodynes, are more necessary than irritating applications', and, returning to the same theme in a later letter, ' I find my dear friend, that a man out of a crowd judges more calmly, as he thinks, than one that is elbowed and shoved about.   You dream of nothing but Craftsmen and Coffee-house talk and I abominate both the one and the other.' [1]   It was good advice, of course, but a bit unrealistic. Ministers who could hear at their backs the rumblings of impatience to be done with European uncertainty, could scarcely act as if they had eternity on their side ; and they were, therefore, at a decided disadvantage in negotiations with Fleury, for example, who had no parliaments to contend with and, in one so old, showed an ex-ceptional reluctance to do things in a hurry.   In the summer of 1729, indeed, the need for an early decision in Europe became so pressing for the British government that Townshend, still in Han-over, was forced by Walpole to surrender complete control of the negotiations for the Treaty of Seville to the Lords of the Council in England, on the grounds that ' being on the spot [they were] better judges of the present temper and disposition of the nation '.[2]

During a parliamentary session ministers were invariably hard

[1] P.R.O., S.P. 43/9 (Regencies—Hanover).   G. Tilson to C. Delafaye, 10/21 June, 8/19 July, 1729.

[2] P.R.O., S.P. 43/10 (Regencies—Hanover), Townshend to Newcastle, 21 July/1 Aug. 1729.

pressed. Debates on foreign affairs or which dwelt largely on foreign affairs were regular and sometimes frequent, at least three or four in any session ; as many as eight or nine in times when things were happening, as in 1729, 1730, and 1731. The debate on the king's speech was always the occasion for a lengthy discussion of foreign affairs, and foreign affairs loomed large frequently in debates on the army and navy estimates and the mutiny bill. Important treaties, such as the alliance of Hanover, merited separate and full-scale treatment, which was also usually given to subsidy treaties, which, because they were attended by expense, had to be laid before parliament by the king.[1]   In the period 1726–31 ministers took very seriously the need to convince parliament and were right to do so. Responsibility for explaining what the government had been doing in the field of foreign affairs was placed upon those most fitted to discharge it. Horace Walpole, the ambassador at Paris, the centre of diplomatic activity for most of the period 1725–31, took the principal role in debates on foreign affairs, and was brought home on leave frequently just before the beginning of the parliamentary session, in order to present the government's case, despite the inconvenience which this invariably caused for the conduct of diplomacy.[2]   And he was brought home, not out of an excess of caution, but from sheer political necessity. In the twenties the two secretaries of state for the north and south, Townshend and Newcastle, were in the Lords. In the Commons, Robert Walpole, although he spoke quite often in debates on foreign affairs, did not like to do so. As he admitted to Newcastle in December 1725, ' You know I do not love to give long opinions nor reasonings upon foreign politicks '.[3]   In such circumstances it was vital for the government to have in the Commons a well-informed spokesman on foreign affairs to assume the labouring oar. Horace Walpole was well-equipped for such a role. He had his defects, of course. He was no orator, and appears to have been almost as long winded in debate as he was in correspondence, which for sheer bulk was only surpassed in his time by that of Saint Saphorin, the British envoy at Vienna from 1718 to 1727, whose verbosity was such as to lead ministers to designate all letters of excessive length as ' St. Saphorins '.[4]   An opening speech of an hour or more came to be expected from him, beginning as did most speeches on foreign affairs in the late 'twenties and 'thirties with

[1] For an account of the alliance of Hanover I refer to my article, ' Britain and the alliance of Hanover,' ante, lxxiv. 404–30.

[2] Coxe, Memoirs of Horatio, Lord Walpole, i. 198, 278 ; Brit. Mus. Add. MS. 32, 748 (Newcastle Papers—Diplomatic), Newcastle to H. Walpole, 10 Nov. 1726 ; Add. MS. 32, 754 (Newcastle Papers—Diplomatic), Newcastle to H. Walpole, 4 Jan. 1727/8.

[3] P.R.O., S.P. 35/60 (Domestic), R. Walpole to Newcastle, 1 Dec. 1725.

[4] Private correspondence of Chesterfield and Newcastle, 1744–1746, ed. by Sir Richard Lodge (Royal Historical Society, Camden 3rd ser., 1930), p. 10.

Utrecht, and did much to earn him the reputation in some quarters of being a great house of commons bore.[1] But he clearly took his duties conscientiously and, as Egmont argued, there was always good sense in what he said.[2] Even Hervey, who could rarely bring himself to say a good thing of anyone, admitted that Horace Walpole was ' a very good treaty dictionary ', and invaluable to his brother in that capacity.[3] Nor did speaking end Horace Walpole's activities in the field of parliamentary management. He wrote pamphlets on foreign affairs, like many others, but he also seems to have acted as a sort of public relations officer for the ministry in parliament, explaining foreign policy privately to members and getting their reactions to particular controversial questions before the ministry committed itself publicly to a definite policy.[4] His activity in this sphere, indeed, appears to have been so well established as to give rise to the rumour that he was drawing an official entertainment allowance for it and, what was more to the point, keeping most of it for himself.[5] Horace Walpole seems to have taken his additional parliamentary responsibilities in his stride, and even enjoyed them, for long after he had ceased to hold diplomatic or ministerial office he continued to speak on foreign affairs and to be heard with respect.[6] As he observed, he was like a great bell that had stopped ringing, but still hummed and buzzed in people's ears.[7]

However, combining a diplomatic post with parliamentary duties was not to everyone's taste. The case of Colonel William Stanhope, nephew to the greater Lord Stanhope, is relevant here. Stanhope was ambassador at Madrid from 1721 until March 1727 when, at the beginning of the Spanish siege of Gibraltar, he returned home. Worried lest he be held personally responsible for the deterioration in Anglo-Spanish relations, he accepted Newcastle's suggestion that he take a seat in the Commons where he could defend himself and the ministry from attack.[8] However, he did not live up to Newcastle's expectations. He appears to have spoken rarely, and without distinction, and quickly developed a strong distaste, if not for parliamentary life, at least for a role which combined the embassy at Madrid with membership of the Commons.

<hr>

[1] Sedgwick, i. 285. For another equally malicious character sketch, see H. Walpole, *Memoirs of the Reign of King George the Second* (1847), 3 vols., i. 140–1.

[2] Egmont Diary, iii. 338.   [3] Sedgwick, i. 285.

[4] Egmont Diary, i. 21, 39, 56 ; ii. 14.   [5] *Ibid.*, iii. 240.

[6] Coxe, *Memoirs of Horatio, Lord Walpole,* ii. 340.

[7] *Ibid.* ii. 299, H. Walpole to Mr. Neville, 19 Aug. 1749.

[8] J. F. Chance, *The alliance of Hanover* (1923), p. 469, Newcastle to Stanhope, 22 Dec. O.S. 1726. Stanhope became M.P. for Steyning, Sussex, in April 1727, and in the general election of that year was returned M.P. for the town of Derby ; Boyer, xxxiii. 402 ; ' An exact and correct list of the Lords Spiritual and Temporal as likewise of the Knights and Commissioners of Shires, Citizens and Burgesses of the 1st Parliament of His Majesty King George the Second,' p. 23. This list is an appendix to Boyer xxxiii. The only mention I have found of Stanhope speaking in debate is on the address of thanks of January 1729 : Egmont, iii. 330.

In 1729 he agreed to return to Spain to conclude the Treaty of Seville with a good deal of grimacing, and at a price. ' Nobody knows better than yr Grace,' he wrote to Newcastle in August 1729,

> the uncertain and dangerous situation of our affairs abroad, and the animositys and discontents of our people at home, and consequently you must be equally sensible of the imminent risks and hazards that any one must unavoidably run that shou'd at this juncture charge himself singly with the weight of so doubtful and dangerous a negotiation, and particularly at the Court of Spain to which place if I went everything would naturally be referred. I say my lord as yr Grace knows all this you won't I hope be surprized at my insisting upon the peerage (in case I be sent to Spain), for a better reason than that of the honour of it, tho I can assure yr Grace that I had rather be without it than to have it upon such terms, and that tho I might look upon myself as secure with it, yet it could never influence my conduct there.[1]

Stanhope got his peerage eventually, becoming Lord Harrington, and led a more restful life in the house of Lords. Much clearly depended on individual temperament and aptitudes, and Harrington, like his uncle, Lord Stanhope, but for different reasons, was not cut out for the at times hectic bustle of debate in the Commons. In any case, however, it is understandable that he should not have relished the prospect of being expected to answer personally to the Commons for failure to achieve satisfaction on matters that were really too intractable for negotiation and depended for their solution on the mutual forbearance of Britain and Spain. From more than one source, indeed, one gets the impression that the embassy at Madrid must have been the salt mines of the British diplomatic service in the eighteenth century. Benjamin Keene, Stanhope's successor at Madrid, for example, found life in Spain laborious, disagreeable and unrewarding. In 1730 he wrote to Thomas Robinson, congratulating him on his recent appointment as minister at Vienna :

> We are here in the same condition you always knew us, a thousand complaints to make without having the necessary documents to found them upon, judge then whether the answers dictated by the good humour of this court will not be vastly satisfactory. If ever I get out of my galley, the next commission shall be in Switzerland, where we have no sea, nor consuls, nor commerce, for on their account am I obliged to be the most plaintif Jeremy that ever lamented.[2]

And Keene was then only at the beginning of his thankless labours ;

---

[1] Brit. Mus. Add. MS. 32,762 (Newcastle Papers—Diplomatic), W. Stanhope to Newcastle, 26. Aug. 1729.

[2] Brit. Mus. Add. MS. 23,780 (Robinson Papers), B. Keene to Thomas Robinson, 15 Dec. 1730.

another twenty years of abuse lay ahead of him.[1]   The only thing
worse than representing British interests at Madrid that he could
envisage, indeed, was defending them in the house of commons,
a job, he admitted near the end of his life, and still in Spain, he would
not have for all the produce of the new Land Tax.[2]

It was common form then in the early eighteenth century for
foreign policies to be explained in parliament by ministers and by
other friends of the government.   Sometimes, however, it was also
considered necessary to provide parliament with papers relating to
foreign affairs, either to furnish additional evidence for an argument
that the government was particularly anxious that parliament should
accept and that otherwise parliament might not accept, or in response to some urgent request of parliament that could not safely
be denied.   A good example of the former occurred in 1717 when
the government was concerned to have parliament believe that
there existed a plot concocted by the Jacobites and Charles XII to
restore the Pretender.[3]   Accordingly a considerable body of correspondence from the Swedish ambassadors in London, Paris and the
Hague, relating to their negotiations with Jacobite emissaries,
was laid before parliament at the opening of the parliamentary
session, and constituted a sort of text to which the ministers could
address themselves.[4]   Whether there existed such a plot appears
doubtful, and appeared doubtful at the time to both government
and parliament,[5] though perhaps more account should be taken
of Charles XII's known capacity for utter recklessness than has
been allowed for in recent examinations of the incident.   What is
not in doubt, however, is that the government would have been in

---

[1] Keene himself in 1752 used the phrase ' thirty years of service and abuse ', *The
Private Correspondence of Sir Benjamin Keene, K.B.,* ed. by Sir Richard Lodge (Cambridge,
1933), p. 315. Having got a ' bad bruising ' from Parliament in 1739, Keene never
forgot it : Lodge, pp. 258, 274, and 369, and *Correspondence of William Pitt, Earl of
Chatham,* ed. by the executors of his son, John, Earl of Chatham (1838–40), 4 vols., i.
50, H. Pelham to W. Pitt, 12 Oct. 1750. Of Keene's immediate predecessors at Madrid,
Paul Methuen was glad to leave, broken in health by the climate, pressure of work, and
lack of success, and his successor, George Bubb, though fortunate in finding Spain,
for her own political reasons predisposed to conciliate Britain, had to fight every inch
of the way for commercial concessions.   [2] Lodge, pp. 392–3.

[3] G. Syveton, ' L'erreur de Goertz ', *Revue d'histoire diplomatique,* ix (1895), 417–44 ;
x (1896), 45–55, 223–52, 509–30 ; J. F. Chance, ' The Swedish Plot, 1716–7 ', *ante,*
xviii (1903), 81–106 ; R. E. Lindgren, ' The projected invasion of Sweden 1716 ',
H[*untington*] L[*ibrary*] Q[*uarterly*], vii (1943/4), 223–46 ; J. J. Murray, ' Sweden and the
Jacobites, 1716 ', *H.L.Q.* viii (1944/5), 259–76 ; J. J. Murray, ' British public opinion
and the rupture of Anglo-Swedish relations in 1717 ', *Indiana Magazine of History,* xliv,
125–42 ; J. J. Murray, ' Scania and the end of the Northern alliance,' *Journal of Modern
History,* xvi (1944), 81–92.

[4] *Journals of House of Commons,* xviii. 474 ; *Journals of House of Lords,* xx. 416. The
correspondence as laid before the Lords is in the House of Lords MS. 1717 (249). I
should like to thank Mr. Bond of the Manuscript Room of the House of Lords for
permission to consult these and other documents.

[5] Brit. Mus. Add. MS. 9149 (Coxe Transcripts), Townshend to Slingelandt, 19 Feb.
1716/7.

serious trouble without it, for its whole northern policy was in tatters and was generally disliked.[1] A measure of the Government's plight, indeed, is that the correspondence itself, where it was not fundamentally ambiguous and open to the interpretation that it showed only that the three ambassadors, rather than Charles XII himself, were engaged in an attempt to obtain funds from the Jacobites, was clearly embarrassing in some respects.[2] From the point of view of the British government, for example, it was unfortunate that people should be able to read in the correspondence, in the same month that the conclusion of an alliance with France had been announced, that the Regent, whatever his public pronouncements, privately favoured the Pretender.[3] And the discrepancy was noticed. The Reverend John Thomlinson, curate of Rothbury, reading the correspondence in March 1717, in one of its several published versions, noted in his diary —'The letters seem to intimate yt ye Regent of France dissembles wth K.G. in ye Triple-Alliance etc. and they know nothing of ye Regent's private sentimts, who think he has been in earnest wth us all this time.'[4] A number of other references in the correspondence to the influence of Hanover must also have been regarded as unfortunate, for it was commonly supposed that Hanover was at the bottom of all the trouble.[5]

Either house of parliament, however, had an indisputable right to ask for papers relating to matters on which it was being asked to give an opinion or which it held to be of public importance. The crown, of course, through its ministers had an equally indisputable right to refuse such requests, and frequently exercised that right.[6] Yet there were occasions when it was deemed wiser to accede to parliament's requests rather than stand on literal right.

[1] Coxe, Memoirs . . . of Sir Robert Walpole, ii. 118, Townshend to Stanhope, 16/27 Oct. 1716. Apart from the articles already mentioned, relating specifically to the Swedish plot, more general accounts of British policy in regard to northern Europe are to be found in Basil Williams, Stanhope. A study in eighteenth century diplomacy (Oxford, 1932), pp. 230–46, and R. Hatton, Diplomatic relations between Great Britain and the Dutch Republic, 1714–1721 (1950), pp. 87–159.

[2] The view that what was really intended was a loan is advanced by J. J. Murray, ' Sweden and the Jacobites ', 1716, H.L.Q. viii (1944/5), 266–7. It was the view of the French ambassador to the United Provinces, and of the Swedes themselves. See P. É. Lémontey, Histoire de la Régence et de la minorité de Louis XV jusqu'au ministère du cardinal de Fleury (Paris, 1832), 2 vols.; ii. 385–6, Chateauneuf to D'Huxelles, lettres des 2, 9, 12 et 19 mars 1717.

[3] Gyllenborg to Goertz, 8 Jan. 1717, which can be found most conveniently in Boyer, xlii. 203. The Regent himself was offended that this letter should have been published : B. Williams, p. 247.

[4] Brit. Mus. Add. MS. 22,560 (Diary of Reverend John Thomlinson), 5 Mar. O.S. 1717. Part of this diary, from 24 July 1717 to 24 July 1722, the end, has been published in Six North Country Diaries, ed. by J. Crawford Hodgson (Surtees Society, cxviii, 67–167).

[5] Boyer, xiii. 171–2, Gyllenborg to Goertz, 4 Nov. 1716, and 7 Jan. 1717.

[6] For an interesting discussion of this question, see the report of a debate in the House of Commons of 1734 in Cobbett, ix. 201–13.

Early in 1727, for example, the houses, about to begin a detailed examination of the events that had led to the conclusion of the alliance of Hanover, asked for copies of memorials and letters which had recently passed between the courts of Britain, France and Spain.[1] The object was to obtain additional, concrete evidence, wherewith to assess the validity of certain statements made in the king's speech and the speeches of ministers concerning the reasons for the recent deterioration in Anglo-Spanish relations.[2] Parliament's requests were granted and the correspondence was duly laid before it.[3] From references in debate it is certain that the correspondence was read and that it proved useful in confirming the government's case, though here again, as in 1717, it also provided material for the critics of government.[4] In this instance the speed with which the relevant documents, together with translations, were provided, suggests that the government had probably anticipated parliament's request.[5] In any case the amount of correspondence to be copied was small, about a dozen letters, and did not constitute a serious clerical problem. Parliament's requests, however, were not always so easily foreseen, or so easily met. In 1729, for example, the government seems to have been caught unawares by parliament's determination to examine closely the state of Anglo-Spanish trade, with special reference to the activities of the naval squadrons which had been sent to the West Indies and the coast of Spain in 1726 to blockade or intercept the Spanish galleon fleet and flota. Addresses were made successively for copies of the instructions of the commanders of the squadrons and of their correspondence with the secretaries of state, for details of attacks made upon British ships since 1725 by Spain, for copies of the instructions given to commanders at Jamaica, with the correspondence which had been

---

[1] *Journals of House of Lords,* xxiii. 11 ; *Journals of House of Commons,* xx. 714.

[2] For the king's speech, see, *Journals of House of Commons,* xx. 707–8 ; for an account of the debate in the Commons on the king's speech, see, Boyer, xxxiii. 96–100 ; and for an account of the same debate in the Lords, see, Brit. Mus. Add. MS. 17677KKK (9) (Dutch transcripts), L'Hermitage, 31 Jan. 1727.

[3] *Journals of House of Lords,* xxiii. 14 ; *Journals of House of Commons,* xx. 725. The correspondence laid before the Lords is in House of Lords MS., 21 Jan. 1726/7.

[4] For accounts of the debate on the correspondence in the Lords on 24 Jan. O.S. 1727, see, Boyer, xxxiii. 497–512, and Brit. Mus. Add. MS. 17677KKK (9) (Dutch transcripts), L'Hermitage, 7 Feb. 1727. The opposition in the Lords entered a number of protests whose general tenour was that Britain's allies, and particularly France, were dragging their feet, an argument based on the report in one of the letters that Spain had attempted to seduce France from the alliance of Hanover : *Journals of House of Lords,* xxiii. 16–17. The equivalent debate in the Commons took place on 6 Feb. O.S. 1727, when the opposition moved unsuccessfully for further information about the reference in another of the letters to Britain's having made at some previous time a specific promise to Spain to return Gibraltar. Reports of this debate are to be found in Boyer xxxiii. 185–6 ; Brit. Mus. Add. MSS. 17677KKK (9) (Dutch transcripts), L'Hermitage, 18 Feb., 1727 ; Paris, Archives Étrangères—Correspondance d'Angleterre, t 358, Joint à la lettre du M. de Chammorel du 20e fevr. 1727 ; ' Knatchbull Diary ', 6 Feb. 1727.

[5] Brit. Mus. Add. MSS. 17677KKK (9) (Dutch transcripts), L'Hermitage, 4 Feb. 1727.

received from them, relating to measures taken against piracy and the interruption of trade since 1713, and for copies of all the memorials, petitions and representations made to George I and George II relating to captures of British ships.[1] Perhaps, as Pulteney argued in the following year, this did not amount to ' wheelbarrows of papers ',[2] but the copying out of over 500 documents, more than half of them in duplicate, severely strained the rather fragile administrative machine.[3] And it was not just a question of copying. The fact that there were things in the correspondence that the government preferred parliament not to know meant that the letters had to be read carefully to remove offending statements. A paper entitled ' chart of omissions ' in the Public Record Office [4] suggests the principles on which suppressions were made, and something of the practical difficulties with which ministers, under-secretaries and clerks were faced by the need to sift and copy so much material. The chart, which bears no date, is arranged in two parallel columns ; on the left appears the title of the document, giving particulars of writer, addressee and date, and on the right is a summary of its contents. It seems to have been the result of an examination of part of the correspondence made by the under-secretaries and their clerks and was drawn up for the benefit of the duke of Newcastle.[5] Beneath the titles of documents are written occasional worried comments, by Newcastle possibly, who certainly spent the whole of one night at least examining the documents,[6] to the effect ' I do not see why this was left out ' or ' I cannot conceive why this was left out '.[7] The most important consideration, it appears, was to remove statements which threw doubt upon the government's public assertions that France was a firm and reliable ally, and in particular to remove those letters in which criticism was expressly made of the fact that

[1] *Journals of House of Lords*, xxiii. 336, 344–6, 350–5, 377–8 ; *Journals of House of Commons*, xxi. 246, 251–3, 261, 284, 286–9, 296–7, 299–300, 303–6, 309. The first item mentioned, the correspondence relating to the naval squadrons, as requested by the Lords, is in House of Lords MS. 1728/9, Mar. 7, 11, Copies of the instructions to the Admirals in the West Indies. I should like to thank Mr. Bond for allowing me to have a microfilm taken of this correspondence which I have compared with the originals in P.R.O. S.P. 42/78, 79 (1 & 2), & 80 (Naval). I should also like to thank Birkbeck College for paying for the microfilm.   [2] *Egmont Diary*, i. 42–3.

[3] For an account of the staff of the secretary of state's office in the eighteenth century, see, M. A. Thomson, *The secretaries of state, 1681–1782* (Oxford, 1932), pp. 128–42.

[4] P.R.O., S.P. 42/79 (2).

[5] From internal evidence in the chart itself. Against the item ' Wager, 17/28 July 1727 ' is written ' I remember Mr. Stanyan told me they [two enclosures] were ordered to be left out and that the P.S. to Sir Charles's letter of 17/28th to your Grace which mentions them is also left out.'

[6] P.R.O., S.P. 36/10 (Domestic), Newcastle to George II, 11 March O.S. 1729.

[7] P.R.O., S.P. 42/79 (2) ' Chart of omissions '. Further evidence of Newcastle's concern with the problem of ' doctoring ' the papers is to be found in Brit. Mus. Add. MS. 32,687 (Newcastle—Home Correspondence), fos. 265–325, which consists of copies of extracts from other sections of the correspondence, with occasional under-linings in red ink of matters which he presumably considered inappropriate to be disclosed or open to parliamentary criticism.

the French ambassador at Madrid had in recent negotiations there contravened his instructions and that the British representative there had incautiously acquiesced in his actions.   Accordingly, eight letters which either referred explicitly to this incident or which hinted at French unreliability or lack of enthusiasm, were suppressed.[1] But this was only the beginning, for the suppression of a document involved the reading of all subsequent despatches to see that it was nowhere mentioned.   Attention was certainly given to this problem and a number of letters were cut about for this reason.[2]   Nevertheless, and not unnaturally, given the magnitude of the task, the small clerical force available to deal with it, and the haste with which it had to be done, there were a good many slips.[3]   Of course, the session of 1729 was unusual in the demands that it placed upon the administrative machine, but in times when things were happening in the field of foreign affairs, nothing could safely be taken for granted.   In the following session, for example, the government was again taken by surprise when, as a result of some clever tactics on the part of the opposition, it found itself obliged to accede to parliament's pressure for a full-scale examination into what had been happening at Dunkirk, where it was asserted, the port had been restored in violation of the Treaties of Utrecht and of Triple Alliance.[4]   On this occasion, however, the government managed to delay the debate by insisting that time must be granted to bring back a vital witness from France and to prepare the relevant papers, and used the postponement to obtain an official assurance from France that the works at Dunkirk had been performed without the authorization of Louis XV and that he had ordered their demolition.[5]   It was perhaps with the memory of this incident still upon

[1] P.R.O., S.P. 42/78, Newcastle to Wager, 2 Jan. 1726/7, 1 June, 12 July, 24 Dec. 1727 ; S.P. 42/79 (1), Wager to Newcastle, 5 June 1727 ; S.P. 42/80, Newcastle to Hosier, 1 June 1727, Newcastle to St. Lo, 24 Dec. 1727, Newcastle to Hopson, 24 Dec. 1727.   For accounts of the incident, which arose out of differences of opinion between Britain and Spain about the fate of the South Sea Company's annual permission ship, ' Prince Frederick ', which Spain had seized at Vera Cruz in 1726, see, A. M. Wilson, *French foreign policy during the administration of Cardinal Fleury, 1726–1743* (Cambridge, Mass., 1936), pp. 173–5, 181, and A. Baudrillart, *Philippe V et la cour de France* (Paris, 1890–1901), 5 vols., iii. 345–84.   A number of other letters in which the naval commanders expressed their impatience or disappointment at not being allowed to attack Spanish privateers and their bases were also suppressed.

[2] The final paragraph in a letter from St. Lo to Newcastle of 19 May 1728, for example, was left out in the letter presented to the House of Lords, because St. Lo had there expressed regret that his instructions did not allow him to attack Spanish privateering bases.   P.R.O., S.P. 42 (80).

[3] For instance, a letter from Townshend to Wager of 5 Aug. 1727, which mentioned the suppressed letter from Newcastle to Wager of 1 June 1727, was not suppressed.

[4] For the opposition's tactics, see, *Egmont Diary*, i. 44.   For a general account of Anglo-French differences over Dunkirk, see, A. R. Saint-Leger, *La Flandre maritime et Dunkerque sous la domination française, 1659–1789* (Paris, 1900), especially pp. 314–23.

[5] For the government's manoeuvres in the Commons, see, *Egmont Diary*, i. 36 ; Sedgwick, i. 116 ; *Journals of House of Commons*, xxi. 437, 439, 449–51, 460 and 469. For the negotiations with France, see especially Brit. Mus. Add. MS. 32,765 (Newcastle—

him that the under-secretary, Delafaye, wrote self-righteously to Newcastle in December 1730 :

> I am doing what I can that things at the office may be in order against the session, and sleep the less, that we may not then be taken napping. I now write with bloodshot eyes, and green spectacles have been in much request. Nor have some fine days we have had tempted me even to take a walk.[1]

Whatever conditions of work may have been like at other periods of the eighteenth century, Delafaye and Tilson, the under-secretaries of the 'twenties, were certainly kept busy when parliament was in session.[2] As Tilson observed in 1731, parliaments were ' terrible task masters '.[3]

So far reference has been made only to the routine measures involved in parliamentary management. Mention must be made finally, however, of certain additional precautions, taken by government in times of crises, to ensure that individual members of parliament should be able to make themselves personally better acquainted with what was happening in the field of foreign affairs. It was not unusual on such occasions for the session to be preceded or accompanied by some written statement justifying the government's policy or supporting it at some particular point, which took the form either of the publication by authority of relevant documents or the appearance of some weighty pamphlet known to have been written either by ministers themselves or upon their instigation. In 1717, for example, a day or two after the opening of parliament a sort of government white-paper appeared, consisting of the intercepted correspondence of the three Swedish ambassadors involved in the so-called Swedish plot ; [4] and such was the degree of public interest that within a fortnight a new edition of the correspondence had been published.[5] Again, in 1726, when parliament

---

Diplomatic Correspondence), Newcastle to Poyntz and Armstrong, 12 Feb. 1729/30 ; Add. MS. 32,766 (Newcastle—Diplomatic Correspondence), Poyntz and Armstrong to Newcastle, 16/27 Feb. 1729/30 ; ' Order from the king of France ', 27 Feb. 1730.

[1] Brit. Mus. Add. MS. 32,770 (Newcastle—Diplomatic Correspondence), Delafaye to Newcastle, 13 Dec. O.S. 1730.

[2] Hume appears to have had an easy life as under-secretary to Conway ; at least he himself said so : E. C. Mossner, *The life of David Hume* (1954), pp. 537–40. Conditions, however, clearly varied from time to time. Addison, for example, certainly did not find his period as under-secretary of state a soft option ; in fact his eyesight failed under pressure of work : P. Smithers, *Life of Addison* (1954), p. 129.

[3] Brit. Mus. Add. MS. 23,780 (Robinson Papers), G. Tilson to Thomas Robinson, 23 Feb./6 Mar. 1730/1.

[4] *Letters which passed between Count Gyllenborg, Barons Goertz, Sparre and others relating to the design of raising a rebellion in His Majesty's Dominions to be supported by a force from Sweden. Translated into English. Published by authority. London 1717.* This is in the British Museum. The date of publication was round about the 25 Feb., O.S., according to the London Gazette of 19/23 Feb. O.S. 1717. See also, J. J. Murray, ' An eighteenth century Whitebook ', *H.L.Q.* xiii (1950), 371–82.

[5] *Daily Courant*, 15 Mar. O.S. 1717, advertised a new octavo edition : Burney collection of newspapers in the Brit. Mus.

was considering the alliance of Hanover, the government authorized the publication of the alliance, with the treaties of Vienna which had given rise to it, and provided every member of parliament with a copy.[1] In the following year, at the beginning of the session, certain correspondence recently exchanged between the courts of Britain, France and Spain was published by authority.[2] In 1727, however, the main statement of government policy was contained in Bishop Hoadly's *The Enquiry*.[3] This lengthy and well-documented pamphlet, which was also distributed to M.P.s,[4] so closely anticipated, in detail as well as in general structure, the arguments of the king's speech of January 1727, that it was commonly supposed that the author had been provided with access to official documents and perhaps received the assistance of Horace Walpole, whose speech to the Commons in the previous February 1726 may have formed the basis of Hoadly's effort.[5] It is impossible to state precisely how many copies of *The Enquiry* were sold, but they were certainly numbered in thousands, perhaps more than ten thousand.[6] Hoadly provoked a considerable discussion which conforms to the classical pattern for this genre detected by Professor Vaucher.[7] It was attacked violently and destructively, but not very effectively, by Bolingbroke in two pieces by the *Occasional Writer*, which were also distributed to M.P.s.[8] Bolingbroke's arguments, which, in so far as they amounted to anything worthy of being called an argument,

[1] *The treaties of Vienna, friendship and commerce. The treaty of Hanover. Printed by S. Buckley. 1725.* This is in the Lansdowne collection of pamphlets at University College, London. I should like to thank the Librarian for permission to consult this collection. Samuel Buckley was at this time editor of the fast declining, and only official, government newspaper, the London Gazette. For the statement about distributing copies to individual members of parliament, see, Brit. Mus. Add. MS. 17677KKK (8) (Dutch transcripts), L'Hermitage, 22 Feb. 1726.

[2] *Letters and memorials which have lately passed between the ministers of the courts of Great Britain, France and Spain. London. Printed by Sam Buckley. 1727 :* Lansdowne tracts. This appeared about the last week in January 1727.

[3] *The enquiry into the reasons of the conduct of Great Britain with relation to the present state of affairs in Europe. London. Printed and sold by J. Roberts 1727. By authority: a sort of political canon :* Landsowne tracts.

[4] Brit. Mus. Add. MSS. 17677KKK (9) (Dutch transcripts), L'Hermitage, 28 Jan. 1727.   [5] As above ; Corr. d. Angl. t. 358, Chammorel, 30 Jan. 1727.

[6] W. T. Laprade, *Public opinion and politics in eighteenth century England* (New York, 1936), p. 294, asserts that over twenty thousand copies were disposed of in three weeks, but, as he adopts the maddening practice of lumping together all his references in one indiscriminate heap at the end of every chapter, there is no means of checking the source for this statement. L'Hermitage estimated some ' thousands of copies ', and this may well have been an under-estimate : Brit. Mus. Add. MSS. 17677KKK (9) (Dutch transcripts), L'Hermitage, 28 Jan. 1727. Some very slight indication of the importance which the government attached to a wide reading of the pamphlet is perhaps provided by the fact that far more copies of it, six, have survived in the Lansdowne tracts than of any other pamphlet in the collection for the period 1715–31.

[7] P. Vaucher, *Robert Walpole et la politique de Fleury, 1731–1742* (Paris, 1924), pp. 15–16.

[8] *The occasional writer. I. London, January 1726/7. Printed for J. Gray* ; *The occasional writer. II. Printed for A. Moore 1727.* For the statement that copies of both these pieces were distributed to members of both houses, see Boyer, xxxiii. 147.

represented a plea for permanent isolation from Europe, were quickly answered by Robert Walpole himself in *A Letter to the Occasional Writer* which was similarly distributed to members of parliament.[1] Soon after, Walpole's retort was republished in full on the front page of the government-controlled *London Journal*, which noted a week later : ' N.B. the demand still continuing for last Saturday's London Journal, containing the answer to the " Occasional Writer ", it is this day re-published '.[2] And a fortnight after this *The British Journal*, devoted its entire issue to a reproduction in parallel columns of both pamphlets, so that ' in a fair and open light' . . . the superiority so evident in the reply may appear in its full force '.[3] The practice thus adopted in 1727 of preceding or accompanying the opening of parliament with an officially inspired pamphlet was repeated in 1729, 1730, and 1731, becoming, as Pulteney noted, an annual custom.[4] At the beginning of the 1729 session, although Hoadly returned to the controversy with *A defence of the enquiry*,[5] the official ministerial defence appeared in *Observations on the conduct of Great Britain*, which included many extracts from unpublished documents relating to the instructions of the naval commanders sent to blockade the Spanish and Spanish American coasts in 1726.[6] The 1730 session was preceded in November or December by Robert Walpole's *Observations on the treaty between the crowns of Great Britain, France and Spain*,[7] which was followed a few weeks later by *The Treaty of Seville and the measures that have been taken for the last four years*.[8] In 1731 two pamphlets appeared just before

---

[1] Boyer xxxiii. 147.

[2] *London Journal*, 11, 18 Feb. O.S. 1727 : Burney collection.

[3] *British Journal*, 11 Mar. O.S. 1727 : Burney collection.

[4] *A short view of the state of affairs with relation to Great Britain for four years past with some remarks on the treaty lately published, and a pamphlet entitled Observations upon it. 1730* [Pulteney], p. 15 : Lansdowne tracts. Boyer noticed the same : xxxvii. 111.

[5] *A defence of the enquiry into the reasons of the conduct of Great Britain occasioned by the paper published in the County Journal or Craftsman on Saturday, Jan. 4, 1728|9. By the author of the enquiry. Printed and sold by J. A. Roberts. 1729* : Lansdowne tracts. Probably published round about the end of January 1729, according to advertisements in the London Gazette of 25/28 Jan. 1729.

[6] *Observations on the conduct of Great Britain with regard to the negotiations and other transactions abroad. London. Printed and sold by J. Roberts 1729* : Lansdowne tracts. Boyer regarded it as the official account : xxxvii 111. It probably appeared early in January, before *A defence of the enquiry*, for it was summarized by Boyer in the January edition of his *Political State* : xxxvii. 112–39, whereas a summary of Hoadly only appeared in the February edition. *The Political State* usually appeared during the second week of the month following that with which it was concerned.

[7] *Observations on the treaty between the crowns of Great Britain, France and Spain 1729. London. Printed and sold by J. Roberts. 1729.* The pamphlet is ascribed to Robert Walpole in Vaucher, p. 16, and that he wrote it seems clear from the venomous things said about its author in *A short view*, mentioned above in footnote 4, and *The observations on the Treaty of Seville examined* [Bolingbroke]. *Printed for R. Francklin 1730* : Brit. Mus.

[8] *The treaty of Seville and the measures that have been taken for the four last years impartially considered. In a letter to a friend. London. Printed for J. Roberts. 1730* : Lansdowne Tracts. This appeared early in February 1730 : Egmont Diary, i. 34.

the opening of the session, expressing the government's point of view, *A defence of the measures of the present administration* and *Considerations on the present state of affairs in Great Britain*, the latter being the joint effort of Horace Walpole and Stephen Poyntz, a man of wide diplomatic experience, formerly ambassador to Sweden and more recently a commissioner at the Congress of Soissons, and concerned principally with the hiring of Hessian troops, a matter over which parliament had showed great concern the previous year and which, it was clear from the attacks of the *Craftsman*, was to be raised in the coming session.[1]

Governments thus took great pains to see that their policies were represented in as favourable a light as possible in open argument by those who could speak with authority. Whether parliament was ever convinced by the arguments it heard and read is, of course, another matter, but that parliament required to be provided with arguments was taken for granted by those best fitted to judge. To ignore this fact, or to admit it only to dismiss it summarily, is to get a seriously distorted picture of parliament and politics in the eighteenth century.

Birkbeck College, London   G. C. Gibbs

---

[1] *A defence of the measures of the present administration, being an impartial answer to what has been objected against it in a letter to . . . London. Printed for J. Peele. 1731* : Lansdowne tracts ; *Considerations on the present state of affairs in Europe and particularly with regard to the number of forces in the pay of Great Britain. London. Printed for J. Roberts. 1730.* The date of the appearance of these pamphlets has been arrived at from advertisements in newspapers, and, although it may not be possible from this source to pinpoint the exact day, the fact that a second edition of each pamphlet was out before 19 Jan. O.S. 1731, the day parliament opened, is enough for my purpose. See *Daily Journal* 18, 19 Jan. O.S. 1731 : Burney collection. For the authorship of the latter pamphlet, see Coxe, *Memoirs of Horatio, Lord Walpole*, ii. 457, and *Egmont Diary*, i. 125.

Index

Peers, etc., will be found under whichever name (title or family name) the bulk of
their career is associated with: e.g. Jenkinson, Charles, 1st Earl of Liverpool, but
Liverpool, Robert Banks Jenkinson, 2nd Earl.